John F. Pile

INTERIOR DESIGN

Second Edition

John F. Pile ▪ Second Edition

Interior Design

Harry N. Abrams, Inc., Publishers

Project Director: Julia Moore
Editors: Cynthia Clark, Kate Norment, Elisa Urbanelli
Designer: Robert McKee
Photo Editor: J. Susan Sherman, with the assistance of Colin Scott
Original artwork:
    Steve A. Broback
    Michael Esposito
    Stuart H. McFeely
    Robert McKee
    Raymond Skibinski

Library of Congress Cataloging-in-Publication Data
    Pile, John F.
    Interior design / John F. Pile. — 2nd ed.
    p.   cm.
    Includes bibliographical references (p.   ) and index.
    ISBN 0–8109–3463–9 (Abrams: cloth) —
    ISBN 0–13–149733–2 (Prentice Hall: pbk.)
    1. Interior design. I. Title.
    NK2110.P55 1994
    729—dc20   94–6342

Printed and bound in Japan

DISCLAIMER: The information and statements herein are believed to be reliable
but are not to be construed as a warranty or representation for which the author
or publishers assume legal responsibility. Users should undertake sufficient veri-
fication and testing of any information or products referred to herein to determine their and safety for their intended purposes.

Page 2: The Opus Restaurant in Santa Monica, California, designed by Grinstein
Daniels in 1992. (Photograph: Tim Street-Porter)

TABLE OF CONTENTS

Preface to the First Edition

Interior design touches the lives of all of us in a very direct way. We all live in interiors, and most of us work, study, shop, and travel inside various buildings, vehicles, and other enclosures. At one time or another, almost everyone has been an interior designer on a limited scale, when choosing a paint color or a rug, when buying furniture, or when arranging furniture in a new living place. For these reasons, interior design is—or should be—of interest to everyone.

A complex and constantly changing field, interior design overlaps and interlaces with related professions—architecture in particular and, to a lesser degree, industrial design, exhibition design, stage design, and other more specialized fields. No one book of reasonable size can deal with every aspect of interior design in full detail at a level that will support professional practice.

This book is concerned with the range of interior design from the modest and everyday experiences at home and at work to full professional involvement in large projects. It is not a collection of decorating suggestions, nor is it a complete "how-to-do-it" book, nor is it a substitute for the level of professional training offered in design schools. It is, rather, a survey of the field as it now exists. Readers interested in learning how to organize residential interiors will find that it presents the basic principles they need to know. It will also provide a useful guide to those who will be dealing with professionals in the field from time to time. Others may find it an introduction to professional study leading to a career in design.

As with any creative endeavor, reading a book, however helpful in learning about a subject and in establishing a point of view, is no substitute for direct, practical experience. Readers who have a real project in mind are urged to augment their reading by trying out some design assignments. Measuring an existing space, making some drawings, putting together color schemes—all these exercises can be done on one's own or in a class with the guidance of an instructor and the stimulation of fellow students doing the same work.

Design schools develop the student's experience through what is often called the *clinical method*. Students are given a *problem*, that is, a space to be designed, with a plan of that space and a set of requirements to be filled. The first problem is usually a single room. As the student gains experience, more complex problems are introduced. The space is never built, but the student receives ongoing criticism and advice from an experienced and skilled critic or teacher and classmates. Putting designs into realized form is the most exciting step of all. It carries its own problems and hazards, but it also promises unique satisfaction.

Earlier books that survey interior design tend to reflect a division in the field that appeared almost from its emergence. There are, on the one hand, *decoration* books that focus on the reproduction of historical styles in interiors that are most often residential. In contrast, *architecturally* oriented interior design is more closely allied to the movement known as modernism that surfaced early in the twentieth century as a challenge to historicism. This orientation is usually more concerned with the larger and more public projects such as offices, hotels, restaurants, and public buildings, although residential work of this character also abounds.

Within the last few years, this polarization into two conflicting approaches to interior design has begun to break down. Modern architecture has taken a turn away from an exclusive focus on the more mechanistic expression of modern life and developed a new interest in historicism, not in terms of imitation, but with a willingness to learn from the past and incorporate historical references into contemporary design. Meanwhile, the general public,

long uninterested in the concepts of modernism, is moving toward an awareness and acceptance of modern design even in residential spaces, for many a last holdout against anything contemporary. Even as these changes in attitude continue to develop and merge, they have given rise to a new design vocabulary less concerned with formal styles as such and more focused on developing good solutions to the real problems of modern environmental circumstances.

At the same time, design, long isolated in the esoteric reaches of art, where it was regarded with suspicion by a large segment of the general public, is becoming more involved with the insights of various non-art fields such as sociology, economics, and psychology. Buildings and the spaces within them are, after all, intended to serve people in some advantageous way, and designers seem to be increasingly willing to seek help from other specialized fields in an effort to bring creative artistic expression and practical service into a stronger unity. In this book, there is no intention to take sides in a conflict of views that is rapidly becoming obsolete. The intention is rather to introduce the reader to the best of past and present thinking and to provide a starting point for further reading, study, studio work, and practice.

Unlike most professions (medicine, law, and architecture, for example), interior design is not regulated by legal restrictions. No license or degree has been required to use the title and to practice. Some regulation to protect the public against incompetents has been introduced in some states, and perhaps such regulation will someday come into general acceptance. For the present, anyone can work as an interior designer, with no limitations except those imposed by one's own levels of skill and experience. Prospective clients, at least those who are knowledgeable, may inquire about training, experience, and certification. For most people with career objectives in interior design, study in a good school is probably the most reliable route to full involvement in the field. It should be noted, however, that some well-known interior designers—including several who are impressively able—have developed their abilities without formal training.

Formal training may begin with a single course or may involve a complete college program. In order to gain full professional status, it is usual to spend at least four years in an established design school that awards a diploma and prepares the student to begin work in a design office. In addition, many professionals elect to take an accrediting examination that leads to a certificate of competence. Designers who wish to join one or another professional organization must demonstrate their skills, after which they can use the organization's name as evidence of a proven level of ability.

Those who wish to learn about interior design outside the professional schools would most reasonably begin with the problems set by their own living circumstances. Most self-taught interior designers have started with a room or two, perhaps designing and redesigning the same space until they find workable, satisfying solutions. As experience develops, a sense of what training will be most helpful may also evolve. Formal study is often more helpful and more meaningful when it follows or is simultaneous with practical experience.

The learning process cannot stop at any fixed point, after reading a particular number of books or after graduating from even the finest of design schools. The identification, observation, and study of good work remain the most useful and significant form of education in any design field. Whether it takes place in school or out, it is essential to the development of a truly personal way of working at the highest possible level of quality.

John Pile

Preface to the Second Edition

This second edition of *Interior Design* includes extensive new text and many new illustrations devoted to issues of particular concern in the 1990s. The revised text not only covers recent legal requirements that affect designers but also reflects a more general shift in design thinking; moving away from work that simply pleases the client or creates a strong visual impact, the design profession is showing an increasing dedication to considerations of social responsibility. The results of this new perspective are no less aesthetically satisfying than the work of the last decade; in fact, as many projects illustrated here demonstrate, responsible design often produces interiors that are more visually admirable than some of the overblown efforts of past years.

In the first edition of this book, the chapter titled "Future Directions" offered suggestions as to what design in the late 1980s and early 1990s might look forward to. Most of those predictions, which were based on the continuation of directions that were already evident, are now largely realized and are documented throughout this book. As in so many areas of contemporary existence, computers and the techniques associated with their use have come to be accepted as essential elements of professional practice. Early fears that individual creativity would in some way be displaced by inhuman intervention have given way to an understanding of how computers, when intelligently used, can simplify and expedite design work, ultimately contributing to superior end results. Young designers entering the profession now take for granted the value of computer technology and accept its use as no more exceptional than the use of the T square, triangle, and pencil.

Computerization is merely one technical aspect of a larger trend in interior design that was also discussed in the first edition, that is, the increasing professionalization of the field. Licensing laws and qualifying examinations are the bureaucratic expression of a growing recognition that interior design is a serious matter, influencing the health, safety, and well-being of a general population that lives and works almost entirely within interior spaces. In the past, designers may have used their conscience to guide their sense of responsibility toward the public, but today more formal requirements and standards are being established to define those responsibilities. The specifics that every designer must be aware of are now a significant part of this book.

It is probably the field's increasing professionalism that has brought it into closer accord with the related design professions, even overlapping them at times. Architects, who in the past have been at odds with "decorators," are increasingly active as practitioners of interior design. At the same time, with their recognized status as professionals, designers are now finding acceptance in cooperation with architects, often working within architectural organizations themselves. The role of the amateur designer also survives, growing and prospering as those who design their own living spaces, perhaps with the aid of books such as this, approach the competence of professionals. The transition from amateur to professional, long a common route into design, is by no means closed, but the field now demands more than just taste and a sense of style.

The interior designer of the 1990s, whether amateur or professional, must face a broadening and deepening sense of responsibility to the complex demands of the modern world. It is no doubt true that the field is more difficult now than it was in past years, but, as compensation, it is now more interesting than ever, offering greater service to its ultimate audience, the users of designed interior space.

John Pile

1.1

CHAPTER

ONE

INTRODUCTION

In our modern, technological world, most of us spend a major part of our lives indoors. In the nature of things, *home* means an indoor place—a room, an apartment, a house, a mobile home, even a trailer or a van. We study in schools and colleges, eat in restaurants, work in shops, factories, or offices. We are born in hospitals and may die there, too. While most of us spend time out-of-doors, walking from one place to another, attending or participating in sports events, enjoying a garden, sailing, hiking, or even camping for a more extended period, these all tend to be brief interludes in lives spent largely inside some human-created structure.

Some working careers still entail being outside—on a farm, on construction sites, or delivering the daily mail. Statistical evidence, however, suggests that work of this kind is decreasing proportionately, while office work and indoor activities are on the rise. Even today's farmer may ride the enclosed cab of a tractor, while the mail may be delivered from a car or truck. When we travel, we say that we are going "out," but cars, trains, buses, ships, and airplanes are almost as totally enclosed as buildings. Even wilderness camping is likely to involve a significant amount of time spent inside a comfortable and often beautiful tent.

If we estimate the portion of an average day spent inside some sort of enclosing space, we will probably find we typically spend about 90 percent of our time inside, with only 10 percent outside (except, perhaps, on vacation, when the balance may tip closer to 50-50). However much we may love nature, most of us must face the reality that modern life goes on, most of the time, inside. If we are to be honest, we must also face the reality that many, perhaps even most, of the inside spaces where we spend our time are unsatisfactory. The rooms, corridors, and lobbies of typical schools, hospitals, offices, shops, and factories are all too often crowded, disorganized, unattractive, and depressing. We commute in trains or buses that are often agonizingly uncomfortable. At home, where interiors should be the way we want them, limitations often lead us to settle for compromises.

It can be an interesting exercise to make a rating chart evaluating the *quality* of the various indoor spaces in which we spend time, with,

for example, a scale of 1 to 10 representing the range from worst experience to ideal. It is a fortunate person who reports an average much above 5. How does it come about that we subject ourselves to being shut up inside so many spaces that are so far from ideal—even downright unpleasant? We have, after all, constructed the enclosures that we live and work in and have done so, presumably, to make life better.

Obviously, any enclosure serves several basic purposes. It protects us against the weather; it provides privacy; it gives us places where we can keep the things we need in some more or less convenient relationship. While enclosure is basic to these needs, it is only a first necessity. Within enclosure we need equipment; places to sit and lie down; surfaces where food and drink can be prepared and served; places for work, reading, conversation, and entertainment. Increasingly, all of these activities demand special technology—for storage and communication; for cooking and refrigeration; for reproduction of sound and image.

THE DEVELOPMENT OF INTERIOR DESIGN

Historically, most interiors were put together, and put together very successfully, as a natural part of the process of building structures. Ancient and still-surviving indigenous societies developed various forms of huts, tents, igloos, tepees, and yurts to solve the problems of shelter in a particular climate with particular available materials. They then simply took their few possessions inside, much as we might arrange our affairs in a tent while camping. The resulting interior was practical and often, in its own way, handsome.

Developing civilizations found appropriate ways of building more elaborate structures, which created their own kinds of interior space. One cannot think of a Gothic cathedral's interior apart from the structure of the building itself, and the glass, additions of carved wood, and

1.1 A variety of elements and objects generate an atmosphere that is comfortable and snug: Classical columns suggest the historic origins of the space; the colors of wood and fabrics convey warmth and comfort; incandescent light from the lamps adds an additional glow of warmth; the curving form of the seating suggests softness

and relaxation. The collected objects reflect the personal interests and history of the occupants. It may come as a surprise to learn that this interior is in the home of a modern designer, Adriano Magistretti of Pediment Designs (New York), in Rome. (Photograph: Isidoro Genovese)

other decorative elements create a consistent whole, inside and out. At least until modern times, cottages and farm buildings have always been designed and built according to traditions that took into account the occupants' way of life. The furnishings evolved from similar traditions, creating interiors thoroughly compatible with both the enclosing structures and the inhabitants' needs and customs.

It is with the development of more elaborate buildings for aristocratic, often royal, owner-occupants that the idea of an interior as a designed unit, comparable to a fashionable costume as an expression of wealth and power as well as taste, emerged. The design professions began to take form in the Renaissance as strictly traditional practices yielded to a more personal way of thinking about design of every sort. Modern industrial society has added tremendous technical complications, both in the nature of buildings themselves and in the variety of specialized purposes that buildings are expected to serve.

Whatever the gains and losses of our modern civilization, we are clearly not likely to turn back to simpler ways of life; our modern habits of living indoors are destined to remain the norm. This gives us a powerful motive for attempting to make the indoor spaces we occupy as satisfactory, useful, pleasant, and generally supportive as possible. Since this seems overwhelmingly obvious, it takes some questioning to discover why we must so often settle for spaces that fall so far short of these goals.

1.2

1.2 A store's design is all important: It can set off merchandise to its best advantage and make shopping an agreeable experience. In Contemporary Porcelain, a shop in New York's SoHo that features the work of ceramicists

Marek and Lanie Cecula, the flexible display elements and lighting make endless variation possible. William Ruggieri designed this store in 1985. (Photograph: © Frederick Charles)

Every situation will suggest its own list of reasons—historic, economic, social, technical, or various combinations of such realistic pressures—but many of these explanations will turn out to be, on close examination, excuses. As a society, we have overcome historical, economic, and technological hurdles to attain all sorts of astonishing achievements. We are able to travel in outer space, communicate instantly over vast distances, manipulate staggering masses of data automatically—in fact, we can, almost as a matter of course, do any number of things once considered miraculous.

We are also able to create spaces in which people can live comfortably, work well, and have pleasant experiences, as a large number of examples can demonstrate. These examples remain extraordinary, however, in a world in which our artificial environments are all too often anything but comfortable and pleasant. We have lost connection with traditions that provide familiar, accessible answers to the problems of living space, and our industrialized civilization has done poorly at providing worthwhile alternatives.

We seem to suffer from some limitations in thinking, from a sort of block that makes us indifferent to our environment or, when we are not indifferent, that makes us inept to a degree that would never be tolerated in factory production, in financial management, or in scientific research. Towns, cities, and (often worst of all) suburbs are allowed to grow in chaos or to fall into decay. Buildings are erected with some care for their technical qualities (structural strength, mechanical systems) but with only the most minimal attention to design in any larger sense. In fact, the primary motivation for building is sometimes quick profit-making rather than any concern for real use over a longer term. The spaces inside such buildings often limit the possibilities for making truly satisfactory settings for living or work.

Even when we build with good motives—schools, hospitals, or other public buildings or houses for our own occupancy—it often seems that the complicated tasks of putting together good interior spaces are botched in any number of ways. Because they are so familiar, the things that make up an interior space—a room, an office, a living room, a bedroom, a kitchen—seem obvious and easy to arrange. All the evidence shows that this is not so. An interior turns out to be a very complex entity made up of many elements that, to be successful in terms of usefulness, comfort, and beauty, must somehow work together.

Probably the great majority of residential interiors are arranged by their occupants. Offices and other working spaces are also designed, at least to some degree, by the people who use them. While this is most likely among the self-employed or among people who work at home, even business offices are frequently designed, or at least modified, by their user-occupants. Quite standard offices often provide for some level of personalization, which allows the user to adjust the interior to his or her own tastes.

It is a reality that a very large number of interiors can hardly be said to have been designed at all. Many people live in interiors composed of rooms left as they found them plus some paint from the painter's standard color card, rugs and curtains inherited, borrowed, or casually picked out at a local store, and furniture acquired in one way or another set about in any way it will fit in. With luck, the results may have

1.5

1.6

1.7

1.8

styles (Colonial, Louis XIV, XV, or XVI, Tudor, Georgian, or even "modernistic," for example) that it became popular to imitate. The term implies a focus on the decorative, ornamental, and movable aspects of interior design: color, furniture, rugs, drapery, and the fixed details of moldings, paneling, and similar small elements that can be introduced into an existing space with relative ease.

Many decorators were also dealers in the elements used in interiors, buying and reselling furniture and rugs and contracting for whatever on-site work needed to be done to pull together a finished project. This latter practice called into question the decorator's status as an independent professional, and with a decline in the emphasis on traditional stylistic work, the term has tended to take on some negative implications. At best, a decorator can produce work of top quality, but self-appointed decorators who may simply be painting contractors or salespeople in drapery outlets have discouraged others from using the term. Most decorators now prefer to call themselves interior designers, although it is more accurate to reserve that term for work approached in a somewhat different way, as described below

Interior Designer

This term describes a professional approach to interiors that puts more emphasis on basic planning and functional design than *decoration*

1.9

1.8 This living space in the New York apartment of the late Billy Baldwin, one of the best-known American decorators of his time, takes a typically eclectic approach. From the early 1960s, it combines such diverse elements as modern painting, a French provincial chair, a carved Chinese teak table,

modern upholstery, and wall-to-wall carpeting. (Photograph: Horst)

1.9 David Salomon designed this richly luxurious traditional space as a Kips Bay Decorator Show House model interior in New York in 1987. The fabric on the sofas and the matching drapery fabric

use a typical kilim pattern. The paneled walls, chandelier, painting, tapestry, decorative vases, and other accessories contribute to the sense of opulence. (Photograph: © Robert Levin, appeared in the New York Times, April 30, 1987)

implies. In Europe, the term *interior architect* refers to designers who deal with the basic organization of spaces, lay out room arrangements, and manage technical issues (such as lighting and acoustics), much as architects design entire buildings. In the United States, where the term *architect* is legally limited (as described below), *interior designer* has become the accepted term for this kind of practice. Interior designers may work as individuals, in partnerships, or in firms that can grow quite large (with dozens of staff members). These last tend to work on larger projects in commercial, institutional, and office areas. The term *contract design* is also used for this type of practice. It refers to the fact that components and construction work are arranged for under contracts, not simply bought at retail.

Specialization is an increasing fact of life in interior design. Some modern design fields, such as health-care facilities, have become so complex as to demand specialization. Other fields, such as office design, do not require specialization but have nevertheless attracted a specialized practice.

1.10

Space Planner and Office Planner

Firms providing space and office planning have surfaced in recent years to handle the development of large corporate and institutional offices that fill whole floors, many floors, or entire buildings with offices and their related services. Since office buildings are usually constructed as floors of open, undivided space, layout planning becomes an important first step in their design. Space and office planners also provide full interior design (or decoration) service.

1.11

1.10 Painted in Canada in 1929 by a house painter who specialized in decorative effects, this box comes from a time when interior design was mostly concerned with surfaces. The scenes on all visible sides of the box advertise the painter's skills at decorating floors, walls, and other surfaces in the latest styles. The box is from the collection of Cullman & Kravis, Inc. (Photograph: Zindman/Fremont, courtesy Susan Parrish Antiques, New York)

1.11 Elegance and reserve, hallmarks of the work of Andrée Putman, interior designer, are evident in this living area of a San Francisco apartment. The rug is a design of Eileen Gray. (Photograph: © Grant Mudford, courtesy House & Garden)

1.12

In addition to these professionals who specialize in interior design, several other design professions overlap the interior field, sometimes providing interior design. These include:

Architect

An architect must have formal training and experience and must pass an examination leading to *registration*, a type of license to practice. Trained in basic building construction, architects are prepared to design buildings from the foundation up. In many cases, the architect's design includes many interior elements: room shapes, door and window locations, details and selection of materials, and such elements as lighting, heating, air-conditioning, plumbing, and related fixtures.

Traditionally, architects provided fairly complete interior design, sometimes stopping short of furniture and decorative elements and sometimes including these as well. In modern practice, architects design some buildings as shells (office buildings, for example), leaving the interior design to others. In other situations—a museum, church, or school, for example—they provide complete interior design. Some large architectural offices (a few employ hundreds of designers, draftsmen, and other specialists) include departments that are actually complete interior design firms within the larger organization.

Industrial Designer

Designers or design firms specializing in industrially manufactured objects typically work on *products*, such as appliances, furniture, machinery, and automobiles. Some products of industrial design, such as furniture, hardware, and light fixtures, become elements used in interior design. Since industrial designers also deal with the interiors of

1.12 In a lounge of the Auberge du Soleil in Rutherford, California, the contrasts between the rough walls and chimney breast and the polished floor and between the unfinished log column and the furniture's classic lines give this space a unique character. The late Michael Taylor was the designer, in 1981. (Photograph: Russell MacMasters, courtesy Auberge du Soleil)

1.19

1.18, 1.19 Residential interiors can express any number of styles or attitudes, as demonstrated here by two bedrooms. The minimalist austerity of a bedroom in the Grotta House in northern New Jersey (fig. 1.18), designed by architect Richard Meier, is softened by a collection of wood bowls by Bob Stocksdale, Del Stubbs, and Tapio Wirkkala. (Photograph: © Scott Frances/ESTO, courtesy HG) Collections of Navajo rugs and model birch-bark canoes in a Maine bedroom (fig. 1.19) add to the warm, rustic quality of the handmade timber house. The 1975 house is the work of builder John McLaughlin and owner/designer Carl Palazzolo. (Photograph: © Michael Mundy, courtesy HG)

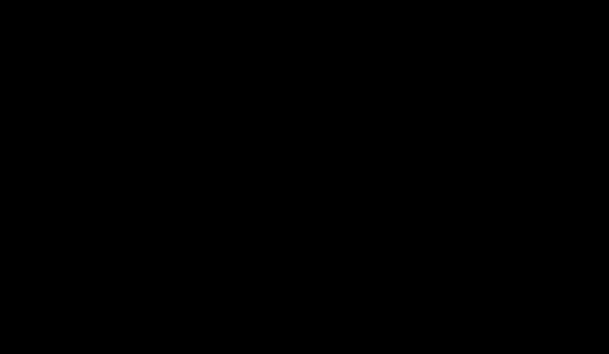

walls and floors. Some consultants are experts in specific types of spaces—hospitals, restaurants (and their kitchens), or theaters. Others deal with certain kinds of problems—furniture design, signs and graphic elements, or, particularly when a major collection is being built up, the selection of works of art. Some large projects may involve almost every one of the specialists and consultants mentioned here, while many small projects may be the work of one designer through-out or may draw on one or two brief sessions with a consultant. Every designer needs to understand these various fields and to know when and where to seek specialized help.

Residential and Contract Design

Interior projects can be divided into two broad classes, each with its own character. Some designers work in both areas, but most choose to concentrate in one field or the other. *Residential* design is concerned with projects that vary from small to medium in size. Even a large apartment or house is within the scope of an individual designer, pos-sibly with an assistant or two. Residential design can be taken up by working on one's own room, apartment, or house, and then moving on to work for friends or relatives before becoming fully professional. Residential work tends to be particularly personal, with rapport between designer and client, a shared taste and point of view, being vital to success. It is work that calls for patience and a willingness to be involved in detail, often detail so small as to be troublesome. Many larger firms avoid residential work, finding the problems of client rela-tionships and the level of detail too demanding in relation to the fees that can be charged. This remains an area in which, under favorable conditions, a designer can find opportunities for personal expression in varied and interesting projects.

Contract design, referring to more public spaces for commercial and institutional use, tends to generate larger projects (fig. 1.20), with clients ranging from individuals to large corporations or institutions. Less personal in their needs and demands, larger organizations are often represented by committees or by various individuals, possibly presenting communication problems to the designer. (The many types of contract design projects are reviewed in more detail in Chapter 18,

1.20 Contract design addresses com-mercial and institutional spaces. These spaces are often large—such as this 1983 multilevel interior, designed by ISD Incorporated for the Continental National Bank of Fort Worth, Texas. (Photograph: Jaime Ardiles-Arce)

implies. In Europe, the term *interior architect* refers to designers who deal with the basic organization of spaces, lay out room arrangements, and manage technical issues (such as lighting and acoustics), much as architects design entire buildings. In the United States, where the term *architect* is legally limited (as described below), *interior designer* has become the accepted term for this kind of practice. Interior designers may work as individuals, in partnerships, or in firms that can grow quite large (with dozens of staff members). These last tend to work on larger projects in commercial, institutional, and office areas. The term *contract design* is also used for this type of practice. It refers to the fact that components and construction work are arranged for under contracts, not simply bought at retail.

Specialization is an increasing fact of life in interior design. Some modern design fields, such as health-care facilities, have become so complex as to demand specialization. Other fields, such as office design, do not require specialization but have nevertheless attracted a specialized practice.

1.10

Space Planner and Office Planner

Firms providing space and office planning have surfaced in recent years to handle the development of large corporate and institutional offices that fill whole floors, many floors, or entire buildings with

offices and their related services. Since office buildings are usually constructed as floors of open, undivided space, layout planning becomes an important first step in their design. Space and office planners also provide full interior design (or decoration) service.

1.11

1.10 Painted in Canada in 1929 by a house painter who specialized in decorative effects, this box comes from a time when interior design was mostly concerned with surfaces. The scenes on all visible sides of the box advertise the painter's skills at decorating floors, walls, and other surfaces in the latest styles. The box is from the collection of Cullman & Kravis, Inc. (Photograph: Zindman/Fremont, courtesy Susan Parrish Antiques, New York)

1.11 Elegance and reserve, hallmarks of the work of Andrée Putman, interior designer, are evident in this living area of a San Francisco apartment. The rug is a design of Eileen Gray. (Photograph: © Grant Mudford, courtesy House & Garden)

1.12

In addition to these professionals who specialize in interior design, several other design professions overlap the interior field, sometimes providing interior design. These include:

Architect

An architect must have formal training and experience and must pass an examination leading to *registration*, a type of license to practice. Trained in basic building construction, architects are prepared to design buildings from the foundation up. In many cases, the architect's design includes many interior elements: room shapes, door and window locations, details and selection of materials, and such elements as lighting, heating, air-conditioning, plumbing, and related fixtures.

Traditionally, architects provided fairly complete interior design, sometimes stopping short of furniture and decorative elements and sometimes including these as well. In modern practice, architects design some buildings as shells (office buildings, for example), leaving the interior design to others. In other situations—a museum, church, or school, for example—they provide complete interior design. Some large architectural offices (a few employ hundreds of designers, draftsmen, and other specialists) include departments that are actually complete interior design firms within the larger organization.

Industrial Designer

Designers or design firms specializing in industrially manufactured objects typically work on *products,* such as appliances, furniture, machinery, and automobiles. Some products of industrial design, such as furniture, hardware, and light fixtures, become elements used in interior design. Since industrial designers also deal with the interiors of

1.12 In a lounge of the Auberge du Soleil in Rutherford, California, the contrasts between the rough walls and chimney breast and the polished floor and between the unfinished log column and the furniture's classic lines give this space a unique character. The late Michael Taylor was the designer, in 1981. (Photograph: Russell MacMasters, courtesy Auberge du Soleil)

take the exam, even in states where no licensing law has been passed, because the NCIDQ certificate attests to qualification in a way comparable to a license. Details of the examination are given in Chapter 19, pages 530–31. As preparation for the exam the NCIDQ offers study materials that also provide a good overview of what full professional qualification requires.

Setting higher professional standards is raising the level of design training and, in turn, the level of expectation on the part of prospective employers and clients. At the same time, clients such as major corporations and hotel and restaurant chains, having learned how much skilled interior designers can contribute, are employing them as *facilities planners*. As mentioned above, larger architectural offices now often include an interior design department staffed by designers whose professional status parallels that of the architects employed by the firm. All of these patterns of professionalism are fairly recent, and they can be expected to grow and spread.

It is also possible to observe a "trickle-down" effect in which the increasing professionalism of the design fields improves the quality of the interior design services offered by some furniture and department stores and by individual designers who work in the traditions of interior decoration, usually specializing in residential work. This has been accompanied by the wider availability of well-designed products, furniture, textiles, carpets, accessories, and other major components of interior design. Not too long ago, such good design was available only through very limited channels, often accessible only to accredited professionals.

Growing Public Interest in Design

Public awareness and acceptance of good design are well established, with books, popular magazines, and newspaper home design pages joining with museum exhibitions to spread information on design excellence. While badly designed home furnishings remain commonplace, good alternatives are readily available. Well-designed automobiles, stereo equipment, appliances, and similar products have wide acceptance, while the success of well-designed home furnishings can be expected to encourage manufacturers to produce and distributors to stock better-designed products.

Computers and Design

Interior design is particularly well suited to computer applications. As computer technology changes and advances, new techniques ever more appropriate to the field will no doubt enter the marketplace and become increasingly essential to the design process. The use of a typewriter keyboard as the primary device for computer control, for example, has served well for applications dominated by words and numbers. For the imagery of drawings, however, the keyboard is now often supplemented by a *mouse* and/or a *slate* with which visual symbols can be manipulated in a manner closer to the familiar processes of drawing. Recent developments suggest that *pen technology*, in which a penlike instrument is used directly on the computer screen, will offer even easier management of visual materials. The ability to read ordinary handwriting will soon augment reading, or *scanning*, of print or lettering by computer. Voice input is also feasible within the near future.

As technological developments allow designers to work on projects by sketching and drawing directly on a computer screen with a "pen" while adding verbal instructions, the mastery and use of electronic technology will become easy and accessible to every designer. The continuing tendency for equipment to simultaneously grow more compact and less costly, as well as increasingly versatile and convenient, suggests that highly sophisticated equipment and techniques will rapidly become as commonplace in design studios as the drawing board and T square are today.

A more detailed discussion of computer applications currently in wide use appears in Chapter 19, pages 535–41.

Types of Future Projects

The future of interior design involves more than computers. As the computer becomes accepted and assimilated, its role as an expediter of work processes is being clarified. End results will remain a matter of the desires and intentions of clients and their designers. A more significant developing change in design practice is in some ways related to the increase in professionalism. This is the movement of interior design work toward two opposite poles that seem to grow farther and farther apart. These poles can be characterized, somewhat simplistically, as large and small projects.

The "large" project end of the scale is dominated by projects with corporate, institutional, commercial, and governmental sponsors. Such work is almost always placed in the hands of larger firms with a staff headed by trained professionals, possibly licensed or accredited in some formal way as architects, engineers, interior designers, or planners. The actual designing is assigned to staff members at various levels of experience and training, often working in areas of specialization such as space planning, design, drafting, materials and color, or specification and purchasing. Some projects may be designed by the interior design departments of large architectural firms, a growing trend as architects become increasingly active in design work. Office planning or space planning, as discussed above, encourages the development of comparably large and specialized design organizations.

The "small" project end of the scale includes residential design and the design of other limited projects, such as smaller retail shops, individual professional offices, and single spaces within larger buildings. Such design work rarely interests larger design organizations, which find dealing with a client, offering supervision, and all of the other complications that go with even the smallest projects too time-consuming in proportion to the fees. The individual private client usually expects a highly personal level of design service, which larger organizations are not equipped to offer even to their large clients.

This increases the opportunities for individual practitioners and very small firms, partnerships or designers with one or two assistants. While this kind of design practice can also be highly professional, it is geared to a different scale and pace of work. Small firms can give individual clients the personal attention they demand, and can do so at fee levels in line with the scale of the work in question. All of this suggests a future in which the medium-sized, all-purpose design firm will become rare, while both large, highly organized firms and individual designers and small firms will flourish.

1.21, 1.22 Although never built, the Hurva Synagogue, designed by master architect Louis Kahn for a site in Jerusalem, has been brought to life through computer graphics. Starting with sketches and a model created by Kahn more than twenty years ago, Kent Larson, a principal in the firm of Peter L. Gluck and Partners, used computer techniques to generate highly realistic images of the space as it would have been built. Photographs of actual materials—wood, travertine, concrete—were scanned to capture colors and textures, while the effects of direct and reflected light were simulated through a software system called INTEGRA. (Courtesy Kent Larson)

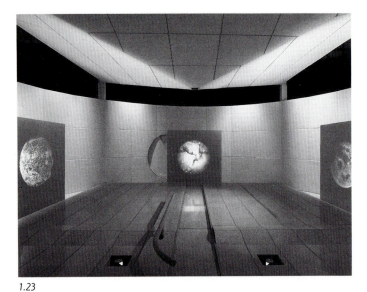

1.23

1.24

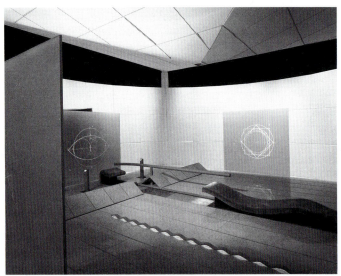

1.25

User Participation in Design

In residential design, there is a tendency for the user of the space, whether apartment, co-op, condominium, or house, not only to show more awareness of design excellence but also to claim a major role in the actual design process. Up to now, good interior design has generally been produced only by the professional decorator, designer, or architect, who could assert total control over a project. The costs of both professional design service and executing the professional's design are usually so high as to make this route available only to the well-to-do, the usual clients of architects and designers.

While this pattern still largely holds true, other forces are at work. Economic mobility in the general population, more widely available education, and an increasing recognition of the benefits of quality design are making design concerns more widely known. The phenomenon of design-oriented magazines, the continuing crowds attending design shows at museums, the sale of design books, and the success of retail shops devoted to home products of a high level of design excellence all point to a parallel trend toward the public's acceptance of a role in improving their home situations.

Self-help materials have been available in the field of interior design for many years, but most have consisted of watered-down versions of the more pretentious approaches of professional decoration. As their audience increasingly sees design as a tool for making life more comfortable and more attractive rather than as a way to display or attain status, authors of self-help books have responded. At the same time, design products have improved. Even well-informed householders are dependent on retail sources for well-designed products. Many of the unfortunate results of self-help owe as much to the badly designed merchandise in furniture and department stores as to any failure of public taste. As well-designed products become more widely available, known, and respected, the quality of the undesigned residential interior is certain to rise.

Even real-estate developers planning apartments, condominiums, and suburban houses (long known for their indifference to design standards) seem to be showing an increasing interest in design quality. Public awareness of design standards leads to demand for excellence. Realization that improved design can be a marketing asset may motivate a rising quality standard in the living spaces available to average occupants.

Consultant Services

In a related trend, consultant design services are being offered to the general public as an aid in smaller, generally residential projects. A consultant of this kind does not attempt to prepare complete plans for a space but offers instead an advisory service on an hourly or per diem basis to deal with aspects of an interior problem that need expert attention. This may include a visit to the space, discussions of how particular problems might be solved, advice about color and materials, suggestions for furniture selection, and any other issues the householder may find problematic. The consultant may provide plans or sketches, access to catalogs and showrooms, and references to tradesmen and contractors known to have a good record for quality performance.

1.23-1.25 Designer Michael Kalil—whose title in this project was Space Engineer—developed this futuristic office. The proposed space is capable of being transformed into almost any configuration to serve whatever function the occupant might wish. The prototype illustrated was built at the Armstrong World Industries Design Center in Lancaster, Pennsylvania.

When not in use, the room is a neutral box, its furniture and features stored beneath the flooring. Display screens can be activated (fig. 1.23); a horizontal, heat-sensor control bar emerges from the floor (fig. 1.24) to accept commands from the occupant's hand touch. A central seat is located between two posts that incorporate controls for lighting and furniture. The intention is

to achieve universal flexibility and adaptability, with almost any imaginable configuration (fig. 1.25) temporarily available. Everything reverts to a neutral state when it is no longer required, just as a radio, TV, or computer becomes inactive when turned off. (Photographs courtesy Armstrong World Industries, Inc.)

1.26

1.27

1.26 Much of the best in contemporary furniture is not available to the public in department stores, but only "to the trade" in the showrooms of manufacturers and importers. These showrooms, although open to the public, are generally known only to professional designers and architects and, through them, to their clients. The showroom illustrated here, Atelier International, Ltd., in New York, is typical. Exposure to such displays is an important factor in acquainting a wider population with high-quality design. Stephen Kiviat, with Skyline Architects, P.C., was the architect; Richard Penney, the designer. (Photograph: © Norman McGrath)

1.27 More and more museums are recognizing well-designed furniture and other interior-related products as works of art, giving the museum-going public an opportunity to study objects to which they might otherwise not have access. This installation of twentieth-century furnishings was designed by R. Craig Miller. It is displayed in the design and architecture gallery in the Lila Acheson Wallace Wing of the Metropolitan Museum of Art in New York. (Photograph: © Peter Paige)

This kind of service can be very helpful when the full services of an interior design firm are unnecessary or beyond the individual's means. It can deal with simple questions (the choice of a color, rug, fabric, or single piece of furniture) or with special problems such as built-ins (shelves or cabinets) or bathroom or kitchen renovations, or it can simply offer advice about practical issues that may be difficult for laymen to deal with. On another level, many people hesitate to turn over a project fully to professionals not only because of concern over costs but also because they wish to retain control of decisions about their own homes. A limited consultant service can be a highly satisfactory middle ground between totally unaided "do-it-yourself" design and full professional service.

Trends

Aside from these issues of how interior design services are offered, provided, and executed, there is also the interesting issue of what future directions will bring to the actual character, style, and look of spaces. Increasing populations will give rise to a greater concentration of people in cities and urban regions, leading to crowding and a reduction in the per capita space available. As resources are consumed faster than they can be replaced, the cost of materials and products will increase. At the same time, computerization and automation promise to make production more efficient and less dependent on manual labor. Office work and work in service fields have already outpaced agricultural and factory production work in developed countries.

Extracting predictions about design from these general trends, it seems that spaces for living and working are likely to get smaller, focusing attention on ways of gaining reasonable comfort in smaller spaces. The costs of materials will probably reverse the long-term trend toward lowered costs for furniture and other products. This may well be offset by dropping costs in technological products whose construction relies more on complex elements suitable to automated production than on materials. Such trends are already apparent in the manufacture of automobiles, which have grown smaller in size while increasing in price. At the same time, new versions of electronic goods,

1.28

1.28 Anne D. McCulley was the set decorator for this set for Ruthless People, a film that popularized the avant-garde imagery of Memphis furniture as only a mass medium can. (Photograph: © 1986 Touchstone Pictures)

such as stereo equipment, television sets, and computers, that are both smaller and functionally improved are constantly being offered at lower prices. Taken together, these directions may help to reverse the long-standing trend toward rapid obsolescence and society's "throw-away" orientation and lead to an increased concern for high quality and long life in the selection of materials and products.

Many commentators have attempted to define recent changes in societal attitudes that seem to promise a fresh thematic character for the final decade of the century. Certainly, a new concern for values beyond the simple desire for luxury and display has emerged. Environmental issues relating to the consumption of energy and resources, the problems of waste disposal, and the protection of the environment cannot be ignored. The special needs of the very young and the very old and the difficulties faced by people who have some sort of disability—temporary or permanent—have been recognized as critical.

Although interior design is only one of many fields that must consider such issues, the profession can have a strong role—for better or for worse—in focusing attention on many basic human problems and in proposing solutions that are humane, reasonable, and practical. Numerous interior design projects of the 1980s seemed to glory in displays of affluence and power: private residences of staggering size and elaboration, corporate headquarters rivaling the royal palaces of the past, and malls and atriums that seemed to celebrate impulsive spending. A general repudiation of these materialistic patterns cannot be expected to bring about a total change of attitudes all at once. Nonetheless, it is clear that an interest in restraint and a broader sense of responsibility are in the minds of many designers and their clients. Although it is sometimes assumed that excellence in design is dependent on the availability of unlimited funds, in reality the demands of economy and simplicity also have created design excellence. The palace of Versailles and the great houses of England unquestionably include elements of outstanding beauty and quality design, but the houses and churches of early American Colonial settlers, the communities of the American Shakers, and the quilts of the Pennsylvania Amish people represent a fully equal, albeit totally different, kind of excellence. If current predictions are valid, we can expect the 1990s to favor design values of an increasingly idealistic nature.

Futuristic thinking rooted in technology suggests that an escape from obsessive materialism might be explored through a group of techniques sometimes called *virtual reality*. *Computer simulation* makes it possible to study a set of alternatives so that the consequences of various actions can be observed and evaluated with great rapidity; the technique can also be used to generate sensory output, allowing consequences to actually be seen, felt, or heard. The best-known examples of such efforts are the flight simulators used in the training of aircraft pilots. The practice of flight maneuvers in real aircraft can be very costly and potentially dangerous; in a simulator, a pilot can use the controls of a specific airplane, with forward view, instrument readings, and so on, artificially but very realistically generated, to practice and perfect landings at various airports, landings on aircraft carriers, and responses to emergency situations without the problems of actual flight. A number of popular computer games offer simplified versions of such simulations.

The concept of virtual reality proposes the use of comparable techniques to simulate environmental circumstances in such a way that a convincing sense of being in a particular place—real or fictitious—is created. The effectiveness of some entertainment formats, including wide-screen film projection from multiple camera images, for example, is well known. Viewers will scream at a roller-coaster ride while sitting motionless in a theater if the visual presentation is sufficiently convincing to give the illusion of movement. The goal of virtual reality is to create a totally synthetic surrounding that would be as persuasive as reality. A participant can visit various locations and seem to look and move about within a setting that does not exist except within the simulation equipment.

Computer techniques that generate realistic perspective views of spaces still in the planning stage—and even permit moving around in such views as if they were real—are already in use. As a method of viewing, studying, evaluating, and presenting design proposals, such techniques have obvious usefulness. An expanded and more adventurous concept of simulation suggests that *reality* could be replaced in a variety of ways. By its very nature, built reality is costly. It takes up space and uses real materials. A virtual-reality environment would occupy no space, use no materials, and have no cost beyond that of its programming. The user would be provided with an illusion of being inside a room, a building, or any other environment, while being capable of looking and moving about and experiencing the visible, audible, and possibly even tactile and kinesthetic aspects of the simulated space.

Such an approach assumes that the physical conditions that real interiors provide—shelter, protection, and air quality, among others—are separable from the visual and other sensory stimuli that comprise the total experience of a real space. If physical reality can be limited to the essential basics, the broader experiential realities could be supplied synthetically. One can imagine, for example, replacing a spacious executive office with a unit that amounted to no more than a seat in a simulator, which might be placed anywhere enclosure was available. The experience of the spacious and attractive room would be generated through virtual reality, disposing of the need to construct the real office. Costly and elaborate suites of offices, now such familiar settings for business and institutional life, could become no more than an empty loft space furnished with simulator units, each able to provide the illusion of a designed environment of whatever aesthetic qualities are desired.

Virtual-reality simulators might be installed in homes, where at will a user could seem to move into offices, conference rooms, or any other spaces. A virtual-reality setting out-of-doors, in the mountains or on the beach, could be available on demand. There are many obvious questions and objections, of course. How would people interact in such simulated settings? What would a virtual-reality store, restaurant, or classroom be like? Would a virtual-reality visit to a museum or gallery be an acceptable alternative to the experience of actuality? Before dismissing such possibilities as pure fantasy, however, we must remember that there is wide acceptance of music broadcast on radio or reproduced on tape or compact disk as an excellent alternative to the experience of the concert hall. Moving pictures and their equivalents on the television screen offer visual and auditory experience surprisingly close to reality. The comfort, safety, and convenience of watching a screen seems to many of us almost equal, perhaps in many ways even superior, to a comparable experience of reality.

If the end purpose of design is to deliver a sensory experience to the user or viewer, does it matter what techniques are used to deliver that experience? Would it be reasonable to select techniques that involve minimal cost and consumption of resources, as well as little or no environmental impact, if the resulting experiences are equal or superior to those encountered in real spaces? Is it necessary to build, furnish, equip, light, heat, air-condition, clean, service, and maintain a building if the same experiences it generates can be created synthetically? These are questions with no currently reliable answers, destined to be topics of concern in the design community within the immediate future.

1.29

1.30

1.29 This temporary conference room for Chiat/Day's Santa Monica, California, offices was designed as a meeting place for the staff of a "virtual office." The system, requiring only an electronic link to the central office, allowed staff members to work almost anywhere. The room (now demolished) was designed in 1988 by Frank O. Gehry & Associates. (Photograph: Bart Bartholomew/NYT Pictures)

1.30, 1.31 In an increasingly densely populated world, spatial compression inspires new design solutions. In a New York City studio apartment, a cooking area (fig. 1.30) is tucked beneath a sleeping loft (fig. 1.31) reached by a short flight of steps. Although the space of this interior is used with maximum economy, individual design details are quite luxurious. Designed by Carl D'Aquino and Paul Laird for Carl D'Aquino Interiors. (Photographs: © 1983 Paul Warchol)

DESIGN QUALITY

All serious designers aim to achieve excellence in their work. While different designers may represent a variety of approaches and aesthetic attitudes, they share an understanding at some basic level of what quality is. An excellent design satisfies three essential criteria: it works well, serving the needs and requirements of its users; it is well made of good, appropriate materials; it is aesthetically successful.

DEFINING DESIGN

Before looking more closely at these criteria, it is necessary, first of all, to define what we mean by *design*. This word has so many meanings and is used in so many contexts that it demands clarification. Many people think of it as meaning pattern or decoration, as, for example, a design for wallpaper or printed textiles. Other people associate it only with fashion design and stage design. In engineering, design may deal with sizing structural members, piping, or ducts, while in the fine arts it deals with the way an artist organizes the formal elements of line, shape, color, and texture in a space.

In interior design, industrial design, and architecture, the term describes all of the decisions that determine how a particular object, space, or building will *be*. It can also be described as determination of *form*, with *form* understood to mean every aspect of every quality, including size, shape, material, structure, texture, and color, that makes one particular physical reality different from any other. When we speak of a house, a living room, an office, an automobile, a chair, or a desk, we call to mind an item that contains certain general characteristics and that serves certain useful purposes, but the word tells us nothing of the specifics that make a particular house, living room, or office unique. It is design differences that distinguish one house from another, one room from another, and that also allow us to speak of one example as better or worse than another.

EVALUATING DESIGN

Evaluation of design can be very complex. The interior designer usually begins with spaces designed by someone else, often long ago, possibly for purposes quite different from those the designer must now satisfy. The client may be an owner, a developer, or a corporation creating space to sell to others or to serve users who have no direct relationship with the designer. The elements that make up the interior—its materials, furnishings, and details—are often designed by others, chosen from among the products available from manufacturers who have no awareness of the project in hand. The finished space, when put into use, may have to serve for years that stretch ahead into times when conditions will change and new generations of users will take over, bringing requirements that may well be different from anything that can be foreseen while design development is in process.

These realities make the interior designer's task more complex than might be suggested by the simple concept of a problem leading to a solution. Nevertheless, the design process can be analyzed in terms of a problem that can be defined and stated with as much clarity and precision as possible. Design proposals can then be viewed as proposed solutions to the stated problem that can be articulated (most often in drawings and models) and evaluated for their success in dealing with the problem.

In order to analyze and evaluate a proposed design, it can be viewed in terms of three closely related qualities: function, structure and materials, and aesthetics.

Function

This is the design world's favorite term to describe the practical purposes that any design is intended to serve. A chair serves as seating support; a living room as a gathering place for varied activities; a dining room as an eating space; an office as a work space; a shop as the arena for buying and selling; and so on. In order to be a success, any design must support its function. This goes beyond mere success or failure, becoming a matter of a scale of value in which the level of functional service can be related to the level of design quality.

Almost any chair can be sat in, and any room will serve for living or dining in some way. A truly well-designed chair will offer appropriate seating comfort for its intended use. A well-designed room will provide a superior setting for its intended function. Such a living room, for example, will provide comfortable settings for conversation, solitary

2.1 Designer John F. Saladino used a heterogeneous array of materials and textures in the living area of his own apartment. The original architectural details—ceiling moldings and fireplace—were retained; textured painted wall surfaces, various textiles, rugs, mirror, and antique furniture relate well in color and scale. (Photograph: Lizzie Himmel)

2.2

reading, music-listening, and TV-watching, as well as a workable setting for entertaining. A dining room will offer space, seating, lighting, and atmosphere suitable to each meal to be taken there, for as few or as many people as may be expected at any one time. An office will provide suitable space for working, equipment, and storage, as well as space to receive visitors and hold small meetings if required. Superior functional performance is the first test of design quality. Failure to function well reflects a larger design failure.

In addition to basic, or *primary*, function, designs must satisfy various secondary functions. Besides providing good seating, a chair should be practical to move, keep clean, repair, and maintain, and its production cost should be appropriate to its intended use. This last issue is so closely linked to the next group of design issues as to leave some uncertainty as to whether it is a functional issue at all. Certainly it ties together matters of function and construction.

Structure and Materials

In order to function, any design must be constructed of specific materials with available techniques of manufacture and workmanship. While closely related to functional issues, quality of materials and construction techniques can be evaluated separately from functional performance. The choice of materials and workmanship greatly influences an object's durability and its initial and lifetime costs, values separate from *function*. A chair can be comfortable and serviceable (that is, serve its primary function)—at least for a time—even if poorly made of inappropriate materials.

An object's materials and construction techniques must be appropriate to its intended use. The longest-lasting and most expensive of

materials do not best serve every situation. A temporary exhibit will be built very differently from a monumental space expected to endure for generations. A paper cup and a cup of solid gold can be equally well designed, as long as each suits an intended use and is well made.

In an interior, wood plank floors, plastered walls, and simple wood furniture may be appropriate to one set of requirements while marble, granite, leather, and stainless steel may suit another situation. In each case, excellence requires logical choices and quality workmanship suited to the materials selected.

Aesthetics

In evaluating design, it is easy to focus on functional performance and quality of materials and workmanship. While these are subject to debate—much as people argue over the best make of car—they offer generally understood criteria by which to judge. Aesthetic values, less easy to spell out, are all too often dismissed as "a matter of taste" that cannot be dealt with in any logical way. Teachers and students of design, as well as working designers, often slip into a belief that design can be evaluated only in terms of its practical aspects, since they cannot explain the aesthetic values at work.

Nonetheless, one can identify levels of aesthetic quality. In the evaluation of design, better is distinguishable from worse, and near-unanimity arises in selecting outstandingly good and bad designs. Such quality distinctions can be made even in the realm of the fine arts, in which the issues of function and structure scarcely apply. "Great art" is identified by a wide consensus that includes critics, historians, dealers, collectors, and sensitive viewers with no special qualifications. All of them recognize high quality even in work that may not be

2.2 In a house in New Mexico designed by architect Charles Foreman Johnson, a sculptural, hand-built fireplace is a dominating element that works well with the adobe walls and wooden pole rafters. All of these features have strong regional associations;

although they might seem awkward or inappropriate in other surroundings, they are clearly at home and logical here. The choice of material helps to place a room in a wider context. (Photograph: ©1985 Michael Skott)

appealing to a particular taste or fit any particular definition of "beauty."

Confusion stems from efforts to define aesthetic qualities in terms of *beauty*. The concept of beauty differs with time and place, with purpose and context. An ornate Victorian parlor, an austere modern living room, the interior of a factory or of a native hut will all be seen as beautiful or as unattractive by various viewers applying different standards. Our definitions of beauty and of unattractiveness may often be no more than our reactions to certain situations that we either like or dislike, attitudes that may arise from extraneous sources. We find it easy to like what is familiar, what is popular or fashionable, what one has learned to like from family, teachers, or friends, from books, magazines, and advertisements. Almost everyone can remember having had different tastes at some time in the past, tastes that have changed with growth, education, and experience.

The values that are usually called *aesthetic* can be better understood at another, more universally comprehensible level. Those aspects of a design that go beyond the functional and the constructional concern the specific way the design presents itself to the human senses. We use an object to serve some need or want, and we expect its physical structure to support that use. We know about an object through looking at it, handling it, and developing a sensory experience above and beyond its simple use. It is the task of the designer to shape an object so as to communicate to any viewer or user the ideas that define the reality of the object. When these ideas are appropriate and clear and when

2.4

they are effectively expressed through the mediums at the designer's disposal (form, shape, color, texture, and so on), we *understand* the design at a deep level and feel satisfaction in seeing, handling, and using it.

It is also true that objects can be made useful and sturdy without exhibiting any particular visual quality. It is the unique role of the designer to form designs in such a way that they come to have a meaning beyond their simple physical reality. Viewing them at second hand, in photographs or other illustrations, is one way to test their success. One can develop a certain rapport with a designed object that one has never actually seen if its visual quality is in itself strong enough to provide satisfaction.

Viewing the work of the interior designer in this way gives us a yardstick for measuring excellence. We expect a space to serve its practical purpose well, and we expect it to be well made of suitable materials. We also expect it to give us a sensory experience that will help us to understand its use and its structure, as well as offer a range of other ideas about its time, location, and the viewpoints of its designer and owner or client. This is the nature of experiencing a visit to a great cathedral, a fine château, or some other landmark building. In the same way, a visit to a more modest office, restaurant, or living room can offer pleasures that go beyond mere practical accommodation. In an ideal world, every space that we enter and use would be designed not only to serve its purpose well but also to offer a visual experience that would be appropriate, satisfying, and even memorable.

DESIGN IN OTHER CONTEXTS

Some confirmation of the validity of these basic design principles can be found by looking at situations outside the worlds of art and professional design. Examples of excellence in design are by no means confined to the works of designers. By examining such examples, we can

2.3

2.3 The interior of this private Lear jet, designed by Herman Miller, Inc., for its own use, is a triumph of design; the severely constricted environment has been made comfortable, even luxurious. Simplicity and the intelligent use of color allow the functional forms of the space and the seating to speak for themselves. (Photograph courtesy Herman Miller, Inc.)

2.4 In a dining area designed in 1992 by Albert Hadley of Parish-Hadley Associates for his own Connecticut home, simple window treatment and traditional Federal-style chairs produce a sense of comfort and ease. (Photograph: John Hall, courtesy House Beautiful)

2.5

analyze the qualities that generate satisfaction and try to define the ways in which we perceive excellence.

We can, in fact, begin with design that can develop without human contribution. It is almost a platitude to say that natural things are beautiful. Almost everyone considers trees, flowers, landscapes, birds, animals, even human beings beautiful. *Design in nature,* while a process that operates very differently from the human design process, only produces objects and settings that work well and satisfy us visually. A second area of design excellence not created by designers is *vernacular*

2.6

design. This term refers to the products of people working in traditional and familiar ways. Their design arises in direct response to needs rather than from a conscious effort to create an individual object in a special way. A third area, one very much within human control, is *technological design,* most often the work of engineers. While engineers use the term *design,* they concentrate on function and structure, giving little or no thought to appearance in their work. Nevertheless, at least some technological design is of outstanding quality.

Nature and Design

Nature normally produces its forms through processes independent of human control. Inanimate, or inorganic, nature can be described as the result of forces acting on materials in ways that follow natural laws that we have come to understand with increasing precision but whose origins remain unknown. A starry night sky, which, scientifically speaking, is simply a display of celestial bodies that rush through space and emit light, is universally viewed as beautiful. The Milky Way, the moon, a spiral nebula—all beautiful elements of the night sky—actually mean little to us beyond our recognition of them as visual traces of extremely remote realities. The earth gives us satisfying images closer to our direct experience—the sea, mountains, polar caps, the patterns of rocks, pebbles, sand, cloud forms, and patterns of moving water—formations and conditions that can be identified and explained by the appropriate sciences.

The evolutionary processes that govern the biological world, or organic nature, have somewhat more kinship to the human design process. Among the great variety of living things, successful forms—in a functional, survival sense—prosper and develop, while less successful

2.5 *Designer Joe D'Urso, long identi-fied with a minimalist aesthetic, turned to a more relaxed approach in this 1991 house on Long Island. While the design retains a certain simplicity, it uses strong, chromatic colors and var-ied materials. The shoji-like screens serve here as room dividers. (Photo-graph: Oberto Gili, courtesy HG)*

2.6 *Simple contemporary design com-bines well with the reserved traditional details of a 1907 seaside house on Long Island. Bentley La Rosa Salasky were the architects and decorators for this 1992 project. (Photograph: © John Hall, courtesy HG)*

variants disappear. This process seems to explain why living things are invariably of excellent design. They are also sources of visual satisfaction, true models for the human design effort. The growth patterns of plant forms, trees, and flowers can be analyzed in terms of geometric and mathematical principles that often parallel patterns in astronomical configurations. Both patterns, organic and inorganic, are responding to the same kinds of physical realities, although on a vastly different scale.

Animal life, from the microscopic forms up to the largest of creatures, is comparably logical and beautiful in design terms. People who object that some living creatures, such as snakes and insects, look ugly are usually simply expressing their fear. Given reassurance against stings, bites, or other forms of attack, one can find design merit in even the most threatening of life-forms. Living species change with the passage of time as conditions change. The great prehistoric reptiles, made obsolete by environmental change, can still be appreciated as superb designs for the conditions under which they prospered. It is interesting to note that some animals also produce objects: webs, nests, hives, dams, even lodges. These creations, the result of instinctive drives rather than of conscious planning, are as consistently excellent as the direct biological products of nature.

2.9

2.7

2.8

Vernacular Design

Vernacular design, produced by human beings, has something in common with the processes of organic nature. The objects made by prehistoric and native populations, like the organic forms of evolution, emerged through trial and error, and then became *traditional* forms, repeated over generations with minimal change as long as they continued to serve the purposes for which they were developed. Simple tools and weapons, huts and tents, containers of pottery or basketry, and basic woven fabrics are not the design of a single creative person but rather *types* that show up in a particular society with only limited individual variation. These things draw our interest because of the excellence of design they often demonstrate, and because we also find them beautiful in ways that more sophisticated design often has trouble equaling.

2.10

2.7 Natural forms have an authority, a rightness, that have inspired design throughout humanity's history. The spiral nebula in Virgo, a vast, unimaginably remote galaxy, is seen here through a powerful telescope. The spiral form is defined by the mathematics of the Fibonacci series. (Photograph: California Institute of Technology, Pasadena, courtesy American Museum of Natural History, New York)

2.8 The pattern of a snail shell's growth recalls, in miniature, the spiral of the Great Nebula (fig. 2.7). This and other natural forms seem to have an almost universal attraction, suggesting that their mathematical basis generates an aesthetic that is intuitively understood. National Museum of Natural History, Washington, D.C. (Photograph: Chip Clark)

2.9 A staircase in the Codd House on Nantucket, Massachusetts, illustrates the spiral shape adapted to human use. The spiral is repeated as a decorative form on the molding (visible at right). (Photograph: Cortlandt V. D. Hubbard, courtesy Nantucket Historical Trust)

2.10 The traditional vernacular designs of native peoples have developed over millennia. These beaded baskets made by the Nevada Paiute tribe are strongly influenced by visual harmonies found in nature. The Denver Art Museum

2.12

2.13

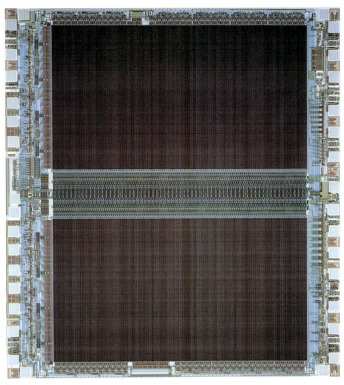

2.14

Vernacular design is by no means limited to the ancient and indigenous cultures. Modern examples surround us in such everyday objects as tools, kitchen implements, bottles, jugs, and jars, sporting and outdoor gear, musical instruments, and the innumerable things for which the question, "Who designed this?" has no answer. The fisherman's dory, the lobster trap, the fireplug, and the telephone pole—all examples of generally excellent vernacular design—like the webs, nests, and hives of the animal world, evolved to fill a specific need without benefit of formal design efforts.

Technological Design

Technology generates design that, while not at all simple or unselfconscious in a technical sense, in aesthetic terms is as *natural* as the products of nature or vernacular design. Indeed, the term *technological vernacular* is sometimes used to describe the design that has its origin in invention and engineering. The designs of ships, aircraft, bridges, and many kinds of machinery, often deemed excellent, are carefully planned in terms of functional performance and structure but not in terms of aesthetics. In other words, aeronautical engineers, naval architects, designers of turbines, pumps, and printing presses design for performance and do not usually concern themselves with questions of beauty.

Nonetheless, their designs often look beautiful to us. In fact, gears, bearings, propellers, and similar technological objects have been gathered together and displayed in museums under the term *machine art*. We find it hard to believe that the designers of such objects do not take aesthetic considerations into account. We also find it surprising

2.11 In a New York apartment of 1984, Steven Holl created a singular environment of related elements. The table, chairs, rug, wall treatment, and hanging light are his designs, developed especially for this space. (Photograph: © Paul Warchol)

2.12 A display of beetles in the National Museum of Natural History, Washington, D.C., exhibits an astonish-

ing variety of color and patterned markings. Their purposes—species recognition, camouflage, warning signals—often elude human inquiry, but their beauty is apparent. (Photograph: Chip Clark)

2.13 Shown here is a detail from a column capital, a feature of the 1986 Saddlery Building in Des Moines, Iowa, by Douglas A. Wells, architect. The

forms and color are clearly inspired by natural patterns—of plants, animals, and insects. Compare this design, for example, with the beetles in fig. 2.12. (Photograph: © 1986 Frederick Charles)

2.14 Technology has generated many aesthetically satisfying designs without benefit of a designer's input. In this computer-generated plot on paper

(42¼ x 44¼") of an erasable, programmable read-only memory chip, microscopic transistors create a colorful pattern with its own inherent beauty. The chip is a 1986 product of Intel Corporation. The Museum of Modern Art, New York. Gift of the Intel Corporation. (Photograph: © 1993 The Museum of Modern Art, New York)

that efforts to improve technological design through the advice of design professionals often do more harm than good.

The design excellence of technological objects comes from the way in which their designs are developed—a way that closely parallels the designs of nature and the vernacular designers. Forms are suggested and guided by functional needs and the practical issues imposed by materials and manufacturing techniques. Each concept, each detail is tested by performance criteria—quite literally in a test laboratory, or in the long-term testing of use—so that better ideas survive while less successful ones fall away.

Designers of both buildings and interiors constantly turn to natural, vernacular, and technological design for inspiration and guidance. Their aim is not to imitate or borrow the forms of these designs, although this is not uncommon. Rather, it is to learn how the practical aspects of designing can lead to visual results that express the intentions behind the design process. We expect an interior space to serve

2.15

2.16

2.17

2.15 A diesel-powered passenger train clothed in a streamlined, stainless-steel skin is typical of the futuristic aesthetic of the 1930s. The Burlington Zephyr of 1934, built by the Budd Manufacturing Company of Philadelphia, was the first American train to replace the steam-driven "iron horse" with technology and design better suited to the modern age. (Photograph courtesy Burlington Northern Railroad, Denver)

2.16 The Zephyr digital clock, designed circa 1933 by Kem Weber for Lawson Time, Inc., Pasadena, California, is made of brass and copper. Both its name and its shape express a national enthusiasm for technological progress—reflected even in such small, everyday products. While streamlining has no functional value in a clock, the recalled form was contemporary in itself (see fig. 2.15). Collection John P. Axelrod. (Photograph courtesy Alistair Duncan)

2.17 Printing, originally a manual skill, was mechanized in the nineteenth century. This Isaac Adams press of 1830, manufactured by R. Hoe and Co., demonstrates the aesthetic possibilities of technology.

its purposes well, that is, to offer comfort and convenience. We expect it to be well made from suitable materials put together with quality manufacturing techniques and workmanship. We also have a right to expect that the space will convey a sense of what it is and what it does and to convey this in a way that is clear and elegant.

A comparison with a written message may be helpful. A badly written paragraph, letter, or newspaper story, even if confusing and ungrammatical, can give accurate information, thus serving its basic purpose of conveying a message. The same content can be expressed in writing that communicates with clarity and ease, even writing that becomes a pleasure to read, or, at best, a form of art that goes far beyond the simple purpose of factual communication.

The old issues of *content* and *form* arise here. In design, purpose and structure make up the *content* of the visual product the designer creates. The *form* in which that content is expressed can be clumsy, confused, inappropriate, and sloppy. It can also be clear, organized, expressive of the design process and its methods, and expressive also of its time and place, its social context, and the ideas of the designer.

ANALYZING EXISTING SPACES

The generalizations offered here become more meaningful when they are applied to actual spaces that can be seen in drawings and photographs or, better still, visited and used. Direct comparison of good examples and bad examples can make theoretical points seem less abstract and more useful in real situations that call for evaluation. It is a helpful exercise to analyze some real interiors, choosing an outstandingly fine example and a distressingly unsatisfactory example in each of several functional categories. A possible list of candidates might include:

> A public space (lobby or concourse)
> A classroom
> An office
> A restaurant
> A living room
> A kitchen

Analysis can then proceed by developing evaluation under the familiar headings of function, materials and structure, and visual expression, as in Table 1.

Many other observations will probably come to mind under each heading in the presence of an actual example. Similar tests can be applied to the various objects that make up a complete interior—the pieces of furniture, furniture systems, lamps and light fixtures, small accessories, and other individual objects that can each be viewed separately as a *design*.

Although the character of design may vary greatly from place to place and is subject to constant change over the passage of time, an analysis of the sort proposed will serve in every case, provided that time and place are taken into account. A castle, a palace, a cathedral, an igloo, or a yurt can be evaluated on this basis as logically and reasonably as can the most recent office, apartment, or loft. These standards apply equally to future directions destined to lead to design different from anything we now know. It is the obligation of every designer to work toward the highest levels of excellence that the realities of problems and the available solutions will permit.

Table 1. Evaluating Spaces

FUNCTION

Excellent Example	*Unsatisfactory Example*
Size and shape of space well suited to purpose	Size and shape awkward and inconvenient
Placement and choice of furniture support use	Placement and choice of furniture inappropriate
Circulation well planned and convenient	Awkward circulation patterns
Good lighting	Unsatisfactory lighting
Satisfactory acoustical environment	Excessive noise and distraction

MATERIALS AND STRUCTURE

Excellent Example	*Unsatisfactory Example*
Choice of materials supports functional performance	Materials unsuitable to intended uses
Adequate durability and ease of maintenance	Materials subject to rapid wear and hard to maintain
Workmanship of good quality	Obvious shoddy workmanship
Appropriate cost of construction	Excessive cost of construction
Consideration of safety and environmental conditions	Dangerous and hazardous conditions possible

VISUAL EXPRESSION

Excellent Example	*Unsatisfactory Example*
Character and atmosphere appropriate to use	Unsuitable atmosphere and visual character
Time and place of design expressed	False or obscure expression of time and place
Character and quality of materials and construction honestly expressed	Materials and structure falsified or obscured
Design intentions clear and strongly developed	Design intention vague or confused

DESIGN BASICS

Interior design is a complex subject involving many related considerations. These include building structure, functional planning, concern with spatial form in three dimensions, the relationships of one space to another, the placement of solid objects (furniture and accessories) within larger spaces, and effects of color, pattern, texture, and light. As a practical matter, these issues are usually thought about one by one, and they can be studied as separate, individual topics. In designing an interior, however, the aim is always to weave them together in order to create a whole that is more than the sum of its parts.

The term *basic design* indicates a body of ideas about design that is so general, so universal in application as to transcend the special and detailed concerns of design projects. Basic design deals with theories and principles that refer to all aspects of *all* design. Many design schools present basic design in introductory courses (sometimes called *foundation* courses) that explore these basic issues in an abstract way, apart from specific design applications.

An understanding of basic design principles can evolve "from the bottom up," through the experience of working on design projects. However, an introductory study of basics viewed "from the top down," that is, beginning with abstract and general concepts, including line, form, space, balance, rhythm, and harmony, can be useful in developing a framework of thought within which to relate the more everyday realities of design practice. Any hope for a set of "rules" that will guarantee design excellence must be put aside. Design, especially interior design, involves so many variables that these concepts can be used only to support the more intuitive ways of designing that have served for thousands of years. This chapter presents some of these basic issues as they might be presented in many design schools. (Since a full treatment of color theory is given in Chapter 9, it is dealt with only briefly here.)

DESIGN AND HUMAN PERCEPTION

Visual Perception

The designer's aim is to make the realities of a designed space—its form, materials, furnishings, accessories, and so on—express in an appropriate way a set of ideas that the designer wishes to communicate. Since vision is the primary sense through which the design and the ideas behind it will reach an audience, basic design must be concerned with the field, both scientific and artistic, called *visual perception*. This study explores the ways in which the visual sense works to build a mental understanding of objects, spaces, and total environments through sight. No verbal description can ever equal the knowledge of reality that comes from actually seeing, although substitute visual images—that is, pictures—can to some extent approach the direct experience. While seeing is such a common experience as to seem to require no explanation, it actually involves many complex processes.

The mind pieces together its understanding of a three-dimensional object from information it receives from both eyes, each of which sends slightly different views. In addition, eye, head, and body movements supply a flow of changing images that, put together, create a mental *model* of the reality. This model can then be held in memory and viewed in the absence of the actual object.

This same process, combined with the physical action of walking, gives us an understanding of space. It is a special quality of space that its experience implies, even requires, movement. We must go *into* a space in order to see it, learn what it is like, and experience its unique qualities. Complex, multispace structures demand that we walk from one space to another, which involves not only motion but also time. Since motion cannot be thought of apart from time, the modern physical concept of space-time becomes useful in designing interiors.

3.1 In a house on Nantucket, Massachusetts, windows and doors in a second-story study allow for maximum light and views, creating an inviting indoor/outdoor space. Mark Hampton was the designer. (Photograph: © William Waldron, courtesy HG)

3.2

This concept is illustrated by a visit to a large building, a cathedral, a museum, or a concert hall, in which a full exploration of the interior space requires passing from room to room and from one level to another. We understand such a space not as a single entity fixed in time but as a sequence of experiences. As we add each new experience of the space in our progress through it, we substitute memories for the actual experience. The smallest of spatial sequences—a small house, a tiny apartment, even a single room—displays this quality to some degree. In order to truly know and understand any space, we must walk into it, look about in all directions—to all sides, up and down—sit down, move around, and spend some time building up a series of impressions that combine into our final idea of the space.

Visual Impressions

In addition to the understanding of reality that comes with vision and movement, a viewer receives impressions of a more abstract, even emotional, character. An object or a place may *look* quiet or lively, cheerful or depressing, solid or vaporous. We learn that a fire or bright sunlight is hot or warm, and so we associate the colors red and orange

with heat. We see the sharp edges of tables and boxes and learn that they also feel hard and sharp, while the soft forms of cushions and draped fabric become associated with the sensation of softness. The horizontal surfaces of the sea, a lake, or a meadow connect repose with horizontality. The sturdy upright of a tree trunk relates naturally to a sense of solidity and stability. The bright colors of birds and flowers carry associations different from the browns and grays of earth and rocks.

All of these associations are reinforced by the kinetic impressions that we receive from our own bodily positions and movements. We learn that a horizontal position *is* restful, while standing upright promotes attention, formality, even resistance. When running, we lean forward in an aggressive diagonal. While we experience bodily *symmetry* as normal and stable, we can move body parts into *asymmetrical* positions, but we learn to do this in a way that maintains *balance*. A person tilted to one side will fall over unless the body is repositioned to maintain balance or support is found by leaning on or holding on to something.

Objects designed by humans also contribute to this buildup of interpretive reactions. We see an automobile or airplane that is capable of

3.2 Soft and curving shapes connote relaxation and ease in a New York apartment living room designed in 1983 by Juan Montoya. (Photograph: Jaime Ardiles-Arce)

3.3 Strong verticals suggest solidity, formality, and dignity in this living room in the Atlanta, Georgia, home of architect John Portman. John Portman & Associates, designer. (Photograph: Jaime Ardiles-Arce)

fast movement, and we come to say that the typical forms *look* fast, even when the object is at rest. When a room strikes us as cheerful, restful, dignified, or businesslike, we may be reacting to memory traces of experiences with rooms that looked a certain way and that turned out to *be* a certain way. It is difficult to say whether this is due to individual characteristics, such as shape, pattern, or color, or whether it comes from a total impression of the sort that the Gestalt school of psychology studies. Basic design begins with a study of the individual elements that go together to form the totality of a *gestalt*.

ELEMENTS OF DESIGN

It is convenient to follow a progression in considering how visual impressions are developed.

Point

As conceived in geometry, a point is simply a location in space having neither dimensions nor substance—an abstract notion difficult to grasp. Two points, however, suggest a beginning and an end and lead to the idea of a connecting line (fig. 3.5). Points in a random scatter

3.4

3.4 In this library of a renovated 1920s Texas home, interior designer Mark Hampton created an atmosphere of comfort and luxury by means of warm colors and rich textures. Objects on display range from pre-Columbian pieces to part of a collection of Austrian bird bronzes. (Photograph: Feliciano, courtesy House & Garden)

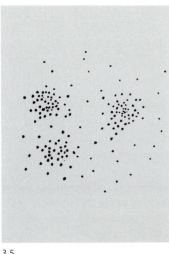

3.5

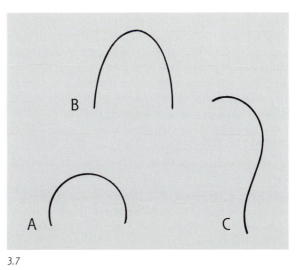

3.6   3.7

seem meaningless, but a cluster of points in a field of scatter suggests a focus or concentration of interest (fig. 3.6).

Line

When a point moves through space or when two points are connected, *line* is generated. Line, which may be straight or curved, has length but not breadth. We seem to see lines where things have edges, where one plane meets another, or where there is a change of color or surface in a plane. Straight lines can be thought of as taking several typical positions:

VERTICAL LINES. These suggest stability and immobility, and, by extension, dignity and permanence. The significance of verticality comes, it seems, from the downward direction of the force of gravity. This force dictates verticals, always perpendicular to all horizontals, as the basic structural support. The vertical columns of a building suggest its solidity and permanence.

HORIZONTAL LINES. These suggest rest and repose. Gravity pulls materials down to a horizontal resting point parallel to the ground in a horizontal line, and earth and sky seem to meet in a horizontal. Human experience of the horizontal reclining position in rest and sleep reinforces these perceptions. Floors and ceilings, normally horizontal, are the surfaces that give spaces their sense of reassuring normality.

OBLIQUE (DIAGONAL OR SLOPING) LINES. These suggest movement, dynamic forces, and activity. Angled lines are always, in a sense, transitional between vertical and horizontal, the positions that gravity tolerates, and are held only through some special means of resistance to gravitational forces. A person leans forward to run, making us associate activity and movement with oblique lines.

While there can be only one horizontal and one vertical direction, oblique lines can take an infinite number of angular slopes. The combi-

nation of oblique lines in alternate directions, called a *zigzag*, gives a sense of restless, rapid hyperactivity. It is used to symbolize lightning, electricity, and radio waves. A sloping ceiling or wall makes a space seem active, lively, even possibly disturbing through its implication of movement.

CURVED LINES. The path of a moving point that continually changes its direction gives a curved line. Curving forms occur more often in nature than rectilinear forms, leading us to perceive curvatures as more natural, freer, and more "humane" than straight-lined forms. Circles and segments of circles, having a simple and clear geometric genesis, appear straightforward. More complex curvatures, such as ellipses, parabolas, and hyperbolas, are more varied and more subtle. *Free curves* that have no geometric controls and combinations of curvatures in S shapes or sinuous relationships suggest increasing levels of complexity, subtlety, and softness.

Two-Dimensional Forms

A *plane* is a completely flat surface, created by intersecting lines. Planes are *two dimensional*, with length and width, as are plane figures—figures that lie completely in one plane—such as the triangle, square, circle, and so on. Planes also contain irregular or free shapes that conform to no particular geometric definition. The human mind seems to be drawn toward recognition of simple geometric shapes, perhaps because, being perfect forms, they can be held in memory and reproduced with ease. In a scatter of points, the eye will seek out a triangle, square, or circle or find an image with a recognizable form (fig. 3.9). The constellations of the night sky are images suggested by the relationships of bright stars seen as points. The Big Dipper, for example, is simply an arrangement of bright points that suggests the form of a long-handled cup. Once that grouping is pointed out and named, it becomes easy to locate and recognize amid the vast number of other stars that surround it (fig. 3.11).

3.5 In a random scatter of points, any cluster becomes a focus of attention. The three clusters here bring to mind the form of a triangle.

3.6 Any two points will generate a sense of relationship (A), which is mentally translated into a connecting line (B).

3.7 Curving lines suggest softness and freedom. Segments of circles (A) carry some stability; segments of parabolas (B) and other more complex geometric forms are both freer and more subtle; free curves (C)—curves that are not parts of circles or any other geometric figures—may be flowing, aggressive, or active.

Design makes wide use of our attraction to perfect shapes, whose completeness and stability we find highly satisfying. Imperfect shapes, such as a square with a corner cut off or one irregular side, a circle with a dent, or a shape not fully closed, cause a sense of tension, which may be used to create a more dynamic, unusual design (fig. 3.1). However, if the "imperfection" is too strong, it leads to outright dissatisfaction and a sense of instability.

More complex forms, such as rectangles of various proportions, other quadrilaterals, polygons, and curved forms, regular and irregular, all have both practical uses and expressive visual qualities of varied sorts.

Surfaces, as they occur in reality—rather than in abstract geometry—also have physical attributes, including:

TEXTURE (ROUGH, SMOOTH, MATTE, GLOSSY, HARD, SOFT)
VALUE (LIGHT, MEDIUM, DARK)
COLOR (HUE AND SATURATION; SEE CHAPTER 9, "COLOR")
PATTERN
TRANSPARENCY, TRANSLUCENCY, OR OPACITY

A surface may be unified, as, for example, a wall painted one color, or it may be subdivided by changes of material, color, or pattern and may also intersect with other surfaces. Transparent and semitransparent surfaces can create complex visual effects, including the spatial illusions resulting from reflections in polished surfaces such as glass and mirror. Surfaces have an almost inevitable relationship with lines since their edges, boundaries of subdivisions, and intersections are seen as lines. In the fine arts, the mediums of painting, drawing, and printmaking are concerned with two-dimensional surface.

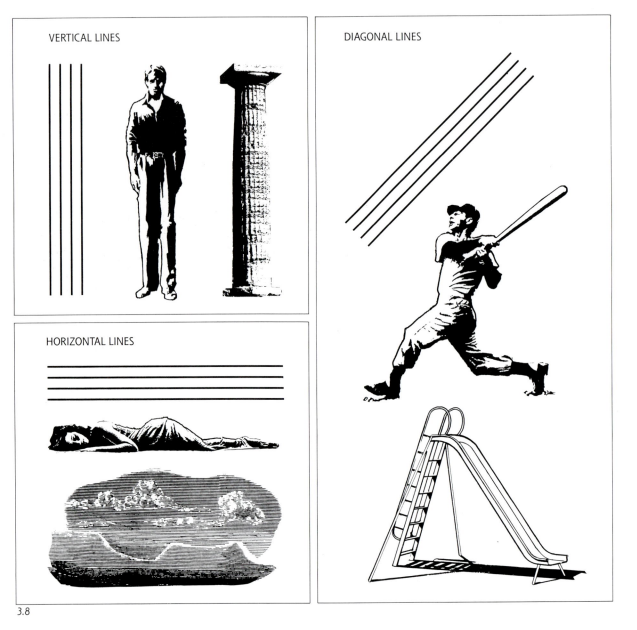

3.8

3.8 Dominant vertical lines contribute to a sense of dignity and solidity. Horizontality relates to feelings of tranquility, calm, and repose. Diagonal forms suggest movement and the dynamic relationship of forces; they promote feelings of activity and motion. In excess, they can be disturbing.

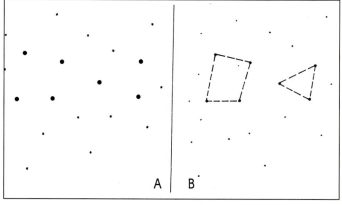

3.9

Three-Dimensional Forms

Adding depth, or volume, to a two-dimensional form creates a *three-dimensional form*. Furniture, some architectural elements (such as columns or stairs), and buildings are three-dimensional solids. Interior design is particularly concerned with hollow three-dimensional form, or space: rooms or other spaces within buildings, which are the primary element of interior design. Hollow space is articulated by planes of enclosure, that is, floors, walls, and ceilings, which separate space inside from space outside and determine the nature of the interior space.

In most interior spaces, the planes of floors, walls, and ceilings are organized in 90-degree, or right-angled, relationships, usually called *rectilinear*, which are considered the most stable of forms. In fact, such boxlike room forms are so common that they have come to be criticized for their monotony and lack of imagination. Small, boxlike enclosed spaces can suggest confinement and restriction or, on the other hand, privacy and intimacy.

Nonrectilinear three-dimensional room forms can be generated by using non-right-angled relationships for one or more of the enclosing planes, as, for example, a sloping ceiling or an angled wall, or by the use of curving planes of enclosure. Curved forms, because they are not

so sharply defined by lines, suggest openness and free space. Round or elliptical rooms have a special character, while domes as a ceiling or roof inspire feelings of grandeur and awe by suggesting the infinite openness of the universe. Domes automatically make an internal space special, even monumental, as, for example, the rotundas of many famous buildings.

Complex hollow space can be developed by connecting several simpler forms (as in the design of Gothic and Renaissance churches, whose plans are usually based on connecting quadrilaterals and semicircles); by opening simple spaces into one another with large doorways, open wells, and similar devices; or by providing more than one level in a single space. Stairways, in addition to offering oblique planes, can be designed in complex three-dimensional terms, such as the helix of the popular spiral stair. These are all common ways to introduce movement, openness, and variety into a space. Complex spaces can also include areas of intimacy without losing their impression of openness, as, for example, when a lowered ceiling is used over a conversation area that looks out to an open space beyond it. (A more detailed discussion of the role of three-dimensional space as a key element in all interior design will be presented below, following the continued discussion of concepts regarded as fundamental to all design activities.)

3.11

DESIGN CONCEPTS

In organizing line, surface, and hollow space, a number of other basic concepts will enter into design decisions. Some of these concepts are:

Size

We think of things as large or small in relative terms, in relation to both the human body and other things. A large living room may be much smaller than a large church, but it appears large in relation to an adjacent small entrance hall. Absolute size is usually less important than relative size.

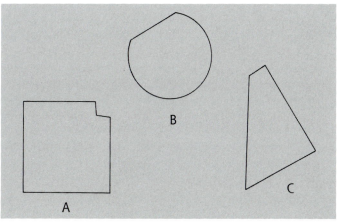

3.10

3.9 In a random scatter of points (A), the mind and eye search out relationships that can be seen as recognizable geometric figures (B).

3.10 Figures that would form a simple geometric shape but for some irregularity are perceived as being defective, cause the mind to struggle to supply a "correction." Figure A is clearly a square, slightly modified. B is seen as an imperfect circle. C appears as a truncated triangle rather than the irregular quadrangle that it actually is.

3.11 In the random scatter of points that stars form in the night sky, the brighter stars seem to form patterns. Once it is pointed out, the Big Dipper becomes a familiar and easily spotted pattern, since its shape suggests a familiar form.

3.12

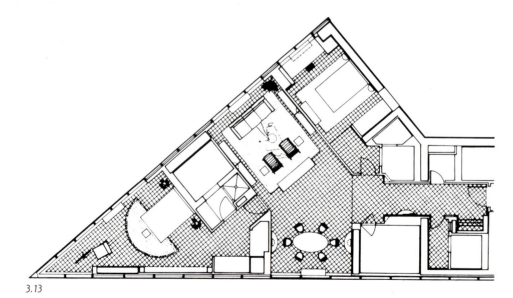

3.13

3.12, 3.13 The diagonal lines and angular and broken shapes of this bedroom give rise to a sense of activity and motion. The plan shows the apartment's unusual triangular layout, which inspired the room's design. The associations with a ship are intentional; the

space is treated as a lookout, with a telescope pointing toward the apex of the triangle. The chair, titled Hell's Angel, is by Patrick Naggar. Andrée Putman designed this 1987 showcase apartment in New York's Metropolitan Tower. (Photograph: © Peter Paige)

3.14 With its curved form and soaring height, a dome lifts a building from the ordinary to the monumental. Many historic religious and government interiors have taken advantage of the monumentality of domes; here, for the lobby of

the Dow Jones office building in New York (1986), architect Cesar Pelli used a domed space to confer a monumental character on a business setting. (Photograph: © 1986 Wolfgang Hoyt/ESTO)

3.15

3.16

Scale

This term is widely used in design and architecture to describe a rather subtle consideration related to size. It refers to the proportion of an object or space to all other objects, to human beings, and to the space to which it belongs. Designers achieve *good scale* by choosing elements that seem to be of an appropriate size for the space they will inhabit, that relate well to human dimensions, and, above all, that look their actual size. Small pieces of furniture often look lost in a large space, while large objects may seem overbearing when crammed into a small room. A large space that appears too small is out of scale. Good scale is indicated when things look so right that the issue does not even come to mind.

Proportion

This concept addresses the relationship of parts of a design to each other and to the whole. Good proportion is a much-discussed concept in the arts and in design and is considered a key requirement in any aesthetic success. It is not hard to tell if an existing space is well or badly proportioned. In the former case, it looks visually "right"; in the latter case, a room may seem too long and narrow, or an element such as a door, window, or piece of furniture may appear awkwardly placed. Achieving good proportions is less easy than recognizing them, although many efforts have been made to develop systems for doing so.

One approach, using mathematical relationships analogous to the rules of harmony in music, suggests organizing proportions according to geometric ratios of simple whole numbers, such as 1:2, 2:3, 3:4, and 3:5. Many Renaissance architects, including Palladio and Alberti, based their structures on such systems (figs. 3.19–3.21). Other approaches, such as the *Modulor* of Le Corbusier (fig. 3.23), base

3.15 Circular forms imply freeness and sometimes even humor. Here, in the Aurora restaurant of 1985 in New York, repeating clusters suggest balls, tops, or, perhaps, soap bubbles. Philip George and Milton Glaser were the designers. (Photograph: © Peter Mauss/ESTO)

3.16 The basic geometric rectilinear shapes—the square, rectangle, and triangle—form the basis for most interior design. A top-floor area in a Santa Monica, California, house of 1982 by Buzz Yudell, architect, with Charles Jencks, juxtaposes all three shapes. (Photograph: Tim Street-Porter)

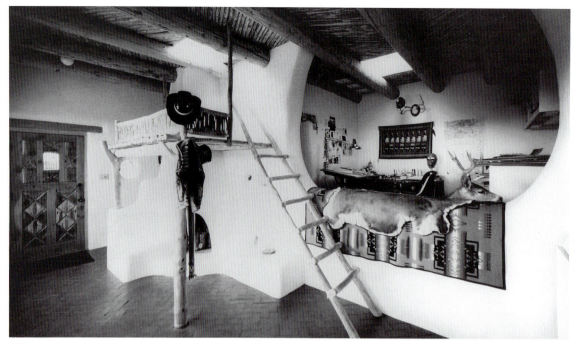

3.17

dimensional units on human body proportions, such as height and arm reach, and extend these through numerical multiplication into a system for controlling dimensions and their relationships.

The *Modulor* also makes use of one particular mathematical relationship, often referred to as the *golden ratio* or *golden section* and designated by the Greek letter phi (φ). It has had so much influence on design throughout history as to deserve some special discussion. The terms *golden mean*, *golden ratio*, and *golden section* all refer to a proportional relationship that satisfies a certain requirement. If one divides a line into two unequal segments so that the ratio of the short segment to the long segment equals the ratio of the long segment to the total line length (the short segment plus the long segment), this requirement is satisfied. The resulting ratio

$$\frac{.618}{1} = \frac{1}{1.618}$$

is expressed in the irrational number .618....

This proportion can be found in the designs of many famous structures and works of art. Various experiments and comparisons of measurements show a strong preference for the golden ratio among human beings and a high level of occurrence in nature.

Harmony, Unity, Variety, Contrast

These terms describe concepts with clear bearing on design, although no precise way of defining an "ideal" measure for *harmony* describes the combination of elements and other principles in a way that produces consonance. In order to achieve harmony, all the varied components of an interior, like the notes in a chord, must relate to each other and to the overall theme of the design (fig. 3.29).

3.18

3.17 A partially enclosing wall with an unusual, horseshoe-shaped opening creates a secluded alcove. John Nieto, an artist, designed this space for his adobe house in New Mexico. (Photograph: © 1985 Michael Skott)

3.18 Small, unusually shaped display cases lighted from within draw attention to the jewelry in Pomellato, a shop in Milan, Italy. Maroon and white detailing on the gray marble walls and

staircase adds a striking visual accent. Marco Duina and Gian Luigi Pieruzzi were the architects. (Photograph: Federico Brunetti/Milano I, courtesy Marco Duina and Gian Luigi Pieruzzi Architects)

3.19 Geometric analysis can demonstrate the mathematical basis behind many classical and Renaissance designs. This plan of Palladio's Villa Foscari (La Malcontenta) at Mira (A) is based on simple arithmetic proportions (B). If the smallest dimensional unit is given a value of 1, the width of the building can be seen to be divided into a rhythmic sequence of 2-1-2-1-2 (mak-

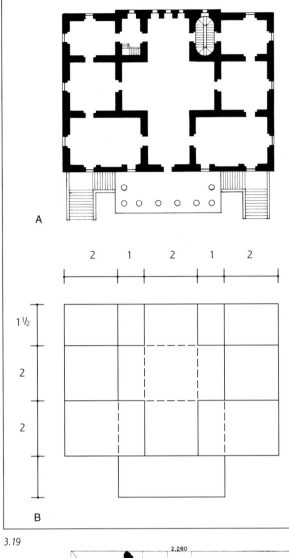

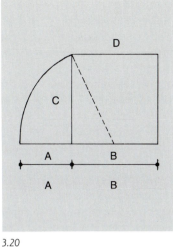

3.20

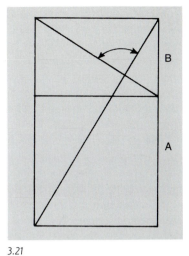

3.21

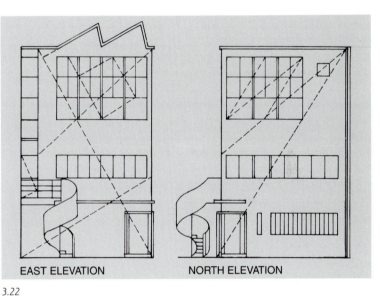

EAST ELEVATION   NORTH ELEVATION

3.22

3.19

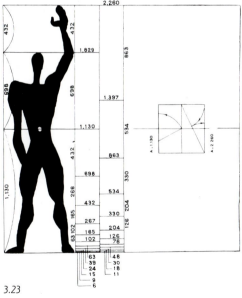

3.23

Unity allows the viewer to experience a design as a whole rather than seeing it as a collection of elements. All the parts of the design will relate so well as to create a unit in which, ideally, nothing can be added, taken away, or altered without changing the totality. Matching or coordinated patterns, closely related colors, and stylistic consistency all lead to harmony and unity, but they also carry the threat of monotony, as in the room in which everything matches everything else in an obsessive way.

Variety and contrast, the countervailing qualities of harmony and unity, can relieve monotony, giving the eye a number of different shapes, textures, colors, or details to look at (fig. 3.30). Contrast heightens values through comparison. A light color will seem lighter if placed near a dark color, a large object larger in contrast with something small. In this context, contrast and variety may be viewed as ways to punctuate harmony and unity, heightening the space's overall impact.

ing a total of 8 units). The length turns out to total 5½ units, divided in the somewhat more complex relationship of 2-2-1½. (The relationships can also be expressed in whole numbers by giving the smallest unit the value of 2. The width is expressed as 4-2-4-2-4; the length as 4-4-3. The totals are then W = 16, L = 11. Reducing these fig-

ures to a ratio gives a proportional relationship of 11:16 or .687).

3.20 To divide a line into golden ratio proportions, a dotted line is drawn from the midpoint of side B of the square to the intersection of sides C and D; then an arc is swung downward to the base line. A/B forms a golden ratio.

3.21 A golden rectangle with a square cut off (A) produces a smaller golden rectangle (B). The diagonals of the larger and smaller rectangles intersect at a right angle.

3.22 In his design for the Ozenfant House in Paris (1922), Le Corbusier used the golden ratio as the basis of his design geometry. This diagram is

based on the illustration he used in Towards a New Architecture (1923).

3.23 Le Corbusier's Modulor is a modern, complex system that uses geometric ratios based on the proportions of the human body to determine the patterns of architectural design.

Balance

This principle concerns the achievement of a state of equilibrium between forces. We are familiar with balance through our direct experience with gravity, which exerts a force on us that we must counter by maintaining an upright position or using a support that holds us up in a secure relationship. Visually, we find unbalanced relationships tenuous and disturbing, while balanced relationships look normal, at rest, and comfortable (fig. 3.24).

There are several ways to achieve balance. The most obvious balanced relationships are *symmetrical,* in which the arrangement of forms on one side of an imaginary central dividing line, axis, or plane is the mirror image of the other side. Such bilateral symmetry is characteristic of the human body and the forms of many living creatures. It is thus associated with the beauty of nature. In design, the identical visual weights and the importance of the center create an effect of repose and dignity. A high proportion of historic buildings, interiors, and objects exhibit the symmetrical balance of bilateral organization. Symmetrical balance can be achieved around a larger number of axes as well. *Radial symmetry* establishes balance around a central point, as, for example, the hub of a wheel, with the design elements radiating out like the wheel's spokes (fig. 3.26).

A more subtle concept, *asymmetrical* balance brings into equilibrium elements that are equivalent but not matching. The principle is demonstrated by a scale of the type in which an object is weighed by moving a weight closer to or farther away from a balance point. A small weight hanging from a long arm will balance a heavy weight placed close to the fulcrum, or balance point (fig. 3.27). This concept, in which different things of different size or weight seem to come into balance through placement, can also apply to shapes, colors, sizes, and other aspects of objects.

Symmetrical and asymmetrical design are often a product of the architectural structure of a space. For instance, a house with a center hall and rooms of similar size to right and left begins with a built-in symmetrical structure that leads naturally to visual symmetry in its design (fig. 3.25). Other building plans and room layouts cannot offer symmetry. A room may have windows on one side only, or an entrance located to the left or right of center. In such situations, asymmetry is best accepted and the room brought into aesthetic balance by means other than strict symmetry. Some historic designs used false elements (a dummy door, for example) to force symmetry where it did not occur naturally. This kind of solution rarely works in modern practice.

In addition, symmetry tends to express a sense of formality, dignity, stability, and conservatism. The more the central axis is emphasized, the more strongly these values will be felt—as in many traditional designs for church and temple interiors, courtrooms, throne rooms, and similar ceremonial interiors. A centered fireplace and mantel or a large central window or door in an otherwise symmetrical room add to the feeling of formality. Asymmetry, in contrast, suggests more openness to change, a more informal and active intention. Many modern buildings and interiors employ asymmetry to express these qualities.

Rhythm

Another concept borrowed from music, *rhythm* relates visual elements together in a regular pattern. It can be achieved by *repetition,* whether simple, as in a rhythm such as 1 1 1 1, or more complex, as in *1* 111 *1* 111 *1* 111 *1*. The number 1 might stand for a window opening, a column, or a subdivision in a paneled wall.

The mind enjoys rhythm, and it is an important element in both historic and modern design (figs. 3.33, 3.34). The classic architectural

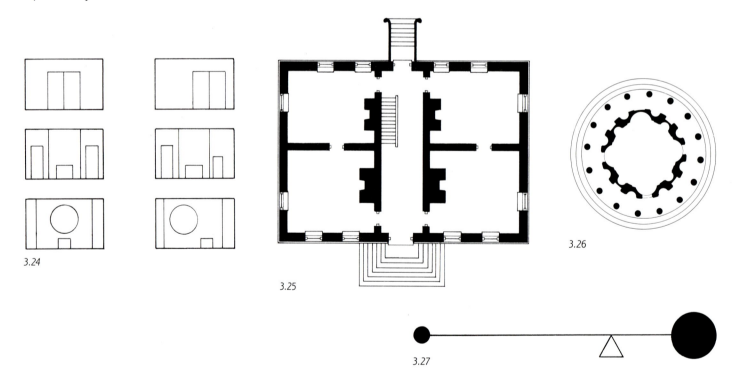

3.24

3.25

3.27

3.26

3.24 *Symmetrical balance demands exact equality between two sides of a composition. A centered doorway seems normal; the same door slightly off-center is disturbing (A). Identical elements on each side of a fireplace are perfectly balanced; a smaller door on the right is perceived as an error (B). The displacement of the central element in C is similarly disturbing.*

3.25 *Bilateral (two-sided) symmetry is familiar as the basis for the planning of many buildings, with rooms, windows, and other elements carefully placed on each side of a central axis to create the kind of balanced pattern that occurs in many natural forms, including the human body. This plan of an American Colonial house is a typical example.*

3.26 *In radial symmetry, elements are arranged around one or more central points like the spokes radiating from a wheel. This plan of Bramante's Tempietto at S. Pietro in Montorio in Rome is radially symmetrical around four axes. Most radially symmetrical plans have two or possibly four axes of symmetry. Other numbers of axes, even odd numbers such as three or five, are possible, if unusual.*

3.27 *The concept of asymmetrical balance relates to the physical laws that make it possible for a light weight on a long lever arm (left) to balance a heavier weight on a short lever arm (right).*

3.28

orders (Doric, Ionic, and Corinthian) are rhythmic systems (see figs. 4.6–4.8), while modern modular furniture and structural systems generate rhythmic patterns. The use of rhythm—the choice of small or large units, close together or widely spaced—should be appropriate to the situation. Since repetition can lead to monotony, it must also be balanced against the need for variety.

Emphasis

One of the ways to transmit meaning in design is through emphasis, which ensures that important elements *look* important while minor and trivial elements look subordinate. This is achieved through balancing size, placement, value, color, and selection of materials. A large door centrally placed becomes a point of focus. A brightly colored object in an otherwise quiet space calls attention to itself.

The designer must decide the levels of importance of all the elements that make up an interior and then find a visual expression for each of these levels, from the most important through the less important to the least important. A handsome fireplace mantel centered in one wall of a room is a natural focal point (fig. 3.31) that is emphasized by placing a fine painting above the mantel. Placing the seating furniture—a sofa and chairs, perhaps—so that it relates to the fireplace while choosing a suitable cover fabric that does not compete with the painting will give the furniture grouping a secondary level of importance. Carpet, ceiling color, and lighting can be treated to appear neutral, almost unnoticeable. Alternatively, a colorful and strongly patterned rug, a strikingly designed seating group, or a spectacular light fixture could be an emphatic focus, in which case the other elements would be deliberately subordinated.

3.29

3.28 In a pre-Revolutionary farmhouse beside the Brandywine River, Pennsylvania, now the home of Jamie and Phyllis Wyeth, contrasting white and navy blue give the bedroom qualities of crispness, some formality, and cool and calm order. Wyeth's painting, Wicker, hangs over the fireplace; an oil study by Rockwell Kent is above the books between the two French provincial chairs. The room was designed by the owners. (Photograph: © François Halard, courtesy House & Garden)

3.29 The repetition of square and rectangular patterns characteristic of the Vienna Secessionist style endows this hotel breakfast room in the Villa Mozart, Merano, Italy, with a sense of unity and harmony. It was designed by the owner. (Photograph: © 1985 Ronny Jacques/Photo Researchers)

3.30

Pattern and Ornament

Smooth surfaces are defined only by their limits, edges, or corners. A patterned surface has visible presence in every part of its extent. The eye focuses on *pattern* and uses it to help measure size and shape, to gain information about material, and to interpret the mood of the design. The fact that pattern is usually repetitious gives it rhythmic qualities on a small scale. Like color—or used in combination with color—pattern can make a surface more or less important or a space seem larger or smaller than it actually is. For example, stripes running vertically make a surface seem narrower and higher, and running horizontally, wider and lower.

At the same time, the elements of a pattern can convey messages. Little flowers and regular stripes create very different moods. Geometric squares and naturalistic curves imply different attitudes. In addition to such expressive qualities, pattern has the ability to hide, or at least minimize, soiling and visible traces of damage. Plain surfaces expose every flaw, while pattern tends to camouflage imperfections.

Ornament refers to visual extras unnecessary for practical reasons but added to show off craftsmanship, introduce variety, and enrich a uniform surface. Ornament played a prominent role in most design of the historical periods. The moldings, eggs and darts, Greek keys, and similar motifs of classical design, and the carved leaves and gargoyles of medieval design clearly express the thinking and the craft skills of their respective eras.

With modern mechanical reproduction, ornament became easier to produce but less meaningful, no longer made by a skilled craftsman for a particular context. The modern movement has often responded by omitting ornament entirely. (Adolf Loos went so far as to say, "Ornament is a crime.") Still, the gleaming edges of glass, chrome, and marble in the modern interior serve some of the same purposes as applied ornament. Recently, ornament seems to have been rediscovered. It now appears in much contemporary work, often quite brashly and aggressively as an expressive tool (fig. 3.35).

In all ornamentation, the key to value is the issue of *meaning*. Why is the ornament there? Does it add something or does it merely cover over and confuse? Good ornament emphasizes what is important, draws attention to what is significant, and tells something about the materials and workmanship involved. The molding around a door or window emphasizes that element's size, shape, and position. Moldings at a cornice or baseboard strengthen the line of intersection of walls, floor, and ceiling. A rosette where a light fixture hangs from a ceiling makes the place of hanging more important. The moldings around panels of furniture or room interiors make the size, shape, and pattern of the paneling stronger, clearer, and more decisive. Carved detail on a chair tells us the place and time of its origin, as well as something about the attitudes and crafts skill of its maker. An object that serves a useful function can at the same time become an expressive carrier of

3.30 *This bedroom in Milan, Italy, combines dramatically diverse styles—antique and modern furniture together with striking modern art within a space of markedly historic character—to achieve both contrast and variety without jarring conflicts. (Photograph: Jaime Ardiles-Arce)*

3.31 *In a New York apartment of 1983 by designer Suzie Frankfurt, the fireplace, mantel, and picture form an emphatic axis, which is balanced by the niche at the left and the arrangement of furniture in an elegantly weighted, asymmetrical relationship. (Photograph: Lizzie Himmel)*

3.32 *In an attic living room of a house in France, daylight enters through the original windows to illuminate a Louis XV writing table. A concealed staircase on the right leads to an upper-level bathroom. Christian Badin was the designer. (Photograph: Roland Beaufre/Agence TOP, Paris)*

3.31

3.32

3.33

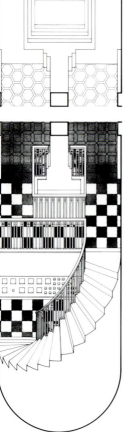

3.34

a message by the addition of meaningful painted surface designs. Ornament fails or clutters when it has no meaning, is introduced only for show, and has no real relationship with the object or space it adorns. However, when its purpose is genuine and useful, it can be a valuable communicative tool.

DESIGN AS AN EXPRESSIVE MEDIUM

The fundamental concern of interior design is how space can be used as an expressive medium. As they create and modify spaces, both architects and interior designers communicate ideas, concepts, and feelings to all those who see, use, and occupy those spaces. Although we may not be conscious of such meanings in any overt way, we can all think of places that have been depressing or inspiring, dignified or cheerful, snug and cozy, or bleak and cold. Many spaces are designed with little or no thought of such matters; created predominantly to serve some functional purpose or to be practical and economical, they

may have an impact on users that is inappropriate. Perhaps this does not matter in a warehouse or an automated factory; in spaces intended for human use, however, it can be disastrous.

Spaces can all too easily be monotonous, confusing, or claustrophobic, even while serving their primary purpose reasonably well. A hospital may house patients and visitors and provide all the special services needed for medical treatment yet still be cold and depressing. An office can provide spaces for desks, chairs, and office equipment but appear confusing and become tiresome. The skilled designer, while planning for functional efficiency, will also evaluate the messages that various forms of designed space can convey and will plan accordingly.

To convey the appropriate messages through spatial elements, the designer must develop a vocabulary of spatial meanings. Although such meanings are grasped by everyone, they are rarely studied or understood with clarity; once pointed out, many may seem obvious. The following survey can help to provide a basis for both creative decisions and design-proposal evaluations.

3.33, 3.34 The repetition of squares of different sizes and in different planes conveys a vigorously rhythmic effect in this 1983 New York project. An intriguing study of a stair hall from the same project demonstrates a similar rhythmic effect. Peter L. Gluck and Partners were the architects. (Photograph: © Norman McGrath)

The concept of space, a specific space, implies enclosure. The most familiar spaces are those we call rooms. Most rooms are boxlike, a quality that can suggest security, define areas of movement, and focus purpose—all positive meanings that have unhappy opposites, such as confinement, isolation, and boredom. A very small room, when properly designed, can be comforting, personal, and private; when poorly designed, it may suggest the claustrophobia of a cell. A large room can be dignified, exciting, even awe-inspiring; it can also be monotonous, confusing, and intimidating. Although size is not in itself a determinant of meaning, *relative size* is. In general, bigger means more important, smaller means less significant. Familiar terms such as "great hall," "master bedroom," or "manager's office" make us think of larger spaces, while "vestibule," "guest room," or "work station" suggest spaces at once smaller and less consequential.

The general rule that large equals important is not invariably trustworthy. It takes some special effort, however, to reverse it. A small space may be given added significance within a surround of larger elements, but it will require further treatment through shape, location, light, color, or some other means to give it real emphasis. A small chapel in a large cathedral, for example, might be given such value, as is the Oval Office in the White House, which gains impact from its unusual shape and central position.

Meanings associated with size can be emphasized by relationships between connecting spaces. A large space seems even bigger when

3.35

3.35 *The home of architect Charles Jencks and designer Maggie Keswick in England contains this architectural library with unusual, Gothic-accented bookcases. There is a symbolic intent: The bookcases speak of the books' con- tents using an ornamental vocabulary that refers to specific historic periods. Jencks and Keswick were the designers. (Photograph: © Richard Bryant, cour- tesy House & Garden)*

entered from a smaller space because the contrast exaggerates its quality, as when stepping into a sizable concert hall or church after passing through a little lobby or vestibule. Height variations are particularly striking in this way A very low ceiling in an access space makes the destination area seem dramatically higher than it may actually be.

Shape involves less obvious values. The familiar "box," or rectangular room, actually occurs in a variety of shapes. A square, the simplest of shapes, is easy to comprehend and so tends to imply stability and order through the identical dimension of each side. If the height matches the side dimension, forming a cube, that impression may be even stronger, suggesting monumentality through simplicity. Rectangles, the most common of shapes, have no particular meaning, although certain mathematical proportions (such as 3:5, or the *golden ratio* of 1:1.618, discussed above) seem to be more readily understandable and hence more aesthetic than random proportional relationships. The *double-cube room* of Wilton House in England is a well-known example of an impressive space whose elegance is augmented through its proportions of 1:2:1, literally double the shape of a cube. Box-form rooms that are longer than four times their width tend to become corridorlike, emphasizing lengthwise movement. A long, narrow living room, for example, seems to lack the central focus so crucial to a comfortable feeling of "together" containment. Such predominant length can be quite appropriate to spaces that are approaches to a destination or that serve as galleries through which people are expected to move. True corridors can become tedious and depressing if they appear to stretch into the remote distance.

Boxlike rooms sometimes seem both commonplace and stiff; curved forms, on the other hand, tend to communicate a sense of specialness, perhaps because they are in fact less common. Round rooms, often called *rotundas,* are favored by architects as monumental spaces; the rotunda of the U.S. Capitol in Washington, D.C., as well as those in numerous state capitol buildings, is but one example. Many churches and chapels are also round; the Pantheon in Rome (see page 70) was an especially valued Roman temple. A round room gives a powerful sense of enclosure and containment whether in a small African hut or in the large church at the Hôtel des Invalides in Paris. The dome, a popular roof for rotundas, adds to the sense of containment and also often provides acoustical effects of echoes or a *whispering gallery,* which further advance the feeling of specialness or even awe.

Rooms that are half round in plan are rare. The combination of a square or rectangular space with a half-round area generates a strong focus on the curved end. Used for a church or chapel, a courtroom, or an entrance hall, the form suggests concentration on a central point. More complex curved shapes, such as the oval and the ellipse, are less readily grasped at a glance and thus seem more subtle, possibly even mysterious. Irregularly curved spatial forms suggest freedom and flowing movement. When carried to extremes they become disturbing and confusing.

Every space, whatever its shape in plan, is strongly conditioned by its height and by the form of its roof or ceiling. Rooms that are low in relation to other dimensions can seem cozy and humane, as in many Frank Lloyd Wright houses, or oppressive, as in countless subway tunnels or in the dramatically claustrophobic interior of a submarine.

Height is generally considered to add an airy sense of openness to a space; at times it may also lead to a loss of desired intimacy. The high ceiling of Victorian parlors may make them seem pretentious. Small but very high rooms are sometimes found to be unpleasant and become targets for a *dropped ceiling,* which is thought to improve proportions. Very tall spaces are impressive locations for stairs and emphasize transitions between floor levels. The atrium spaces popular in many modern hotels and shopping spaces attempt grandeur through height; although they sometimes achieve it, more often than not the result is oppressive and meaningless.

The various types of vaults (the tunnellike *barrel vault,* the complexities of *groin vaults*) are important factors in the development of the special characteristics of many spaces in historic architecture. A curved ceiling, or a curved *cove* that softens the transition from wall to ceiling, can relieve the confining sense of boxiness in simple room shapes. Ceilings that stop at a distance away from walls to create a cove also add the impression of a *floating ceiling,* which deemphasizes the intersection of walls and ceilings. The reverse, a band of lower ceiling surrounding a higher middle area, can give a sense of differentiation between the central space and its edges, as is frequently seen in ballrooms, where the inner dance floor and the outer area of seating or tables are each related to their own height dimension. The triangular form generated by the common gable roof creates an internal space that repeats the associated external shape of the house, resulting in the familiar (although misnamed) *cathedral ceiling.* Sloping ceilings can also free spaces from boxiness, as occurs under a pent roof or an asymmetrical gable (see fig. 3.32).

As spatial forms are combined, the emerging complex spaces may express ideas with clarity or they may generate confusion. A clear shape slightly modified tends to introduce uncertainty and stress. A classic example is a room with a corner cut off with rectangular or diagonal planes. Sometimes such a form explains itself—the diagonal may accommodate a fireplace. A rectangular closet built into a corner, however, may explain itself but also suggests a makeshift concept of planning. A room with an added-on subsidiary space, such as a living room with a dining alcove or sleeping area, is a familiar combination that appears generally ambiguous unless the alcove has defined limits at each side (see fig. 3.17).

More complex spatial combinations can be studied in many well-known historic buildings, including churches with elements such as aisles, higher spaces with balconies or mezzanines, and round spaces with radiating or surrounding secondary spaces (see fig. 3.14). The Gothic cathedral, with its high central spaces, lower aisles, extending transepts, and choir, often with chapels clustered about, is a superb example of spatial complexity. It cannot be comprehended from any one position but must be explored by walking about, thus generating a kinesthetic or space-time experience.

As spaces are grouped, other meanings emerge. A row of identical spaces implies similarity of purpose (hotel rooms, offices, or hospital patient rooms) whether in a common straight line along a corridor or in staggered placement. Many small spaces combined with one or more larger areas implies a hierarchy of importance. Narrow and overly complex circulation paths generate confusion and annoyance. In

3.36

space relationships, as in all design, symmetry suggests equality of function, while asymmetry suggests a relationship having a single orientation. Stairs at each side of an area or the frequently encountered balanced placement of men's and women's restrooms typify the logic of symmetry. The relationship of a kitchen to a dining area is characteristic of an asymmetric relationship. Overlapping spaces occur in many modern plans where complexity and ambiguity are sought as goals. Unusual spaces imply unique or extraordinary intentions and can be quite successful in their very specialness. One thinks of I. M. Pei's triangular plan for the East Wing of the National Gallery of Art in Washington, D.C. (see fig. 4.79) and Frank Lloyd Wright's hexagon-based house plans or the helical interior space of his Guggenheim Museum (see fig. 4.64).

Spaces are rarely completely closed. Windows, doorways, and other openings not only relate spaces to one another but also communicate meanings about the nature of the relationship. A room with a door suggests potential isolation. A wide opening implies easy connection. Spaces such as balconies facilitate a relationship between two levels in which an observer on the upper level is both within and yet separated from the space below. Stairways and ramps provide actual movement between levels, as well as a transitional relationship that the use of elevators denies. Large windows forge a strong link with the exterior environment, pushed in some modern examples to an extreme in which

all-glass walls are used to escape from the enclosed quality of conventional spaces (see fig. 3.36).

Whatever their form, spaces are further modified by their contents and by the treatments of their surfaces. A room crowded with an excess of large furniture can seem small, and a low ceiling may seem even lower if painted a dark color. A glass wall can suggest expansiveness, openness, or, in a less positive context, a loss of privacy. A heavy door that closes with a firm sound suggests security and isolation. Massive, seemingly immovable furniture gives a feeling of permanence and stability but also communicates rigidity and even stodginess. Light, easily moved, portable, and demountable furniture, in contrast, communicates openness, flexibility, and activity but may also imply impermanence and instability.

The relationship of occupants to the spaces they use has become a stimulating field of study within environmental psychology. Issues of privacy and territoriality, the desire of individuals to modify or personalize a given space, and the ways in which space can influence behavior have all been the subjects of investigations by psychologists and anthropologists. Such much-discussed publications as E. T. Hall's *The Hidden Dimension*, Robert Sommer's *Personal Space*, and Corwin Bennett's *Spaces for People* have been influential in broadening designers' understanding of the interaction between people and the spaces they occupy.

3.36 A dramatic, unobstructed view of distant mountains becomes the primary design feature of an otherwise simple bedroom in a Colorado house. The 1990 project is by designers Ettore Sottsass and Johanna Grawunder. (Photograph: Antoine Bootz, courtesy Metropolitan Home)

4.1

CHAPTER

FOUR

DESIGN HISTORY

The history of interior design draws upon several different fields of scholarly study. It is based in architectural history, but incorporates elements of the decorative arts, including furniture, metalwork, glass, ceramics, and textiles, which are often collected and displayed separately. Many books deal with one or another of these subjects, often emphasizing the interests of antiquarians and collectors over those of the practicing designer. For the interior designer, such fragmentation hampers an understanding of the unified way in which all of these things developed together in a particular historic period. Current interest in interior design history emphasizes understanding design as an expression of its own time and as a resource for stimulating new ideas.

A different approach treats historic interior design as a basis for modern imitation. This view of history, which has an extensive literature, was dominant from the end of the nineteenth century until well into the twentieth century. During that period, the study of interior design was largely a matter of learning the historic periods in order to adapt or imitate them in the interiors of the eclectic buildings of the time. While the leaders of modernism rejected this approach, they were usually devoted students of historical design. However, over-enthusiastic followers, in their rebellion against imitative design, often seemed to encourage an indifference to historical study. The many educators among these followers passed this attitude down to their students.

Recent years have witnessed a renewed interest in historic design, not as a basis for imitation but as the foundation for a broad understanding of the lines of development that have led to current ways of thinking about design. Designers now demonstrate a fresh willingness to make references to historic elements in a new, modern context. Even if references are sometimes picked up quite literally, the intention is never the direct imitation of whole rooms or even whole buildings of the past. At the same time, there is heightened interest in preserving and restoring historic buildings and interiors, work in which a detailed and precise knowledge of history is vital.

In the space available here, it is not possible to do more than give a general outline of the essential development of interior design in the Western tradition, with names and terms important in describing historic work and the significant people who have influenced its direction. Several traditions of non-European design are also represented because they have influenced European and American design. Reading in the specialized literature of architectural and design history—increasingly available in scholarly and well-illustrated books—is an important part of every designer's education. Visiting actual historic interiors, in museums and, especially, in surviving buildings, is the best as well as the most enjoyable way to become fully aware of historical design development.

PREHISTORIC AND INDIGENOUS DESIGN

It is not uncommon for the modern viewer to find greater interest in prehistoric and indigenous design than in many of the period works of the more familiar cultures of the "civilized" world. Modern art has been strongly influenced by native art. While modern design may not have felt as deep an influence, there are often strong affinities between the directness of design by indigenous peoples and the most respected of modern work. Weavings such as rugs and blankets, pottery and baskets, and smaller household utensils from Africa, Oceania, and the Arctic and American Indian cultures are familiar examples of the kind

4.1 The eruption of Mount Vesuvius in A.D. 79, buried the city of Pompeii in lava, which preserved a remarkable variety of ancient Roman remains. The atrium of the house of Menander, circa A.D. 70, is an excellent example of Roman residential design, with its cen- *tral pool and opening to the sky, its fine Roman Doric columns, and its partially surviving wall frescoes. Private living spaces open off the atrium on all sides. (Photograph: Deutsches Archäologisches Institut, Rome)*

4.2

of design that seems as vital and significant as the best contemporary equivalents. There is little access, directly or through photographs, to the total interior in which such objects belong, but a sense of their complete environment can be generated from looking at both the individual objects and illustrations of the typical house structures.

ANCIENT WORLD

Egypt

The first major historic civilizations appeared in Egypt and in the Tigris–Euphrates valley of Mesopotamia. Knowledge of interiors from the latter region is fragmentary because the primary building material was unfired mud brick of poor lasting quality. Egypt, however, has left enduring visual evidence of its design because many temples and tombs were built of stone, some even cut into solid rock, and have survived well. The great pyramids at Giza (fig. 4.2) are remarkable not only for their great size but also for their purity of form and subtle geometry making use of the *golden section* proportion (see Chapter 3). The internal spaces of the pyramids, of minimal significance, are ingeniously arranged passages and chambers, tiny in relation to the total mass of these structures. Temples are characterized by the vast *hypostyle hall*, a large space filled with rows of columns to support stone roofing, the forms of the stone columns based either on earlier columns of bundled reeds plastered with mud or other plant forms. The Egyptian custom of carving and painting walls with written and illustrated inscriptions gives further information on the ancient Egyptian environment.

4.3

4.2 The pyramids of Egypt are among the oldest surviving and most impressive of all stone constructions. About 2,300,000 stone blocks, weighing approximately two and a half tons each, make up the largest of the three pyramids at Giza, Egypt. (Photograph: Hirmer Fotoarchiv)

4.3 The throne of Tutankhamen, from circa 1300 B.C., was discovered in the Pharaoh's tomb in 1922. Although it is elaborately carved and decorated to suit its ceremonial purpose, it exhibits the features of a classic Egyptian chair—most notably, the carefully joined wood-frame structure and seat.

The open seat frame supports a woven-rush surface. The animal feet of the chair are raised slightly in order to remain visible above the rush floor covering used in most Egyptian interiors. Egyptian Museum, Cairo. (Photograph: Jean Vertut)

4.4

Tombs have yielded up a wide range of objects, including furniture in good states of preservation, placed inside to accompany the body into an afterlife (fig. 4.3). The interiors of more everyday structures, such as houses, do not survive, but miniature models found in some tombs give an idea of the setting of Egyptian daily life (fig. 4.4). They suggest spaces with only minimal furniture, lively color in wall decoration and woven materials, and, where they occur, the treatment of columns as strong decorative elements. Interiors were closely connected with the out-of-doors through open loggias and courtyards, even parts of rooms open to the sky with only cloth awning protection. The light and simple furniture, much of it folding and portable, could be extremely elegant, with fine proportions, restrained carved ornamentation, and, sometimes, colorful painted details.

Greece

Greek art and design is widely admired by Western cultures as a high point in aesthetic achievement. The Greeks built important buildings in stone but used wood for roofing, with the result that ancient Greek buildings survive only as ruins. Combined with such artifacts as pottery decorated with painted imagery, these ruins give a sense of early Greek interiors. The restored portions of the palace at Knossos on Crete

4.5

4.4 Our knowledge of the typical Egyptian house is derived from beautifully detailed and painted models that were sometimes placed in tombs. This model of the house of Meket-Re, from circa 2000 B.C., shows a mud-brick house at the rear of a walled garden with a central pool. The columns, of bound papyrus reeds plastered over

with mud, are painted in strong, bright colors. A hanging cloth and painted walls round out a characteristic color scheme. Metropolitan Museum of Art, New York. Museum Excavations, 1919–1920; Rogers Fund, supplemented by a contribution of Edward S. Harkness

4.5 The Queen's Chamber in the Palace of Minos at Knossos, Crete, dating from circa 1500 B.C., has been extensively restored. The columns, originally of wood (now replaced with stone), exhibit the downward tapering form typical of this time and place.

They are painted black with red capitals. The Doric order, which emerged much later, may have evolved from this type. The restored wall paintings are based on traces of the original frescoes. (Photograph: Hirmer Fotoarchiv)

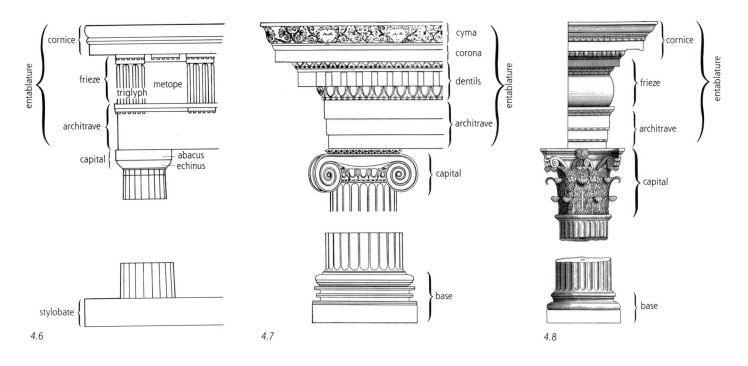

4.6　　　　　　　*4.7*　　　　　　　*4.8*

(circa 1600 B.C.), including the great staircase with its columns and the throne room with wall painting decoration, present a vivid picture of early Greek design (fig. 4.5).

It is the later historic, high civilization of Greece that produced the famous temple architecture that has had such extensive influence throughout subsequent design history. The typical Greek temple is a simple, windowless, rectangular enclosure either surrounded by columns on all sides or with a front portico using columns designed according to a codified system called an *order*. The three major orders, Doric, Ionic, and Corinthian (each named for the supposed place of origin), are characterized by a particular column design and a well-standardized system of detailing the cornice (or *entablature*) above, which ornaments the stone lintels spanning from column to column (figs. 4.6–4.8). The details seem to be based on a translation into stone of an earlier system of wood building.

The simple Doric order has an austere column with no base and a plain block capital. It is usually considered strong, pure, dignified, perhaps the most beautiful of the orders. The Ionic order, with its spiral, voluted capital, is sometimes described as feminine, gracious, and charming as compared to the sturdy and restrained Doric. The Corinthian order displays a more elaborate capital with acanthus-leaf decoration. In comparison with the others, it seems rich and elaborate.

Plans of ancient Greek houses can be reconstructed from excavated ruins, while knowledge of Greek interior design and furniture is surprisingly complete as a result of its frequent, precise representation in vase paintings. A typical Greek house had rooms arranged around a central courtyard, a plan that became the norm of residential design in Mediterranean regions until modern times. The generally simple rooms used restrained moldings and details borrowed from the architectural systems. Strong color appeared in textile elements such as hangings, cushions, and coverings. Lesser utilitarian objects such as cups, dishes,

4.9

4.6 The three orders of architecture developed by the Greeks are systems of columns and related details. The Greek Doric order, the simplest of the three, is often regarded as the most beautiful. The column has no base and rests on the three-stepped platform stylobate (continuous base). The entablature, which spans from column to column, is

made up of three sections called, from top to bottom, cornice, frieze, and architrave. (Drawing after Grinnell) The Greek Doric frieze alternates panels called triglyphs and metopes. The famous Elgin Marbles (British Museum, London) are the carved metopes from the Parthenon.

4.7 The Ionic order is characterized by the spiral volutes of the column capital. Each column has a square base as well. In this example, from the Temple of Athena Polias at Priene, Turkey, circa 440 B.C., the entablature omits a frieze. The use of dentils and egg-and-dart moldings as decorative details is typical. (From Priene, by T. Wiegand and H. Schrader, 1904)

4.8 The third Greek order, called Corinthian, became a special favorite of Roman architects. This example is a Roman version from the fourth-century S. Giovanni Laterano in Rome, as illustrated in Palladio's The Four Books of Architecture of 1570.

4.10

and vases probably provided important decorative accents. The chair type called a *klismos* is characteristic of ancient Greece (fig. 4.9). Its outward-curving legs suggest that animal horns may have been a precedent, a form that is inappropriate structurally when translated into wood. Extended, the same basic design generated a couch or a bed. Tables and chests were of simple form, with unostentatious, often colored decoration.

Rome

After their military conquest of Greece, the Romans took over Greek concepts of art and design and, with their typical energy, practicality, and engineering skill, made them their own. Roman architecture employed the Greek orders with certain changes, especially in the Doric order, modifying its proportions and adding a base. The Romans seem to have preferred the rich Corinthian order, and they adopted it

as a favorite part of Roman design. Among their constructional innovations were an extensive use of good-quality brick and concrete, arch construction, vaulting, and domes, which, for the first time, permitted buildings roofed over in masonry. Many Roman temples survive in good condition; the domed interior of the Pantheon (A.D. 120–124) remains a fine example of a monumental Roman interior (fig. 4.11).

The eruption of Mount Vesuvius in A.D. 79 served to preserve, by burying, entire neighborhoods in Pompeii and Herculaneum, providing an extensive knowledge of more modest Roman interiors. Houses were planned with rooms surrounding a central courtyard, or atrium, open to the sky (see fig. 4.1). Larger houses may have had more than one such court, which supplied all or most of the building's light, since rooms had few or no windows. The more luxurious houses commonly displayed elaborate wall decoration using both marble inlays and painting, typically in black, gilt, and the shade of red often called

4.9 *Accurate knowledge of ancient Greek furniture design comes from the detailed images that appear on painted vases and plates. The chair here, with its curved and splayed front and back legs, is a typical example of the klismos. The vase dates from circa 440 B.C. (Photograph: Alison Frantz)*

4.10 *Perhaps the most admired building ever constructed is the Greek Doric temple on the Acropolis in Athens known as the Parthenon; built circa 447–432 B.C. The architects were Iktinos and Kallikrates. (Photograph: Alison Frantz)*

Pompeian (fig. 4.12). Wall paintings were generally realistic, and their representation of everyday scenes gives information about furniture and other decorative details. The technique of mosaic became highly developed and provided decorative treatment of floors.

The books of Vitruvius—the first systematic handbook of architectural practice, written in the first century B.C.—were translated during the Renaissance and provided codified data about the orders of architecture. Roman architectural design, known from the surviving (and ruined) major buildings, from the excavation of lesser, domestic buildings of Pompeii and Herculaneum, and through Vitruvius's books, has had a recurring influence in the design work of Western societies, an influence that continues to be exerted, through both direct imitation (in buildings such as the old Pennsylvania Station in New York City; see fig. 4.58) and a more subtle and indirect incorporation of such concepts as symmetry and order into the basic approaches to architectural thinking.

MIDDLE AGES

The decline and eventual breakup of the Roman Empire led to a comparable collapse in the Roman classical traditions of design. The lack of a strong central governmental force left Europe in a state of political anarchy and social misery. Religion took over as the central focus in almost every aspect of life, and design was almost exclusively at its service.

Medieval developments can be considered under four stylistic designations, the first two relating to the remaining aspects of Roman traditions, the latter two representing the formation of a new tradition destined to lead gradually toward the modern world.

Early Christian Design

As Christianity gained official acceptance, churches began to appear as a significant building type. The Roman court building called a *basilica* became the model for the Early Christian church, a central space with flanking aisles permitting a clerestory (a high, windowed wall) to light the central space. Arches and columns based on Roman practice were used, but their detail is less classical (in the sense of academically accurate) and systematic, with fragments of Roman orders used in an improvisational way; some of the fragments were bits of carving simply taken from older Roman buildings. The art of mosaic became a major decorative device for geometric floors and walls and in pictorial representations of religious subjects. The best examples of Early Christian work are in Rome.

Byzantine Design

Byzantine architecture developed from the Roman model after Constantinople became the capital of the Roman Empire in A.D. 330. It, too, is primarily a church-building development that employs Roman structural techniques and details along with an elaborate mosaic decorative art. Byzantine building includes major domed structures, such as the famous Santa or Hagia Sophia in Constantinople (532–37), and reaches a level of elaboration and richness beyond the characteristic austerity of Early Christian work (fig. 4.13). The Byzantine style

returned to Italy to produce such buildings as the churches and tombs at Ravenna and San Marco in Venice (1063–94).

Romanesque Design

In spite of its name, Romanesque design has less connection with Roman architecture than do the styles described above. It is the style of the early Middle Ages, from about A.D. 800 to 1200 in Europe and, under the name Norman, in the British Isles. Surviving buildings, built in stone, are mostly churches, monasteries, and castles, the last the new building type so characteristic of the Middle Ages.

The typical feature of Romanesque stone structures is the semicircular arch and vault, a remnant of Roman structural technique (fig. 4.14). Monasticism produced a large number of building complexes, many surviving in reasonably good condition. In these, simplicity became a matter of religious conviction as well as a practical necessity, creating churches, chapter houses, cloisters, and dormitories with interiors of great beauty, emphasizing spatially impressive structure, minimally decorated.

Early medieval castles were often simple tower houses built in easily defended locations (fig. 4.15). Existing interiors with stone floors and roofs reveal such details as stone window seats at the small slitlike window openings, fireplaces for heat and cooking, and the generally unornamented functional character of Romanesque design. Furniture was minimal, partly because of undeveloped standards of comfort and partly because castle occupants moved from one location to another, maintaining their authority in the territory under their control through presence. Thus, the typical inventory of household fittings included plank-on-trestle tables, benches and stools of simple design, demountable, portable beds, trunklike chests for storage, and tapestries as wall coverings. Average people, the peasantry, had even less in the way of possessions and furniture of only the simplest sort.

Toward the end of the Romanesque era, larger churches began to show more elaborate decorative detail, and structural experiments in buttressed vaulting moved the style toward the development of Gothic architecture. Many buildings from the gradual transition period have earlier portions in the Romanesque style and later elements in the Gothic style.

Gothic Design

Gothic building is widely regarded as one of the great achievements of the Middle Ages. The characteristic feature of Gothic architecture is the pointed arch and vault, a technical development that made it possible to raise the height of the building and fill the walls with large window areas. The multiple ribs used in the vaulting of some Gothic cathedrals, such as Exeter in England (fig. 4.16), created the rich visual patterning known as *fan vaulting*. At its peak, the Gothic cathedral became a skeletal stone cage with wall areas largely filled with stained-glass windows, which served as both decorative art and illustrations of religious narratives. Sculptural carved detail was often used in the same way.

Castles and town fortifications survive in many locations, and some houses and other buildings of wood-frame construction, often with the exposed framing called *half-timber* work and with interiors more or less as they were in the twelfth to fourteenth centuries, still stand. The

4.11 The Pantheon in Rome of A.D. 118–25 is one of the earliest domed, all-masonry structures with a vast interior space. Beneath its coffered rotunda, the interior of the Pantheon, 142 feet high and 142 feet wide, is one of the most impressive of all domed masonry constructions, shown here in a painting by Giovanni Paolo Pannini of circa 1750. The bright disc on the wall is sunlight shining down through the oculus, the unglazed opening at the top of the dome. National Gallery of Art, Washington, D.C. Samuel H. Kress Collection

4.12

4.12 The walls in the Ixion Room of the House of the Vettii in Pompeii (A.D. 63–79) are decorated with frescoes, including some highly realistic perspective effects of architectural subjects. The dominant colors are the typical Pompeian red and black. (Photograph: Ludovico Canali, Capriolo)

4.13 The most spectacular of Byzantine interior spaces, the vast nave of Hagia Sophia in Istanbul, circa 532–37, is crowned by a 100-foot dome on pendentives. The pendentive is a curved, triangular element, introduced to fit a round dome over a square space beneath it. The original gilded and mosaic wall decoration, with its typical intricate and complex motifs, has been partially obliterated, but the overall richness and complexity remain impressive. (Photograph: Hirmer Fotoarchiv)

Guild Hall at Thaxted, England, used half-timber construction; its upper floors are cantilevered out beyond the floors below so that each floor is larger than the one underneath—one way of gaining interior space in a crowded medieval town (fig. 4.18). There is no typical medieval house plan. Layouts seem to have been improvised to suit site and function. Although complete rooms with furniture and lesser decorative details rarely survive intact, depictions of rooms in medieval art are frequently detailed and realistic in a way that makes it possible to visualize the Gothic interior quite accurately.

Decoration of Gothic stylistic character, with its ubiquitous pointed-arch forms, appeared in door and window moldings, around fireplaces, and in ceiling construction in a degree of elaboration that reflected the wealth and position of builders and owners. Wood furniture of increasing quality, elaboration, and functional variety began to appear. Chairs and benches with designs that seem to derive from the simple box chest were made in considerable assortment, usually with a frame of heavy members and thin inserted panels, generating the familiar appearance of *rail-and-panel* construction (fig. 4.17).

Substantial local variation in details gives Italian, French, German, and English medieval design their own unique qualities, while the Islamic influence makes Spanish work distinctive. The Crusades carried Gothic architecture and design into the Middle East and, in return, brought back into Europe an awareness of the art, design, materials, and techniques of that region. These varied influences combined to create the foundation on which all subsequent European design development has been based.

These influences are detectable even in America since the first settlers in the New World colonies brought with them traditions of European architecture and design that were formed in medieval times. The

4.15

early Colonial house in America, with its heavy braced frame, similar to the typical North European half-timber building, and its minimal windows with leaded glass in small panes, is essentially a European late-medieval structure.

RENAISSANCE TO ROCOCO

Various changes and developments touching every aspect of Western culture and society led Europe away from medieval ways of thinking toward the Renaissance. The Renaissance involved a new interest in the classical traditions of ancient Rome and Greece, a withdrawal from the domination of the Church and its mysticism, and a movement toward humanism, a belief in the human ability to solve problems and deal with life in a rational way. A new, experimental attitude led to the beginning of modern science, the voyages of the early explorers, and progressive ideas about trade and economic issues, all of which laid the foundations for the industrialized, technological society of the twentieth century.

In design, these developments had several direct results. Interest in surviving classical Roman structures and study of Vitruvius's text on architecture resulted in the introduction of classical ideas (including the orders) into design. The more rational, scientific way of thinking,

4.14

4.14 The stone barrel vaulting of the nave of the church of Saint-Sernin in Toulouse, France (1080–1120), demonstrates the most advanced structural techniques that were available to the builders of the early Romanesque era. (Photograph: Jean Roubier)

4.15 Although built near the end of the Middle Ages (circa 1519), the great hall at Cotehele, England, designed by Sir Piers Edgcumbe, retains the characteristics of the halls of earlier castles and manor houses, serving as the main

living space for both domestic and ceremonial uses. Only minimal furniture and window detail soften the exposed structural stone walls and floor and wooden roof construction. (Photograph: © James Pipkin)

4.16

4.17

applied to construction, initiated a series of technological innovations that led to the modern understanding of engineering as a basis for structural design. The invention and development of firearms made medieval defensive systems obsolete, eventually causing the castle to give way to the palace, château, and England's *great house*, although the houses and shops of the masses remained medieval in all but a few

minor decorative details. The invention of printing, accompanied by an increase in literacy, accelerated the transfer of knowledge and made changes in the world of design increasingly rapid and extensive. At the same time, the changeover from the feudal system to more modern political and economic practices increased the variety of design requirements, with an emphasis on luxury and individuality of design.

4.16 *The Gothic cathedrals of the Middle Ages used masonry construction—vaulting supported by exterior buttresses—to create interior spaces of great beauty and spiritual impact. To an observer facing east in the nave of the English cathedral of Exeter (circa 1280–1370), the many ribs of the vaults create patterns characteristic of fan vaulting, used in several English cathedrals. The screen with an organ above interrupts the view into the choir, engendering a sense of mystery through spatial complexity. (Photograph: Copyright A. F. Kersting)*

4.17 *In the Middle Ages, the chair was an object with specific symbolic and ceremonial significance, denoting status or rank. This fifteenth-century French example is built up in a wood rail-and-panel construction derived from box construction. The tracery at the top relates the piece to Gothic architecture. Metropolitan Museum of Art, New York. Gift of J. Pierpont Morgan, 1916*

4.18

Italy

The Renaissance began in Italy around the beginning of the fifteenth century and gradually spread north to France and England, then to other parts of Europe, including Germany, the Low Countries, and Spain, with a time lag roughly proportionate to the geographic distance. Art history customarily divides the Renaissance into three phases: early, middle (or High), and late (Baroque and Rococo). The term Mannerism, borrowed from the history of painting, is sometimes used to describe the transition from the High to Baroque phases in Italy.

EARLY RENAISSANCE. Early Renaissance work is characterized by a rather cautious application of classical Roman detail to buildings that are largely medieval in overall concept. Symmetrical planning appears in such buildings as the Florentine palaces (the Palazzo Medici-Riccardi of Michelozzo di Bartolomeo or the Palazzo Strozzi of Benedetto da Maiano, for example), which display a restrained use of classical moldings externally but a full use of Roman orders in the interior central courtyards. The interior of the small Pazzi Chapel (begun circa 1442), usually attributed to Filippo Brunelleschi (1377–1446), gives a clear example of the way in which the detail of rediscovered Roman classical

orders was used in Renaissance design. Such cautious introduction of Roman detail appears only in exceptional (and, in their own day, trend-setting) interiors such as those of Brunelleschi.

While ordinary houses remained untouched by Renaissance ideas, the wealthy began to add decorative moldings, doors and door frames, and other details borrowed from Roman antiquity to the interiors of their houses and *palazzi*. Elaborate ceilings with structural beams made into patterns of squares (coffered ceilings), painted wall and ceiling decoration, and classical molding were often the main decorative elements in an otherwise simple room. Ceilings frequently included paintings, perhaps by major artists. Sculptural plaques or rondels (such as those of Della Robbia) appeared as wall decoration. Elaborate fireplace mantels began to include classical detail in their carving.

HIGH RENAISSANCE. The fully developed or High Renaissance moved toward a more sophisticated understanding of the concepts of Roman architecture with such consistently classical projects as the plan for St. Peter's in Rome by Donato Bramante (1444–1514), which would be altered and expanded over the following century. The modest-size

4.18 *The Guild Hall at Thaxted, in Essex, England, was built in the second half of the fifteenth century. It is a fine example of half-timber construction, in which a structure's framework is exposed. (Photograph: John Pile)*

Massimi Palace in Rome (1535) retains interiors in fairly complete states of preservation, while older engraved illustrations of these spaces give even more complete detail as to their design (fig. 4.21). Furniture was still used rather sparsely, in a manner reminiscent of medieval austerity, but there was a gradual increase in the variety and richness of furniture types (fig. 4.19). Classical detail, used with skill and confidence, provided wall decoration, moldings at doors and windows, fireplace mantels, and elaborately decorated ceilings.

The clarification and near-standardization of Renaissance design practice, as well as its geographical spread, were encouraged by architect-theorists such as Leon Battista Alberti (1404–1472) and Andrea Palladio (1508–1580). Both not only produced important work but also wrote illustrated books explaining their working methods. Alberti emphasized the mathematical and geometric basis of his designs, while Palladio offered practical instruction along with illustrations of his own works, such as the Villa Rotonda (or Capra) at Vicenza (begun 1550) and the "Basilica" (begun 1549) in the same city, and accurate drawings of Roman architecture that formed the basis of his church designs, such as S. Giorgio Maggiore (begun 1566) and Il Redentore (begun 1576), both in Venice.

Palladian interiors are developed with the same sense of order and devotion to classical detail that governs the overall concepts of the

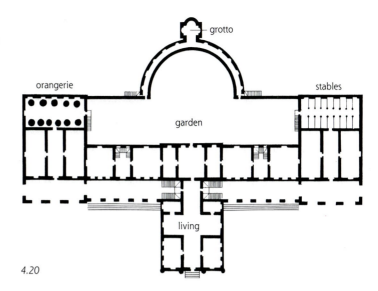

4.20

4.19

buildings that house them. The churches use Roman architectural details for pilasters, cornice moldings, and door and window trim, usually in gray marble to contrast with the generally white wall and ceiling surfaces, thereby accenting form. The effect suggests that Palladio was trying to re-create, or at least make reference to, the great baths of ancient Rome.

Palladio's villas include many well-preserved interiors, which give an overview of his domestic work. The Villa Barbaro at Maser (circa 1555–59) has a main living area with a spacious cruciform central hall dividing the square plan, creating four large rooms in the four corners (fig. 4.20). The spaces are architecturally simple, but the walls are richly decorated with illusionistic paintings by Paolo Veronese in which architectural elements (arches, balustrades, doorways, trellises) frame scenes of distant landscapes. In the Villa Foscari at Mira (circa 1556), Giambattista Zelotti's frescoes include some doorways standing open with family members and servants, even a pet bird, looking in—all in *trompe l'oeil* painting (fig. 4.23). This kind of painted wall decoration suggests stage scenery.

Taken together, Palladio's work and books formed a demonstration of High Renaissance practice that became a basic model for classically oriented design for the next several centuries. Palladian influence can easily be traced to the American colonies, continuing to appear even today.

The urge toward systematic perfection so strong in the work of the High Renaissance gave way toward the end of the period to an interest in more experimental and personally expressive ways of designing. The term Mannerism is often applied to the style that marks a transition from the reserve and order of the High Renaissance to the elaboration of the Baroque, the third and final phase of Renaissance design. Mannerism is exemplified by such works as Michelangelo's Laurentian Library in Florence (begun 1524), with its extraordinary entrance hall and stairway. The architect used a classical order but pressed the columns back into recesses in the walls and filled the space with a great, exuberant stairway creating a dramatic sense of movement. Other inte-

4.19 Renaissance furniture developed to suit the needs of an aristocracy with new and specialized functional demands—for the storage of varied objects of value and personal significance—and a taste for elaborate surface decoration. This sixteenth-century Florentine walnut stipo, or cabinet, is made up of separable upper and lower sections for easy transport. The figures carved in relief are bambocci, or urchins. (Courtesy Sotheby's, New York)

4.20 The plan of Palladio's Villa Barbaro at Maser appeared in a woodcut illustration in his influential The Four Books of Architecture, first published in Venice in 1570. The central living block houses a cross-shaped hall space with enclosed rooms (and stairs) at the four corners. The wings extend outward to farm buildings at left and right.

riors, such as the Palazzo del Te (circa 1526–34) of Giulio Romano (circa 1499–1546) at Mantua, similarly employed classical detail but introduced oddities, what seem to be mistakes (but are deliberate), and curious fresco paintings.

BAROQUE. The rich, sometimes excessive decoration of Baroque spaces led art historians of the last century to dismiss this work as decadent. Modern art historians have reinstated the Baroque as a significant phase, being especially attracted to the Baroque interest in space, movement, effects of light, and sense of drama rather than its details of decoration. While classical detail was still used extensively, it was altered, even distorted, as in the spirally twisted columns of the Baldachino in St. Peter's in Rome (begun 1624; fig. 4.22) by Gianlorenzo Bernini (1598–1680). In smaller Roman churches, such as S.

Carlo alle Quattro Fontane (1638–41) and S. Ivo della Sapienza (circa 1642–60), Francesco Borromini (1599–1667) carried Baroque ideas of spatial complexity to a further extreme.

The simple shapes—squares, circles, and rectangles—of the earlier, more restrained phases of Renaissance design gave way to more complex forms—ellipses, trapezoids, and spirals—in Baroque design. As these forms are developed in three dimensions and overlapped and interlaced, Baroque space takes on qualities of mystery and theatricality. It gives the effect of a richness that cannot be clearly comprehended but that vividly expresses drama, movement, and action. These design directions were encouraged and supported by the Counter-Reformation movement in the Catholic church, where they joined with the other arts (including music) to make churchly events exciting and dramatic.

4.21

4.21 In the grand salon on the second floor (piano nobile) of the Massimi Palace in Rome (by Baldassare Peruzzi, 1535), the Roman Ionic pilasters, the elaborate frieze and ceiling, and the details of mantel and door frames combine to suggest a re-created interior of ancient Rome. The classical statuary adds to the effect, while the sparse use of furniture is typical of such ceremonial Renaissance interior spaces. From Letarouilly on Renaissance Rome by John Barrington Bayley.

4.22 The Italian Baroque at its most flamboyant is demonstrated in the huge baldachino, or canopy, under the dome of St. Peter's in Rome (begun 1624). Bernini's gigantic Corinthian columns are twisted and covered with decorative detail that almost conceals their Roman classical derivation. (Photograph: Copyright by Leonard von Matt, Switzerland)

4.23

4.23 The Renaissance architecture of the interior of the Villa Foscari—also called La Malcontenta—by Andrea Palladio at Mira, near Venice, circa 1556, is elegantly simple, while Giambattista Zelotti's elaborate frescoes wittily introduce rich architectural detail in illusionistic perspective. Balancing the real door on the left is a painted open door at the right, from which a figure seems about to step into the room. The furnishings are modern. (Photograph: Evelyn Hofer)

4.24

4.24 The Baroque fascination with
movement and drama made monumental stairways, such as this Johann Lukas
von Hildebrandt design for the Upper
Belvedere Palace in Vienna (1700–23),
favorite subjects for the sculptural elaboration of architectural basics. Color is
an austere white except for the blacks
of the metalwork. (Photograph: Foto
Marburg)

Central Europe

Over the next hundred years, Baroque ideas traveled north, reaching northern Italy in the work of Guarino Guarini (1624–1683) at Turin, in both churches and in secular buildings such as the Palazzo Carignano (1679–92), with its curving stairs and elliptical domed rotunda. Still later, Baroque concepts reached southern Germany and Austria and spread into Hungary and Czechoslovakia on the east and Switzerland on the west. Baroque churches by such architects as Johann Michael Fischer (1692–1766) and Johann Balthasar Neumann (1687–1753) are astonishingly complex and elaborate. German and Austrian palace architecture at the end of the seventeenth century and the beginning of the eighteenth combined Italian Baroque influences with the comparable French stylistic development, Rococo; Johann Lukas von Hildebrandt's Upper Belvedere Palace in Vienna (1700–1723; fig. 4.24) and Neumann's Residenz at Würzburg (1719–44) serve as good examples of this style.

France

In France, the Renaissance passed through the same three phases as in Italy, each occurring about fifty to a hundred years later than the Italian equivalent. The Early Renaissance in France appeared first in small details of ornament, door and window frames, and fireplace mantels in châteaux that are otherwise medieval in concept. Chambord (1519–47), the giant royal hunting lodge in the Loire Valley, is full of classically derived detail and has a generally symmetrical plan, pointing toward growing acceptance of the Italian conceptual formality. The double spiral central staircase is a remarkable demonstration of geometric planning ingenuity. The much smaller château of Azay-le-Rideau is remarkable for its intact interiors, with furniture in place much as it must have been when the building was new (fig. 4.25).

With its square plan around a central court, symmetrical about both axes, the château Ancy-le-Franc, the work of the Italian architect Sebastiano Serlio (1475–1554), marks the arrival of a developed Renaissance style in mid-sixteenth-century France. By 1657 Louis Le Vau (1612–1670) was building the château of Vaux-le-Vicomte outside Paris (fig. 4.26). This building served as something of a model for the same architect's work for Louis XIV at Versailles, which was begun in 1661. Work continued there with Jules Hardouin-Mansart (1646–1708) succeeding Le Vau. The palace is a vast complex with many spectacular interiors, including a chapel, an opera house, and the famous Galerie des Glaces, or Hall of Mirrors.

Toward the end of the seventeenth century and in the eighteenth, French Renaissance design took on some of the character of Baroque design, particularly in the free and flowing use of curves. However, the last phase was more restrained in France than in Italy and Germany, meriting a different stylistic term, Rococo, to describe the elaborately

4.25

4.25 A room in the château of Azay-le-Rideau (1518–27) in the Loire Valley retains a basically simple, medieval quality conveyed by the exposed wood ceiling beams. Italian Renaissance ideas are evident in the ornately carved fireplace with its classically inspired details. Fabric-draped walls and a curtained and canopied bed represent concessions to comfort. The demountable furniture could be adapted to specific circumstances. (Photograph: John Pile)

4.26

decorative but classically ordered character of French Late Renaissance design. Such buildings as the Petit Trianon (1762–68) by Ange-Jacques Gabriel (1698–1782), among the finest examples of Louis XVI design, display a restraint and classical discipline characteristic of the Rococo style. The preserved salon from the Hôtel de Varengeville demonstrates how Rococo elaboration was adapted by aristocratic French society of the time (fig. 4.27).

Following the French Revolution of 1789, Rococo design shifted toward a more reserved and less florid direction (see discussion of Neoclassicism, below). The interior styles called Directoire and Empire (after the political developments of the time) introduced references to the styles of ancient Rome, partly as a result of interest in the findings of the excavations at Pompeii and, in the case of Empire work, partly to celebrate the exploits of Napoleon's era (fig. 4.28).

French Renaissance furniture and decorative elements are usually described with a terminology based on royal reigns, a reminder that these styles almost exclusively served royalty and the aristocracy, having relatively little impact on a wider public. French provincial furniture design, however, is a partial exception. In the seventeenth and eighteenth centuries, furniture makers of provincial France began to make everyday wooden furniture in simplified versions of French Renaissance "high style" prototypes. Such furniture, which struck a

4.27

4.26 This overwhelming, elaborately decorated bedroom was meant for the king, should he spend the night at the château of Vaux-le-Vicomte near Paris, built in 1656–61 by Louis Le Vau. The painter Charles Le Brun and a team of plasterworkers and other artists produced an interior clearly based on Italian Baroque influences. (Photograph: Caisse Nationale des Monuments Historiques et des Sites. © ARCH. PHOT. PARIS/S.P.A.D.E.M.)

4.27 This room from the Hôtel de Varengeville, a town house on the boulevard St.-Germain, Paris, is a fine Rococo interior of about 1735. The soft color of the wood paneling and the rich gilded surface decoration are typical of the style. The central table, with its japanned lacquer finish and elaborate gilt decoration, was made in 1759 by the famous royal cabinetmaker Gilles Joubert (1689–1775) for Louis XV's private rooms at Versailles. Metropolitan Museum of Art, New York

pleasant balance between simplicity and elaboration, has remained popular in France and is still widely collected elsewhere. (Unfortunately, the style has been abused by modern mass-produced imitations of poor quality, causing the term French provincial to become almost meaningless.)

The term Biedermeier designates German and Austrian furniture of the early nineteenth century based on French Empire design and interpreted by local craftsmen, who modified French design in the direction of traditional German peasant furniture. At its best, Biedermeier furniture can be simple, elegant, and handsome, with its use of various lighter woods and occasional painted (often black) detail (fig. 4.30).

England

English design of the Renaissance developed in a series of styles identified, as in France, with the reigning monarchs. Royalty did not influence design in any direct way, but designers, cabinetmakers, and other craftsmen seem to have felt that a change of rule offered a reason for introducing stylistic change that was already in the wind. Renaissance ideas first appeared in England in the sixteenth century during Tudor and Elizabethan times. Awareness of the new design developing in Italy came to England with travelers, with Italian craftsmen, and, indirectly, with craftsmen-designers from the Low Countries, where a somewhat modified version of Italian and Spanish design had appeared.

The great house of Longleat (circa 1568–80), with its external symmetry and Italianate interiors, provides a complete example of Elizabethan Early Renaissance design. Robert Smythson (circa 1535–1614), one of several builder-craftsmen who seem to have acted as architects in this period, was probably responsible for Hardwick Hall of 1590–97, one of the finest of Elizabethan buildings to have survived (fig. 4.29).

4.29

4.28

4.30

4.28 The French Empire style found its way to America with such craftsmen as the French-born and -trained Charles-Honoré Lannuier (1779–1819), who settled in New York and is believed to be the designer of this griffon-support console table (circa 1811). It is made of rosewood and ebony, with secondary parts of pine, poplar, and ash, and has gilded ornamentation and a marble top. The Napoleonic decorative elements (eagles, wreaths, fasces) that give the Empire style its name were readily translated into symbols appropriate to the new federal government of the United States. (Photograph: Helga Photo Studio, courtesy Bernard & S. Dean Levy, Inc., New York)

4.29 The Long Gallery of Hardwick Hall, Derbyshire, England (1590–97), is a fine example of an Elizabethan great house interior, with its tapestried walls and strapwork plaster ceiling. The room runs the full length of the building, and the many large windows on the right flood it with light. The architect's identity is uncertain, but stylistic similarities to other buildings suggest Robert Smythson (circa 1535–1614). (Photograph: © 1985 James Pipkin)

4.30 An oval library table of circa 1830 in the German Biedermeier style displays the style's characteristic combination of light, yellow-toned fruitwood and black edge trim. (Courtesy Didier Aaron, Inc., New York)

A more sophisticated and consistent High Renaissance direction appeared in the work of Inigo Jones (1573–1652), who had visited Italy and was familiar with Palladio's work. He used a Roman temple concept for the English church of St. Paul at Covent Garden, London (1631), which presents an interior of classic simplicity characteristic of his other work as well.

Sir Christopher Wren (1632–1723) moved the Renaissance in England a step closer to the Baroque spirit. After the great fire of 1666 in London, he built a new cathedral of St. Paul, with its famous dome, and many small city churches. For these, Wren employed the classical vocabulary in a surprisingly varied way, each one a unique study in interior space and detail. St. Stephen's Walbrook (1672–79) is a particularly fine example (fig. 4.31). The building is crowded in among neighbors so that its exterior is scarcely visible, but its beautifully domed interior is one of Wren's greatest successes. Wren's work also included secular buildings; the Chelsea Hospital in London (1682–85), with its quiet brick exterior and handsome chapel and dining hall interiors, clearly influenced design in the American colonies.

Overall, the eighteenth century in England moved toward a more restrained and academic classicism, represented in buildings such as Lord Burlington's house at Chiswick (circa 1725–30), clearly based on Palladian precedents. The eighteenth-century style called Georgian developed a restrained and elegant way of using classical detail in large houses and in rows and squares of smaller city houses as well. Interior detail and furniture design exhibited some of the most admired of all historic work.

4.31

4.31 In St. Stephen's Walbrook (1672–79), one of Sir Christopher Wren's many London churches, a simple rectangular space becomes complex and visually rich, as the arrangements of columns, arches, and domes transform its plan into, in rising sequence, a square, a Greek cross, an octagon, and a circle. This design may have served Wren as a preparatory study for St. Paul's Cathedral, Wren's largest and most famous work. (Photograph: Edwin Smith)

4.32   4.33   4.34

The famous English cabinetmakers Thomas Chippendale (1718–1779), George Hepplewhite (d. 1786), and Thomas Sheraton (1751–1806) became known for their fine products (figs. 4.32–4.34). The books they published illustrating examples of their work led to the development of styles in both England and America that take the names of their originators. The Adam brothers (James and Robert), working as architects, interior designers, and furniture designers, developed a personal style within the Georgian tradition based, in part, on Roman work as it was discovered in the excavations at Pompeii (fig. 4.35). (The excavation of Pompeii in the eighteenth century attracted wide attention in Europe and led to considerable imitation, more or less literal, in the decorative design fashions of that time.) Adam interiors such as the library at Kenwood (London, 1767–69), the drawing room at Home House (1772–73), or the sequence of great rooms at Syon House (1760–69), in their richness of color and delicate decorative detail, are among the most spectacular of eighteenth-century works.

Neoclassicism

The complexities of late Renaissance design, the elaboration of Baroque space, and the flowing decoration of Rococo surfaces led to an inevitable reaction, not so much a return to the simplicity of the early Renaissance as an effort to look back to the origins of classicism in Greece and Rome. Although the term Neoclassicism did not come into use until the 1880s, the work that is now so called appeared in France as early as the mid-eighteenth century. Ange-Jacques Gabriel,

mentioned above as the designer of the Rococo interiors of the Petit Trianon, turned, in the exterior of that building, to a restrained classicism, using, on each of the building's four sides, four Corinthian columns or pilasters centered between matching bays with a simple cornice and balustrade at the level of the flat roof. Gabriel's larger twin buildings that front on the Place de la Concorde in Paris have a similar classic sense identifiable as Louis XVI or Neoclassic in style (fig. 4.36). Étienne-Louis Boullée (1728–1799) is known for a number of fantastic building designs of Neoclassic character. His unbuilt proposal for the Bibliothèque Nationale in Paris as it appears in an engraving would have been a vast monumental space both austere and original (fig. 4.38). Boullée and Claude-Nicolas Ledoux (1736–1806) have become known in recent years for works that seem to hint at the direction Postmodernism has taken. Ledoux developed a highly personal style in which simple arch forms combine with classic columns, often with heavy rustication, to generate powerful masses, sometimes embellished with elements of fantasy. Images of the Royal Saltworks at the French town of Arc-et-Senans (1775–79; fig. 4.37) and the surviving tollhouses at the old gates of Paris have been sources of direction for many current Post-modernists. A small boudoir now installed in the Victoria and Albert Museum in London is believed to be a Ledoux interior of the 1770s or 1780s. It suggests that Ledoux, like Gabriel, could combine a Rococo and Neoclassic vocabulary as a particular project might suggest. Contemporary engravings of the interior of his theater at Besançon, France (1778–84), now unfortunately destroyed, suggest a magnificent Neoclassical space.

4.32 This fine example of Thomas Chippendale's "ribband-back" side chair, of mahogany, dates from about 1755. The simple structure accommodates strong joints—for example, the section where the front legs meet the seat frame is larger than in other designs, allowing amply for joining. The carving, based on Rococo influences, converts the pristine form into something rich and elaborate. (Photograph courtesy Stair & Company, New York)

4.33 George Hepplewhite made this dining chair in London about 1785, in both arm and armless versions, for a matching set of ten. The shield back is characteristic of Hepplewhite's work and that of his followers. The chair is finished in black with polychrome decorative details. (Photograph courtesy Stair & Company, New York)

4.34 The style of Thomas Sheraton was more reserved than that of Chippendale, suggesting the Neoclassic influence of the Louis XVI style. His book The Cabinet-Maker and Upholsterer's Drawing Book of 1791–94 helped to make his style widely known. This mahogany chair was made about 1790. (Photograph courtesy Stair & Company, New York)

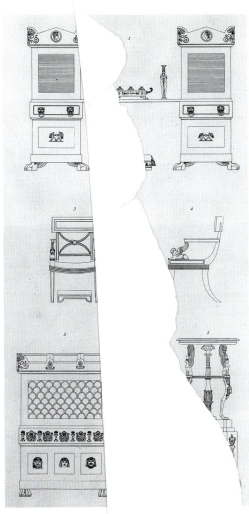

4.40

NORTH AMERICA

Colonial Style

On the American continent, early settlers brought with them the design ideas from their former homes in Holland, France, Spain, and, of greatest importance, England. Colonial houses were generally modest and simple, almost medieval in character in that they were direct and functional with a minimum of decorative detail (fig. 4.44). Gradually, as the settlers became established and more affluent and were joined by newcomers of more aristocratic background, this early Colonial design vocabulary gave way to a version of more elaborate English style.

An American equivalent of eighteenth-century English Georgian design developed in which the influence of Wren and the great English cabinetmakers can be traced quite readily (fig. 4.42). Large houses such as Westover, in Virginia (circa 1730), and the Governor's Palace in Williamsburg, Virginia, and churches such as Philadelphia's Christ Church (1731–44) adhered closely to the models provided by Wren and his contemporaries (fig. 4.43). Palladian details and academic classical design, learned from books imported from England, began to appear in buildings such as Thomas Jefferson's house at Monticello (1796–1809), clearly based on Palladio.

Federal Style

The term Federal style describes the furniture and interior design paralleling the architectural Greek Revival style in the newly independent United States around the beginning of the nineteenth century. The people of the young nation realized their government was the first democracy since the Athens of Pericles, inspiring an interest in the design of ancient Greece. While photographs were not available and

Regency Style

The work of the English Adam brothers (... orporated both Rococo and Neoclassical tendencies ... 769–1831) was an active traveler and collector who t ... designed by the Adams) with antiques and eventually ... he public (for a fee) as a kind of museum; his well-illustra ... l Furniture and *Interior Decoration Executed from Designs b* ... pe (1807) further encouraged the spread of the Neoclassica ... 4.40). The English Regency style takes its name from the per ... during which George, Prince of Wales, became Regent i ... succeeded George III as George IV (he died in 1830). ... d not only from Neoclassical design but also from other m ... lirections, including Egyptian, Greek, Gothic, Chinese, and ... les of decoration. The work of Sir John Soane (1753–1837) in ... s of his own house (1812–13) and the Dulwich Art Galle ...), both in London, remains close to Neoclassicism. The R ... at Brighton (1815–21) by John Nash (1752–1835), on t ... d, is an eccentric agglomeration of various exotic styles a ... create a fantasy palace for the Prince Regent himself (fig. 4 ...

4.36

4.41

4.40 A plate from Thomas H ... 1807 book, Household Furni ... Interior Decoration, illustrate ... ing table, an armchair, and a ... representative designs of the E ...

4.35 ... *Regency period. The illustration at the* has a *lower left is a side view of the writing* and a *table above. The Metropolitan Museum* room *of Art, New York. Harris Brisbane Dick* Lansd *Fund, 1930 (30.48.1)* 68) to t

4.41 In the kitchen of the Royal Pavilion at Brighton, England, remodeled by John Nash in 1815–21, the eccentricity of English Regency design achieves its ultimate expression: although the structural columns are of iron, the tops are ornamented to look like palm trees.

4.42

travel to Greece was rarely attempted, such books as James Stuart and Nicholas Revett's *The Antiquities of Athens* (1762–95) made fairly accurate information about Greek architecture available. An effort to revive Greek architecture and adapt it to nineteenth-century needs produced many templelike churches, public buildings, and even private houses (fig. 4.45). The interior design followed suit with related interior detail and furniture design suggested by images of Greek vase paintings. The American cabinetmaker Duncan Phyfe (1768–1854), well known for his designs based on the English Sheraton style, modified his pieces to reflect the Greek influence. Along with the revival of Greek architectural elements, influences from the Empire and Directoire styles in France and the Adam and Regency styles in England entered into American design. The term Neoclassical becomes applicable to many aspects of the Federal Style.

The Greek Revival was not confined to the United States. A parallel direction appeared in Germany and in England, with the work of Karl Friedrich Schinkel (1781–1841) and Sir Robert Smirke (1781–1867); Schinkel's Altes Museum in Berlin (1822–30) and Smirke's British Museum in London (1823–47) rival one another in the display of Greek columns (fig. 4.46).

Gothic Revival Style

Before long, the Greek Revival led to a desire to revive other ancient styles. A Gothic Revival in both England and the United States followed on the heels of the Greek Revival, with many of the same architects simply shifting the sources that they imitated.

4.43

4.42 This highboy cabinet, made in Boston circa 1725 in the English Queen Anne style, is veneered in walnut and maple; the body is made of pine. The ornamental detail is restrained, but the carefully matched veneers on the drawer fronts generate flowing, symmetrical patterns. (Photograph courtesy Bernard & S. Dean Levy, Inc., New York)

4.43 Many American Colonial houses exhibited Neoclassical details based on the Georgian architecture of England. This example, the Vassau-Longfellow House in Cambridge, Massachusetts, was built in 1759. (Photograph courtesy Essex Institute, Salem, Mass.)

4.44 A bedroom of the Peter Wentz farmstead, built in 1758 in Montgomery County, Pennsylvania, and restored in 1971, exhibits the simple plaster walls, exposed wood structural ceiling, and uncurtained, double-hung window of its time and place. Below the chair rail, a surprising spotted pattern has been created with a paint-dipped sponge. (Photograph: Oberto Gili, courtesy House & Garden)

4.45 A watercolor rendering circa 1845 by the prominent New York architect Alexander Jackson Davis shows the double parlor of a New York City row house as it was to be furnished and decorated in the then-fashionable Greek Revival idiom. The Ionic columns and entablature have Greek echoes in the furniture; the side chairs are of the klismos form seen in ancient Greek vase painting (see fig. 4.9). New-York Historical Society

4.44

4.46

4.47

While Gothic architectural styles did not look out of place for churches, their application to hotels, public buildings, and houses produced many odd results (fig. 4.47). Gothic Revival furniture and interior design tended toward the curious and quaint. Its extension into simple country building led to the naive style called Carpenter Gothic. The term refers to country building with supposedly Gothic decorative detail added in the interest of fashion, with results sometimes charming, often simply amusing. The forms of pointed arches, tracery, and crockets ornamented ordinary household furniture. Houses and barns were decorated with forms vaguely resembling Gothic tracery cut out of wood by the increasingly popular scroll saw.

VICTORIAN ERA

The drastic changes wrought by the Industrial Revolution affected every aspect of life. In design, the modern world of mechanized production began to push aside the traditions of handcraft production in which design was an integral part of the making of things. Factory-made products were designed not by the people who made them but by managerial or professional sources only indirectly aware of the actual processes of manufacture.

At the same time, the efficiencies of industrial production began to create a new class of consumers, a middle class able to afford a certain level of luxury, especially at the modest cost that industrial production made possible. This pattern of cheap industrial production feeding markets that sought out elaborately ornamented objects, now easily produced by mass-production techniques, fueled the typically Victorian middle-class love for decoration.

Victorian design is characterized by a kind of flamboyant elaboration borrowing from any and all historical origins in order to create interiors that were rich and crowded (fig. 4.48). There can be a certain naive charm in Victorian decoration, especially as it merges, now, into nostalgia, and its frequent originality somewhat offsets its excesses. Gothic, Renaissance, even Moorish and Oriental influences jumbled together coincided with the development of clever inventions (folding, reclining, and convertible furniture) and new uses of materials such as cast iron and metal tubing. The swivel chair, the brass bed, iron lawn furniture, and bentwood products are all Victorian developments.

4.46 The façade of the British Museum in London by Sir Robert Smirke was built in 1823–47, at the height of the Greek Revival in England. It used an extraordinary number of Greek Ionic columns to create an impressive street-front for a building whose exterior was otherwise unremarkable. (Photograph: Edwin Smith)

4.47 Lyndhurst (built 1838, renovated from 1864), a Gothic Revival mansion overlooking the Hudson River near Tarrytown, New York, is a markedly different example of the work of Alexander Jackson Davis, who designed the Greek Revival interior in fig. 4.45.

The occupants of this dining room could imagine themselves to be characters in one of Sir Walter Scott's Romantic novels set in the Middle Ages—even though the atmosphere, with its dark, rich clutter, is more Victorian than Gothic. (Photograph: Bob Bishop)

4.48

4.48 In 1894, this Victorian gallery in the New York home of Mrs. William Astor housed her collection of paintings. Far from being a neutral setting in which the art collection stands out, it is filled with lamps, a large chandelier, rugs, draperies, and furniture—all intended to create a sense of opulence. The actual paintings, displayed in tiers that rise far above eye level, seem to be no more than additional accessories. (Photograph: Museum of the City of New York. Byron Collection)

4.49

4.50

4.51

Although the term Victorian brings to mind a surplus of clutter and a confusion of decorative styles, many of the trends that were to lead to the modernism of the twentieth century first surfaced in the Victorian era. While architects and designers were inclined to treat decoration as something quite apart from functional realities, Victorian engineers, inventors, and manufacturers, who had little contact with the stylistic tastes of the design world, were developing a strong functional aesthetic. The first great bridges designed by engineers such as Thomas Telford (1757–1834) and Robert Stephenson (1803–1859) in England and the visible iron structural systems designed by Henri Labrouste

4.49 *The reading room of the Bibliothèque Sainte-Geneviève (1844–50) in Paris, designed by Henri Labrouste, uses iron columns and arches within a building of generally classical character—an early effort to introduce modern materials in architectural construction. (Photograph: Marvin Trachtenberg)*

4.50 *William Morris's firm, Morris & Co., produced the Green Dining Room in 1867 for the newly built Victoria & Albert Museum in London. The inclusion of stained-glass windows by the Pre-Raphaelite English painter Edward Burne-Jones demonstrates the Arts & Crafts movement's aim to unify art, design, and craft. (Photograph courtesy Victoria & Albert Museum, London)*

4.51 *Sir Joseph Paxton (with contractors Fox and Henderson and glaziers Chance and Company) produced, in 1851, what is often considered the first truly modern building, with its elegantly functional, prefabricated iron-and-glass structure. The Crystal Palace housed the extravagant Victorian dis-play that made up the Great Exhibition, an early type of world's fair, held that year in London. The illustration, a contemporary lithograph of Joseph Nash, shows the exhibition in progress. Victoria & Albert Museum, London.*

4.52

4.53

4.52 Gustav Stickley's Craftsman workshop, United Crafts, at Eastwood, New
York, built this sideboard (circa 1906–
10) from quarter-sawn white oak.
Morris's Arts & Crafts ideals are evident
in the clean lines of this honestly made
furniture, with only hand-hammered
copper hinges and pulls for decoration.
(Photograph courtesy Jordan-Volpe
Gallery, New York)

4.53 The R. R. Blacker House of 1907
in Pasadena, California, was designed
by Charles Sumner Greene and Henry
Mather Greene, leading American
architects of the time on the West
Coast. The influence of the nineteenth-
century Arts & Crafts movement can be
clearly traced in the Greenes' work.
(Photograph: John Jacobus)

(1801–1875) for the Bibliothèque Sainte-Geneviève and the Bibliothèque Nationale, both in Paris, suggested a new direction dominated by structural rather than decorative issues. Railroad locomotives and the engines of steamships came to be recognized as having visual qualities that could equal those of historic architectural structures.

The Great Exhibition of 1851 in London, a showcase for Victorian overdecoration, was, surprisingly, housed in a structure that pointed the way to modern architecture. This was the Crystal Palace, designed by Sir Joseph Paxton (1803–1865), built with a structural framework of iron and a glass skin in prefabricated parts, factory-made and assembled rapidly on site (fig. 4.51). This famous structure bore no resemblance to any earlier building, and it was a great popular success. After the exhibition ended, the building was dismantled and reassembled at Sydenham on the (then) edge of London, where it remained until destroyed by fire in 1936.

Arts & Crafts Movement

While visiting the Great Exhibition, William Morris (1834–1896) found himself distressed by the quality of the objects exhibited there, and he felt impelled to become something of a design reformer. He believed the degradation of Victorian design lay in the separation of the design process from handwork in the industrial production of goods and the resulting elimination of the craftsman. He urged a return to handwork using materials honestly and with restrained and artistic decorative detail. Morris's critical writings and lecturing interested a group of followers who made up what came to be known as the Arts & Crafts movement.

Morris established a firm that sold Arts & Crafts products and took on interior design assignments (fig. 4.50). He himself designed textiles, wallpapers, some furniture, and many small objects. For textiles and wallpapers, Morris tended to concentrate on decorative surface designs. He used dense, allover patterns based on leaf, flower, and, occasionally, bird forms that were unusually respectful of their natural origins and accurate in their representation of detail (see fig. 8.32).

Morris's followers included architects and artists, as well as what would now be called interior designers. Some of his disciples concentrated on simple, well-crafted furniture and accessories while others were fine artists whose work was often incorporated into furniture designs. A chest or cabinet might carry a large and richly detailed pre-Raphaelite painting as frontal decoration. As these elements were combined in interiors, the effect often suggested the medieval style, but the work was never strictly imitative in the manner of the Gothic Revival.

In post–Civil War America, Morris's Arts & Crafts movement, its name shortened to Craftsman movement, formed the basis for what is often called the Mission or Golden Oak style, typified by the furniture of Gustav Stickley (1858–1942), which found wide popularity around the turn of the century (fig. 4.52).

A similar aesthetic can be seen in the California work of the brothers Greene and Greene (Charles, 1868–1957, and Henry, 1870–1954) whose development of a personal style based on the use of natural wood as structure, exterior surface, and interior detail produced such masterpieces as the Blacker House in Pasadena, California (fig. 4.53).

Frequent hints of Oriental influence appear in the details of interior woodwork, stained glass, metalwork, and furniture—even a unique upright piano—all meticulously designed by the architects.

Charles Eastlake (1836–1906) promoted some of Morris's ideas in his book *Hints on Household Taste,* published in England in 1868 and soon circulated in the United States as well. It is a manual urging the householder to accept quality and simplicity in preference to Victorian elaboration. Curiously, Eastlake's illustrations showing his own designs now seem as ornate as any other Victorian work. Many American interiors of the era display Eastlake-style woodwork in such elements as door and window frames and fireplace overmantels.

Morris's views, which continue to be influential, were eventually adapted by later designers involved in the development of modern design. The work that he and his followers produced remains some of the best of the Victorian age.

Shaker and Adirondack Design

A source of simple and restrained design that ran counter to the general Victorian love of ornamentation came from the religious communities of the American Shaker sect. From the latter part of the eighteenth century through the nineteenth, this group formed colonies that built villages of great simplicity and beauty. Interiors were furnished with products designed and made by members in a functional, direct, and dignified style that hints at the direction that modern design was to take in the twentieth century (fig. 4.54). Shaker furniture and other products were sold to outsiders and gained considerable popularity, suggesting that Victorian taste was not restricted to the overelaborate style of the more commercial products of the time. Shaker products are now admired and valued antiques.

Another furniture design direction that stands outside the main line of development has come to be known as Adirondack furniture. The term describes rustic designs, usually of hickory left as natural sticks or logs—even, perhaps, with the bark left on—manufactured primarily by the Old Hickory Chair Company of Indiana, founded in 1898. The stylistic term emerged from the popularity of the furniture for the rustic summer homes and lodges built in the Adirondack region by wealthy city dwellers.

TURN OF THE CENTURY

Art Nouveau in Europe

In continental Europe, an aesthetic movement known as Art Nouveau surfaced at the end of the nineteenth century. Its primary bases were in Belgium, with such designers as Henri Van de Velde (1863–1957) and Victor Horta (1861–1947; fig. 4.55), and in France, with Hector Guimard (1867–1942) While the movement included art and architecture, it was particularly in interior design and in the design of furniture and smaller objects that it came into its fullest development. Art Nouveau is characterized by the abandonment of all historical references (which made it the first truly original style in a very long time), by adventurous exploration of new forms, and by the use of a rich and original vocabulary of decoration based on the curves and flowing

4.54

lines of natural forms. Art Nouveau, like the Arts & Crafts movement in England, revealed an awareness of Japanese design in its simple, flowing lines and freedom of form.

The movement spread rapidly, becoming known as Jugendstil in Germany and the Scandinavian countries, and it influenced the work of Charles Rennie Mackintosh (1868–1928) in Scotland (see fig. 12.1) and Antonio Gaudí (1852–1926) in Spain. Each of these men developed a highly personal style quite unlike anything else that was being produced in their respective home cities of Glasgow and Barcelona, but with visual qualities that can now be seen to parallel closely the Art Nouveau of Belgium and France.

Art Nouveau design was strongly fashion-oriented, and its sudden rise in popularity was matched by its sudden decline and virtual disap-

pearance by the dawn of World War I. Subsequently, Art Nouveau was generally dismissed as an eccentric fad; only in recent years has it been rediscovered and become an object of study and admiration.

Vienna Secession

In Vienna, a parallel new style directed toward the modern world arose. The Vienna Secession movement was begun by artists and designers who found the policies of the traditional academy too restrictive. In response, they set out to establish their own gallery. Josef Olbrich (1867–1908) designed their building, built in Vienna in 1898–99, in a style that mixed a certain symmetrical classicism with an original decorative vocabulary similar to Art Nouveau, although generally less curvilinear and more geometric in feeling. The work of Otto

4.54 *The inspired simplicity of American Shaker design, exemplified by the Elders' Room of the Brick Dwelling House, Hancock Shaker Village, Pittsfield, Massachusetts (circa 1825–50), derived from religious belief rather than design theory. The bare floors, white walls, and hand-crafted, solid-*

wood furniture evince an aesthetic that is surprisingly modern in spirit. The peg strips allow the broom, clothing, and even chairs to be neatly stored. The small iron stove is remarkably fuel-efficient. (Photograph courtesy Hancock Shaker Village, Pittsfield, Mass.)

4.55 *The Art Nouveau designer Victor Horta developed every element and detail of the dining room of the Hôtel Solvay in Brussels (1895–1900) in the original Art Nouveau style, with forms based on nature's flowing curves. Furniture, fireplace mantel, window frames, and light fixtures are all Horta's work, designed specifically for this project. (Photograph: Dotreville, Brussels)*

4.56 *The dining room of Vienna Secessionist Josef Hoffmann's Palais Stoclet in Brussels (1905) incorporates Hoffmann's own designs for rug, furniture, lighting, and ornamental silver pieces, with twin mural mosaics by Gustav Klimt. The Wiener Werkstätte shops produced the decorative elements used throughout this elaborate mansion. (Photograph: Studio Minders, Ghent)*

4.58

Eclecticism

The ideas of Sullivan and Wright did not find wide acceptance in the United States of the early twentieth century. At the Chicago World's Fair of 1893, Sullivan's Transportation Building was considered more strange than beautiful, while the other buildings, of pseudo-Roman classical design, were greatly admired. American architects often went to France to study at the École des Beaux-Arts and came home trained to produce buildings designed in the style now called Beaux-Arts in recognition of its origin; the Paris Opera House by Charles Garnier, built in 1861–75, is a fine example, with its rich overlay of florid, classically inspired decorative detail inside and out.

Most important buildings designed in America before World War II were influenced by the Beaux-Arts imitative way of working, often called Eclecticism. The word means "borrowing from many sources," and this was the leading characteristic of eclectic design. A museum or courthouse might be Roman in origin, a church Gothic or Romanesque. New York's Pennsylvania Railroad Station (1904–10; fig. 4.58), for instance, was designed by the firm of McKim, Mead and White in imitation of the Roman Baths of Caracalla. A style was chosen to suit each project; banks were often Greek or Roman, schools Tudor Gothic, clubs Renaissance palaces, private homes small châteaux or Georgian

4.58 The majestic main concourse of the original Pennsylvania Railroad Station, New York, was inspired by the ancient Baths of Caracalla in Rome. Built in 1904–10 from designs by McKim, Mead and White, the terminal incorporated functional iron-and-glass train sheds (out of sight through the arch on the left) and eclectic borrowings from historic precedents. (Photograph: Geo. P. Hall & Sons, 1911, courtesy Museum of the City of New York)

4.59

4.60

4.59, 4.60 The pioneer professional decorator Elsie de Wolfe, in an 1898 renovation, brought about a dramatic change in the New York row house she occupied with Elisabeth Marbury. In 1896 the dining room was the picture of late-Victorian and Edwardian elaboration (fig. 4.59). With only fresh paint, some new furniture, and the elimination of bibelots, the 1898 interior (fig. 4.60) achieved the relatively clean, simple look that de Wolfe favored throughout a long career. (Photographs: Museum of the City of New York. Byron Collection)

mansions. Modern steel structure was often concealed by the period-style exterior.

Interior design was expected to follow along, providing historically believable decoration in whatever style suited the building or the taste of the owner. The profession of interior decoration became focused on the ability to create rooms furnished with antiques (genuine or imitation) and related details in one of many styles. A diluted version of American Colonial interior design became a particular favorite in residential works.

The most positive development of the eclectic era in interior design was the emergence of a specialized profession called, at the time, interior decorating. Elsie de Wolfe (1865–1950) is often considered to be the first truly professional decorator (figs. 4.59, 5.60). Her clients were mostly wealthy New Yorkers, her work generally confined to tasteful borrowing from the historic periods. Her 1913 book *The House in Good Taste* served to popularize her thinking, which went far beyond stylistic imitation to probe more basic questions about aesthetic goals, even suggesting simplicity as a design objective. Her work opened the way for other decorators, such as Nancy McClelland (1876–1959), Ruby Ross Wood (1880–1950), Rose Cumming (1887–1968), and Dorothy Draper (1889–1969), who similarly adapted traditional styles to their clients' modern needs. The work of such designer-decorators as T. H. Robsjohn-Gibbings (1905–1976), Edward Wormley (b. 1907), and William Pahlmann (b. 1900) in the 1930s and 1940s had its roots in the style-oriented professional practice developed by the first wave of eclectic decorators.

Frank Lloyd Wright

Wright (1867–1959), building on the guidance of Sullivan, began early in the century to produce houses such as the Roberts House of 1908 and the Robie House of 1906–9 (figs. 4.62, 4.63) that, with their total rejection of historical references and their introduction of open and flowing interior space, define some of the primary directions of modern design. Concerned with every detail of the interiors of his buildings, Wright designed built-in furniture and lighting and, where the client would permit, movable furniture (fig. 4.61), even rugs as well. His interest in and respect for the character of materials recall the Arts & Crafts movement. He always used wood in a natural finish and had plaster painted in its own cream-white color tones. These colors, along with those of brick and stone (where they occur), created a soft, warm, natural color tonality, often enlivened by a strong, bright red, Wright's favorite accent color. He introduced more bright colors through inserts of stained glass in windows, in geometric patterns. Wright did not hesitate to use ornamentation in an abstract, geometric vocabulary.

Wright might be said to have had two careers, one up to 1915, when he left the United States for Japan to work on his Imperial Hotel in Tokyo (completed 1922), the second after his return to the United States. Much of his later work exhibits his awareness of traditional Japanese design. He produced a large body of work, including many houses (Fallingwater, a country house in western Pennsylvania of 1937, is probably the best known) and a variety of larger buildings with extraordinary interior spaces. The S. C. Johnson office building in Racine (1936–39), the Price office tower in Bartlesville, Oklahoma (1953–55), and the Solomon R. Guggenheim Museum in New York (1956–59; fig. 4.64) suggest the scope and variety of Wright's later work.

As in his earlier work, Wright controlled, insofar as possible, every detail of interior design. His interest in ornament, while it grew more restrained, set his work apart from the International Style developing in Europe, giving it a much more personal, occasionally even eccentric feeling. The selection of materials, each used in its particular natural color, still controlled the interior's overall character, with the tones of brick, stone, plain concrete, and natural woods dominating (see fig. 9.36). A strong, bright red continued to be used as an accent color. Some of Wright's furniture designs move away from the craft-related use of wood. For example, the office furniture for the Larkin Building (see fig. 4.61) employed painted steel as a primary material, a striking innovation in 1904.

4.61

4.61 Frank Lloyd Wright's swivel chair designed for the Larkin Company Administration Building (Buffalo, 1904), of painted metal and oak, represents an early effort to develop a chair suited to the modern office in both functional and aesthetic terms. Height 37½". The Museum of Modern Art, New York. Gift of Edgar Kaufmann, Jr.

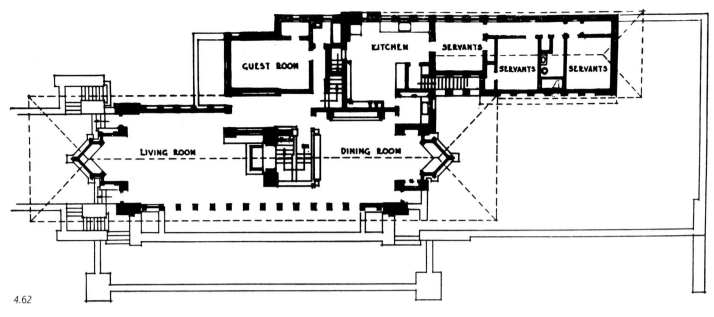

4.62

4.63

4.62, 4.63 Whenever his clients permitted it, Frank Lloyd Wright acted as his own interior designer. In the dining room of the Robie House (Chicago, 1906–9), his extraordinary table and chair group, built-in cabinets and shelves, lighting, ceiling treatment, carpet, and stained-glass windows together create a harmonious unity (fig. 4.63). While this early photograph suggests a gloomy massiveness, light and bright color actually prevail. In the plan of the Robie House (fig. 4.62), the dining room appears at one end of the main living space. A continuous ribbon of windows stretches across the front of the building; living and dining areas flow into one another, divided only by the freestanding fireplace and stairway. Decks and roofs on either side extend the long horizontals of the building. (Photograph: Chicago Architectural Photo Co.)

4.64

Walter Gropius

In Europe, meanwhile, modernism emerged in the work of three pioneers, all of whom had worked around 1911 in the office of the German premodernist Peter Behrens (1868–1940) and had probably become familiar with Wright's early work through its publication in Holland and Germany. Gropius (1883–1969), one of this famous threesome, is best known through the influence of the German design school called the Bauhaus, established under Gropius's direction at Weimar in 1919 (fig. 4.65). The Bauhaus taught design in conjunction with modern art. In Bauhaus designs, spaces took on a quality related to the abstract character of the current painting and sculpture (Cubism and related movements). Ornament came solely from the visual effects created by combinations of materials and colors. The goal was to unify art and technology, creating an aesthetic suited to the modern mechanistic world by relating materials, form, and function in an abstract visual vocabulary.

The Bauhaus was a key influence on architecture, interior design, and industrial design in the 1920s and 1930s and, through the continued influence of its teachers and students, onward into recent times (fig. 4.66). The austere and unornamented "functional" modern interi-

or with its tubular metal furniture and color palette of black, white, neutrals, and primary colors can be traced to Bauhaus origins.

After the closing of the Bauhaus in 1932, Gropius's influence continued through his work in England and, subsequently, in the United States, as well as through his leadership of the architecture department at Harvard University from 1937. Under Gropius's direction, Harvard became the first American design school to accept the ideas of the modern movement.

De Stijl

The Dutch movement called De Stijl (after the name of the magazine that was its mouthpiece) defined directions similar to those of the Bauhaus and had close connections to the work of the painter Piet Mondrian and the sculptor Theo van Doesburg. Gerrit Rietveld (1888–1964) is the best-known De Stijl designer, with his constructivist sculptural Schroeder House of 1924 in Utrecht (fig. 4.67) and his geometrically abstract furniture (see fig. 12.8). The furniture of Marcel Breuer (1902–1981), developed at the Bauhaus, seems to parallel De Stijl thinking, although there was no direct link between the two centers (see fig. 12.56).

4.64 The Solomon R. Guggenheim Museum in New York (1956–59) is a famous late work of Frank Lloyd Wright. The great spiral ramp forms the main exhibition gallery of the building. (Photograph: Robert Mates © The Solomon R. Guggenheim Foundation, New York)

4.65

4.66

Ludwig Mies van der Rohe

The second major pioneer of modernism, who knew Gropius through their shared tenure in Behrens's office, Mies van der Rohe (1886–1969) followed Gropius as director of the Bauhaus in its final years. Mies tended to relieve the austerity of his work with rich materials, including onyx marble, travertine, chrome-plated steel, and natural or black leather. The term Bauhaus style refers to either the austerity of Gropius or the richness of Mies's vocabulary of interior color, finish, and detail, or it can include both.

Mies van der Rohe's influence stemmed less from his academic positions than from his architectural design. The German pavilion at the

4.67

4.65 The director's office of the Weimar Bauhaus, designed by Walter Gropius in 1923, was furnished with a rug, wall hanging, and lighting created in the Bauhaus workshops and furniture of Gropius's own design. Here, the abstract qualities of modern art met the machine-inspired, unadorned simplicity of the Bauhaus aesthetic to create a

space characteristic of the developing International Style. (Photograph: Bauhaus Archiv)

4.66 This nickel silver and ebony teapot, designed and made by Marianne Brandt in 1924 at the Bauhaus, combines the clean geometry of machine production with a craft aes-

thetic (in the flowing form of the handle). Height 7". Manufactured at the Bauhaus metal workshop, Germany. The Museum of Modern Art, New York. Phyllis B. Lambert Fund

4.67 The upper level of the Schroeder House, its main living floor, in Utrecht (1924), is one of the few complete

examples of a De Stijl interior. It is the work of Gerrit Rietveld, an architect best known for his constructivist approach to furniture design. As in a Mondrian painting, the colors are restricted to white, black, and the three primaries. (Photograph: Die Neue Sammlung, Munich)

Barcelona Exposition of 1929 (fig. 4.68) and the Tugendhat House of 1930 in Brno, Czechoslovakia, gave striking demonstrations of the modern view of interior space as open and flowing, without division into boxlike rooms, and without historical reference or applied ornamentation. Mies moved to the United States in 1938 to head the architectural school of the Illinois Institute of Technology, at Chicago. His phrase "less is more" is often quoted to summarize his design philosophy. He continued to influence modern design, producing a number of the major buildings of the 1950s and 1960s.

Le Corbusier

Although actually Swiss, Le Corbusier (Charles-Édouard Jeanneret, 1887–1965) is usually thought of as a French modernist since most of his career was based in Paris. His influential book *Towards a New Architecture* of 1923 made him the primary theorist and publicist of the ideas of the modern movement, even before he had produced any major body of work. In his work of the late 1920s and 1930s, he demonstrated his conviction that the aesthetic of engineering (of ships, airplanes, and industrial buildings) formed a sound basis for all design in the modern era. His work was always regulated by an orderly, mathematical modular system that gave a special power and dignity to his design.

The Villa Savoye at Poissy-sur-Seine (1929–30), with the main block of the house elevated to the second-floor level on columns, is a good example of his work, shocking when it was built but now a respected key monument of the modern movement (figs. 4.69, 4.70). Le Corbusier's early interiors generally shared the simplicity, austerity, and Cubist geometrics of Bauhaus design, although his use of color was somewhat more adventurous, perhaps drawing on his distinguished work as an abstract painter. He used not only strong primary colors but also tints (pink and blue) and secondaries—greens and oranges—and applied them in large, simple areas.

Because no modern furniture was available when the first Le Corbusier projects were designed, older, simple products, such as bentwood café chairs and plain restaurant tables, were often selected. Later, in cooperation with Charlotte Perriand (b. 1903), Le Corbusier developed furniture designs using steel tubing, leather cushions, and table tops and cabinet fronts of solid color (see fig. 12.55). Some of these designs continue in production and have come to be called *classic modern*.

After World War II, Le Corbusier's work changed in character, becoming less geometric and more sculptural or organic. The pilgrimage church at Ronchamp (1950–55) demonstrates this shift and also offers one of the finest religious interiors of the twentieth century (figs. 4.71, 4.72).

4.68

4.68 Perhaps the most famous of all modern interiors, the German pavilion at the 1929 Barcelona Exposition was demolished after the fair but was reconstructed from the original plans in 1986. Shown here as originally built to Ludwig Mies van der Rohe's design, the pavilion combines travertine marble floors, polished-steel columns, and screen walls of glass and polished marble, rich materials characteristic of Mies's style. The Barcelona chair and ottoman are regarded as classic pieces of the modern era. (Photograph courtesy Mies van der Rohe Archive, The Museum of Modern Art, New York)

4.69

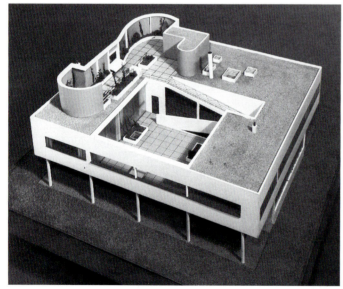

4.70

The term International Style came to be used for the geometrically based, unornamented, and rather mechanistic work of the European pioneer modernists.

Art Deco

At about the same time that the International Style was developing, a more commercial and fashion-oriented kind of modernism was appearing, now usually called Art Deco. It had its origins in post–World War I France, where influences from primitive art and Cubist painting and sculpture combined with modern motifs, such as electric power, radio, and skyscraper building (figs. 4.74, 4.75). Ornament was accepted, but it was a modern ornament of stepped and zigzag forms often associated with the rhythms of jazz music. This style became a favorite for theaters and exhibition buildings and was often used for public spaces, office building exteriors, and apartment buildings (fig. 4.73). New York's Chrysler Building (1930) and the structures of Rockefeller Center, including Radio City Music Hall (1931 and after), are rich in Art Deco detail. This style also had some popularity in

4.69 In the Villa Savoye, Poissy-sur-Seine, France, of 1929–30, Le Corbusier (Charles-Édouard Jeanneret), with Pierre Jeanneret, created a vastly influential example of International Style modernism. The main living space unifies outdoor and indoor areas by means of a rolling glass wall that allows the resident to define the flow of space. The nondescript original furnishings in this rigorously modern building reflect the unavailability of anything more appropriate at the time the house was built. (Photograph: Lucien Hervé, Paris)

4.70 The main block of the house is lifted on columns, while the garage, entrance, and service space make up the small enclosed portion of the lower floor. A finely detailed exhibition model was made of the house, in wood, aluminum, and plastic, 25 x 22½ x 11⅛". The Museum of Modern Art, New York. Exhibition Fund

4.71

4.72

4.71, 4.72 Notre-Dame-du-Haut in Ronchamp, France (1950–54), is one of the most important of Le Corbusier's late works. The sculptural exterior, with its upswept roof and pattern of window perforations, includes a towerlike form enclosing a chapel, one of three. (Photograph: Marvin Trachtenberg) Inside, Notre-Dame-du-Haut is as modern as its exterior, yet it suggests earlier architectural traditions. The lighted rectangles on the right are funnel-shaped apertures in the thick south wall, each filled with stained glass. All of the interior details were designed by Le Corbusier. (Photograph: Lucien Hervé, Paris)

England and, to a lesser extent, in other European countries. It was the decorative style of the interiors of some of the last great ocean liners, such as the *Normandie*, the *Queen Mary*, and the *Queen Elizabeth*.

Another influence in the 1930s came from the introduction of streamlining in dirigible and airplane design. The rounded shapes of streamlined aircraft were taken up by the practitioners of the new profession of industrial design and adapted to trains, automobiles, furniture, and even such unlikely objects as refrigerators and pencil sharpeners (see figs. 2.15, 2.16). Industrial designers produced interior design work—most often for trains, ships, retail stores, and showrooms—using some mixture of Art Deco and streamline styles.

Postwar Modernism

After World War II, professional design work by both architects and interior designers settled into a vocabulary of modernism largely based on the work of the prewar pioneers. The influence of Gropius and Mies as teachers combined with a widening acceptance and admiration of modern work led to the adoption of *functionalism,* or the International Style, as the basis for most public and commercial work (fig. 4.78). The availability of furniture design classics by the European leaders and a full range of more recent furniture and related products by postwar designers made the modern interior readily available everywhere. The famous Glass House (with four walls of floor-to-ceiling glass) at New Canaan, Connecticut, designed in 1949 by Philip Johnson (b. 1906) for his own use, carried the aesthetic of Mies's minimalism to a dramatic

4.74

4.75

4.73 *The meticulously preserved Art Deco lobby of the Pantages Theater, Hollywood (1929–30), displays the flamboyant forms and color of architect E. Marcus Priteca's decorative fantasy. Such modernistic design stands in striking contrast to the streamlined reserve of the International Style then developing. (Photograph: Carl Iri)*

4.74 *The Skyscraper bookcase, designed circa 1928 by Paul Frankl in black-lacquered wood with silver-lacquered front edging, refers explicitly to the skyscraper architecture of the period in its nonsymmetrical center element with active setback forms. Setback and zigzag motifs are favorite elements of Art Deco design. (Photograph courtesy Phillips, New York)*

4.75 *This Art Deco bedroom by Paul Ruand (Paris, 1933) is furnished with semicircular Bibendum armchairs, a cube bed, and a decorative screen, all designed by Eileen Gray. With its African stool and zebra skins resting on a glass floor, the room exhibits an imaginative mix of Art Deco and more puristic, abstract geometric modern trends.*

4.76

4.77

4.76 Philip Johnson's own Glass House at New Canaan, Connecticut, was built in 1949. The glass perimeter wall of the house allows an unimpeded view of the interior, causing inside and outside to merge. (Photograph courtesy Philip Johnson)

4.77 Despite the glass exterior walls, the interior of the Glass House has a surprisingly sturdy character of its own, deriving from the discrete, simple elements: the brick drum, which encloses the bathroom (not visible here); the brick flooring, rug, and classic modern furniture; and the works of art displayed. (Photograph: Alexandre Georges)

4.78

extreme (figs. 4.76, 4.77). In spite of the praise granted such examples in professional circles, modernism was not widely accepted in residential interior design, which, for the most part, clung to imitations of traditional styles, with some limited inclusion of the craft-oriented Scandinavian furniture design often called Danish Modern.

RECENT DIRECTIONS

In the 1970s and 1980s, several challenges to modernism surfaced. Since this is a field for ongoing development, even struggle, it is not surprising that the differing directions in competition for domination of future design work have engendered considerable conflict and confusion. Although the rather illogical term Post-modernism has been coined to describe whatever develops beyond the modernism of the recent past, the term has in fact come to be attached to a particular direction, which is only one of several quite different approaches. Whatever term is ultimately chosen, a number of distinct directions, each developing in a lively way, can be recognized and defined.

Late Modernism

Late Modernism is a new term to define the most conservative of these directions. This work is firmly based on the modernism of the four famous pioneers, but it attempts to move forward into new forms, more adventurous and aesthetically more varied than the formulaic designs of the later generations of modernists. The work of I. M. Pei

(b. 1917), such as the East Building of the National Gallery of Art in Washington, D.C. (1978), belongs to this category (fig. 4.79). The houses and other interior work of Richard Meier (b. 1934; fig. 4.80) and Charles Gwathmey (b. 1938; see figs. 8.30 and 12.4) also fall in a direct line of development from early modern roots.

High Tech

A somewhat different direction with a basis in modernism has come to be called High Tech. It places more emphasis on the exploitation and visible display of elements of science and technology, particularly the advanced technologies of the computer-oriented, aerospace, and automated industrial fields. Early modernism was closely allied with technology in its interest in the machine and its intention to create a design vocabulary suited to the modern, technological world. Devotion to the machine has gradually come to seem somewhat dated, a rather naive and romantic view of mechanization as the solution to every problem. High Tech design moves forward into the post-machine-age technology of electronics and space exploration to learn from the advanced technology of those fields and to search out an aesthetic in their products.

Prior steps in this direction can be found in the work of Buckminster Fuller (1895–1983), best known for the development of the geodesic dome structure, which has been used in many ways, including as the American exhibition pavilion at the Montreal World's Fair of 1967 (see fig. 18.16). Charles Eames (1907–1978) also hinted at this direction in

4.78 In the 1950s, modernism's diverse influences came together in America in a widely accepted idiom easily adaptable to the facilities of large corporations. Florence Knoll Bassett, head of the Knoll Planning Unit, designed this executive reception area (1954–57) for the offices of the Connecticut General Life Insurance Company in Bloomfield, Connecticut. Skidmore, Owings & Merrill were the architects. (Photograph: © 1957 Ezra Stoller/ESTO, courtesy Skidmore, Owings & Merrill, New York)

4.79

his own house of 1949 (see fig. 6.3), assembled from industrial building components, and in his well-known and widely popular furniture designs of 1946 onward (see figs. 12.16 and 12.40).

The mature style uses industrial materials, furniture, and equipment of technological character, simple forms, and little decorative or ornamental details. Its identification with advanced technologies tends to make High Tech work look futuristic. Architects and designers of this style include Renzo Piano (b. 1931) and Richard Rogers (b. 1933), whose Centre Pompidou in Paris (1971–77; see fig. 8.14) has become an emblem of High Tech, and James Stirling (1926–1992; fig. 4.81) and Norman Foster (b. 1935) in England.

Post-Modernism

The general term Post-modern has now come to identify the recent direction that grew from the theoretical position taken by Robert Venturi (b. 1925) in his influential book of 1966 *Complexity and Contradiction in Architecture*. In it, Venturi challenges the emphasis on logic, simplicity, and order characteristic of modernism, suggesting that complexity and ambiguity have a place in design. Following this dictum in his own work, Venturi has produced designs that sometimes seem eccentric, disturbing, or banal (fig. 4.84; see also fig. 8.1).

4.80

4.79 The 1971–78 East Building—popularly called the East Wing—of the National Gallery of Art in Washington, D.C., was designed by I. M. Pei & Partners. Stairs, landings, and decks lead to the various exhibition galleries, which overlook the main entrance area and central atrium. The simple geometric forms combined in complex angular relationships are typical of this architect's work. An Alexander Calder mobile forms a colorful focal point. (Photograph: © 1978 Ezra Stoller/ESTO)

4.80 Richard Meier was the architect and interior designer for the Smith House in Darien, Connecticut, built in 1965–67 in the style now called late modernism. The simple, geometric forms and absence of ornament exemplify modernism's continuing dynamism. (Photograph: © Ezra Stoller/ESTO)

4.81

Post-modern design also departs from modernism in its willingness to include ornamentation and elements referring to historical styles. Such traditional elements are not intended to imitate past building styles but rather to act as references used out of context, often with humorous impact. Such *metaphors,* as these designers' figures of speech are often called, seem to question the seriousness of mainstream modernism. If the realities of the modern world sometimes seem to approach absurdity, Post-modernism offers us absurdities as serious creativity or, to look at this work in another way, presents serious work that can be viewed as absurd.

The American designer best known for Post-modern work (although he dislikes the term) is Michael Graves (b. 1934), whose early designs for witty and odd furniture and interiors were later joined by major architectural projects (see fig. 8.64). His Portland (Oregon) Public Service Building of 1980 was one of the most controversial projects of the period, attracting both extravagant praise and bitter condemnation. It is interesting to note that Philip Johnson (b. 1906), long a proponent of modernism in America, moved toward Post-modernism in such projects as the A.T.&T. (now Sony) headquarters office building in New

York (1984), with its references to Roman, Romanesque, and Georgian design elements (see figs. 4.76 and 18.9).

In Italy, the group that uses the title Memphis has been energetic in developing furniture and interior design that share the Post-modern inclination toward arbitrary and whimsical uses of color and form (see figs. 8.51 and 12.57). Many designers in the United States have enthusiastically adopted this style.

Deconstructivism

The term *deconstructivist* describes the work of a number of architects and designers whose designs are quite varied. However, when this work is shown in a group exhibition, as it was in 1988 at the Museum of Modern Art in New York, the cumulative impact is one of a distinct emerging style or direction. The characteristics of deconstructivism include an emphasis on elements that seem torn apart and reassembled in an apparently illogical or chaotic manner. Once such a tendency is recognized, given a name, and made the subject of exhibitions, publications, and critical comment, it takes on a life of its own, leading to increased interest and acceptance.

4.81 *The work of the late British architect James Stirling is often described as High Tech. However, the Neue Staatsgalerie in Stuttgart, West Germany, by James Stirling, Michael Wilford and Associates, architects (1984), eludes* easy classification: *It is unique in its combination of High Tech, Postmodernism, and independent, creative directions. (Photograph: Timothy Hursley, © The Arkansas Office, courtesy House & Garden)*

4.82, 4.83 *In the Parc de la Villette project, architect Bernard Tschumi has created a series of small bright red pavilions that seem to be fragments of a larger whole. These "follies," as he calls them, are complex and eccentric* in form, as demonstrated by both the exterior and the interior of one pavilion. Tschumi's work is representative of the recent deconstructivist direction in architecture. (Photographs: © Peter Mauss/ESTO)

4.82

4.83

4.84

In deconstructivist projects, design elements—instead of being constructed into unified wholes—are de-constructed, separated, and pulled out from a whole in ways that frequently result in sharply angled, overlapping, and interpenetrating forms that deliberately deny the traditions of architectural and design aesthetics. External elements seem to break into interior space, while interiors, often not clearly bounded, break out from containment. The term *deconstructivist* has been chosen in part to describe these qualities, in part to recall the term Constructivism, which in art history describes the work of a movement of the 1920s centered in the Russian avant-garde, before the Soviet government suppressed all modernism in exchange for a propagandistic "realism." The creations of such artists and architects as Alexander Rodchenko (1891–1956), Vladimir Tatlin (1885–1953), and Kasimir Malevich (1878–1935) had an emphasis somewhat similar to deconstructivism in that the assembly of elements appears disjointed and unrelated except as it is put together in a particular work.

The American architect Frank Gehry (b. 1929) has produced designs that have often been classified as Post-modernist but have not fit this identification comfortably. His own house, originally a nondescript suburban building in Santa Monica, California, has since 1978 undergone a series of remodelings in which spaces have been torn and fractured, while elements taken from banal construction practice have been added to exterior surfaces in an effort to fragment existing forms. Another American, Peter Eisenman (b. 1932), is the designer of a vast as yet unbuilt complex for the University of Frankfurt in which units that seem ripped apart are distributed along a linking spine to create complex and disturbing relationships (fig. 4.85).

In Paris, a new park, the Parc de la Villette, is studded with a number of small pavilions—each different but each related to the others in dimension (a small cube) and in color (bright red)—that seem to be fragments of some larger whole (figs. 4.82 and 4.83). Although the forms of these follies (as the designer calls them) are eccentric and

4.84 In the dining room of Robert Venturi's Philadelphia home, which dates from the turn of the century, the owners have chosen to keep the original woodwork and leaded-glass cabinet doors. The stenciled walls and whimsical display of famous names above, the chairs of uncertain period, and the eclectic collection of pictures and objects confer an inclusive, multifaceted personality on the space—a theme in the Venturi design theory that has informed the development of Post-modernism. The design was done by Venturi, Rauch and Scott Brown, architects, in 1983. (Photograph: © Paul Warchol)

complex, their effect is playful and cheerful rather than forbidding. They are the work of the Swiss-born but now New York–based Bernard Tschumi (b. 1944).

Underlying all deconstructivist work is a clear challenge to any design that strives for formulas of complacent charm and acceptability. The arches and pinnacles so obligatory to the Post-modern skyscraper and the replay of traditional elements that make so many suburban houses appealing to a large public seem, like television entertainment and junk food, too simplistic. Deconstructivism has taken up a search for more meaning and more strength.

The variety of different and often conflicting currents now running in the design world is characteristic of a period of change in which established norms seem to have outlived their usefulness while new norms have not yet taken clear form, similar to the Mannerist developments in Italy in the sixteenth century, when the established ascendancy of classical design systems came into question while the Baroque of the seventeenth century had not fully emerged. Mannerism was a style in transition, permitting experimentation, the testing of new and sometimes outrageous or extreme ideas, confusion, and rich

development. If the present is also such a time, it is not surprising that untried and disturbing forms are evident.

Living and working in design at such a time may not be as easy as it is in the middle of a well-established period, but the level of excitement and interest is higher. Public awareness of design issues and involvement in controversy increase at such a time and make design a lively and vital field rather than a settled craft. The close of the twentieth century promises to become one of the most interesting of all historical design periods.

NON-EUROPEAN TRADITIONS

Until the last few centuries, geographical regions separated by long distances had little means of communication. European traditions developed over the past 5,000 years, independent of remote civilizations that were largely unknown. Each of the great non-European ancient civilizations not only has a history but also a *design* history that can become a lifetime study. Here, it is possible only to provide some general comments, with emphasis on the ways in which non-European

4.85

4.85 The Biocenter at J. W. Goethe University in Frankfurt, Germany, represented here in model form, is a 1987 project, yet unbuilt, by architect Peter Eisenman. Like other deconstructivist work, this structure is made up of elements that seem to have been torn apart and reassembled. (Photograph: Dick Frank Studios)

4.86

design has from time to time been valued in Europe and exerted some degree of influence. The cultures of particular interest for these purposes are those of the Far East (primarily China and Japan), of the Islamic world, and of pre-Columbian America.

China

Civilization in China developed in the Stone Age, and Chinese written history begins around 3000 B.C. Although Chinese artwork has survived from very early periods, our knowledge of Chinese architecture and interior design extends only a few centuries into the past. The preferred building materials, wood and bamboo, are not long lasting, so few ancient structures survive; stone, an available building material in China, has generally been used solely for platforms, understructure, and enclosing walls. Nonetheless, because Chinese culture has been, until very recent times, extremely conservative, the traditional design of the last few centuries is believed to differ little from earlier practice.

Marco Polo's visit to the Far East occurred in the thirteenth century,

allowing access to Chinese art and decorative design. However, information concerning built structures remained scant until the eighteenth century, when the development of the tea trade and the importation of artwork, landscape paintings, and wallpapers illustrating Chinese architecture brought fresh knowledge to the West. Paper was invented in China, and wallpapers were made there as early as 200 B.C. In the first part of the sixteenth century, hand-painted papers, made in small sections (about 12 by 16 inches) and decorated with flowers, birds, and landscape motifs, began to be imported into Europe (fig. 4.87). By the eighteenth century, *Chinoiserie,* a fashion for Chinese motifs based on a fascination with the exotic products of a distant culture, had become widespread in France and England. Actual imported objects—porcelains, teak tables, and other small pieces of furniture and artwork brought by the ships of the tea trade—led to the use of Chinese motifs in the furniture designs of Thomas Chippendale and other English cabinetmakers of the Georgian era (fig. 4.88). Photography, a still later development, has offered detailed imagery of Chinese architecture and

4.86 *The Peacock Room was designed by artist James Abbott McNeill Whistler in 1876–77, when the influence of Oriental art and design was at its peak in England. The painting in this detail of the room, now installed in the Freer*

Gallery of Art, Smithsonian Institution, Washington, D.C., is Whistler's The Princess from the Land of Porcelain. (Photograph courtesy the Freer Gallery of Art, Smithsonian Institution, Washington, D.C.)

interiors only in relatively recent years. Efforts to create complete interiors in a Chinese idiom have predominantly been restricted to spaces with a highly exotic character, as in some theaters of the 1920s.

The typical traditional Chinese building uses a framework of wood posts and beams assembled into a cage structure in some ways similar to the framing of modern Western structures. The parts of a wood (or bamboo) frame were locked together with ingenious joints that required no nails or screws, generating a structure that has good resistance to earthquakes but only moderate resistance to fire, rot, and insect damage. Although often used as a base, masonry was only occasionally used for wall panels inserted between posts, somewhat in the manner of European half-timber work. Sloping roofs surfaced with thatch, shingles, or tile have been used since the earliest times, but the support of roofs does not use the Western system of rafters that form a triangular gable; instead, a beam spanning the width of an interior space supports short posts that support a shorter beam that in turn supports another, still shorter post-and-beam assembly, creating a stack of diminishing rectangular units that hold the sloping roof. It is probably this system of construction that has given rise to the most obvious characteristics of traditional Chinese architecture. Roof surfaces are generally curved in a concave line that continues outward beyond the enclosed space to form broad eaves. Several successive levels of eaves are frequently formed, generating a highly distinctive building silhouette.

Inside, the connections between supporting posts and beams are made with complex interlocking brackets that form intricate and high-ly decorative patterns. Palaces, temples, pagodas, and houses were all built with variations on this general scheme. Towerlike pagodas use a succession of typical bracketed roof structures to generate the picturesque multiroofed form. Interior spaces are usually open halls of varied size with the posts, beams, and brackets all painted in strong and bright colors, creating a richly ornamental effect. The favored colors are vermilion red, deep green, black, and gold. Windows, doors, and wall panels may be perforated screens having elaborate, small-scale decorative patterns.

Houses are often composed of several pavilionlike units arranged around an open court. Other plans weave open courts and garden spaces into more complex groupings. In general, strict symmetry is valued; larger temple and palace complexes are frequently made up of a sequence of larger central pavilions and paired smaller units arranged symmetrically along a lengthwise axis, most often carefully oriented along a north-south line. Movement is generally blocked along the center axis—it becomes necessary to move to one side or the other to pass a barrier and progress to the next centrally positioned pavilion.

Traditional Chinese furniture, as made for the more affluent, is of fine quality in both design and construction. Many examples from the seventeenth and eighteenth centuries are of simple but elegant form made up from wood members that combine straight lines and subtle curves. Chairs, usually with arms, are made in a variety of shapes (fig. 4.89). Tables may be square or oblong, at writing height or low. Cabinets are often beautifully decorated with lacquered surfaces and decorative hardware.

4.87

4.87 Hand-painted Chinese wallpaper imported into Europe and America in the eighteenth century helped fuel the Western enthusiasm for Chinese art and design. This example is from Westbury House at Old Westbury Gardens, Old Westbury, New York. (Photograph: Zindman/Fremont)

4.88　　　　　　4.89

Beds consisted of a low platform that could be covered with soft padding for sleeping but that in daytime could be used as a seating area. In the colder climate of north China, such a bed was often built of brick, accommodating an arrangement under the platform for heating by a fire that could be tended from outside the bed. In the south, carved screening might surround such a raised bed, creating a kind of room within a room.

Japan

Japanese design has exerted an influence on Western practice through several lines of contact. In the nineteenth century, Japanese prints became known in England and were admired by the artistically inclined who made up the Aesthetic movement that linked fine art with the Arts & Crafts movement. The painting of James Abbott McNeill Whistler (1834–1903) has an obvious connection with Japanese art, while his Peacock Room (1876–77), now preserved in the Freer Gallery of Art in

4.90

4.88 An engraving from Thomas Chippendale's book The Gentleman & Cabinet Maker's Directory of 1762 shows a chair in the Chinese style that was fashionable at the time.

4.89 The great delicacy and elegance of traditional Chinese furniture can be seen in this eighteenth-century chair, which combines straight lines and subtle curves. The Metropolitan Museum of Art, New York. Seymour Fund, 1967

4.90 The main building of the Ise shrine in southwest Honshu, Mie prefecture, Japan, was first built in A.D. 478 and, with only a few exceptions, has been reconstructed every twenty

years since. The structure consists of a basic frame of wood posts, beams, and rafters enclosed by plain wood planks; the roof is of thatch. (Photograph: © Yoshio Watanabe, Tokyo)

4.91

Washington, D.C., was clearly an effort to absorb Japanese traditions into Western design (fig. 4.86). By the 1870s, Londoners could, and often did, acquire screens, boxes, ceramics, and other decorative objects from shops specializing in such imports. In France, Siegfried (later Samuel) Bing (1838–1905) was drawn into the fashionable interest in Japanese art and design stimulated by the Japanese exhibits at the Paris World's Fair of 1878. His Paris shop, called L'Art Nouveau, opened in 1895 and included Japanese imports among its offerings. The mixture of work from the European Art Nouveau movement with actual Japanese works shows a clear intention to absorb Japanese aesthetic concepts into Western design. Awareness of Japanese architecture and interior design was developed through such publications as Edward S. Morse's 1885 book *Japanese Homes and Their Surroundings*. With the coming of modernism in the twentieth century in Europe and America, traditional Japanese design came to be regarded as predictive of the directions appropriate to current thinking.

Although the design and architecture of Japan has early links with Chinese sources, these influences came to Japan by way of Korea. Certain Shinto shrines—built to house the spirits of deities and supernatural beings of Japan's indigenous, pre-Buddhist religion—have been rebuilt at regular intervals for nearly 1,500 years. These replicate the originals in form and material, and they display the affinity for the natural world that characterizes so much of traditional Japanese design. Izumo shrine, first built before A.D. 550, survives in rebuilt form. It is a simple single interior space defined by wood posts resting on an elevated wood platform reached by a stair. A gabled roof extends out to the edge of the platform, forming a surrounding porch. Although the structure is symmetrical, the stair and entrance are not centered but placed in the right-hand half of the structure. Ise shrine, originally built in A.D. 478 and rebuilt every twenty years since, is made up of several similar structures placed within a fenced enclosure (fig. 4.90). The basic frame of wood posts, beams, and rafters is enclosed by plain wood planks set into grooves in the posts. With no applied decoration, the austere simplicity that characterizes so much of traditional Japanese design is clearly evident.

Beginning in the eighth century, shrines, temples, and pagodas were built in a style strongly influenced by Chinese practice. Roofs with curving profiles, upturned eaves, and multiple-level "stacked" roofs; bracketed-wood interior construction; and rich decoration came into use, with the result that many of these buildings are almost indistinguishable from Chinese buildings of the same period.

The concept of a wood frame supporting a sloping roof with all structure internally exposed and with a minimum of applied decoration came to be much admired by Western visitors to Japan and exerted considerable influence in the development of modern twentieth-century Western design. A typical Japanese house has a floor raised off the ground on posts bearing a pavilionlike area with regularly placed wood posts supporting a wooden roof structure. The plan layout is modular, with the basic module the dimensions of the tatami straw mats made in a uniform size—about three by six feet. Room

4.91 The Shoin of the seventeenth-century Detached Palace at Katsura, near Kyoto, Japan, is an example of traditional Japanese architectural design in its most perfected form. (Photograph: Okamato Shigeo)

4.92

4.93

areas are defined by the arrangement of mats, and room arrangement is often quite free and asymmetrical, creating linked pavilions with open courts and gardens interwoven with enclosed spaces. Most walls are sliding screen panels, or shoji, that make it possible to open up or divide interior space at will.

Zen Buddhism, with its ideas of simplicity, its respect for nature, and its emphasis on an aesthetic developed on the basis of a philosophy that might be called minimalist, was a strong influence in the development of Japanese design traditions. The ceremonial drinking of tea was honored in special rooms in houses, and in special teahouses, where a small hearth sunken in the floor served for heating water, but there was no furniture.

Traditional Japanese practice, in fact, did not call for furniture to any significant degree. Cushions were placed on the floor for seating, and small charcoal heaters called hibachi provided portable heat. A fixed charcoal burner called a *kotatsu*, sunk into the floor and with a low raised top, was also used; cloth quilts could be stretched over it and over the feet and legs of those sitting around it to gain warmth. A bed could be made up anywhere by placing soft pads on the floor mats. Small drawer chests, cabinets, and low tables were normally kept put away, to be brought out only as needed and then put away again, out of sight. A clear alcove called a tokonoma could hold a hanging scroll painting and flower arrangements set on a slightly raised floor platform. Other alcoves could include some shelves or built-in cabinets. Shoji screens were basic and geometric in decoration or bore more complex patterns. Portable folding screens, some richly embellished with landscape or other painted art, appeared frequently. Candle holders, lanterns, and lamps using oil and wicks provided nighttime illumination. A kitchen might be no more than an area surrounding an open

4.92 The spirit of traditional Japanese design survives in the interior of this modern (1981) residence, where concrete replaces wood as the primary material. The house, near Kobe, Japan, was designed by Tadao Ando. (Photograph: Gilles de Chabaneix)

4.93 "Oriental" rugs have been popular elements in European and American interiors since the Renaissance. Pictured here is a portion of an Islamic carpet, a Persian "garden rug" from Kurdistan dating from the first half of the eighteenth century. The Metropolitan Museum of Art, New York. Gift of James F. Ballard, 1922. The James F. Ballard Collection

4.94

hearth or a fireplace where cooking could be done with simple pots and utensils. Bathing called for great wooden tubs, often with an integral arrangement for heating at the bottom. A latrine was a neatly edged floor opening serving a box placed below, accessible from outside.

The patterns of wooden grid structure and sliding wood-and-paper shoji, along with the openness of plan and the absence of furniture, suggest a precursor of the qualities that were to develop in the modernism of Europe and America in the twentieth century. Certain historic examples, such as the great Katsura Detached Palace complex at Kyoto (early seventeenth century), a vast and superbly refined example of the typical traditional house, have become the focus of interest for Western moderns who find in them a special order of perfection (fig. 4.91). It is clear from his later work that during his long stay in Japan, Frank Lloyd Wright became strongly influenced by the culture's traditional designs.

The flow of European influence into Japanese culture has tended to overwhelm aesthetic traditions and replace them with a somewhat diluted version of Western styles. The fact that the traditional architecture of Japan never placed great emphasis on comfort and convenience—never developing any practical system of heating, for example—has probably contributed to its decline. Some modern Japanese architects have moved toward an integration of some aspects of traditional work, such as its abstract visual forms, into modern practice using Western technology. Kenzo Tange (b. 1913) is the best-known representative of this direction, while Tadao Ando (b. 1941; fig. 4.92) and Arata Isozaki (b. 1931) have developed an international practice based on a fusion of the best of Eastern and Western traditions.

The Islamic World

The spread of Muslim religious belief, beginning with Muhammad's revelations of A.D. 610 to 620, carried with it architectural and design ideas that became varied as they developed in differing geographical regions. The text of the Koran and the common use of Arabic established a core of consistency in spite of the variety generated in the

stretch from Moorish Spain across North Africa, the Middle East, and Turkey into India and what is now Pakistan. With its vast reach in both time and geography, it is not surprising that Islamic design is so diverse as to make characterization difficult. Still, certain themes can be recognized. The mosque is the significant building type on which design effort has been focused. Although mosques differ greatly in concept, as a prayer hall the emphasis is always on interior space rather than external massing. The technology of building is concentrated on arch, vault, and dome construction in masonry, with arch forms including the pointed arch, the wider four-centered arch, and, particularly in Spain and Portugal, the horseshoe arch. The tall pointed forms of European Gothic design and the directional, lengthwise orientation of the Gothic church contrast with plans that are predominantly nondirectional, grouping repeated bay units in clusters that expand in all directions, with only certain internal elements oriented toward Mecca. Buttressing is not a significant visual element, and great heights are rarely attempted except in minaret towers.

The Sunni rejection of the representation of living things—human, animal, and plant—encouraged the development of a vocabulary of abstract decoration, small in scale and rich in elaboration. Walls and arches were often built with alternate bands of stone in contrasting colors (most often red and white), and surface decoration in ceramic tiles and mosaics in bright and varied colors were common. The undersurfaces of arches and domes were often treated with many brackets and niches called *muqarnas* (or stalactites), forming a complex cellular surface. Although representational art was permitted in Shiite regions, building decoration remained generally abstract. The decorative use of Arabic calligraphy in Islamic art was of paramount importance. Arabic is the language Allah chose for his revelations to Muhammad, and the Koran, to the Muslim, is the record of those revelations and contains the actual words of God. Calligraphy appears as a design element in all forms of Islamic art.

4.95

4.94 The courtyard of the Great Mosque at Damascus, Syria (circa A.D. 706–15) is part of a walled precinct, a not-uncommon feature of Islamic religious architecture. At Damascus, a former Roman precinct was appropriated as the basis of the mosque. The courtyard is framed by arcaded galleries; the sanctuary's north side and façade form one wall of the courtyard, seen to the left.

4.95 Decorative tilework above the arches of the Lion Court of the Alhambra palace at Granada, Spain, built in the thirteenth and fourteenth centuries, is characteristic of Moorish (Islamic) work in that country. (Photograph courtesy Spanish National Tourist Office)

A mosque such as the Great Mosque at Damascus (A.D. 706–15) is made up of an open courtyard with a vast adjacent arcaded prayer hall (fig. 4.94). The *mihrab*, a niche oriented toward Mecca, and the *minbar*, a pulpit for preaching, are the only elements that stand within a columned prayer hall. In Spain, the Mosque at Córdoba (A.D. 784–86, with later additions) is made up of a court and another vast prayer hall with two tiers of arches resting on a huge number of columns. The lower arches are of the characteristic horseshoe form, while the upper semicircular arches are raised on square "stilts" that rest, in turn, on columns. The *mihrab* (A.D. 962–66) is topped by a dome made from a complex grid of intersecting arches. Later mosques, such as that of Sultan Süleyman I at Istanbul (1550), have an open interior hall topped by a high dome with half-domes on either end, a concept clearly based on such Byzantine structures as Hagia Sophia, also in Istanbul (see fig. 4.13).

4.97

4.96

The palace called the Alhambra at Granada, Spain, of the thirteenth and fourteenth centuries, is a complex cluster of open courts with fountains and ponds and adjacent halls with columns supporting arches and domes, all elaborately and colorfully decorated (fig. 4.95). Although much Islamic design concentrates on interior space with minor concern for exterior form, tombs, especially those built in India, are well known for their external mass. The most famous of such buildings, the Taj Mahal (1630–53) at Agra, is made up of a central domed chamber surrounded by passages that link four smaller chambers at the corners of the symmetrical square plan. An upper dome rises to a height of almost 200 feet. Marble wall surfaces, both inside and out, are carved and ornamented with gold and color detail.

Islamic design has exerted influence on European practice through various exchanges. The Moorish invasions of southern Europe and the long presence of the Muslims in Spain exposed a wider population to a largely unknown culture. Further contacts with North African and Indian design resulted through the activities of colonialism, which reached a peak in the nineteenth century. The most direct link between Islamic and Western design has turned out to be the carpets and rugs made in

many Islamic regions; these products frequently exhibit the abstract forms of Islamic ornamentalism at their best. Rugs, both antique and of recent or current manufacture, are readily transportable and have served to make this aspect of Islamic art a familiar element of interior design practice even up to the present day (fig. 4.93).

Pre-Columbian America

Although Native American design as it developed before the arrival of European colonizers is commonly known through such artifacts as rugs and pottery, these objects are generally viewed as isolated artworks to be collected or displayed, with little or no direct impact on the design of complete interiors. North American cultures either were nomadic or built with fugitive materials, so that scarcely any surviving interior spaces are available for study. In the southwest regions of North America, Navajo, Hopi, and Zuni builders of adobe structures have left a somewhat more complete legacy of vernacular architectural forms, and here, too, interiors are of simple character, with portable artifacts the primary evidence of unique, creative achievement (fig. 4.96).

In Mexico as well as in Central and South America, the highly developed civilizations of the Toltec, Aztec, Mayan, and Inca populations created great cities that included monumental structures. The Spanish conquerors who devastated these cultures left only the great stone structures that were too massive to destroy or plunder, such as the temples at the Mayan site of Chichén Itzá dating from the fifth to thirteenth centuries A.D. Almost none of these surviving monuments include significant interior space (fig. 4.97). Many pre-Columbian structures are covered with carved abstract and fantastic images that seem connected with religious beliefs, mythology, and magical concepts. The impact of this work on later design has thus far been minimal. Mayan or Aztec decorative detail is sometimes imitated in a superficial way to generate novelty in a theater or restaurant. The work of Frank Lloyd Wright in the 1920s (in the Millard, Storer, and Ennis houses in California, for example) is sometimes related to Mayan themes; it seems more likely, however, that the use of patterned concrete block, a constructional system that Wright was experimenting with at the time, generated wall surfaces whose ornamental resemblance to Mayan precedent was purely fortuitous.

4.96 The simplicity and logic characteristic of pueblo architecture, the vernacular building type of the Native American populations of the southwestern United States, are suggestive of modern design. Photographed circa 1887–96, this cluster of houses at Taos Pueblo, New Mexico, is known as South House. (Photograph courtesy The Southwest Museum, Los Angeles)

4.97 The Upper Temple of the Jaguars, overlooking the Ball Court at Chichén Itzá, Mexico (1000–1200), is typical of the monumental structures created by the highly developed pre-Columbian civilizations in America. (Photograph: Jeffrey Jay Foxx, New York City)

5.1

5.2

THE DESIGN PROCESS

When visiting an interior space or looking at photographs of completed projects (such as those in this book), it is often hard to imagine how the many elements present were brought together in an organized and pleasing totality. The ability to manage this process is one of the key skills of the interior designer, equal in importance to the aesthetic capability that determines the success of a project in visual terms. Until the nineteenth century, formal training for designers scarcely existed—designers were either trained by apprenticeship or entirely self-taught. The apprentice learned every step of the design process by working closely with a master, seeing actual projects through from beginning to end. The self-taught designer learned from experiment and mistake, with the mistakes often painful to designer and client alike.

In the mid-nineteenth century, design and architecture became subjects for formal training at the famous École des Beaux-Arts in Paris. The system of teaching devised there has, with minor modifications, become the method used in virtually all design schools. The "Beaux-Arts method" is based on the simulation of an actual project as it might present itself in professional practice. A written *problem* is prepared, describing the specific requirements that a client might bring to a designer. All of the students in a class are given the problem and asked to develop a *solution* in a limited period of time, usually five or six weeks. Students work under the direction of an instructor or *critic*, who offers advice and suggestions as sketches are made and developed into formal presentations of finished drawings (and sometimes models as well), which are then evaluated and graded by a *jury* of several professionals and instructors. The design problems assigned increase in complexity as the student advances.

This remarkably successful method of teaching is the basis for the skills of almost all currently practicing design professionals. It has, however, some obvious limitations. Each project begins with a written problem that must substitute for a relationship with an actual client.

Although the space to be worked on may be real or imaginary, the student encounters it as a given condition, most often to be known solely through drawings. As the design is developed, there is no interaction with a real client; instead, the critic, a trained design professional, offers direction based on standards and attitudes that may be quite different from those of a lay client. While the completed project is presented in drawings similar to those that might be shown to a client, the reaction to it that is offered the student again comes from professionals and does not allow for the interaction, revision, and further development crucial to projects undertaken with bona fide clients.

The student project ends with the presentation and response. The steps that would be involved in moving forward to execution of the project, the details of construction, purchasing, supervision, and completion, are not experienced because there is no way to carry through these steps in the school setting. As a result, the graduating student is fully trained in a key stage of the design process yet has only general knowledge of the many steps that come before and after the central phase. Professional designers will usually admit that their formal training dealt with only a small part (perhaps no more than 10 to 25 percent) of the process that a real project involves. Learning about the remainder of the design process must then take place on the job, usually as an employee of a professional design firm. It is the *total* process of design projects, from beginning to completion and beyond, that is the subject of the following discussion.

SEQUENTIAL OUTLINE

Every interior design project must be taken through a number of working steps in a logical order. The size of the project and the designer-client relationship will determine what steps are necessary. The simplest of projects—a single room, perhaps with the designer as his or her own client—may hardly require any formal organization of work

5.1, 5.2 As demonstrated by these perspectives produced with DesignCAD 3D, software developed by American Small Business Computers, computer-aided techniques can generate schematic images that simplify the planning process. Elements of an interior, including even minor decorative details, can be drawn, placed, colored, shaded, and detailed with convincing realism. Reflected, diffused, or ambient lighting from various sources can be simulated. The luxury bathroom (above) and windowed kitchen (below) can be repeatedly modified on the computer screen until design, color, and details are exactly as the designer intends. (Photographs courtesy American Small Business Computers) and may omit some steps that might seem overelaborate. Larger projects and projects that require client approval of design decisions call for more organization and systematization. In extensive projects involving many spaces and serving many people, orderly working methods are essential. They not only ensure efficient work processing, they also reassure corporate and institutional clients, who will certainly expect such methods.

One of the striking differences between the amateur interior designer and the skilled expert is that the amateur tends to approach the project without any work plan. Making decisions without reference to a clear sequential order leads to revisions and mistakes. The end result often looks makeshift and poorly planned.

Some of the sequential steps common to many design projects may at times be omitted. Construction drawings may not be needed if there will be no new construction. Estimates and bids may not be involved when items to be purchased are few and of known price. Steps are sometimes combined—programming may include space allocation, for example—and steps are often overlapped in time sequence. It is nevertheless useful to consider a listing of typical steps and to examine what each step involves in some detail. (In the following checklist an asterisk is used to identify the steps included in a typical school design problem.)

CHECKLIST OF DESIGN STEPS

PROJECT BEGINNINGS
Establish contact with client
Outline scope of project
Outline time schedule and budget
Determine need for specialized consultants
Agree on designer-client contract relationship
Schedule design work
Select space(s) to be dealt with

PROGRAMMING
Obtain or prepare a survey of space(s)
Conduct interviews and collect data on requirements
Develop preliminary program
Review preliminary program with client
Prepare final program
Obtain program approval from client
Develop space allocation
Prepare adjacency studies

PRELIMINARY STEPS
*Develop preliminary design
Review preliminary design with client
*Revise and finalize preliminary design
Obtain client approval of preliminary design

DESIGN DEVELOPMENT
*Develop detailed design
*Make material selections
Select purchased items

*Select colors and finishes
Estimate costs
*Prepare final design
Prepare detailed budget
*Prepare presentation
*Make presentation to client
Review budget with client
Make revisions as necessary
Obtain client approval of design and budget

WORKING DRAWINGS AND BIDDING
Prepare construction drawings
Prepare detail drawings
Prepare specifications
Make cost estimates and obtain bids
Make time schedule for construction and installation
Select contractors and issue work orders
Prepare and issue purchase orders

SUPERVISION
Supervise construction (including demolition where required)
Coordinate and expedite construction and deliveries
Supervise installation and completion
List defects and errors and supervise correction
Supervise move-in

POST-COMPLETION
Make needed adjustments and changes
Prepare post-move-in evaluation

Many projects present further complications when they are comprised of a number of units, each one of which is, in a sense, a separate design project. Various rooms of a building, for example, or floors of a multifloor project may call for individual design treatments and may be *phased* so as to progress on different time schedules.

Although many of the details involved in the steps listed above are discussed in greater detail in various chapters of this book, an overview of the entire design process as outlined here can be beneficial.

PROJECT BEGINNINGS

ESTABLISH CONTACT WITH CLIENT. Designers find clients in various ways, including reputation from previous projects, recommendations of satisfied clients, social contacts, and aggressive sales efforts. The best situation is when a prospective client approaches a designer with a desire to assign a project. Many prospective clients contact several designers and ask them to present their method of work and examples of previous projects. The making of sketches or design proposals as a means of attracting a client is generally regarded as unethical. Ideally a degree of rapport and trust between designer and client-to-be should be established at the very beginning of a relationship.

OUTLINE SCOPE OF PROJECT. While it is the prospective client who must tell the designer what work is contemplated, the designer very often has an active role in helping the client define what is called for. Clients often have only a vague (or even mistaken) idea of what a project calls for and what possibilities exist. Discussion at this stage will form the basis for the next steps.

OUTLINE TIME SCHEDULE AND BUDGET. It is important that designer and client have a shared understanding of what is desired and what is possible in these important areas. Clients are frequently quite unrealistic in their expectations. It is generally unwise to go along with accepting goals that cannot be realized even if this seems to be necessary to obtain an assignment. Trouble will surface later if a client begins a project with expectations that seem certain to lead to disappointments.

DETERMINE NEED FOR SPECIALIZED CONSULTANTS. Most larger projects, and some smaller ones, call for the involvement of various professionals in addition to the interior designer. There may be an architect already enlisted before an interior designer is selected, or the services of an architect or engineer may be required to deal with aspects of the interior project. Consultants in the specialized fields of lighting, acoustics, and code compliance may be necessary as a project progresses. It is best to reach an understanding about how these services will be obtained and paid for at the beginning of a project. The relationship between interior designer and architect is particularly important—there must be mutual respect and a clear understanding about the areas of responsibility of each if a project is to proceed satisfactorily.

AGREE ON DESIGNER-CLIENT CONTRACT RELATIONSHIP. Whether a standard form of contract or a simple letter of agreement is used, it is important to negotiate fees, schedule of payment, and other business matters at the beginning of a project. It is unwise to proceed with any further steps until an agreement has been reached and put into writing. Details of business issues are the subject of Chapter 19; client contracts are discussed beginning on page 544.

SCHEDULE DESIGN WORK. Scheduling is the responsibility of the designer together with whatever assistants or staff are to be employed. Target dates need to be set for beginning and ending each step, with an eye to meeting the expectations of the client. To be realistic, a schedule must consider not only the time the designer and staff will need to spend on the new project but also the time required by any other projects that may be in the works. Charts are often helpful in showing the relationship of steps that may overlap or be dependent on one another. Scheduling through the use of such sophisticated techniques as PERT (Project Evaluation and Review Technique) and CPM (Critical Path Method) can be of great assistance in large and complex projects (figs. 5.3 and 5.4).

SELECT SPACE(S) TO BE DEALT WITH. This step is not required when the project is to deal with an existing space; many projects, how-ever, begin before a space has been selected. A client who is about to rent a new apartment, buy a house, or lease floors in an office building can often be helped to make a wise choice through the advice of a designer. Different possibilities may be more or less suitable to a client's needs and may involve greater or lesser costs in ways that will be more evident to the experienced designer than to the client. The selection of a particular space is, of course, a necessary step before more detailed design can begin.

PROGRAMMING

OBTAIN OR PREPARE A SURVEY OF SPACE(S). Architectural plans may be available for either an existing space or a space not yet constructed. It is necessary to check plans of existing space against the actual reality, since built space often does not comply with available plans as a result of changes made during construction or later alterations. If no plans for existing space are available, the designer must make a carefully measured survey so that drawings can be prepared. Even small projects that involve only furniture and color selection require accurate plans for intelligent design decisions. Taking photographs of existing space can make small details available visually, eliminating the need to revisit the space.

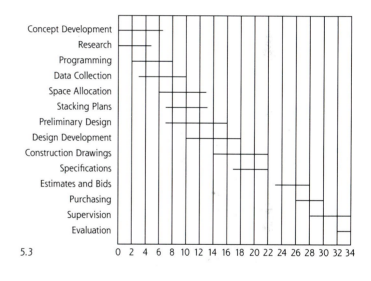

5.3

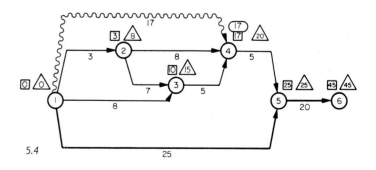

5.4

5.3 A PERT (Project Evaluation and Review Technique) chart in bar (or Gantt) form shows the time required for the various steps of a project. Overlapping bars suggest that certain steps of the project may occur at the same time. Comparing the actual time for the completion of a step with the planned time shown in the chart helps monitor the development of a project.

5.4 In this CPM (Critical Path Method) chart, lines represent activities or processes, circles, or nodes, represent the beginnings and ends of processes. Numbers indicate the duration of each step (in days or weeks). The critical path that gives the system its name is the route through the chart, from left to right, that adds up to the longest total time. This represents, therefore, the shortest possible time in which the project can be completed if each stage remains on schedule, and thus is the sequence most attentively monitored. Other paths allow some leeway in time—the float, indicated by numbers in boxes—and are not critical. (From Critical Path Method by A. T. Armstrong-Wright)

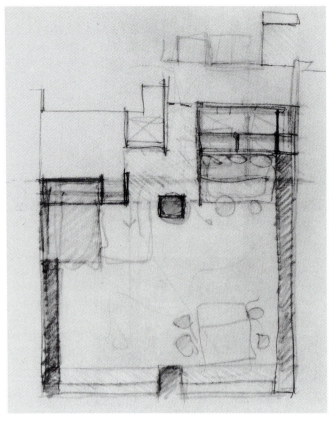

5.5

CONDUCT INTERVIEWS AND COLLECT DATA ON REQUIREMENTS. For simple projects information on requirements can often be obtained from a client in some of the earlier meetings listed above. For complex projects it is usually necessary to interview many individuals, department heads, managers, workers, or typical users of the projected spaces to discover what detailed requirements may exist. Data collection is discussed more fully in Chapter 6.

DEVELOP PRELIMINARY PROGRAM. Programming is a vital part of interior design work. A full discussion appears in Chapter 6, beginning on page 156. The preliminary program is a draft describing the general requirements of the project and listing the spaces called for, with their functions and specific needs. It is prepared as a basis for the next step.

REVIEW PRELIMINARY PROGRAM WITH CLIENT. At this time the client has an opportunity to add or subtract information, make changes, and correct errors. When the client is a large organization, this review may be done by a committee or by a number of individuals who have detailed knowledge of particular parts of the project.

PREPARE FINAL PROGRAM. Any revisions required after the preceding step are made at this time, so that the program becomes a "bible"

to guide all further design work. Specialized consultants offer programming services independent of the work of a designer. Some clients may have commissioned such programming and may come to a designer with a complete project program already in hand.

OBTAIN PROGRAM APPROVAL FROM CLIENT. Confirmation of full agreement between designer and client regarding the program requirements must be secured before work progresses.

DEVELOP SPACE ALLOCATION. This step may have been partially or completely included in the program described above. Many programs leave open the exact allocation of space. The assignment of space in terms of square-foot areas is detailed in Chapter 6, page 158. A graphic chart or *block diagram* (see fig. 6.29) makes space allocations visually accessible.

PREPARE ADJACENCY STUDIES. Drawing information from the program and possibly from additional survey data, the relationship of spaces is studied and charted using matrix charts, link-value charts, and bubble diagrams (see figs. 6.30–6.35).

5.5 *This rough sketch, done in soft pencil on thin tracing paper, represents a living and dining area under development by interior designer Norman Diekman. Many such sketches are generated in the course of elaborating design ideas. (Courtesy Norman Diekman)*

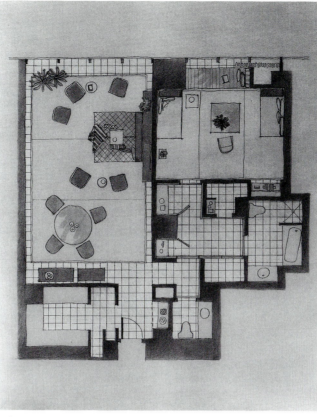

5.6

PRELIMINARY STEPS

DEVELOP PRELIMINARY DESIGN. This is the most crucial point in the design process. Creativity, the subject of fuller discussion in Chapter 6, page 145, comes into play in the effort to find approaches that will be original, aesthetically satisfying, valid solutions to the problems defined through programming. Even experienced and highly skilled designers often find it difficult to explain how this aspect of the design process works. They will say that they "think about" the problem until they are "hit by an idea." One method of defining this process suggests that the designer holds in memory a stock of data consisting of innumerable bits of information, abstract shapes, forms, colors, awareness of historical materials, places seen, experiences, and philosophical concepts that the mind searches in an unconscious effort to find elements that can be combined into a new construct, a proposed solution to the problem at hand.

Education, whether formal or informal, can be viewed as a matter of building up the store of data held in the mind, the *vocabulary* from which fragments of ideas can be drawn to create a new set of relationships. In *Notes on the Synthesis of Form*, Christopher Alexander has suggested the idea of "fit and mis-fit variables." The problem is viewed as a set of demands that calls for related elements that will fit the requirements, much as one piece of a jigsaw puzzle fits into the matching forms of adjacent pieces. One assembles the puzzle picture by searching for fits; piece after piece is picked up, tried, and found to be a misfit until, finally, the right piece slips into place. Something like this goes on as the designer's mind searches memory to find elements that meet the needs of the given problem.

During this phase of the process, a designer will spread out the accurate, scale plans of the space in question and overlay these with thin yellow tracing paper on which sketches of the interior in plan form can be drawn. Many such plan sketches can be made to test alternatives as ideas develop; they provide an ideal way to study space allocations, placement of walls and openings, and location of major furniture elements with generally fixed locations (figs. 5.5, 5.6). Movable furniture can be shown in typical locations. Plans make it easy to see patterns of movement or circulation, using overlay diagrams to analyze these patterns and find ways to make them orderly, simple, and nonconflicting. At least one elevation or section at the same scale as the plan creates a sense of the three-dimensional proportion of the space being worked on.

Preliminary design most often serves the designer, alone or with colleagues, while he or she considers alternative ideas and moves toward specific proposals. The concept of *feedback* can help to describe how this process works. Each sketch or group of sketches suggesting a preliminary design can be regarded as an effort to fit a maximum number

5.6 *In this neatly drafted plan of a city apartment by Norman Diekman, the furniture and all other interior elements are drawn to scale. Color has been added in pencil, pastel, and marker pen to suggest the way the interior will actually look. (Courtesy Norman Diekman)*

5.7

of variables to the requirements of the problem. Once drawn on paper, the proposal can be criticized by the designer alone or with coworkers in an effort to retain and develop the aspects that work best and to identify ways in which improvements can be made. This feedback or evaluation forms the basis for the next sketches, which will attempt to find an even better fit to the problem requirements. The idea of solving a problem through *successive approximations,* borrowed from mathematics, helps to describe the way in which successive sketches, each improved through the feedback of evaluation, can approach the goal of a best solution. It should be recognized that in design, unlike mathematics, there is no one "best" or perfect solution to a problem. Many different approaches can lead to a high level of success. A designer will often pursue different directions for a time in order to make a choice through comparison of various proposals, any one of which could lead to an excellent conclusion. The designer may make the selection of the best direction alone, or may want to involve the client in the decision.

REVIEW PRELIMINARY DESIGN WITH CLIENT. The point at which sketches should be shown to a client is a matter of judgment. Some people may find design sketches hard to understand and become confused at seeing alternatives. Others may enjoy being included in the design process and indicate preferred directions to follow. In either case, the designer should assemble sketch plans that will give the client a clear idea of the design approach being taken.

REVISE AND FINALIZE PRELIMINARY DESIGN. At this time the designer incorporates whatever adjustments may have been suggested in the preceding client conference. This step may also include many cycles of revision as ideas develop and, in larger design firms, as colleagues discuss design ideas with one another informally or in meetings and reviews. When preliminary design has reached a point satisfactory to the designer or design team, the following step is appropriate.

OBTAIN CLIENT APPROVAL OF PRELIMINARY DESIGN. An affirmative approval is needed at this point. Also at this time, the designer might present preliminary selections of color and materials to be looked at together with sketches. The goal is to gain the client's general approval before moving ahead to the next step.

DESIGN DEVELOPMENT

DEVELOP DETAILED DESIGN. Once the design approach has been determined, the designer develops and refines it in more detailed design drawings, plans, elevations, sections, and, possibly, perspectives (fig. 5.7). These will be carefully drawn in black and white (pencil or ink), with a straightedge and instruments where appropriate, perhaps on sturdy white tracing paper. Such drawings can be reproduced as prints—which convey a quality of authority—suitable for mounting, pinup display, or mailing for client review.

5.7 Here, the three-dimensional effect of N. M. McKinnell's accurate, measured perspective drawing is enhanced by shading in pencil. It shows the main entrance area of the Boston City Hall, a 1968 project of Kallmann & McKinnell. (Courtesy Kallmann & McKinnell)

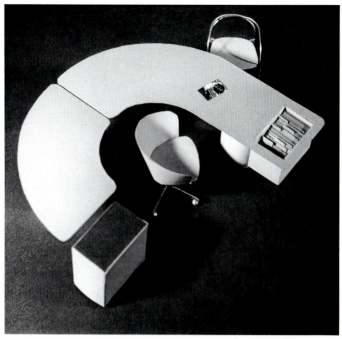

5.8

5.9

5.8 A model in cardboard and paper shows a grouping of custom-designed office furniture at a scale of 1″ = 1′-0″. Model and design by John Pile for Cosco Office Furniture, Inc. (Photograph: John Pile)

5.9 A model is most often built without a ceiling in order to view it from above easily. It is one of the most convincing ways of illustrating a planned interior space. The example here, of cardboard, is a ¼″ = 1′-0″ miniature of the office area of a bank. Because it is to scale, even the diagrammatic indica-tion of furniture is accurate; colors and finishes are rendered very much as they will appear in the completed project. The model (and the design) for the Essex County Bank headquarters in Peabody, Massachusetts, is by John Pile, consultant designer to J. F. N. Associates. (Photograph: John Pile)

5.10

5.11

5.10, 5.11 Two watercolors illustrate alternative color schemes for a living room in Robert A. M. Stern Architects' Villa in New Jersey, 1983–87. The base sheet is a carefully constructed perspective drawing in pencil by Thomas A. Kligerman, the associate in charge of the project. The watercolor was then added by William T. Georgis, also of the Stern office. (Courtesy Robert A. M. Stern Architects)

MAKE MATERIAL SELECTIONS. Some materials may be implied by design decisions, others may require a choice among alternatives. It is advisable to collect samples of materials as they are considered.

SELECT PURCHASED ITEMS. Items such as furniture, light fixtures, and appliances are selected at this point. Illustrations from catalogs or brochures can be assembled, using folders to group items that will be in particular spaces.

SELECT COLORS AND FINISHES. Color studies may take the form of drawings or charts. Samples of paint colors, colored materials (such as wood, stone, or tile), and textiles and carpets must be assembled and grouped according to spaces where they will be used. In preparation for presentation, color may be added to original drawings or prints with colored pencil or marker. Another way to combine color scheme and design is to make a kind of color collage on the plan, pasting down swatches of actual materials or colored paper slips to furniture or other items pictured in the plan.

ESTIMATE COSTS. As decisions are made, their impact on costs can be determined. Preliminary estimates can be obtained from contractors on the basis of designs that are still subject to some revisions.

PREPARE FINAL DESIGN. With all of the decisions made in the preceding steps, final design can now be completed.

PREPARE DETAILED BUDGET. Cost estimates can also be refined and incorporated into a budget for presentation to the client.

PREPARE PRESENTATION. In design circles, the term *presentation* describes a formal showing of design proposals to a client for approval. Preparation may be a simple matter of collecting drawings and samples, or it may involve considerable special effort.

MAKE PRESENTATION TO CLIENT. The materials prepared above are now presented to the client for approval. Presentations must sometimes be made to several groups or committees at different times. There may be a question-and-answer period of a formal sort, or more informal discussion may take place. The skill of the designer in verbal communication is an important part of any presentation. Many clients have trouble understanding drawings and rely on explanations offered in words. Notes should be taken on any suggestions or requests for revisions. If designer and client have a close working relationship, the presentation may be managed informally or omitted entirely. Corporate clients, accustomed to the presentations made by advertising agencies, generally expect a similar performance, including an element of salesmanship, from the designer. Drawings of the design development stage are usually suitable for presentation. Some rendered color perspectives, possibly the work of a specialist, may be added (figs. 5.10, 5.11). Color and material charts are usually carefully organized and assembled for showing. Large samples of actual materials, even examples of actual pieces of furniture, may also be shown.

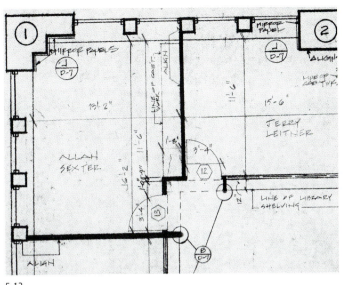

5.12

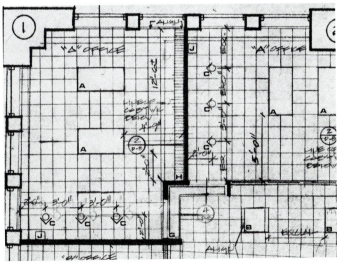

5.13

5.14

5.12–5.14 A complete set of working drawings may include many sheets, each providing particular information. These details come from a set by Forbes-Ergas Design Assoc., Inc., interior designer, for a suite of law offices. Fig. 5.12 is from a portion of a basic construction plan giving dimensions, door sizes and types, and similar struc-tural information. Fig. 5.13 shows the same area as it appears in a furniture layout sheet, with the locations and identity of each type of furniture item. Fig. 5.14 is from the reflected ceiling plan sheet, which details the layout of acoustic tile and the locations of ceiling lighting fixtures. (Courtesy Forbes-Ergas Design Assoc.)

Architects frequently use models as presentation elements; similarly, interior models can be effective presentation tools (figs. 5.8, 5.9). Although elaborate models can be very costly, they often prove the best means of putting across a design proposal. Some designers make their own models, others commission special model-making craftsmen.

In recent years, designers have come to make increasing use of audio-visual techniques for presentation, particularly to groups that must approve larger projects. Slides, films, and videotapes all aid the viewer in understanding complex drawings and models. Photographs of models create an illusion of reality (and convey a certain charm, as well) that often helps to convince clients of a design proposal's success. The goal of a design presentation is securing approval to go ahead with the execution of the project.

REVIEW BUDGET WITH CLIENT. This step may be formally incorporated into a design presentation or it may more informally follow the presentation in response to the common question, "What will all this cost?" It may also be the subject of a separate meeting following a generally successful presentation.

MAKE REVISIONS AS NECESSARY. Revisions may be requested even if a presentation has met with general approval. Concerns over budget frequently produce requests for changes that will reduce a total expenditure considered excessive.

OBTAIN CLIENT APPROVAL OF DESIGN AND BUDGET. It is important to obtain a clear and affirmative approval. Given that approval, possibly with some minor adjustments, the remaining steps can proceed.

WORKING DRAWINGS AND BIDDING

PREPARE CONSTRUCTION DRAWINGS. *Working drawings*, as they are often called (*blueprints* to laypeople), will be used first to obtain final cost figures and then by contractors and workmen constructing the project (figs. 5.12–5.15). Working drawings include scale plans, elevations, and sections, using notes and symbols together with large-scale details to spell out every particular of the work to be done. Written specifications give details of materials and methods of workmanship that drawings cannot fully show.

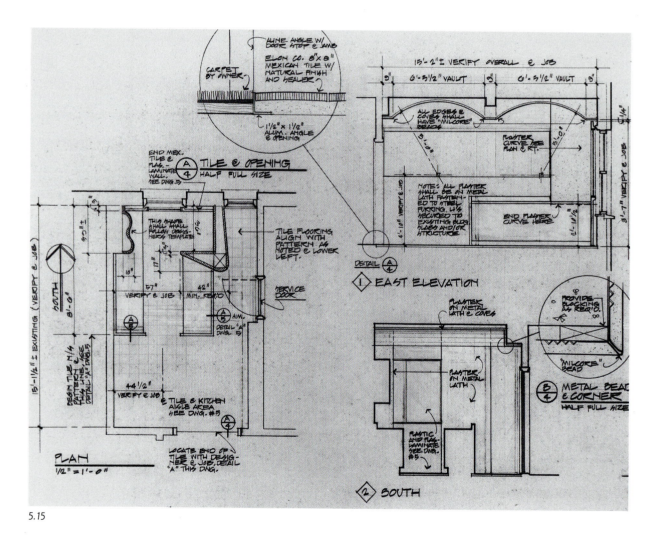

5.15

5.15 In a portion of a working, or construction, drawing for a complex interior project, a plan appears at the left and two elevations, at the same scale, at the right above and below. Details within the elevations are circled, then drafted at one-half full size within connected circles. A large project requires many such enlargements. Design and drawing by Norman Diekman. (Courtesy Norman Diekman)

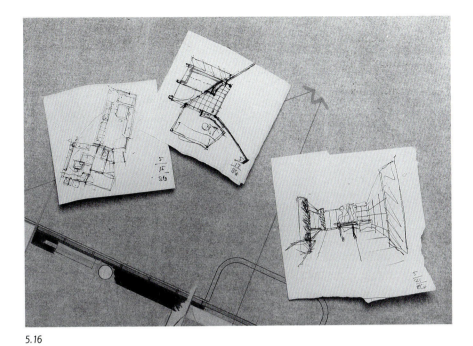

5.16

5.17

CASE STUDY 1

DESIGN DEVELOPMENT
AS PROCESS

A City Apartment
Design and Drawings by Norman Diekman

The clients, sponsors of the American craft movement, were a couple who own houses elsewhere and wanted a city base where they could keep and display objects in their collection. They selected this condominium apartment in a Manhattan high-rise building primarily for its twenty-fifth-floor location, which provides a flood of afternoon light and spectacular day- and nighttime city views from the ample windows.

The design process is traced here in a sequence of drawings, a representative selection from the large number of studies produced in the course of devising concepts and communicating them to the clients for discussion and, ultimately, approval.

Many projects and many designers employ fewer drawings. Norman Diekman is particularly interested in the technique of this medium and in its use as a primary design tool. It is this combination that makes this project an appropriate showcase of creative interior drawing.

5.16 The legendary "first sketch on the back of an envelope" is, in practice, not uncommon. These sketches include initial notes made on paper napkins over lunch in a restaurant; the ideas were then developed in the office. They represent the following stages: During a lunch meeting with the client, an overall concept emerged (left) that placed the design emphasis upon the light and views that determined the choice of the space. The image of a summer pavilion in the sky takes shape verbally and visually. Another napkin sketch (center), made a few days later, illustrates the treatment of the entrance at an angle where the foyer opens into the living space. A thumbnail perspective sketch (right) captures the space as it will be with afternoon sunlight pouring in. The designer likes to call such a sketch "a Xerox of the mind"—that is, the visual trace of a thought in the course of development.

5.17 This complete color plan of the apartment is a study for both designer and client. The background is a black-and-white Ozalid print made from a pencil line drawing on yellow tracing paper showing only the walls and other fixed elements of the plan. A dark print provides the background tone for the drawing with Prismacolor and ordinary black pencils, used to indicate furniture and other elements with partially realistic, partially diagrammatic shading.

5.18

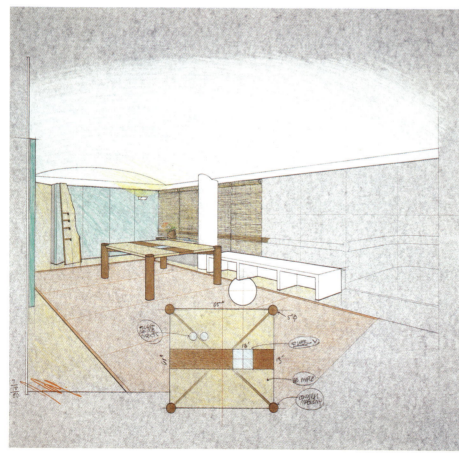

5.19

5.20

5.18 After the concept and plan have received general approval, the cost estimates must be addressed. This sheet combines a plan, elevations, and a perspective in order to assemble the requisite details. The lower elevation, the plan above it, and the perspective at upper right focus upon the entrance area.

5.19 This perspective drawing focuses on the large table omitted from the study in fig. 5.20. The table is designed to serve two purposes. For dining, it seats six to eight or can be used for buffet meals; as a display surface, it allows craft objects from the owners' collection to be viewed and studied. A plan of the table appears at

the bottom, overlapping the perspective. The designer had originally intended to fill in a nighttime sky and skyline visible through the windows at the right, but decided instead to leave the drawing as it is. As in all creative work, one of the most important skills in drawing and rendering is knowing when to stop.

5.20 The theme of a summer pavilion in the sky appears here in fairly precise detail, in a perspective clearly evolved from one of the napkin sketches. The high, curved ceiling suggests vaulting and spreads the afternoon light up and into the space. The daytime view is accurate; another could be drawn as it would be at night to show the space under different lighting conditions. Compare the banquette seating and the brown cylindrical wood table here and in the plan view. The square table is omitted here: not yet fully developed as an element, it would appear too distracting.

Interior design working drawings follow the general practice of architectural draftsmanship; indeed, architectural and interior drawings are often combined. At this point, coordination between designer, architect, and engineer is vital to avoid duplication and conflict. At the same time, this cooperative effort extends to all the specialists involved—lighting, acoustical, and other consultants. Electrical and plumbing details and, occasionally, heating and air-conditioning details must also be coordinated. The interior designer must now prepare special charts of color chips and plans marked to show color locations for the painting contractor.

The way in which the project is to be contracted somewhat influences how complete the working drawings must be. If competitive bids are to be taken, drawings and specifications must be very complete and as precise as possible to assure that all bidders will be figuring on an identical set of requirements, leaving nothing to the imagination. For example, the indication "wood" can refer to softwood, hardwood, plywood, or even particleboard. Only totally specific drawings and/or specifications that clarify every such issue will serve to ensure that competitive bids are based on an identical set of requirements. If a contractor (or several contractors) is employed on a time and materials (or *cost-plus*) basis, drawings can be somewhat less inclusive, leaving details to be resolved later with the designer giving instructions on the job, verbally or in sketches. Good drawings can protect against later misunderstandings.

The process of making working drawings by hand, with pencil and instruments, is gradually being replaced by computer-based techniques known as CAD (computer-aided drawing) or CADD (computer-aided design and drawing). Equipment (hardware) and software are constantly being improved while costs continue to drop. More details concerning computer drawing are given in Chapter 19, pages 535–41.

PREPARE DETAIL DRAWINGS. Construction drawings often do not include details of such items as special furniture, cabinetwork, or other items that will be separately contracted for. These details must be prepared well in advance of the times when they will be needed.

PREPARE SPECIFICATIONS. Specifications are written descriptions of materials, workmanship, and other details not easily made clear in drawings. When bids are to be taken, specifications are combined with drawings to form a complete set of *contract documents* on which bids are to be based.

MAKE COST ESTIMATES AND OBTAIN BIDS. Final estimates are gathered on phases of the work that are not to be put out for bidding. Taking of bids involves sending drawings and specifications to possible contractors (usually at least three) who submit bid prices, which are amounts for which the bidder guarantees to perform the work specified. One general contractor may bid on all aspects of the work, or separate bids may be taken from different trades (masonry, plumbing, electrical, and so on). The bidder who offers the best price usually wins the contract. For smaller projects and projects with tight deadlines, it is increasingly common to select one contractor without bidding and to enter into a cost-plus contract in which payment is made on the cost of materials and workmanship plus a fixed percentage for overhead and

profit. Besides being simple and convenient, this basis facilitates making additions and changes in a project as work progresses. While many people fear that an open-ended arrangement leads to higher costs than a fixed-price arrangement, experienced designers know this is not necessarily true.

MAKE TIME SCHEDULE FOR CONSTRUCTION AND INSTALLATION. Accepted bidders and suppliers of purchased items can now provide firm schedules for their parts of the work in question.

In the design stages, the project probably progressed with informal schedules or instructions to advance "as rapidly as possible." Before actual work begins, the designer must make firm schedules to ensure that construction work proceeds without delays or conflicts. Scheduling also involves the architect (if there is one) and the contractor. Since interior design is the last phase of work, following schedules is crucial to the designer's success in delivering a job on time. Clients consider this the most important aspect of a project; they will sooner forgive cost overruns than a late completion date.

Trades must work in a logical sequence and purchased items must arrive when needed for the job to go smoothly. For example, when new stud or block walls are to be built, door frames (called *bucks* in the trade) must arrive and be set in place before the partition walls can go up. Plumbing and electrical work come before any surface finishes, but plumber and electrician must return to install fixtures *after* walls and ceilings are finished. Carpet is best installed last, although a painter may have to return after carpet installation to touch up any damage to walls that may have occurred. The interior designer has the additional task of providing a follow-up service to see that work schedules are maintained. Sophisticated management techniques such as PERT and CPM, often using computer data management and display, can aid in handling the schedules of large and complex projects with their overlapping and intricate complexities (see figs. 5.3 and 5.4). A simple CPM chart can help in working out schedules for more modestly scaled interior projects.

SELECT CONTRACTORS AND ISSUE WORK ORDERS. Selected bidders are now asked to sign contracts or accept work orders to proceed with work.

PREPARE AND ISSUE PURCHASE ORDERS. Many of the elements that go into a typical interior are not made to order or made on site but are purchased from manufacturers or dealers as standard items. These include rugs and carpets, wallpapers, furniture, light fixtures and lamps, and various accessories. Even antiques and unique works of art fall into this category. Making catalog selections, checking prices and delivery schedules, and issuing written orders for these purchases form a significant part of the interior designer's work. Complexities arise when, for example, upholstery fabric ordered from a supplier must go to a furniture manufacturer to cover particular items, and the finished pieces have to be delivered on a precise schedule. When clients prefer to do their own purchasing, the designer must still prepare the information on which the orders will be based. Coordinating delivery schedules usually remains a design responsibility.

Supervision

SUPERVISE CONSTRUCTION. Projects require on-site supervision to ensure the proper following of drawings and specifications and the quality of workmanship, as well as to resolve any unanticipated problems that may arise. When a project site is close to the designer's base of action, frequent visits can provide adequate supervision without much difficulty. When a project is beyond the designer's travel range, it may be wise to make arrangements with a local designer to provide regular supervision. Supervision becomes crucial in the final phase of a job, when paint colors need to be checked (and sometimes revised), when furniture is being delivered and needs to be put in place, and when small details require constant attention.

COORDINATE AND EXPEDITE CONSTRUCTION AND DELIVERIES. Careful effort must be made to ensure that the phases of construction and deliveries of purchased items are scheduled to avoid delays and conflicts.

SUPERVISE INSTALLATION AND COMPLETION. This extension of the preceding step requires coordination of all work to bring about project completion on or before the scheduled date.

LIST DEFECTS AND ERRORS AND SUPERVISE CORRECTION. Any project of any size will include various unfortunate mistakes that must be corrected. A *punch list* is usually prepared listing all such issues, to be crossed off as each is dealt with.

SUPERVISE MOVE-IN. This is a crucial time in the history of any project. The designer should take a role in assuring that all goes smoothly and that confusion and errors are kept to a minimums.

Post-Completion

MAKE NEEDED ADJUSTMENTS AND CHANGES. However carefully planned and supervised, every project includes some problems that surface only after the completed project is put into use. The designer must be ready to deal with whatever problems may emerge and to make any needed changes as promptly as possible. Client satisfaction is strongly influenced by the effectiveness and promptness of this final phase of work.

PREPARE POST-MOVE-IN EVALUATION. Responsible designers carry out follow-up evaluation of completed jobs at reasonable intervals—for example, six months, one year, and two years—to determine how well the project is serving its users and meeting its goals. Many designers omit or ignore this step. This may be one reason why some well-known projects that photograph well and win praise from critics leave users with major dissatisfactions. Honest evaluation, together with a plan to provide revisions and corrections as needed, contributes to a project's success and to the designer's improved performance on future projects.

It often seems that *design* as the term is usually understood turns out to be a minor part of the total performance of the interior designer. It is important to be sure that the demands of project management never overwhelm design creativity and push it into the background. Nevertheless, a design success combined with poor management can leave behind an unhappy client and dissatisfied users who judge an aesthetic success inadequate compensation for assorted everyday complaints. The combination of poor design and good management is far more likely to satisfy clients. However, this is a choice that need not be made; excellent design and good project management together express a designer's concern for delivering high-quality design work.

6.1

CHAPTER

SIX

PLANNING

Planning is a primary aspect of interior design. The very term *design* implies planning of a thoughtful and organized nature. Design professionals offer as one of their most important skills the ability to plan, creating spaces that will be practical and comfortable and will serve their intended purposes. Amateurs tend to use available furniture placed according to chance or habit and to rush into choices of new furniture, color, and materials without taking the time to plan methodically. Poor planning—or no planning at all—is probably the most common cause of disappointing interiors. While not as apparent as unsuccessful color or lighting, it is more fundamental to basic performance.

CREATIVITY IN PLANNING

For every human situation there are routine ways of acting that provide satisfactory results in conventional situations; it is not necessary, for example, to invent a new way of tying shoelaces or brushing teeth every day. Many design problems, in turn, can also be dealt with through routine—standard plans for houses, schools, medical offices, kitchens, and bathrooms abound. Yet a key difference between dull or mediocre design and work of real excellence is precisely the level of creative thinking that the designer has generated. Designers therefore must consider, for each project, where routine proposals will serve and where a creative approach can lead to better results.

When routine approaches dominate, a designer's work may be practical and may serve certain functional needs, but it will lack the spark that can push design work to a higher level of excellence and make a positive contribution to the lives of those who encounter it. For a designer, the excitement and satisfaction of producing outstanding work stem from the creative process.

There has been much discussion in recent years over the question of whether creativity can be learned. It is said that all human beings are born with creative abilities and that this can be recognized in the behavior of young children, who are typically highly inventive in their play, their speech, and, when given the chance, their art. Unfortunately, much of education involves replacing such creativity with routines

and rules. The three Rs, for example, specify correct ways to read words, form letters, and deal with arithmetic problems. Developing creativity can be considered largely a matter of rediscovering abilities that have been dormant since childhood.

Design schools have organized various courses, programs, and exercises intended to develop such abilities. Group brainstorming sessions, free sketching (sometimes called "empathic" sketching—that is, related to empathy with a particular problem), and encouragement of fantasy proposals are all techniques that can help to bring forth imaginative approaches to a given set of requirements. Our memories are stocked with images of work that is currently popular, avant-garde, or trendy, and it is easy to draw on such sources without realizing how much influence they are exerting. All designers by necessity draw on memory and on knowledge of what has already been done and proven successful. The goal is to make *creative* use of such knowledge without mindlessly repeating past or current routine practices.

Being creative, however, does not mean that every problem and every situation must have a totally new and radically adventurous approach. Inventiveness does not call for an effort to be different just to be different—that route too often leads to forced, eccentric, and pointless design. The objects that come to be regarded as classic gain that reputation because they have an excellence that bears up with much use over a long period of time. The effort to create design that has such classic excellence involves originality of a more subtle nature. It is a fortunate reality of interior design practice that, although the problems to be worked on fall into familiar patterns, no two problems are ever identical. When there are numbers of truly identical spaces (rooms in a hotel or motel, for example), they constitute only one design problem. Even in this situation, rooms facing in different directions or at different floor levels may suggest a variety of designs. It is more usual to find that each project calls for new thinking. Each house, each apartment, each living room, and each office is in some way unique if only because its occupants have unique requirements. It is the discovery of the issues that are specific to a particular project that can become the starting point for a truly creative approach.

6.1 Situated on a balcony overlooking the bedroom below, this private reading spot in the Atlanta home of architect John Portman affords lofty privacy. John Portman & Associates was the designer. (Photograph: Jaime Ardiles-Arce)

6.2

It is helpful to look for some element in any project that can serve as a springboard for imaginative thinking. It may be some aspect of the given space—its shape, structure, light, and view (or lack thereof), some special functional requirement, something about the character of the client, whether an individual or an organization—that can set off a line of thinking. Is the building old or new, handsome or unappealing? Is its structure visible and interesting; is there good daylight or none; are window views attractive or depressing? Is there something special about the intended occupants, their business, their organizational style, their tastes and interests? Noting such matters may lead to an intriguing approach to what at first may have seemed a routine problem. Might good light but an unattractive view lead to a new way to treat windows? Can the structural elements be made interesting and exciting, or should they be hidden in a clever way? Do the occupants have special interests, hobbies, collections, strong color preferences? If such matters are not simply viewed as requirements (possibly troublesome requirements) to be dealt with but are instead exploited as a basis for an imaginative approach, creativity can be stimulated.

Rather than beginning a project with an effort to find a "solution," an acceptable plan, or an overall scheme, it is more useful to start with loose sketches, allowing free association to guide fantasy without strict concern for the practical realities of the client's needs. Letting the problem simmer, "sleeping on it," or otherwise leaving it in the back of the mind while dealing with other matters are all means to discover an approach that will be both original and realistic. The aim is to put aside the constraints that so often lead to routine approaches so that other possibilities have a chance to come forward.

Concept Development

One route to design that will rise above mediocrity is to search out an overriding concept, an idea, a theme that will guide thinking and bring all of the diverse parts of a design into a strong relationship. A guiding concept is not a program of detailed requirements; it is a statement of an overview—something that can be expressed in a sentence or two—written or sketched on the proverbial back of an envelope. Although the theme that guided design development may be difficult to identify in a finished project, it is invariably present in outstanding work. Students in design schools are painfully familiar with the teacher's question, "What is your *concept* here?" usually asked before

6.2 The glass pyramid designed in 1983 by architect I. M. Pei of Pei Cobb Freed & Partners to form a new entrance to the vast complex of the Louvre museum in Paris generated extensive controversy when it was first proposed, raising questions about how it would relate to the ornate architec-ture of the famous building. When unveiled in 1988, however, it was clear that the architect's strong concept made the addition exceptionally suc-cessful—beautiful in itself but also an enhancement to the expansive court and its rich historic architecture. (Photograph: Owen Franken/Stock, Boston)

"C L O V E R L E A F"
T Y P I C A L   L I V I N G - R O O M
LOOKING IN THROUGH WINDOWS

SHEET II
USONIAN HOUSES FOR THE U S A PITTSFIELD MASS
QUADRUPLE   SUN-DECK   TYPE
F R A N K   L L O Y D   W R I G H T   A R C H I T E C T

6.5

looked at guidebooks, real-estate brochures, and similar materials. In a plan, a space is drawn out to scale with lines representing walls, doors, windows, and columns in their proper relationships. (See Appendix 1, "Architectural Plan Symbols.") A completed interior design plan includes furniture and any other significant elements drawn in their intended locations. The most vital of all architectural and interior drawings, plans usually come first and can convey almost all of the information about a project that needs to be drawn.

ELEVATION. This term describes a view that shows one face (front, side, or rear) of its subject projected onto a vertical plane, as if the face had been transferred onto paper in scale (fig. 6.4B). Exterior elevations

of a building resemble a picture of whatever face of the structure is shown. Interior elevations of rooms show one wall surface at a time in scale, usually with whatever furniture or other objects will be on or close to that wall.

SECTION. Sectional drawings show an object, a space, or a building as if it had been sliced through to reveal internal spaces and construction (fig. 6.4C). Two kinds of sections are useful in interior drawings. The first discloses, in addition to the internal spaces and constructions, the hidden structure and materials within the thicknesses of the subject being sectioned (for example, the ducts and wiring placed between walls or above ceilings). A section of a window or a door frame or a

6.5 Perspective drawing helps planners—and users—to visualize spaces as they will appear in reality. Frank Lloyd Wright developed a unique and beautiful style for his architectural perspectives. This drawing illustrates the living space of one of the Usonian Houses he designed to be built in Pittsfield, Massachusetts, in 1942. (Photograph courtesy The Frank Lloyd Wright Memorial Foundation)

6.6

cabinet belongs to this category. The other type of section shows the hollow spaces of rooms within a building, making clear their shapes and relationships, without disclosing the composition of thickness. A variation of this type of section (sometimes called a *sectional elevation*) slices the structure so as to reveal the appearance of distant walls or any other elements that would be visible if the near or front wall were removed. Detail sections (often drawn at large scale) are particularly useful in showing how materials are to be put together in actual construction. (See Appendix 4, "Material Indications in Section.")

Perspective Drawing

This technique, familiar in representational art, manipulates line on a two-dimensional surface to show three-dimensional space as it actually appears from a given viewpoint, with lines converging toward a point or points on a horizon and objects at a distance drawn smaller than those close up (fig. 6.5). Since it can give a virtually photographic view, perspective has become a favorite device in interior sketches and formal *presentation drawings* to indicate how a space will look when

completed (figs. 6.12 and 6.13). A fine-arts training usually includes some instruction in perspective, at least at the level of drawing observed space "by eye" as it is seen in perspective. To draw an unbuilt space in perspective, either from orthographic drawings or from imagination, takes a special skill that is usually acquired only with some study and practice. A *measured perspective* can be as accurate as a photograph in depicting a space's actual appearance, and it offers the advantage of showing a space yet to be built—which, of course, a camera cannot do. Elaborate perspective renderings are usually made by specialists who devote all their time to this work. Most interior designers will find an ability to sketch and draw in perspective a valuable skill. Classroom work with a teacher and self-teaching from books are both possible ways to become proficient in perspective drawing. A short summary of the basic technique is provided in Appendix 5.

While all of the types of drawing will be used by the interior designer, the plan is the primary tool of planning. Once a space is built and occupied, we do not see the plan as such, but it controls how well that space serves us. A good plan is basic to the production of a well-

6.6–6.9 In this interesting and complex space, ingenious planning has provided for private and semipublic functions within a limited area. A floor plan (fig. 6.8) helps understanding of the design. Such plans are the designer's major tool. In fig. 6.9, the same plan is axonometrically projected. This type of drawing enables professional—

and nonprofessional—designers to picture three-dimensional relationships. The drawing is made to scale for the three axes, height, width, and depth, but with the width and depth drawn at a 45-degree angle to the horizontal. Comparing the plan, the axonometric projection, and photographs of the

realized space, one can easily visualize the design and comprehend the concept behind it. Buzz Yudell, architect, and Tina Beebe, color consultant, designed the space, in their own home in Santa Monica, California, in 1985. (Photographs: © Henry Bowles, courtesy House & Garden)

6.7

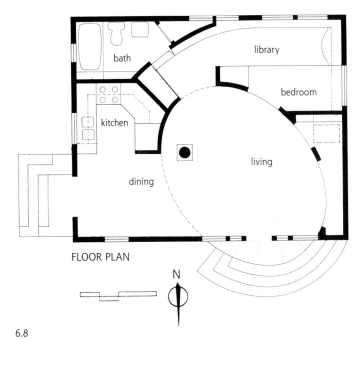

bath

library

bedroom

kitchen

living

dining

FLOOR PLAN

N

6.8

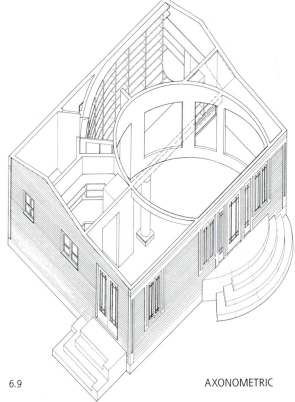

6.9

AXONOMETRIC

6.10

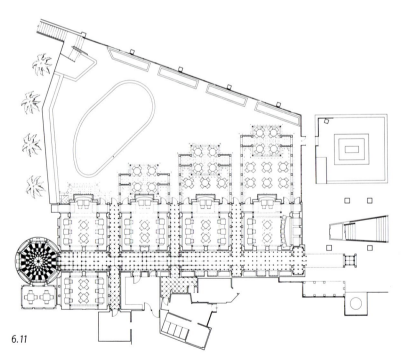

6.11

6.10, 6.11 The plan of a northern Italian town, with its main street, octagonal piazza, and side streets, inspired the architects of an imaginatively conceived 1985 hotel restaurant. The vaulted ceiling design is derived from the breakfast room of Sir John Soane's eighteenth-century house in London. Fig. 6.10 shows one of the "side-street" dining areas of the Cardini restaurant in the Los Angeles Hilton Hotel; its modest scale generates an atmosphere of intimacy. The floor plan (fig. 6.11) shows the total planning concept of the designer, Voorsanger & Mills Associates Architects. (Photograph: © 1986 Peter Aaron/ESTO)

designed interior. Seeing a space in plan on paper makes it easy to analyze the way the built space will perform. Planning makes it possible to try out, study, and revise various possibilities in seeking a satisfactory scheme.

PRELIMINARY STEPS IN PLANNING

Under some conditions one may begin planning freely on blank paper. However, most planning must take account of existing circumstances and other *constraints*, or limitations, such as building code requirements, that restrict what can be done. The interior designer is most often limited by the more or less fixed elements of architecture in the space. This obviously applies when the designer works with an existing space. It also applies when architectural planning has been completed before interior design begins, even when the new construction will provide only an unpartitioned shell.

Ideally, interior design planning should begin along with the architectural planning of fixed elements. This is possible when the interior designer is part of the design process from the beginning. It can also occur when the given architectural space is open and clear, as in lofts and office space rented without preexisting partitions. Most houses and apartments are built from plans made before the owner or occupant, much less the interior designer, has any input. By having a house custom-built, the owner can influence the architect or builder and participate in the planning process and can also bring the interior designer into the process.

Selecting Space

A designer can be very helpful before the planning process begins, when a client is looking for space—to rent an office in an office building; to rent or buy an apartment in an apartment house; or to purchase a house. The building or house may be existing or still unbuilt. A client will usually have in mind certain criteria, such as general location, size, and cost, but often finds it difficult to choose between alternatives or to evaluate an available possibility. A designer can bring a practiced eye to observe the potential strengths and weaknesses of an available space and offer disinterested advice about how well the given conditions will suit the client's requirements.

The first step is to spell out the client's requirements in a program. The term *program* in the world of architecture and design describes a statement of objectives and requirements that is best written out to form what is sometimes called a *project brief* or *problem statement*. It is axiomatic that a good statement of a problem is basic to finding a good solution. Indeed, the solution to a problem may become almost self-evident once the problem is stated with clarity. Conversely, unclear objectives and uncertainty about requirements typically cause confusion and delays and, all too often, lead to disappointing and unsatisfactory final results.

The program lists, with as much precision as possible, these requirements: the kinds and numbers of spaces to be provided; the relationships of the spaces; any specific needs for equipment, storage, or special furniture; and other specific needs. After the space is selected, this program will form the basis for the new interior design.

Whether the designer accompanies the client on visits to different spaces or evaluates spaces, built or unbuilt, from plans, it is important for the designer to notice and call attention to such things as:

- *WINDOW ORIENTATION IN RELATION TO LIGHT*, at various times of day and in various seasons.
- *OUTLOOK FROM WINDOWS, FOR GOOD VIEWS OR OBSTRUCTION*, including the possibility of future obstruction.
- *QUALITY OF PLAN LAYOUT*, including convenience of spatial shapes and locations. In house and apartment plans, awkward or wasteful spaces often appear. Note potential problems with noise and privacy. Check closets, baths, and kitchens for adequacy and quality of layout. In apartment, office, and loft buildings, check adequacy of elevators and stairs.
- *POSSIBLE NOISE PROBLEMS*, from elevators or adjacent spaces or from out-of-doors. City street noise and aircraft noise are particularly problematic.
- *ELEMENTS THAT CAN OR SHOULD BE CHANGED: Can walls be added or removed and doors or windows added, eliminated, or changed to improve a space? If closets, kitchens, or baths require change or improvement, will this be possible?*

Designers often note changes that will greatly improve a space at small cost. With an unbuilt structure, a change may be possible at no cost. On the other hand, some desirable changes may be very costly or even impossible. Removing a partition wall, for example, may be relatively easy, but removing a *bearing wall* or column that is part of a building's structure will be difficult and expensive, if not impossible. Changes that affect plumbing and ductwork may be easy but will always be costly. They may also be very difficult or impossible where, for example, pipes come from below and continue upward into spaces occupied by other people, preventing the relocation of a bathroom or kitchen.

Legal restrictions relating to safety may rule out certain changes in layout. Window and door locations may be restricted by zoning that regulates exterior appearance. An owner might not permit some changes in rented space. All such issues are best explored before the final selection of a space.

In comparing spaces, the designer may notice that seemingly identical spaces are actually quite different. The same apartment plan, for example, may be better or worse on various floors of a building or with different orientations because of the difference in light and view. In an office building, two plans with the same area may differ in window size and location, in light and view, and in convenience of access from corridors and elevators. Identical houses on opposite sides of a street, because of their orientation, may differ greatly in terms of light, view, and privacy. Clients are often unobservant of such factors, particularly when evaluating space from plans alone, and can benefit greatly from intelligent design advice when making decisions that can be difficult, even frightening, and that often involve large sums of money.

Analyzing and Evaluating Space

Once a space has been selected (or if no selection is required, as when a space in current use is to be altered, renovated, or refurbished), the designer must analyze and evaluate every aspect of it. In this process,

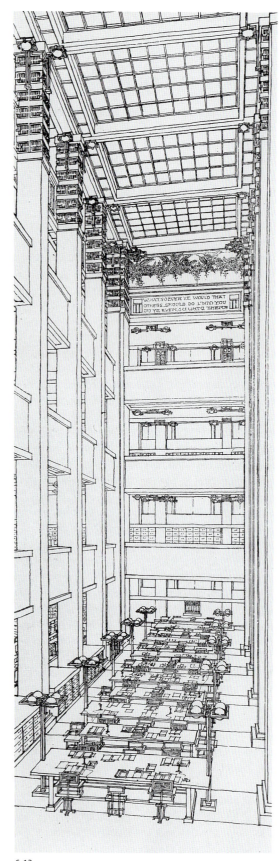

6.12

6.13

it is helpful to categorize elements or characteristics of the space as:

- *GOOD OR EXCELLENT ELEMENTS—probably the features that led to the selection or decision to keep the space—that should be retained, emphasized, and exploited in design development.*
- *NEUTRAL QUALITIES that are satisfactory but offer no special merits or attraction.*
- *PROBLEMS AND UNSATISFACTORY FEATURES that must be altered, eliminated, or at least neutralized or minimized.*

6.12, 6.13 A perspective drawing of a particular space can be even more informative than a photograph, as demonstrated by a highly detailed Frank Lloyd Wright perspective for the interior of the 1904 Larkin Company

Administration Building (fig. 6.12). Fig. 6.13 is a photograph of the space as built. The building, now demolished, was located in Buffalo, New York. (Photograph: The Frank Lloyd Wright Memorial Foundation)

Such attractive features as good daylight or a fine view from windows are easy to recognize and should be exploited. Modern residential and office spaces tend to be largely neutral in character, with smooth floors, walls, and ceilings; windows and doors without ornamental detail; unobtrusive heating and air-conditioning outlets; and no fireplaces, molding, paneling, or other special details. Problems sometimes do not present themselves until planning begins—or even after moving in.

Spaces already divided into rooms usually cause more problems than open space. Since houses and apartments are laid out to suit an imagined "typical" occupant or family that may be quite different from the actual one, their plans may well be unsuitable to a particular occupant or have serious faults that would be troublesome under any circumstances. Common problems are:

- *SOME OR ALL OF THE ROOMS ARE TOO SMALL. Kitchens and bathrooms are particularly likely to be inadequate.*
- *ROOMS RELATE POORLY TO ONE ANOTHER. For example, the dining room is not adjacent to the kitchen, or the bathroom is poorly placed.*
- *ROOMS ARE BADLY SHAPED. They may be too long and narrow, have awkward notches or cutoff corners, or make furniture placement difficult.*
- *CORRIDORS ARE LONG, NARROW, DARK, AND UNPLEASANT. This not only wastes space, it is usually inconvenient as well.*
- *OPENINGS (DOORS AND WINDOWS) ARE BADLY PLACED. For example, an entrance door opens directly into a major space, or openings are so placed that they take up wall space and make furniture layout difficult.*
- *CLOSETS ARE INADEQUATE, BADLY SHAPED, OR POORLY LOCATED.*

Once such problems are recognized, it is possible to consider steps that will minimize or eliminate them. Moving a partition or removing it may improve a plan layout and alter room size. Doors can be relocated or blocked up. Some spaces can be enlarged by taking space away from adjacent areas. A dining room, for example, can often be eliminated and its space given partly to an enlarged kitchen and partly to adjacent living space.

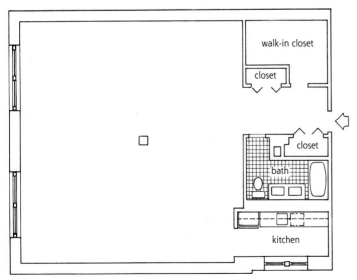

6.14

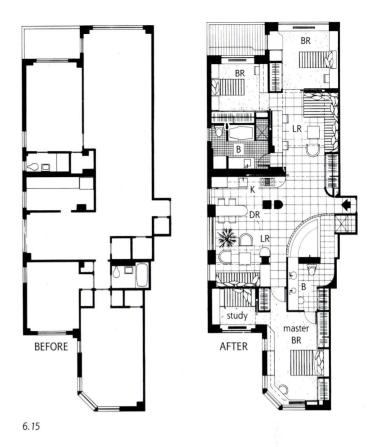

6.15

At a more detailed level, poorly placed or awkwardly shaped windows can often be dealt with through drapery or blinds. The appearance of poorly shaped spaces can be improved through choice of wall colors and materials. Color and lighting (each the subject of a subsequent chapter) can make spaces seem larger or smaller, as desired. The size, character, and placement of furniture can help to minimize planning problems. Even a small kitchen or kitchenette can usually be made more workable with suitable choices of equipment and better layout. Corridors can often be improved through lighting and color and by using them for book storage or a gallerylike display of art.

Collecting all such information about existing conditions or other limitations constitutes the preliminary basis of planning. The designer's main planning tool is a scale plan showing what exists or what is to be built, along with any other data about fixed elements. Such a plan may come from a real-estate firm or architects' drawings. These can be used as a starting point, but an on-site check should be made to ensure their accuracy. Plans provided by real-estate agencies are often small in scale, unclear in details, and inaccurate, at least in minor ways. Building plans may not have been followed exactly or later changes may not be shown in the plan.

On site with ruler and measuring tape, the designer (or an assistant) should check available plans, obtain heights of ceilings and openings that may not be shown in the plan, note any significant details, and, possibly, take some photographs for reference. If no plans are available, the on-site job becomes larger, requiring careful measurement of

6.14 *This is the floor plan of a loft space as provided by the rental agent who offered the apartment. The only fixed elements are the kitchen, bathroom, closets, and single central column. These, plus the locations of windows and door, are the only design constraints. The final layout can be as open or as intricately subdivided as the new owners and their designer may decide.*

6.15 *Knowledgeable replanning was used to customize a space for a particular owner of a Manhattan apartment. The apartment as purchased is shown in the plan at left. As replanned (right), it now provides a two-bedroom suite, a luxury bath, and a living area for two teenagers (upper portion of plan); common rooms—kitchen, dining, and living area—near the entrance; and a bedroom, study, and luxury bath suite for the parents (lower portion of plan). A curving glass-block wall surrounds the large tub of the master bath, separating it from the living area. Bromley/Jacobsen Designs was the designer.*

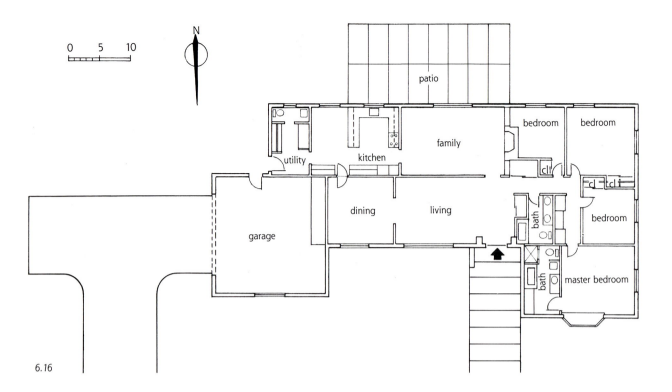

the space in question so that accurate plans of existing conditions can be drawn up.

The task of *measuring up* an existing space is often the first assignment given to a junior designer. As a test of accuracy and thoroughness, it is good practice for any beginner. When only one or two rooms are being considered, this is a fairly simple matter. Plans of a whole house or larger building may take considerable time and effort to prepare, but it is vital to have accurate plans before starting design work. The usual procedure is to make a roughly drawn plan on a pad and note down complete dimensions (fig. 6.24). Back at the drafting board, these are drawn up to scale as a basis for further design work (fig. 6.25).

Planning the Space

Planning can now move to its primary task, the fitting of the project's requirements to the plan.

Research

The usual first step in preparation for planning is to survey available information relating to the kind of project to be undertaken. This is particularly helpful if the project is of a kind that the designer has not previously dealt with or if it is of a highly specialized nature. It is hardly necessary to do background research in relation to such familiar material as the design of a residential space, but a retail shop, a restaurant, or a medical facility involve significant issues that go beyond the obvious. Even residential spaces may involve special requirements (for

an elderly person or a person with a disability, for example) or may be intended to incorporate solar heating or an unusual facility for exercise, music, or some other activity. No designer can hold information on every possible issue in mind and keep up-to-date on an infinite number of changing materials and methods.

Research involves seeking out whatever books, technical reports, journal articles, and manufacturers' data may relate to a project. There are many good books devoted to the design of such specialized spaces as schools, hospitals, auditoriums, offices, and so on, while other publications deal with such matters as barrier-free access, current lighting practices, and energy-conservation issues. A scan of relevant material and of recent magazine articles can lead the designer to a body of data relating to the project that will be fresh and readily available. Critical review of published reports of recent projects can suggest what other designers are doing in a given field, providing guidelines about what to consider and what to avoid. Visits to actual projects of a parallel nature can also be helpful. Before starting work on a hospital interior, for example, it may be useful to visit several recent hospital projects to observe their successes (or limitations), while on-site conversations with users can often bring out realities that are not apparent in articles and illustrations. Research can begin to make the designer an expert in a particular project type before undertaking actual design work.

Programming

If the *program* has not already been prepared in order to select space, it is prepared at this time. (Since the designer usually begins with an existing space to be redesigned, the program is most often prepared at this stage.) It may seem unnecessary to prepare a program for a small

6.16 This plan of a suburban house contains a number of serious problems: Several major rooms (family room, two bedrooms) and the patio face north—the least desirable orientation. Major rooms (living, dining, and master bedroom) face the street, resulting in limited privacy and a less-than-ideal outdoor view. The prime southern ori-

entation will usually be blocked by the window treatment required for privacy. The front door opens directly into the living room, with no vestibule or other transition. Access from the garage to utility and kitchen areas is only through outdoors, with no convenient access from the garage to the main living spaces. The living room contains the

passage route to dining, kitchen, and family room. The traffic route to kitchen and patio goes through the family room, whose fireplace is close to the circulation path. Furniture arrangement in living and family rooms will be difficult due to traffic paths and architectural constraints. All rooms except the two corner bedrooms lack good cross-ventilation. All four bedrooms

have a partition wall adjacent to another bedroom, resulting in the loss of acoustical privacy. Master bedroom closet space (in bath and hall) is poorly planned. The bay window of the master bedroom, apparently added for external effect, is poorly placed in relation to the interior. The master bath general layout and shower placement are awkward.

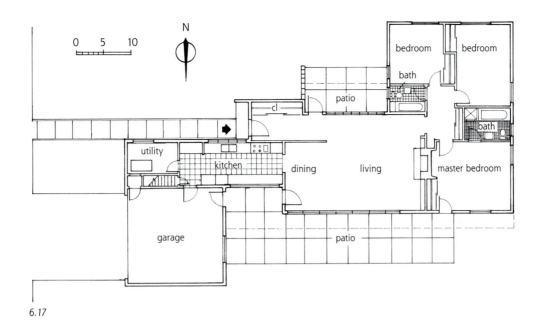

6.17

project (such as a living room, a kitchen, or an office), but requirements need to be specified, whatever the project size.

When work is being undertaken professionally for a client, a clear
program must be developed to ensure that client and designer share a
common point of view about their goals. This applies equally to individual clients and to corporations or other large organizations. In the
latter case, where the designer must deal with and satisfy many people, clear lines of communication become even more important. A
committee is always more difficult to deal with than an individual, and
clarity of objectives is best determined through agreement on a written statement.

Designers typically begin programming by developing a *general project statement.* This may be no more than a sentence or two outlining
the work to be done—its extent and purpose—in the most general
terms. They usually follow this by a *survey* organized to collect complete specific details about the clients' requirements. Such a survey will
ask such questions as the following: How many people are to be seated
in a living room? Will there be books, a piano? Will the kitchen be
used by one person or several? Will it be used to prepare only snacks
or full dinners for a crowd? Is a dishwasher wanted? A microwave
oven? A restaurant range? How is the office to be used? Does it need
conference seating, files, a computer? Are there color preferences or
other special personal requirements to be taken into consideration?
Even when designing for one's own use or for one's own family, it is
helpful to note down all such data, in part because the process will
raise questions that should be answered before planning begins.

For large, many-faceted projects, such as corporate offices, hospitals
and other medical facilities, school and college buildings, and airport
and other transportation facilities, programming of a highly organized
sort becomes an important and complex need. Specialized consultants
other than the interior designer are sometimes retained to develop a
program even before a designer is hired. Other design organizations

are prepared to develop complex programs using specialized personnel
for that purpose.

In projects accommodating a number of people, each must be inter-
viewed to learn individual practical needs, habits of living and work,
tastes, and personal preferences. For larger projects it may not be necessary or appropriate to interview every person involved. Department
heads and a few representative individuals should be able to give data
on behalf of the others. It is important to remember, however, that
managers often have mistaken ideas about what their subordinates
really need and want. Their information should be cross-checked by
conducting some individual interviews.

In addition to ascertaining space and furniture requirements, it is
important to collect data on activities and processes, asking such questions as the following: Where is privacy important, and where does
interaction occur? Data may be recorded on a simple lined pad or on
forms developed for the purpose. It is wise to remind those inter-
viewed that the designer cannot guarantee to satisfy every item on
each "wish list"; compromises may be necessary to resolve conflicts
and to accommodate budgets. Data must also be collected about general needs—for example, storage requirements and facilities for group
use.

A printed form is often developed for data collection on larger projects. Data can then be entered into a computer so that a numerical
count of spaces of a given type, equipment needs (how many files of a
particular size, for example), and other information can be obtained as
planning proceeds. Data collection will also usually include information
on *adjacency* needs to help identify, for each person or each function,
which other persons or functions need to be located nearby. Although
it does not require a survey to know that a dining room should be
close to the kitchen that will serve it, in office planning there is no way
to know which people need to be near one another, who uses a conference area often and who does not, and which groups work together in

6.17 *This well-planned modern house
displays the following desirable features: The major rooms (living room
and master bedroom) face south. No
major rooms face the street (on right).
The main entrance is sheltered, opens
into a vestibule, and is close to coat
and general-storage closets. The garage*

*has direct access to the kitchen and
utility areas and easy access to the
principal living space. The kitchen follows a logical corridor work-flow plan.
The dining area has direct access to the
kitchen and an open, natural relationship to the living space. The living area
is not cut by a major traffic path. The*

*living spaces and bedrooms all permit
reasonable furniture layouts. All major
rooms have good cross-ventilation. The
second bath is accessible to all living
spaces and to the smaller bedrooms.
No two bedrooms share a partition
wall or a wall with a living area, thus
assuring good acoustical isolation and*

*privacy. Enough closets are provided
for each bedroom and for linens and
general storage. At least two outdoor
living spaces—patios or terraces—are
provided. A good house plan should
offer all, or most, of these advantages.*

6.18

6.19

teams unless this information has been collected through a survey. The uses to which this information can be put are discussed below (page 162). Some furniture manufacturers offer survey forms and a computerized data-collection service as aids to designers working on projects in which their furniture systems are to be specified. Use of a manufacturer's service has, of course, the disadvantage of making designer and client captive to that maker's products.

Any program is subject to question and to revision. Testing the program's validity is useful, especially when the designer was not the person who prepared the program. Items may have been included out of habit; questionable assumptions may have been made. Other elements may have been left out because no one thought about them. Such program testing can take place before planning begins and will often continue throughout the planning process. The designer must also evaluate the program's requirements and ensure that they do not lead to unwise planning. If they do, the issues should be discussed and the program revised.

With simple spaces, the preparation of the program can lead directly to designing (see page 165). In a simple project, the number of rooms and their uses probably have already been established. The designation of rooms as living room, bedroom, kitchen, and so on rarely comes into question. The designer must still decide whether to combine some rooms (separate living and dining rooms, for example), whether any rooms can or should be made larger or smaller, or whether some room uses should be changed (a bedroom to a study, or even a garage to a new living room), but such changes can usually be kept in mind quite easily. More complex projects, in which many spaces and functions need to be provided, call for several preliminary steps, including the following.

Area Assignment

This involves estimating for each space, meaning each function and/or room, an approximate size expressed in square footage. Arriving at appropriate area assignments is partly a matter of common sense and experience, and partly a matter of consulting various data handbooks

Table 2. Room Areas in Square Feet (Typical)

ROOM	SMALL	AVERAGE	LARGE
RESIDENTIAL:			
LIVING ROOM (OR SPACE)	150	400	800
Dining room (or space)	75	250	400
Kitchen	50	125	450
Bedroom (master)	120	200	500
Bathroom	30	60	200
OFFICE:			
Executive	250	350	600
Managerial	100	200	250
General office staff	55	100	120
Clerical (minimum)	50	80	100
Circulation space (as percent of total)	15%	25%	35%
HOSPITAL ROOM	75	90	125
HOTEL/MOTEL ROOM	100	175	400
AUDITORIUM (PER PERSON)	6	7.5	9
RESTAURANT (PER PERSON)	7	12	24
ELEVATOR	20	55	120
GARAGE (ONE PASSENGER CAR)	150	200	250

6.18, 6.19 A renovated attic in an older house greatly expands a house's useful space. An attic before (fig. 6.18) and after (fig. 6.19) conversion by Bill and Juanita Sharpe in their own home in Grand Rapids, Michigan, in 1987. (Photograph: B. Sharpe, courtesy Metropolitan Home)

6.20

6.21

that list commonly accepted area rules for various functions (see Table 2). One can work out an appropriate area for a bedroom, for example, by evaluating similar rooms. The minimum size for a bathroom is found in many handbooks. Suggested sizes for offices of various sorts are often listed in tables. Areas for an auditorium, a conference room, or a restaurant can be calculated on the basis of the number of seats to be provided and the type of use.

Once footage has been estimated, a list of spaces and their proposed areas, with allowances for circulation spaces, storage, and so on, can be prepared, and the total area added up. Obviously, the aim is to

6.20, 6.21 A mezzanine level in New York's Barbizon Hotel served as a visitors' reception area from the 1930s to the 1950s (fig. 6.20). Today, the same space is the mezzanine level of the hotel's restaurant (fig. 6.21). As designed by Judith Stockman & Associates, interior designers, with Milton Glaser as conceptual director, it has a fresh and modern feeling that replaces the older flavor of a bygone day. (Photograph of fig. 6.21: © Langdon Clay)

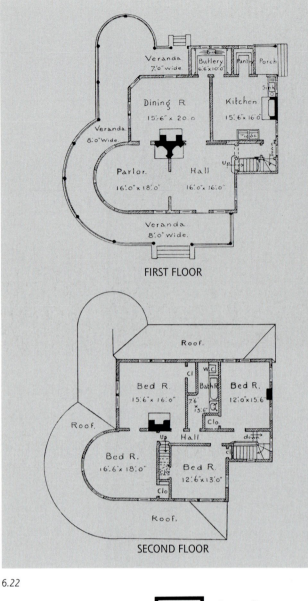

FIRST FLOOR

SECOND FLOOR

6.22

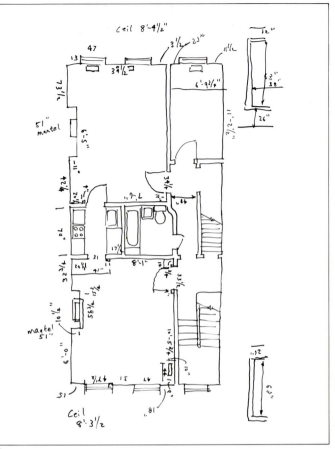

6.24

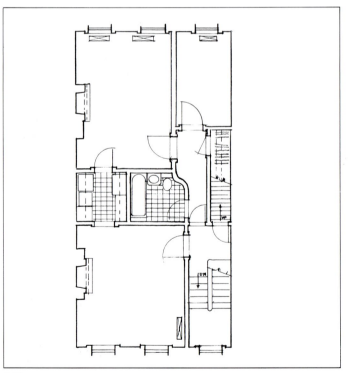

6.25

6.23

6.22 Older houses in sound condition often make good candidates for conversion—if the projected result is cost-effective. Antiquated kitchens and baths and some room arrangements need replanning in order to adapt the spaces to modern life and to the new occu-pants' special needs. In this 1890s house, for example, a designer would provide a more modern kitchen layout and additional and better bathroom facilities and better closets and other storage.

6.23 This apartment plan is typical of those offered in the advertisements of real-estate firms. A designer can help clients evaluate the plans of apartments that they are considering renting or purchasing.

6.24, 6.25 Rough, freehand field notes (fig. 6.24) accompany the mea-suring that precedes the actual interior design. The data collected in the field notes are then organized into a neatly drafted plan drawn to scale (fig. 6.25). For a small area such as this, the usual scale would be ¼" = 1'-0". The space is a compact, top-floor apartment in an 1830s Brooklyn, New York, brownstone.

6.26

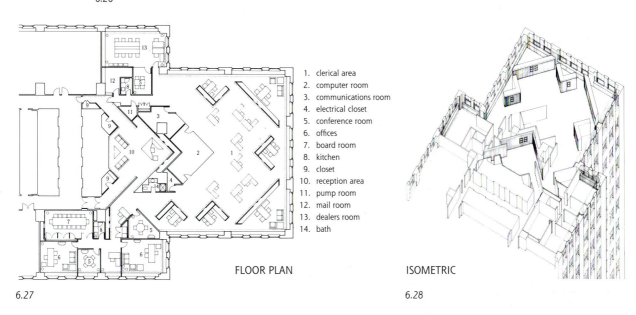

1. clerical area
2. computer room
3. communications room
4. electrical closet
5. conference room
6. offices
7. board room
8. kitchen
9. closet
10. reception area
11. pump room
12. mail room
13. dealers room
14. bath

FLOOR PLAN

6.27

ISOMETRIC

6.28

match the total area available fairly closely. If the mismatch is too great, area assignments may have to be adjusted or the available space reconsidered.

For larger projects that will occupy two or more floors, it is next necessary to assign each functional unit to a particular floor. This step is called *stacking,* meaning the preparation of a *stacking plan* or diagram. Stacking is discussed in detail on page 164. For projects on one level, work can proceed to the following steps.

Block Diagramming

In this step, which presumes that area assignment has been made, each area is drawn to scale in the form of a block or a box of arbitrary shape, usually a convenient rectangle, unless a more special shape is called for by the function of the space. A requirement of 4,800 square feet, for example, is drawn as a block of 48 by 100 feet, or perhaps 40 by 120 feet, to scale. All of the blocks representing all of the required spaces make up a chart that gives a clear visual idea of how the space requirements relate in size (fig. 6.29).

6.26–6.28 Imaginative design transformed a neutral area in a modern office building for Banque Bruxelles Lambertf, New York, into an interior with style and wit—the "windows" are inserted elements that mask the structural walls and windows. A floor plan (fig. 6.27) and an isometric drawing (fig. 6.28) of the space clearly show the inserted elements. Isometric views show width and depth to scale at 30- and 60-degree angles. Verticals are drawn at the same scale. An illusion of space similar to that of perspective *drawing results, although—because each dimension is equally foreshortened—the isometric view is proportioned differently from a perspective. Emilio Ambasz & Associates was the designer, in 1984. (Photograph: © Paul Warchol)*

Adjacency Studies

Adjacent means side by side or adjoining. In interior design, the term has been extended to describe a full range of relationships from close to far apart. Rather than describing adjacency needs in terms of yards or feet, the designer usually makes a scale that gives simple numbers or letters to different levels of closeness. Such a scale might be:

1 = *Adjoining*
2 = *Near*
3 = *Medium distant*
4 = *Far*
5 = *No contact*

The designer next makes a chart showing all of the spaces to be planned, arranged as in a map mileage chart so that a blank is shown for each relationship of one space to another. This is called a *matrix chart*. For example, a house or apartment made up of

LR = *Living space*
DR = *Dining area*
K = *Kitchen*
BR 1 = *Bedroom 1*
BR 2 = *Bedroom 2*
B = *Bathroom*
would be charted thus:

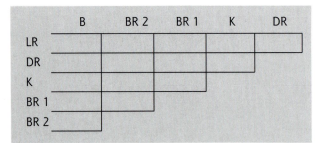

As the designer decides the suitable level of closeness between each pair of spaces, he or she assigns it a corresponding number from the scale and places it in the appropriate box of the chart. The chart above might be completed in this way:

	B	BR 2	BR 1	K	DR
LR	4	4	5	4	2
DR	4	5	5	1	
K	4	5	5		
BR 1	1	3			
BR 2	2				

In such a simple situation, the designer could probably determine the needs for adjacency by common sense and common usage, as well as by asking the intended occupants of the space a few questions, such as: Should bedroom 2 be close to or far from bedroom 1? In more

complex problems with many spaces and complicated relationship needs, the designer would take a survey of individuals or key people in various areas, asking them to specify their needs for contact with each unit in the project. These data may be displayed numerically or with graphic symbols in a matrix chart.

Once this information has been collected, the designer makes a chart combining the block diagram with adjacency data. Lines of different thicknesses represent the levels of adjacency, the broadest line indicating the greatest need for closeness. These lines are drawn to connect the various blocks of space. The designer rearranges the blocks in an effort to make the heaviest lines as short as possible. The result is called a *bubble diagram,* with the blocks shown rounded and connected by link lines representing adjacency needs (figs. 6.30, 6.31). Such a diagram begins to suggest spatial relationships that would be efficient, even though it is not realistically indicative of any actual layout.

While these steps may sound complicated, they are very helpful, even for small projects involving more than two or three spaces. Although it may seem expedient to bypass these steps when planning a house or small office, designers and clients may find that preliminary area and adjacency diagrams clarify the needs and decisions of each and can prevent later problems and misunderstandings. In planning such complex projects as modern hospitals, airports, or large corporate office buildings (figs. 6.34, 6.35), they are indispensable. For multistory projects, further diagramming is used to aid *stacking,* that is, locating the elements on various floors.

Stacking Plans

In modern practice, many larger projects occupy a number of floors in a building. The decisions about what functions to place on each available floor must be made before the planning of each floor can be undertaken. The steps involved in making a stacking plan are:

1. Determine the usable floor area of each of the floors the facility is to occupy.
2. List the area required for each functional unit of the facility as determined through the area-assignment step described above.
3. Note any special characteristics of particular floors (ground level, top floor, adjacent to usable roof space, and so on).
4. Note any requirements or preference for specific functions to be on a particular floor. Loading dock or ambulance access at ground level, for example, or cafeteria or lounge to be adjacent to an open area.
5. From the adjacency studies described above, extract needs for location on the same floor and needs to be on a near floor. Where elevators provide vertical transportation, the levels of closeness can be considered to be only three:
   Same floor
   Next floor (by stairs, one flight up or down)
   Remote floor (elevator access)
   A matrix chart similar to that described above can be made showing each function and displaying at each intersection point the desired level of closeness using only the three levels: 3 = same, 2 = next, 1 = remote.
6. Prepare a stacking diagram in which each floor is shown as a bar

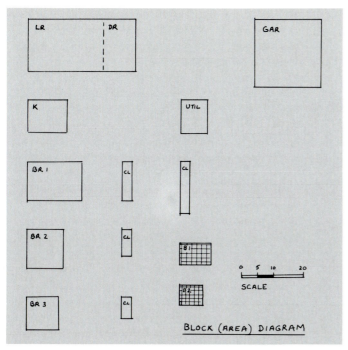

BLOCK (AREA) DIAGRAM

6.29

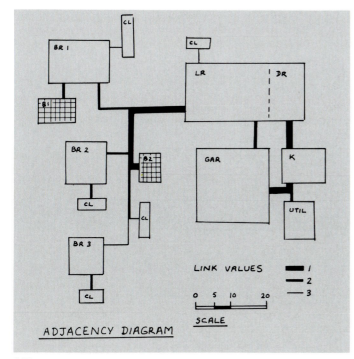

ADJACENCY DIAGRAM

LINK VALUES
■■■ 1
■■ 2
— 3

6.30

Adjacency Matrix Chart for a Three-Bedroom House

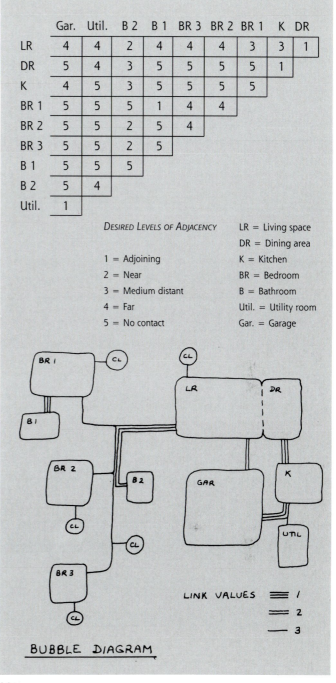

	Gar.	Util.	B 2	B 1	BR 3	BR 2	BR 1	K	DR
LR	4	4	2	4	4	4	3	3	1
DR	5	4	3	5	5	5	5	1	
K	4	5	3	5	5	5	5		
BR 1	5	5	5	1	4	4			
BR 2	5	5	2	5	4				
BR 3	5	5	2	5					
B 1	5	5	5						
B 2	5	4							
Util.	1								

DESIRED LEVELS OF ADJACENCY

1 = Adjoining
2 = Near
3 = Medium distant
4 = Far
5 = No contact

LR = Living space
DR = Dining area
K = Kitchen
BR = Bedroom
B = Bathroom
Util. = Utility room
Gar. = Garage

LINK VALUES
≡ 1
= 2
— 3

BUBBLE DIAGRAM

6.31

6.29 This block (area) diagram for a simple, three-bedroom house shows the square footage of the spaces to scale, but the shapes are arbitrary. These diagrams, preliminary planning steps, convert numbers into graphic form.

6.30 The bubble diagram is here more carefully drafted as an adjacency diagram, preparatory to discussion and review with the client. The house plan in fig. 6.17 is derived from this diagram.

6.31 A matrix chart (above) shows the desired relationships among the spaces of the block diagram (fig. 6.29). The information from the block diagram might next be reorganized into a bubble diagram (below) to show graphically the relationships in the matrix. The term "bubble" describes the appearance of such plans: when drawn freehand, the shapes are soft and bub-blelike. The weight of the lines that represent relationships varies in proportion to the density of traffic; the bubbles are moved about until their arrangement uses the shortest and most direct links possible—with the most important links the shortest of all. When the process is completed, the diagram will suggest an appropriate floor plan.

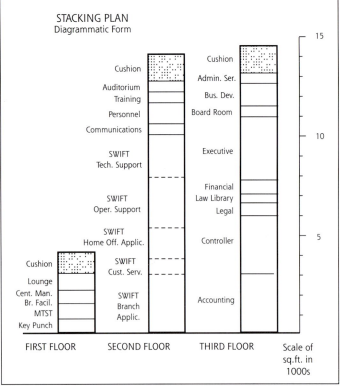

STACKING PLAN
Diagrammatic Form

FIRST FLOOR · SECOND FLOOR · THIRD FLOOR

Scale of sq.ft. in 1000s

First floor (right bar): Cushion / Lounge / Cent. Man. / Br. Facil. / MTST / Key Punch

Second floor: Cushion / SWIFT Cust. Serv. / SWIFT Branch Applic.

Third floor / second bar: Cushion / Auditorium / Training / Personnel / Communications / SWIFT Tech. Support / SWIFT Oper. Support / SWIFT Home Off. Applic.

Right bar: Cushion / Admin. Ser. / Bus. Dev. / Board Room / Executive / Financial / Law Library / Legal / Controller / Accounting

6.32

with a length measured to indicate total available area at a convenient scale. Reserve a portion of each floor for circulation (10 percent is a usual allowance). Draw a bar for each functional area with a length measured at the same scale.

Where there is a specific requirement for a function to be on a particular floor, place those function bars on the appropriate floor-area bars. Now place function bars requiring same-floor locations next to the bars already placed. Continue to place function bars, progressing from same-floor functional units to next-floor units and finally to remote-floor units, to achieve the desired relationships to a maximal degree. Large units may have to be broken onto two adjacent floors. Although it may not be possible to achieve every required relationship within the given space, by making a number of trial arrangements a stacking plan that achieves optimal results can usually be found.

7. An evaluation of the proposed stacking plan can be made using the matrix of functional areas. At each intersection point, enter a figure (3, 2, or 1) indicating placement of the two functions at same, next, or remote floors. Add the numbers in the matrix to obtain a total *figure of merit*. If the figure obtained is the same as the comparable total from the matrix of requirements described under step 5 above, the proposed plan can be viewed as *perfect*, having satisfied all of the desired relationships. If no perfect plan can be achieved, proposed plans can be evaluated by comparing the figure of merit for each proposal, with the highest figure indicating the most successful stacking arrangement.

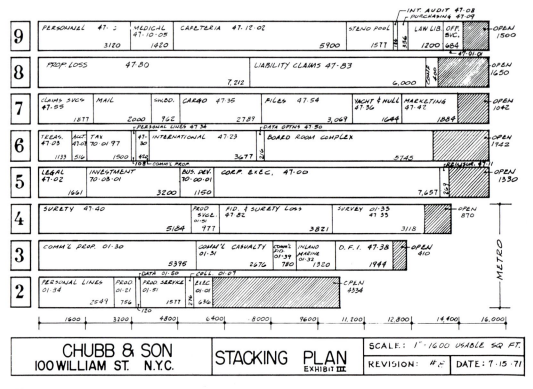

6.33

6.32, 6.33 Two types of stacking plans for a five-story project are illustrated here. The diagrammatic form (fig. 6.32) is a graph in which required areas are grouped to form bars representing the respective floors of the total project. In the chart form (fig. 6.33), appropriate for review with a client, the bars representing the project's floor levels are divided to indicate the areas occupied by various departments. The bars are then drawn horizontally in a "stack" to show the floors arranged from bottom to top, as they would be in the actual building. (Courtesy John Pile)

When a "perfect" stacking plan proves impossible and a "best" plan must be selected on the basis of a figure of merit, it may be problematic that all functional units are given equal weight in the matrix. This means that a unit with few occupants receives the same weight as one with many. When this becomes an issue of concern, a further modification of the matrix can be introduced by multiplying each number in the matrix by the total number of persons to occupy the two units that the matrix intersection represents. Thus two units with ten persons in each generate a multiplier of 20. If these two units should be on the same floor, 3×20 gives a number of 60 as the figure to be multiplied into the total figure of merit. If two units on the same floor have populations of 5 and 80, that will generate the number $(5 + 80) \times 3$ or 255, far outweighing the two units of ten each when the total figure of merit is added up. Stacking plans can best be studied by following other examples (figs. 6.32, 6.33).

After a satisfactory stacking plan has been developed and accepted, the planning of each floor becomes a separate matter, with work proceeding according to the steps that would be applicable to a single-level project. For each floor, area assignments, block diagramming, adjacency studies, and matrix studies can progress, as discussed above.

Designing the Space

Once the program and preliminary diagramming have been prepared, the actual designing begins. In this first phase, commonly known as "making sketches," the usual procedure is to place yellow tracing paper over the plan showing existing conditions and limitations and sketch out proposals, starting with general space allocations and gradually moving to finer detail (see Case Study 2, page 177). As described above, freehand sketches may be made on any medium and may include floor plans, sections, elevations, or perspectives. Preliminary design, of course, can also develop mentally, without any drawing, but such design thinking can be hard to hold in memory, and it is often misleading in the way it relates to real spatial limitations. Design ideas are best put on paper as soon as possible so that they can be looked at, compared, and saved as design progresses.

Exactly how the planner arrives at a completed design is difficult to describe. It seems to involve a special talent for visualizing geometric possibilities. The planner looks at the space available and at the information about needs embodied in block diagrams and adjacency charts and derives from this a rough solution, which is sketched out on paper. Then the first proposal is evaluated and improvements suggested. This leads to a next proposal, and a next, and so forth, until a plan emerges that seems to resolve the space allocation problem.

In real situations, this process is modified by any number of pressures that contend with one another for dominance. What elements will be given locations with good daylight and view? What spaces must be close to the point of arrival? How are the conflicting needs of residents, visitors, workers, and other identifiable groups to be reconciled? These concerns, while typical of large and complex problems, come up in small projects as well. How large should the kitchen be when every foot allocated to it must be taken away from some other space? Is an extra bathroom worth its cost in space and in money? If necessary, rooms can be combined and doors can be moved, closed

up, or cut out, but are such steps worth their cost and complication? The planner must consider all these issues while developing a basic plan assigning space locations, sizes, and purposes and positioning walls and openings to achieve a completed project that works well and is visually satisfying.

Plan Types

Although any conceivable arrangement of spaces may be considered in developing usable plans, it is often helpful to consider some typical ways of grouping spaces. A plan may be based on one of these arrangements, may use different types in different areas, or may use combinations of types within a particular grouping. The units making up a plan may be rooms, spaces more or less open to one another, or functional units within an entirely open space (fig. 6.36). Arrangements in frequent use include:

- UNIT WITH ADJACENT SUBSIDIARY UNIT. Typical examples include a living room with adjacent dining area, a dining area with adjacent kitchen or kitchenette, a bedroom with connected bath or dressing area, and an office with adjacent lavatory or storage area. Smaller subsidiary spaces can often be placed in an interlocking arrangement that works well for rows of hotel, motel, or hospital patient rooms.
- IN-LINE (LINEAR) BANDS OF SPACES. A line of rooms each opening into the next is a frequent arrangement of the galleries of a museum or for an exhibition where visitors are to follow a planned circulation path. An in-line arrangement with a parallel corridor is typical for rows of offices and hotel or hospital rooms. Rooms with adjacent subsidiary units are most often placed in line with parallel circulation.
  - SINGLE-LOADED CORRIDORS have the spaces they serve on one side only, often with services on the other side.
  - DOUBLE-LOADED CORRIDORS serve rows of in-line spaces on both sides. Double-loading is space efficient since one corridor serves two rows of spaces, but, where daylight is desired for the primary spaces, is possible only within a building unit of the appropriate width.
- IN-LINE INNER AND OUTER UNITS. Units placed in line may be made up of an outer space that must be passed through to reach an inner space, a common arrangement for private offices accessible only through an outer secretarial and/or waiting space.
- CLUSTERS. Spaces grouped around a common area that may serve for access or another significant function are called cluster arrangements. Private offices are often grouped around a central clerical space. Work that involves team cooperation is well served by cluster arrangements that may be made up of bands of in-line units around a shared space or may be in a radial relationship around a compact center. A radial grouping may take circular form, but it can also be developed in straight-line patterns. A cluster may be open to other spaces on one side or may be entered through a circulation path. An entire floor plan may take a cluster form, as in a museum where galleries open off a

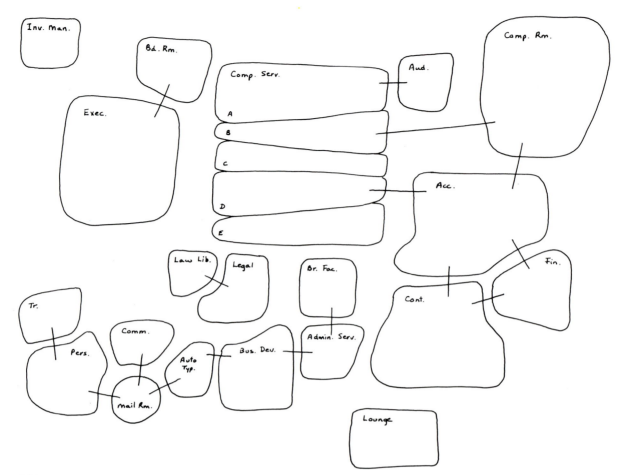

6.34

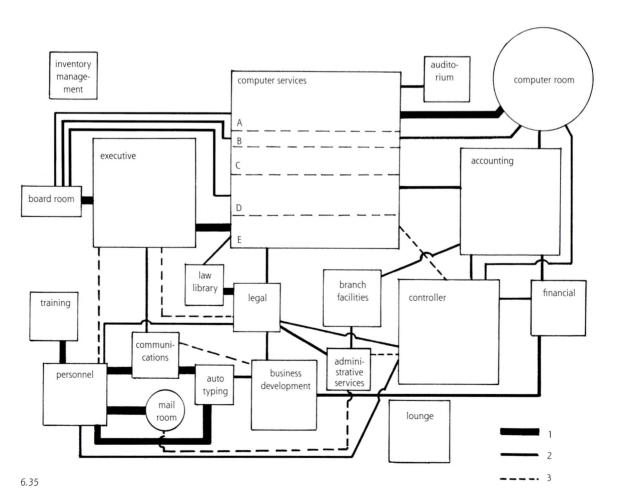

6.35

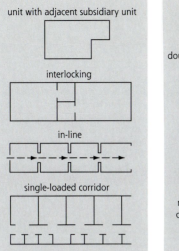

unit with adjacent subsidiary unit

interlocking

in-line

single-loaded corridor

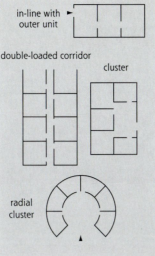

in-line with outer unit

double-loaded corridor

cluster

radial cluster

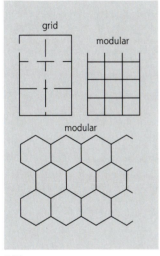

grid

modular

modular

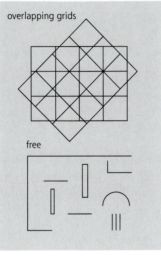

overlapping grids

free

6.36

court or an atrium. The cluster arrangement was the basis of the typical ancient Greek and Roman courtyard house plan, as well as of some similar modern houses.

- GRID PLANS. This organizational form packs spaces together in patterns that involve groupings of either similarly or variously shaped areas. Museum or gallery plans that offer visitors free or flexible circulation are often of this type. When openings between elements of a grid are limited, a grid plan can generate complex and confusing patterns of circulation. An irregular grid of various spaces packed together with irregularly placed openings can become a labyrinth of complexity.
- MODULAR PLANNING. Based on a grid of regular geometric elements such as squares, rectangles, or other repeated units, modular planning is a basis for organization greatly favored in architectural design. Structural design tends to call for repeated identical units (bays) that are economical to construct and that

establish an orderly basis for planning. On a modular grid, spaces may be laid out in any of the arrangements discussed above, with elements of the plan falling on the modular lines or relating to them (at half, third, or fifth points, for example). Elements may also depart from the module in some positions while still maintaining a relationship to its pattern.

- OVERLAPPING GRIDS. A means of introducing complexity and enrichment to plans that have a regular module, overlapping grids can offer subtle variations on the geometry of a simple grid without total abandonment of a geometric basis.
- OPEN, OR "FREE" PLANS. Elements are placed within a space that may be totally unobstructed or that may be based on a structural grid that is unobtrusive. Such classic modernist plans as that of the Barcelona Pavilion of Mies van der Rohe (see page 107) place screen walls within an open area in a way that modulates space without enclosure or obvious pattern. The modulating elements may be set in rectilinear patterns (as in the Barcelona Pavilion) or in more irregular geometric or free relationships. Open plans are often adopted for gallery or exhibition spaces and are the cornerstone of open or "landscape" office planning.

Circulation

A matter that needs special attention in planning, usually called *circulation*, is an aspect of any layout. People using a built space do not stay fixed in unchanging locations. They move about, and the ease and convenience of their movement have a very strong impact on the sense of comfort that a space provides. When moving from one place to another, a simple and direct route feels better than a roundabout and awkward path. Squeezing through narrow openings and bumping furniture when moving about is unpleasant and irritating. The more frequently a line of movement will be followed, the more important it is that the route be direct and ample. A space that will hold a number of people needs routes of movement that interfere as little as possible and that have generous paths. A space serving few people allows more minimal passage that will serve one person at a time.

An *overlay circulation diagram* aids the planner in resolving circulation patterns (fig. 6.37). In this chart, lines are drawn to show the paths of movement that will be followed most frequently. The planner may vary the line thickness to indicate frequency of movement or the number of people expected to follow each path. A circulation diagram makes it easy to spot problems. A good circulation pattern will show short, direct routes, particularly for the most used paths. A problematic pattern will generate a complex and confused circulation diagram, with winding and contorted paths passing through bottleneck points of constriction. When using a built space, one does not ordinarily think about circulation patterns as an abstract concept, but the success of circulation planning will make itself felt in the space's sense of ease and comfort, as compared with other spaces that arouse annoyance and discomfort.

Circulation patterns can be described as falling into a number of types that can be used alone or in various combinations. They interact with space-plan arrangements to generate, ideally, plans that organize

6.34 In contrast to the simpler sketches on page 163, this bubble diagram reflects the complexity of an office project that must incorporate a number of departments with an intricate pattern of relationships. This draft lacks many of the secondary links that have been added to the diagram in fig. 6.35.

6.35 In this drafted bubble diagram, all projected links have been drawn in with line weights developed from a matrix chart of adjacency requirements. Note that two areas (inventory management and lounge) were found to have no regular business communications with other units. The largest depart-

ment (computer services) has five internal subdivisions, one of which, C, has no links to any other department but only to the adjacent subdivisions B and D.

6.36 Various types of plans are illustrated here in diagrammatic form.

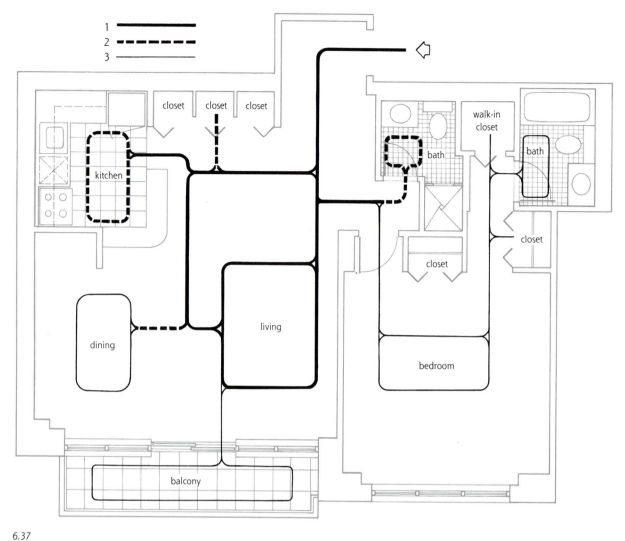

1 ━━━━━━
2 ▬▬ ▬▬ ▬▬ ▬▬
3 ━━━━━━

6.37

spaces well and provide logical access and movement. Typical circulation patterns include the following:

- STRAIGHT-LINE. The most common pattern is a direct route from an access point to destination(s) at an end, on one or both sides of the line of movement. Its end may be an exit or alternative access point. Although the line may not actually be straight—it may turn corners or curve—the movement remains along a single route.
- LINE WITH BRANCHES. This elaboration of the linear pattern offers alternative paths that branch off or fan out to give access to various possible destinations.
- RADIATING CIRCULATION. Here alternative paths move out from a central access point.
- RING CIRCULATION. A circular path moves through the spaces it serves and returns to a starting point. It provides two alterna-

tive paths to any destination and can provide access or exit at two or more points. It has special value where safety regulations require two exit routes.

Circulation patterns within a single space also need study. In planning any room it is useful to make a diagram of the way in which movement can take place from any access point to any destination. Are the available routes direct; do furniture groupings obstruct movement; will circulation routes cut through furniture groups in a way that will be inconvenient to those moving about or disturbing to those using any group? A plan with diagrammatic lines tracing usual paths of movement is the best test of circulation patterns (fig. 6.38). All lines of circulation should ideally be direct, as short as possible, visually obvious, and independent of other "cross-traffic" lines of circulation, as well as free of conflict with functional groupings that call for cohesion.

In any planning, spaces located at a dead end, where circulation is

6.37 A circulation diagram drawn over a plan often helps to evaluate the plan's practicality and can serve for the design of the furniture layout as well. This plan of a rental apartment was provided by a real-estate firm. The projected normal circulation has been dia-grammed clearly and neatly, with varied line weights indicating the anticipated level of traffic along each path. A poorly planned layout, by contrast, exhibits a confused and tangled circulation pattern with many points of overlapping cross-traffic.

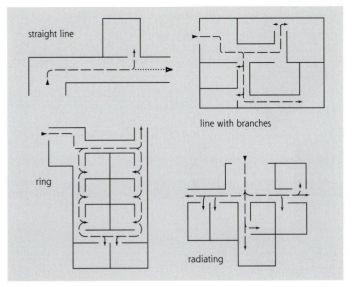

straight line

line with branches

ring

radiating

6.38

brought to a stop by the absence of any further possible destination, have a special value. They imply privacy and a sense of arrival and offer a feeling of repose or containment. A private office, a residential bedroom, or a private dining room can all provide this special quality. It is often noted that people at a party tend to move toward such dead-end spaces and group there, sometimes at the expense of crowding, even when other more generous spaces are available. It is not uncommon to find a crush of people in a kitchen, for example, while the dining and living spaces are quite empty. The feeling of arrival at a destination seems to have an attraction that is lacking in a space that is also a circulation route to other spaces beyond.

Furniture Layout

Furniture layout, a form of detailed planning, usually follows more general space planning, but it is wise to have furniture placement in mind while planning spaces. Most people can come up with examples of rooms almost impossible to furnish because of their basic plan: the bedroom with no wall broad enough to permit placement of a bed; the living room with so many doors and windows that furniture has no place to rest. When an interior design project involves a room or rooms that are not to be changed, planning begins with furniture layout. Wherever it fits in the sequence of planning, furniture layout must follow a pattern comparable to that of space planning.

The first step is to list the furniture required. The designer returns to the program to learn what activities are to take place in the space in question and then decides what furniture clusters will serve those activities. Many other questions arise. What are the needs for storage or for the display of objects? Are there existing pieces of furniture (a treasured antique, perhaps, or a favorite chair or sofa) to be retained? Will any or all existing pieces be appropriate to the new space? Will new built-in units be best for dealing with some furniture needs, such as placement of books, TV and stereo equipment, and kitchen utensils? How many people will use a particular space and how many will need

to be seated, both in normal situations and on special occasions? All such questions need to be explored in an effort to arrive at furniture planning decisions that will serve user needs at the best possible levels of satisfaction. A short checklist will often prove useful.

In completing such a checklist, additional details about sizes and any other specifics that may be significant should be noted. While many entries may seem obvious, it is surprising how often a methodical review of such a list will reveal needs not previously recognized. Like the program and earlier charts, this is another tool to clarify the client's needs and desires and the designer's approach. Using it can avoid future problems and misunderstandings.

With a list of furniture requirements in hand (or in mind), the designer can place the necessary pieces on the floor plan (see fig. 6.41). The guiding basis for placement must be an understanding of the activities being provided for and a consideration of people's movement into and around the space. The program will list these activities, both everyday and special.

Furniture Planning Checklist

NUMBER OF PEOPLE USING SPACE
    Normally_____
    Maximum_____
NUMBER TO BE SEATED
    Upright_____
    Lounge_____
    Reclining_____
TABLES
    Low_____
    Work_____
    Conference_____
    Dining_____
    To seat (number)_____
        Normally_____
        Maximum_____
DESKS OR OTHER
WORK SURFACES
    Size(s)_____
STORAGE NEEDS
    Clothing_____
        Hanging_____
        Folded_____
    Books_____
    Records, tapes, CDs_____
    Dishes, silver, other tableware_____
    Other_____
SPECIAL EQUIPMENT
AND STORAGE
    TV, stereo, video cassette
        recorder_____
    Film/TV projection_____

Music (instruments such as
    piano, music stand,
    printed music,
    and so on)_____
Bar and serving needs_____
Files_____
Typewriter_____
Computer equipment_____
Other_____
BEDS
    Single_____
    Double_____
    Queen_____
    Convertible_____
    Other_____
BATHROOM
    Standard_____
    Toilet_____
    Sink_____
    Bathtub_____
    Lavatory_____
    Shower_____
    Bidet_____
    Vanity_____
    Linen storage_____
OTHER REQUIREMENTS
    Display_____
    Artworks_____
    Hobbies_____
    Plants_____
    Workshop_____
    Miscellaneous_____

6.38 The dotted lines on these plan layouts represent typical circulation patterns.

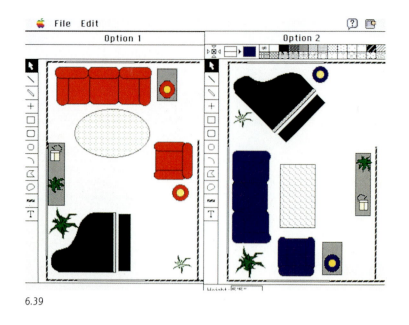

6.39

When drawing furniture in plan, it is important to use correct sizes, properly scaled. With practice, it becomes easy to draw furniture to scale without measuring or consulting catalogs for dimensions, but developing this skill takes some effort. Templates with cutouts to scale representing commonly used furniture types in typical shapes and sizes are available for various spaces (home, office, kitchen, and bathroom). While some furniture types are fairly consistent in size (chairs, sofas of given capacity, beds, file cabinets), others vary greatly. Tables and office desks come in a range of sizes and in various shapes. Even pianos range from upright to concert grand.

Exact sizes of existing furniture can be obtained by measurement, of course, while sizes of new furniture are given in manufacturers' catalogs and price lists. A chart of sizes drawn to scale, such as the one provided in Appendix 2, "Furniture Symbols," can be photostated to any desired scale and kept at hand to aid in drawing. It is sometimes suggested to amateur home decorators that they cut out pieces of paper or cardboard, possibly color-coded, at scale sizes to represent furniture. These can then be moved about on a plan, representing different arrangements. Experienced designers prefer to work with drawing directly, regarding cutouts as an unnecessary planning aid.

The following notes offer some suggestions for furniture planning for the most frequently encountered space functions.

LIVING AREA. The living area varies widely, from the formal parlor-like space used only for an occasional ceremonial event to the all-purpose space of a studio apartment. In almost every case, the primary uses will call for a furniture grouping suitable to conversation and various types of entertaining. Conversation demands seating that will accommodate an adequate number of people arranged at suitable distances and in comfortable configurations. A sofa on one side of a room and chairs far away on the other side make communication awkward. Distances between 4 and 10 feet are most comfortable for normal con-

versation. A primary seating group for four to six people is the normal core, usually arranged around a low coffee or cocktail table. Larger numbers of people tend to break up into separate groups. Movable seating works best in such situations.

The same seating will probably serve for music-listening and television-watching, for one person or several, making the location of the TV screen, stereo, and TV controls important. A fireplace, even if it is rarely used, becomes an important focal element. For a while, the television had come to replace the traditional fireplace as a focus of attention in the living space. However, it is becoming increasingly common to relegate the TV to a special viewing area, perhaps in another room, or to conceal it when not in use. Windows with an attractive view offer an alternative focal point. In any case, windows will probably influence furniture layout according to their placement and the amount and intensity of light they admit.

Many living areas are expected to serve secondary functions as well, for example, as library, office, study, music room, or guest sleeping room. The combined living-dining room demands furniture for the dining function, often a minimal everyday provision that can be expanded for an occasional larger gathering, which leaves more space for the living area's other functions, such as entertaining large numbers of people. Circulation is of special importance at large gatherings, especially if there will be buffet service of food and drink. If normal furniture placement does not allow easy movement, an alternate arrangement should be planned for such occasions (see figs. 6.41 E, F).

DINING AREA. Whether located in a separate room or in an alcove or other part of a general living space, dining spaces call for a table of suitable size to meet the range from minimum to maximum number of diners to be seated with the appropriate number of chairs available. It is particularly important to leave sufficient space around the table for

6.39 A computer program called Abracadata, available to professional designers as well as to the general public, makes it possible to develop room plans on a computer screen with a wide range of furniture layouts and color choices. In this image, the same living room appears in two schemes. (Photograph courtesy Abracadata)

chairs to be pushed back for access and for serving. Table shape—rectangular, square, oval, or round—strongly influences the degree of formality that will be associated with dining. Circles and squares, having no obvious head or foot, favor informality, while rectangles and ovals are the norm for formal dining. In the larger or more formal dining room, a buffet, sideboard, or other extra serving surface and provision for storage of dishes and serving pieces may be considered.

FAMILY ROOM. Family rooms—or television rooms, recreation rooms, or playrooms—have become common in larger houses, particularly for families with young or teenage children. Such an extra room permits the living room to retain some formality and relieves it of an excess of multiple functions, as well as giving children their own social space. The furniture selected for the room depends upon the family's habits. Almost all families require TV and stereo systems, along with comfortable seating in related locations. Other choices may be recreation equipment and space to store it, table tennis or other game tables, a bar, barbecue cooking provisions, or space for hobby or craft activities. Since family needs change as children grow, flexible furniture selections and space planning should permit adjustment as time passes and adapt to alternative functions, such as media room, studio, office, or workshop, after the children have grown up.

BEDROOM. Bedrooms are inevitably planned around the bed or beds they contain. Furniture for sitting, reading, dressing, storage, and other functions may be considered if there is space for it. Many bedrooms will be expected to offer facilities for such quiet or semiprivate purposes as office work, sewing, or hobby activities. Children's rooms should be planned to adjust to children's changing needs as they grow. Provisions for play, entertaining a friend, study, possibly music and TV, plus storage for clothes and belongings are essential. Shared rooms need to offer some individual territory to each child. A study, sewing room, or hobby room can often be furnished to serve as a guest room as well.

NONRESIDENTIAL SPACES. Nonresidential spaces are so varied as to make discussion of the furniture planning problems of each type impractical. In general, layout must always begin by considering the primary function and the items needed to support it, with some thought given to secondary functions as well. After the size of the

6.40

6.40 Frank O. Gehry was the architect for a 1978 renovation of his own 1930s-vintage clapboard house in Santa Monica, California. This living area is organized in a conversation grouping, but books, telephones, and stereo equipment are also at hand. Note the open framing and the seemingly unfinished studs and joists that give the space an almost improvisational quality, typical of Gehry's work. (Photograph: Tim Street-Porter)

required pieces of furniture and the number of people who will use them regularly or occasionally are determined, placement then proceeds, relating the pieces to the size and shape of the space, as well as to the location of fixed elements such as doors, windows, alcoves, or bays. The way people move around within the space while engaged in their customary activities, as well as their movement in and out of the space, will also guide logical furniture placement.

Many spaces relate closely to residential parallels. A hotel, dormitory, or hospital room functions much like a home bedroom. A private office in an office complex shares some qualities with a library or study. While larger spaces such as restaurants, conference rooms, hotel lobbies, and the public spaces of clubs, airports, and museums do not have direct parallels with residential spaces, the same basic issues arise: furniture planning will be guided by the functions of the space and the furniture; the relation between furniture shapes and the layout of architectural spaces; and the patterns of movement that normal and special usages will generate.

The example of one functional type can serve to suggest the approach to furniture planning for any space. *Private offices* vary greatly in size and intended function. A minimal private office or cubicle may be sized to hold no more than a minimal work surface and a chair. Larger offices usually contain seating for one or more visitors and some extra work and storage provisions. The largest offices have space for both formal and informal meetings and often serve as conference areas. Expressing status level through the amount of space and the size, quantity, and opulence of furniture may be as important as ensuring the office's actual work functions.

Although a desk is usually a key item of office furniture, the term *work surface* better describes the variety of arrangements, whether desk, work counter, table, or other, that may be used to suit particular patterns of work. If windows offer daylight and view, furniture placement should take their location into account. Traditionally, a desk is placed centrally, with the office occupant seated behind it and facing the chairs provided for visitors. A low storage unit (called a credenza) is often placed behind and parallel to a desk, giving the user an extra work surface in back, as well as storage. A modern variant is the L-arrangement, in which the secondary work-surface unit is placed at one side of the desk to form an L. This layout first emerged to provide a location for a typewriter or other office machines that would keep them off the main desk top but leave them readily at hand. This arrangement satisfies the common desire for a clear desk top by placing gadgets and clutter off to the side, where the user can easily reach them simply by turning.

Many offices are now planned to suit a less formal view of work functions. A work surface may be placed along a wall to accommodate the solitary functions of reading, writing, and telephoning. A table will then provide a focus for meetings and conversations with visitors. Storage drawers, files, and shelves can be grouped at one side of the primary work surface along with space for business machines, often including a computer. Larger offices may have a full lounge seating group and low table, similar to the living room core conversation group, intended for informal and extended meetings.

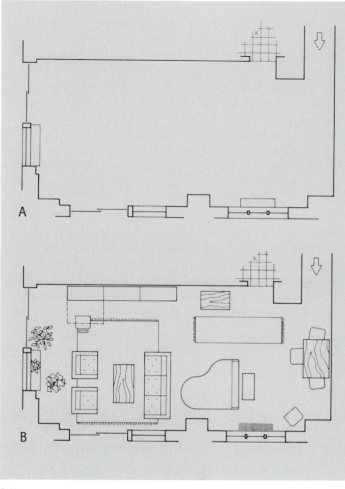

6.41

Offices planned for a particular individual can accommodate personal work habits and expressions of personality. Offices planned as part of the larger installations serving corporations and other large organizations are usually developed in standardized patterns that recognize the reality of the rate of employee turnover. An office that will serve many occupants over a period of years should require only minor adjustments.

LEVELS OF MOBILITY. In planning furniture placement, it is customary to draw all furniture in plan using normal or typical locations for pieces that can be easily moved about. It may be helpful to consider, in order, levels of mobility for furniture.

FIXED LOCATION. This includes objects that are to be built-in, such as bookshelves and dressing-room closets, and objects that are impractical to move, such as major kitchen appliances. Some objects that are, strictly speaking, movable may be considered fixed when the space plan permits only one location. This might be true of the bed in a bedroom that has only one wall space that permits bed placement.

6.41 This series of furniture plans shows the same living-dining area planned in several different ways.

A. This plan shows the unfurnished space; the entrance is at the upper right, indicated by an arrow; the kitchen access (labeled K) is close to the entrance. Two sets of sliding doors (upper left and lower left) lead to two different terraces.

B. The dining table at far right can be opened up to seat as many as six. In the living area, the seating group is placed to relate both to windows and views and to the unit along the upper wall that houses a music system, a bar, and a small drop-front desk. The piano is an obvious visual focal point.

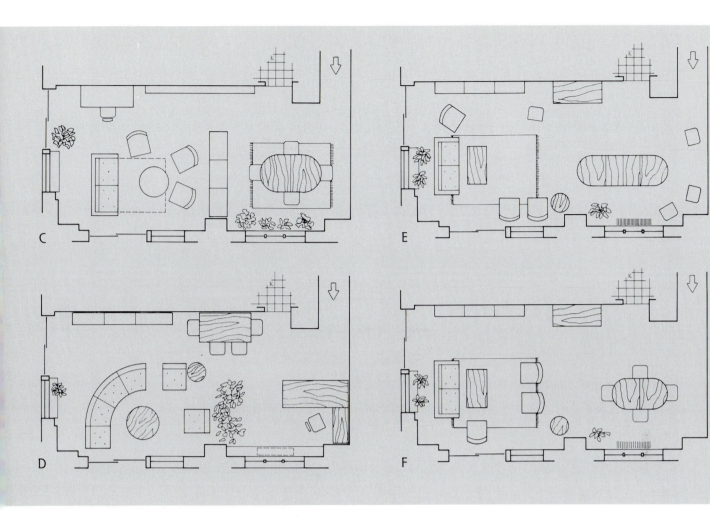

SEMIFIXED LOCATION. This refers to furniture that is so large and heavy as to be difficult to move. It is normally kept in a single location. This is often true of a large sofa or sectional seating group, a large storage piece, or a wall-unit grouping. Although a piano on casters can be shifted about, a fixed location is usual both because of its weight and mass and because there is often only one location that is possible or satisfactory.

MOVABLE FURNITURE. This includes most chairs, tables, and smaller desks, storage units, and lounge furniture. A furniture plan usually shows such furniture in normal locations. Sometimes it is helpful to draw alternate plans to show how furniture can be rearranged for special situations. A living room, for example, may have a normal layout and a planned rearrangement for large parties. A conference room with a center table and surrounding chairs may be converted to a classroom or auditorium plan, with all chairs facing the front of the room.

PORTABLE FURNITURE. This is a special class made up of folding and stacking chairs, folding-leg tables, and furniture on wheels such as tea carts, roll-around files, and projector stands. Typical locations for such furniture and places for storage when not in use need to be considered.

Resolving Conflicts in Planning

Throughout the planning process, whether of extensive spaces or of one room, the designer must always balance conflicting values and requirements that pull in different directions. The designer deals with these by assigning levels of importance to conflicting requirements and finding ways to resolve the conflicts. Typically, the total space available is insufficient to provide ample room for all the various activities the client may wish to pursue. Which activities are to take precedence and which are to be limited? Are there ways to overlap or share activities so that each will be served at an optimum level? A small dining room, for example, might use a large table to serve many guests and permit uncrowded serving space, but the large table may leave limited room for chairs, which will have to be pushed up close to a wall or to adjacent furniture. Generous space for seating and circulation may leave room for only a small and skimpy table. Which value should have priority, or should a compromise be made? What functions in an office require the best light and view—executive offices used by a few important people or general work space used by many? Is there any compromise that will give maximum advantage to all users of the space?

C. A room divider is used in this plan to create a separate dining area. The table will seat two to six as placed and can be extended to seat eight. The convertible sofa is situated so as to be opened easily to become a guest bed. There is a large desk or worktable along the upper wall, as well as a long shelf upon which to display art.

D. In this plan, primary lounge seating is imagined as a curved sectional group with related chairs. The wall unit and dining table are located along the upper wall. A generous home office occupies an area near the entrance, for an occupant who makes major business use of the space during working hours.

E. This is a temporary furniture arrangement for a party where there will be a large number of guests. The dining table has been extended to its maximum length for buffet food service; drinks are on the table near the kitchen entrance. All seating has been pushed close to the walls for easy circulation.

F. The same furniture shown in E is here repositioned for everyday use.

6.42

The most common conflict involves costs. All too often, the list of requirements outruns the available budget. In this case, what features are to be given up? The route of compromise between conflicting values usually appears to be the most reasonable choice, but compromise sometimes results in a situation in which no values are well served and overall mediocrity takes over. In the small dining room mentioned above, a decision to use a medium-sized table may still leave the seating and circulation crowded while making the table inadequate as well. One of the extremes—to provide a generous table at all costs or give up table size entirely in favor of better seating and open space—may well be preferable. Similarly, when it comes to the budget, it is often best to give up some desired feature: to omit a separate dining room, for example, or make do with existing furniture, in order to provide a spacious living room, an all-new kitchen, or a valuable Oriental rug. Ultimately, such decisions rest with the owners, clients, and users, but the designer can aid the decision-making by articulating the choices and by proposing one or more solutions, often in plan form.

At another level, all design involves making choices that imply points of view about what is important and what is not. Although owner, user, or client can contribute to many such decisions, the

6.43

6.42 Juan Montoya designed this media room for a New York apartment in 1983. The family enjoys video viewing and listening to music, and these pastimes determined the formulation of a room that is, in effect, a home the-ater. Adjustable lighting, the wide screen, and inviting seating make the space particularly effective for its special purpose. (Photograph: Jaime Ardiles-Arce)

6.43 In this simple, virtually all-white bedroom, the mirrored wall visually doubles the small space. Stephen Shubel was the interior designer for this San Francisco project. (Photograph: John Vaughn, courtesy Metropolitan Home)

designer must accept responsibility for making a vast number of small decisions in which the values to be taken into consideration are hardly major enough to be thought about as separate issues. When the sofa is placed here or there, a few inches forward or back, the decision implies some view about the relative importance given to the ways in which the sofa and the space around it are to be used. Every plan is based on innumerable decisions of this sort, and the plan's success reflects the quality of such decisions.

EVALUATING THE PLAN

Effective planning is aided by another special skill that all designers need to develop. This is the ability to visualize in three dimensions what is being drawn out in plan, to imagine a completed space, even though the details have not yet been considered, and to live in that space in the imagination. This skill can be practiced when looking at plans published in books and magazines or plans drawn by others. One can imagine oneself a tiny person existing at the scale of the drawing and enter the space. When actually planning, each proposal can be tested by this kind of mental visit to the place that exists, at this point, only on paper. The aim is to make of the mind something like a motion picture or television camera that makes it possible to see—and to feel and sense in every way—what the built space will be like. In this kind of mental visit to the unbuilt space, the designer can enter, look about, move along the various possible lines of circulation, turn right and left, stop, perhaps even sit down where some real occupant of the space might do so. This permits the designer to make a running evaluation of appearance, convenience, and practicality. "How would I like to be here, move thus, sit in this location?" These questions and their answers form a critique of the sketched plan.

In making such a mental visit to a proposed space, a number of points call for special attention. It should become habitual to check

6.44

6.44 A complex space incorporates a bedroom in a renovated older building in Tuscany, Italy. The stairway almost doubles back on itself as it winds up, in a limited space, to a gallery landing that accommodates a private work area. The stairs continue upward at upper left. The art, furniture, and furnishings are part of an eclectic and personal collection. (Photograph: Jaime Ardiles-Arce)

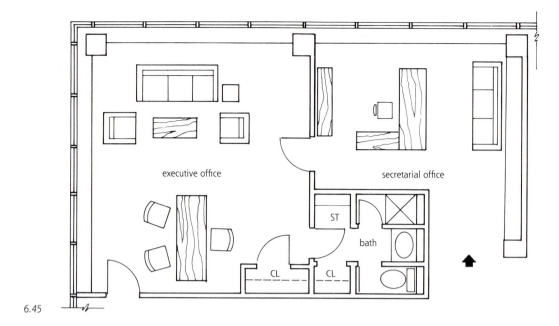

6.45

6.46

6.45 This floor plan shows an executive office suite of a major corporation in a modern New York high rise. The corner office (at left), designed for a senior executive, includes a desk work area and a spacious, informal conference seating group, as well as closets, storage units, and a private washroom, complete with shower. Primary access is through a secretarial office (at right) that has its own storage wall. The door at lower left provides secondary access.

6.46 Louis Frye, designer, conceived this executive office in Tech Center, a 1987 office complex in San Diego, California, for its developer's headquarters. Floors of polished marble tiles, glass block for the corridor wall, and shoji that soften the intense sunlight together form a pure background for the Bauhaus-inspired furniture, much of it created by Frye for this project. There is an informal seating area at right, as well as the traditional across-the-desk arrangement. (Photograph: © 1987 William Gullette)

Case Study 2

Office Floor in a City Building

Offices for Wheel-Gersztoff Associates, New York
Forbes-Ergas Design Assoc., Inc.,
Interior Planning and Design
Wheel-Gersztoff Associates, Inc.,
Lighting Consultants

A full floor in a Manhattan loft building was developed for a lighting design firm with a staff of sixteen. Because most of the firm's clients are architrects or designers, a strong design quality was important, both to display the firm's design standards and to demonstrate excellence in lighting design. The flavor of the original building is maintained in the hardwood floors and the metal ceiling, which recalls the pressed-metal ceiling characteristic of the period—although this is, in fact, a modern reproduction in cast aluminum. The overall impact of the space is modern and elegant, yet simple and efficient. It serves the partners and staff well, while also signaling an appropriate message to visiting professionals and their clients.

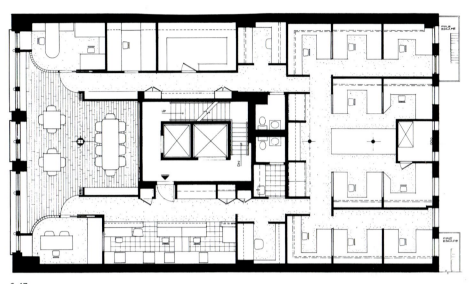

6.47

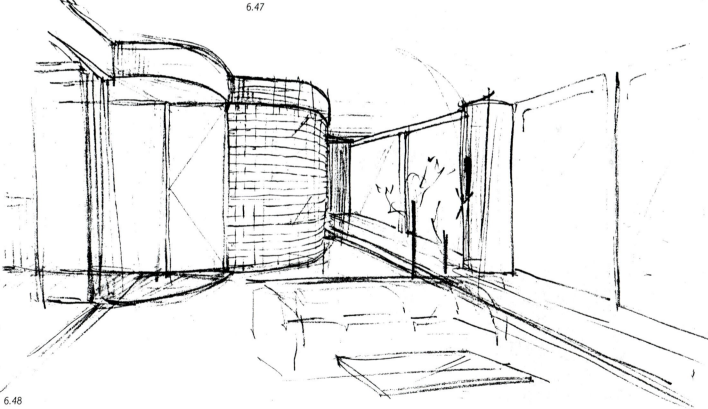

6.48

6.47 This plan of the entire floor was intended for presentation to the client. The elevators and stair occupy a central core. The conference area, which can be subdivided by folding partitions as desired, and the partners' offices are at the left; the drafting room, its work-stations defined by low screens, is at the right. Note the generous provision for storage, files, and samples in a number of locations.

6.48 This rough pencil sketch by Susan Forbes is typical of those made during the design process. It depicts the public space at the front of the building, where large windows illuminate a central seating and conference area. The curving glass-block wall defines one of the two identical private offices used by the partners.

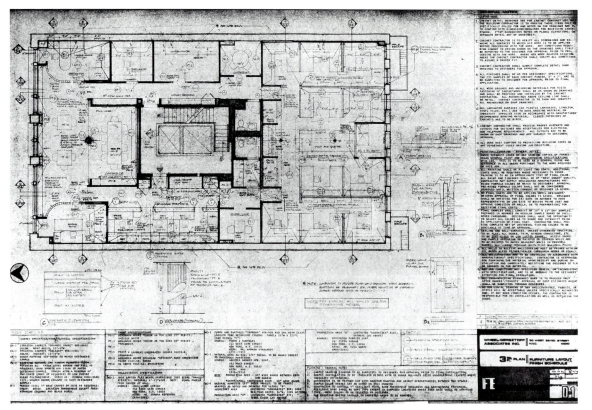

6.49

6.50

6.49 Shown here is a sheet of construction drawings (often called blueprints). These plans include complete details of all the structural tasks to be done, with separate sheets for lighting, air-conditioning, and other mechanical work. In this set, the finish schedule, all specifications are found on the plan as well; an additional sheet includes elevations and sections. The result is a complete information package that will serve both for obtaining estimates and for actual on-site construction.

6.50 The drafting room incorporates workstations designed and constructed specially for this project. Notice that the lighting has been sensibly planned: The general, or ambient, light is projected upward from the storage elements, while task downlighting illuminates counters and adjustable cantilever lamps can be focused over drafting boards as required. (Photograph: © Norman McGrath)

6.51

6.51 The front area that appears in the sketch in fig. 6.48 *is here shown completed; note the metal ceiling. The larger conference area is at the left; folding partitions can close it off. This photograph is taken from one partner's office* and looks across to the other private office opposite. Although unobtrusive, the lighting is at the same time practical and pleasant, demonstrating the client firm's expertise in this area. (Photograph: © Norman McGrath)

these issues as a plan is being drawn, even to consider them when planning ideas are just forming in the mind. Not every issue will apply to every project, but the following lists the more important.

ENTERING. The moment of arrival in a space, the transition from being outside to being inside a house, an apartment, a suite of offices, or a room, is always significant. First impressions are, traditionally, of major importance, and repeated arrivals at the same location only intensify the impression. How does the arriving person move? What does that person see? How are the practicalities (removing coat, placing packages, umbrella, and so on) dealt with? In a home, the impact of the entry is mostly visual and spatial. Everyone knows a house where the front door bursts into the midst of a living space or where there is no convenient place to hang coats. A public space such as an office, shop, or restaurant may require a reception control point, waiting space, or directory information to aid orientation. A cramped waiting room with a tiny wicket window guarding a receptionist is all too familiar a depressing introduction to many professional offices. A handsome, spacious, and suitably furnished reception area suggests, in contrast, a well-organized and confidence-inspiring organization.

MOVING INTO DESTINATION SPACE. This is the next step of experiencing a space. Are there halls, corridors, stairs, elevators, lobbies, doorways to be passed through? How will they look and feel to a first-time visitor, to a regular visitor or user, to a resident or owner? Going down a long, narrow, twisting hall is not the best introduction to a living room, classroom, office, or guest room. While familiarity can blunt the impact, an unpleasant access still leaves a negative impression. Passing through a low, narrow, or dim transition space can be offset by arriving at a large, bright destination space, the contrast heightening the favorable experience of arrival. Most often, direct, simple, and open access, with its implications of ease and welcome, is best.

ARRIVAL AT OBJECTIVE AND ACTIVITY PROVISION THERE. In a living room, where and how does the arriving person greet others or find a place to sit or stand? What is seen as one looks about? Comparable questions can be asked of a dining location, a bedroom, an office, or a shop. Is it possible to move about comfortably? Does the space offer different situations to suit different times, people, moods?

UTILITY SPACES. Kitchens, bathrooms, workshops, and other such spaces need to be planned to make the activities that go on in them as efficient as possible. They also should offer easy movement and a sequence of satisfactory visual impressions. Too often, a kitchen planned for strict efficiency turns out to be cramped and inflexible. A workshop need not be less pleasant than a living area in order to be practical.

CIRCULATION. Not simply a matter of abstract planning charts, circulation is a sequence of experiences, visual and kinetic, that can be imagined while studying a plan. It is important to consider the different patterns that may apply to the resident, the visitor, the employee,

6.53

6.52 In a sedate and traditionally formal entrance hall, Oriental rugs and a crystal chandelier relate to period furniture in this 1985 residential setting in Austin, Texas, designed by Kenneth Jorns. (Photograph: R. Greg Hursley)

6.53 Flowing space, warm color, and a strong relationship with the outdoors work together in this living room of a house in Okusawa, near Tokyo, Japan. The classic upholstered chair and sofa— 1929 designs by Le Corbusier—and a modern lamp by Joe Colombo seem well suited to the spirit of the space, designed by architect Mayumi Miyawaki. (Photograph: Gilles de Chabaneix)

and other kinds of users, all of whom may use the same space in different ways. In planning a hospital or an airport, the experiences of many different kinds of users, each with different patterns of movement and varied needs, should be traced in order to discover and minimize conflicting patterns.

DAYLIGHT AND VIEW. When planning, a designer needs to take daylight and view into consideration. Windowless spaces, while common in many modern buildings, are generally found to present problems. Where will light and view be available, and how can their absence be offset? On the other hand, glare can be unpleasant, and a view, under some circumstances, can be distracting. These situations can be controlled, but wise planning to avoid awkward relationships between people and window areas works best.

DEAD-END LOCATION. While people value freedom of movement within a space, a quality that good, open circulation provides, they also seek out and enjoy cozy spaces at the end of movement paths.

Such dead ends, or culs-de-sac, where no further movement through is possible, may suggest some sort of primitive security or stability and will suit certain spaces, including bedrooms, private offices, and bathrooms. Provision of intentionally planned dead ends is important in serving some of the social inclinations of the space users.

ACOUSTICAL ISSUES. Usually thought of in technical terms of materials and even electronic devices, acoustical issues actually respond best to sound planning. The easiest way to deal with these issues is to place sources of noise as far away as possible from places where quiet will be important. If this cannot be done, barriers of some sort can isolate noise to some extent. In practice, placing a family room with TV as far as possible from bedrooms seems only logical. A wall of closets in between two adjacent bedrooms serving users of different age levels can help to minimize cross talk. In offices, layout can do more to provide *acoustical privacy*, that is, inability to hear conversation from one space to another, than any available materials. The planner, by placing elements so that sound must either travel a long distance or be

6.54

6.54 The dramatic spatial quality of an austerely handsome foyer and stair hall of a house in Uruguay is enhanced by the simplicity of the plank door, plant bench, and slab stair landing. (Photograph: Jaime Ardiles-Arce)

6.55

blocked by natural sound-absorbing barriers, will eliminate the most troublesome acoustical problems (see also Chapter 14, pages 421–24).

SAFETY AND SECURITY. Control of access, surveillance, and safe exit routes, often thought about only after problems appear, are all best dealt with through planning. A few minutes spent imagining various emergency situations (fire, vandalism, theft, and so on) will suggest simple ways to minimize what can otherwise be difficult problems to control. Safety against accidents is also closely related to planning around such elements as glass doors and partitions, steps, stairways, and ramps, and in such high-risk areas as bathrooms. When imagining such problems, the designer should seek to envision the experiences of children, the elderly, and people with disabilities (see also Chapters 7 and 15).

All of these points may seem obvious, and thinking about them can—and certainly should—be second nature to the skilled planner, but our everyday observation of the interior spaces we use makes it clear that good planning for all of the building user's needs cannot be taken for granted. Planning is too often viewed as a matter of applying familiar formulas or of staging formal visual effects, whether or not these really serve intended purposes. Consider how many houses have a front door that is seldom or never used, while family and visitors alike go around to the side or back. How much space is given to formal parlor living rooms, used once or twice a year, while normal life is crowded into a family room often located in a dark basement? Public buildings are equally given to main entrances leading to little-used lobbies, while most visitors come from underground subway concourses or parking garages. Good planning avoids these absurdities and concentrates on serving real needs with both efficiency and elegance.

6.55 A broad corridor sweeping through an open office area of the ARCO Chemical Company at Newtown Square, Pennsylvania, seems to invite progress toward a distant destination. Davis, Brody & Associates was the designer. (Photograph: Robert Gray, courtesy Davis, Brody & Associates)

7.1

HUMAN FACTORS AND SOCIAL RESPONSIBILITY

It is generally taken for granted that all design is concerned with the creation of objects and places that will satisfy the uses to which people will put them. Designers, without even realizing that they are doing so, often assume that they know how to do this on the basis of personal experience, thinking that their own requirements are typical of those of all others or that their observations of people provide an adequate foundation for deciding what "most people" will need. Some designers may become so focused on abstract concepts of form or on technical issues of function that the realities of human needs are neglected or forgotten. To avoid the mistakes that such attitudes can engender, the design professions have become increasingly involved¯ with the methodical study of the specific ways in which their work affects individual people and the public at large.

Such studies can be divided into two major areas. The first, known as *human factors*, deals with the needs of individual people. In interior design this involves the many issues that directly influence the comfort and convenience of those who will be the occupants and users of the spaces being designed. The second, designated as *social responsibility*, is concerned with both the immediate and long-term impact of design on society. Although these two areas are closely connected, each deserves thoughtful consideration. This chapter offers an overview of the ways in which an interior designer may engage these issues.

HUMAN FACTORS

Since all buildings are designed to serve some human purpose, it may seem strange that the study of human factors in relation to design has become a specialized field. Many buildings and many interiors, however, including some by skilled designers, fall far short of serving human needs in an optimal way. This can hardly be considered a recent problem. Throughout history, there have been cold and cramped cottages,

depressing and comfortless temples and churches, mansions and palaces that must have been miserable to live in. Such problems, long viewed as inevitable evidence that "nothing is perfect," have been accepted more or less without complaint.

Over the years, a number of forces have emerged in protest against antihuman design. One such force, the theoretical school on which modern architecture is based, is *functionalism*. First developed in the 1930s, functionalism insists that the serving of function is the primary goal of all design efforts. Oddly, it has been the failure of many projects designed in the name of functionalism to deliver the promised satisfactions that has stirred up a new interest in understanding the relationship between human beings and the buildings that they build and use.

Several related disciplines, each with a highly specific interest in designing for human needs in a more careful and methodical manner than has been common in the past, have pulled together in recent years. Their first task has been to study existing buildings, to see how they work or, more often, fail to work for their users. Many modern offices, shops, restaurants, apartments, and houses are inconvenient, uncomfortable, or unsatisfactory in one or more ways (for example, poorly lighted, badly ventilated, or noisy). More and more stories circulate about widely published projects that photograph well—that even win awards—but have turned out to be unsatisfactory in use, some even bitterly disliked.

The causes of such failures are varied and often difficult to pin down. In some cases, design simply has not caught up with the complexities of modern building technology, or technology may have been relied on for performance beyond its current capability (as with windowless buildings totally dependent on less-than-perfect air-conditioning and other environmental controls). In other cases, design may have been directed by people or agencies with little awareness of the actual needs

7.1 A play area for children is provided in the "ballroom" of the IKEA store in Elizabeth, New Jersey. Attracting and entertaining the children of potential customers is an effective means of displaying a commercial establishment's concern for a customer base that includes all ages. (Photograph courtesy IKEA)

of users. Modern apartment houses and office buildings are designed more for the profit of the developer than for the satisfaction of occupants. Economic forces that run counter to users' needs (for taller buildings, perhaps, or smaller rooms) exert formidable pressures, and mistaken assumptions about "what the public wants" take the place of genuine information about actual requirements.

A particularly disturbing accusation suggests that designers are often more concerned with using projects as vehicles to further their own careers than with designing for users' needs. In a world in which media exposure has become vital to success, there are certainly temptations to try for startling, spectacular, or glamorous effects, whether or not they coincide with the goal of serving real human needs.

Increasing criticism of the design professions, from both without and within, has stimulated a new level of attention to the aspects of design that directly affect the user. The design profession has become open to the studies of other professions that deal with human needs, particularly to research findings from psychology, sociology, anthropology, and other disciplines that tend to be more rigorously scientific in their approaches than the largely empirical world of design. Since, however, this is not as yet a defined field but an interdisciplinary approach drawing on a number of specialized fields, there is some confusion of terminology. Such terms as *environmental psychology, architectural psychology, ergonomics, spatial behavior,* and *proxemics* have come into use, each defining one way of investigating the relation of design to human use.

The term *human factors* is something of an umbrella term intended to include all such specialized studies, which share the realization that human beings are powerfully affected by their environment and the related conviction that human behavior is in turn influenced by the environment in which it occurs. Although it is widely believed that people feel, work, rest, eat, and think better in some spaces than in others, there is surprisingly little ex*act* knowledge of what makes one place so much more satisfactory than another. Precise scientific knowledge about any issue generally comes from research involving carefully controlled experiments in which only one factor is varied while all other factors are kept constant. Controlled research of this sort is rarely possible in the complex situations of built environments, where too many factors interact and prove difficult to control.

For these reasons, research in human factors is usually based on observation and such techniques as surveys rather than on controlled experimentation. While the results are therefore less precise, they yield general guidelines that can significantly aid the designer in avoiding serious mistakes and increasing user satisfaction. Many of the insights in the area of human factors research have come from sociology and psychology, fields that work in similar ways in much of their methodology. At the same time, the movement called *consumerism* has increased public awareness of the need to evaluate the performance of products of every sort, including buildings and their interiors, in terms of both service to and protection of consumer-users.

Every designer should be familiar with the studies of such pioneers as anthropologist Edward T. Hall and psychologist Robert Sommer, as well as with the constantly growing literature that examines the relation between designed artifacts and spaces and their human users. Hall, in *The Hidden Dimension,* studies the ways in which different cultures have developed differing attitudes toward space between human bodies in various social contacts. He extends this to the ways in which people use rooms and furniture (see Table 3). In various articles and several books, including *Personal Space* and *Tight Spaces,* Sommer has related similar observations more directly to the planning of buildings and rooms. His observations of territorial behavior in public and private spaces have provided new insights for designers. In addition, ergonomic data provide more specific details about human bodily dimensions, muscular and sensory functioning, safety and security matters, and the special needs of certain segments of the population. (Children, the elderly, and people with disabilities present particular requirements for the designer; for a discussion of these special needs, see Chapter 15.)

The ways in which a designer may use the study of human factors will vary with the nature and scope of individual design problems, but some typical applications can be listed to suggest the range of possibilities.

Background

Traditionally, design education has focused on aesthetic issues, frequently relegating functional matters to a secondary role. Even the designs of avowed functionalists more often seem aimed at creating a strong visual effect than at serving specific user needs. The study of environmental psychology or any other discipline in the field of human factors directs design attention to the specific ways in which design affects human life and makes the union of aesthetics and practical service a design goal.

Visually exciting design that runs counter to human needs can be seen as wasteful, harmful, and destined to failure when put to use. The notorious Pruitt-Igoe housing project in Indianapolis won design awards but finally was demolished in response to its disastrous inade-

Table 3. Personal Distances

	Close	Far
Intimate	0"–6"	6"–1'6"
Personal	1'6"–2'6"	2'6"–4'
Social	4'–7'	7'–12'
Public	12'–25'	25' and over

The four terms are fairly explanatory in defining kinds of relationships. *Intimate* indicates the closest of personal relations—family members or lovers. *Personal* contacts are one-to-one conversational relationships. *Social* contacts are those at parties, conferences, business meetings, typically with more than two people involved. *Public* contacts are those between speaker and audience, teacher and class, and similar person-to-larger-group relations.

Based on E. T. Hall, *The Hidden Dimension,* 1966.

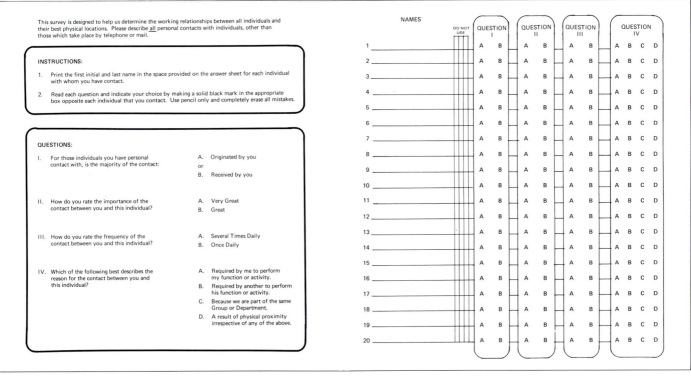

7.2

quacy as a living environment for its residents. A handsome building may contain offices or laboratories that are inconvenient and inefficient. A fine winding staircase may be the scene of dangerous accidental falls.

On the other hand, users' efforts to make spaces comfortable by rearranging furniture, introducing personal clutter, and similar modifications can undermine the visual quality of a designed space. Occupants are often quite content with houses of banal exterior and interior design. The thoughtful designer will make every effort to create a space that works for its users without sacrificing visual quality.

Programming

In this phase of design work, the specific needs that a design project is meant to serve are spelled out in detail (see Chapter 6). Too often, programs are developed by designers and clients without direct contact with end users. Managers of businesses and organizations may assume that they have sufficient knowledge to develop programs without any firsthand exploration of user needs. This leads to housing that is hated by its occupants; offices that are depressing and inconvenient to workers; hospitals that frustrate patients, visitors, and medical staff; schools and colleges that act as inhibitors to learning; and airports built for aircraft and airlines rather than for travelers.

Better programming demands the methodical observation of existing projects of a comparable nature to discover what aspects work well and where problems and failures occur. Surveys can go directly to users to discover what real needs and desires exist (fig. 7.2). Office workers will often have specific complaints about noise, lack of storage space, poor lighting, and similar issues. Vandalism and crime in a housing project have many causes, but design that avoids dark, hidden spaces and provides access routes in full public view has a favorable impact on such problems. It is, of course, not possible to reach every future user of a hospital, airport, or office building, but some sampling of potential users can be undertaken.

Since surveys can only discover opinions and desires based on the experience of those surveyed, their results require interpretive study. Motivations should be questioned and unrealistic desires separated from genuine needs. A desire for "more closets," for example, may indicate a need for other kinds of storage that will be more serviceable. A wish for a windowed corner office may come less from any practical need than from a desire for heightened status—a value that may or may not deserve consideration. All needs and desires must be brought into some realistic relationship not only with the project's budget and priorities but also with the underlying economic forces.

User Participation

Clients of designers and architects who will be occupants and users of the projects they commission (as in the case of a private house or apartment) are almost inevitably participants in the design process, which means they discuss proposals and approve plans. In larger projects where the clients are managers, officials, developers, or others without direct user roles, it may take a specific effort to obtain any user participation in the design process. In fact, designers frequently

7.2 This programming questionnaire was administered to collect data for the design of a large corporate office facility. (Courtesy J. F. N. Associates)

resist such participation as troublesome, time-consuming, or a needless interference in their professional work.

Actually, user participation in design, accomplished through review groups, worker committees, and/or sessions with sample groups of potential users, will often aid design by discovering real needs in detail, and sorting these out from assumed requirements. It may even lead to better design and direct economies. Just as worker participation in factory management has been found to improve production, user participation in design can contribute to developing projects that improve the user's quality of life.

Participatory design depends on establishing a relationship between designers and users in which each educates the other. The resulting design should satisfy many sets of values. While participatory design can take some extra time and trouble, it has proven worthwhile in many projects. Among its benefits is the higher level of users' acceptance of the end result. When compromises must be made (for example, between desires and economic realities), users involved in the process find it easier to accept the result than if they had simply been presented with a solution over which they had no influence.

Giving choices of equally satisfactory alternatives is another technique through which participation can improve user satisfaction. Choosing a color scheme, furniture, or furniture arrangement makes users feel that the resultant space is their own in a way that a fixed scheme mandated by remote authority does not. Designers' work is often defeated or sabotaged by users who resent having had no input into what is provided; involvement in some aspect of the design process can disarm such hostility.

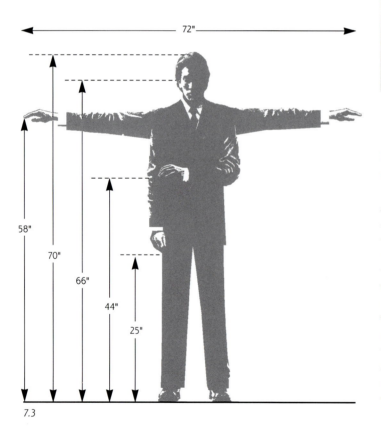

7.3

7.4

Use of Research Data

Many design decisions can be aided or guided by information developed by researchers in the fields dealing with human factors. *Anthropometric* data deal with bodily dimensions to establish clearances, heights of tables, counters, and shelves, and similar useful guidelines (fig. 7.4). To this, *ergonomic* data add a concern with body mechanics and sensory performance, thereby guiding the designer on such issues as seating comfort and ease of seeing and hearing, and thus lighting and acoustics as well (figs. 7.5–7.7). (It is important to remember that the data concerning averages for the general population, so often used as bases for design, ignore the reality that most people are not average: the unusually large or unusually small; the very young or very old; and people with temporary or permanent disabilities comprise major segments of the total population. The design issues that consideration of these facts generate are the subject of Chapter 15.) *Experimental psychology* studies sensory perception and

7.3 *This diagram shows typical human dimensions for an adult male of 70 inches in height. Average dimensions for people of other heights can be determined by multiplying the figures given here by the person's height (in inches) and then dividing by 70.*

7.4 *Ergonomic furniture provides for maximum comfort at a computer workstation. The keyboard is set in a recess lower than normal desk height to make typing easier; the CRT screen, set below the work surface, is placed at an angle*

to favor natural sightlines and minimize head movements and neck discomfort. This workstation was designed by Nova Office Furniture. (Photograph courtesy Nova Office Furniture, Inc.)

deals with the ways in which spaces are experienced and the impact of color and light on both senses and emotions. *Anthropology* and *sociology* study human behavior in various cultures and contexts.

Even studies in animal behavior have been useful in understanding human attitudes toward privacy and communication and have aided understanding of territoriality, the desire for space defined in terms of individual and group privacy. *Proxemics* deals with the impact of spatial realities on social grouping and behavior. For example, crowding is known to increase levels of irritation and frustration, leading to interpersonal friction, arguments, and even crime. Human beings require suitable levels of privacy for work, meditation, and rest, as well as adequate settings for personal contacts, in both work and social situations. Appropriate spaces, walls, doors, and furniture selection all contribute to making daily life comfortable, satisfying, and productive.

Research in all of these fields is quite specialized, often pursuing observation or study of specific, narrow questions. Many designers seem impatient with such studies, feeling that they do not deal with practical questions relating to particular projects. Actually, some studies have yielded very precise and useful "how-to" information concerning, for example, the design of good lighting and physiologically satisfactory seating. In other areas, such as the emotional impact of color or the role of space in influencing behavior, research data can have only a more general impact in promoting better understanding of these matters.

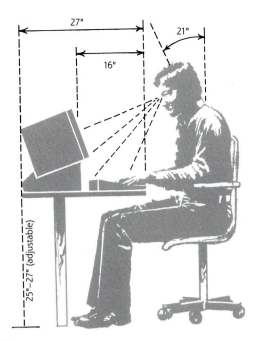

7.5

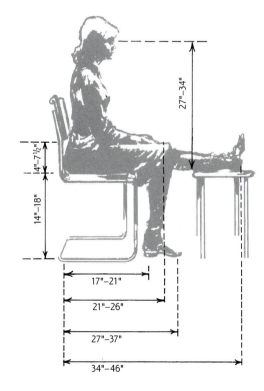

7.6

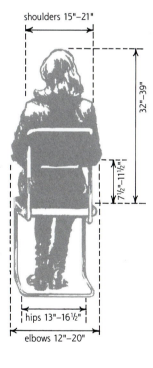

7.5 *Office tasks involving computer operation call for furniture thoughtfully sized and preferably adjustable to make the workplace ergonomically suitable.*

7.6 *This diagram illustrates the basic dimensions required for satisfactory seating.*

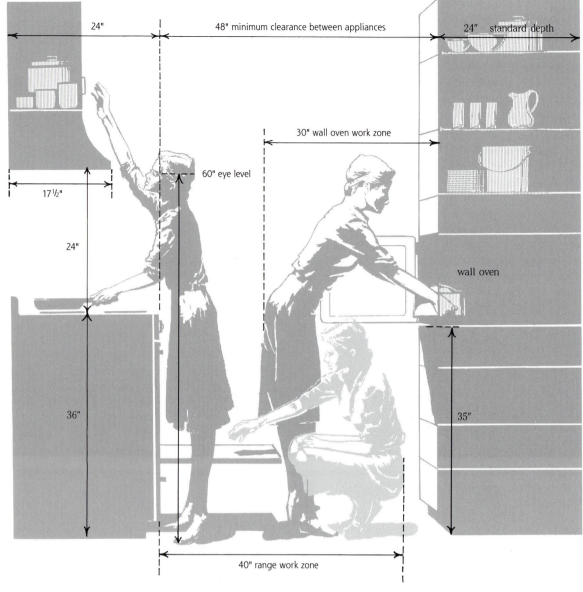

24"

48" minimum clearance between appliances

24"   standard depth

30" wall oven work zone

60" eye level

17½"

24"

wall oven

36"

35"

40" range work zone

7.7

It is not unusual to find that research data yield findings that may appear to be obvious; everyone knows something about the impact of warm versus cold colors or can guess that avoiding dark, hidden spaces in public areas will discourage crime and vandalism. Still, even such seemingly obvious issues are so often ignored that it seems important to focus attention on them. Designers also find that in presenting design proposals to clients and committees, documented research findings offer support when the obvious becomes a matter for dispute.

Employment of Consultants

In many larger projects it is helpful to employ specialists in the fields of environmental psychology, sociology, or ergonomics. This transfers some responsibility from the designer to an expert with greater experience and more specialized knowledge in areas that lie somewhat outside the normal concerns of the designer. Just as specialists in engineering, lighting, or acoustics can be helpful to the overall success of a project, the specialist in human factors can function as a kind of spokesperson for a particular set of considerations.

7.7 These clearances, applied to kitchen design, are derived from studies of human proportions and movement, such as reach.

Scanning the available literature for studies and data germane to a project, setting up and conducting surveys or interviews, organizing user participation in design—these are all functions that a specialist can be expected to perform with a concentration that the designer can rarely achieve. Finding consultants who have expertise in their special fields as well as an adequate understanding of the goals and problems of design is not always easy, but current interest in this field is encouraging more and more qualified people to enter it.

The increasing use of interdisciplinary teams in the design of larger projects opens the way for including a specialist in environmental psychology as one of the team. Some localities legally require such a specialist, and this trend may well become general before too long. In the meanwhile, and in working on smaller projects, designers will have to continue to rely on their own knowledge and judgment about when to call on specialists.

Performance Evaluation

It is a curious reality that after design projects are put into use, they are seldom evaluated in any methodical way. Interesting projects may receive publication, commentary, and even criticism in the design press, but such comment is usually concerned primarily with aesthetic values. Furthermore, it is often based on information gleaned from drawings and photographs, sometimes supplemented by a brief visit to a space too new to have developed any clear user points of view. Designers themselves tend to move on to new projects, losing interest in jobs already completed. They may even avoid asking for evaluation for fear of stimulating complaints and criticisms that would otherwise be overlooked or suppressed.

This pattern has tended to inhibit the process of learning by experience, a process that has the potential to improve the levels of satisfaction delivered by the work of a particular designer and the work of the design professions collectively. The environmental fields have begun to make a practice of taking a formal evaluation after a project has been in use long enough to weed out problems related to the stresses of moving in and the resistances often set up by the strangeness of a new place. Making an evaluative study at intervals such as six months or one year can generate information about what has worked well and what has not that provides a foundation for future improvement in design performance.

An evaluative study can be made on the basis of questionnaire or survey techniques, a more informal observation and report by a consultant with some experience in such evaluations, or firsthand observation and interviews undertaken by the designer. The last approach has the obvious disadvantage of introducing the possibility of bias on the part of the designer, who is more likely to accept favorable comment than unfavorable criticism—although it is the latter that is most important in limiting future mistakes. Ideally, evaluation reports on a wide variety of projects should be made available to the entire design community, enabling all to learn from a common and growing pool of experience. At present, such general availability is unusual. However, from time to time journal articles provide some evaluative information of greater depth and seriousness than the rumors that frequently travel in design circles.

Human Factors in Relation to Smaller Projects

The outline offered above may seem to apply only to larger projects, such as airports, hospitals, and housing projects, and large design organizations. It is certainly true that the need for formal and specialized study of human factors issues is greatest in such projects, in which direct user-designer contact is difficult and the bureaucratic management style adopted from conception to completion results in a rather inhuman organizational routine. Human factors issues are, however, every bit as important in small projects, even down to the design of a single room.

While room designations such as *living room* or *bedroom* or project descriptions such as *private office* or *cafeteria* may suggest a full and detailed program of "usual" functions, probing real user needs may lead to the discovery that the intended use is not at all standard. A living room may be used as a studio, a place for group meetings, or a conservatory for growing plants—or it may hardly be used at all, but kept as a showplace or parlor. A bedroom may also serve as a study, a TV room, or an extra living room; it is vital to learn how many people will use it and what their relationships are. Many offices are conference rooms, TV-viewing rooms, or studios as well as offices. A cafeteria will often serve as a social club and lounge as well as for regular meal service.

While the design of spaces should respond to their intended use, it may also influence what the actual use will be. A dining room may impose formality or encourage relaxation. A cafeteria may impose a sense of rush, permit some ease and comfort, or turn into a "hangout" to what may be an undesirable degree. The planning of home kitchens has been found to be a factor influencing family relationships for better or worse. A cramped layout in which two people who share meal preparation constantly collide and get in one another's way puts nerves on edge and can even cause arguments, while a more accommodating layout might encourage cheerful cooperation.

Members of a family need to have suitable privacy and suitable gathering places to support pleasant relationships. Furniture arrangement can aid and encourage conversation or inhibit it. Color and lighting establish moods in a space and influence the events that take place there in subtle ways that often go unrecognized.

Many such issues may seem to be only what any competent designer would consider in the normal course of a design project. It is, however, the long history of their neglect that has made the subject of human factors a special field. In small projects where elaborate research and the employment of consultants is out of the question, the designer has a particular obligation to remember that the aesthetic aspects of a design must be related to the practical aspects that users will have to live with.

Human Factors in Relation to Specific Issues

In addition to the general planning and design considerations related to human factors, a group of more technical issues deserves attention. Both large and small projects can benefit from a concentrated review of the following matters:

7.8

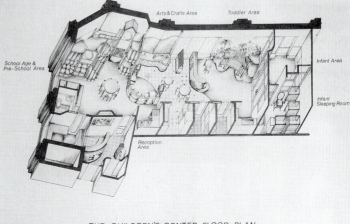

THE CHILDREN'S CENTER FLOOR PLAN

7.9

7.8, 7.9 Social consciousness combined with enlightened self-interest has
persuaded many businesses to provide
day-care facilities for the children of
their employees. The Wall Street firm of
Goldman, Sachs & Co. retained Sherry
Robbins of SDR Design to develop this
1993 children's center. In the preschool
and school-age area shown in fig. 7.8,
nets provide safety at the balcony
edge, as well as create a sense of openness. (Photograph: © Howard Barash
Photography 1993, courtesy Goldman,
Sachs & Co.) Other parts of the center,
shown in an axonometric drawing (fig.
7.9), include an arts and crafts area
and spaces for toddlers and infants.
(Drawing courtesy SDR Design)

SAFETY. The threat of accidents is generally associated with automobiles, travel, and public streets, but indoor accidents, particularly at home, are a major cause of injuries and death. Stairways and steps pose real dangers (see Chapter 8, page 247). Bathrooms, with their slippery surfaces, hard projections, mirrors, glass, and hot water, are notorious accident locations. Kitchens, with open flames, gas or electric elements, boiling water, heated fats, and sharp objects, present other risks. High locations, balconies, windows, and platform edges need the best possible guardrails or bars, marking, and lighting. Glass always poses a danger, particularly in the form of large windows and doors that can sometimes be virtually invisible (fig. 7.10). Polished floor surfaces are a hazard, especially outdoors or near entrances where water, snow, or ice can add to the risk. Nonskid surfaces will minimize these risks. Small rugs and mats and the edges of larger rugs can cause falls. Furniture edges, projecting legs, and objects that roll or overturn easily are also involved in a surprising number of accidents.

Fire safety is a special matter that calls for the observance of building code regulations concerning exit routes and equipment such as smoke detectors, fire alarms, extinguishers, sprinkler systems, and hose connections, and for the choice of materials for maximum fire-resistance. Many designers feel that fire-safety consideration stops at the minimal observance of legal requirements, yet code compliance is not in itself assurance that all safety issues have been fully addressed. Reports of actual fires make it clear that a far higher standard of fire safety is both easily obtainable and highly desirable. Many modern synthetic materials present risks because they give off toxic fumes when burning that can be more deadly than the fire itself. The dangers are multiplied by modern closed spaces with artificial ventilation, often on high floors where rescue access is difficult. More detailed discussion of safety issues as dealt with in code restrictions is included in Chapter 14, beginning on page 426.

SECURITY. This is an issue closely related to safety and, unfortunately, an increasingly important consideration, particularly in urban areas where social conditions have brought about an increase in robbery, vandalism, and even terrorism. Design cannot control every aspect of such problems, but both basic planning and suitable details and equipment can help to minimize risks. Dark halls and hidden areaways invite trouble, while open and visible access points are to some degree self-protecting. Oscar Newman's book *Defensible Space* explores the ways in which design and planning can discourage crime and vandalism in apartment buildings and public housing projects. Most of the recommended steps may seem to be obvious, common-sense precautions, but a systematic review of the risks that are inevitably present and the design steps that can be taken to control them is a commendable routine.

HEALTH HAZARDS. In addition to safety hazards that create possibilities of injury, building interiors can create other problems that may impinge on occupants' health. Many materials in common use, as well as certain practices, can have an unfavorable impact on air quality within a building. Asbestos, long a favorite insulation material and an ingredient in various building products, is now well known as a car-

cinogen. This and other hazards associated with specific materials are discussed in Chapter 8, page 259. The recirculation of air in air-conditioned interiors may favor both the short-term danger of infection and the long-term risks related to continued exposure to low levels of air pollutants. Tobacco smoke is an air pollutant being brought under control by increasing regulation of indoor smoking.

Concern has recently developed for hazards that may be associated with exposure to electromagnetic fields (EMF). Such magnetic fields are created wherever electrical devices are in use. Where small currents are involved, the strengths of the fields are not great and their levels fall off short distances from the sources. The large currents which flow through high-tension power-transmission lines and transformers, however, do create electromagnetic fields of significant levels. The discovery of concentrations of cancer cases and other related illnesses among people who have had long exposure to strong electromagnetic fields

7.10

7.10 Glass doors tend to prevent collisions between people entering and exiting but can become dangerous when certain lighting conditions render the glass virtually invisible. Here, a decorative pattern of dots on a frameless glass door solves the problem. The entrance to the offices of A. G. Becker, Inc., in New York was designed by Jack L. Gordon Architects. (Photograph courtesy Jack L. Gordon Architects)

Table 4. Safety and Security Problems

	TYPE OF HAZARD	DESIGN PRECAUTIONS
FALLS	SLIPPERY FLOORING	Avoid slippery materials, especially near outdoor access.
	SMALL RUGS OR MATS	Avoid when possible. Use rubber antislip underlay.
	BATHROOMS	Provide grab bars and use nonskid surfaces. Consider positioning the door to open outward in order to easily reach an injured person who may be blocking the door.
	STEPS	Avoid level changes and single step if possible. If not, mark level change clearly through contrasting colors, material, or design. Provide rail and/or safety light.
	STAIRWAYS	Plan moderate (normal) angle of slope. Break long runs with landings. Provide handrails on both sides and, for wider stairways, in the center as well. Provide good lighting. Avoid slippery materials. Provide nonskid treads and/or nosings. Avoid winders. Mark beginning of stairway clearly through design.
	WINDOWS	In high (upper-floor) locations, consider safety bars or rails. Use window type that restricts opening (but see fire safety problems below). Avoid low sills.
	BALCONIES, ROOFS	Provide adequate railings. Restrict roof access.
	KITCHENS	Place all provisions and materials within easy reach if possible; if not, provide a secure step stool. Store knives and sharp objects well out of reach.
	DARKNESS	Provide adequate lighting and emergency light at key locations. Provide double switches at top and bottom of stairways. Install a light switch near the bed in bedrooms. Install a night-light in bathrooms. Consider placing proximity or sonic switches in appropriate locations.
FIRE	PREVENTION	Avoid highly inflammable materials. Store dangerous substances in fireproof enclosures. Use fire-safe materials near fireplaces, heating stoves, and kitchen ranges. Provide adequate and safe electric wiring.
	CONTROL	Provide extinguishers, smoke alarms, alarm signals, or bells where appropriate. Consider providing hose cabinets and sprinklers, particularly for high-floor locations, exit routes, and high-risk areas.
	EXIT AND ESCAPE	Provide safe exits, including two independent routes for upper floors and hazardous locations. Provide ample exits from public spaces using out-swinging doors with panic-bolt hardware. Provide exit signs and lights. Provide fire-company access (avoid fixed windows and fixed window bars). Consider outdoor escapes, ladders, and so on. Provide emergency lighting.
ELECTRICAL	FIRE	Provide adequate and safe wiring. Also see "Fire" above.
	SHOCK	Avoid placing outlets near water. Provide ground-fault interrupt circuitry for bathroom and other wet locations.
WATER	BATHROOMS	Provide safe (thermostatically controlled) mixing faucets for tubs and showers. Avoid slippery floor surfaces (see "Falls" above), tubs, and shower bottoms.
	POOLS	Control access. Consider installing railings or antiskid flooring.

has led to the investigation of possible EMF dangers. Although there is strong disagreement among researchers about the levels of risk involved in EMF exposure, prudence suggests that exposure to this possible hazard should be minimized until there is a resolution of these disagreements. Avoidance of proximity to outdoor high-tension power lines is an obvious precaution. Less obvious are the underground lines, power feeders in larger buildings, and the transformers that are used in many buildings to convert high-voltage currents to service voltages. Building occupants should not use spaces close to these EMF sources for extended periods of time. Compact meters are available that measure levels of EMF in terms of the gauss unit. Checking suspect locations with such a meter allows easy identification of potential dangers.

Other health hazards have been traced to the presence of lead in paints and in water that comes from pipes or plumbing devices, such as faucets that contain lead. This danger is of special concern in projects where children will be users/occupants. Radon gas in interior air and even very small amounts of mercury that might come from fluorescent lighting tubes or from discarded batteries are additional sources of health problems associated with interior occupancy. Health hazards related to the deprivation of full-spectrum light resulting from the use of many types of modern artificial lighting are discussed in Chapter 10, page 314.

	Type of Hazard	Design Precautions
Air quality	Smoke	Provide adequate ventilation. Use smoke venting for enclosed meeting spaces. For spaces that carry special hazards (restaurant kitchens, theaters, and so on), consider smoke venting for use in case of fire.
	Cooking	Provide hoods and vents to remove cooking fumes.
	Chemical, bacterial	Check ventilating and air-conditioning systems to avoid retention and spread of pollutants. Provide adequate ventilation. Provide natural ventilation as backup in case of failure of mechanical HVAC systems.
	Materials	Avoid materials that may give off air pollutants (plastics and other synthetics call for particular care). Avoid materials that produce toxic fumes when burning or smoldering.
Material	Glass	Avoid glass and mirror in locations where collisions are possible. Mark or pattern glass walls and doors to aid visibility. Avoid sharp edges and corners in furniture applications. Avoid glass shower and tub enclosures. Consider use of tempered or shatterproof glass or nonshattering plastic alternatives where appropriate.
	Metals	Avoid sharp edges and corners in hazardous locations.
	Other	The location of all hard materials (tile, slate, stone) and rough materials (exposed concrete, rough wood boards) should be carefully considered, as well as all their possible safeguards.
Miscellaneous	Furniture	Avoid small, low, and easily overturned furniture items, including chairs. Consider safety issues for movable furniture (on casters or rollers) such as low tables, plant stands, and so on. Furniture with rounded or padded edges and corners is safest.
	Children	Check bars and railings on stairways, furniture, and so on to avoid spacing that may catch a head, arm, or leg or allow the child to slip through. Steps, stairs, windows, and balconies all require safeguarding to prevent falls.
	Garage	Isolate to prevent possible exhaust pollution. Provide fireproof enclosure and good ventilation.
	Elevators and escalators	Check safety provisions, emergency stop, alarms, and control of access.
Security	Intrusion	Provide suitable locks, gates, bars, and so on. Consider TV surveillance, intercom, or computerized access control systems when appropriate. Plan to avoid hidden (blind) corridors, stairways, and vestibule locations, and light these areas well.
	Burglary	Provide suitable locks, bars, automatic lights, and so on. Consider installing an alarm system.
	Pilferage and theft	Provide lockable storage, locking for individual rooms, and access and exit control points. Consider magnetic or other merchandise control systems for shops and stores.
	Vandalism	Consider use of resistant materials. Plan for maximum surveillance of risky locations.

NOISE. Noise, defined as unwanted or excessive sound, can be a source of major discomfort. Moderate levels of sound appropriate to a particular space use are tolerable and may even be desirable. The buzz of conversation in a restaurant and the low-level hum of activity in a large office space are not objectionable, but when such sounds rise to an excessive level they set up reactions of irritation and strain that can be tiring and unhealthy. In spaces intended to be quiet, such as a bedroom, even very low levels of unwanted sound can be objectionable. A neighbor's radio or late-night music practice can be profoundly disturbing. Mechanical noises from air-conditioning equipment or other machinery within a building can also introduce what has sometimes

been called noise pollution. Outdoor noise from traffic or aircraft operation provide additional examples of sounds that need to be minimized. The discussion of acoustics (Chapter 14, pages 421–24) deals with some of the problems associated with noise control.

SPECIAL NEEDS. Human factors issues regarding the needs of population groups considered "special" in a number of ways, including those people who may differ substantially from the average in size or strength, children, the elderly, and those with various disabilities, are the subject of Chapter 15.

SOCIAL RESPONSIBILITY

It may well be that the prevalent values of the 1980s, when pursuit of financial profit and individual gain seemed to be of primary importance, have given rise to a heightened sense of responsibility for the social and environmental impact of the projects with which designers work. Buildings consume land and air space, materials, and energy for construction. In use they continue to consume energy and produce waste products. They exist to provide the interior spaces within, the spaces that interior designers plan, detail, and furnish. Interior designers and architects have traditionally understood their obligations to serve the needs and desires of their clients but have tended to feel that their responsibilities end at that point. For projects where the commissioning individual, family, or organization will be the only occupant or user, this assumption may seem valid. It ignores, however, the reality that every project, no matter how small or how personal, as it consumes space, resources, and energy and generates wastes, affects society as a whole. A project that is used by a population beyond the owners who commissioned it has a further social impact. The students in a school or college and their teachers; the patients, staff, and visitors of a hospital; the workers in an office; the customers in a store; the guests and staff of a hotel; and the patrons and workers in a restaurant are all users of interior spaces they do not own and did not commission. What is the responsibility of designers to these people and to society in general?

In a commercial society, a large proportion of the projects that call for designers' services are generated to make a profit for their owners and developers. Certainly, providing a useful service need not conflict with generating a profit for the project's developer and owners, but the goal of maximizing profit can readily come into conflict with some of the interests of both a project's users and the general public. Primary responsibility in these matters must lie with owners and developers, who decide what is to be done and who have veto power over every aspect of the projects they initiate. Designers, however, as they carry out the wishes of their clients, have numerous opportunities to influence the ways in which a project will relate to the concerns of both users and the public. To exert influence in the direction of responsibility, to find ways to resolve possible conflicts between the interests of clients and the public, and to avoid involvement in actions that are grossly irresponsible are obligations that every designer must accept.

It is helpful to summarize the issues facing designers that embody elements of social responsibility; although some may be quite obvious, others are subtle and easy to forget or to ignore, and yet others are complex or troublesome to deal with.

Quality versus Profit

The clients who employ architects and interior designers, who accept or reject their proposals and finance the execution of designed projects are frequently not the users and occupants that such projects will serve. Projects generated for profit demand that the designers minimize costs in order to optimize profitability. Excellence in uses of space, in structure, in selection of materials and finishes, and in provision of convenience and comfort is commonly more costly than inferior provi-

sions. Minimal space allocations result in crowding; shoddy structure, materials, and equipment reduce user satisfaction and may contribute to actual safety and health hazards. While higher standards are adopted for many projects, this is most often true of luxury facilities that serve a limited, affluent population—the VIP lounge at an airport terminal, for example, contrasts strikingly with the typical city bus terminal. So-called affordable housing is inferior to luxury housing not only in luxuries that may be regarded as optional, but also in the basics of space, convenience, and accommodations for the occupants' well-being.

The pressures to minimize costs through design decisions that favor economy over excellence affect nonprofit-sponsored projects as well. Public housing is a notorious case in point. The clinics and hospitals that serve a less affluent public differ markedly from private hospitals and medical-office facilities. Legal requirements regarding structural solidity and safety establish bare minimums that are regularly accepted as adequate standards in public and other nonprofit institutional projects.

Environmental Concerns

LAND USE. Interiors are in buildings and buildings occupy land. Although issues concerning land use may seem remote from interior design concerns, an awareness of the consequences or benefits of poorly considered or well thought out land use will aid the designer as such topics become increasingly urgent over the coming years.

Unplanned use of land has created the urban sprawl that surrounds most cities and towns, with shoddy and chaotic structures edging highways while the land beyond is either left isolated or developed as suburban housing of inferior design quality. In cities, older buildings of good quality are often demolished to make way for larger structures of lower quality. The combination of crowding in city centers and strip development around cities has generated problems associated with excessive dependence on automobile transportation. Loss of agricultural land, forests, and wetlands vital to the survival of various plant and animal species is among the results of unplanned and wasteful land use. Zoning laws (see Chapter 14, page 429) intended to control land use according to rational plans are largely insufficient.

Examples of intelligent land use exist in a number of planned communities where single-family houses are grouped to minimize the building of streets while providing automobile access separate from pedestrian circulation. In place of small lots surrounding each house, communal open land is treated to form a parklike setting that serves all residents. In some communities, well-spaced high-rise apartment towers are included for residents (such as single people, couples without children, and the elderly) who prefer to avoid the responsibilities of a house.

European examples of planned communities invariably draw admiration from visitors. In England, the concept of a *garden city*, proposed by Robert Owen and Ebenezer Howard, was realized at Letchworth in 1904 and at the Hampstead Garden Suburb (at the edge of London) in 1908. In Sweden, the city of Stockholm has for many years purchased surrounding farmlands as they become available. When population growth calls for additional housing, *new towns* are designed to make efficient use of land and provide living settings of very high quality. Direct high-speed rail lines connect these communities to the center of the city, where automobile traffic is restricted. Among the successful results of this type of planning are the suburbs of Vallingby and Farsta. Tapiola, near Helsinki in Finland, is another distinguished example.

In the United States, as early as 1924 several well-planned communities—such as Sunnyside Gardens in Queens, New York, and Radburn, New Jersey—were built. Greenbelt, Maryland, a 1934 project of the U.S. Resettlement Administration, and the more recent privately financed communities of Columbia, Maryland, and Reston, Virginia, are additional instances of planned land use. Many smaller projects have adopted the concepts of *cluster housing* and *planned development;* unfortunately, such thoughtful approaches to land use remain exceptions to the more common norm of unplanned suburban sprawl.

ENERGY CONSUMPTION. From broader issues relating to the ecology of the total environment to the microlevel of waste disposal at each space occupancy, awareness of the potential environmental impact of project elements should be a design concern. Every interior consumes energy. Heating, air-conditioning, lighting, cooking, and the range of modern appliances, conveniences, and entertainment equipment all use power, fuel, or both, each with attendant problems of fuel supply, waste disposal, and ecological damage. Socially responsible design that seeks ways to minimize energy consumption through efficient heating and cooling, dependence on natural ventilation, solar heat, and daylight illumination can have a highly favorable impact on energy dependence and the creation of harmful wastes.

WATER USE. Like energy consumption, water use involves drawing on resources that are finite. Limitation of water use for air-conditioning and reduction of water use for lawn watering, fountains, and pools are matters in which designers can have a favorable impact through provision for recirculation and modification of demand. Even the specification of flushing tanks and valves that minimize water consumption per flush can have a significant impact on water use.

SELECTION OF MATERIALS. All materials consume energy and resources in the process of manufacture. Metallic ores, fuels, and energy are used in the production of iron, steel, aluminum, and other metals and generate related waste products and pollutants. Masonry materials consume clay, sand, and rock and use energy in conversion to cut stone, brick, tile, and concrete. Although wood is a renewable resource, the cutting of slow-growing trees is depleting forests more rapidly than new growth can develop. The rare woods of tropical trees, much admired for their fine appearance, are disappearing along with the rain forests (see Table 9 in Chapter 8, page 258). Cutting and processing wood into products (lumber, plywood, and wood-based manufactured products such as paper and many types of wallboard) consume energy and generate wastes. The manufacture of plastics, often considered replacements for natural materials, also requires resources converted from their original forms through the use of energy, and most plastics are based on synthetic resins derived from petroleum, the fossil fuel being depleted most rapidly.

By choosing materials that will have the least undesirable impact on the depletion of resources, on energy consumption, and on waste production, interior designers can readily contribute to ecological and environmental health. Cement, sand, and clay—the basics of concrete, glass, brick, and tile—present fewer environmental problems than do plastics, aluminum, and exotic hardwoods. Selection of wool rather than nylon or vinyl, common softwoods rather than fine hardwoods, and glass rather than acrylic are all examples of ecologically sound design decisions.

WASTE DISPOSAL. As it nears crisis proportions, particularly in industrialized countries, the problem of waste disposal can be confronted on several levels. Organic materials, paper, kitchen garbage, and human wastes are easily biodegradable, but many other forms of waste are not. Much discarded packaging material, bottles, cans, and larger objects such as furniture, appliances, and construction debris present problems of disposal. Recycling rather than destruction is an efficient approach to the reduction of waste-disposal problems. Glass, most metals, and many plastics can be recycled into new products. Wastepaper can be reused or made into other paper-based products. Factory wastes such as sawdust and wood scraps can be used to make particleboard and similar products. Even biodegradable materials, however, can be problematic when their quantity outruns the available methods and places for disposal.

Although reduction in waste production may be outside the immediate concerns of many interior designers, provision for efficient disposal and appropriate recycling may encourage improved ways of dealing with wastes. Interior designers may suggest to clients the selection of materials and construction techniques that produce minimal waste, including those that generate the least on-site wastes during installation.

ADAPTIVE REUSE. The most spectacularly wasteful activity that falls within the consideration of architects and designers is the frequent demolition of older buildings that could better be put to new uses through intelligently planned repair and replanning, usually called *adaptive reuse.* A well-constructed older building can often be reworked for a modern use at far less cost than new construction would involve. Disposal of demolition wastes is reduced or eliminated, wasteful consumption of new materials is minimized, and a superior end result can often be achieved. Case Study 3 in this chapter describes a fine example of the ways in which design can approach such areas of responsibility. (For further discussion of adaptive reuse and historic preservation, see Chapter 17, pages 489–97.)

ROLE OF THE DESIGNER

Confronting these large and difficult issues, it is easy for any designer to feel discouraged, even hopeless. Even with the best of intentions, what can one do that will have any significant impact on so many intractable problems? It may be helpful to sort the issues into categories of responsibility that suggest differing approaches, as follows.

MATTERS WITHIN DIRECT CONTROL OF THE DESIGNER. Many design decisions related to issues of responsibility are entirely within the designer's domain. Planning the placement of elements in relation to windows, for example, can determine how much lighting and ventilation can be naturally provided and how much must be dependent on energy-intensive artificial systems. The choice of materials, normally made on the basis of aesthetic preference, can be modified by an awareness of which materials are drawn from resources subject to rapid depletion. The extent of demolition and reconstruction as compared to preservation and reuse is very much within the field of designers' recommendations. The designer's willingness to investigate and consider the needs and preferences of actual users and occupants, instead of relying on assumptions that may be inaccurate, will have a positive effect on the project's social responsibility.

One of the most difficult positions for a designer may be the decision to refuse involvement in a project that seems too drastically at odds with concepts of responsibility. The rejection of an assignment that appears destined to lead to an irresponsible product may be a hard choice when it seems clear that others will be only too happy to take on the work. The justification that "If I turn it down, someone else will do it anyway" is all too often the excuse offered for proceeding with questionable efforts. Each designer must confront such issues at one time or another and make his or her own decision. In the long run, involvement with projects that are hurtful to broader social goals does nothing to enhance the reputation of a designer. The extra effort involved in acting responsibly, on the other hand, can draw favorable attention and will certainly contribute to any designer's sense of self-esteem.

ISSUES REQUIRING COOPERATION BETWEEN DESIGNER AND CLIENT. Even the decisions that a designer may make alone demand at least the passive approval of a client before they are put into execution. Many larger decisions come to a client's attention in very specific ways: where will a project be located (where will a building be built, or what rental space will be occupied); what space allocations will be established; what weight will be given to the needs and preferences of users and occupants? In all such areas designer and client must arrive at agreement about the level of responsibility that will be acceptable. Designers can find that their role becomes that of an educator. Irresponsibility often comes forward in the guise of economy. Bad lighting costs less than good, and crowding and discomfort may seem economically favorable when compared to the expense of adequate space and superior levels of comfort and convenience. Fortunately, there is extensive evidence to support the idea that "better" is often advantageous as compared to "worse" in the long run. Many socially responsible courses of action can even be shown to be financially beneficial in immediate terms. Natural light and ventilation cost less than their artificial alternatives. Reuse of older structures is frequently a better bargain than new construction. Workers' efficiency rises—and absenteeism and turnover decline—in facilities planned responsibly, with consideration for workers' needs, health, and well-being. Insurance rates drop and liability suits are less likely in facilities that are safe, afford universal access, and reduce health hazards. Responsible design is also likely to increase the life span of a project, minimizing the need for costly upgrades to new standards as they become accepted and legally mandated.

Although many of these concepts become obvious to any thoughtful designer, they may seem strange to individual clients and to client organizations that tend to focus on limited goals and the lowest possible first cost. There is a clear obligation on the part of every designer to make a case for social responsibility in terms of the economies that some decisions can offer, as well as the broader benefits that accrue to client, owner, and developer through the long-term satisfactions realized by users, occupants, and the general public.

CONCERNS OUTSIDE DESIGNERS' IMMEDIATE CONTROL. However responsible the individual designer may be, alone and in cooperation with clients, it cannot be denied that many issues cannot be solved within the limits of any project or any design practice. Irresponsibility generated by ignorance, greed, and carelessness will continue to be a common circumstance of modern life. It is overly optimistic to assume that good design, even when widely accepted, can cure the intractable problems of poverty, unemployment, inadequate housing, drug dependency, crime, and disease that remain so damaging to modern society. Yet the designer can confront these problems like any other citizen, searching for favorable strategies and encouraging their adoption through whatever personal, economic, or political means may be available. The role of designers as experts in matters that relate to the environment and to many economic issues creates a responsibility to use that expertise not only in the projects assigned to them directly but also as a means to further educate the general public. Professional organizations that speak for designers in larger groups have a particularly valuable role to play in pressing for the recognition of issues of social responsibility on the parts of both individual designers and the public.

CASE STUDY 3

OFFICES FOR A NONPROFIT
ORGANIZATION
NATIONAL AUDUBON
SOCIETY HEADQUARTERS

Croxton Collaborative, Architects
Randolph R. Croxton, Director of Architecture
Kirsten Childs, Director of Interior Design

The National Audubon Society came to the planning of its headquarters with a strong commitment to "socially conscious" concerns. The chosen designers, Croxton Collaborative, were already known for similar interests, expressed in earlier, smaller projects. Together the client and the design firm developed a project that served to demonstrate what a broad range of environmental concerns might suggest for future design projects.

Early on, a major decision was made to reject the planning of a new building or the leasing of space in a recently built high rise. Either of these approaches would indicate a wasteful bypassing of older, existing structures in favor of new and technologically elaborate alternatives that tend to consume resources and energy. Audubon House, as it is now known, was originally the Schermerhorn Building, an 1891 work of the respected architect George B. Post (1837–1913), in the style known as Romanesque Revival, which relied on handsome stonework and semicircular arches. The purchase and renovation of the old loft building, which had become shabby and neglected, cost only about two-thirds of what comparable facilities in a modern high rise would have cost. The Audubon Society offices occupy five floors and the roof level of the eight-story building; two floors are rented to tenants, as is the retail space at street level. Audubon Society scientists worked with the designers to develop strategies for energy efficiency, environmentally sound materials, superior interior environmental qualities, and

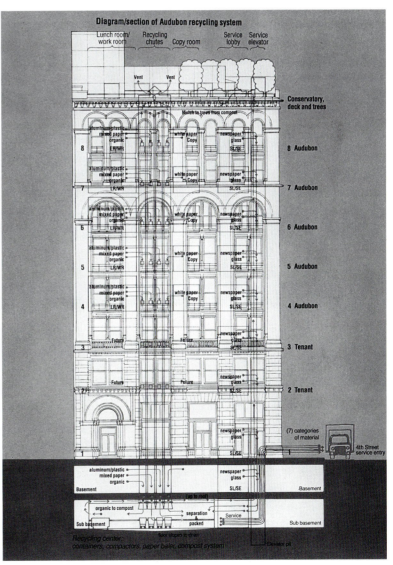

7.11

7.11 An elevation of the National Audobon Society Headquarters building includes a diagrammatic chart of the innovative recycling system. Chutes for various kinds of recyclable materials run vertically through the eight floors of the building to the bins in the building's subbasement. (Courtesy Croxton Collaborative Planning, Architecture & Interior Design)

an unusual waste-disposal system designed to support recycling of trash.

The basics of energy conservation were approached through enhanced lighting and mechanical systems; the use of efficient mineral insulation to line the external masonry walls; and new double-glazed windows incorporating a film insert that acts as a wavelength filter, minimizing ultraviolet and infrared heat radiation in summer and retaining heat in winter. The reduced requirements for heating and cooling are met by a highly efficient gas-powered chiller/heater with an exceptionally low net output of environmentally harmful emissions. The equipment conserves floor space by requiring less area than conventional HVAC installations and uses a refrigerant that does not deplete the ozone layer.

Artificial lighting is kept to a minimum, reducing the energy requirements for the lighting itself as well as for the summer cooling required to dispose of heat produced by the fixtures. Ambient light is provided at a low, 30 footcandle level, while task lighting at each workstation is provided at an intensity of 70 footcandles where and when it is needed. The large windows, particularly those on the upper floors, and the skylights that serve the top two floors further reduce the demand for artificial lighting during daylight hours. The strategic placement of low partitions near windows and the use of glass partition walls for windowed perimeter offices allow additional natural light to find its way to interior spaces. The building is projected to require a maximum of 0.6 watts per square foot of floor area, compared to the 2.4 watts that is the current standard for office buildings under the New York State Energy Code. Interior colors were chosen for high reflectance to gain maximum effectiveness from the lighting, and motion-sensing proximity switches in certain spaces automatically turn lights off when the area is unoccupied.

The selection of interior materials was made with attention to two goals: avoiding wasteful resource consumption and minimizing materials that give off air pollutants. Paints, wallboard, furniture finishes, and carpet adhesives that give off formaldehyde, benzine, and toluene were avoided or minimized. The drywall surface material used in construction is made from recycled newspaper; countertop materials use recycled plastic packaging as an

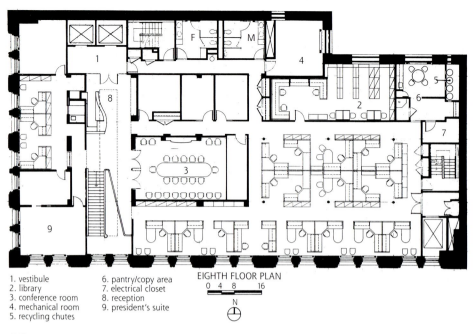

1. vestibule
2. library
3. conference room
4. mechanical room
5. recycling chutes
6. pantry/copy area
7. electrical closet
8. reception
9. president's suite

EIGHTH FLOOR PLAN

0   4   8   16

N

7.12

ingredient; ceramic tiles incorporate recycled industrial-waste glass; and natural fiber carpet is laid on a Homasote underlayment without adhesives. Exotic woods from endangered species were consciously used to support rain forest groups who are managing these resources in a sustainable way; and plastic materials that consume fossil fuels in their production were avoided.

Interior air quality, a notorious problem in the modern building, where the recycling of air gradually concentrates fumes, bacteria, and other pollutants, was of primary importance in this project. In addition to the material selections mentioned above, several other factors contribute to the exceptional air quality of the buildings. The air-conditioning system, which delivers six air changes per hour with an unusually high ratio of fresh outside air, exceeds the highest current recommended standards by 30 percent, and air is drawn from the top of the building rather than from street level. Most unusual is the fact that windows in the offices can be opened whenever desired.

An especially interesting element is the building's system of trash disposal, which uses four tubular chutes that run from top to bottom of the building. Each chute is designated for a specific type of presorted waste—white paper, mixed paper, aluminum and plastic,

and organic material—which is delivered to separate bins in the subbasement. Organic waste will be composted and used to fertilize trees in the rooftop conservatory.

In addition to the attention to environmental concerns, the designers provided for barrier-free accessibility throughout; the entrance door and lobby floor, for example, were lowered by 14 inches from the original level to provide direct, front-door access at sidewalk height without a step.

It is particularly striking that such an environmentally and socially responsible program has not led to any compromises in the aesthetic aspects of design. The qualities of color and light, the character of furniture and equipment are as pleasant and comfortable as anything achieved through conventional approaches.

It is even more remarkable that there has been no economic penalty for the responsible nature of the program. In first cost, by using an existing structure, the scheme represented savings of approximately 30 percent over a conventional new building. Operating costs have been similarly reduced by more than 60 percent through energy efficiency, so that savings will be realized year after year as the offices remain in use. There are also the less quantifiable savings that can be expected through the reduction of lost work time due to

7.12 The corner office illustrated in fig. 7.13 is labeled 9 on this plan of the eighth floor of the National Audubon Society Headquarters; the skylit lobby in fig. 7.15 is labeled 8. The semi-open offices that occupy most of this floor are typical of the building's other floors. (Courtesy Croxton Collaborative Planning, Architecture & Interior Design)

CHAPTER

EIGHT

MATERIALS AND ELEMENTS

The *elements* of interior design are the separate parts or components that make up a space. The term comes from the long-used phrase *elements of architecture*, referring to the basic building components—walls, floors, ceilings, columns, doors, windows, and similar items. Every building is made up of *structural* elements, those that actually support the building and enclose it, and *nonstructural* elements, additions that do not affect the building's basic structure. Unless the interior designer participates in the planning of a new building, he or she will find the structural elements fixed in place, and thus difficult or impossible to change or remove. Outside walls, *load-bearing* walls that carry the weight of the roof or ceiling, floors, roofs, and structural columns fit into this category, as do many windows, outside doors, stairways, and other elements that compose the basic architecture of a building. Nonstructural elements, such as interior partition walls, which carry no load, some steps and stairs, doors, and openings, are usually subject to change, addition, or removal, and are therefore more likely to be within the control of the interior designer.

All elements are made of *materials,* such as wood, stone, plaster, paint, and paper. A floor can be stone, brick, wood, or tile, all appropriate to the function of this element. A wall might be built of brick, stone, wood, or plasterboard on studs, but this material may then be covered with plaster, paint, fabric, tile, paneling, or any number of other materials. An important part of interior design work is the selection of suitable materials for the various elements that make up a particular interior space.

A typical interior consists of several elements and a surprising number of materials. It is an interesting exercise to list, for a few familiar spaces, every element and every material, including even the small details of hardware and trim. Such lists may turn out to be much longer than might be expected. Organizing the selection of materials demands knowledge of what is available and an awareness of what is best suited to specific needs and uses. Collecting information about

materials, both in memory and in a data file of catalogs, literature, and samples, is a vital part of preparation for interior design work. This chapter offers an introduction to the wide range of possibilities, but cannot begin to cover the huge variety of materials and products currently available. The materials of textiles and furniture, because of their special importance, are covered in separate chapters (11 and 12).

STRUCTURAL AND INTERIOR MATERIALS

Every interior exists within a structure made up of materials organized in a way that provides an enclosure envelope and a supporting system of elements having an architectural or engineering basis. The degree to which this structural context affects interiors is quite variable. In a medieval cathedral, the vast stone structure is internally dominant; one might say that the structure *is* the interior. In many other interiors, structure may appear in the form of an exposed brick or stone bearing wall; in the wood framing of walls, ceiling, or room; or in columns that support floors or a roof above. Structure may also be totally invisible, as in spaces within a modern high rise where columns, beams, and slabs are out of sight, hidden within partition walls, hung ceilings, and other elements of finish. Even in such cases, although the occupant or user may be unaware of structure, the designer will be aware of column locations that cannot be changed, bearing walls that cannot be removed with ease, and beams and girders that must be either concealed or exploited as visual elements in the completed space.

Awareness of architectural structure is essential to any interior design work that goes beyond the level of surface decoration. Understanding of structure can best be organized in terms of the basic structural systems that are each based on a particular family of materials. The traditional materials that have been in use for thousands of years are wood (timber)

8.1 The combination of wide, pine-plank flooring and cedar siding, both inside and out, generates a rustic quality in this ski house in Vail, Colorado, designed by Venturi, Rauch and Scott Brown in 1977. The house is furnished *mostly with a collection of Gustav Stickley Mission oak pieces from the turn of the century, with wicker chairs of the same vintage. (Photograph courtesy Venturi, Rauch and Scott Brown)*

and masonry (stone, brick, tile, and various manufactured forms of block). In the modern world, beginning in the nineteenth century, two other major types of materials have come into importance. These are metals—primarily iron and steel—and the special form of concrete known as reinforced concrete.

Although such structural materials may appear in interior spaces, many other interior materials are nonstructural. They may cover over structure, they may be added to structure to modify function and appearance, they may be used quite independently of structure to modulate interior space (as with partition walls, hung ceilings, and such inserted elements as stairways), or they may simply be surface materials used for a vast range of practical and aesthetic purposes.

TYPES OF MATERIALS

While all materials originate from natural sources, human needs impose certain levels of modification on materials as they are found in nature.

NATURAL MATERIALS. These remain unchanged except when they need to be superficially modified for use. Stone and wood, for example, can be used in their natural forms, but they are usually cut into standard shapes. Quarried stone is most often cut into blocks, in which form it is called ashlar, and trees are cut first into logs, then into boards, or lumber, of standardized forms and sizes.

PROCESSED MATERIALS. These are the result of converting natural materials into special forms for practical use. The natural material clay takes on different properties and uses when fired into brick and tile. Sand and small stones (called aggregate), when bonded together with cement, form concrete, a kind of artificial stone that can be poured in mass, reinforced with embedded steel rods, or made up into blocks similar to cut stone. Wood may be sliced into thin sheets of veneer, and layers of veneer may be glued together to form plywood. All metals require processing to extract them from ore, refine them, and possibly combine them into alloys. Then they are formed into sheets, tubes, rolled sections, castings, or other shapes.

SYNTHETIC MATERIALS. These do not exist in nature but have been brought into being, or manufactured, through artificial processes. Glass is an ancient synthetic made from sand and various other elements fused by heat. Plastics, the most familiar of modern synthetics, are made from various chemicals, most of them derived from petroleum. Synthetics themselves can be combined, leading to the creation of hybrids such as fiberglass.

In practice, many materials result from combinations of these levels of processing. A natural fiber such as wool may be processed through spinning and weaving to make a textile. A core of solid wood may be surfaced with a synthetic plastic laminate. Rolled steel beams or columns may be enclosed in poured concrete and covered in turn with metal lath and plaster, plasterboard, solid wood boards, plywood, tile, or any number of other materials.

WOOD

Structural

Timber is the most widely available, simplest, and most familiar of structural materials. Wherever there are trees, the use of wood for building becomes commonplace. For their huts and houses, native peoples used branches, poles, and logs in ways that minimized the need for precise joinery. As better tools became available, wood was worked with more precision into beams, planks, boards, and panels, creating characteristic historic building patterns.

Wood is limited by its source, trees, to a lengthwise strip material. This in turn limits timber building structure to a *frame*, that is, a cage or grid of long members put together with diagonal bracing members to form a sturdy structural support for whatever wall and roofing materials will be used. Walls and roofing may also be wood (in the form of vertical planks, clapboards, or shingles) or other materials, such as plaster and rubble for walls, tiles or tar paper for roofing.

Wood makes a reasonably durable, but not permanent, building material, being subject to decay, rot, insect damage, and fire. Wooden buildings over a few hundred years of age are rare, and none from ancient times survive, although we have knowledge of wood construction in ancient Egypt, Greece, and Rome from secondary sources such as paintings, written materials, and physical evidence in ruined structures.

Because of its lengthwise structure and comparatively light weight, wood was a favorite material for floors and roofs even when walls were made of stone or other more lasting materials. Many ancient ruined structures exhibit surviving masonry walls and columns, while wood roofing has been lost through one or another form of damage. Surviving wood roofing used for medieval barns, churches, and other large spaces often displays large wooden members assembled into triangular arrangements called *trusses* in order to span spaces wider than the longest available beams. The frames of heavy timber used for many smaller medieval structures are often exposed externally, creating the visual patterns of *half-timber* construction (fig. 4.18). In America, since exposed framing proved impractical because of climatic conditions, such framing in Colonial houses and other buildings was usually hidden by an external covering of shingles or boarding (fig. 4.43). However, if it was not covered by paneling or plaster, the framing was often visible inside.

The development of power saws and planers in more modern times has led to the practice of converting timber into neatly cut and sized units, referred to as *lumber*. Modern wood construction uses sawmill-cut lumber for the heavy framing or, for smaller buildings, smaller members placed close together to form a light but strong frame. Small houses are commonly built with a structure of 2-by-4-inch studs placed 16 inches apart to form wall framing. Joists for floors and rafters for roofs are also 2 inches thick but 8, 10, or 12 inches deep. They are also placed at the same 16-inch spacing. An outside sheathing and an interior finish together create a hollow "sandwich" assembly that provides reasonable strength with minimum material and labor costs. This

Table 5. Basic Materials

MATERIAL	TYPES		COMMENTS
MASONRY	ROUGH STONE (FIELD-STONE, FLAGSTONE) CUT STONE, OR ASHLAR (LIMESTONE, MARBLE, GRANITE, SLATE) BRICK TERRA-COTTA, BLOCK	TILE (QUARRY TILE, MOSAIC, VITREOUS CERAMIC) GYPSUM BLOCK CONCRETE BLOCK PRECAST CONCRETE REINFORCED CONCRETE MASS CONCRETE	Masonry materials need to be sized and shaped to suit their planned use. Rough stone can be selected to fall within a desired range of size and shape. Cut stone is sized and shaped according to the designer's plans. Brick, tile, and block come in a limited number of standardized sizes and shapes. The shape of poured concrete elements is determined by each design.
WOOD	SOFTWOODS (FROM EVERGREEN TREES) SUCH AS PINE, SPRUCE, FIR, CEDAR, REDWOOD HARDWOODS (FROM THE NUT, FRUIT, AND OTHER DECIDUOUS TREES) SUCH AS OAK, MAPLE, BIRCH, WALNUT, CHERRY, POPLAR, AND MANY MORE EXOTIC WOODS	VENEER PLYWOOD (SOLID CORE AND VENEER CORE) LAMINATED WOOD (SUCH AS BUTCHER BLOCK) PARTICLEBOARD	Wood is characterized by a lengthwise grain structure, which results from the growth of the tree. Size is limited by the dimensions of available trees of a given species; the dimensions of width and thickness are strictly limited, while lengths of over 16 feet present problems in both availability and handling. Veneer is thin sheet, available only in limited widths and lengths. Plywood and particleboard are made in sheets of standard size, most frequently 4 by 8 feet.
METALS	STEEL (STRUCTURAL OR MILD IN VARIOUS FORMS SUCH AS SHEET, ROLLED SECTIONS, AND TUBING) STAINLESS STEEL (IN SIMILAR FORMS)	ALUMINUM (IN SIMILAR FORMS AS WELL AS IN EXTRUSIONS AND CASTINGS) COPPER, BRASS, AND BRONZE ALLOYS FOR DIE-CASTING	Metals other than stainless steel all require finishing to protect them from rust and corrosion. Steel can be painted or plated. Aluminum can be anodized in its natural color or in various other colors. Brass, copper, and bronze can be constantly polished to maintain their natural color, lacquered to avoid polishing, or left to weather to the tones of green that oxidation produces. Chromium plating is a widely used finish for steel and die-cast alloys.
SYNTHETICS	GLASS PLASTICS (IN SHEET, MOLDED, EXTRUDED, AND OTHER PROCESSED FORMS)	MANUFACTURED PRODUCTS SUCH AS LINOLEUM, RESILIENT FLOOR TILE, OR SHEETROCK (WALLBOARD)	Glass is available in flat panes or sheets of various thicknesses and sizes. Usually clear, glass can be made in various tints and colors as well. Curved sheets must be made to special order. Tempered glass, of great strength, cannot be cut, so it must be made to the desired size and shape. Glass block is glass in hollow, bricklike form. Plastics can take many forms; they appear most often in interiors as flat sheets of clear or tinted acrylic or Lexan, used as an unbreakable substitute for glass, and as thin sheets of melamine laminates, used as a tough surface applied over other materials. It is possible to obtain plastic sheet with bends or curves, but it must usually be ordered from the factory. The most common sheet size is 4 by 8 feet.
HYBRIDS AND MISCELLANEOUS	WOVEN FIBERS LEATHER, CORK, RUBBER ROPE, CORD, NETTING AIR-SUPPORTED MEMBRANES	PAPER HARDBOARD, CHALKBOARD, AND TACK BOARD CEILING TILE	Woven fibers, both natural and synthetic, are the materials of carpeting and rugs and of wall-covering materials, including special carpeting and woven sheet material (applied like wallpaper). (See also Chapter 11, which discusses drapery and upholstery textiles.)

Table 6. Interior Materials

			Floors	Walls	Columns	Ceilings	Stairs	Doors	Window Frames	Window Treatment	Movable Furniture	Built-in Furniture	Bathroom Fixtures*	Kitchen Fixtures*	Fireplaces	Mantles	Trim	Hardware
WOOD		SOFT	⊡	▣	▣		⊡	●	●		○	●	○	○			●	●
		HARD	●	○		○	●	○	○		●	○	○	○			○	○
		PANELING		●				●										
		PLYWOOD	○	●		○	○	●			●	●	●	●				
		BOARDING	○	○			○	○										
METALS	STEEL	MILD			▣		▣	●	●		●	○	○	●	○			●
		STAINLESS		○							○		○	●				○
		ENAMELED		○									●	●				
	IRON	CAST			□										○			○
		ENAMELED											○	○				○
	ALUMINUM	CAST									○						○	○
		EXTRUDED							●		○							
	BRONZE																	○
	BRASS										●						●
	COPPER																○	○
	DIE-CAST																	●
MASONRY	STONE	FIELDSTONE	▣	⊡											⊡			
		LIMESTONE		⊡											⊡			
		TRAVERTINE	○	○			○				○							
		MARBLE	●	▣	⊡		⊡				○		○		○	●		
		GRANITE	○	⊡			⊡				○		○					
		SLATE	●				○				○		○					
	CONCRETE	MASS	⊡															
		REINFORCED	▣	⊡	●	○	●								⊡			
		BLOCK		●											⊡			
	GYPSUM	BLOCK		▣														
	BRICK		○	▣	⊡		○								▣	○		
	TILE	CERAMIC, VITREOUS	○	●	○								○	○	○		○	
		PORCELAIN		○	○													
		QUARRY	●				○											
		MOSAIC	○	●	○								○	○				
		TERRA-COTTA		○	○													
	TERRAZZO		●				○											

*The word "fixtures" includes plumbing and appliances

KEY □ Structural use • Nonstructural use (frequent) ○ Nonstructural use (occasional) Empty position: Unsuitable or rarely used

Table 6. Interior Materials (continued)

		Floors	Walls	Columns	Ceilings	Stairs	Doors	Window Frames	Window Treatment	Movable Furniture	Built-in Furniture	Bathroom Fixtures*	Kitchen Fixtures*	Fireplaces	Mantles	Trim	Hardware
GLASS	WINDOW							●				○					
	PLATE							●		●		○					
	TEMPERED						●	○				○					
	MIRROR		○	○	○					○	○	○					
	BLOCK		○														
PLASTIC	TRANSPARENT		○					○		○							
	LAMINATE		○	○			○			●	●	●	●				
	SHEET WALL COVERING		●	●													
	EXTRUSION					○		●		○	○			○		○	
	TILE	●	○				●										
TEXTILES	DRAPERY		○				○		●								
	UPHOLSTERY		○							●	●						
	WALL COVERING		●														
	CARPET	●	○														
MISCELLANEOUS	LATHE AND PLASTER		●	●	●												
	DRYWALL		●	●	●												
	ACOUSTIC TILE				●												
	LINOLEUM	○	○			○								○			
	ASPHALT TILE	●				●											
	CORK	○	○														
	RUBBER	○															

system, called *balloon* or *western* framing, is characteristically American and is still in very common use for the construction of small houses (fig. 8.2). *Braced framing,* using heavy timber and bracing, also continues in use and has become popular with modern architects to form the structure for houses and other small buildings, particularly where large areas of walls are given over to glass

The industrial processing of wood has added plywood and particleboard to the list of timber materials. Both of these convert wood into large sheets that minimize solid wood's tendency to warp, shrink, and split. Plywood is made up of layers of thin wood veneer, particleboard of wood chips and sawdust bonded together with an adhesive and pressed into flat sheets. Both materials make economical use of wood, and both are most useful for sheathing walls, roofs, and floors rather than as primary structural materials.

Although its use as a major building material is limited in modern practice by the combination of rising cost (resulting from diminishing supplies, as forests are cut more rapidly than they are replaced with new growth) and restrictions introduced to reduce fire risks, wood seems assured a continuing role in the architectural construction of smaller buildings and as a secondary material in building using other materials for primary structure. Although wood structure is usually hidden, it influences the location and size of openings. When wood-frame members are exposed, they may become major visual design elements.

Interior

Along with its role as one of the primary materials of architectural construction, wood is used in many interior applications as well as for furniture construction (see pages 373–77). A table detailing the characteristics of the most-used furniture woods appears on page 378. All wood has characteristics that relate to its origin in the trunks of trees: a lengthwise grain; limitations on available length and width;

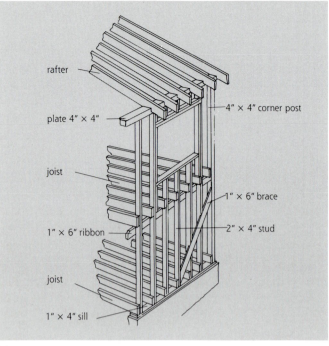

rafter

plate 4" × 4"

4" × 4" corner post

joist

1" × 6" brace

1" × 6" ribbon

2" × 4" stud

joist

1" × 4" sill

8.2

and visible grain patterns that relate to the ways in which logs are cut to produce usable lumber. The following general information is applicable to wood in all of its many uses:

SOFTWOOD. The term refers to the woods of evergreen trees (conifers) that are generally fast growing and therefore sufficiently "soft" to cut with a handsaw and be assembled with hammer and nails. Pine, spruce, fir, and other softwoods are the materials of carpentry. Redwood and cypress are valued for their oil content, which allows them to last well out-of-doors even when left unpainted. "Wide-board" floors, some interior paneling and the tongue-and-groove boarding often used for wainscoting and other wall surfacing, and the moldings used for the majority of trim are of softwood milled into standard forms readily available at lumberyards. Natural finishes, stains, or paints are usually applied to softwoods to provide surface protection.

HARDWOOD. The wood from deciduous trees, including fruit and nut trees as well as others that lose their leaves annually, is denser and "harder" than the softwoods. Hardwoods are of good appearance and take finishes well, rendering them suitable for fine cabinetry and furniture making. Birch and maple are often used for wood flooring and for furniture. Mahogany, oak, and walnut are familiar hardwoods in wide use. Other hardwoods are less available and their use is confined to furniture and decorative applications. Cherry, ash, hickory, satinwood, zebrawood, and ebony are used in limited applications for decorative effect. Poplar is frequently used in concealed locations, as in a plywood core.

PLYWOOD. This widely used material is made by bonding together a number of layers. Veneer plywood is made of many thin layers, most often of fir. The outer layer may be fir (suitable solely to utility applications) or it may be a veneer of better appearance, such as birch or walnut. Plywood is also made with a core of solid wood (often poplar) plus two outer layers, cross-banded with the grain running across that of the core, and a surface layer of attractive face veneer. Both faces of plywood must have the same layering in order to achieve "balanced construction" and discourage warping. Particleboard can also be used as a core for plywood, requiring only one layer of face veneer on both sides.

VENEER. Wood can be cut into very thin slices (usually $\frac{1}{28}$-inch thick), making sheets that are somewhat flexible. Successive layers sliced from one log or slab form a *flitch*, with each layer repeating the grain pattern of the adjacent layers. When veneer is glued to its backing or core, the arrangement of adjacent strips can create various patterns, including the symmetry of *book matching*, the repetition of *slip* or *end matching*, and the diamond shape of *quarter matching* (fig. 8.3).

PARTICLEBOARD. This is a sheet material made by pressing together wood chips and sawdust with an adhesive to make a board or panel that has most of the qualities of wood but is grainless. A similar board made with higher pressures to create greater strength and smooth surfaces is called *hardboard;* Masonite is a familiar trade name.

LAMINATION. Strips of solid wood can be laminated together to make large surfaces, such as the widely used *butcher block*.

BENTWOOD. Strips of certain woods, when subject to steam heat and moisture, can be made sufficiently flexible to be bent around forms. When dried and cooled, the bent shapes are retained. The furniture manufacturer who developed this process, Michael Thonet, created in his Austrian firm an extensive line of bentwood furniture during the mid-nineteenth century (see fig. 12.41).

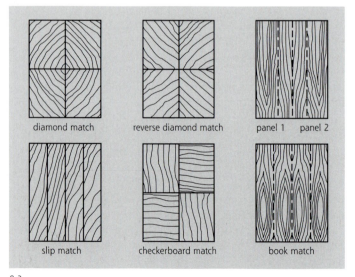

diamond match

reverse diamond match

panel 1   panel 2

slip match

checkerboard match

book match

8.3

8.2 The structural system of wood framing known as balloon framing was developed in Victorian America. Small, lumberyard-sawed wood pieces are assembled in a frame that is easy and economical to construct. When they are vertical, these elements are called studs; when horizontal, joists; and when roof supports, rafters.

8.3 When veneers are sliced from a solid block, the successive sheets laid to make up a flitch have virtually identical grain patterns. The arrangement of veneers can generate a wide variety of patterns, some of which are shown in this chart. (Drawing courtesy Hardwood, Plywood & Veneer Association)

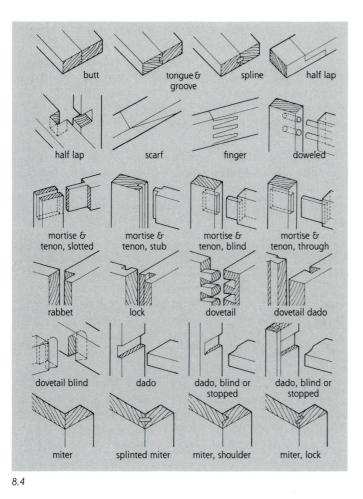

8.4

 contains labels: butt, tongue & groove, spline, half lap, half lap, scarf, finger, doweled, mortise & tenon, slotted, mortise & tenon, stub, mortise & tenon, blind, mortise & tenon, through, rabbet, lock, dovetail, dovetail dado, dovetail blind, dado, dado, blind or stopped, dado, blind or stopped, miter, splinted miter, miter, shoulder, miter, lock

MOLDED PLYWOOD. If layers of veneer are pressed between molds while being glued together to form plywood, the finished product will retain the form of the mold. Molded plywood is often used for parts of furniture, including chair seats or backs.

Because wood is available in boards or sheets of limited size, most applications for the material require the assembly of a number of separate pieces. The term *joinery* describes the great variety of wood joints that are used in making furniture, paneling doors, and manufacturing windows and other items of *millwork* (fig. 8.4). Wood joints and other woodwork details have been developed over hundreds of years to deal with the following issues:

SHRINKING AND SWELLING. Changes in humidity make it necessary for larger expanses of wood to be put together with some allowance for movement, as in *rail-and-panel* construction.

WARPING. This condition is also largely controlled in rail-and-panel construction, as thicker rails hold thinner panels flat.

END GRAIN. The exposed surface where wood is cut across the grain is of unsatisfactory appearance and takes finishes poorly. Miter joints and special edge treatments are used to hide not only end grain but also the layering of plywood and core panels.

GLUES. Some adhesives, particularly older types of glue, may not hold joints when stressed. Many joints are intended to hold parts together through interlocking so that glue need not be depended upon. Although modern resin glues usually develop joints of high strength, traditional joints are often still used both for their good appearance and their usefulness in holding parts in place while glue is drying.

Many wood joints have an attractive appearance and can enhance the aesthetic quality of objects where they are used. Dovetails, mortise-and-tenon joints, and exposed dowel joints are among those that can be ornamental and suggestive of fine craftsmanship.

Wood requires finishing to seal open grain structure and create attractive and durable surfaces. Various paints, varnishes, lacquers, and oils can be used to create finishes of varied appearance. (Table 7 on page 229 lists the most popular finishes for wood and other materials.)

MASONRY

Masonry is the general term for a family of materials that played a major role in historic building and that continues in modern use. The term refers to construction with stone and manufactured materials such as brick, tile, concrete block—even the mud brick used in some ancient and indigenous buildings. With the exception of mud brick, masonry materials offer excellent durability. The oldest surviving buildings are all of stone (the pyramids of Egypt, fig. 4.2, and Stonehenge, for example), and the ruins of ancient structures are usually the remaining stone portions of buildings that used timber roofing.

Use of stone requires available quarry resources and involves the tools and labor required to cut, transport, and erect this heavy material. Bricks and tiles are invented materials that have many of the qualities of stone, except that they can be made when and where needed and in sizes convenient to handle.

Masonry materials offer good strength under *compressive* loads (as in walls and columns), which tend to squeeze or crush the material in use. However, they have poor *tensile* strength for resisting stretching and are therefore not very satisfactory for use as beams or rafters in floor or roof construction. A *beam* is a structural member stressed in *bending* by the loads placed upon it. Bending stress combines compression at the top of a simple beam with tension at its bottom. Materials such as wood and steel make good beams because they are strong in both compressive and tensile stress. Masonry materials are strong only in compression.

A short stone beam called a *lintel* may be used to span a door or window opening in masonry construction, but the opening must be kept narrow in order to prevent the lintel from cracking under its own weight and the weight of the wall above. *Post-and-lintel construction* (fig. 8.5), in which columns are placed fairly close together to support lintels, creates an enclosure with the internal space filled only with columns, as, for example, in the hypostyle halls of Egyptian temples. Ways to roof over large open spaces with masonry did not come into

8.4 Woodworkers have developed many ways of joining wood to aid strength and govern appearance. Some commonly used woodworking (often called millwork) joints appear in this chart.

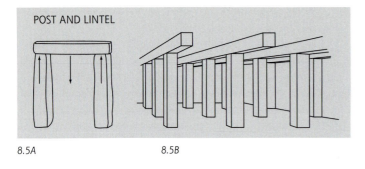

POST AND LINTEL

8.5A   8.5B

wide use until the ancient Romans developed systems of arches and vaults that made possible the building of such structures as the Roman baths or the Pantheon (fig. 4.11). Domes and vaults remained the only feasible and durable structural devices for enclosing large spaces until the development of the modern materials discussed below (fig. 8.7).

The building techniques of both domes and vaults require carefully cutting stones into complex shapes; using a temporary (usually wooden) structure called *centering* to support the structure while it is under construction; and erecting massive walls or buttresses to resist the outward pressure, or *thrust*, exerted by arched forms as they convert the downward pull of gravity to an outward push (figs. 8.6A–8.6D). The Gothic cathedrals are spectacular exercises in masonry construction using vaulting and buttresses to produce lasting and dramatic buildings (fig. 4.16).

Vaulted construction has now generally become obsolete, replaced by newer materials that span large openings and spaces more economically. For bearing walls and columns, brick and concrete are in wider use than stone, which is often restricted to the exterior surfaces of walls in monumental buildings. Brick remains in wide use for walls of small

buildings with wood floor and roof construction. Exposed brick (sometimes painted) has become a widely used interior surface. Exposed rough stonework is also still quite common for walls and chimneys, particularly in buildings in rural or suburban settings.

Stone

Stone may be in the rough form of rubble or fieldstone or neatly cut from a quarry as *ashlar* (fig. 8.9). When used for bearing-wall construction, stone is usually *bonded;* when used as a surface treatment, larger units of thin stone may be joined in other patterns that do not imply bonding. The types of stone in wide use include the following:

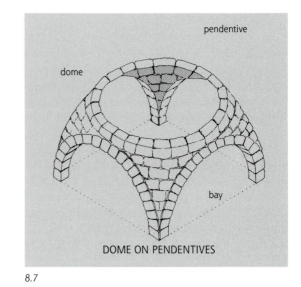

DOME ON PENDENTIVES

8.7

GRANITE. An igneous rock, very compact and hard, generally of dark colors ranging from pink to dark browns and near black.

LIMESTONE, SANDSTONE, SLATE. Sedimentary rock of medium density, light to darker grays, brown, and, in the case of slate, in grays ranging from bluish to near black.

MARBLE. Many types of metamorphic stone in varied degrees of hardness, typically with strong patterns of veining and a wide range of colors, from white and gray to strong greens, reds, and yellows. Travertine, a soft marble with a creamy color and a surface with open holes or pits, may be filled to give a solid surface. Many decorative marbles have little strength and require backing to hold together.

Brick

Brick is a modular material made by firing special clays into units usually in a nominal size of 2 by 4 by 8 inches. Mortar is used to hold brick together to make up walls or surface treatments for walls of other materials (fig. 8.10). Bricks are most often in shades of red or brown. Glazed brick can be made in a range of colors. Mortar joints may be white, gray, or toned in other colors. The patterns of bonding used with brick are diverse and can create textural and visual effects of considerable interest (fig. 8.11).

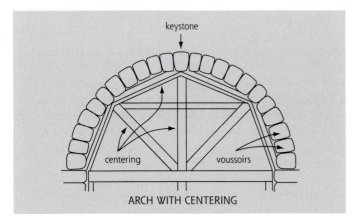

ARCH WITH CENTERING

8.6A

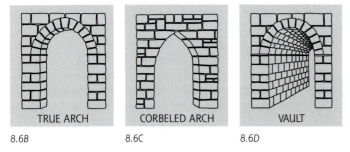

TRUE ARCH   CORBELED ARCH   VAULT

8.6B   8.6C   8.6D

8.5A, 8.5B In the most basic structural system, post-and-lintel (sometimes called trabeated) construction (A), vertical posts, or columns, support horizontal members (the lintels). When the material used is wood, the system is described as post-and-beam construction. To enclose a space with a ceiling or roof, a series of post-and-lintel groupings can be used to support slabs of stone or planks of wood (B). (Drawings: Copyright © Farrell Design Associates)

8.6A-8.6D The construction of an arch or vault requires centering (A), a temporary wooden structure on which the stones are supported in position until sufficient buttressing is in place. (Drawing A by Marilyn Boyle) In a true arch (B), each wedge-shaped stone, or voussoir, presses against its neighbors, creating outward pressure, or thrust. In a corbeled arch (C), although the shape

of the opening is archlike, the stones are simply stacked vertically, each successive stone cantilevering beyond the stone below. There is no thrust, only downward pressure. A vault (D) is an arch form extended in depth to create a roof over a deep space. (Drawings B, C, D: Copyright © Farrell Design Associates)

8.7 Curved, triangular masonry surfaces called pendentives form the transition between a dome and the supporting walls or columns. Pendentives make it possible to fit the circular form of a dome over a square space (bay) with supports at its four corners.

8.8

8.8 In modern use, stone is a popular material for country houses. Architect Marlys Hann chose rough fieldstone for her 1985 house in the Catskill Mountains. (Photograph: Paul Warchol)

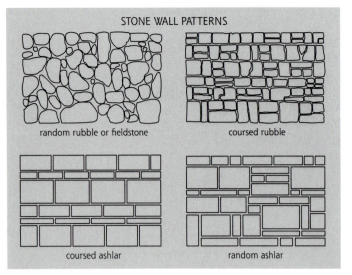

STONE WALL PATTERNS

random rubble or fieldstone

coursed rubble

coursed ashlar

random ashlar

8.9

Concrete Block

Concrete block (also called cement block) is a manufactured masonry material popular for its strength and low cost. Concrete blocks are usually made hollow to save material and reduce weight (see fig. 8.10). The common modular size is a nominal 8 by 8 by 16 inches. Two-inch-thick block is also frequently used. The gray tone of concrete block is generally hidden with a surface treatment of plaster, tile, or paint. Concrete block can be cast with a surface pattern of special design.

Plaster and Stucco

These materials are prepared in a semifluid state to be applied to a backing of brick, block, or *lath* of wood or metal. A common modern

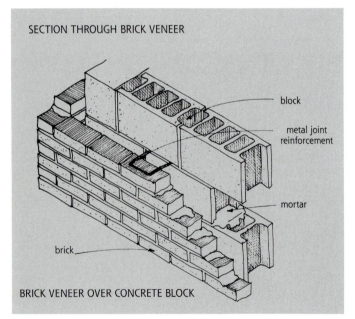

SECTION THROUGH BRICK VENEER

block

metal joint reinforcement

mortar

brick

BRICK VENEER OVER CONCRETE BLOCK

8.10

substitute for plaster is plasterboard or gypsum board (often called Sheetrock)—a sheet material with a plasterlike core surfaced with a special paper. It is attached to an underlying wall structure of block or studs of wood or metal.

Tile

Tile is made in many forms: ceramic tiles with glazed surfaces in varied colors and patterns; small mosaic tiles in many colors; larger, sturdy *quarry tiles;* and tiles made from the fired clay called *terra-cotta* (fig. 8.12). Terra-cotta tile can be made with decorative sculptural forms, as well as in special shapes for various architectural uses. It was once used extensively as a means of fireproofing iron and steel structures and to form floor arches between metal structural members. Although now obsolete, terra-cotta arch construction may be found in renovations of historic structures.

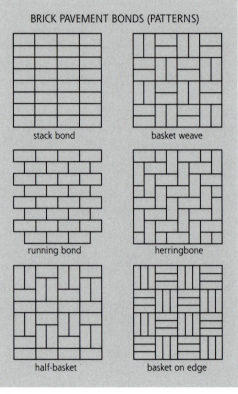

BRICK PAVEMENT BONDS (PATTERNS)

stack bond

basket weave

running bond

herringbone

half-basket

basket on edge

8.11

Concrete

The material concrete was known to the ancient Romans but then forgotten and not rediscovered until the eighteenth century. Made up of cement, sand, and small stones mixed with water, it hardens into a stonelike solid. This is *mass concrete,* the material of road surfacing and of concrete block, a favorite modern masonry material (see below). Mass concrete, however, has little value as a major structural material because of its weakness in dealing with tensile stresses. Only with the

8.9 When used as a wall material—either for the entire wall or as a surface veneer—stone has strong visual character. The random patterns of fieldstone or rubble (A) suggest a rustic ambience, an effect that can be made more subdued by arranging stone in horizontal bands of coursed rubble (B). Ashlar, stones cut in rectangular shapes, may be laid in regular horizontal bands to create coursed ashlar (C) or in more irregular patterns of random ashlar (D).

8.10 Brick may appear as an external veneer over concrete block or as an interior wall material, left exposed on the inside of an all-brick wall. Concrete block is also sometimes left exposed as an interior wall material. Both brick and concrete block walls are assembled with mortar for the joints. (Drawing: Copyright © Farrell Design Associates)

8.11 Brick used for paving or flooring can be laid in a wide variety of patterns, which can be either minimized or accentuated by the selection of mortar color.

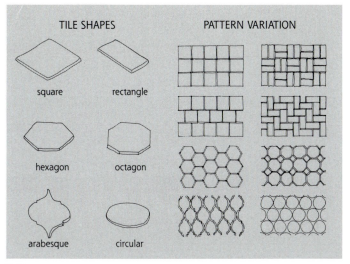

TILE SHAPES		PATTERN VARIATION	
square	rectangle		
hexagon	octagon		
arabesque	circular		

8.12

invention (in 1849) of *reinforced concrete* did concrete become a major modern structural material. Reinforced concrete is a hybrid material using steel rods embedded in concrete; the rods take tensile stresses while the concrete accepts compressive stress (fig. 8.13). This combination uses each material in the role for which it is best suited, resulting in economies and permitting structural design to exploit the variety of shapes that concrete can assume to suit each particular problem.

The first step in making reinforced concrete is building hollow, temporary, boxlike *forms,* usually made of wood, as molds into which concrete will be poured. Steel rods are placed in carefully engineered locations where tensile stresses are anticipated, and concrete is then poured into the forms surrounding the steel. When the concrete hardens, the forms are removed, leaving a structure of great strength, good economy, and inherent fire-resistance.

Reinforced concrete, rather than steel (see below), is likely to be chosen as the primary structural material where large special shapes spanning wide spaces are required; where planning calls for the irregular placement of columns in high-rise buildings; and wherever labor costs are low compared with the cost of steel (for example, in less industrialized parts of the world). Even in buildings using steel as the primary structural material, reinforced concrete is often employed for certain elements, such as floor or roof slabs or foundation walls.

When concrete is used to fireproof steel members, it can be difficult to tell by simple inspection whether the structure is steel or reinforced concrete. Columns, beams, and slabs appear much the same in both systems. The architectural and engineering drawings used in the construction of all major modern buildings will, of course, reveal what structural system is in use.

Such striking open and flowing building forms as Frank Lloyd Wright's Solomon R. Guggenheim Museum in New York (fig. 4.64) or Eero Saarinen's TWA terminal at Kennedy Airport, New York, could hardly have been conceived without the availability of reinforced concrete.

METALS

Structural

In the nineteenth century, the Industrial Revolution brought metals into wide use to make machinery. Iron in both cast and wrought forms began to be employed for bridge building, for columns in mill structures, and then as a major structural material for the frames of train sheds, market halls, and other utilitarian buildings. Iron finally began to replace masonry in many types of large buildings, and was itself replaced by stronger steel (iron alloyed with carbon) as the latter became generally available. The high strength and moderate cost of steel made it an ideal material for railroad rails, engines and other machinery, and shipbuilding. Toward the end of the nineteenth century, it was recognized as the best available material for the structural frames of tall buildings.

The *skyscraper* came into being with the rising values of city real estate, but its technical realization depended on the development of the elevator and the use of steel framing. In steel construction, walls do not ordinarily carry any weight (they exist strictly to provide enclosure), while columns at the wall line or standing freely support a grid of beams and girders that in turn support floor and roof-deck materials (fig. 8.15). The familiar I or H shapes of steel members provide a maximum of material where maximum compressive and tensile stresses at the top and bottom of beams occur, while the thin connecting web uses a minimum of material. Steel structural members are cut and drilled at the mill and assembled on site with rivets or welding with

8.13

8.12 *Tiles of various shapes can be arranged to form many different patterns, as illustrated here. (Drawing: Copyright © Farrell Design Associates)*

8.13 *A reinforced-concrete building is shown under construction. The lower portion of the columns can be seen encased in poured concrete; the steel rods above are in place, awaiting the* pouring of the concrete into forms, *which hold the material until it hardens. (Photograph courtesy Associated Builders and Contractors, Inc.)*

8.14

8.15

surprising speed and seeming ease. While steel will not burn, the heat of a fire can soften it enough to lead to structural failure. Therefore, in multistory buildings steel is always fireproofed by covering it with masonry, concrete, or, in modern practice, sprayed-on insulating material.

In addition to forming a cagelike frame construction, steel can be used to make roof trusses to span wide openings. It is also the material for other types of constructions, including domes and *space frames*, roof structures in which many small members create a grid using the rigidity of triangular forms to provide high strength with minimal material. Steel is a key material for some new and still experimental structural techniques, such as suspended structures using steel cable to support roofing in much the same way that cables of a suspension bridge carry a roadway over a wide open space.

Steel is currently the primary material for the structures of large buildings and is often used in small and light forms for parts of smaller buildings. *Open-web joists*, using steel rods to connect top and bottom steel elements, commonly form the roof structures for one-story

8.14 The Centre Georges Pompidou in Paris exhibits its exposed steel structure, as well as mechanical systems and escalators, on the exterior. The building was designed in 1976 by Richard Rogers and Renzo Piano, who were selected in an international competition. (Photograph: Marvin Trachtenberg)

8.15 When a steel-frame building is under construction, the cagelike structure of slim steel vertical columns and horizontal beams can be clearly seen. Later, the steel will be wrapped in insulating fireproofing materials and will disappear as outer wall surfaces enclose the inner structure. (Photograph courtesy Associated Builders and Contractors, Inc.)

garages, shops, warehouses, and factories. In small houses, steel may show up as a single floor beam or in the form of the tubular columns often used in a basement to support a main floor beam. Steel construction offers minimal obstruction to interior space and has been a primary force in the increased openness of modern planning. The only major rival of steel in modern building is reinforced concrete.

Interior

In low buildings metal structural members may be visible elements in an interior. Many small items of trim and details make use of metal, generally in a manufactured or prefabricated form. Metals can be worked in many different ways to produce materials for additional fabrication or to make finished objects. Rolling, stamping, casting, extruding, and machining are among the processes used in working with metals. Connections can be "mechanical," using rivets, screws, nuts and bolts, or threaded elements, or they can be welded, by applying heat or electric power to bring about partial melting to fuse parts together. Metals in general interior use are listed below:

STEEL. Many small elements such as door frames, doors, window sash, handrails, and items of hardware are made of steel. Most steel requires a protective finish, such as paint, or plating with a nonrusting metal, such as chromium. Stainless steel resists rusting but, because of its high strength, is difficult to cut and work.

IRON. Wrought iron is sometimes used for decorative railings and grillework. Cast iron is an economical material formerly used for structural and decorative parts of buildings. Its poor tensile strength makes it brittle and easily damaged. It may be found in historic buildings and was quite commonly used for furniture (or parts thereof) in the Victorian era.

ALUMINUM. The light weight and resistance to rusting characteristic of aluminum have made it a popular material for many architectural details, such as storefronts, window frames, and exterior wall cladding. It can be made into continuous ribbons of varied form by the process of *extrusion* (squeezing through a die that determines cross-sectional shape). Detail elements such as handrails and hardware items are often made of aluminum. Surfaces will develop a gray oxide surface unless finished by *anodizing* (a form of plating) or with some other coating. Anodizing can produce a color tone while preserving the metallic glitter of aluminum surfaces.

BRASS AND BRONZE. These are nonferrous alloys, much used in decorative detail in historic design. Brass has a yellow gleam that makes it a popular material for hardware and trim. Bronze has a deeper brown metallic color and will weather to the green tone familiar in statuary.

COPPER. The special orangy metallic color of copper is well known for its decorative possibilities. Copper must be protected with a lacquer coating if it is not to turn a green oxide color, frequently seen as the tone of copper roofing. Interior uses in hoods over fireplaces, stoves, or bar counters are not uncommon.

Glass

Although this familiar material is most valued for its transparency, it can also be produced in opaque and mirror form. Glass is most often used in windows, doors, and partitions where transparency is essential; it has also come into use as a primary material for buildings where "curtain walls" of windows become the exterior sheathing of the entire structure (fig. 8.16). Common "window glass" and "plate glass" are subject to easy breakage, introducing a variety of hazards when used in walls, doors, or furniture. Special types of glass have been developed to limit such problems. These include:

LAMINATED OR SAFETY GLASS. One or more layers of a plastic sheet are sandwiched between sheets of ordinary glass to create a material that resists the tendency of plain glass to shatter into sharp-edged shards.

TEMPERED GLASS. Glass is treated by heat processing to gain extra strength. Tempered glass is resistant to breakage and shatters into small, harmless pieces. It is a favored material for frameless glass doors, shower doors, and similar applications. Tempered glass cannot be cut and must be factory produced in desired sizes and shapes.

WIRE GLASS. Made with an embedded mesh of wire that holds a sheet of glass together even when breakage occurs, wire glass is particularly useful for its ability to resist shattering from fire heat. It is therefore a code requirement in locations where a fire barrier is needed.

SPECIAL GLASSES. A number of glasses with special properties are available. Some offer heat insulation by means of multiple layers with air space between, some feature resistance to heat transmission through coloring that blocks infrared radiation, and others block heat by means of semimirrored reflectivity.

MIRROR. This form of glass is silvered on one side to create a reflective surface. Partial mirroring makes "one-way" glass that, when lighting is appropriately balanced, permits vision in one direction but blocks it in the other.

DECORATIVE GLASSES. These include a wide variety of textures and surface treatments that permit light passage but distort image transmission. Glass is also made in a full range of colors, clear or textured, suitable to many decorative uses, among them the well-known "stained glass" in which separate pieces of glass are joined with metal strips to generate patterns.

Plastics

Plastics all are synthetic materials made by chemical combination of various basic ingredients, most derived from petroleum. A type of plastic may be known by several names—a generic or chemical name and one or more trade names given to it by manufacturers. Acrylic is a generic name, Plexiglas and Lucite are trade names for acrylics. The

8.16

8.17

character of a particular plastic can vary greatly according to the way it is processed. Nylon, for example, appears to be totally different when knitted into a stocking, woven into carpet fiber, or made into a solid glide or roller. There are two main families of plastics, and they differ in their basic qualities:

THERMOPLASTICS. Soft and moldable when heated, thermoplastics become stiff and solid when cooled. Thermoplastic objects are made by molding, rolling, or extruding the heated material. Familiar groups of thermoplastics include acrylics (transparent and clear, colored or opaque), polystyrenes (much used for everyday household items), and vinyls (common as floor tiles and as alternatives to leather in upholstery).

THERMOSETTING PLASTICS. These are made from a liquid resin and a second liquid called a catalyst that when combined and subjected to heat harden and become solid. Once formed, objects of thermosetting plastic cannot be softened or melted. Thermosetting plastics can be processed by rolling, molding, or foaming to make sheets, objects of complex forms, or light foam slabs of varied densities ranging from soft cushioning to firm board. The melamines are a strong thermosetting plastic. Phenolics (Bakelite is a well-known trade name) are weaker but inexpensive and good insulators. Polyesters and urethanes are used to make foams, soft or rigid. Glass fibers are embedded in polyester to make the hybrid, high-strength material usually called by the trade name Fiberglas. Plastic laminates are made from layers of special paper bonded together and surfaced with melamine plastic to make a

8.16 The glass portions of an outside wall open up an unconventional space in a Los Angeles, California, house to light and views. Every level of the curving stair provides glimpses of the outside. The seating is from Dialogica; the coffee table was designed by the architect Eric Owen Moss. (Photograph: © Scott Frances/ESTO)

8.17 Regional traditions lead to design developed around locally available materials. Bamboo is an exotic material in Europe and America, but in this house near Sanur, Bali, Balinese designer Putu Suarsu makes it the dominant material, giving the space its special

character. The natural materials tile and brick add their warmth to the space. The house dates from 1986; many of the objects are antiques from the Indonesian islands. (Photograph: Tim Street-Porter)

thin sheet material of great strength and excellent resistance to scratching or other damage. Plastic laminates are generally bonded to an understructure of plywood or particleboard.

MATERIAL SELECTION

For any given use, a short list of widely accepted materials will usually come to mind, making selection of the specific material for a particular purpose a matter of common usage, personal preference, or habit. Unfortunately, this often leads to unimaginative or cliché selections, to the neglect of less familiar possibilities that may offer real advantages, or, at worst, to downright mistakes when a chosen material fails to perform as desired. Many of the most common complaints about interior projects relate to materials that fail in one way or another—that break, wear out, attract dirt, prove hard to clean and maintain, or in some other way create problems that could have been avoided.

Evaluating Materials

These problems can be guarded against by using a mental (or actual) checklist in evaluating each choice. Materials are usually chosen to satisfy their primary role—a floor material to be practical to walk on; a window material to admit light; a door material to provide closure. Problems are most likely to arise in connection with *secondary* criteria, which may be overlooked if one focuses on primary function and appearance alone. An otherwise satisfactory floor material may become dangerously slippery when wet; an attractive wall surface may become marred easily and be hard to clean; carpet selected for its surface appearance and color may show dirt and wear. It is an important part of the interior designer's work to be alert to such issues and to deal with them by learning all of the characteristics of the materials chosen.

The following is a checklist of criteria for material selection:

FUNCTIONAL CRITERIA
 Primary: Suitability to basic utilitarian purpose
 Secondary:
  Durability in anticipated use
  Ease of maintenance, repair, cleaning
  Resistance to damage and vandalism
  Safety characteristics (accidents, fire)
  Acoustical performance
AESTHETIC CRITERIA
 Availability of desired natural or applied colors
 Textures
 Possibilities of pattern
 Visual suitability to intended function
ECONOMIC CRITERIA
 First cost
 Lifetime cost in relation to expected durability and estimated
  cost of maintenance, cleaning, repair, and future
  replacement

These matters are interrelated in complex ways, making judgment and selection difficult. For example, the desired appearance may conflict with the material's functional practicality or cost. The relative importance of various criteria will change with the intended use. Fire safety may be of minor importance in a one-story residence but significant in a high-rise office or hotel. The presence of a sprinkler system can reduce fire safety to an incidental value. The impact of cost will vary with available budget, while lifetime cost will weigh more strongly on a project planned for long use than on one destined to have a shorter span of usefulness. Vandalism, a factor in public spaces in modern cities, rarely impinges on a private home or office. Acoustical qualities may be vital in a concert hall, significant in an office or home, but of little importance in a shopping center. Durability can influence aesthetic values, as some materials wear or age in a way that is visually acceptable (wood, wool, natural leather) while other materials grow unattractive and shabby long before they actually wear out (some carpets of synthetic yarns).

Materials in Their Setting

Along with all the practical matters involved in material selection, some intangibles affect the concept of appropriateness. The impacts of climate, regional traditions, and location, for instance, can be strong influences. Rough white plaster walls, tile floors, and a wood-beamed ceiling suggest a Mediterranean or other semitropical location. Sliding screens, mats on the floor, and austerely simple forms and natural colors suggest Japan (fig. 8.19). A country cottage or farmhouse calls for material choices different from those customary for a town house or city apartment. It is possible, of course, to create the look of a Mediterranean villa in a northern city high rise or a Scandinavian modern space in California or Mexico City, but such unexpected concepts raise questions about their suitability.

There are also traditional usages for certain spaces in relation to their materials. Dark wood paneling, with its air of sober formality, has often been adopted for a conservative boardroom or law office or for the library in a rather formal home; for the same reasons it would seem out of place in a children's playroom or a fast-food restaurant. Glittering materials (brass, mirrors, crystal) suggest a casino, an opera house, or a shopping center; in a library, a hospital, or a country cottage they would seem inappropriate.

It is a useful exercise to develop material selection (and color choices, since the color of materials will influence the color scheme; see Chapter 9, "Color") for various kinds of spaces without reference to actual design. In the process, ideas about what is appropriate will emerge quite strongly. A list for this experiment might include:

 A LIVING ROOM IN A COUNTRY HOUSE IN MAINE
 THE BOARDROOM OF A MAJOR CORPORATION
 A SMALL KITCHEN IN A CITY APARTMENT
 A HOSPITAL PATIENT'S ROOM IN A SMALL SOUTHERN CITY
 A JAPANESE RESTAURANT
 AN OFFICE FOR AN EXECUTIVE OF A COSMETICS FIRM
 A BEDROOM FOR A YOUNG CHILD
 AN IRS TAX-AUDIT SERVICE OFFICE
 A FASHION BOUTIQUE

8.18

8.19

Many others may come to mind as devices for demonstrating the visual impact of material selection. While it is important to avoid cliché material choices, total disregard for widely accepted traditions of usage may lead to bizarre results.

Genuine versus Imitation

The idea that materials should be what they appear to be has wide acceptance as a basic value in design. Some designers even insist that *all* materials be used only in their own natural color; they develop color schemes through choosing materials with their natural colors in mind. This may be problematic in the case of synthetics. Plastic laminate, for example, can hardly be said to have a "natural" color; its use requires acceptance of an artificial color and perhaps of texture or pattern as well.

Most designers prefer to avoid materials that attempt to imitate some other material in an artificial way. Fake materials tend to degrade the quality of the space where they are used. Many modern materials are made with the specific purpose of mimicking some other, usually superior (and more expensive) material. Linoleum is produced in patterns that imitate tile, wood boards, parquet, or marble. Wallpaper can be found that imitates wood boards, marble, tile, or brick. Some plastic sheeting is embossed to imitate the texture and mortar joints of brickwork. Imitation wood beams of plastic can be glued to ceilings to suggest structure that does not exist. Serious design work of good quality rejects all such imitations as cheap, shoddy, and generally of such poor appearance as to fool no one.

Every designer has to make decisions about where to draw the line on the issue of imitations. Is a plastic laminate that imitates a wood veneer satisfactory as a tabletop or desktop material? Are paper-thin wood tiles that imitate parquet acceptable since they really *are* made of wood? Is a plastic material that imitates leather a satisfactory alternative to the real thing? What about false wormholes in the *distressed* finishes applied to some antique reproductions? Such questions may have to be decided on a case-by-case basis, but it generally makes sense to minimize or avoid imitations wherever possible.

Some imitations can be seen in another light. We know that painted imitations of marble were often used in Baroque churches and that Early American floors were sometimes painted in patterns to suggest tiles. The aim in these instances, however, was not so much to deceive as to elicit delight in the maker's skill, as is the case with *trompe l'oeil* painting (see fig. 4.23) and the art of theatrical scene painters.

If plastic is to replace leather, a plain surface or texture is preferable to one that tries to mimic pigskin or elephant hide. Laminates come in plain colors and in patterns that are purely geometric rather than imitative. Plastic butcher block or knotty pine, linoleum marble or flagstone, simulated brick and tile, fake fireplaces, and plastic plants have no place in a well-designed interior.

On the other hand, the changing of color through dyeing (of textiles, carpets, and similar elements) and the changing of a surface through materials such as paint and wallpaper have come to be widely accepted. Most surface materials have appearance characteristics that make it clear that they *are* surface. A tiled wall does not suggest that the wall is tile all the way through. Wood paneling looks very different from struc-

8.18 The gleaming marble of the majestic Ionic columns echoed in the carved fireplace mantel, the hardwood parquet floor, the generous reading tables, and the Windsor armchairs all set a tone of dignity consistent with the main reading room of the New York Bar Association library. The building was originally designed by Cyrus L. W. Eidlitz in 1895. James Stewart Polshek and Partners, Architects, were responsible for the 1984 renovation that introduced lively wall colors and modern lighting. (Photograph: © Elliott Kaufman)

8.19 The special aesthetic of the traditional Japanese interior is defined by the use of natural materials left in their own subtle, natural colors. For the Urasenke Tea Ceremony Society of New York (1981), Jeremy P. Lang Architects employed wood, sliding paper-and-wood shoji, and woven tatami on the floor in simple geometric forms to develop a serene visual harmony with its basis in Japanese aesthetic traditions and philosophy. (Photograph: © Stan Ries, courtesy Jeremy P. Lang Architects)

8.20

tural woodwork. Even stone used as a surface material (in large, thin sheets) looks quite different from the smaller blocks of actual stone construction. The idea that structural and surface materials *should* look different has been a recognized design principle for many years.

MATERIALS IN RELATION TO ELEMENTS

Each element, whether structural or nonstructural, is composed of one or more materials. As previously mentioned, the structural elements in a space are usually the result of architectural decisions over which the designer has little control. However, since elements can be modified through surface treatment, which can make drastic changes in appearance, the designer has a wide range of choices:

> LEAVE MATERIAL EXPOSED in its natural, unfinished state or, if already covered, uncover to expose it. (Brick, stone, wood, even concrete are often used in this way.)

> TREAT EXPOSED, NATURAL MATERIALS with a finish chosen to preserve their natural appearance while protecting against wear and dirt. In practice,

such natural finishes will change the color and appearance of the material to some degree, usually darkening the color somewhat. (Typical finishes of this kind are wax, oil, and various clear varnishes and lacquers.)

> COAT EXPOSED MATERIALS with a finish that covers and seals the surface and hides it with a colored pigment (usually paint). Even when the color is changed, the texture of the material shows—that is, a red brick wall painted white (or any other color) still looks like brick. Paint tends to hide construction details, such as mortar joints, and may change texture.

> COMPLETELY COVER OVER MATERIALS with a layer of a second covering material. (Examples are wood veneered or covered with plastic laminate; wallpaper or plastic sheet material on walls; carpeting on a floor.)

> In many situations, a basic, often structural material is hidden by another structural layer. Such a covering layer of material may then be finished with still another coating. (In a wooden house, the wood studs and joists of wall, ceiling, and roof construction are usually covered by lath and plaster or, in modern practice, plasterboard, which is then finished with another material such as paint. Steel structural columns are wrapped with an insulating material for fire protection, which is in turn covered by a material chosen for its finished appearance.)

8.20 *The cool gray of concrete and the warm colors of natural wood set off the spectacular natural landscape surrounding a bedroom of the Post Ranch Inn, a luxury resort in Big Sur, California. Mickey Muennig was the architect and Janet Gay Freed the interior designer for this 1992 project. (Photograph: © Larry Dale Gordon 1992)*

8.21 *Interesting results can be achieved when materials are used in unorthodox ways, as in this balcony railing made of perforated steel, a material typically associated with High Tech design. A kitchen can be seen in* the background. Hodgetts + Fung Design Associates were the architects and designers for this California residential project. (Photograph: Tim Street-Porter)

8.22

The following survey discusses the major interior elements, and the most common materials and finishes used for each.

WALLS

Load-Bearing Walls

Since they support floors and roofs, load-bearing walls must be of considerable structural strength. Their material has usually been determined by the architectural design of a building. The primary material, often covered and concealed by finish materials, can be an important interior element when left exposed. Common examples are:

- BRICK
  Exposed or painted.
- CONCRETE BLOCK
  Exposed or painted. It is usually left exposed only in utilitarian spaces such as garages or basements.

- CONCRETE
  Mass or reinforced.
- STONE
  Available in varied colors and textures. Fieldstone (figs. 8.8, 8.22), laid up, or constructed, in a variety of ways, from very rough to more regularly patterned courses, or layers. Ashlar, or neatly cut stone, is often used in monumental architectural spaces.
- WOOD
  Large frame members and planking of post-and-beam construction, exposed or finished (see fig. 8.1). Most common carpenter-built construction is usually concealed.

Partition Walls

Partition walls (or simply partitions) typically have an inner, hidden support structure and an outer surface which, in turn, may be covered with a surface finish. The same combination of materials that makes up a partition is often used to line (and thus conceal) bearing-wall materials (see fig. 14.20).

8.22 The wall and fireplace here are of rough-cut limestone. The exposed stonework in this 1849 house in Castroville, Texas, establishes an informal, rustic quality. (Photograph: Copyright © 1985 Michael Skott)

8.23 Office partitions of several heights and with stepped profiles give various levels of privacy in these offices designed by Gensler and Associates/ Architects for the Computer Systems Development Facility of the Crocker

National Bank in San Francisco in 1982. The partition units are of conventional drywall construction. Glass panels can be added to make a full wall, providing additional privacy. (Photograph: Jaime Ardiles-Arce)

8.24 Privacy in open-plan offices can be achieved as needed by means of flexible office partition systems. The solid, opaque, and clear-glass panels of this partition are part of a system that includes furniture designed by William Stumpf for Herman Miller. (Photograph: Peter Kiar, 1985, courtesy Herman Miller, Inc.)

8.23

8.24

8.25

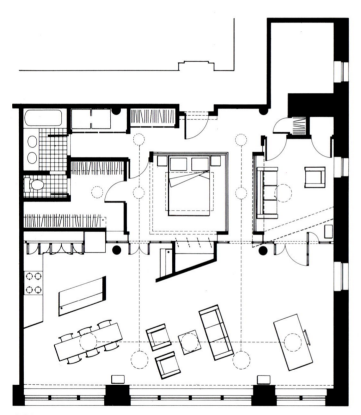

8.26

8.27

8.25, 8.26 In a New York residential loft, a dividing wall using alternating panes of clear and translucent glass offers a wide variety of options. The French doors on the left can be opened or closed to provide more or less privacy; the door on the right pivots on a third point and can be opened to form a 90-degree angle to the wall. In addition, some of the individual glass panels swing open to provide ventilation. (Photograph: © Andrew Garn, courtesy Metropolitan Home) In the floor plan (fig. 8.26), the wall, can be seen to bisect the space from left to right, separating the open living-dining area from the more private, subdivided areas of the loft. Design was by William McDonough Architects and designer Robert Currie. (Plan courtesy William McDonough Architects)

8.27 Sliding glass doors can convert a space from an open garden pavilion into an enclosed room. A new owner required that an existing (1955) house by the famous architect Mies van der Rohe be expanded to provide entertaining and guest rooms. Peter L. Gluck and Partners, architects for the 1981 project, left the original house untouched, adding instead a two-pavilion complex adjacent to the original building. In his Tugendhat House of 1930 in Brno, Czechoslovakia, Mies himself set the precedent for entire walls of sliding doors. (Photograph: © Paul Warchol)

8.28

8.29

WOOD STUDS. Wood strips, usually 2-by-4-inch studs spaced 16 inches apart, are the most common partition structure in nonfireproof construction. They provide space for pipes, wiring, and ducts. Where drainpipes are to be run within a partition, 2-by-6-inch studs are used. A double wall with two separate sets of studs can improve acoustical isolation between spaces.

METAL STUDS. Steel studs are used in place of wood to offer improved fire-resistance while still providing hollow space within a partition's thickness for pipes, ducts, and wiring.

GYPSUM BLOCK. This light masonry material, used only in partition-wall construction, gives superior fire-resistance and acoustical control and provides a sturdy surface for plaster or other surface treatment.

CONCRETE BLOCK. (Usually cinder-concrete block.) A masonry block even heavier and more solid than gypsum block, it is used for spaces that need particularly good isolation, such as fire stairs, elevator shafts, and machinery rooms.

LATH AND PLASTER. The traditional partition surface of older construction is wood lath supporting a covering of plaster applied by hand, wet, in several coats. More modern lath may be a perforated gypsum board or an expanded metal mesh. Metal lath is usually used over metal studs to provide good fire-resistance. Lath and plaster may be used to line bearing walls as well. Plaster may be applied directly (without lath) to gypsum or concrete block. High labor costs and slow drying time have tended to discourage the use of plaster walls.

DRYWALL. This is the term given to the most common alternative to stud and plaster partition construction (fig. 8.23). Studs (wood or metal) are covered with sheets, usually 4 by 8 feet, of plasterboard, a factory-made sheet composed of gypsum plaster sandwiched between sheets of a special heavy paper. This wallboard can be cut and nailed in place quickly and easily. Joints are covered with a special tape and both joints and nailheads are covered with a plasterlike compound, producing a fairly smooth wall. Drywall partitions often show some bulges or waves, and the marks of joints and nailheads may also show up. Cracking is, however, less likely than in lath and plaster surfaces.

MOVABLE PARTITIONS. These are factory-made products available as complete systems that incorporate doors, glass panels, and, usually, provision for wiring. The prefabricated elements can be taken apart and reused in new locations and arrangements as necessary. Metal or metal and glass are the most usual materials. Movable partitions are most widely used in office installations (fig. 8.24).

FOLDING PARTITIONS. Also factory-made products, these use panels or accordion-folding elements that slide on ceiling or floor and ceiling tracks to make it possible to combine or separate adjacent spaces at will. Both appearance and acoustical performance of folding partitions tend to be problematic, but their use is common where a special functional need requires this kind of flexibility, as in making dining or conference rooms larger or smaller to suit the needs of various groups.

TOILET PARTITIONS. Another factory-made system product, these provide panels and doors for the stalls and screen elements used in public toilet facilities. Metal with baked enamel finish is the most usual material, although slate and marble were once common and are still used occasionally.

GLASS. In addition to its use in movable partitioning (figs. 8.25–8.27), glass can be used with wood or metal framing to create walls that offer transparency or translucency in varying degrees. Glass is

8.28 Large-scale glass block is used in this restaurant for an internal screen-partition wall. The area beyond can be seen, but the ripple texture of the block distorts the visual image in a way that adds interest to the sense of space. The 72 Market Street restaurant in Venice, California, is a 1983 design by Michael Rotondi and Thom Mayne of Morphosis. (Photograph: Tim Street-Porter)

8.29 Glass blocks are produced in a variety of sizes, shapes, and textured patterns. Their hollow construction makes them good insulators; they block vision but admit light and generate interesting patterns. (Photograph courtesy Pittsburgh Corning Corporation)

available in a wide range of colors and textures and in shatterproof form. Glass partitions can also be built up of *glass block,* a masonrylike material providing translucency and a unique appearance (figs. 8.28, 8.29).

Wall Finishes

Surface or finishing materials applied to bearing walls or partitions usually become important ingredients of any completed interior. Because many of these finishes can be renewed and changed with ease and at modest cost, they are adaptable to frequent redecoration schemes. Table 7 on page 229 lists the primers and finish coatings most commonly used in interiors.

PAINT. This is probably the most widely used of wall (and ceiling) finishes. An infinite range of color possibilities and some variety in available texture, along with low cost and easy renewal, make paint endlessly adaptable. Top-quality paints justify their extra cost because of their ease of application and durability. Better paints offer a wide choice of ready-mixed or custom-mixed colors. Special colors can be mixed on the job by skilled painters.

WALLPAPER. This surface material offers a vast variety of textures, patterns, and imagery, making it a popular alternative to paint. Wallpaper was widely used during some historic periods, and reproductions of many excellent historic designs continue to be available (fig. 8.32). Color and pattern coordination with printed textiles is offered by some manufacturers. Intelligent use of wallpaper can avoid some of the mistakes of unsuitable use and inferior patterns that have sometimes given this material a bad reputation with modern interior designers.

WOOD. Paneling, whether in designs using elaborate moldings and joinery or in simple flush designs, is a valued wall surface treatment (fig. 8.33). It usually suggests opulence and luxury. Traditional paneling is assembled from rails and panels of solid wood. Plywood is often used for modern paneling, but simulating traditional designs by applying moldings to plywood leads to unfortunate visual results. The simple paneling of solid boards, tongue-and-grooved together or with moldings or reveals at joint lines, is also in wide use. Prefinished paneling tends to be of poor appearance, especially in the more inexpensive forms. Simulated wood finishes are particularly objectionable, and knotty pine, whether genuine or simulated, has been so overused as to become a cliché.

Natural finishes or stains that show the grain of the wood are most often used for paneling, but paint finishes are also appropriate and have been widely used in traditional interior design.

TILE. A vast variety of tiles, from tiny mosaic to large squares and rectangles, in many colors, textures, patterns, and materials, can be used as wall surface treatments. Tile is particularly suited to wet, humid locations with water splash and steam, typically kitchens, bathrooms, areas around pools, and similar spaces. Decorated and painted tiles can approach an art form. Spanish or Dutch painted tiles suggest specific

periods and countries; at their best, they are objects of collectors' interest.

MIRROR. This form of glass has a special interest as a wall material because of its ability to create the illusion of increased space. Floor-to-ceiling and wall-to-wall mirrors double space visually (fig. 8.30). Parallel mirrors placed opposite each other generate an illusion of endlessly continuing space. Tinted, *antique,* and small squared mirrors create other visual effects. As mirror has been overused and misused, its selection should be considered carefully.

PLASTIC. Vinyl and other plastic sheet materials are in wide use as wall coverings, both for their ability to resist damage and for the variety of color and textural patterns they offer. Many plastic wall coverings simulate other materials, such as grass, cloth, canvas, suede, even metals. Once damaged, plastic materials are more difficult to repair than painted surfaces.

FABRIC. A traditional material for wall covering, fabric offers a fine variety of colors and textures. Silks, satins, and brocades were often used in luxurious interiors of traditional design. Simple canvas can be used as a base for paint, providing a reinforced wall surface and a subtle texture. Genuine grass cloths and varieties of burlap, although now widely imitated in plastic, remain fine wall-covering possibilities.

8.30

8.30 Large areas of mirror visually repeat an interior, effectively doubling its space. This high, narrow room appears more spacious than it is, with the glass-block wall and marble-topped desk extending into their mirrored doubles. Gwathmey Siegel & Associates were the architects for this 1981 executive office for the Evans Partnership, Montvale, New Jersey. (Photograph courtesy Gwathmey Siegel & Associates)

8.31

8.32

8.33

Table 7. Interior Primers and Finish Coatings

Interior Primers

Primer	Description	Frequent Use
Wall primers		
Latex	Quick-drying, offers excellent alkali resistance. Provides for ease of equipment cleaning.	Drywall, brick, metal
Alkyd	Made from odorless alkyd, somewhat slow drying.	May be applied over partially cured plaster and metal.
Alkali	Alkali-resistant content based on butadiene-styrene copolymer or chlorinated rubber.	Masonry, but do not use below-grade.
Wood primers		
Enamel undercoat	Provides a low gloss and a hard film that prevents penetration of the enamel paints that may be applied as top coats.	Excellent on surfaces that require a smooth finish.
Paste wood fillers	Made from transparent and coarse pigment held together with a binder.	Used on open-grain woods. Provides added color and smoothness.
Clear wood sealer	Transparent pigment often added to reduce penetration and improve sealing.	Often used under clear wood finishes.
Masonry primers		
Cement grout	A thin mortar applied with a brush or trowel.	Used to provide a smooth surface to rough masonry.
Block fillers	Composed of either latex or a solvent-thinned epoxy-ester. Relatively thick and applied with a brush or roller.	May be applied to damp surfaces. Provides resistance to alkali.

Interior Finish Coatings

Finish	Description	Frequent Use
Gloss enamels		
Enamels	Usually alkyd enamels that are very resistant to yellowing and alkaline cleaners.	Brick, wood, particleboard, metal, plywood
Floor enamels	Alkyd enamels are abrasion-resistant but will blister and peel if wet. Alkali-resistant enamels are abrasion-resistant but provide poor resistance to solvents. Epoxy or urethane enamels are abrasion-resistant and not affected by water or solvents. Latex floor paint provides good abrasion resistance.	Masonry, wooden floors
Dry fallout spray gloss	Similar to gloss enamels, but dries very rapidly.	Walls
Semigloss		
Semigloss enamel	Alkyd-based product with good gloss retention, also grease and alkali resistance.	Woodwork, trim
Semigloss latex	Has moderate hiding power, ease of application and clean-up, rapid cleaning, low odor.	Drywall, plaster, wood, plywood
Dry fallout spray semigloss	Provides a moderate gloss level.	Walls, ceilings
Flat finishes		
Alkyd flat	Superior to latex paints in hiding power and washability. Odorless, but should be used in well-ventilated areas.	Drywall, brick, wood, metal, plywood
Latex flat	Good hiding power, spreadability, odorless. Requires special primers prior to application on porous surfaces. Do not apply in extreme temperatures.	Plaster, drywall, brick, masonry

8.31 In a house on the island of Nantucket, Massachusetts, the structural elements—walls, floor, and ceiling—are all surfaced in wood. The furniture, although not of the rustic character that might be expected, relates well to the setting. The four-poster beds are in the Federal style popular in America in the early nineteenth century. Design was by Denning-Fourcade, Inc. (Photograph: © William Waldron, courtesy HG)

8.32 William Morris, a founder of the Arts & Crafts movement, created many richly ornamental designs for wallpaper. This 1875 pattern, called Marigold, was used for both wallpaper and textiles.

8.33 Interior designer Mark Hampton made modern use of dark wood paneling in the library of a brownstone apartment in 1985. The contrast between the colorful Oriental rug and upholstery and drapery fabrics and the dark wood dispels any hint of heaviness or gloom. (Photograph: © Robert Levin)

Table 7. Interior Primers and Finish Coatings (Continued)

TRANSPARENT FINISHES

FINISH	DESCRIPTION	FREQUENT USE
VARNISHES		
FLAT OR SATIN	Flatting agent added that makes it less glossy in finish than glossy varnishes. Mar-resistance is inferior to gloss varnish.	All types of wood surfaces
COUNTER OR BAR VARNISH	Dries very hard and is resistant to alcohols. Made from polyurethanes sand polyesters.	Bar tops
PENETRATING SEALERS	Very thin varnishes that are applied and removed while the surface is still wet. Fair resistance to marring.	All types of open-grain woods
SHELLAC	Often used as a "wash" coat on wood surfaces before final sanding. Fast-drying, light-colored, but has a poor resistance to abrasion, water, and alcohols.	Wood, plaster, drywall, brick, plywood
LACQUERS		
STANDARD	A coating material with high nitrocellulose content that is modified with resins and plasticizers. Good durability, but little resistance to chemicals. Dries quickly and is easy to repair. Increases flammability of surfaces.	Wood furniture and paneling
CATALYZED	Superior to standard lacquer in resistance to chemicals.	Wood furniture and paneling
VINYLS		
CATALYZED	A clear converting catalyst vinyl coating. Fast-drying and highly resistant to abrasion.	Wood furniture and paneling

STONE. Although usually thought of as a structural material, stone in thin sheets is a possible wall covering. Marbles in varied colors and veining patterns are particularly appealing. Travertine, either filled or with an open, porous texture, is often used as a wall surface in monumental spaces.

DOORS

Walls require openings for access. Doorways provide access to a space, and doors control access. Door frame and door, usually thought of as a unit, are often manufactured and sold together. The selection and specification of a door can be more complex than might be expected. In addition to the door itself and its frame, the designer must choose a knob, a lock, and hinges. Optional items include the saddle (threshold), push and kick plates, closer, panic bolt, alarm gear, and other items that may affect fire safety, security, and performance.

Door Materials
Most doors are made of the following materials:

WOOD. Doors may be of panel construction (composed of *stiles*, or vertical members, and *rails*, or horizontal members, into which are inserted thinner panels) or *flush* (that is, smooth of surface and seemingly of one piece). Flush doors may be of solid (heavy) or hollow-core

8.34 This medieval, nail-studded door is, in fact, a fantastically successful trompe l'oeil done on an ordinary plain panel. David Fisch was the artist. (Photograph: © Jeff Blechman)

8.34

8.35

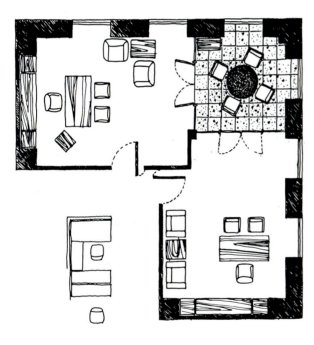

8.36

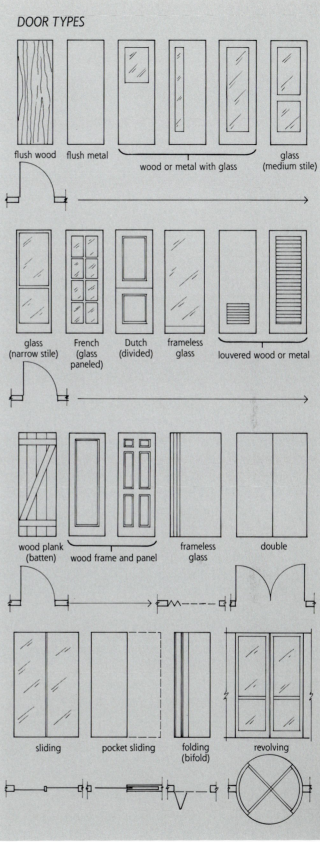

DOOR TYPES

flush wood   flush metal   wood or metal with glass   glass (medium stile)

glass (narrow stile)   French (glass paneled)   Dutch (divided)   frameless glass   louvered wood or metal

wood plank (batten)   wood frame and panel   frameless glass   double

sliding   pocket sliding   folding (bifold)   revolving

8.37

8.35, 8.36 A conference dining area located at a corner between two adjacent executive offices (fig. 8.35) is accessible to both through double, hinged doors (one is visible at left), while blinds over the glass partition safeguard each office's privacy. In the plan of the space (fig. 8.36), the con-ference-dining area is at the upper right corner; the adjacent executive offices are below it and to its left. Charles Kratka Associates designed the offices for Times Mirror, New York, in 1984. (Photograph: Jon Naar, courtesy Charles Kratka Associates)

8.37 Various types of commonly used doors, including solid, all-glass, and partial-glass types, are shown in elevation above, with the architectural plan symbols that represent them below.

8.38

8.38 This Spanish-style California house of the 1920s was renovated by designers Sussman & Prejza in 1986 for their own use. The steel-framed window and French doors now boast red-painted frames that pleasantly modulate the view into the garden beyond. Related color in the floor, upholstery fabric, accessories, and the window and painting on the right unify the space. (Photograph: Tim Street-Porter)

8.39

(lighter) construction. Surfaces may be of genuine wood veneer or the more durable plastic laminate. They may be finished with stain (leaving the natural look of wood) or paint. It is possible to design wood doors of unusual shape, size, or surface design. Where heavy two-way traffic is anticipated, a small glass window in an otherwise solid door is often introduced to discourage collisions.

METAL. Metal doors, usually of hollow steel construction with a solid fiber infill, are sturdy and have been rated for fire safety. Finish may be paint or plastic laminate.

GLASS. Glass doors are usually framed in wood or metal (fig. 8.38), although frameless tempered glass doors are also widely used (these require safety precautions; see Chapter 7, page 194). Glass may be colored or patterned; frames may be simple or decorative in design.

Door Types

Special types of doors (fig. 8.37), which may be of any appropriate materials, include:

DOUBLE DOORS (fig. 8.35).

SWINGING DOORS. Hinged doors swinging inward or outward or in both directions.

SLIDING DOORS. These avoid the space-consuming outward swing of a hinged door. A single sliding door requires a *pocket*, or hollow space in the thickness of the adjacent wall, to slide into. Paired sliding doors (or a grouping of more than two) can slide over one another. While this requires no pocket, it limits the opening to 50 percent of the total

8.39 Levelor vertical blinds are used in the 1980 guest bedroom of a Coconut Grove, Florida, apartment. The designer, Juan Montoya, explained that the blinds "were used to create blades of light and shadows at night." The construction of the Italian beds allows the slipcovers to be easily removed for cleaning. The chair is a replica of the desk chair used on the French liner Normandie of the 1930s. (Photograph: Norman McGrath, courtesy Juan Montoya)

width. Such doors run on tracks that place the alternate doors in different planes. Special hardware permits setting paired sliding doors flush when closed and then angles the tracks slightly to allow the doors to slide. Aluminum-framed sliding doors are popular for outside window-door uses. Sliding *shoji* screens, adapted from traditional Japanese practice, can be considered a form of sliding door that permits a flexible subdivision of space.

FRENCH DOORS. Actually long casement windows that extend to floor level, these are simply double, hinged doors of framed glass.

LOUVERED (OR JALOUSIE) DOORS. Usually made of wood, these permit air circulation. They have become popular for closets that require some ventilation.

ACCORDION FOLDING DOORS. A kind of compromise between swinging and sliding doors, they permit full opening but when open do not project into adjacent space as far as conventional swinging doors do.

REVOLVING DOORS. Widely used to control drafts and loss of heat at entrances that handle large numbers of people, they are usually standardized factory-made products which come in many different designs and with varied details.

GATES. These may be regarded as a special type of door. They come hinged or sliding and of various materials and designs. Special forms of roll-up and sliding gates, available for security closure, are often used in addition to more conventional door types.

WINDOWS

An important element in basic architectural design, windows are also important elements in the interiors that they serve. Since windows greatly influence the nature of an interior, designers often change or replace them as part of their design schemes. This alteration concerns both the window itself and the *window treatment,* any additions to the window, such as shades or curtains, that can modify both the appearance and the function of the actual window.

Glass is obviously the primary window material, in the form of *window* (thin) or *plate* (thicker) glass, clear or patterned or *obscure* (not transparent). Virtually unbreakable Lexan plastic has come into use as a glass substitute where breakage is a major problem.

Window Types

Types of windows can best be classified according to how they are framed to hold glass (fig. 8.43).

FIXED GLAZING WINDOWS. Fixed into place, these cannot be opened. They require only simple frames and are widely used where opening capability is not required, as with shopwindows and windows of air-conditioned spaces, or in combination with windows that open.

Fixed glazing requires consideration of means for cleaning, of impact on fire safety (access and escape), and of provision for alternative ventilation in the event of mechanical ventilation system failure.

DOUBLE-HUNG WINDOWS. This type uses the most familiar sash, two up-and-down sliding units giving a 50 percent opening in any combination of top and/or bottom.

CASEMENT WINDOWS. These swing outward or inward like small doors and most often appear in pairs. *French windows* (listed above as doors) are casement windows that extend to floor level (fig. 8.40).

AWNING AND PROJECTED WINDOWS. These have framed units hinged horizontally to swing in or out in various configurations.

JALOUSIE WINDOWS. A special form of awning window, these use many small hinged louvers of glass.

SLIDING WINDOWS. These move sideways on top and bottom tracks. Floor-to-ceiling versions opening to the outdoors are widely used.

All of these window types may use frames of wood, steel, or aluminum. Double-hung and casement windows may use large panes of glass filling each movable unit or have a number of smaller panes set into small frame members called *muntins*. The pattern of windowpanes has a strong impact on the visual effect of windows and can suggest a particular style or period of design. For example, the small panes of Colonial windows are very different from the plate glass of Victorian windows.

Window Treatment

Window treatment (fig. 8.44) serves a variety of purposes, including:

> *CONTROL OF EXCESSIVE LIGHT, SUN, AND GLARE*
> *SCREENING OF THE BLANK NIGHTTIME "BLACK-GLASS" EFFECT*
> *OF EXPOSED WINDOWS*
> *LIMITATION OF HEAT GAIN FROM SUMMER SUN*
> *LIMITATION OF WINTER HEAT LOSS TO COLD GLASS SURFACE*
> *SCREENING OF INDIFFERENT OR UNPLEASANT VIEW*
> *SCREENING FOR PRIVACY OF OCCUPANTS*
> *HIDING OR MODIFICATION OF UNSATISFACTORY WINDOW SHAPE,*
> *LOCATION, OR DETAIL DESIGN*
> *IMPROVEMENT OF BARE OR UNFINISHED-LOOKING WINDOW OPENING*
> *INTRODUCTION OF DESIRED COLOR AND TEXTURE*

Most window treatment calls for adjustability to deal with night and day, summer and winter, and changing conditions of use. A wide variety of blinds, shutters, curtains, and drapery techniques have been developed to deal with these problems. Some of the most useful include:

ROLLER BLINDS (OR SHADES). A piece of cloth or heavy paper on a spring roller, these usually pull down from the top. Variations exist that pull up from the bottom or that have a roller suspended by pulleys, permitting any desired opening, top or bottom. Special roller blinds

8.40

effectively block out light, making them a good choice for spaces used for slide or film projection or where daytime darkening of a bedroom is desired.

ROMAN AND AUSTRIAN BLINDS. These types, which pull up with a cord into accordion folds, are well suited to some traditional interiors.

MATCHSTICK OR SLAT BLINDS. Blinds of thin bamboo or wood strips, they pull up by cord into a roll and make a somewhat informal, as well as inexpensive, simple window treatment.

THERMAL SHADES. Special energy-saving shade materials use plastic sheet or special weaves to provide sun control through tiny microlouvers. Mechanized systems use motors to raise and lower blinds in response to conditions measured by light- or heat-sensitive sensors.

HORIZONTAL VENETIAN BLINDS. These familiar and useful controllers of light and view come with slats of wood, plastic, or aluminum in a wide variety of colors and finishes. Heat- and light-limiting/conducting materials can be added as an energy-conservation measure.

Contemporary design has favored blinds with very narrow slats (about ⅝ inch), which give a particularly neat look.

VERTICAL VENETIAN BLINDS. Widely used in modern interiors, these blinds pull to the side (fig. 8.39). Their louvers come in various widths, materials, and colors.

DRAPERY. This refers to loosely hung fabric, usually heavy and opaque, that can cover an entire window or extend from floor to ceiling or wall to wall. A vast range of fabrics can be used, and fabrics in combination with linings can provide any desired degree of light and privacy control. Sheer fabrics permit light transmission and some degree of see-through vision. Several layers of drapery make different levels of light and view control possible. Since drapery introduces textiles at window openings, it offers color, pattern, and various kinds of trim, making possible a great variety of aesthetic effects (figs. 8.42, 8.45, 8.46). (See Appendix 6, "Estimating Material Requirements.")

CURTAINS. A more modest form of drapery, curtains are usually placed within the window frame, possibly attached to the actual

8.40 In this 1870s residence in Remsenberg, New York, renovated by Hagmann Mitchell Architects in 1985, French doors flank an alcove with double-hung windows on each side of a central, fixed-glass window surmounted by a small lunette window. The bench, side chairs, and table in the alcove are all Biedermeier. The upholstered chairs at the left are Villa Gallia designs by Josef Hoffmann from about 1913. The rugs are contemporary washed Tibetan. (Photograph: © 1985 Frederick Charles)

8.41

window sash. Simple sash, café, lace, and net curtains offer limited light and vision control, often in ways appropriate to historical stylistic treatments.

SHUTTERS. Often also called blinds, these come solid or louvered and appear in many traditional interiors (figs. 8.41, 8.47). They can be used alone or in combination with shades, curtains, or drapery.

SHOJI SCREENS. Screen panels sliding on tracks not only function as shades but also give the window area a special character.

METAL CHAIN DRAPERY. A recent development, links or beads in long strands provide some degree of security protection in the event of glass or breakage.

8.42

8.41 The complex arrangement of shutters in this dining room, in which the upper section can be tilted outward to control daylight, is a traditional Turkish window treatment. The owner/ designer of the 1991 interior in Bodrum, Turkey, was Mica Ertegün of MAC II, New York. (Photograph: Marianne Haas, courtesy Elle Decoration)

8.42 Simple swags of drapery frame windows and introduce overtones of opulence and tradition into an otherwise simple, even austere space. Robinson Mills & Williams of San Francisco were the designers for San Francisco's Fairmont Hotel. (Photograph: Nick Merrick, Hedrich-Blessing)

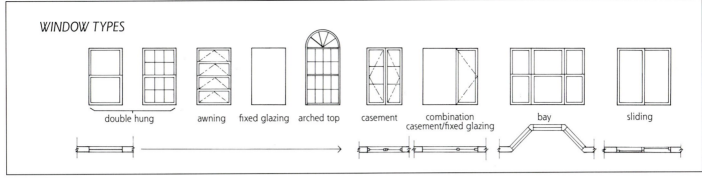

WINDOW TYPES

double hung   awning   fixed glazing   arched top   casement   combination casement/fixed glazing   bay   sliding

8.43

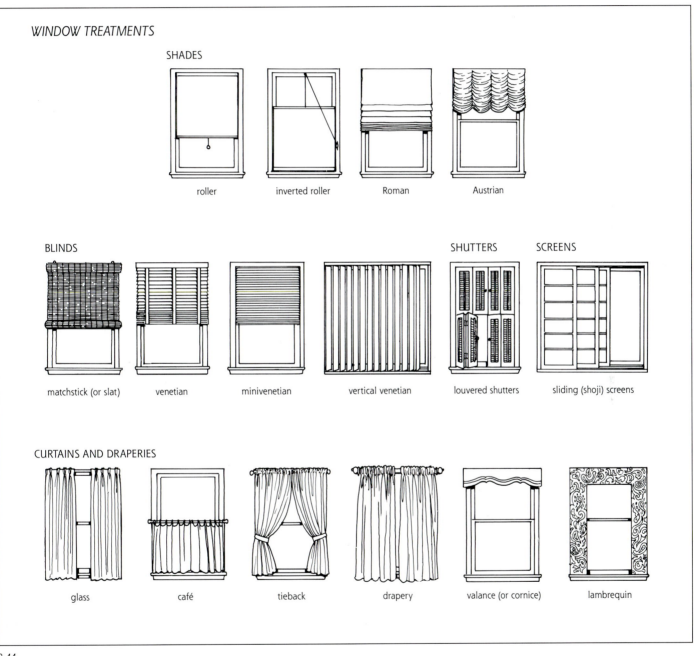

WINDOW TREATMENTS

SHADES

roller   inverted roller   Roman   Austrian

BLINDS

matchstick (or slat)   venetian   minivenetian   vertical venetian

SHUTTERS

louvered shutters

SCREENS

sliding (shoji) screens

CURTAINS AND DRAPERIES

glass   café   tieback   drapery   valance (or cornice)   lambrequin

8.44

8.43 Various types of windows are shown in elevation above, with the architectural plan symbols that represent them below.

8.44 Various types of commonly used window treatments, both hard and soft.

8.45

8.46

8.47

8.45 Photographer Chris Mead conceived this ultrasimple window treatment for his Long Island, New York, home. A rectangle of canvas, used as a shade, is simply buttoned up to admit light. (Photograph: © Chris Mead)

8.46 Mario Buatta designed this elaborately festooned window treatment for a Kips Bay Decorator Show House of 1987 in New York. Formal and highly decorative but of questionable utility, it draws attention to the rich fabric used. (Photograph: © Robert Levin)

8.47 Traditional shutters with adjustable slats, a favorite tropical window treatment, are used in a 1760 house on Martinique. The four-poster beds are equipped with mosquito netting that doubles as ceiling-suspended canopies. Note the tile floor, with its small and simple rugs. (Photograph: Gilles de Chabaneix)

8.48

COLUMNS

Totally bearing-wall structures, including most houses and small buildings, do not require columns. In large modern buildings with frames of iron, steel, or concrete, structural columns that carry the building's weight often stand free in interior spaces. They can be hidden by partitioning, but the large open spaces of stores, offices, lofts, and similar large interiors often leave them exposed.

Columns in older buildings often make use of decorative motifs from historic architecture. Whether plain or decorative, columns invite various treatments, ranging from simply painting the exposed column to wrapping it with materials that cover the original, changing its form and providing it with a surface of any desired materials, textures, and colors.

Steel columns, most often tubular or of H-shaped cross section, may be exposed only in buildings where strict fire-protection rules do not apply. Otherwise, they must be enclosed in insulating materials, which gives them a simple boxlike appearance similar to that of concrete columns. Wood columns (or *posts*) and brick piers also have simple rectangular or square shapes. Their surfaces may be left exposed or covered or wrapped as desired. Many of the techniques for wall treatment apply to columns as well, including paint, wallpaper, wood paneling, metal sheathing, and combinations of such treatments. Columns are sometimes covered with mirror to minimize their visible impact, although the resulting glitter may make the column appear *more* rather than less important.

FLOORS

Along with ceilings, these elements of the interior represent the largest shares of area. Since a space's users come in direct contact with floors, they are usually far more important than ceilings as major design elements. Floors are ordinarily flat, but may include level changes created by raising a false floor in some areas or by depressing floor areas as a part of basic construction. This has been an accepted way to provide a sense of separation between spaces and to introduce spatial variety for aesthetic reasons.

Changing the floor level can present problems, however. A dropped area will reduce the height of the space below and is therefore usually practical only in new construction or in total renovation. In the latter case, it is also likely to be costly, since the old floor must be removed and replaced at the lowered level. A raised area is less problematic, since it requires only the building of a false raised floor on top of the existing floor. There must be sufficient ceiling height to give satisfactory headroom after the raised level is in place.

All floor-level changes require steps or ramps at access points, making them potential accident spots. Small level changes of one or two steps, because they are easy to overlook, cause the most accidents. These should be avoided in public spaces and wherever crowds of people gather. Railings, edge markings, lights, and similar devices at level changes and at edges of raised floor areas offer some protection from accidents.

8.48 A 97-foot-long loft space, now a residence in a reinforced-concrete loft building, gains a special quality from the gargantuan mushroom columns. The columns, typical of warehouse construction, have bush-hammered surfaces that exaggerate their integral texture. The panel leaning against the wall at the right is an acrylic plank sculpture by John McCracken. Frederick Fisher and Eric Orr were the architects for this Los Angeles project. (Photograph: © Timothy Hursley, courtesy House & Garden)

Floor Materials

Most floors are composed of a basic structural material such as wood or concrete, which may be left exposed, treated, or totally covered with a special flooring material. Some heavy flooring materials, such as stone, brick, terrazzo, and ceramic tile, are suitable only to ground-level locations or over heavy subfloors, such as concrete. Lighter floor materials may be considered in almost any location, with selection determined by functional and aesthetic considerations. Widely used flooring materials are:

CONCRETE. This is the basic structural material of floors in most modern buildings, including the *slab on grade* ground floors of many houses. Bare concrete can be troweled to a smooth surface, but is still generally regarded as acceptable only in utility spaces. Concrete floors are usually surfaced with one of the floor coverings or other treatments listed below.

MASONRY MATERIALS. These are widely used to give floors a hard and durable surface. These materials are usually laid over concrete or another subfloor that provides structural support. Typical materials include brick, slate, flagstone (fig. 8.49), marble (including travertine), and granite.

TERRAZZO. A special form of masonry floor surface, it uses marble chips mixed into a cement mortar (fig. 8.51). The mix is then ground and polished to a smooth surface after setting. Metal divider strips subdivide areas to discourage cracks and to create patterns or designs. A wide variety of color and textural effects is possible.

WOOD. A common flooring material, wood may be used as the basic construction and left exposed; as a subfloor and covered with another material; or as a surface material applied over a subfloor. Although not very durable, softwoods are often used for simple board floors, includ-

8.49

8.49 *The massively scaled flagstone flooring, part of Marcel Breuer's original design for his 1967–69 house in Lawrence, New York, dominates and stabilizes the space. The more recent (1981–83) interior design, by Juan Montoya, uses African urns and a coffee table of Montoya's own design. (Photograph: Peter Vitale, courtesy Juan Montoya)*

8.50 *The artist Miriam Wosk used tiles in dazzling colors and patterns suggesting rugs in the floors and stairs of her home in Beverly Hills, California. The interior design is largely her own; the space, a penthouse renovated by Frank O. Gehry, was built onto the roof of an older building. (Photograph: © Grant Mudford, courtesy House & Garden)*

8.53

WOVEN SOFT FLOOR COVERINGS. Matting, rugs, and carpeting are special types of textiles and are made in a bewildering variety of weaves, fibers, colors, and textures.

The term *rug* describes a movable unit of carpet, usually smaller than the room in which it is used. *Area rugs* are often used to help group items of furniture within a larger space, thus defining an area for conversation, dining, or other activities. Rugs are made in a great range of sizes, from very small (often called *mats*) up to room size.

Many popular types of rugs come from particular regions and are made in locally characteristic styles and colors.

Oriental rugs are handmade in various regions of the Near and Far East. Antique and *fine,* or high-quality, Orientals can be very costly; museum-quality examples are viewed, and priced, as works of fine art (fig. 8.52). The names of various types refer to the place of origin and to pattern. Full knowledge of types, quality, and value of Oriental rugs involves extensive study, but a basic ability to recognize quality can be

8.53 *In the home of the late Charles Moore in Los Angeles, California, designed in 1978 by his firm, Moore Ruble Yudell Architects & Planners, antique Oriental plants and rugs soften the modern living space. The ceramic-tile floor can be seen continuing into the garden beyond the sliding glass doors. (Photograph: © 1981 Glen Allison)*

8.54

developed through examination of examples in museums and in the displays of recognized dealers and auction galleries.

Genuine Oriental rugs are handmade in the slow and painstaking process of knotting. A warp is stretched on a loom, the weft threads are woven across at the starting end, and then the yarn tufts that give the rug its pattern and color are inserted and knotted to the warp, one knot at a time. After each row of knots, from one to four weft strands are woven through to build up the rug base before the next row of knots is begun. These knots are visible on the rug's underside and can be counted. Generally, the more knots per square inch, the finer the rug. In a fine rug, there may be as many as 800 knots per square inch—in a 9-by-12-foot rug, 12,441,600 knots! A skilled weaver can tie something like 12,000 knots per day, but even at this rate, such a rug represents about one thousand days of handwork of a highly skilled kind. Oriental patterns are sometimes printed on factory-made rugs, creating a reproduction, usually of inferior quality, which should be clearly distinguished from genuine Orientals.

The Indian *dhurrie* is an inexpensive modern rug type available in simple stripes and patterns and in varied and excellent colors.

Scatter rugs are small units used over other floor materials such as wood, tile, or even carpet. Many types are available in a range of sizes, extending up to area or near-room dimensions. Familiar types include hooked and braided rugs, rya rugs made in Scandinavia, modern handweaves, and rag rugs.

Carpet is the term for floor covering made in continuous rolls, with widths from as little as 27 inches up to *broadlooms* as wide as 18 feet. Modern carpeting is factory-made and is widely used *wall-to-wall* over a floor that need not be of finished appearance. Carpet is made from a number of fibers, both natural and synthetic, and with a variety of con-

structions or weaves. Color and pattern possibilities are almost unlimited, with a wide range of quality and price. The soft texture, feel, and appearance of carpeted floors, their acoustical effectiveness in absorbing sound, and their relative ease of cleaning and maintenance have made them very popular for residential, office, and commercial spaces. Even schoolrooms, hospital rooms, and bathrooms, traditionally thought unsuitable spaces for carpeting, are now often carpeted.

The disadvantages of most older types of carpeting have to do with their absorbent and hard to clean surfaces, which hold spots and odors and form an unsanitary harbor for the growth of bacteria. Modern synthetic fibers and carpet constructions minimize these problems; they can be maintained by simple vacuum cleaning, quite as effective as the washing and waxing required by hard-surface floor coverings and less costly. The ability of carpet to minimize noise from footsteps and furniture movement together with its absorption of sound from other sources makes it an asset in the acoustical ambience of hospitals and schoolrooms. Where sanitation, soiling, and moisture are significant problems, only carpet specially developed for such service should be specified. (See Appendix 6, "Estimating Material Requirements.")

Carpet tile (also called carpet squares) is a recent development in which carpet is made and laid in small units of one to two feet square rather than in wide rolls. Easy replacement of damaged areas, access to underfloor wiring where it is in use, and the possibility of a pleasant tilelike visual pattern are among the reasons for selecting carpet tile. Both glued-down and loose-laid types are in current use.

Underlayment, or cushion, is suggested for use with many carpet types. Special-purpose materials provide additional softness, help to protect and thus extend carpet life, and facilitate the removal of the

8.54 In this living room in the resort town of East Hampton on Long Island, New York, the checkerboard pattern of the linoleum flooring acts as a foil to the simple furniture and the white walls. The painting is by Jack Ceglic, who also designed the room. (Photograph: © Mary Harty/Peter DeRosa, courtesy House & Garden)

carpet itself for relocation or replacement. Various types, made from natural fibers or from rubber, exist. Advice of the carpet manufacturer or supplier about choice of underlay or padding is usually a sound guide to selection.

Table 8 is a guide to the great variety of fibers, constructions, and other characteristics of carpets in current use.

Carpet selection presents a complex problem in which cost and durability must be balanced against one another and related to aesthetic decisions about color, pattern, and texture. The high cost of wool as a fiber has encouraged the acceptance of synthetic fibers, with new forms constantly appearing. New fibers have not had a chance to demonstrate durability over time, but the performance of synthetics has been, to date, disappointing in terms of wear, resistance, ease of cleaning, and the ways in which appearance changes with use. Fire-safety issues also are a cause for concern with many synthetics. In evaluating costs, it is wise to consider life-span cost, including maintenance

Table 8. Carpets

CARPET AND RUG FIBERS

FIBER		CHARACTERISTICS
NATURAL	COTTON	Soft fiber with limited durability. Inexpensive and often used for informal area or scatter rugs. Often dyed in strong colors, as in Indian dhurries.
	WOOL	Best-quality natural fiber. Excellent texture and appearance. Good resistance to soil and wear, appearance survives wear well. Dyes well in wide range of colors. Expensive, standard for top-quality carpeting.
	CELLULOSICS	Hemp, jute, sisal, various grasses. Generally used for informal matting of natural color and texture. Fair to poor durability and resistance to wear and soiling. Inexpensive.
SYNTHETIC	ACRYLICS	Warm, soft textures imitative of wool. Good resistance to soil and wear. Color and texture may be harsh and glossy. Pile subject to crushing. Moderate price.
	NYLON	Most-used fiber for commercial carpet. May be dull to glossy with good color range. Best moderate-price alternative to wool. Resistant to mold and mildew. Static-resistant treatments available where required.
	OLEFIN	Limited color and pattern, some gloss, waxy texture. Water-resistant. Good soil-resistance.
	POLYESTER	Good resilience and texture, soft quality resembling wool. Good soil- and wear-resistance, wide color range. Some crushing possible with wear.
BLENDS		A wide variety of blends combining wool with synthetics or different synthetic fibers is available. The aim is to obtain the best qualities of each fiber while arriving at moderate costs. Wool and nylon and acrylic-nylon blends are most widely used.

CARPET TEXTURES

TEXTURE		CHARACTERISTICS
CUT PILE	PLUSH OR VELVET	Dense pile with surface cut at level height (usually less than one inch). Smooth, velvetlike surface of luxurious appearance. Wears well under moderate traffic.
	SAXONY	Similar to plush but with two or more yarns twisted together to form pile tufts more distinguishable in the surface texture. Pile may be deep but less dense than in high-quality plush or velvet. Medium wear characteristics.
	FRIEZE	Similar to plush but with tightly twisted yarns forming a strongly textured pile with a pebbly appearance. The tight yarn twist generates good wear-resistance, making it suitable for heavy traffic areas.
LOOP PILE	LEVEL LOOP	Uncut loop pile with uniform height loop. When made with quality yarn in high density, this is the most durable and wear-resistant carpet. Suitable to public spaces and other heavy-service contract applications and for areas of the home where heavy use is anticipated (as in kitchens, baths, and family or recreation rooms).
	MULTILEVEL LOOP	Uncut loop pile with loop of varied heights, producing a random or patterned (sculptured) surface.
	TWEED	Uncut loops, larger and with less density than level loop, producing a rougher, more informal or tweedy texture. Usually a lower-cost and less durable carpet type. Yarn tufts of different colors are often mixed to form a pattern.
SHAG		A term for carpet with a very long (over one inch) pile loop (usually cut, but may be uncut or mixed) and with low density, so that the pile lies on its side to give a rough, shaggy appearance. Not suitable for heavy wear applications.
TIP-SHEARED		Mixed cut and uncut pile loops, also called random-sheared. Various textures and patterns are possible. Usually of medium wear qualities.

Table 8. Carpets (Continued)

CARPET CONSTRUCTIONS

CONSTRUCTION		CHARACTERISTICS
WOVEN	WILTON	Woven on a Jacquard loom, permitting up to five or six colors in a pattern design. Top-quality construction, particularly when woven of worsted yarn. Density (and quality) are defined by the number of warp lines per inch, called the pitch. Older Wilton was woven on a 27-inch loom with 256 warp lines, called full pitch. Warp lines (rows or wires per inch) may vary from 13 for top quality to 8 for medium quality. Cut pile is normal. A Wilton with an uncut pile may be called a Brussels carpet. Broadloom widths have been produced.
	AXMINSTER	An industrial weaving technique (now obsolete) permitting great variety in color and pattern, with some similarity to handweaves. Quality is defined by the weft count, given in rows to the inch. The range is from 11 rows (top quality) to 5 rows (lower quality) per inch. Widths up to 12 feet (broadloom) have been produced.
	VELVET	Normally a cut-pile carpet industrially produced in varied color and pattern. (A similar uncut pile weave is called tapestry.) Quality is similar to Axminster, but inferior to Wilton weaves.
TUFTED		This is now the most widely produced type of carpet. Industrially produced in broadloom widths with yarn pushed up through a backing to form tuft loops, which may be cut or left uncut. A latex backing may be added to secure the tufts. The density of the yarn and the height of the pile influence appearance and durability.
NEEDLEPUNCHED AND NEEDLEBONDED		A manufacturing technique using hooked needles to insert fibers into backing. First developed for production of kitchen, bath, and outdoor carpeting of polypropylene fiber, now also used for general-purpose carpet.
KNITTED		Construction superior to tufting in durability, but inferior to weaving. Multiple needles knit pile and backing together, usually with an added latex backing. Loop pile in solid color or tweed is most common.
FLOCKED		Short fibers are stood on end electrostatically and adhered to a backing. Surface resembles a cut-pile velvet. Patterns may be printed on flocked carpet. An economy construction producing carpet of inferior wearing qualities.
HANDMADE	KNOTTED OR TIED	The construction of Oriental rugs, in which the yarn is tied into a woven backing with individual knots. Up to 800 knots per square inch are used in high-quality Orientals. The ends of knots may be cut off to form a pile or the surface may be formed of knots, giving a flat, durable surface.
	WOVEN WITHOUT KNOTS	Kilims and Soumaks are fine Oriental weaves handwoven without knotting. Kilims are thin and light but durable. The Soumak adds a third element to the warp and weft and forms a smooth surface. Soumaks are also sometimes called Cashmeres.
	HOOKED	Tufts of yarn are pushed through a woven backing to form a pattern or pictorial design. A traditional craft technique producing durable rugs or mats, usually of traditional design types.
	BRAIDED	Developed as a means of using discarded fabric remnants by braiding narrow strips together into strips that can be sewn into rugs or mats. Often called rag rugs. A traditional handcraft technique capable of producing work of lively color and charm. Commercially produced imitations are also available.

and repair costs along with estimated durability, before accepting substitutes for wool on the basis of assumed economy. For large projects, laboratory and use testing is advisable before specifying a particular carpet.

ACCESS FLOORING. This is a relatively recent kind of raised floor system often used in modern office design. It involves lift-out floor panels supported by an understructure (see fig. 14.24). The purpose is to provide an underfloor space for wiring and, in some cases, for air and water supply, providing easy access for changes and repairs. Access flooring is most appropriate for computer rooms and office spaces where the use of computers and other electronic devices will be extensive.

STEPS AND STAIRWAYS

These elements can be considered a special form of flooring, since they make use of many of the same materials and surface finish techniques. Stairways may be constructed from wood, concrete, or steel, in accordance with the overall structure of the building in question. Steel stairs may have treads of cement or composition, and exposed surfaces can be covered and finished to suit the intended use. Many steel stairs are factory-made and supplied in prefabricated form for installation on site. Spiral stairs, a favorite for fitting a stair into a limited space, are also available in prefabricated form.

Designing Stairways

Where new steps or stairs are to be constructed, it is necessary to observe the basic dimensional limitations that control the convenience and safety of all stairs. A step is made up of a riser (the vertical surface between stepping surfaces) and a tread (the horizontal step surface). The riser and tread dimensions together establish the slope of the stair and, therefore, the ease and convenience of its use. Riser height should fall within a range of 6 to 9″, 7″ being desirable.

Since all risers in a flight (or *run*) of stairs must be equal, the exact riser height is determined by dividing the total level change into equal units. For example:

GIVEN A LEVEL CHANGE OF 9′8″ (116″) AND TRYING TO GET A RISER HEIGHT
CLOSE TO 7″, DIVIDE 7 INTO 116:

$$\frac{116}{7} = 16.57$$

SINCE THE NUMBER OF RISERS MUST BE A WHOLE NUMBER, EITHER 16 OR 17
RISERS MIGHT BE SELECTED:

$$\frac{116}{16} = 7.25 \quad \text{and} \quad \frac{116}{17} = 6.82$$

THIS GIVES THE CHOICE OF A RISER 6.82″ HIGH OR 7.25″ HIGH.
THE LOWER RISER WILL YIELD A STAIR THAT IS EASIER TO CLIMB.
THE 7.25″ RISER WILL PRODUCE A SLIGHTLY STEEPER STAIR, BUT IT WILL TAKE
UP LESS SPACE BECAUSE THE FEWER RISERS WILL REQUIRE FEWER TREADS.

The number of treads is always one less than the number of risers, since the topmost riser requires no tread.

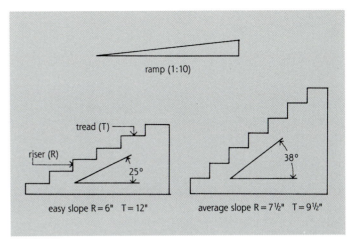

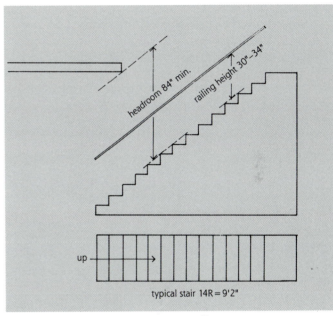

8.55

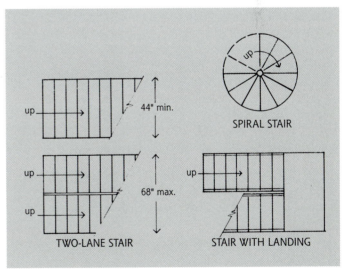

8.56

8.57

8.55 Slopes and riser and tread dimensions for a ramp and typical stairways are given here.

8.56 Railing height and headroom clearance for a typical stairway are shown.

8.57 These drawings represent architectural symbols for several stairway examples.

8.58

Tread dimension is determined in relation to riser dimension. Old rules of thumb for this relationship (which are still in general use) are:

RISER PLUS TREAD SHOULD EQUAL *17 TO 17½"*.
RISER MULTIPLIED BY TREAD SHOULD FALL BETWEEN *70 AND 75"*.

In the example above, if a 7.25-inch riser had been chosen:

$$17-7.25 = 9.75 \text{ and } 17.5-7.25 = 10.25$$

$$\frac{70}{7.25} = 9.66 \quad and \quad \frac{75}{7.25} = 10.34$$

Applying the first rule yields a tread dimension between 9.75" and 10.25", while the second rule gives between 9.66" and 10.34".

Averaging this out, a tread of 10" (a comfortable tread length) might be selected. The total length of the run of stairs, or the amount of space the stairway will actually use, would then be 16 (the number of risers) minus 1, or 15 (the number of treads) times 10", or 150" (12'6"). Treads are often designed to overhang the riser below with a projection called a *nosing*. This overhang dimension is not considered in calculating stair dimensions.

Having established the slope of a stair through tread and riser calculation, the width must be established and the overhead clearance worked out. One person using a stairway needs a width of at least 26"; a stairway permitting two users to pass needs at least 44", although a wider dimension up to 68" is more comfortable. Stairways wider than this must be subdivided by railings so that every user has a rail to grip.

8.58 *In the central rotunda of the Opus One Winery in Oakville, California, a winding stairway provides access to the caves on the lower level. Light pouring into the upper level of the space dramatizes the transition to the cool, dim areas below. The designers were Johnson Fain and Pereira Architects and Planners. (Photograph: Tim Street-Porter)*

8.59 *In spite of their imperfect safety record, spiral stairs continue to be popular for their compact dimensions and their interesting—sometimes spectacular—appearance. This decorative spiral designed by Richard Himmel rises from the corner of the living room of a Chicago duplex apartment to the gallery above. (Photograph: Feliciano, courtesy House & Garden)*

Headroom calls for at least 84" of clearance. The length of a stairwell, or the floor opening through which a stair passes, is determined by the line of headroom as it passes through the structure of the floor above.

All stairways need railings. Stairways that are open at the side require some form of rails or banisters that prevent people from falling. Rail or baluster elements should be carefully spaced so that young children can neither slip through and fall nor catch their heads between elements. Long runs of more than 20 to 24 risers should be broken up into shorter runs with landings. *Winders,* the wedge-shaped treads used in curving stairs, have such a bad record in causing accidents that they are best avoided, especially in public spaces. Objects of breakable materials such as glass and mirror should not be placed close to stairs, and materials that can be slippery, in normal circumstances or when wet, should not be used on or near stairs. Nonslip nosings and tread materials can minimize the risk of slipping.

Ceilings

Inevitably, ceilings form an important aspect of all interiors, at least in terms of square footage. Many ceilings are simply blank, neutral areas, often, like the sky out-of-doors, providing a simple overhead for more complex elements at eye level and below. However, thought and design effort may make the ceiling a more active part of an interior.

A simple and basic issue in ceiling design involves the decision to keep a ceiling as a single plane or to introduce lowered areas (usually called *soffits*) in portions of a space to contrast with areas of full height. The term *cove* is often used for a curved transition from wall to ceiling or for a curved profile where a lowered ceiling makes a transition to a higher ceiling level. A cove is often formed in a pocketlike profile, providing a space where *cove lighting* strips can be concealed to form a source of indirect lighting. Ceiling planes can also slope at an angle, as seen in many attic spaces and spaces with dormer windows. The term *cathedral ceiling* is a rather misleading designation for ceilings that are high and introduce sloping surfaces.

The ceiling plane establishes the height of a space and therefore its volumetric proportions. A maximum height is usually established by structure, but a lower ceiling, called hung or *furred,* can be introduced down to whatever level may be considered minimum headroom (8 feet 2 inches is a commonly accepted minimum, although heights as low as 7 feet 2 inches will not create any physical problem). In setting ceiling height, it is often necessary to consider what is to be placed above the ceiling, since the space between ceiling and structure is commonly used to house ducts, wiring, and plumbing (including sprinkler pipes, when they are used); in addition, many architectural lighting fixtures are recessed up into the *plenum,* or cavity above the ceiling. Dimensional clearances must be sufficient to avoid any interference between these elements and any structural elements, such as beams and girders.

The visible ceiling surface may be smooth and blank, but it may also be studded with such functional elements as lighting fixtures, air-conditioning outlet louvers, sprinkler heads, and audio loudspeakers. It may also take on the functional demands for specific acoustical perfor-

mance. Ceilings of open louvers, slats, or *egg-crate* create a visual overhead plane while permitting easy access to ducts, sprinklers, and other functional elements for economic or technical reasons. Another approach, which finds particular favor in interiors of High Tech character, is to expose all piping, ducts, and other technical elements, possibly painting them with strong colors to make them decorative features rather than offensive necessities to be hidden (see Chapter 14, "Technical Matters").

For purely visual reasons, a ceiling may be ornamented with peripheral moldings, one or more decorative rosettes, or even rich sculptural and painted decoration, as in many historic interiors. Structural elements such as beams may be exposed and, in turn, decorated. Coffered ceilings (with a wafflelike pattern of squares) and the varied and often complex patterns of vaulting, domes, and modern shell structures all form alternative kinds of ceilings. In spaces under the roof level of a building, skylights can be introduced into ceiling design for both practical and visual reasons.

Ceiling Materials

A listing of widely used ceiling materials includes:

PLASTER. A primary traditional material, this is applied wet on lath to achieve both plain and decorated ceilings (fig. 8.61). Plaster moldings and trim are important elements in many historic interiors. As with walls, the scarcity and high cost of the plasterer's skilled labor combined with the plaster's slow drying time discourage its use in modern practice. Moldings of wood or plastic are now sometimes used to patch, repair, or simulate the decorative elements characteristic of plaster. Paint and wallpaper are common finishes.

SHEETROCK OR WALLBOARD. This is now the most common inexpensive material for plain, smooth ceilings similar in appearance to plaster. Its treatment is similar to the same material on walls.

WOOD. This appears as a ceiling material when the beams or joists and planks of wood construction are left exposed. Natural or painted finishes are possible. Wood paneling similar to wall paneling is occasionally used in more traditional interiors (fig. 8.62). An unusual but effective ceiling results from the use of narrow tongue-and-grooved boards of the sort supplied for hardwood flooring, normally used with a natural finish.

ACOUSTICAL CEILING MATERIALS. Special ceiling tile and panels of pressed paper, fiber, and mineral composition have holes or pores that trap and absorb unwanted sound (fig. 8.63). Small tiles (usually one foot square) may have clearly visible round holes or a less noticeable texture of pores suggestive of travertine stone. Bevel-joint lines accentuate the pattern of tiles; flush joints are less visible and suggest a smooth ceiling plane. Similar materials are also made in larger panels (commonly 2 by 4 feet) for use with a system of support structures that can coordinate with lighting fixtures and heat, ventilation, and air-conditioning (HVAC) outlets on the same dimensional module.

8.60

CEILING SYSTEMS. Panel materials (usually with acoustical value), supporting structure, which may be visible or hidden, and, often, lighting and HVAC elements are all integrated into a factory-made product system. It may include visually striking elements such as coffers or other forms. Such integrated systems most often find use in office and other contract or commercial interiors (fig. 8.64).

METAL CEILINGS. Some systems use spaced metal strips with the intervals open to the acoustical material above. Metals such as stainless steel, aluminum, copper, or bronze also find occasional use as surface materials for ceilings. Pressed-metal ceilings (erroneously called *tin* ceilings), once popular Victorian elements, have now been rediscovered.

GLASS. The usual material for skylights, glass is normally set in a framing of wood or metal (fig. 8.60). As skylighting expands to become a total ceiling, it is possible to speak of a glass ceiling—a feature of some famous architectural structures. Glass, mirror, or a plastic substitute as a ceiling material can create spectacular and startling visual effects.

8.60 *The entire ceiling of a kitchen has been turned into a skylight. Cooking thus becomes an almost outdoor activity, particularly pleasant in the southern California climate. Frank O. Gehry was the architect for this Los Angeles project. (Photograph: © 1986 Tim Street-Porter)*

8.61

MISCELLANEOUS ELEMENTS

Of the surprising number of components in an interior, many may seem minor or incidental, but each calls for design attention in terms of material selection and specification. The following is a very condensed list of such elements with some notes on the material selection issues that they involve.

BUILT-IN ELEMENTS. As these usually function as furniture pieces, they are discussed in Chapter 12. Wood, both solid and plywood, is the most commonly used material. Where toughness and durability are of primary importance, plastic laminate is frequently employed as a surface material.

FIREPLACES AND HEATING STOVES. Although more or less obsolescent in a functional sense, fireplaces are still widely valued and used for aesthetic and nostalgic reasons. The materials and designs of fireplaces, hearths, and mantels remain a significant aspect of both traditional and modern interior design. Since the public has become concerned with energy conservation, heating stoves have been rediscovered as economical heating devices and as objects with strong aesthetic appeal. A wide variety of both traditional and modern designs is available.

8.62

8.61 In converting a large mansionlike town house in New York into a group of medical offices, interior designer John F. Saladino retained the ornamented plaster ceilings. The 1986 waiting-room interior displays a compatible, traditional, and rich character in dramatic contrast to the usual drabness of doctors' offices. (Photograph: Peter Vitale)

8.62 The Social Saloon in the transpacific paddle-wheel steamship China, designed and built by William H. Webb in New York in 1867, displays an elaborate, gilded ceiling. The skillful woodwork of ships' joiners and the rich decorative carving seen here were typical of the interiors of nineteenth-

century passenger ships. This relic of what is said to have been the largest wooden ship ever built has been restored (1986) and is now preserved by the Belvedere-Tiburon Landmarks Society in California. (Photograph: Philip L. Molten)

8.63

8.64

8.63 Acoustical ceilings absorb noise in spaces where sound may otherwise reach disturbing levels. In the Merchant & Main Bar & Grill in Vacaville, California, designers James and Robert Tooke used a system ceiling: A grid of metal supports holds squares of sound-absorbent material, which reduces restaurant noise generated by hard, sound-reflective surfaces to a comfortable level. (Photograph courtesy Chicago Metallic Corporation)

8.64 A complex ceiling design uses stepped, recessed panels to create a decorative pattern that incorporates lighting fixtures and air-conditioning supply diffusers. The interior is the Diane von Furstenberg store in New York designed in 1984 by Michael Graves, architect. (Photograph courtesy Michael Graves)

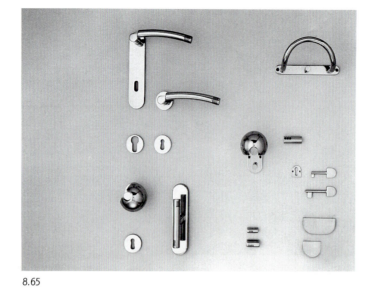

8.65

8.66

TRIM. This is a general term for moldings, cornices, reveals, base-boards, nosings, wainscots, railings, and similar elements used for functional and/or aesthetic reasons. Wood, metals, and plastics are all common materials for elements of trim, which usually are ordered from catalogs but can be custom-designed to fill a particular need.

HARDWARE. This is an important part of every interior. It is customary to distinguish between *builders'* and *cabinet* hardware. Builders' hardware includes doorknobs, hinges, latches, lock sets, and similar items used on architectural elements (figs. 8.65, 8.66). Cabinet hardware includes the hinges, latches, pulls, and many minor devices that are part of furniture and built-in components. The design, materials, and finish of hardware elements form important details of the interior design. Components of fine quality and aesthetic merit are available, but it takes some effort to seek them out and assure their use.

SIGNS AND GRAPHICS. Residential interiors may need no more than a house number or nameplate, but many contract interiors require a large number of directional and identification signs, exit signs, and sometimes sign elements that relate to advertising and display. If left unplanned, these elements can grow chaotic and be distracting. A list of requested sign elements should be drawn up for every project and a careful effort made to design and coordinate their use. A number of sign systems offer materials of high design quality. A fuller discussion of signage and graphic design appears in Chapter 13, pages 406–409.

8.65, 8.66 Serie Otto G hardware by Italian designer Vittorio Gregotti (fig. 8.65) and Serie Otto A hardware by Italian designer Gae Aulenti (fig. 8.66) include door hardware and coat hooks in cast brass, chromium, or nerox plate, which present excellent design alterna-

tives to the bland, largely banal hardware generally available. Because they are in daily use, these objects—usually considered minor design details—have significant influence. (Photographs courtesy Fusital)

8.67 These escalators add a dynamic visual element to the vast, dramatic atrium in the Hong Kong Bank, a 1986 project of the British architectural firm Norman Foster Associates. (Photograph: © Richard Bryant)

MECHANICAL SYSTEMS. HVAC, electrical, and plumbing systems introduce visible elements, such as air louvers, grilles and convectors, switches and outlets, and filters and plumbing accessories, all of which need to be carefully chosen. At worst, these necessities can be unpleasant intrusions into designed space, while at best they can become fine details that enhance the total quality of a completed interior. Detailed coverage of mechanical systems is included in Chapter 14.

SAFETY AND SECURITY EQUIPMENT. Like the visual elements of mechanical systems, fire-alarm boxes, extinguishers, hose cabinets, panic bolts, TV scanners, and similar equipment too often look like afterthoughts and clutter the spaces where they are required. Planned locations and equipment selection are an interior design responsibility. Systems that relate to matters of safety and security are dealt with in Chapter 14, pages 426–28.

VERTICAL TRANSPORTATION. Elevators and escalators (fig. 8.67) are part of many large-scale interior projects. Small elevators are available as possible adjuncts to stairway circulation in residences and other small buildings. Concern with issues of barrier-free access (see Chapter 15) has brought fresh attention to the provision of elevators in both new construction and in renovation of older spaces. Because elevators are costly, demand space, and require regular maintenance, they have in the past been viewed as a luxury needed solely in buildings of more than three-story height. As the only fully practical way of providing barrier-free access to interiors on more than one floor level, however, the use of elevators must be considered in many projects and will become mandatory for most public multistory locations under the provisions of the Americans with Disabilities Act (ADA). If an elevator is to be provided, it should be sized to accommodate an occupied wheelchair (68 inches wide by 51 inches deep, minimum), and call buttons and controls in the elevator cab should be accessible to wheelchair users, with markings in braille or otherwise manually understandable coding for sight-impaired users.

The minimum area occupied by an elevator is determined by the interior dimensions of the cab plus allowances for the cab structure, the tracks and counterweight space in the shaft outside the cab, and the thickness of the shaft walls, making the total plan dimensions of elevator and shaft almost 7 by 9 feet. Space must also be provided for the elevator machinery above or below the top or bottom elevator shaft doors. Because an elevator shaft forms an open vertical stack, special fire precautions are required under building codes. In addition to its size, plan location for an elevator must take into account the fact that the shaft must rise vertically through the floor levels it serves in the same location on each floor. In new construction this obvious need can be readily recognized, but in an existing facility finding a suitable elevator location may be quite difficult and disruptive to other layout considerations.

A number of new types of elevators have appeared in recent years, among them all-glass cabs and shafts, as well as arrangements that permit shafts or cabs to rise in open space (without shafts) in exposed positions in multistory open space. Such open elevators and "bubble" elevators have become spectacular elements in atrium spaces, attract-

ing attention as they move and offering the occupants open views that can make an elevator ride a form of entertainment.

Although elevator manufacturers provide standard designs for doors and cab interiors, designers frequently prefer to substitute special designs to make the experience of elevator use interesting and pleasant. Since the elevator is so often a key step in the transition from arrival in a building to a destination within it, visitors' experiences are strongly affected by elevator design. A shabby and claustrophobic elevator establishes a tone of depression and indifference, while an elevator that is attractive as well as smooth and efficient in operation can make a strongly positive impression.

To aid in planning elevator installations where large numbers of users are to be accommodated, as in tall office buildings, department stores, and concert halls, elevator manufacturers provide highly sophisticated services. Calculations are used to convert estimates of numbers of people to be served into proposals for number and size of elevators and speed of travel. The goal is to minimize waiting—a particularly difficult problem during periods of peak loads, such as the beginning and end of a business day. Minimal waiting may call for an excess of elevators that will be little used at slack hours. Elevator controls are available to improve service through favoring up or down directions, avoiding unnecessary stops, and otherwise expediting operation automatically or with responses to control settings made by a supervisor.

Television surveillance of the interiors of elevator cabs in situations where the confined space of the elevator may attract problems of crime or vandalism is another accommodation to be considered. Elevator security may also be tied into the overall building security systems.

Escalators are more efficient than elevators in moving large numbers of people and are therefore a preferred vertical transport device in such public locations as train and bus stations, air terminals, department stores, access points to underground concourses, and upper and lower levels in shopping malls and similar facilities. Escalators pose hazards to some users with disabilities and are not effective for wheelchair occupants, necessitating supplemental elevator service as a backup alternative. Escalators occupy large areas (in part because of the need for separate up and down units), are costly to install and to operate, and present problems in terms of circulation planning and fire safety. They are nevertheless in wide use in the situations where their performance outweighs all such considerations. Manufacturers provide a variety of standard designs, including use of spectacular materials, transparent side walls, and other features that add to the visual attractiveness of an installation. Special detailing can also be developed to make a particular escalator bank unique to a certain space.

People movers are similar to escalators but provide mechanical transportation on a horizontal plane (with the ability to deal with small level changes). They are useful where large numbers of people must move along long horizontal distances that seem excessive for walking. Airline terminals use people movers to aid passengers in reaching distant gates. Passengers are frequently in a hurry, loaded with baggage, and tend to arrive and depart in "bunches" related to flight times; in such situations people movers can be especially helpful. Although they serve some people with disabilities quite well, for others (including wheelchair users) they are hazardous or unusable.

ENVIRONMENTAL ISSUES

The materials used for an interior design project may have an impact on the environment in a number of ways. In the past, designers have given little thought to such matters, assuming that legal restrictions took care of any issues of importance. However, deepening concern over environmental issues has been propelled by a revitalized awareness of the increasing magnitude of some problems and by dramatic reports of specific cases of unfortunate situations that have been traced to certain materials in common use. A conscientious designer must be alert to environmental issues and will find that a growing number of clients will want to ensure that their own projects will not turn out to be problematic in unanticipated ways.

The environmental issues most pertinent to interior design can be divided into two categories. The first has to do with the impact of material selection and use on larger environmental concerns affecting the population as a whole, such as depletion of resources, consumption of energy, and production of excessive or problematic waste. The second group of issues relates to the actual interior environment that the project will create and the impact that that environment will have on the health, safety, and well-being of the occupants and users of that space. Although the impact of any one project on the general environment will, of course, be relatively small, each project makes its own contribution, for better or for worse, on the total environment. Each designer and each client must make an individual determination as to how far to go in striving for minimal negative impact on the environment. The most responsible course of action may involve giving up certain desired features and incurring financial costs. Decisions about how to react to the pressures of conflicting aims may be difficult, but they are inescapable. Fortunately, doing what is best for the environment will often turn out to have specific benefits for the owners, occupants, and users of a particular project.

Consumption of Resources

All materials used in architectural and interior construction must come from somewhere. Certain resources are so plentiful as to create little concern over consumption, at least at present levels. Sand, for example, the basic material of concrete and of glass, seems an almost endlessly available resource. Stone (except for some rare marbles), slate, and the clays from which brick and tile are made are not in short supply. Iron ore, the source of iron and steel, is not in danger of depletion in the foreseeable future. Also, iron and steel are recyclable into the production of more iron and steel. Glass, brick, and concrete revert to "rubble" and, eventually, to sand. Some other resources are renewable if care is taken to replenish them. Wood, for instance, comes from cut trees, but new trees will grow if reforestation is routinely undertaken. Wood timbers saved during building demolition can often be reused, and scrap or discarded wood can be reduced to sawdust and used in making wood-based synthetic materials. Wood is also the common material of paper, which can be recycled in various products.

Unfortunately, the consumption of wood and forest renewal are not always well regulated. Hardwood trees are slow-growing—a century-old oak or walnut may be cut and not replaced. This pattern has result-ed in many fine woods rising in price through scarcity. Some exotic woods (rosewood, zebrawood, ebony) from tropical regions are becoming rare as rain forests are cleared and the best trees sold for consumption (see Table 9). Even softwoods are threatened when ancient trees are cut and not replaced and when clear-cutting eliminates whole forests. White pine, a favored material of Colonial America, has virtually disappeared. Giant redwoods are consumed faster than replacements can grow. Even Douglas fir, the material of construction lumber and plywood manufacture, increases in price, and scarcity looms.

Forest depletion has further ecological impact when the habitats of small plants, many animals, insects, and birds are wiped out. Changes in ecosystems have extended influence on water supply, climate, damage to the ozone layer, the greenhouse effect, and potential global warming.

Plastics, often mentioned as a manufactured and therefore endlessly available replacement for wood, actually consume petroleum-derived resins and chemicals. Petroleum is an irreplaceable resource being rapidly depleted as a fuel and energy resource. It must also be remembered that the production of materials—conversion from their original form in nature into building materials—consumes energy. The cost of aluminum derives not only from the ore from which it is made (bauxite) but also from the cost of the electricity consumed in the refining process. Energy production consumes coal, gas, and oil, all resources destined for depletion if present rates of consumption continue. Energy production and consumption result in by-products that contribute to the formation of acid rain, with resultant damage to plant life and the ecosystems dependent on it.

Natural fibers produced from plants such as cotton and linen have constantly renewable sources, as do many materials with animal origins, such as wool, horsehair and goats' hair, leathers, and silk. Only the products obtained from endangered animal species—furs and certain skins, such as leopard and zebra, and the now-outlawed ivory from elephant tusks—threaten the natural world through possible extinction of wild animal populations.

Pollution and Waste

Among the by-products of the processes of energy generation and manufacturing are air pollution and other wastes. Atomic energy plants are an obvious source of waste that has no known practical means of disposal. Materials put into use in structures and products will generally turn to waste as the uses made of them become obsolete. Although the materials of surviving great historic buildings remain in use, many modern buildings have short lives and are demolished to make room for replacements. Demolition turns a large share of the materials of a structure into waste—a steel frame may be worth selling for scrap and so is recycled, but the glass, concrete, smaller wood, and synthetic elements typical of modern buildings are ground up, burned, or transported to landfills where space is running out. Fine antique furniture hundreds of years old retains the use of the wood from which it was constructed, but tables and chairs only a few years old are commonly scrapped, with their materials—metals, wood, and plastic—adding to

Table 9. Endangered Status of Tropical Hardwoods

Trade Name *Scientific Name (in italics)* *	Source	Main Uses
ENDANGERED		
Afrormosia *Pericopsis elata*	Africa	Furniture
Ebony *Diosporos spp.*	Africa, Southeast Asia	Musical instruments, inlay, brush backs
Iroko *Chlorophora excelsa, C. regia*	Africa	Veneer, furniture
Mahogany *Khaya spp.*	Africa	Furniture, paneling, turnery, door frames
Paduak *Pterocarpus soyauxii, P. spp.*	Africa, Southeast Asia	Joinery, veneer, furniture
Rosewood *Dalbergia stevensonii, D. nigra, D. latifolia*	Latin America, Southeast Asia	Joinery, handles, musical instruments, furniture
THREATENED OR OVER-EXPLOITED		
Sapele *Entandrophragma cylindricum*	Africa	Veneer, furniture, cabinetry, joinery
Mahogany *Swietenia macrophylla*	Latin America	Furniture, paneling, turnery, door frames
Teak *Tectona grandis*	Southeast Asia	Shipbuilding, joinery, furniture, flooring
Utile *Entandrophragma utile*	Africa	Veneer, cabinetry
Lauan/Meranti/Philippine mahogany *Shorea spp., Pentacme contorta*	?	Plywood, furniture parts, light structural work
Ramin *Gonstylus spp.*	Southeast Asia	Furniture, interior joinery, moldings, plywood, picture frames
Okoume *Aucoumea klaineana*	Africa	Furniture components, joinery, paneling

Trade Name *Scientific Name (in italics)* *	Source	Main Uses	Comments

Note: It is difficult to know if tropical hardwoods sold in the United States have been responsibly produced because no system currently exists to identify such products and their origin. For the woods listed below, harvesting involves little or no damage to natural tropical forests.

Trade Name *Scientific Name (in italics)* *	Source	Main Uses	Comments
Rubberwood *Hevea spp.*	Malaysian plantations	Furniture	Good replacement for ramin
Teak *Tectona grandis*	Javanese plantations	Shipbuilding, joinery, furniture, flooring	Hard to distinguish from other teak
Virola *Dialyanthera, Virola sp.*	Amazonian swamp forests	General utility	No road building required; not managed but regenerates well

*Some family names contain numerous species (spp.)

landfill overload. Other waste is developed at construction sites when materials are cut and assembled and packaging (used to aid shipment from production factories) is removed and discarded. Disposal of construction waste is costly and troublesome, adding to the overuse of landfills and incinerators, while the latter in turn contribute their share to air pollution.

Interior Environment Impact

Materials can also influence interior air quality in potentially undesirable ways. The odors associated with many familiar materials—the smell of freshly cut wood, fine leather, and other natural materials—are reminders that materials give off fumes and vapors over long periods of times. Fortunately, the vapors coming from the traditional natural materials are generally harmless, but modern synthetics, plastics, and solvents used in paints, other finishes, and adhesives can be insidious and harmful, especially when used in spaces without ample ventilation, such as the typical sealed interior common to many modern buildings.

Contemporary sealed interiors, unfortunately, are all too likely to make use of a high percentage of synthetic materials. Wall paneling of manufactured boarding; plastic fibers in carpets, drapery, and upholstery fabrics; plastic foams in upholstery; and many synthetic finishes for floors, walls, and ceilings have all been found to give off fumes over a long period of time in a process called "out-gassing" that pollutes interior air. Air-conditioning systems in these buildings commonly recycle air to limit energy consumption, so that the so-called fresh-air supply is actually recirculated air in which a concentration of pollutants gradually builds. Bacterial concentrations may accrue in ducts and other parts of air-conditioning systems, encouraging the spread of infectious diseases. Many complaints of nose, throat, and eye irritations, headaches, and other less specific ailments have been traced to pollutants in the air of enclosed spaces. Formaldehyde, a chemical much used in adhesives and in the making of particleboard and similar construction materials, has been found to have a direct relationship to various physical ailments; its use is now generally forbidden by various health codes. Benzine, xylene, and toluene are also carcinogens often present in wall and floor coverings and in the adhesives used with them.

Many older materials have been found to be associated with health hazards little suspected when they were in widespread use. Removal or containment of such materials is a continuing problem in the renovation of existing building interiors. Lead, until recently the most common base for paint pigments, is a hazardous substance that can cause brain injury, particularly to young children. Removal of lead-based paints and avoidance of lead pipe or other lead plumbing parts (such as faucets) are important environmental concerns. The mineral asbestos, long a favorite material for insulation and fireproofing, is a highly dangerous carcinogen. Although the disastrous health risks experienced by asbestos workers have brought about a general ban on asbestos in most uses, it remains present in pipe and duct insulation in numerous older buildings. Asbestos was also extensively used in the making of floor tile and various sheet products, flat or corrugated, that were popular a decade or two ago. Removal or containment of asbestos is essential, but the very process of removal can be extremely hazardous.

Fire risks involve additional concerns discussed more fully in Chapter 14, page 427. Most of these hazards arise when materials give off highly toxic fumes during smoldering or burning. Although fire-control systems are a primary defense against such dangers, the selection of materials that resist ignition, do not support combustion readily, and give off less harmful combustion by-products is prudent. Certain interior spaces, such as the passenger cabins of aircraft, are particularly problematic because of the prevailing use of all-synthetic interior materials in an environment where accidents are often accompanied by fire. In such accidents, toxic fumes may account for more fatalities than actual bodily injuries.

Sick-Building Syndrome

This phrase has come into popular use to describe buildings in which indoor air quality is so unsatisfactory as to cause serious illness and lesser physical complaints among users or residents. The term is somewhat misleading, since it is not, of course, the building itself that is "sick" but rather the occupants who suffer from maladies created by the environmental problems that the building generates.

The best defenses against sick-building syndrome are removal of all known hazardous materials, care in specification of new materials to avoid potential pollutants (natural materials most often are the least offensive), air-conditioning and ventilation systems that offer ample input of outdoor air (ideally six changes of air or more per hour, with an intake of outdoor air in a ratio exceeding 24 cubic feet per minute), and wherever possible windows that can be opened to permit free air circulation. In general, minimizing the use of synthetic materials, care in checking the health certification of all materials, and provision of ample ventilation and air cleansing are the principal lines of defense against material-related hazards. (Further discussion of these issues can be found in Chapter 7, pages 193–95.)

9.1

CHAPTER

NINE

COLOR

Among all the aspects of interior design, color is one of the most important—perhaps *the* most important element. A successful interior invariably includes color that creates a strong and satisfying impression. Badly chosen color will make any space, however well planned otherwise, seem unpleasant. Unsatisfactory color is probably the most common source of failure in interior design. The depressing effect of "institutional green" in offices, hospital rooms, and classrooms is well known. Harsh, random, and clashing color is commonplace in living rooms in which rugs, paint colors, and furniture have been brought together by chance or by separate purchases without thought for color relationships. A room with a rosy red rug, pea-green walls, blue-and-yellow striped curtains, a brown leather sofa, and a yellow-and-orange flower print hanging on the wall offers a great deal of color, but it is more likely to disturb than to please.

Changing the color scheme is one of the easiest ways to improve a space. Even if one existing color element is retained, the intelligent selection of new colors for other items will often transform an unattractive space into something much more agreeable. In the room described above, white or beige paint for the walls and new curtains in related, subtle tones might make the rug, sofa, and flower print acceptable by bringing all of the colors present into a better relationship. Color is an important design tool as well as a major element of the designed space. An aspect of color that does not get much attention is its ability to affect space visually. Color can make a small space look larger or can camouflage bad proportions.

Color planning involves complex issues that require some study in order to master good color use. Color planning has, moreover, become surrounded by a certain mystique—beliefs that stand in the way of dealing with color directly and successfully. Too many people, including otherwise competent teachers of design, assert that color cannot be taught, that skill in using color is an inborn talent possessed by only a few people. Others suggest that it cannot be taught systematically, that learning to use color can be managed only through experience.

Neither of these views matches reality. Certainly it is true that some people seem to have a special sensitivity to color and that its use is easier for them than for others, and no one can doubt that experience is helpful in developing color usage skills. It is equally certain that the study of color can make what at first seems confusing and mysterious become clear and understandable. While there are no absolute rules that govern color use, accumulated experience has led to a variety of suggestions that anyone can follow to arrive at good color schemes that will be comfortable, satisfying, stimulating, even exciting.

Our ability to see color, besides being useful, gives us a tremendous amount of pleasure. People who disclaim any artistic interests appreciate the colors of flowers and trees, water and sky, and the human uses of color in costume, graphic materials, architecture, and interior design. Even those with the physical problem known as color blindness (which causes confusion only between certain pairs of colors) are not prevented from enjoying color. Color blindness is not even a significant handicap in working with color. A designer with this condition can easily compensate by using name identification of the problem colors. Otherwise, color work is no different than it is for those with fully normal color vision. Working with color is almost universally enjoyed. Putting together a color scheme is probably the most pleasurable aspect of design work. Developing skill in using colors begins with the study of color systems, which are based on the scientific principles of light and color.

LIGHT AND COLOR

Human vision depends on the presence of light, and the effect of color results from some special properties of light. Light is a form of radiant energy. The eye distinguishes different wavelengths of the radiant energy, or light, and interprets them, in the brain, as different colors. Light energy at the extremes of wavelength—infrared at the long end and ultraviolet at the short end—becomes invisible.

THE COLOR SPECTRUM. Daylight, or white light, is a random mixture of light of all wavelengths. (Artificial light that appears to match the color of daylight is also called white light, although it usually has a

9.1 Pale greens and mustard complement the natural wood tones in a house in Paris designed by the owner, American photographer David Seidner. The room's furnishings are an eclectic mix, including upholstered furniture by Jean-Michel Frank, and an African stool and table. (Photograph: © David Seidner, courtesy HG)

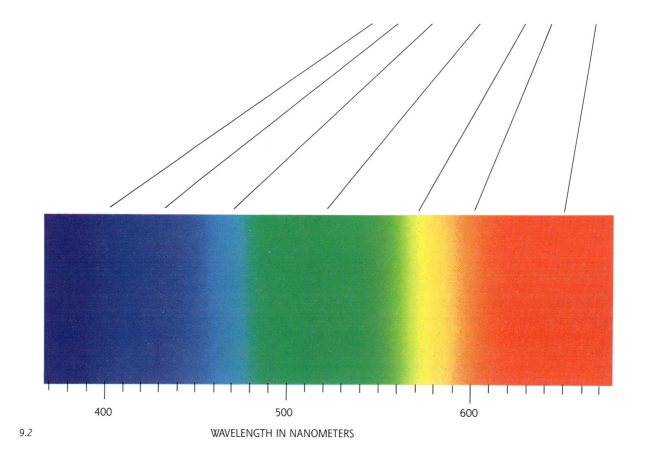

9.2

WAVELENGTH IN NANOMETERS

somewhat different color makeup.) When white light passes through a glass prism, its different wavelengths become sorted into colors, creating the familiar rainbow, or spectrum, arranged according to wavelength (fig. 9.2). The longest is red, followed by orange, yellow, green, blue, and violet. Their measure in nanometers (formerly designated millimicron), or one-millionth of a millimeter, is generally assigned as follows:

RED	700–650 NANOMETERS
ORANGE	640–590 NANOMETERS
YELLOW	580–550 NANOMETERS
GREEN	530–490 NANOMETERS
BLUE	480–450 NANOMETERS
VIOLET	440–390 NANOMETERS

The various wavelengths of daylight are not always balanced. At dawn or sunset, daylight tends to be short of blue-green components, thus appearing reddish. Incandescent lamps share this characteristic. On cloudy days, daylight is weak in red-orange, so it appears bluish. In such situations, the brain introduces a compensatory bias. The mind soon adjusts to the varying tints of daylight and the quite different color content of artificial light sources (firelight, candlelight, incandescent light, or fluorescent light), quickly accepting them as "normal," so that colors appear quite recognizable under any of these different kinds of light.

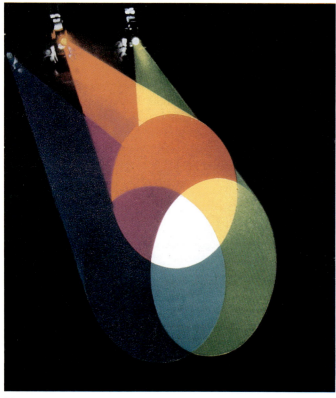

9.3

9.2 When white light passes through a prism, it is broken up into a spectrum, or rainbow, of colors—red, orange, yellow, green, blue, and violet—whose order is determined by the wavelengths of the radiant energy they represent. (From Theory and Use of Color by Luigina De Grandis)

9.3 Additive color is the term used to describe the mixing of colored light. The primary colors of light are red, green, and blue. Yellow results, as demonstrated here, by adding red and green light. All three primaries combine to form white light.

ADDITIVE COLOR. Colored light, produced by filtering white light so that only one color can pass through the filter (a colored glass or gelatin), makes normal color vision inoperative: everything appears as a tone of the colored light. For example, in pure red light, white and red objects appear bright red, green objects almost black, and other colors as intermediate tones of red. Colored light is used in stage lighting and sometimes in lighting displays but rarely in lighting interiors, since it distorts real color and the single color soon becomes irritating and monotonous.

Color mixing of light, used mostly in the theater, is called *additive* color, because mixtures are obtained by adding together the wavelengths that represent the three colors considered *primary* since they cannot be made up by mixing other colors (fig. 9.3). Any other color can be produced by mixing the three additive primaries—red, blue, and green (yellow is produced by adding red and green). All three produce white or normal light.

SUBTRACTIVE COLOR. In interior design (as in painting, printing, and any other situation using pigments and dyes as the colorants), one is usually working with *subtractive* color. That is, the object or material absorbs, or subtracts, all the colors of light *except* the color of the object, which is the color we see. A red object is actually one that absorbs all colors but red and reflects back only red light. If we mix two colors, for example red and yellow, as paint or pigment, the red pigment is subtracting all but red light reflection, the yellow all but yellow, so that the mixture reflects back some red and some yellow, producing the visual impression of orange color.

THE COLOR WHEEL. When dealing with subtractive color, the colors that cannot be produced through mixing turn out to be red, yellow, and blue. Given these three *primaries* (fig. 9.4), any other color can be produced by mixture. On the color spectrum, with the band of colors arranged according to wavelength, the primaries alternate with *secondaries,* which can be mixed from the primaries that are their neighbors on either side. The spectrum begins with red. Its neighbor, orange, results from mixing red with the next color of the spectrum, the primary yellow. Yellow is followed by green, a secondary made from yellow and blue, the next primary. The visible spectrum ends with violet (or purple), a secondary that can be made by mixing blue with red, the color at the beginning of the rainbow band.

This has led to arranging the band in a circle, so that its end meets its beginning. In the resulting *color wheel* (fig. 9.5), the primaries and secondaries are equally spaced, with each secondary between the two primaries that can be mixed to create it. This wheel arrangement is the basis for the various color systems that organize the confusing realities of color into an understandable entity.

COLOR SYSTEMS

Color systems are extremely helpful in any discussion of color because they clarify the terminology used in everyday conversation about color and suggest organized ways of arriving at visually satisfying color schemes.

Once ordinary color names go beyond the primaries and secondaries, they become more and more imprecise. Modifiers such as light,

9.4 *The three primaries of subtractive color—red, yellow, and blue—are here shown as blocks and arranged in a color wheel. Blending each pair of primaries generates the secondaries, orange, green, and violet. When each of these is placed between the pair of primaries that creates it, the six-color wheel results—the spectrum in its natural order.*

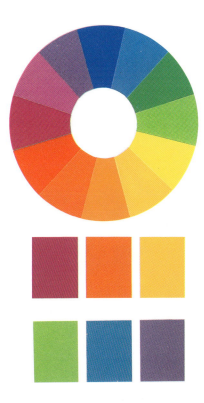

9.5 *Mixing each primary and the adjacent secondary produces an intermediate, tertiary color. The six shown here—violet-red, red-orange, orange-yellow, yellow-green, green-blue, and blue-violet—make up a spectrumlike band that has shifted slightly from the primary-secondary position. When the tertiaries are placed between their components, a twelve-color wheel results.*

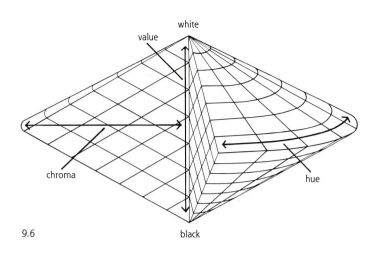

9.6

white

value

chroma

hue

black

bright, deep, dull, and dark are used in various and confusing ways, and many color names, such as tan or buff, suggest a wide range of color tones. Color names drawn from real objects are equally imprecise. Just what color is rose, cream, or sky blue? Manufacturers of paints, textiles, and other materials deepen the confusion by designating their products with such names as flame, champagne, and colonial blue, which defy precise identification.

Efforts to understand color in a systematic way go back at least as far as Johann Wolfgang von Goethe's study of the early nineteenth century. Modern systems vary somewhat in detail, but each provides an organized way to arrange and name colors. The best-known systems are those developed by Friedrich Wilhelm Ostwald (1853–1932; fig. 330) and Albert Munsell (1858–1918). The Munsell system, widely used in dealing with colors produced by dyes and pigments, is the system most generally accepted in interior design work and forms the basis for the following discussion.

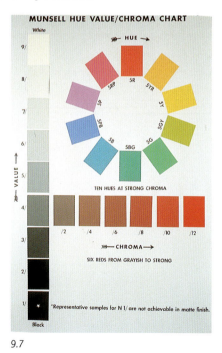

9.7

Munsell Color System

In the *Munsell* system, any color is described in terms of three attributes. By noting these three qualities according to a standardized system, any color can be exactly described and specified. Understanding the three dimensions of color is the key to dealing with color problems in an organized way.

HUE. The first (and most obvious) characteristic of a color is its position in the spectrum, the quality that gives it its basic name. In the Munsell system, this is called *hue,* and it is designated by a letter identification. Munsell chose to recognize *five* basic hues, a decision that goes against the normal understanding of primaries and secondaries. In practice, the Munsell system is usually modified to use six hues, three primaries and three secondaries, which can be identified by the letters R, O, Y, G, B, V (red, orange, yellow, green, blue, violet). Intermediate hues between these six are then identified by two-letter combinations: RO for red-orange, OY for orange-yellow, and so on. These hues are often called *tertiaries.* Still finer gradations of hue (*quaternaries*) can be inserted between the first twelve with three-letter designations (OOY, OYY, YYG, and so on). This subdivision can be continued indefinitely.

VALUE. The second characteristic of any color is its lightness or darkness, called its *value.* The value of a color depends upon the amount of light it reflects (lighter) or absorbs (darker). Adding white, which reflects all light, lightens a color without changing its hue; similarly, adding black, which absorbs all light, darkens a color without changing its hue. Munsell measures value by means of a scale of tones ranging from light to dark (fig. 9.8). White, placed at the top of the scale, is designated 10; black, at the bottom, is designated 0. The value scale between them has nine equal steps of grays ranging from dark to light. The value of any color can be found by matching its lightness or darkness with one of the steps of gray. In mixing color, a sample of a particular hue can be moved upward on the value scale by adding white or downward by adding black. Light values, above the middle of the scale, or 6 through 9, are called *tints*; dark values, below the middle, or 1 through 4, are *shades* (fig. 9.9).

Values strongly affect the perception of a color. The same color, or hue, placed at opposite ends of the value scale has greatly different effects. For example, the lightest tint of violet, often called lavender, is a delicate, light color that might be used in a summer home. Its darkest shade is a very deep purple that might appear heavy and oppressive in the same setting.

In the Munsell system, the value number of a color follows the hue designation. For example, YG/7 is a yellow-green with a value matching step 7 of the gray scale.

CHROMA. The third aspect of color is its intensity or purity, called its *chroma* in the Munsell system. *Saturation* is also a commonly used term for this quality. Steps of chroma are numbered up to 14, from low chroma to maximum chroma, although different hues reach maximum chroma at different step numbers (fig. 9.10). Maximum chroma signifies a particular hue in its purest form. Adding the hue opposite to it

9.6 In the Ostwald system, a central axis is a scale of grays, from white at the top to black at the bottom. A color wheel is arranged around it, with each hue's maximum chroma, or saturation, at the circumference. The hues become gradually less saturated as they near the central axis, where they reach neutral gray. Above and below the wheel, the hues parallel the gray value scale

(upward for tints, downward for shades) in disklike steps. These circles become smaller as the number of steps to maximum saturation decreases toward the upper and lower points. When all the possible colors are placed, forming a geometric solid, the result is a symmetrical figure—a pair of identical cones meeting at the center plane. (Courtesy U.S. Department of Agriculture)

9.7 In an illustration from the most recent version of the Munsell color system, a value scale of grays at the left runs from white at the top to black at the bottom. From a middle gray, a line of steps runs to the right in increasing

levels of saturation for a particular hue—in this case red, the hue at the top center of the color wheel, as shown. (Courtesy Macbeth, New Windsor, New York)

9.8

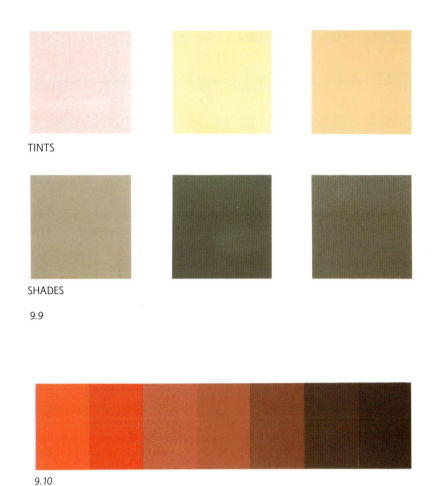

TINTS

SHADES

9.9

9.10

on the color wheel lowers the chroma, making the color less pure and intense. Mixing equal amounts of the colors opposite to one another on the wheel produces a neutral gray, identified as chroma 1. The intensity of a color usually affects its value as well. In Munsell's notation of colors, the chroma number comes last. Thus, YG/7/4 indicates a yellow-green hue at a value of 7 and chroma of 4.

THE COLOR SOLID. Arranging colors using the gray value scale, which is neutral, as a central axis, the circular arrangement of hues as a ring with the axis at its center, and all possible steps of chroma connecting the axis (low chroma) with the hue on the rim of the wheel (high chroma) like spokes gives a three-dimensional cluster, or *color solid,* with every color in a logical place. Because various hues reach maximum chroma at different value levels, the Munsell color solid does not form a neat sphere or any other perfect geometric shape. Yellow, for example, becomes most intense at a high-value level, blue and red at a lower value. The color solid is therefore somewhat irregular and lumpy. Some color systems force a perfectly symmetrical color solid by imposing different ways of spacing and annotating actual color specimens.

Although the Munsell system is generally recognized as the most useful and practical color system for interior designers' use, a number of other systems are of interest for the differing ways in which they organize the complexities of color relationships. A simplification of the Munsell color wheel with its five hues into a wheel of three primaries and three secondaries has already been mentioned. The logic of this approach can be understood in two ways:

In the color wheel, the secondaries orange and green are positioned between the primaries that, when mixed, create them. Violet is positioned at the end of the spectrum, beyond blue. If the spectrum is bent into a circle with violet placed next to red, violet then falls between red and blue, the primaries that make it, and a logical color wheel emerges.

A second basis for the logic of the six-hue color wheel arises from the physical measurement of the wavelengths of colored light. The colors at the ends of the visible light spectrum, red and violet, have wavelengths of 700 and 400 nanometers (angstrom units), respectively. If this range of 300 nanometers is divided equally into five parts of 60 nanometers each, the resulting values of 640, 580, 520, and 460 will be found to correspond with the hues orange, yellow, green, and blue,

9.8 *The gray scale of values from white to black in ten tones (A) is shown adjacent to a value scale of reds (B), with the clear primary near the center. Adding white to produce the lighter tints or adding gray or a complemen-* *tary to produce darker shades reduces the chroma of the pure color. The equivalent gray tone is shown adjacent to each color tone. It is not possible to produce a tint as light as pure white or a shade as dark as solid black.*

9.9 *When tints and shades become discernibly different from the pure colors on which they are based, they are given new names. Pink, cream, and beige (above) are tints of red, yellow, and orange. The shades (below) may be called tan, olive, and taupe. They are derived from yellow, green, and orange.*

9.10 *Here a scale of chroma moves in seven steps from the fully saturated pure color to a least saturated neutral, while maintaining the entire scale at a constant value.*

indicating that the primaries and secondaries of the color wheel are spaced in accordance with their measured wavelengths. Various names have been given to this six-part color wheel since it was first defined by Goethe in 1810. When intermediate steps are added between the six primaries and secondaries, these hues, called tertiaries, generate a twelve-step color wheel sometimes referred to as the *Brewster system* (after David Brewster) or the *Prang system*.

Other Color Systems

The *CIE* (Commission Internationale de l'Eclairage) is an international scientific organization concerned with establishing standard means for expressing color characteristics of light sources and the reflection and transmission of light by objects in numerical terms. It is of primary use in scientific applications dealing with the precise matching of colors, taking into account both light sources and the color qualities of materials and objects. It offers a level of exactitude beyond the needs of practical applications, suitable only to laboratory measurements.

The *DIN* (Deutsches Institut für Normung) offers a system that classifies colors in terms of hue, saturation, and relative lightness. The DIN color wheel is divided into twenty-four parts, with the four basic (or primary) hues of red, yellow, green, and blue. About nine hundred standard colors are identified in this system.

The *Gerritsen system*, first presented by Frans Gerritsen in a book published in 1975, is based on the color-perception behavior of the human eye. Because the cones of the human retina sense and distinguish red, green, and blue, these hues are designated as primaries, while the hues magenta, cyan, and yellow, each sensed by two of the three primary receptor cones, are designated as secondaries. In practice, this corresponds to the phenomenon of additive color in which the addition of red and green generates the secondary yellow. The Gerritsen system arranges the three primaries and three secondaries in a circle. Two intermediate colors are then developed between each pair of the basic six, creating a ring of eighteen colors. Additional intermediate steps produce a ring of fifty-four colors, approaching continuous hue variation (fig. 9.11). Values are defined in steps created by reducing the intensity of the primaries. Any color at any level of value can be defined in these terms. Because of its use of the light sensitivities of the eye as the basis for establishing primaries, the Gerritsen system is more adaptable to work with colored light (as in stage lighting, for example) than to work with dyes and pigments. In this system, the complementary pairs (see discussion below, page 267) are blue and yellow, green and magenta, red and cyan. It is interesting to note that the three chromatic hues used in color printing are yellow, magenta, and cyan (black is the fourth ink color), the three secondaries of the Gerritsen system.

In the *Kuppers system*, six primary colors are defined: red, yellow, green, cyan, blue, and magenta. These six primaries arranged in a ring are, of course, quite similar to the basic color wheel of the Brewster or Prang system. Kuppers also makes use of a "color solid" in which all possible colors are arranged in a six-faced form similar to a cube but with faces of diamond rather than square shape. As with Gerritsen's work, the Kuppers system attempts to account for the phenomenon of additive color and thus is more appropriate to work with color lighting and color printing than to interior design.

The *OSA* (Optical Society of America) *Uniform Color Scales* (OSA-UCS) are based on a theoretical color solid in which spheres of colors are packed together in contact with other spheres most similar in color sensation, so as to build up a three-dimensional polyhedron. This system has been used to generate 558 standard sample colors intended to be spaced in uniform steps of difference in terms of each color attribute. The theoretical basis of this system is complex and difficult to visualize, although its practical application does not differ greatly from that of the Munsell system.

The Swedish *NCS* (Natural Color System) is based on studies of color perception, by Ewald Hering, that define as "natural" the six color sensations of red, yellow, green, blue, black, and white. A color wheel of the four chromatic colors is developed with nine intermediate steps between each of the four basic colors (fig. 9.12). For each hue, colors are arranged in a triangle with the basic hue, black, and white placed at the vertices. The sides of the triangle are divided into ten steps, making a scale from hue in tints to white and in shades to black. A grid of colors in intermediate steps fills the triangle (fig. 9.13). There are forty such triangles for forty steps of hue, ten steps between each of the four chromatic hues. Each triangle contains sixty-six colors, for a total of 2,640 colors, each with a specific identification. Of these colors, 1,412 have been made available as colored papers, convenient for designers' use. An *SIS* (Standardiseringskommissionen) color atlas based on the NCS system identifies each sample with a notation on the relative presence of the four chromatic hues plus whiteness and blackness. The atlas offers samples in forty hues and five gray scales described as achromatic, yellowish, reddish, bluish, and greenish.

A number of other systems have been developed by manufacturers of such color-related products as paints, printing inks, and textiles. The system developed by the Container Corporation of America (CCA) is based on the Ostwald system. It incorporates loose-leaf pages holding small, removable sample chips of colors, each with an identifying nota-

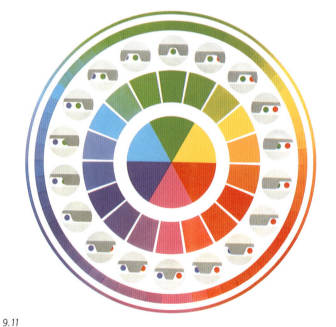

9.11

9.11 The Gerritsen color system is represented by a color circle from the 1975 Theory and Practice of Color by Frans Gerritsen. Each color in the wheel (and outer ring) relates to the small diagrams that show the relative presence of the additive (light) primaries used in this system. (Courtesy Uitgeverij Cantecleer bv, The Netherlands)

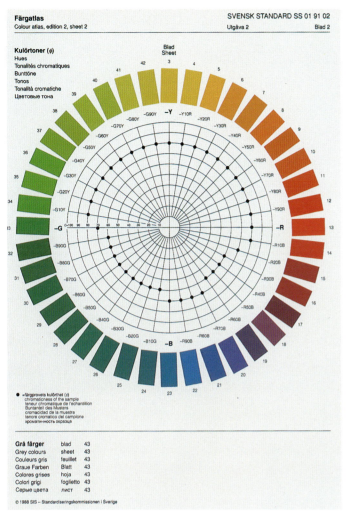

Kulörtoner (ø)
Hues
Tonalités chromatiques
Bunttöne
Tonos
Tonalità cromatiche
Цветовые тона

● =färgprovets kulörthet (ø)
chromaticness of the sample
teneur chromatique de l'échantillon
Buntanteil des Musters
cromacidad de la muestra
tenore cromatico del campione
хроматичность образца

Grå färger	blad	43
Grey colours	sheet	43
Couleurs gris	feuillet	43
Graue Farben	Blatt	43
Colores grises	hoja	43
Colori grigi	foglietto	43
Серые цвета	лист	43

© 1988 SIS – Standardiseringskommissionen i Sverige

9.12

tion. Replacement chips can be obtained, allowing chips to be removed for inclusion in color charts or for the use of suppliers or contractors. Paint manufacturers offering color systems include Martin-Senour (Nu-Hue Custom Color System) and SCM Glidden Coating and Resins (Glidden Professional Colors), among others, each providing a large variety of color samples suitable for interior designers' use with specific instructions for mixing paint to give accurate matches for the samples. Although the specification of colors through the use of such systems has obvious advantages of convenience, it requires becoming "captive" to the products of a particular manufacturer. Other color systems, such as the Color-Aid system of papers and the Pantone system of papers and transfer transparencies, relate to the uses of colored inks or papers.

Complementary Colors

In practice, it is most useful simply to bear in mind the concepts of value and chroma while working with a color wheel that places the strongest possible chroma of each hue in the rainbow-order ring. In this arrangement, each hue will be found to be directly opposite

9.12, 9.13 The NCS system of the Scandinavian Color Institute of Stockholm is presented in the Natural Color System Color Atlas. Sheet 2, reproduced in fig. 9.12, shows samples of high chromatic values—one of each from a range of forty specified hues.

(across in a straight line from) a hue that we think of as opposite in character: red across from green, orange from blue, yellow from violet. Thus each primary stands across from a secondary made up by mixing the two other primaries. Such opposite colors are called *complementary.* Mixing two complementaries—in effect, adding together the three primaries—results, in the subtractive color of dyes and pigments, in a neutral gray. (In reality, the actual color may be a brownish or bluish neutral rather than the theoretical neutral gray of the color systems.)

Warm and Cool Colors

Looking at the color wheel, we see that the circle is divided through its center into two families of color that make strongly different impressions. Red, orange, and yellow are described as *warm* colors, green, blue, and violet as *cool.* A clear mental association between the colors themselves and the temperature sensations of hot and cold has been established. Warm colors actually seem to raise the apparent room temperature, making spaces feel cozy and pleasant indoors in winter, while cool colors provide relief on a hot day or in a warm climate. Notice that a complementary pair is always made up of one warm and one cool color.

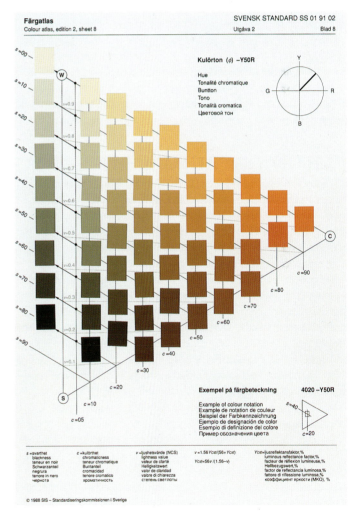

Kulörton (ø) −Y50R

Hue
Tonalité chromatique
Buntton
Tono
Tonalità cromatica
Цветовой тон

Exempel på färgbeteckning   4020 −Y50R

Example of colour notation
Example de notation de couleur
Beispiel der Farbkennzeichnung
Ejemplo de designación de color
Esempio di definizione del colore
Пример обозначения цвета

© 1988 SIS – Standardiseringskommissionen i Sverige

9.13

Sheet 9 from the NCS atlas (fig. 9.13) gives color notation within one of the forty specified hues. (Photographs: Reproduced with permission of the NCS-Scandinavian Color Institute, Stockholm)

9.14

Neutral grays, black, and white are neutral in relation to the warm-cool range, as one might expect from their position as the central axis of the Munsell color solid. Tints and shades close to neutral, located near but not at the axis, can be spoken of as warm or cool according to which side of the color wheel they lie on. They are sometimes hard to identify in terms of hue, partly because we use different color names for colors of low values and low chroma. A dark red or orange of low chroma will usually be called a shade of brown. A blue in a similar position in the color solid will be seen as a cool gray. Colors with names such as tan, olive drab, or taupe at the darker end of the scale or pink, cream, or beige at the lighter end are examples of hues given new names when of low chroma and either high or low value.

PSYCHOLOGICAL IMPACT OF COLORS

It is widely recognized that colors have a strong impact on human moods and emotions. Even some physical sensations can be modified by the presence of colors. However, the exact nature of these influences is not well understood, and the confusion is compounded by the complex ways in which color interacts with spatial perception, as well as the ways in which colors influence each other.

It is generally agreed that warm colors convey a sensation of warmth, both physical and emotional. Well-documented cases demonstrate that complaints about inadequate heat have been silenced by a change of color scheme, with no change of actual air temperature. The idea of a cozy room is strongly identified with the use of warm color and lighting that emphasizes the warmth of the colors present (see fig. 9.21). In contrast, cool colors suggest formality and reserve and communicate a sense of physical coolness as well (see fig. 9.18).

Many attempts have been made to identify the impact of the various hues, but it cannot be ascertained whether these reactions are innate or cultural. For example, death and mourning are associated with the color black in Western traditions, whereas in China and other Oriental civilizations the color of death is white. The response may also differ according to the context. Red is commonly associated with danger and the meaning *stop*, yet it is used for exit signs that indicate a route out

9.15

9.14 In a 1990 Mediterranean-inspired villa in Montecito, California, designer John Saladino used a palette of greens, pale yellows, and beige with accents of coral. The color scheme relates well to the trompe l'oeil ceiling painted by Christian Granvelle. The furniture is a mix of antiques and contemporary designs by Saladino. (Photograph: © Langdon Clay, courtesy John F. Saladino)

9.15 Bold colors—contrasting in both value and hue—create an atmosphere that is vibrant, active, even aggressive. Frank Gehry, architect, remodeled the Los Angeles home of artist Miriam Wosk, who created the interior design. (Photograph: © Grant Mudford, courtesy House & Garden)

9.16

of danger to safety. A color that may communicate excitement of a pleasurable sort in one context may be irritating in another; a hue that is calm and soothing under one set of circumstances may be depressing in another. With these cautions in mind, it may be useful to review the generally accepted associations for the various hues:

Reds are seen as warm, even hot, exciting, and stimulating. They are associated with tension and danger (heat and fire). Limited amounts of red can augment and balance blues and greens in a color scheme, adding life and cheer. Strong reds and greens together in large areas can generate unpleasant tensions.

Oranges share the qualities of reds to a slightly reduced extent. Small areas of red-orange are a useful, stimulating modifier in otherwise neutral or cool color schemes.

Yellows, the mildest of the warm colors, are usually associated with cheerfulness, even humor (in theater lighting, it is traditional to use yellow for comedy scenes). They give a strong effect of brightness while suggesting less tension than reds and oranges. Yellow tints (creams and beiges) are known as safe colors, with no negative implications, but their overuse subjects them to insipidity.

Greens are the cool colors closest to warm. They have become a favorite for balanced color schemes seeking to be calm and restful, peaceful and constructive, associations stemming from green as the color of grass and leaves. The color theorists of the 1930s so successfully promoted green as the best color for offices, classrooms, and hospital interiors that its overuse has made "institutional green" an objectionable cliché. However, green remains a good color to impart serenity, especially when used with limited areas of red or red-orange to counter any sense of drabness.

Blues are the coolest of the cool colors, suggesting rest and repose, calm and dignity. Overused or in too strong a chroma, blues can generate depression and gloom, as evident in the phrase "to have the blues." Intense blue in small areas can be a helpful accent in warm and warm-neutral color schemes.

Violets, along with their stronger versions called purples, have a reputation as problematic and unsafe colors. At the borderline between cool and warm, they seem to convey uncertainty (in contrast to borderline green, which communicates strength from both families). Violets are often seen as artistic, suggesting subtlety and sensitivity but

9.16 *In their "Thematic House" bedroom, Charles Jencks, architect, and his wife, Maggie Keswick, designer, have restricted color to a monotone except for a few small accents. The result is that attention is focused on the symbolic motif of this "Foursquare Room"—repeated in ornamental details in the* design of the ceiling, mirrors, lighting elements, and the four-poster bed. Although the color is limited to tones close to ivory white, the effect is still richly colorful. The house is in London. (Photograph: © Richard Bryant, courtesy House & Garden)

at the risk of conveying ambiguity. Purples even more strongly intimate tension and depression, although they also project dignity (the "royal" purple). Violets can be highly expressive but must be used with caution.

Neutral colors—grays, more or less warm, cool, or exactly neutral, as well as browns and tans—tend to convey, in milder form, the impressions of the hues that they contain in dilute form. The truly neutral grays make good background colors, easy to live with over long periods. However, they are subject to dullness and an impression of monotony. When used with limited areas of more chromatic color, grays can be very useful. Browns and tans, which are actually somewhat neutralized reds and yellows, have a traditional association with a snug, clubby atmosphere. They appear homelike in their milder tones, masculine in their heavier values.

Whites and near-whites suggest clarity, openness, and brightness. White is always a safe color and can be used in large areas to highly satisfactory effect if offset with small areas of chromatic color. The association with cleanliness and sanitation is an obvious one. All-white schemes can seem forced and empty, but whites used with appropriate accents imply modernity and high style, perhaps in part because whites were so widely used by early modernist designers.

Black is a powerful accent color, depressing if used to excess. It suggests weight, dignity, formality, and solemnity. Extensive use of black is best limited to spaces occupied for brief periods of time (elevator cabs, vestibules, bathrooms). As dark grays share some of these qualities to a reduced degree, they can be used more safely where strong, dark accents are required.

While these generalizations seem to have considerable value, it must be remembered that colors are rarely used alone and that colors used together interact in ways that are very complex. One cannot simply mix a bit of red for excitement, some black for dignity, and some green for calm and expect to achieve a scheme with all of those qualities. Almost any color can work in certain situations, and almost any combination can be successful, given balanced relationships of hue, chroma, and value and sound choices of location, area, texture, and other variables. In practice, all of the systematic knowledge of color reviewed above is best absorbed as background for creative work that proceeds in ways that have no dependence on formula or routine.

COLOR SCHEMES

The concept of *color harmony* is one of the keys to understanding the theory that lies behind the development of various color schemes. This concept has its origins in a comparison of colors with musical tones. It is well known that certain musical notes sound well together, while others make a discordant or clashing sound. There is a basis for this in the physics of sound, which explains the reasons for harmonious chords in music. While the physical basis of color harmony is not so easily explained, it is commonly observed that some colors clash in a harsh relationship while other combinations, whether soothing or exciting, subtle or aggressive, are pleasant.

Planned color schemes can be classified into a number of types, regardless of the actual hues used or whether warm or cool colors dominate. These types are discussed here in order of complexity, beginning with the simplest. Not unexpectedly, this parallels the order of difficulty involved in producing a successful scheme. The most complex and difficult types can be extremely beautiful, but putting them into practical use takes more experience and skill (or perhaps special talent) than working with the simpler types of scheme.

9.17

9.17 *Soft brown wicker, green plants, and turquoise glass stand out against the pale tones of this living room's blue-and-white furniture and light-colored walls. The color scheme is well suited to the setting, a summer house in Southampton, New York, designed by Stephen Sills in 1990. (Photograph: Oberto Gili, courtesy HG)*

Monotone (Neutral) Color Schemes

These use a single color of low chroma in one value or a very limited range of values (fig. 9.16). Typical colors used are grays, tans, and tinted whites. It is almost impossible for such a scheme to fail through harsh or clashing effect, but monotony—as the name suggests—is a risk. Monotone schemes are ideal for situations where strong color will enter in some transitory way—in the costumes of occupants, the display of colorful art or merchandise, or dramatic views through large windows. In practice, the monotone scheme is often modified by the introduction of some stronger color in minor accent elements. A strictly monotone scheme can seem somewhat forced, as in the case of the all-white room, which has become something of a decorating cliché. All-beige or almost all-beige schemes are very safe and, if monotony is relieved by some changing element not strictly a part of the scheme, can be fully satisfactory.

Monochromatic Color Schemes

Similar to monotone schemes, these use a wider range of chroma and value in a single hue. The familiar ideas of a red room or blue room exemplify schemes of this type. Such schemes also can be developed using the natural colors of materials that fall in a narrow range, such as red-orange tones ranging down through browns and tans, all of the same hue. Like monotone schemes (which may be considered a special case of monochromaticity), these schemes tend to be easy, since harsh clashes are almost impossible. Monochromatic schemes likewise risk monotony or a certain artificiality.

Problems arise when every item—carpet, walls, furniture, curtains—is given a strong version of the chosen hue, such as a particular blue. Rooms with a single strong color can be dramatic and often look good in photographs, but they can be hard to live with over an extended period of time. Such schemes may work best for spaces that people occupy only briefly.

Analogous Color Schemes

These schemes achieve harmony by using hues that are close together on the color wheel (fig. 9.18). The typical analogous scheme uses one primary or one secondary plus the hues adjacent to it on either side. Two examples are blue with its neighbors blue-green and blue-violet and green plus blue-green and yellow-green. An adjacent primary and secondary plus the tertiary hues between them (blue and green plus the blue-greens between them, for example) also generate an analogous scheme. In each case, the hues included fall within a segment of the color wheel that spans no more than about 90 degrees. As long as hue is restricted to one-quarter of the wheel, a range of varied value and chroma may be used.

Once again, because of its restriction, the analogous scheme virtually guarantees harmony. Because of its greater color range, monotony is less of a hazard than with monotone and monochromatic schemes. Complementaries from across the color wheel are often introduced as accent colors; however, if these become important elements in the scheme, it is no longer truly analogous but a species of complementary schemes.

Complementary Color Schemes

As the name implies, these schemes use contrasting hues from opposite sides of the color wheel: reds with greens, oranges with blues, yellows with violets (fig. 9.21). The basic hues may be more subtle intermediate colors rather than primary or secondary colors, as long as they face each other across the wheel. Complementary schemes, which tend to seem bright and balanced, are generally well liked when skillfully assembled. The danger in complementary schemes is that they may become overbright, even garish. Flags, sports costumes, display advertising, and some stage design make good use of such sharply contrasting complementaries, but interiors in strong bright reds and greens or blues and oranges may appear unpleasantly harsh or tiring.

Successful complementary schemes usually use a color of low chroma and either high or low value (tints or shades) from one side of the wheel to cover large areas and stronger colors from the opposite side of the wheel for smaller areas. Neutralizing each color by adding the complementary to it helps to unify complementary schemes. For example, a room might have floor and wall areas of a light green, grayed (reduced in chroma) by the addition of red. Some objects, perhaps upholstered furniture, would display the complementary red in strong but not full chroma, reduced by a small addition of green.

Complementary schemes are more difficult to plan than the simpler scheme types discussed above, especially if one considers the range of variations on basic complementary color. It is possible to widen the band of hues used on either one or both sides of the color wheel while still maintaining a complementary balance. Both red and the adjacent red-violet on one side of the wheel might be used with the slightly yellowed green opposite or with a range in the yellow-green to green band. Once again, such schemes require care and subtlety to avoid garishness.

A further variant of complementary schemes, sometimes classified as a totally different type, is the *split-complementary scheme*. In this scheme, a hue on one side of the wheel is used with the two hues that fall on either side of the directly opposite complementary. With red, for example, both yellow-green and blue-green could be used, omitting the true green between them (hence the term *split*). This scheme also works best using lower levels of chroma for the hues from one side of the wheel in larger areas and more intense color from the other side of the wheel in smaller areas and accents. Effective split-complementary schemes look lively and colorful. They make a subtler and more varied impression than simple complementary schemes.

Triad Color Schemes

Choosing three hues approximately equidistant from one another on the color wheel—red, yellow, and blue; orange, green, and violet; or slightly shifted versions of these combinations—creates triad schemes (fig. 9.24). These are the most difficult of all the color schemes discussed so far, and the most likely to slip into harshness and confusion. Successful triad schemes generally employ reduced intensities of all hues or all but one hue. Triad color is often used in small areas in an otherwise mostly neutral scheme. An interior following this scheme might have mostly white surfaces, with flooring in one hue of the triad

9.18

9.19

9.20

9.18 The color scheme for this living space in a Lake Tahoe residence is described as analogous because the colors used are adjacent in the spectrum—primarily a range of blue and its neighbor green, the green reaching over to its other neighbor, yellow, in the yellow-tans of the wood and rush chairs, stools, and wooden wall finish. It is also, by virtue of the dominant blues and greens, a cool scheme, suitable to a hot climate. The late Michael Taylor was the designer. (Photograph: Timothy Hursley, © The Arkansas Office, courtesy House & Garden)

9.19, 9.20 The strongly chromatic colors in the scheme illustrated in fig. 9.18 are all blues and greens; the more neutral tones are tans and beiges, or desaturated yellows. The chart (fig. 9.19) thus shows a range from blue-gray through blue and green to yellow. When charted on a color wheel (fig. 9.20), all tones are adjacent, staying within one-third of the full spectrum.

9.21

9.22

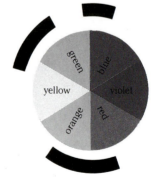

9.23

9.21 Complementary colors were chosen by Mrs. Henry Parish II, designer with the firm of Parish-Hadley, for her own home in New York. Such schemes are rich in color and, when warm tones dominate—as they do here—endow a room with an inviting, comfortable charm. (Photograph: Oberto Gili, courtesy House & Garden)

9.22, 9.23 The strong orange and yellow tones that compel one's attention in the space shown in fig. 9.21 are balanced by smaller areas of color from the opposite side of the wheel, making a complementary scheme. The color chart (fig. 9.22) demonstrates that the greens of the painted panels, however, are close to yellow, while those of the plants—a significant element in this scheme—are closer to blue; the result is a split-complementary scheme. The dark brown wood finishes may seem to fall outside the main color range, but they are, in fact, very deep tones of orange. On the wheel chart (fig. 9.23), the split tones are slightly shifted from a position exactly opposite one another.

9.24

9.25

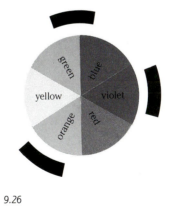

9.26

9.24 A triad scheme uses chromatic colors that are more or less equally spaced around the color wheel. The most common, or major, triad is red, yellow, and blue. Shown here is a minor triad, made up of the secondaries orange, green, and violet. Because they are based on saturated hues, triad schemes tend to have great impact—so it is not surprising to find this example in the showroom of a paint company, Janovic Plaza in New York, designed by Voorsanger & Mills Associates Architects. (Photograph: © 1982 Peter Aaron/ESTO)

9.25, 9.26 The triad scheme in fig. 9.24 is illustrated here in chart form (fig. 9.25). A neutral color acts as background for the triad. The three secondaries that make up the dominant chromatic colors are about equally spaced on the color wheel (fig. 9.26).

9.27

9.28

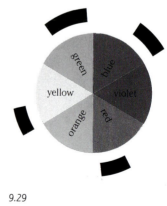

9.29

9.27 A tetrad color scheme is composed of four hues equally spaced around the color wheel. In this living area in a Houston home, built circa 1919–21 by Harrie T. Lindeberg, Mark Hampton has used a subtle tetrad scheme in a 1983 remodeling to generate a feeling of ease in familiar, traditional terms. (Photograph: Feliciano, courtesy House & Garden)

9.28, 9.29 Although the color tones are muted, the four hues that form a tetrad scheme are distinct here (fig. 9.28). The greens of the upholstery and the blue of the rug are prominent values. The red and pink of the sofa and the browns of the wood finishes represent the third hue, while the creamy yellow lampshades and the beige-tan of the painted wall surfaces complete the tetrad. The tetrad color scheme diagrammed on a color wheel (fig. 9.29) shows the four hues at even intervals around the circle.

at reduced value and chroma plus accents in the other two hues of the triad.

Tetrad Color Schemes

These use four hues equally spaced around the color wheel (fig. 9.27). The comments offered for triad schemes are even more strongly applicable to tetrad color. Examples are, in practice, fairly rare, but, difficult though they may be to produce, lively and satisfactory schemes of this type remain a possibility.

SPECIAL COLOR EFFECTS

A number of circumstances alter the appearance of color. In the theoretical consideration of color schemes, all colors are thought of as uniform, solid, and flat (nonglossy). In practice, real materials have characteristics that modify the way color is seen. A glossy finish often alters the apparent color of an object due to its high reflectance. Light reflected from its surface tends to dilute and weaken the visible color, while adjacent colors (such as floor color) reflected on it may actually cause a shift in its apparent hue.

Effects of Texture, Pattern, Metallic Materials

TEXTURE. Textured surfaces alter apparent color by introducing shadow or gloss at a microscale. Under a microscope, the texture may be seen as tiny hills and valleys, a series of pores, pits, flakes, shreds, or slivers that may have glossy surfaces, or may cast shadows or do both. The color seen is then the color of the material modified by these textural elements. Due to these effects, many textured materials will shift color when observed at different angles or when rubbed or stroked in one direction or another. Suede, many solid-color carpets, and textiles exhibit the latter effect. Even wood, if it is left unfinished or is finished to preserve its natural color and texture, may change color according to the angle of view and the angle of lighting. Textiles and carpets with strong texture shift the visual appearance of the actual dye color in ways that are hard to predict. Textures of surfaces (plaster, brick, stone) can alter the appearance of paint color. In order to take texture into account, color effects should be judged from actual samples of the material to be used.

PATTERN. Color also appears in patterns, from the slight pattern of some woven fabrics up to the large-scale, highly visible designs of some printed textiles and wallpapers. When viewed at a distance, small-scale patterns appear as a solid color, the result of visually mixing the colors that make up the pattern. Larger patterns should be categorized as sets of colors grouped together, each component having a separate identity.

METALLIC MATERIALS. Metallic materials show color in a way that can be confusing. Polished metals act as mirrors, reflecting adjacent colors. The white metals—namely, silver, stainless steel, aluminum, and chromium—reflect colors back with little change. Brass, gold, copper, and other colorful metals act much as a tinted mirror, tinting the adja-

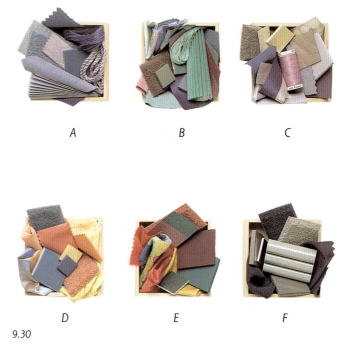

A   B   C

D   E   F

9.30

cent colors they reflect back yellow, orange, or reddish brown, according to the metal in question. This effect is also influenced by the finish. Glossy, or mirror-polished, finishes have a very high reflectance. Textured metallic finishes (also called satin or brushed) combine the reflectivity of polished metals with a microtexture (of tiny roughnesses) that breaks up sharp or smooth reflectivity. Metallics, like patterns, can be considered special cases, best evaluated in actual or simulated* samples.

Colors in Relation to Each Other

The actual space will also influence how colors appear. When seen against a larger background, small areas of color may alter in both value and hue. Light colors will appear lighter than they are when seen against a darker background; darks become darker against a light background (fig. 9.32). A medium tone can be made to seem either light or dark through contrast with its surroundings (fig. 9.33). Similarly, hues will seem to shift in relation to surroundings. A neutral gray will appear warm when placed on a blue background and cool when placed on red (fig. 9.34). Stronger colors will seem to shift in hue in relation to background, with a small sample seeming to move toward the complementary of the background color. For example, a small area of strong green will seem more intensely green when placed on a reddish (pink) background; placed on a violet background, its hue will seem to shift toward yellow-green.

---

*Metal foils, metallic papers, and plastic sheeting are often convenient substitutes for actual pieces of metal that may be unavailable or too difficult to use in color planning.

9.30 One of the initial steps in working with color is to collect material samples, as demonstrated by Martin-Senour Paints. Here materials are organized to illustrate various types of color schemes: (A) monochromatic, (B) analogous, (C) complementary, (D) split-complementary, (E) tetrad, and (F) neutral with accents. (Photographs courtesy Martin-Senour)

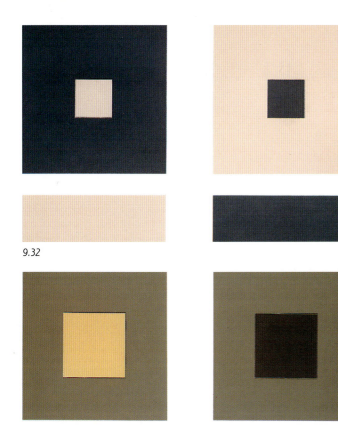

9.32

9.33

9.34

the sides move away. A dark ceiling will tend to seem lower than the same ceiling in a light tone. A dark floor *and* ceiling can greatly reduce apparent height and may even seem oppressive. A door painted to match the color of the wall around it or a window curtained in a tone matching its surround will blend into its environment. The same elements treated in contrasting colors will be emphasized.

Similarly, furniture can be made recessive or prominent according to whether it matches or contrasts with its background. An ebony black grand piano will be striking on a light floor with a light wall behind it. It will appear smaller and less assertive against a floor and wall in dark tones. Trim moldings (baseboards, cornices, window and door frames) stand out and define form when painted to contrast with walls in hue, value, or both. Trim painted to match walls tends to be less noticeable, deemphasizing the shape and contributing to an effect of spaciousness.

Effects of Light on Color

For every use of color, it should be remembered that color and color effects are influenced by the presence of light, which is what makes it possible to see color at all. When working with color in developing interior schemes, it is important that the light used match the light that will be normal in the actual built space. Working at the drafting table with daylight illumination when the built space will normally be artificially lit can lead to some distressing surprises. Conversely, a desk lamp can falsify a scheme that will most often be seen in daylight. Many interiors must serve with both daylight and artificial light. In such cases, proposed color schemes should be evaluated under both types of lighting and under combinations that simulate the light that will be present in the real space.

Daylight and incandescent light have enough in common to be almost interchangeable, keeping in mind that incandescent light is warmer, making cool colors appear more neutral and warm colors stronger than they appear in daylight. The human eye and brain accept this shift quite readily, since the relationship of colors remains otherwise unaltered. Fluorescent lights, HID (high-intensity discharge),

9.35

Effects of Color on Space

Conversely, color itself creates some surprising effects. Warm colors are said to *advance*, that is, appear closer than they actually are, while cool colors *recede*, appearing farther away. Light colors make objects look larger and lighter than they are, while darker colors make them look smaller and heavier. Placing sharply contrasting hues (that is, one advancing, one receding) together can cause a sense of *vibration* as the colors seem to move in opposite directions (fig 9.35).

These effects can be used to advantage in interior design. A small space can be made to seem larger, an oddly shaped space to seem better proportioned by a judicious use of colors in ways that exploit these effects. A long, narrow room will seem more normally shaped if the end walls are of a strong, warm color while the sides are lighter and cooler in tone, so that visually the ends seem to come closer and

9.31 *Used together, strong red and blue suggest excitement and activity in this house in Mexico designed by George Woo, architect. (Photograph: © Balthazar Korab, courtesy House & Garden)*

9.32 *A small sample of a light tone on a dark background appears lighter than a larger sample of the same color. Similarly, a small, dark sample on a light background appears darker than a larger sample.*

9.33 *A dark background with a medium, light sample appears darker*

because of the contrasting tone than the same background with a dark sample.

9.34 *Identical neutrals look different when placed on different backgrounds. The red makes the gray seem cooler and darker, while the blue background shifts the gray to a lighter, warmer tone.*

9.35 *Because the eye cannot focus simultaneously on an intense green superimposed on an intense red, the edge where the colors meet appears to vibrate. Since strong complementaries juxtaposed tend to produce this phenomenon, they are usually used only when an effect of intensity and tension is desired.*

and other light sources are much less predictable in their impact on color. Inspection of a scheme under the actual light source is essential when such illuminants are to be used.

PRACTICAL APPROACHES

Having absorbed as much of the theoretical views of color as possible, actual work with color comes down to some methodical steps that can be applied to virtually any interior problem. A preliminary step involves collecting an adequate assortment of color samples, including samples of materials, in ranges of colors, that may become part of actual schemes. (Putting together such a sample collection is discussed in more detail later in this chapter, beginning on page 287.) Assuming that samples are at hand, the steps to be taken are:

1. Note down in an orderly list the factors that will influence the scheme. *These might include such items as:*

    The orientation and extent of windows or other daylight supply to the space.

    The type and location of artificial lighting to be used; the hours that the space will be used and the purposes it will serve.

    The character or atmosphere desired, expressed in such general terms as calm, restful, stimulating, exciting, dignified, playful, and so on.

    The personal preferences of users, if they can be ascertained. In residential design, the occupants can easily be queried about the colors they like and dislike. In public spaces, such individual preferences are not a factor, but generally accepted preferences of a whole population can often be identified through observation of common regional color usage.

    Geographical location, both in terms of climate and in relation to regional preferences in color use.

2. Establish the general character of the scheme in relation to the factors outlined above. *This may include choosing among warm, cool, or neutral color, selecting the type of color scheme in theoretical terms (analogous, complementary, and so on), and deciding the dominant hue or hues. This step can be developed in words alone or together with color images. These may be actual color samples; imagery from color photographs of existing interiors; or other color materials, such as paintings or color combinations in natural objects or settings.*

3. Make selections of color for one or two of the major large areas, *such as floor, walls, and ceiling. Any major areas of predetermined color should be noted at this first step—existing furniture to be retained, for example, or large areas of material of a known color (brick, stone, or natural wood to be left unpainted), or any other color elements not subject to change.*

4. Add color selections for secondary items: *furniture, drapery, and other elements with significant color impact.*

5. Add selections of small areas of color that will act as accents. *These may be strong values of color already selected, in a contrasting color, or materials of a special nature, such as metallic elements, tinted glass, or mirror, that will have a significant impact on the total scheme.*

Once these basic selections are made, the scheme can then be adjusted, changing one or more items to improve or fine-tune the scheme. It is often wise to make several alternative schemes for comparison; sometimes elements from one scheme can be exchanged with those of an alternative as an aid in arriving at the optimum solution.

In going through this process, it often seems that choices can be extremely arbitrary—that one color can be as good (or as bad) as another and that the difficulty of arriving at good color can arise as much from this freedom as from any other problem. If that is so, several approaches that effectively limit or guide choices in what may otherwise seem a totally unstructured realm of possibilities may be considered. The following three approaches have a record of proven usefulness.

Natural Color

A decision to keep all materials in their own natural, unaltered color will generally produce a pleasing and harmonious result. Each material, whether brick, stone, wood, plaster, tile, or other, has a natural color that results from its growth or manufacture, a color that will be visible as long as no colorants, paints, or dyes are used to alter the basic color of the material itself. Such a scheme finds support from a certain school of thought that connects it to the issues of honesty and expressivity in design. The idea that all materials are best left in their natural color relates to the belief that the nature of materials should be central to the visual character of any constructed space.

In practice, most materials have natural colors in a warm neutral range, from the grays of stone and slate to the browns and reds of brick and tile, from the light grays and whites of plaster to the lighter browns and tans of woods. Textile fibers fall in a range of light neutrals (light grays and tans). Wool ranges from black and brown through grays and tans to near-white. A naturally colored interior will usually have a color character defined by these values. Stronger color can come from the greens and flower colors of plants or from the colors introduced by the clothing of occupants.

This kind of color can be seen in the work of Frank Lloyd Wright (fig. 9.36), his one-time student Harwell Hamilton Harris, and many modern architects and designers. It is also the color of many historic interiors, medieval castles and churches, and European and American Colonial cottages and farmhouses. The introduction of strong accent color is a frequent modification of the strictly natural color scheme. Wright liked to use his favorite vermilion red in small spots, perhaps on some cushions or upholstery fabric, or on a small area of tile or paint. The stained glass of the medieval stone cathedral has a similar impact.

Modern synthetic materials that can hardly be said to have a natural color introduce quandaries into the natural color scheme. What is the natural color of the plastic of floor tiles, laminate furniture tops, or plastic chair shells? What of surfaces, such as steel, that require paint for protection? In the all-natural color scheme, the usual answers are to select plastic colors that use a minimum of artificial colorants—grays, tans, and neutrals like those of so many natural materials—and to select paints that are basic pigments, such as white lead and red lead, choosing them for their durability and protective qualities rather than for their varied color. White plaster may be painted white for protection without altering its color. Red lead primer and the rustlike finish of Cor-ten steel are relatively natural choices for steel that must be fin-

9.36 In all his work, Frank Lloyd Wright respected the intrinsic qualities of his materials, including color. The pleasing, warm, and humane atmosphere of his interiors derives in large measure from this commitment to natural hues. Here, in the 1929 Storer House in Los Angeles, the tones of only the rug and couch do not derive from their materials; however, they remain largely within the color range set by the natural materials. (Photograph: Carlos von Frankenberg/Julius Shulman Associates)

9.37

ished. Wax, oil, and some clear lacquers protect wood with minimal change in color.

Natural color is generally very safe since its colors are basically neutral, precluding harsh, unpleasant, or clashing combinations. Its record of success in both historic and modern interior design is impressive. In spite of its rather limited range, it rarely seems monotonous, perhaps because it stays close to the natural color range of the outdoor landscape, a range that has an almost universal appeal.

All-Neutral Color

This approach, which might also be called the neutral-plus color scheme, has much in common with the all-natural color approach but is arrived at without specific concern for the natural colors of materials. It is a type of monotone or monochrome scheme (see page 272) based on the idea that neutral colors, those close to the central gray axis of

the Munsell color solid, are always safe and nonclashing, generally acceptable in any situation. A neutral scheme may be based on true neutral grays in the white-to-black range or may be warm, using beiges and tans as dominant colors, or cool, using grays of greenish, bluish, or violet tint. Of all the neutrals, white is probably the most useful and most widely used. Whites too can be cool or warm or, with colored pigment added, tinted toward cream, as in the many paint colors offered with names such as off-white, linen white, or oyster white. Schemes using white, grays, and black are of this type.

The notion of *neutral-plus* adds to the neutral scheme some limited areas of strongly chromatic color, often one or more true primaries. Such schemes were favorites of early modernism, suggesting the paintings of Mondrian and the work of various designers connected with the De Stijl and Bauhaus movements. White and neutrals plus primary accents remains a useful formula for color schemes that can hardly go

9.37 Neutral colors are usually thought to be safe in that they avoid any risk of harsh clashes—a fundamental consideration in exhibition spaces, where objects on display often present strong color. The Tilghman Gallery in Boca Raton, Florida, developed by Rex Nichols Architect & Associates, Inc., in 1986, furnishes an ideal setting for the artworks there. The chair in the foreground is a design of Robert Venturi. (Photograph: © Steven Brooke)

wrong while offering possibilities for varied color through the use of strong color tones in the accent areas. An all-neutral scheme with only plants as a source of accent color is also frequently adopted.

Neutral schemes are very satisfactory in places where strong color will come from sources other than basic interior color, as in museums and galleries (fig. 9.37), where a neutral surround best sets off paintings or objects. They are similarly useful in restaurants, where the table settings and costumes of diners will provide color, or in transport design (vehicles, such as airplanes or trains, and terminals), where an environment of quiet neutral color character provides the most restful setting for the changing light, view, and occupants.

Functional Color

This is probably the approach most widely used in developing color schemes. It is based on an analysis of what color is expected to *do* for the interior space in an active sense. Overall color tonality is chosen to enhance or offset environmental factors of climate or orientation. Warm color is welcome in cold climates or spaces with a northern orientation that will never receive direct sun. Cool colors are helpful in hot and sunny locations. Difficult spatial shapes can be modified, with small spaces made to look larger and oddly shaped spaces made more reasonable through color distribution, based on the known facts of color perception. Elements can be emphasized or visually diminished through color, and messages can be subtly conveyed through selection of colors that attract, repel, or express specific attitudes. A white door in a white wall will seem to disappear. A bright red door invites attention and suggests importance.

In general, a functional approach to color permits, even encourages, a very free use of color elements, demanding only that every color decision be purposeful in one or another specific way. Functional use of color can interlace with the concepts of color theory and can overlap neutral and natural color use. It is particularly appropriate to modern concepts of overall design rooted in functional intentions.

COLOR IN SPECIALIZED INTERIORS

Although the basics of developing color schemes apply to every type of interior space, it is possible to define recommendations suitable to specific interiors. Considerable research has been done in an effort to discover the "best" color schemes for various space functions, with highly inconclusive results. Because many variables interact with color in complex ways, no fixed rules can be established for dealing with color use. The sizes and shapes of spaces, the anticipated duration of typical occupancy, the impact of climate and local (or national) traditions—not to speak of changing tastes and styles—all lead to the often contradictory suggestions developed by researchers and writers. Out of this confusion, however, arise a number of generalizations and a few specifics that can be helpful in planning color schemes for assorted types of occupancy.

It is sometimes stated that "modern" color for interiors of all kinds can be characterized by the use of white as a dominant color with accents of bright primary colors or black. While this image may relate to some modern design of the 1920s, as mentioned above, the leading

figures of modernism were, in fact, users of strong and varied color. It may be that familiarity with black-and-white photographs of early modern work (taken before the development of color photography) has promoted the idea that black, white, and chrome were the colors of modernism. The frequently stated conviction that modern interiors are "cold" is probably based on this misunderstanding. Le Corbusier (who was a talented modernist painter as well as an architect) used strong tones of green, orange, warm browns, red, and blue in his interiors. Visitors often express surprise on visiting his famous Villa Savoye (see fig. 4.69) to find that it is richly colorful. The reconstructed Barcelona Pavilion of Mies van der Rohe (see fig. 4.68) has been similarly surprising with its green and orange marbles, scarlet red curtains, and other strong color elements. Current practice encourages designers to use color in varied ways while avoiding the clichés of modernism or any other stylistic rigidities. More detailed discussion of color and some common interior uses follows.

Offices

Commonly occupied for long periods of time on a daily basis, offices deserve color schemes that will be of optimum help to their users. For many years recommendations for the use of a bland buff or tan, or the green tones thought at one time to be "eye-savers," led to office interiors with a depressingly institutional character. Modern practice suggests the use of livelier colors in limited areas with related quiet tones for larger spaces. Because it is important to limit brightness contrast within the field of vision of the office worker (see Chapter 10, page 298), dark tones and black become problematic and work surfaces need to be of fairly light tones to minimize contrast with task materials, typically print on white paper. Floor colors should not be so dark as to introduce excessive brightness contrast between tasks or work surfaces and floors. Intense colors such as bright reds, yellows, purples, or violets are best restricted to secondary spaces passed through briefly, such as corridors or service areas. For the milder colors appropriate to work spaces, it is generally believed that cool colors encourage concentration whereas warmer colors best suit activity. Southern orientation with natural light and warm climate locations support the use of cool colors, while colder climates and northern orientation suggest warm color tones. In multifloor office projects, each floor can be given an identifying color tonality, with strong color in lobbies, corridors, and entrance points and quieter versions of related hues in general office areas.

Private offices tolerate more aggressive color schemes, especially when occupants can be identified and personal color preferences considered, as with many executive offices. Office personnel may change or be moved about with the passage of time, however, rendering overly personal or eccentric color schemes inappropriate even in private offices. Natural color schemes, discussed above, featuring the tones of materials such as wood, leather, and masonry, are usually successful. The popular "modern" color practice of using white for walls, a neutral tone for floors, and accents of intense, saturated, and primary or near primary color is regarded as unacceptable by many researchers, who find the white surfaces to be sources of excessive brightness, contrast, and glare. Studies indicate that user-occupants are frequently dissatisfied with such color schemes, regarding them as harsh and cold. Black,

9.38

white, and sharp colors are thus best used in lobbies, corridors, and other spaces that are not occupied for long periods of time (fig. 9.38).

Schools and College Facilities

Typically afflicted with drab institutional color schemes, educational facilities are well served by many of the same criteria that apply to offices. Students in a classroom alternate attention between desktop tasks and forward vision toward teacher and chalkboard. Mild color schemes for floor and side walls, cooler or warmer in tonality as orientation and climate may suggest, can be relieved by stronger color on the end wall related to or contrasting with chalkboard color. The black of the traditional chalkboard, which in practice actually appears as a medium gray, is less satisfactory than other chalkboard tones now available. The intense green chalkboard and brown tones of many tackboard surfaces also take on an institutional drabness that can be avoid-

ed or relieved through the use of contrasting color surrounds.

Classrooms for young children profit from the use of brighter colors, usually in warm tones; the use of primary colors, however, is an undesirable cliché. Auditoriums, gymnasiums, and large lunchrooms are best served by light tones, especially warm colors that minimize brightness contrast. Corridors and stairway areas can use stronger colors to offer variety and stimulation during transitions from one area to another.

Restaurants and Other Food-Service Areas

A restaurant offering excellent food and service can fail if color and materials generate a depressing or unpleasant atmosphere. Grays and black as well as stronger tones of blue and violet are unadvisable, and yellow-greens have unappetizing implications. Although red and other warm tones tend to stimulate appetite and create a cheerful

9.38 Brilliant color is generally most appropriate in spaces that are passed through quickly. In this reception area in the Campbell, California, center for Apple Computers, red, blue, and black are all present in saturated intensity. Simon Martin-Vegue Winkelstein Moris were the designers. (Photograph: Charles McGrath)

atmosphere, they are best used with restraint and with stronger accent colors that may be analogous or complementary. Floor coverings are frequently chosen in tones that tend to hide dirt; fussy patterns in dull colors, however, can be unappealing. Good maintenance is preferable to hiding soil. In restaurants where they are used, table linens contribute an important color element within the diner's field of vision and need, of course, to be selected in relation to the overall color of the restaurant.

Various traditional associations of color with style of food service can provide valuable suggestions for restaurant color as long as they do not lead to cliché treatments. Natural wood for floors and tabletops—possibly for walls as well—relates well to seafood cuisine. The national colors of red, white, and green in an Italian restaurant, red and white in a Danish dining room, or blue and yellow where Swedish food is offered are acceptable if not presented in overpowering excess. Softer warm tones suit luxury restaurants serving traditional menus; the glitter of silver and glassware supplies a lively accent to the restrained color, which suggests a leisurely pace.

Cafeterias and dining accommodations provided in office or industrial facilities can use brighter colors to stimulate a rapid pace and to provide contrast with the colors of work settings. Black, gray, strong cool colors, and yellow-greens are to be avoided. In fast-food outlets, intense color is often deliberately adopted to encourage quick customer turnover; since a brisk pace is one of the attractions of these restaurants, such schemes can still be attractive in overall impact.

In these, as in all food-service facilities, the level and type of lighting are critical (see Chapter 10, page 309). Fluorescent light is generally unsuited to dining areas, whereas warm light concentrated on tabletop areas maximizes the attractiveness of food. Light levels can vary from low in luxury restaurants to bright in facilities favoring a speedier pace. If fluorescent light must be used for reasons of economy, warm-tone tubes should be specified and accent incandescent light provided at food-service areas. Restaurant color schemes must always be developed under the type of lighting that will be used in the completed facility.

Stores, Shops, Showrooms

Retail and sales facilities present color problems similar to those of restaurants. Choice of color must be favorable to the goods on display and must relate to the price levels, pacing, and general character of the store. Acceptance of certain traditions helps customers to feel right in a particular shop and thus to find selection and purchase of goods easy. Menswear, for example, is appropriately offered in settings of brown wood tones and subdued color, while women's shops benefit from pastels and warm tones. The "high-tech" vocabulary of white, black, and chrome (possibly with bright accent colors) befits products with technical associations, such as electronic or photographic gear; bright colors in general suit sports equipment; and restrained color complements the sale of expensive jewelry.

In many shops, the colors of merchandise and packaging furnish so much color that a neutral, noncompeting setting may serve well. In an automobile showroom the strong colors of the cars on display provide all the color needed. Discount outlets and clothing shops featuring "plain pipe racks" use little color and bright lighting to create a neutral environment appropriate to an image of fast pacing and low prices.

Retail food stores call for color coordinated by area to the various kinds of food for sale. Because of its associations with freshness and cleanliness, white suits the display of dairy and frozen-food products. Meats show well in either white surroundings or with blue or blue-green tints that accent the red tones. Special warm-tone lighting is also often used to accent the color of meat both on display and at service areas. Bright accent colors can become part of an overall color theme that aids the identification of supermarkets and other chain retail outlets. Signs, packaging, and advertising materials, if color coordinated, assist each other in projecting the character of a particular business to encourage customer satisfaction and loyalty.

Medical and Healthcare Facilities

The complex, interrelated needs of doctors, nurses, patients, visitors, and staff—groups with overlapping but varied relationships to the spaces they use—present special problems in color selection. Patients enter a hospital with concerns and worries, and their stays will include periods of discomfort and boredom. Visitors have another set of concerns as they come to cheer, observe, and attend to the patients they see. Doctors and other staff put in long working hours under circumstances that can be tiring and stressful. Of these groups, the needs of patients should be primary, and, fortunately, serving these needs generally will be advantageous to each of the other constituencies. In terms of color, the basic requirement is schemes that will be at once restful and calming while projecting a level of optimism and good cheer that supports recovery and health (fig. 9.39).

A number of recent research studies have reported findings suggesting that environmental ambience plays a significant role in the rate of recovery among hospital patients and in the well-being of nursing-home occupants. The specific elements that can make a favorable difference include visual contact with the out-of-doors and the use of warm color tones, along with materials, such as natural wood and fabrics, that relate to residential interiors. Some hospital patients may occupy a room for an extended period of time, during which the wall opposite the bed and the ceiling above will be major background elements in the field of vision. White, institutional green, or tan in these areas contributes to a depressive atmosphere. Cool colors, although believed to be calming, are of questionable value in patients' rooms because they can also be interpreted as depressing; strong greens or blues are best avoided or used as accents in a warmer context. The practice of alternating warm and cool schemes for patients' rooms, sometimes suggested as a means of providing for differing personal character and taste among patients, is also of dubious worth since patients are usually assigned to rooms with no opportunity to express a preference. Patients' bathrooms call for mild, warm colors that flatter users' skin tones when reflected in mirrors.

In intensive care units, however, cooler colors, which offer a calming ambience, are appropriate. Bluish green has become a standard color treatment for operating rooms because it provides visual relief from the brightly lighted red tones of blood and tissue that occupy the visual field of the surgeon and other personnel at work. Examination and treatment areas may use cooler colors wherever a calm atmosphere is indicated and warmer tones in areas such as dermatology and obstetrics; in all cases, color should be restrained to avoid any possibility of environmental color reflection interfering with patient diagnosis. Nurseries, for example, should not use strong colors (proposed in an effort to enhance these spaces for visiting adults) because they may distort evaluation of infants' skin color and impede appropriate care.

Hospital corridors, with their extreme length and heavy use by many, sometimes conflicting, types of traffic, are problematic. Active color schemes can add to a sense of confusion and clutter, while white, buff, and institutional green contribute to a depressive tone. Mild warm tones for side walls, with stronger accent colors for end walls, doors, and any other locations that can provide relief from monotony, may be considered. Lobby and reception areas can use stronger color schemes developed to project a sense of quality and good organization. Laboratories, staff offices, lounges, and cafeterias in hospitals can be approached in the same ways that such areas are treated in other contexts.

Environmental circumstances have a strong impact on the behavior and recovery of patients being treated in psychiatric hospitals and the psychiatric-care facilities of general hospitals, where lengthy stays are common. Attractive color treatment has been shown to have a favorable effect in such conditions. In general, color schemes suggesting pleasant residential environments, colorful and warm but calming rather than overactive, are most beneficial. Strong tones of blue (depressive) and of red and orange (exciting) are best avoided, and violet, purple, and black should never be used. Highly reflective finishes

can generate images that may be disturbing to some patients, making polished floor surfaces, shiny tiles, and gloss paints inappropriate.

Nursing homes call for color treatment paralleling that of general hospitals. Because patients are often long-term residents, emphasis on a calm and homelike atmosphere is important. Not surprisingly, elderly patients tend to express conservative taste in colors and decorative treatment, so that natural wood tones, warm paint colors, and traditional decorative patterns in upholstery, bed covers, and other details are most effective in relieving any sense of institutional bleakness.

Medical and dental offices, clinics, and group-practice facilities can follow color recommendations for office systems in combination with those for hospital treatment, laboratory, and other work spaces. Medical-office waiting rooms are notorious for their unpleasant character, the result of shabbiness and neglect or, in a misguided effort at betterment, overdecoration with excessive color and pattern. These reception and waiting areas deserve special attention, as patients must frequently endure long waits in states of tension and anxiety; a pleasant and optimistic tone can be conveyed through the use of lively color, either warm, cool, or a balanced combination thereof, as climate and orientation may suggest.

Hotels and Motels

In addition to providing lodging for their patrons, hotels and motels can offer an element of entertainment. Even the business traveler who must use a city hotel hopes for some degree of pleasure in the stay. Vacationers regard the hotel as a major factor in making a visit to a

9.39

9.39 The warm tones of simple wood details enliven a patient's room in the Reisman Building of Beth Israel Hospital, Boston, Massachusetts. Design was by Rothman Rothman Heineman Architects with Crissman Solomon Bauer Architects and Lloy Hack Associates. (Photograph: © 1984 Steve Rosenthal)

city pleasurable, and resort hotels exist solely as settings for enjoyment. Although the public lobbies of hotels are occupied only briefly by a guest, they make a first impression that sets the tone of a stay and is reinforced with each entrance and exit. Color is a significant element in expressing efficiency, dignity, luxury, relaxation, playfulness, or any combination of such qualities. The dark woods and rich marbles of many older hotels suggest solidity and tradition, whereas the bright saturated colors and whites of a resort hotel imply informality and entertainment. Hotel dining rooms are, in effect, restaurants and should use color with the care discussed above.

Guest rooms, because they are temporarily a private home to their occupants, are notably demanding of color that will please and cheer the occupants. Hotel managers must decide on whether to adopt a standard scheme for all guest rooms of a particular type (making for economy and efficiency) or whether to use a number of varied schemes for similar rooms. The latter approach ensures that repeated stays in a certain hotel will not be monotonously uniform and allows the arriving guest to make a choice among rooms to favor personal taste. Offering choices, however, can complicate the assignment of rooms. Although some hotels attempt to simplify this process by having color photographs of rooms available at the registration desk, this too can lead to confusion and delay. When an assortment of schemes is offered, each must be sufficiently agreeable to any reasonable guest. The general suggestions for selecting color on the basis of climate and room orientation (warm or cool dominant tones as appropriate) can be enlivened by the introduction of colors characteristic of the location or region. This is especially applicable to resort hotels in exotic locations, where the guest has come with a desire to experience "local color." Brightly colored tiles and fabrics combined with white or near-white wall surfaces may suggest a tropical island; textiles or wall coverings in small patterns using red and green typify the coziness associated with British residential interiors; and natural teak, white, and bright (probably red) details distinguish "Danish modern." Although such color schemes may be used in the actual locations mentioned, they may also be used elsewhere to evoke a particular style and atmosphere. While an emphasis on high style or fashion color might suit some big-city hotels, a more modest and homelike character may be more appropriate to a tourist motel. An estimated average duration of guests' stays can guide color selection: in facilities where guest stays are relatively brief, more aggressive color can be used to make an impression that will not have time to become boring; where longer stays are typical, as in many resort locations, color that is pleasant but calm will be less likely to become a source of irritation to any guest. Strong accent colors in bed coverings and draperies, rather than in more fixed elements, allow replacement from time to time to adjust to changing fashion and to inject an element of freshness over a period of years.

Industrial Settings

Frequently cluttered with equipment, machinery, and materials, industrial settings can profit from the use of color in setting the tone of work spaces to reduce fatigue and annoyance and to promote efficiency and safety. As with offices, brightness contrast needs to be carefully considered to ensure that materials and tools in use are readily distinguishable from backgrounds but that excessive contrast does not promote eye fatigue. Glossy surfaces that produce reflected glare are undesirable. Areas of bright, pleasant color that offer relief from eyestrain may be strategically located. Problems associated with various work processes can to some extent be offset by appropriate color choices. Excessive heat, for example, is countered by dominant areas of blues or greens. Conversely, warm reds and oranges reduce discomfort associated with cold. Irritation generated by high noise levels can be lessened by the presence of light colors, especially greens.

Color use to aid safety in industrial settings has come to be widely accepted. Greens are commonly used as a general color for machinery and equipment, forming a background for contrasting color according to the following rules:

Yellow indicates potential hazards, including moving equipment such as forklifts and cranes.

Red indicates fire-safety equipment, containers of dangerous materials, and control switches and buttons on machinery.

Blue indicates electrical controls and repair areas.

White indicates trash containers, drinking fountains, and food-service locations.

Black-and-white striping indicates traffic areas, aisles, and stairway locations.

Another color code is used to identify piping according to function. The bright colors of the coded pipes often inject a lively color element into industrial settings.

WORKING METHOD

Putting together a color scheme at the drawing board involves making color charts and material charts. These convert color scheme ideas into visual forms that can be evaluated and, when accepted, realized.

Collecting Color Samples

The process requires a readily available stock of color samples that can be viewed, placed in trial relationships, and then pinned down to form visual records of schemes as they develop. Preparing a collection of such samples is a key preliminary step in color work.

It is generally most convenient to work first with abstract color schemes, that is, representing all colors with flat paper swatches devoid of texture, pattern, and other special characteristics of real materials. Colored papers, which come arranged in systems, offer a suitable medium. Available index booklets of such color paper systems are an ideal means of bringing a full range of color to the worktable.

The color stock can be augmented with large sheets of color papers and color paper samples cut from packages, printed brochures, advertisements, and any other sources that may turn up. The habit of clipping and filing colored papers and cards leads quickly to a highly useful collection of samples ready for use in working on color schemes. Metallic papers, glossy flint papers, and textured papers can be added to a sample collection to increase its range. In addition, one can mix colors (using tempera, gouache, or designers' colors) in small quanti-

9.40

9.41

9.42

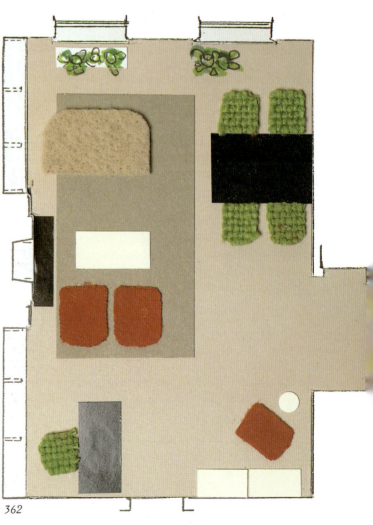

362

9.43

ties and brush the mix onto cards to create additional color samples. Preparing samples in this way was standard practice some years ago, when color materials were less widely available. With modern color systems in general use, this method has become a last resort.

Preparing Color Charts

USING COLORED PAPER SAMPLES. With an adequate sample collection at hand, it is a simple matter to begin making up any desired color scheme by grouping together sample swatches to represent the chosen colors (fig. 9.40). In doing this, it is important to lay out the samples so that each color covers an area roughly proportionate to the actual space it will take up, so that large sample areas represent large areas and appropriately small swatches stand for small accents. Again, it is essential that the work of color charting be done under light having the same color characteristics as the light that will be normal in the real space, including all the types of light to be used, alone and in whatever combinations may occur in the actual space.

Insofar as possible, color samples should be arranged in the same order that they will occupy in the actual space, that is, floor color should go at the bottom of the chart, walls above, colors for furniture and other objects in corresponding relationships, and ceiling color on top. It is important to include samples of *all* colors that will be present; a white ceiling, for example, should not be ignored but should be represented with an appropriate area of white sample. As it is developing, the scheme should be viewed against a neutral background—white, black, or, best of all, a neutral gray. Samples should be placed side by side, leaving no background visible between them. As a scheme is brought together into a final color plan, samples can be glued down to a mount to form an established record (fig. 9.41). Such an abstract color chart can be used for review with a client or as a basis for color sketching or rendering.

Another method of color charting uses a floor plan, usually at ¼" = 1'-0". An extra print of the furniture layout plan works best as the basis for a color chart. Actual colors of flooring, furniture, and built-in elements are shown by pasting down samples cut to fit the plan indication of the element in question. Wall colors and the colors of drapery and other materials on vertical surfaces are indicated by diagrammatic color lines (in pencil or marker), which are then keyed to sample swatches placed adjacent to the plan (fig. 9.43). In this way, color is seen more or less in position as it will occur in the real space.

A further extension of this technique places a plan with wall elevations adjacent to the plan indication of the wall surfaces. Plan and elevations then both become the basis for pasting in color samples (or pencil or marker indication of colors), displaying all colors in correct relative location and area. By cutting out such a plan and elevation drawing chart and folding the wall elevations up into a vertical position, a kind of abstract model of the space, called a *maquette*, is created. Traditional decorators often made such a color presentation by rendering (usually in watercolors) the floor plan and each wall surface. While lacking the full three-dimensionality of a model, this maquette is often helpful in visualizing how colors will actually relate in the completed space.

Still another technique of color charting uses a perspective drawing, usually only a geometric layout without detail, as a basis. Color samples cut to fit the areas in the layout are pasted down to form a collage color chart that approximates the appearance of the constructed space as seen from a certain viewpoint.

USING ACTUAL MATERIALS. The color chart can be taken a step further by translating the abstract colors into real materials and finishes (fig. 9.42). Once again, a collection of samples is extremely useful. Wood and laminate finishes available from furniture makers and samples of basic material colors (brick, concrete, terrazzo, metals, woods, and so on) are needed along with samples of tiles, floor coverings, and other materials. For materials not easily kept on hand, such as brick, stone, and other bulky materials, color illustrations may be substituted. It is important to have samples of the actual carpet and textiles in order to take into account the impact of textures and patterns. Large samples of carpets, textiles, and other major material areas should be viewed together because tiny samples, viewed only at the drawing table, tend to be misleading.

Large *memo square* samples of textiles, usually a yard of whatever width the fabric is produced in, large samples of carpet, and panels of wood finish are available from manufacturers. It may be necessary to carry the more portable materials to a showroom where a more bulky item is on display in order to observe the relationship. Textiles, carpet, and paint color samples, for example, might be taken to a furniture showroom or to a supplier of brick or marble. Larger design firms often operate a sample room storing large samples of frequently used materials, which can be spread out on a table and viewed under suitable lighting.

Sample Boards

Charts called *sample boards* can be made up using real materials along with color swatches representing paint and other solid color areas. Such charts, like the abstract charts, should show materials in areas proportional to their real use and in appropriate relationships. The accepted chart becomes a record of the color selections for items to be purchased and for paint and other colors to be applied on site. A written record of pattern and color numbers should be made and a set of samples should be put away in a folder or envelope representing the scheme settled on for each space of a total interior project.

Realizing the Color Scheme

Realization then becomes a matter of placing orders for products (furniture, draperies, and so on) with correct color specifications, relaying specification information for materials and items that are built-in (architectural materials, hardware, and light fixtures), and, for the painter, preparing a plan color chart showing where each color is to be applied, with a key to a set of sample swatches.

SPECIALLY MIXED COLORS. It is important to remember that color choices are not limited to the available standard colors offered by the makers of paints, fabrics, carpet, and other products. Carpets and textiles can be dyed to order and paints mixed to match any sample

9.40 This color scheme was initially developed using a selection of colored papers.

9.41 Here, the same scheme shows the papers arranged with their areas proportionally equivalent to their final organization in the interior and ordered to correspond roughly to their ultimate placement. Thus, the rug color occupies the bottom of the chart, the ceiling color the top, and the wall, upholstery, and drapery colors the area in between. The papers have been taped down in a neat band because the scheme will be presented to a client for discussion.

9.42 In this stage, the scheme takes the form of a chart of the actual materials laid out as they will be used in the completed space.

9.43 The same scheme is shown here in a paste-up, or collage, floor plan. Fabrics are cut out and fixed in place to represent upholstered furniture. Papers are used to show the floor color; the colors of furniture materials (wood, marble) and other elements (such as walls) are usually indicated in colored pencil. This type of plan does not portray the total, three-dimensional impact of wall, ceiling, drapery, and other colors, and it should be studied along with other color charts for a balanced impression of overall color. Nevertheless, it helps to analyze the effect of color on certain key features of a space.

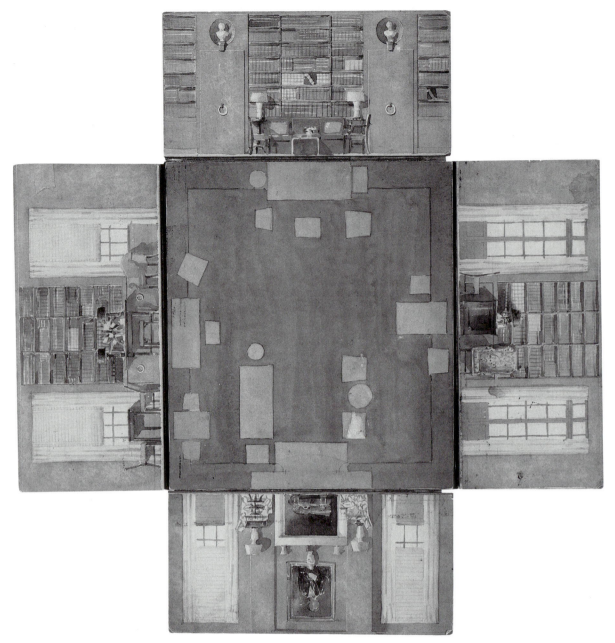

9.44

swatch. Ready-mixed paints are usually limited to a range of banal tints, although some paint color systems offer a much wider range, including strong colors often identified as decorator colors. A competent painter can mix color to match any requirement, except, perhaps, color desired at an extreme level of intense saturation (very high or full chroma). Dyeing carpet and fabric to order offers only the limited risk that a large area matched to a small sample may be a visual surprise—for better or for worse.

EVALUATING COLOR ON SITE. In following a project on site, it is important not to be upset by the impression given by one or another color or finish before all the related elements are in place and seen under the specified lighting. Colors influence one another so strongly that it is quite common for one color, perhaps a painted area or a floor color, to look all wrong until the other elements that make up the total color scheme are in place. Some on-site adjustments of color can be made, although only to certain elements, the most flexible being paint color. A prime coat can be viewed and changes considered before a

9.44, 9.45 A room of a New York apartment of 1948 is here presented in the form of a maquette. The floor plan (in the center) is surrounded by elevations of the four walls, all realistically rendered in watercolors. If each wall is folded up to form a box, the result suggests the three-dimensional view given by a model. Any one or two walls can

be folded down so that the interior can be studied at eye level. This example is the work of the late Grace Fakes of McMillen, Inc. The actual room as constructed (fig. 9.45) closely matched the scheme proposed in fig. 9.44. (Photograph: Hans van Nes, courtesy McMillen, Inc.)

9.45

final coat is applied. Still, it is important to remember before making adjustments to paint color that the color areas to be delivered later (carpet, upholstery) will influence the way painted areas will appear. Hasty changes and adjustments made on site when the total scheme is not yet in place are often unwise. In general, if a well-proportioned color chart viewed under appropriate light has seemed satisfactory, the finished space will probably look as good. Sticking to a well-conceived plan until all elements are in place is usually the sensible course of action.

Common Color Problems

The following lists common problems in color use that cause disappointing color results:

- RANDOM ACQUISITION OF ITEMS AND COLOR DECISIONS NOT RELATED TO A CAREFULLY CONCEIVED COLOR PLAN.
- TOO MUCH AND TOO VARIED COLOR. Restricted color schemes are usually safe; schemes using many hues run greater risks. A full rainbow scheme using many or all hues will almost certainly fail, appearing as chaotic as the random color arrived at without planning.
- TOO INTENSE COLOR USED IN LARGE AREAS. This may work in spaces used only briefly; otherwise, it is likely to become tiring over a period of time.

- TOO MUCH CONTRAST IN LARGE COLOR AREAS. In complementary schemes in particular, near-equal areas of contrasting color in near-equal intensity set up a tension that is usually unpleasant. It is best if one or the other color is dominant in intensity or in area. Most often it is best if small areas of high intensity are used in relation to larger areas of lesser intensity.
- DRABNESS AND MONOTONY. This potential problem is at the opposite extreme from the problems mentioned above. Institutional-green color schemes and use of beiges, tans, and browns may carry safe color too far, producing depressing results. In restricted color schemes, strong accent color is useful in avoiding this kind of problem.

Successful color depends, above all, on the planning of a total scheme with all elements, in swatches or samples of whatever sort, viewed in relationship to one another in proportional areas and under appropriate light. The amateur's failure to create a well-conceived color relationship is usually the result of piecemeal color decision-making. Whether the planned scheme is derived from some form of color theory or simply improvised intuitively, it will have a basis in systematic coordination. This is the only reliable way to approach color planning.

10.1

CHAPTER

TEN

LIGHTING

Vision is the sense we find the most useful—in learning about our living spaces, in moving around those spaces and locating objects we need for our comfort or use, and in forming the mental images, impressions, and emotions that make those spaces understandable and memorable—and vision is dependent on light. Because we cannot see in the dark, and because electricity is so readily available, we have come to take it for granted that interior spaces will be lighted. It is not surprising, then, that lighting is one of the most important aspects of successful interior design. Good lighting supports convenience, comfort, and favorable emotional reactions. Improving the lighting of a space can be more effective than any other single factor in increasing overall sense of satisfaction. Bad lighting hampers utility and may produce depression and displeasure with the space, making an otherwise attractive room dismal and unattractive.

Stage designers are well aware that the lighting of a set can do more than anything else to establish a mood, focus attention, even create illusions. In addition, lighting is easy to control and, in comparison with solid materials such as walls, furniture, or carpets, highly economical. It is all too common to plan an interior in terms of such substantial elements and treat lighting as an afterthought, to be provided by routinely chosen fixtures and lamps. Intelligent interior design recognizes lighting's ability to influence the way in which occupants see a space and considers lighting a primary means of giving a space special character.

A glaring light bulb or two actually gives enough light to see clearly, but such light is painfully unflattering to the space, its contents, and its occupants. Its uniform level and unconsidered placement reveal every defect and show everything equally, offering no variety or subtlety. A room considered ugly almost always turns out to be badly lit. Switching off a glaring ceiling light and substituting a few well-chosen and well-placed lamps or fixtures can make a startling, instantaneous improvement, often at very little cost.

Good lighting can achieve the following effects:

- *SET A DESIRED MOOD OR ATMOSPHERE.* Dim light usually makes a space seem intimate and cozy, bright light businesslike and energetic. Restaurant designers and managers are well aware that bright, even light encourages quick turnover in a fast-food outlet but that it works against a mood of leisure and comfort.
- *DIRECT OR CONCENTRATE ATTENTION.* Brightly lit areas within an otherwise dim space draw visual focus. Strong light on a dining table within a generally dimmer room renders table settings, food, and drink more attractive. A brightly lit wall or spotlights clearly display artwork. A good light at a desk, with the surround at a lower light level, helps to concentrate attention on work. Merchandise on display under strong spotlights draws attention in a showroom or store.
- *CONTROL SHADING AND SHADOW TO AID THE VIEWER IN SEEING FORM AND TEXTURE.* Diffuse, even light tends to flatten objects. Sharp shadows emphasize forms, and strong cross light coming from one side brings out texture. These effects are obvious outdoors—the light of a bright and sunny day makes objects seem sharp and crisp, while a cloudy sky, with its more even light, suggests a dullness that can set a somber, even depressing tone.
- *EMPHASIZE OR MODIFY SPATIAL PERCEPTION.* A dark ceiling appears lower, even oppressive, while a brighter ceiling can seem to float upward, almost like the sky. Bright windows draw attention to their size and shape. Using blinds or curtains to diminish their brightness makes them less important; lighting other areas more strongly makes them almost unnoticeable.

Until modern times, daylight was the primary source of light everywhere; the design of buildings had to take into account the lighting of interiors through windows and such alternatives as skylights. Auxiliary light came from open fires, candles, and the various types of lamps developed over the years. Simple in nature, these gave a limited amount and quality of light and were difficult to control. Electric light can be so efficient and effective that it has taken over all night lighting service and has become the primary source of light in many spaces. Windowless spaces—even buildings—in which daylight is insignificant have become common, especially in large stores and offices. Artificial light again becomes primary in homes, where most people spend much of their time after dark. Since we now so rarely experience daylight as an important source of lighting, we may even overlook it.

Modern electric light can be produced by a variety of sources (incandescent, fluorescent, and so on), each quite different from the others.

10.1 A group of the popular Tizio cantilever, adjustable desk lamps designed by Richard Sapper are displayed in the New York showroom of Artemide, Inc., an importer of Italian lighting elements. The showroom (now closed) was designed by Massimo Vignelli. (Photograph: © Paul Warchol)

10.2

Portable lamps and fixed lighting fixtures give a wide range of control over the location, intensity, and quality of lighting output. Daylight is also subject to control from a variety of kinds of window glazing and window treatments, such as blinds, shades, and curtains. Since light is a form of basic energy, lighting interacts with heating and air-conditioning in a way that can be quite complex.

With so many options, lighting has become a complicated subject that can be studied from a technical point of view. At the same time, it is something of an art and involves creative thinking and imagination. Illuminating engineers and professional lighting consultants, specialists in these matters, are often employed to assist in interior design projects in which lighting will be both important and complex. Every interior designer needs to have a basic understanding of lighting issues in order to deal with simpler situations directly, as well as to work effectively with lighting specialists when they are involved in a project.

VISION AND LIGHTING

It is an unfortunate reality that bad lighting is all too common. It may result from simple carelessness or indifference, but it can also come about in planned situations, even when handbook recommendations or manufacturers' advice is followed. The design of lighting is too often limited to providing a high level of light, with the assumption that this will take care of all users' needs. However, seeing depends on many additional factors—shading and shadow, limitation of brightness contrast, color quality—that, along with level of intensity, make seeing easy and satisfying. To understand the complexities of these issues, it is necessary to consider the basics of human vision, the sense that lighting is, after all, intended to serve.

Almost everyone has at some time studied, at least briefly, the physiology of the human eye and can recall something of its mechanism (fig. 10.4). The familiar analogy with a simple camera still serves to

10.2 Daylight, ambient light from hanging overhead fixtures, and task lighting from table-mounted lamps work together in a barrel-vaulted former assembly hall, now the Kaskel Library, of the Hackley School in Tarrytown, New York. This conversion project won a lighting award in 1986 for its designers, Keith Kroeger Associates, architects, with Cline Bettridge Bernstein, lighting consultants. (Photograph: Adam Bartos, courtesy Keith Kroeger Associates)

explain it. The eye itself is the dark chamber comparable to the box or bellows of the camera; the retina at the back of the eye is the light-sensitive surface comparable to the film or plate of photography. The pupil of the eye is a lens that can change focus to form a sharp image on the retina of objects near or far away. The retinal image is transmitted through the optic nerve to the brain, which interprets the image to create the mental picture that we see. The image is, of course, in color, and it is in sharp focus only at its center. Through movements of the eyeball, head, and body, the eye scans the scene before it and builds up a mental image that includes a wider, more sharply focused field of view than the eye itself can generate at a given moment.

As it focuses on individual objects, what the eye sees depends on the kind and quality of light available. Light bouncing off objects reflects back to the eye variations in brightness and color that correspond in a complex geometric way with the size, shape, distance, color, and texture of those objects. This creates on the retina the picture in perspective that we learn to understand as being the appearance of whatever we look at.

10.3

10.3 In the social context of residential and restaurant settings, candlelight still generates a special, intimate aura as no other light source can. This dining area in a New York apartment is by John F. Saladino, designer. (Photograph: © Peter Vitale)

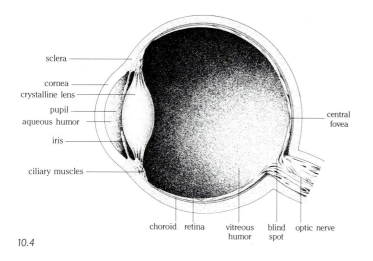

Considerations for Good Lighting

The goals of lighting are to promote good visibility and to generate qualities of atmosphere, the aesthetic and emotional impressions that convey a mood appropriate to the space in question. These goals may be in conflict, as in the restaurant where the dim "candlelight mood" lighting creates a pleasant atmosphere but makes it difficult or impossible to read the menu or cut the steak. Many spaces demand that lighting deal with varied tasks and moods. A living room may be used for reading, conversation, TV-watching, and a range of other occupations. No single lighting setup will answer each of these activities. Therefore, means of varying the lighting must be found. For every task and every situation, the following issues must be faced:

LIGHT LEVEL. This is the simple quantity of light at a task, which is easily measured. The eye, which developed through millions of years as a device to aid adaptation to the totally natural environment, is equipped to adjust to the extremes presented by natural light, from the brilliant noonday sun to dim starlight or less. Two devices deal with this adjustment. One is the iris, the ring around the pupil that gives the eye its distinctive color. According to the brightness of the scene viewed, the iris automatically enlarges or contracts to admit more or less light, exactly as the iris of a camera does.

A second level of control, in the retina–optic nerve–brain system, is called accommodation. Over a period of minutes, it becomes possible to see better in dim light (as in a darkened auditorium) or to adjust to beach or snow brightness. Together, the adjustments of the iris and accommodation make possible satisfactory seeing through a surprisingly wide range of conditions. Therefore, light level is actually less important than many other factors. Still, one candle cannot provide sufficient light for reading, while too much light may create glare and will certainly cost more than necessary. Since older people and people with vision problems need more light for a given task than others, it has become customary to provide an ample light level for reading, writing, sewing, drafting, or other demanding seeing tasks. A generous excess of light is appropriate for such tasks as industrial inspection, medical examination, or surgery.

10.5

10.4 The human eye is the receptor that all lighting is designed to serve. The iris varies the size of the pupil, controlling the amount of light that reaches the retina, thereby enabling the eye to adjust to a wide range of conditions. The cross-sectional drawing is by Giorgio Brunelli. (From Theory and Use of Color by Luigina De Grandis)

10.5 Imaginative lighting brightens a windowless auditorium. Jointed panels of acrylic plastic diffuse light from bulbs set along a track; the result is a soft, overall illumination. A motor lowers the tracks for relamping. Hidetoshi Ohno, architect, principal of A.P.L.

Sogokeikaku Jimusho of Tokyo, designed the lighting; Endo Planning provided the interior design. The space is the International Conference Hall of YKK 50 of the Yoshida Kogyo Company, Kurobe, Japan. (Photograph: Taisuke Ogawa)

CONTROL OF BRIGHTNESS CONTRAST AND GLARE. The adjustments of the iris and retina–optic nerve–brain system cannot deal with a visual field that includes bright and dim areas that both demand attention, as when trying to read while facing a bright window. The iris of the eye struggles to open up to aid seeing the book but is forced to close down to control the bright window light. Tired eye muscles and difficulty in seeing inevitably result. Such excessive brightness contrast is one of the most troublesome of lighting situations.

When the difference between the brightest and dimmest points within a visual field is not extreme, the eye need not struggle to find a compromise adjustment. This entails shading direct sources of light, such as unshielded bulbs, fluorescent tubes, or windows letting in bright sunlight; avoiding dark backgrounds behind bright objects (desktops and tabletops and floors are frequent offenders); and providing *fill light* to keep less lighted background areas from contrasting with bright visual areas. (Further discussion of brightness contrast continues on pages 304–305.)

Excessive brightness, called *glare*, comes from such familiar situations as an unshaded ceiling light bulb or from ceiling-mounted fluorescent light fixtures that form bright spots in an otherwise dim ceiling. Both situations are common because they provide a high level of light economically.

One special form of glare, called *veiling reflection*, comes from looking at somewhat glossy material placed so as to reflect a source of illumination, such as a window or light bulb. A person reading print on glossy paper will move the paper around in an effort to find a position that kills the glare. Special efforts to deal with this problem (discussed on page 306) are called for wherever reading, writing, or other close seeing will take place for an extended time.

CONTRAST AND DIFFUSION. Shade and shadow emphasize form but conceal detail in the shaded areas. Light that comes from a concentrated source, or point source, tends to create strong shade and shadow, while diffused light tends to diminish or block out shading. The sun, a point source, casts strong shadows that make objects look crisp and sharp. A cloudy sky gives a soft, diffuse light that reveals detail in shade but may seem dull or depressing in mood. Actually, sunny daylight is a mixture of point-source direct sun and diffuse light from the sky. A pure point source, such as a theater or photo spotlight, accents form by creating even sharper shadows, but its light may seem harsh.

High-contrast point-source lighting draws attention and accents form and texture. Diffuse light promotes good general vision but may seem drab and characterless. The absence of shadows can make some tasks harder because shadows aid three-dimensional depth perception. When writing or drawing, the shadow of pen or pencil as it is lifted and lowered aids in seeing and control. For most situations, a suitable mix of point-source and diffused light will serve best.

ECONOMIC ISSUES. Daylight is free, but windows and skylights are not. Moreover, windows and skylights admit summer heat and allow winter heat to escape, effects which must be offset with mechanical equipment that is costly to provide and operate. Artificial light requires the purchase of lamps, fixtures, and wiring, as well as the ongoing cost of maintenance, replacing bulbs and tubes, and power. In addition, the heat generated by lighting calls for additional summer air-conditioning, which is rarely balanced by comparable savings in winter heating. This is usually a minor factor in residential lighting design but a major concern in stores, offices, and factories, where artificial light is required on a nearly full-time basis. Given the present high cost of energy, it becomes important to design lighting that offers the best possible results with the minimum first cost and operational expenses.

DAYLIGHT

In recent years, there has been a tendency to ignore daylight as a significant source of illumination. Although it costs nothing, it varies with the season, weather, and time of day, and it requires building design that places windows (or skylights) to make light available where needed. Still, in many ways, daylight remains the most attractive form of illumination. It is the lighting for which the eye was developed, and its variability actually helps to make it pleasant and satisfying. Interior designers often seem to neglect the possibilities of using daylight, first, because they take windows for granted as a given condition of interior space and, second, because they think of windows as elements to be "treated" in some decorative way rather than made functionally useful.

Admitting Daylight

The nature of daylight in the interior is determined by the architecture of the space, as well as by the location and orientation of the building. It is worthwhile to study those given circumstances and to consider how they might be exploited to make the best use of natural lighting. Windows vary in size and shape, in details of framing and opening. Latitude and climate affect the light they admit, as does external shading (through overhangs, sunshades, awnings, nearby trees, and buildings). Skylights, encountered less often in existing buildings, are subject to some of the same variables. Where the space under consideration is already built, it is wise to observe and make note of the way windows perform—in what direction they face, their height and position, what view and shading they offer, and, incidentally, if they present problems with noise, heat loss or gain, or privacy. Where design work concerns a space not yet built or undergoing a major renovation, the same issues must be considered based on the facts available from drawings and on-site observation.

Windows can be changed—blocked up if badly placed, enlarged, combined, or reshaped—although this is likely to be a costly step. The effect of any changes on the exterior of the building must, of course, be considered, and permission must be obtained when the building owner is not the tenant of the space. Major changes in windows may require the help of an architect to deal with structural details and any applicable building code limitations. In general, changing frames or glazing within a window opening is fairly simple, as is cutting down a small window to make it larger (or to make it into a door). Cutting an opening for a new window of moderate size is also usually fairly simple. Large windows present more problems because the new opening requires supporting structure above it. Combining several windows,

10.6 Besides admitting an appreciable amount of sunlight, this window wall establishes a spectacular presence in a residential space. The duplex apartment in Chicago was designed by Richard Himmel. (Photograph: Feliciano, courtesy House & Garden)

sun on summer afternoons. South orientation has the advantage of receiving sun consistently for most of the day, at an angle that changes with the season. In winter, the low sun angle gives maximum heat and light, while in the summer the high angle reduces the sun's penetration. Careful planning of sun shading can control sun penetration precisely, a technique used as a basis for the design of solar houses that exploit the sun's energy to a maximum. Since sunlight is not available on cloudy days, only north-facing openings can offer consistent lighting. A south orientation is generally considered the most favorable in terms of light, pleasantness, and controllability.

Given a particular orientation and opening of known size, shape, and location, it is possible to predict the light patterns in summer and winter, at different times of day, and on sunny or dark days. This information will aid in determining window treatments, artificial light backup, and, sometimes, furniture placement and color schemes.

WINDOW TREATMENTS. While windows can provide excellent light, direct sun can be a problem and must be controlled. With east or west orientations, early morning or late afternoon conditions always call for sun control. Shades or blinds, with or without curtains, offer fully controllable adjustability, which curtains alone cannot give. (See Chapter 8, pages 234–37, for a full discussion of window treatment.) Using daylight requires artificial backup light, even in spaces used by day only, for dark days and winter afternoons. For spaces used at night, the artificial lighting planned for that use will usually serve as the daytime backup.

When placing furniture, it is important to keep bright windows out of the field of vision of a person doing any task involving close work, such as reading, sewing, or desk work. Seating for visual tasks with the back to the window can also cause problems because of the shadow cast forward. Thus, the traditional "light coming from over the left shoulder" remains ideal, although light from the right is also satisfactory for most tasks and best for left-handed people.

Artificial Light

Barring remote wilderness cabins and atmospheric candlelit restaurants, artificial light in the modern world means electric light. Since Thomas Edison introduced his pioneering invention, a wide variety of electric light sources and lighting devices has been developed, making electric light marvelously useful and controllable. To the designer, artificial light has the potential advantage of being totally controllable in terms of brightness, color, placement, and quality. For these reasons, it is actually preferred in many situations (for example, restaurants, stores, showrooms, and exhibition spaces). At its best, it can compete favorably with daylight when used in offices, residential spaces, and many special-purpose spaces such as classrooms, lobbies and lounges, waiting rooms, and many utility and work spaces.

Planning Lighting

Planning lighting for an interior normally means planning the electric lighting. Since daylight is at best a part-time source of lighting, artificial light is generally planned to do a total job.

Many people tolerate lighting planned on a hit-or-miss basis, following habitual routines—they accept a central ceiling fixture in each room and plug an occasional lamp into some convenience outlet. Good results are hardly to be expected from this approach. Good lighting for a given space depends on careful planning, starting with an analysis of needs, followed by the intelligent selection of lighting devices to suit those needs, and ending with fixture spacing and location to achieve the lighting levels and effects desired. Observing lighting installations in use, both good and bad, will build up a memory stock of examples to follow and errors to avoid. Typical planning steps are:

- *DEFINE THE GENERAL AIMS IN TERMS OF CHARACTER AND ATMOSPHERE.* Is the space to be businesslike, efficient, restful, cozy?
- *CONSIDER THE SPECIFIC PURPOSES FOR WHICH LIGHTING IS REQUIRED.* Is the space used for working, dining, reading, watching television? Does it combine several purposes, necessitating varied or changeable lighting? Most people want their living spaces to be pleasant and relaxing, but they also demand good light for reading or writing, as well as efficient light for cleaning. A store must use lighting to set a tone suitable to its style and quality level and, at the same time, to flatter and feature merchandise.
- *ASCERTAIN THE INTENSITY LEVELS FOR PROPER VISION AND BALANCE THESE AGAINST ENERGY AND FIRST-INSTALLATION COSTS AND OTHER FACTORS TO DECIDE ON LIGHTING TYPE.* Efficiency plays a major role in determining lamp type and fixture location, particularly in large installations. For example, the efficiency of fluorescent light favors its use in factories and other large spaces requiring bright light. However, it is important to plan carefully to avoid the visual and psychological problems associated with its use.
- *SELECT FIXTURES BASED ON GENERAL AIMS AND SPECIFIC NEEDS.* Once a decision is made to have brightness in one place, subtlety in another, variety for stimulation, or uniformity for efficiency, actual products should be chosen to create those effects, such as ceiling lights fixed in place for general illumination, indirect lighting for softness, concentrated spot lighting for emphasis and variety, and portable lamps for local accent and easy individual control.
- *PLACE FIXTURES.* This can be dealt with on an ad hoc (improvisational) basis in typical residential projects and similar situations where variety and atmosphere outweigh efficiency. In most larger projects, such as offices, restaurants, and stores, placement is determined by calculation, using formulas that yield the desired light levels along with the satisfactory quality of light.

Lighting is usually planned on overlay sheets placed over floor plans. A *reflected ceiling plan* (fig. 10.10) is the usual final drawing in which most lighting is indicated, although portable lamps are indicated on furniture plans. Plans and drawings detail the specifics of lighting location, but they give no idea of the *visual effect* of lighting. This remains an aspect of interior design almost impossible to present visually in advance of actual installation. Efforts to develop computer programs that will produce images illustrating a space as illuminated by a partic-

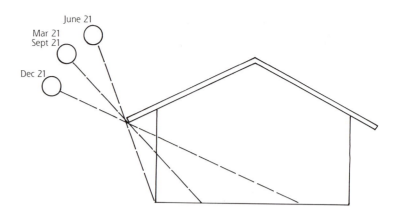

ular lighting installation have met with considerable success. In general, however, it is the informed imagination of the designer that serves as the primary means for planning and predicting how lighting will really look.

LIGHTING NEEDS

The first step in making a lighting plan is an orderly assessment of lighting needs. These will normally fall into three categories:

1. Light for specific visual functions, now often called *task lighting*. This means providing adequate and suitable light for every activity that depends on good vision. The typical tasks that call for special light are:

 Reading
 Writing
 Sewing

10.9

10.8 In the temperate zones, the sun's path across the sky is low in winter, high in summer. Properly shaded, southern exposure admits the light and warmth of the deep winter sun but blocks the strong summer sun—thereby reducing air-conditioning costs.

10.9 Strong task lighting above work surfaces and a much lower level of ambient (general) light provide comfortable visual conditions at minimal energy cost. These New York University library study carrels are by Voorsanger & Mills Associates Architects. (Photograph: © 1983 Peter Aaron/ESTO)

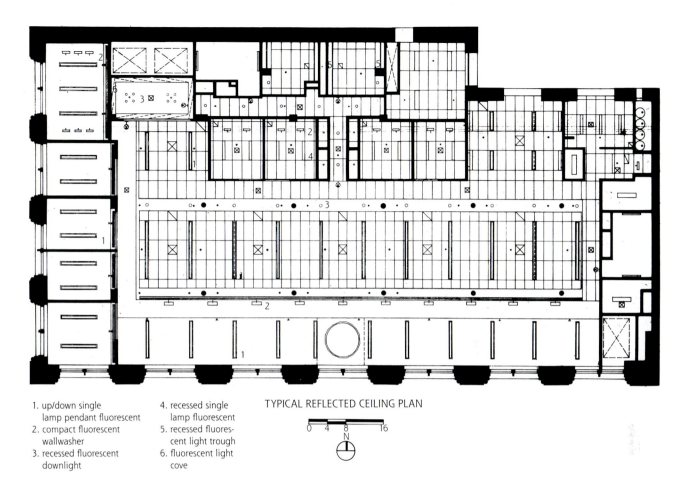

1. up/down single lamp pendant fluorescent
2. compact fluorescent wallwasher
3. recessed fluorescent downlight
4. recessed single lamp fluorescent
5. recessed fluorescent light trough
6. fluorescent light cove

TYPICAL REFLECTED CEILING PLAN

0 4 8   16

N

10.10

Drafting

Food preparation and cooking

Eating

Dressing

Washing, shaving, and makeup

plus any number of special tasks that may arise in a particular home environment (music practice, for example), in workplaces such as offices, factories, and hospitals, or in such special-purpose interiors as theaters, museums, galleries, gymnasiums, or pools.

2. In addition to lighting for specific tasks, good lighting calls for *general lighting*, which provides a comfortable level of light for finding one's way around a space, locating objects, and seeing people and objects. This general or background lighting, often called *ambient light*, should be strong enough to avoid excessive brightness contrast between it and bright task lighting.

3. *Special lighting* focuses attention on specific objects or areas and generates variety and contrast to make a space lively and interesting, even to add aesthetic impact. Attention is always drawn to brightly lit areas and objects, a phenomenon exploited in store and showroom display lighting. This is often called *accent lighting*, to describe the strong light concentrated on a painting, a display of objects, or simply on a wall.

Level of Illumination

Once the kinds of light needed in various locations have been identified, it is helpful to gain an idea of the desired light levels. Lighting measurements are based on a unit called a candlepower, the amount of light given by a standard candle of controlled size and composition. To avoid the seemingly inexact concept of a standard candle, a unit called the candela has been created for use in technical studies of lighting. A candela is defined as an international unit of luminous intensity equal to one-sixtieth of the luminous intensity of one square centimeter of a blackbody surface at the solidification temperature of platinum. For all practical purposes, one candela is equal to one candlepower. The level of light delivered to a surface one foot away from a standard candle is designated as one footcandle (fc). Light meters measure light levels in terms of this unit. A laboratory light meter gives very precise readings but is an expensive device. Many photographic exposure meters measure footcandles with sufficient accuracy for most practical purposes.*

The meter known as the Sekonic Studio Deluxe Model L-398 is particularly suitable for use as a footcandle meter; it is an excellent exposure meter as well.

10.10 A typical reflected ceiling plan shows the layout of ceiling tiles for the central areas, as well as the location of all lighting fixtures. Symbols indicate the different types of fixtures, which are identified by a number key. The plan is for a floor of the National Audubon Society Headquarters (see Case Study 3, Chapter 7), designed by the Croxton Collaborative. (Courtesy Croxton Collaborative Planning, Architecture and Interior Design)

Tables of recommended illumination levels for various purposes appear in lighting handbooks. For many years, recommendations have tended to move upward, but, in view of rising energy costs, recent reevaluation has led to lower light level recommendations, with the increasing understanding that other factors may be more important than the simple intensity of lighting.

Carrying a light meter to measure the footcandle level in familiar situations leads to the surprising conclusion that a very wide range of levels can be acceptable for many tasks. One can see reasonably well with as little as a footcandle level of 5, although somewhat more will help with demanding tasks (reading fine print or sewing on dark materials, for example). At the other extreme, full daylight can reach levels of 6,000 footcandles without causing discomfort. A table such as the following should, therefore, be regarded as no more than a general guide or suggestion:

Table 10. Recommended Light Levels

TASK	RECOMMENDED FOOTCANDLE LEVEL
Movie theater (during picture)	1
Passages and storage areas	5
Stairways, shipping areas, TV-watching	10
Cooking, washing, cleaning, playing games	10–20
Intermittent reading or writing	20
Reading fine type (for example, a newspaper)	25
Typing, bookkeeping, switchboard operation	30
Prolonged reading, study, business-machine operation, close work	50
Drafting	50–100
Sewing black thread on black material	500
Surgery	2,000

A light source, that is, a lamp of a certain wattage, has a light output measured in lumens. The lumen is the unit of light that will deliver a level of one footcandle to a surface one foot square at a distance of one foot. Illumination level varies with the distance from a light source, in accordance with the inverse square law familiar in many physics experiments. A light source that delivers 20 footcandles to a surface two feet away, when moved to a distance of one foot, will deliver not twice as much light, as might be expected, but four times as much, or 80 foot-candles. When moved further away, to four feet, illumination will fall to one-quarter the level, or 5 footcandles (fig. 10.11). In practice, the illumination level delivered by a particular source will also be influenced by its age and cleanness, by the design of the fixture used, and by the characteristics of the space where it is located. White or light-color surfaces nearby reflect and conserve light; dark surfaces or open space do not.

Brightness Contrast

Another important lighting issue involves limitation of brightness contrast, mentioned above. When the eye adjusts to the general level of light in a given field of view, it can tolerate some areas brighter and some dimmer than the average, but extremes of contrast are uncomfortable; for comfort, therefore, the brightness of what is in view needs to be limited.

The brightness of any visible surface is influenced by the light that falls on it and by the percentage of that light that it reflects. Even in bright light, for example, a black or dark brown surface will appear dark, while white paper or paint will seem bright. The quality of surfaces that controls the appearance of brightness is called *reflectance,* which can be measured as a percentage. If 80 footcandles fall on a surface but only 60 footcandles are reflected back, the surface has a reflectance of 75 percent, or .75. Footcandles refer to the level of light arriving on a surface; the light reflected back is measured in footlamberts (fL). The footlambert is the unit of measurement of brightness. The brightness of the surface mentioned above would be 60fL (fL = fc × percentage of reflectance or, for the example, 80 × .75 = 60).

To see comfortably, it is important that the brightness of surfaces within the field of vision is kept within certain limits. Suggested ratios are:

> BETWEEN A VISUAL TASK AND ITS IMMEDIATE SURROUND, NO MORE THAN 1:3.
> BETWEEN A VISUAL TASK AND ITS MORE DISTANT (GENERAL) SURROUND, NO MORE THAN 1:5.
> BETWEEN A VISUAL TASK AND A REMOTE DARK SURFACE, NO MORE THAN 1:10.

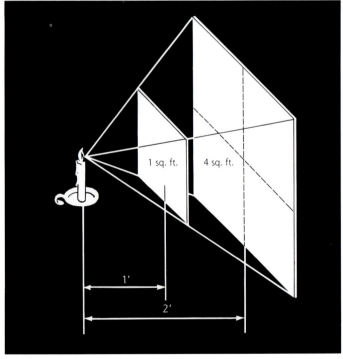

10.11

10.11 This diagram illustrates the inverse square law: the light of one candle falls on one square foot at a distance of one foot, but from two feet away, the same pyramid of light falls on four square feet—providing one-quarter the intensity of light.

10.12

To reach these goals and keep brightness contrast to acceptable levels, surface reflectances in interiors should be limited to the following ranges:

CEILINGS	.70 TO .90
WALLS	.40 TO .60
FURNITURE (TOP SURFACES)	.25 TO .45
OFFICE EQUIPMENT	.25 TO .45
FLOORS	.20 TO .40

Charts citing samples of typical surface finishes, with their reflectance values shown as percentages, are available. Some paint charts, for example, show this information for various paint colors. If the standards listed above are accepted, ceilings painted in dark colors and walls paneled in dark wood are ruled out. While this is probably reasonable in offices and other working environments, exceptions can be made for certain residential spaces and locations where visual comfort may be secondary to aesthetic considerations.

10.12 Lighting can play an important role in minimizing safety hazards. On this winding stairway, in addition to a sturdy handrail and a nonslip carpet to reduce possible hazards, lighting units are placed low to illuminate the wedge-shaped stair treads. Stanley Tigerman was the architect of this residence in a northern suburb of Chicago. (Photograph: Howard N. Kaplan © HNK Architectural Photography)

Lighting for the Aging Population

Visual acuity declines with advancing age, and visual problems become more common among members of older age groups. The recent increase in the average age of the general population, combined with the trend toward older people remaining active both in the work force and in their homes, calls for an awareness of adequate light levels to serve the needs of older people and of the visually impaired of any age.

Light levels in selected locations that can be adjusted on demand can deal with some of the needs of older and visually impaired persons in an economically and environmentally sound manner. One simple and obvious possibility is the provision of lighting devices that will accept lamps of varied wattages. A reading light normally lamped with a 60 or 75 watt bulb, for example, can be given increased output with substitution of a 100 watt bulb. Substitution of one of the newer "bulb"-shaped fluorescent lamps can provide increased output with no increase in wattage and related power consumption. An even simpler approach is the increased use of lighting devices that can be moved within close proximity for specific visual tasks. An ordinary table lamp might be replaced by an adjustable lamp with a lamp head that can be pulled close for reading, writing, or sewing tasks. In many situations, it is appropriate to supply fixtures and switching that permit multiple tiers of light level—"normal" for general use and "high" for those with special needs.

While such arrangements may be difficult to provide in many public areas (such as stores, restaurants, or hotels), they are appropriate to workplaces and residential locations where visual tasks may be demanding and where the probability of older or sight-impaired users is high. Certain environments virtually guarantee a user population with a need for higher light levels, including hospitals and other medical establishments, retirement-community residences, and social-service facilities for the elderly. In these accommodations, light levels should be set higher than the "normal" recommended in standard references.

Elevated light levels should also be planned for areas with special safety problems, such as stairways and bathrooms, where use by older people is anticipated (fig. 10.12). Provision of extra lighting activated by automatic switches (proximity switches operated by sound or movement sensors) should also be considered. Manual switches for extra lighting should be located at a lower position appropriate for wheelchair users.

Special-Purpose Lighting

OFFICES. Because modern office buildings often allow little or no daylight to reach major interior areas, artificial lighting becomes the primary illumination source. In the past, it was considered satisfactory to simply provide overall lighting adequate to deliver a desired standard desktop level. Tests showing that increased levels of lighting tended to improve efficiency (speed of work and reduction of errors) gradually led to the acceptance of very high levels for office lighting, generally supplied by ceiling-mounted fluorescent fixtures. In recent years it has been recognized that such standard office lighting of the 1950s and 1960s is far from ideal.

High levels of uniform lighting, often delivered from fixtures of poor design, tend to create glare both from fixtures and from reflections on task materials at desktop level. Such lighting is also wasteful of energy and therefore costly because areas that have no need for high light levels (such as seating, circulation, and storage spaces) are receiving the same levels as actual work surfaces. Realization of such problems has led to the development of alternative approaches, such as *task-ambient lighting*, in which higher levels of light are provided at desktop or "task" areas, while overall or "ambient" light is set at much lower levels (fig. 10.9). Such lighting is now available in many office-furniture systems, with task lighting set close to work surfaces and ambient lighting supplied indirectly from fixtures aimed upward to reflect off the ceiling or from ceiling fixtures that provide only the lower levels needed for circulation and other nontask areas.

The effects of glare from ceiling lights can be eliminated by the use of fixtures incorporating lenses or parabolic reflectors that cut off light exiting the fixtures at certain angles, which would otherwise appear as bright spots in a ceiling. Suitable fixtures appear as dim or dark when viewed by workers seated at work surfaces. Glare can also come from task lights, especially in the troublesome form known as *veiling reflections*, where glossy materials—papers and even pencil lines on paper— reflect light sources in a way that "washes out" the material being viewed. When the angle of view toward task material is equal to the angle of incidence of the lighting in use, such veiling reflections occur (fig. 10.13). Positioning of task-lighting sources at the sides of work surfaces or the use in fixtures of special lenses made up of tiny prisms that direct light sideways can reduce or eliminate reflected glare. Task lighting can also be locally switched so that lights remain off at workstations that are not occupied, resulting in energy savings.

The computerization of modern offices has made video display terminals (VDTs), comprising keyboard and screen, ubiquitous items of office equipment, often in continuous use throughout working hours. Visual comfort at computer workstations is extremely important in min-

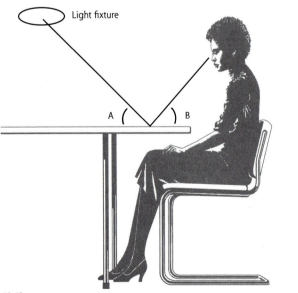

Light fixture

A ( ) B

10.13

10.13 When angle A (the angle of a sightline to a work surface) equals angle B (the angle from that surface to a light source), glare and veiling reflections will result at the task area, making seeing difficult. Control of this problem involves the proper placement of lighting fixtures and/or the shielding of light sources with suitable louvers or lenses.

10.14

10.14 In the Opus Restaurant in Santa
Monica, California, ambient light comes
from coves wrapped around columns,
while sharper accent lighting is provided by exposed tubes angled from walls
to ceiling. The soft green of the upholstery serves as a contrast to the warm
color of the pearwood walls. Grinstein
Daniels were the architects of the 1992
project. (Photograph: Tim Street-Porter)

imizing work stress and physical complaints among office workers, and proper lighting is a key factor in avoiding such problems. Lighting that creates glare on the glass of screens is a common problem that requires careful placement of fixtures and shielding the screen from glare. Light levels must be carefully set, or made adjustable, at individual workstations to ensure that the brightness of the screen and of related visual materials are balanced. The brightness level of nearby surroundings and of task materials close to a VDT screen should be no more than three times that of the screen itself.

Private offices and conference rooms require the same attention. In these spaces, as well as in general offices, some accent light is often desirable to relieve monotony by providing an alternative visual focus, so that a brief look away from work materials offers visual relaxation and stimulus.

HEALTHCARE FACILITIES. Lighting in hospitals, clinics, and medical offices involves a complex variety of issues concerning the comfort and well-being of patients and visitors and the working needs of doctors, nurses, and staff. Waiting areas and circulation spaces require moderate light levels (30–50 footcandles), while medical-office consulting rooms, like other private offices, are best served by similar ambient light levels with increased desktop levels (60–100 footcandles). Examination and treatment rooms require higher levels (100 footcandles or more) with additional high-intensity lighting available for specific examination and treatment routines. Surgery requires very high light levels from specialized fixtures designed exclusively for operating rooms. Nurses' stations need 100 footcandles or more of illumination at work surfaces.

Patients' rooms, often illuminated in older facilities with drab general lighting at low levels, actually call for lighting adjustable to several differing intensities. A low level of lighting is suitable for nighttime and a second, medium level (30–50 footcandles) is needed for daytime. In addition, a higher level should be available, from portable or otherwise movable light units, for examination and treatment. Reading lights are also needed for the use of patients in bed. In semiprivate rooms and wards, separate lighting controls should be placed at each patient's area to assure only minimal disturbance of other patients in the same room.

Well-designed lighting can help to reduce anxiety and discomfort in medical facilities. Families and other visitors, as well as patients, are

10.15

10.15 Peter L. Gluck and Partners used a variety of lighting types in the 1990 New York shop of Stuart Moore Jewelers. Concentrated light from tiny spots in cases, recessed ceiling lights, and indirect lighting spilling over the curving ceiling surfaces work together to create atmosphere and to focus attention on the displayed items. (Photograph: © Norman McGrath)

strongly influenced by the overall appearance of such establishments and tend to interpret comfortable and appropriate lighting as an indication of competent, professional care management.

RETAIL STORES AND SHOWROOMS. Store managers understand that the ambience of a store and the appearance of merchandise on display strongly affect customers' decisions about purchasing. Lighting plays a major role in communicating the character of a store and must be in accord with the sales policies of a particular firm. Shops that feature low prices and rapid turnover of merchandise are best served by high-intensity light levels with little concern for aesthetic subtleties. Bright, even glaring light is typical of discount houses, supermarkets, and similar mass-merchandising facilities. A basic level of 100 footcandles is common, with special displays using levels as high as 500 footcandles supplied by directed spotlighting.

In stores offering increased customer assistance and an emphasis on better-quality merchandise rather than bargain prices, a moderate level of ambient light is appropriate (50–70 footcandles), with possibly lower levels for circulation spaces and higher levels for merchandise on display. Brightly lit accent displays combined with the lighting of perimeter walls and displays (100–300 footcandles) help to enliven the character of selling spaces and can focus attention on items featured seasonally or in special promotions.

Specialty shops stressing style and quality are best served by lower light levels, approaching those of residential lighting. The desired atmosphere may suggest a private club or fine hotel. General lighting of 20 to 40 footcandles is appropriate, with higher levels (up to 60 footcandles) on actual merchandise. Here, too, focal displays can use higher light levels (up to 100–200 footcandles).

In addition to these generalizations, one must consider the specific merchandise to be displayed in order to choose suitable light sources and fixtures. Uniform general lighting can wash out highlights and make goods look soft, even dull. Point-source lighting tends to develop highlights and emphasize texture. Although some highlighting is desirable for almost any merchandise, it is especially favorable to products that "glitter." Jewelry, photo equipment, and small appliances look best under high-contrast, concentrated lighting (fig. 10.15). Furniture and rugs are better served by softer lighting, although rugs and textiles (including the fabrics of clothing) look most attractive when a "wash" of higher-intensity light falls on surfaces from above or from the sides to emphasize texture. The lighting of automobile showrooms is a particular problem since the glint of highlights is an important factor in making the forms of car bodies appear handsome and exciting. Point sources, as well as other fixtures, must be placed so that they can be adjusted and directed to provide the gleaming effects that make new cars attractive.

The color of the illuminants selected also serves to make merchandise look its best. Fluorescent lighting, although economical, is unflattering to colors. The economical "daylight" fluorescents are often tolerated in bargain outlets where the bright glare of bare tubes is associated with the low prices implied by pipe racks and massed merchandise. While fluorescent lights with better color correction are serviceable in many merchandising situations, incandescent, halogen, and high-intensity discharge (HID) lighting (see page 312) are usually more flattering to merchandise in which color is a significant element. The attractiveness of displays in supermarkets and other food shops depends largely on the color quality of the lighting. Meat displays are notably sensitive to light-color characteristics. Because standard fluorescent light makes meat look gray and unappetizing, special warm-color lights are often installed over meat counters to bring out the pink and red tones associated with freshness. Outdoor daylight, of course, is the most flattering lighting for the majority of products, and an effort to simulate it in both color and direction is a sound decision in almost all merchandise display.

RESTAURANTS. Restaurant lighting parallels store lighting in many respects, with the character of the lighting playing an important role in communicating price level, quality, and speed of turnover. Restaurant selection is strongly influenced by appearance, and the level of customer satisfaction, although obviously affected primarily by the food and service, is also determined by visual impressions, among which lighting is of ultimate importance. Bright, uniform light suggests a briskly paced atmosphere usually associated with luncheonettes, diners, and fast-food chain outlets where speed and low prices take priority over quality and service.

In restaurants with table service, a mid-range ambient light level (30–50 footcandles) makes circulation easy and is adequate for table illumination. Hotel dining rooms and mid-level restaurants are generally well served by such overall lighting. Dimmers make it possible to alter lighting levels as the season and time of day suggest. Fluorescent light, unflattering to both food and patrons, is best avoided in favor of incandescent and halogen sources.

More expensive restaurants featuring specialized cuisine and gourmet quality are most advantageously lit at lower levels to suggest an elegant or "romantic" atmosphere. Stronger light levels at tables will help to avoid an atmosphere so dim as to be inconvenient to diners. An ideal balance results when lighting can be directed onto the table (to aid menu reading as well as food consumption) while leaving the seated diners in dimmer light. Unfortunately, this may be possible only for booths or banquettes, where fixed table positions are assured. Wall illumination can raise the ambient level of light while preserving a mood of restraint. Wall decoration, helpful in establishing restaurant character, and its illumination can also add accent and variety in an otherwise low-level light ambience. Candlelight is traditionally associated with romantic dining and can be effective in a space with dim ambient light; in actuality, however, it is often quite uncomfortable in terms of the diners' real need to see. Small lamps with appropriate shading are sometimes used as an alternative, although this approach presents problems in providing outlets and creates inconvenience in table setting and clearing.

Bars and back-bar areas invite strong lighting directed onto the bar top and back-bar displays, where the glitter of bottles and glassware generated by point-source lighting adds to a milieu of lively but intimate comfort. Auxiliary strong lighting should be provided in any dimly lit restaurant for cleaning and maintenance work done before or after serving hours.

SELECTION OF LIGHTING

The selection of lighting devices involves several decisions, all of which entail choosing among a vast range of possibilities. The basic light source—called the *bulb* or *tube* by laymen but known professionally as the *lamp,* the term that will be used here—may be any one of a number of types, including incandescent, fluorescent, and HID. It may be mounted in any one of a wide variety of fixtures, which may be located and spaced in many different ways. Controlling intensity, contrast, glare, and visual effect while juggling these variables in combination can become quite complex.

Selecting lighting devices begins with consideration of the type of light source, the lamp to be used. The most familiar sources are the incandescent bulb and the fluorescent tube, both in wide use and both available in a great variety of sizes, shapes, and types. In recent years, several other sources, less familiar to the general public but increasingly used in architectural lighting, have become available, in bulbs or tubes and in portable lamps. These sources include cold cathode, neon, and, particularly useful, the family of sources called HID. Each of the basic source types has its own set of advantages and disadvantages.

Incandescent Light

Incandescent lamps, invented by Thomas Edison, are the oldest and most familiar of sources (fig. 10.16). Incandescent light is by nature a point or near-point source, which tends to cast sharp shadows and form bright highlights. These characteristics can be modified to offer some diffusion, by frosting the lamps, by using certain shapes such as the T or tubular form, or by employing various shades or fixtures. Like sunlight, candlelight, or oil-lamp light, incandescent light has a continuous spectrum that includes all colors of light to form a white. However, the white of incandescent light contains more red and yellow and less green and blue than daylight, making it much warmer. This warm color tends to be attractive, flattering to human coloring, and suggestive of coziness and comfort (see fig. 1.1).

Incandescent light can be made to serve virtually all lighting needs, but it presents economic problems. It uses much of the electrical energy it consumes to produce heat as an unwanted by-product of light. This makes it costly in terms of power consumption per lumen produced and can also create an extra load on summer air-conditioning. As a result, it is rarely used in factories, office buildings, and other structures that require large amounts of electricity. Smaller consumers need not be as concerned with economic factors, so incandescent light is popular for most home uses. It is also widely used in places that

benefit from its point-source characteristic, as in store displays, where it is flattering to merchandise; in restaurants, where it renders both people and food maximally attractive; and in other locations where aesthetic considerations take precedence over economics.

Tungsten-halogen lamps are a special type of incandescent lamp that gives a higher light output than standard incandescents for a given wattage. They are made in several forms (bulbs, tubes, and mushroom-shaped reflector types) and are generally very compact in relation to their output. They operate at high temperatures and therefore usually use a quartz (heat-resistant) glass envelope. Because of their high heat output, their need for protective shielding to guard against possible injury in case of breakage, and the unusual size and shape of the lamp envelopes, halogen lamps are usually not interchangeable with standard types and require a specially designed fixture or lamp holder.

The typical tungsten-halogen lamp is a small quartz glass tube in wattages from 50 to 5,000. The halogen gas that fills the tube retards the burning of the filament, so that high-temperature operation is possible with long lamp life. Reflector-type halogen lamps (PAR types) use a halogen quartz tube within a reflector surround to project an intense, directed "spotlight" beam. They are widely used in display lighting because their small size and easy directional adjustability make them convenient for highlight illumination of merchandise. Low-voltage halogen lamps are very small reflector units in 20- to 75-watt sizes. They provide a highly concentrated and compact source of light with cooler color quality than other incandescent and halogen sources. A transformer is required to provide the low-voltage operating current. Halogen lighting generally shares the continuous-spectrum characteristics of incandescent light, with slightly cooler color that is closer to daylight than other incandescent types. Halogen light is flattering to foods, people, and most types of merchandise. Its somewhat better efficiency, compared to incandescent sources, places it between fluorescent and incandescent light in terms of cost versus quality of light.

Fluorescent Light

Developed in the 1930s for general use, fluorescent lighting is a highly economical alternative to incandescent light. Its power consumption for a given light output, at about one-third to one-quarter that of incandescent lamps, soon pays off the higher cost of the lamps and their fixtures to produce major economies. This has made fluorescent lighting the norm for factories, offices, and classrooms and for restaurants and stores that strive for lower operating costs.

The typical fluorescent lamp is a long tube and therefore gives off

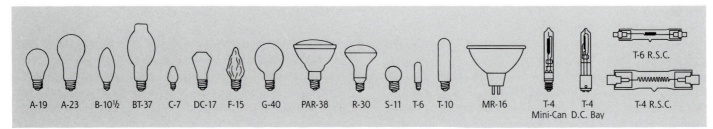

10.16

10.16 Incandescent (tungsten) and tungsten-halogen bulbs and tubes (both called lamps in the industry) are available in a variety of sizes and shapes. The standard industry system for designation of incandescent lamps uses a letter to indicate shape and a number to indicate size (diameter, in eighths of an inch).

10.17

diffuse, shadowless light. While this promotes good general vision, it makes certain kinds of detail harder to see and tends to create a bland and monotonous lighting effect, rather like outdoor light on a cloudy day.

Fluorescent light has another troublesome characteristic, its color quality, which does not receive as much attention as it deserves. Part of the light from a fluorescent tube is full-spectrum light, that is, light with all colors present. However, this is true only of the portion of light output that comes from the glowing phosphors on the inside of the tube that fluoresce to give the source its name. The gases in the tube (mercury vapor, xenon, and others) emit light of a single, pure, one-frequency-number color. When viewed with a laboratory instrument called a spectroscope, this can be seen clearly as a dim rainbow band with superimposed brilliant lines of sharp color. While giving the illusion of normal white light, this spectrum does odd things to color perception, distorting the natural coloring of many objects. This makes fluorescent light aesthetically unpleasant—and possibly the source of various physiological discomforts. (See also the discussion of full-spectrum lighting, page 314.)

This problem has been addressed by introducing fluorescent tubes in a great variety of white colors, such as *warm white* and *deluxe warm white,* some of which certainly improve color rendition. Unfortunately, when fixtures are relamped, there is no guarantee that the maintenance staff will use a particular color tube. Most often, they install the basic daylight tube, which is the cheapest, most widely available, and least desirable tube, generating the cold, blue-greenish "daylight" that makes people and objects take on an unattractive color cast.

To provide fluorescent light in forms readily interchangeable with conventional incandescent bulbs, manufacturers have introduced a variety of lamp types with compact shapes and integral ballasts so that the new units can be simply screwed into a regular lamp socket. Available types include compact U-shaped tubes in two- and four-tube clusters (see fig. 10.18) enclosed within an envelope of bulb or globe shape. Some versions have a base that contains a ballast while others plug into a ballast base that is in turn screwed into any regular lamp socket. Among other versions are a straight tube mounted on a compact strip that includes the ballast (ideal for closet and under-cabinet lights) and a circular tube mounted on a center ballast that screws into any socket. Although all of these units have a high first cost, their energy-saving abilities make them economical over a period of time. Most of these lamps have an improved, warm-color output visually close to that of incandescent lighting despite the fact that they share the discontinuous-spectrum component of fluorescents.

Fluorescent lights use special starters of several types. The familiar *preheat* starting requires pressing a special switch for a short interval before the cathode heats sufficiently to permit the lamp to light. *Instant start* (also called "Slimline," after the tubes used in this circuit) requires no separate starter and lights at once, like incandescents. *Rapid start,* widely used in large office and commercial installations, requires no starter and lights after a very brief delay.

10.17 Fluorescent light diffused by plastic sheeting creates a luminous ceiling that provides even, almost shadowless illumination. The Manufacturers Hanover Trust Company Building, New York, is a 1954 project by Skidmore, Owings & Merrill, architects. (Photograph: © 1954 Ezra Stoller/ESTO)

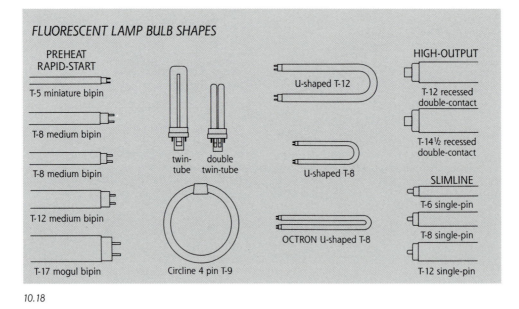

FLUORESCENT LAMP BULB SHAPES

PREHEAT RAPID-START

T-5 miniature bipin

T-8 medium bipin

T-8 medium bipin

T-12 medium bipin

T-17 mogul bipin

twin-tube   double twin-tube

Circline 4 pin T-9

U-shaped T-12

U-shaped T-8

OCTRON U-shaped T-8

HIGH-OUTPUT

T-12 recessed double-contact

T-14½ recessed double-contact

SLIMLINE

T-6 single-pin

T-8 single-pin

T-12 single-pin

10.18

The transformers, or ballasts, associated with fluorescent lighting present certain problems. They produce a humming sound that can be troublesome (some newer electronic ballasts minimize this problem), they create heat (somewhat offsetting the promise of a cool fluorescent tube), and they are subject to eventual burnout or failure that may require inconvenient (and costly) service. The heat generated by a fluorescent tube and ballast is directly proportional to the wattage consumed, so that in view of the less-wattage-for-equal-light-output equation, fluorescent light is inherently economical. Still, in estimating lifetime cost, the first cost of fixtures and tubes, as well as the cost of relamping and repairing fixtures and ballasts, should be taken into account.

In spite of the problems associated with fluorescent lighting, its economic advantages keep it in general use. Where it must be used for economic reasons, lamping with tubes of improved color characteristics, selecting good fixtures (which means avoiding the least expensive tube and fixture), and, whenever possible, mixing its use with incandescent light or daylight will help to make fluorescent light a more satisfactory choice.

High-Intensity Discharge Light

HID lighting combines some of the advantages of incandescent and fluorescent light. The lamps, of bulb shape, give point or near-point light; the economy of operation is excellent; and it offers lamp types with acceptable color characteristics—not, however, full- or continuous-spectrum light. First cost is high for both lamp and fixture, the latter of a special type, with a bulky and expensive transformer. HID lights have a slow starting characteristic, coming up to full light output only gradually over some minutes.

HID lamps have a long life (15,000–24,000 hours), and their poor color characteristics can be offset by pairing the mercury vapor and

high-pressure sodium types, effectively balancing their respective cold and warm color characteristics. Available HID lamps are of three types:

MERCURY VAPOR in 40- to 1,000-watt sizes, with 20–60 lumen-per-watt efficiency ratings but with cold color quality, somewhat improved in deluxe white and deluxe warm-white versions, albeit with some loss of efficiency.

HIGH-PRESSURE SODIUM in 50- to 1,000-watt versions, with superior (50–125 lumen-per-watt) efficiency, but with an orange-yellow color quality.

METAL HALIDE in 15- to 1,500-watt lamps, with a 100 lumen-per-watt efficiency; these have the best HID color quality and, in smaller sizes, are suitable for a greater variety of interior uses.

HID lighting is now in extensive use in public spaces, as an ambient (general or background) light source in offices, where it is often installed in special upward-directed fixtures to provide indirect light reflected from the ceiling, and in portable lamps and uplight fixtures for home and other general uses.

Other Lighting Sources

NEON. These tubes, familiar in illuminated signs, are available in a full range of colors, including several tones of white. The thin neon tube can be bent to any shape, including decorative and fanciful forms. Although its tube life is very long (many years), a transformer is required. Neon is limited mainly by a low efficiency; it is usually considered only for special, decorative applications.

COLD CATHODE. Cold cathode lighting is somewhat similar to neon, using a thin tube bent to desired forms. Because it is permanently

10.18 Fluorescent tubes (lamps) are made in a variety of shapes and sizes, including a number of types that can be directly interchanged with incandescent units. Most commonly used shapes are illustrated in this chart.

installed, it is sometimes useful in such special situations as indirect lighting coves (pockets in which the light source is hidden) of irregular shape. It has the same efficiency characteristics as neon.

MERCURY AND SODIUM. These lights of the gaseous discharge family are highly efficient in terms of lumens produced per watt of current consumed, but their one-color light (bluish for mercury, orange for sodium) makes them unsuitable for general use. They are often used for street and highway lighting, and mercury lamps have been used in industrial plants.

LASER LIGHT. This is a special process in which light is amplified or intensified so as to be emitted in a highly concentrated, intense beam. Laser beams have various applications in medical and scientific equipment. As illumination sources, laser beams are hindered by their color limitation and by their intensity, which makes them dangerous when viewed directly. Although laser beams can serve in decorative or display applications when played on a reflecting surface or directed across open space, where they are visible as linear bands, they have as yet no extensive practical applications in lighting.

FIBER OPTICS. Strands of glass fiber can transmit light internally, much as water can flow through pipes. Bundles of such glass fibers can convey light from any source to one or more remote locations, where the light emerges from the fibers. Various experimental applications in which light is delivered from central sources to many positions are under development, but the only uses currently available in interior lighting are decorative. A "spray" of light coming from thin strands of fiber optics can create ornamental effects without the complications of many small lamps and the associated wiring that might otherwise be necessary.

Color Characteristics of Artificial Lighting

Comparing the color characteristics of the many types of artificial light with one another and with natural light is difficult because of the discontinuous, line-spectrum components of fluorescent and HID sources. A continuous-spectrum light includes all wavelengths (that is, all colors) visible to the eye. When passed through a prism, this light is broken up into its separate wavelengths into a rainbow with all colors present (fig. 10.15). A discontinuous spectrum includes only certain wavelengths, possibly a single color (for example, red neon) or a number of colors that together give an impression of white light. Such light passed through a prism turns out to consist of sharp lines of intense color. Mercury vapor and sodium lights have a discontinuous spectrum. Fluorescent and HID lights combine the two types of spectra (fig. 10.16); daylight and incandescent light have continuous spectra.

Continuous-spectrum light (daylight, incandescent light) can be compared in terms of its warmth or coolness quite readily. To make this comparison orderly and consistent, the concept of color temperature, expressed in degrees Kelvin (°K) or, in recent terminology, simply kelvins (K), is used. High K numbers indicate cool light, low numbers warm.

In order to deal with fluorescent and other discontinuous-spectrum sources, an equivalent color temperature figure is used, that is, a number describing a continuous-spectrum light that *appears* to match the discontinuous source in question. It must be remembered that although the apparent color may match, the effect of discontinuous light on color matching and on vision can be quite different from that of its similar continuous-spectrum source. See Table 11 for color temperatures of some common light sources.

Different brand sources of similar types may vary somewhat. The term *deluxe* is used for modified versions of certain fluorescent and HID types to indicate altered (improved) color rendition. Color temper-

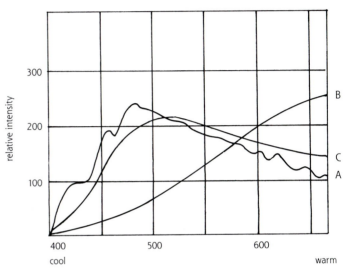

10.19

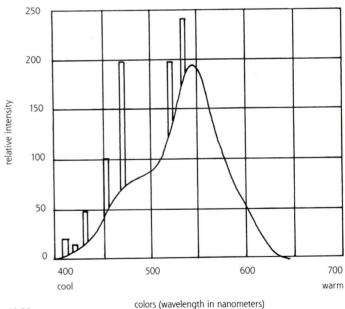

10.20

10.19 This chart graphically displays the wavelengths of the colors of various full-spectrum light sources. Both sunlight (A) and incandescent light (B) contain all colors, forming a continuous spectrum. The red, orange, and yellow (warm-color) wavelengths are some- what stronger in B than in A, which accounts for the noticeably warmer quality of incandescent light. A special "full-spectrum" fluorescent called Vitalite (C) includes invisible as well as visible wavelengths and approaches the color balance of daylight.

10.20 This chart of fluorescent-light spectra shows that this source includes both a continuous-spectrum component—similar to that of incandescent light—and discontinuous components. The continuous spectrum is generated by the glowing phosphors on the fluo- rescent tube and the discontinuous spikes by gases in the tube that produce pure color light at certain wavelengths. The resulting mix appears as white light but is quite different from sunlight in its makeup—and in its effects.

ature shifts as lamps age; new lamps are cooler, aged lamps warmer than average values. The use of a dimmer always shifts color toward warmer (lower kelvin number) values.

Lamps are usually rated by the manufacturer in kelvins with a number that appears in manufacturers' literature and, often, on the actual lamp carton. For comparison purposes, lighting engineers have agreed to a "standard daylight" of 4,870 K. Mixtures of light from various sources will, of course, have a color temperature between those of the sources resulting from the relative intensity of the types of light making up the mix.

To simplify the evaluation of color characteristics of various types of lighting, an index has been developed that attempts to rate a given light source in terms of its color quality. The CRI (Color Rendering Index) for a light source is a single number in a range from zero to 100, with 100 representing perfect color rendition. Incandescent and tungsten-halogen sources have a CRI of 95 or better. Fluorescent light ranges from a CRI of 48 to 90. Lower color temperatures have the best CRI values: 2,700 K lighting yields a CRI of 90, while 6,300 K sources have a CRI as low as 48. Among HID sources, metal-halide lamps fall in a CRI range from 60 to 70. The CRI ratings of mercury vapor and high-pressure sodium, 32 and 21, respectively, suggest their very poor color qualities and corresponding unsuitability for most interior installations.

FULL-SPECTRUM LIGHTING. For many years, various scientific research projects relating to the physical effects of light on human health have suggested that the human body makes use of light in a variety of ways, of which sight is only the most obvious. Light deprivation causes physical and psychological problems such as feelings of

depression. These effects have been observed in general populations in extreme northern climates with long, dark winters and in coal miners and other workers who spend long hours in environments with minimal light. The human organism seems to require light with the full mixture of spectral qualities typical of sunlight—light including the invisible components of infrared and ultraviolet, as well as the full range of visible light colors. Concerns about the health effects of many forms of artificial light, particularly those with discontinuous spectra, have been raised. Very serious undesirable effects have been observed when people have been restricted to light of only one wavelength (sodium light is a typical and extreme example) for extended periods of time. Sodium light used in some schoolrooms (where its economy led to its introduction) is reported to have been connected with a number of health problems, including disturbed behavior and even increases in dental cavities.

For people whose lives include frequent and extended exposure to daylight and who live and work under artificial light that has a content largely of continuous spectral characteristics, light deprivation is probably not a significant problem. Yet the expanse of time now commonly spent working entirely under artificial light, combined with the introduction of new light sources of limited spectral characteristics, calls for increasing recognition of the need for full-spectrum light. Incandescent and halogen lighting come close to full-spectrum output of visible light, although they remain lacking in invisible spectral output. Special lamps are now available with spectral output closely matched to sunlight. As acknowledgment of the human need for full-spectrum light exposure increases, it is probable that such special lamps will enter general use. Fortunately, full-spectrum lamps are readily interchangeable with standard incandescent screw-base lamps and thus can be put into use experimentally or on a regular basis in a variety of applications. Although the color characteristics of full-spectrum lamps are noticeably different from the usual incandescents, the light quickly comes to seem "normal" and pleasant to most users because it is so similar to sunlight.

Economic Issues of Lighting

In considering the economic impact of the selection of a light source, some fairly complex issues must be faced. They include:

FIRST COST OF FIXTURES AND LAMPS (MANUFACTURER'S LIST PRICE)

COST OF FIXTURE INSTALLATION AND WIRING (ELECTRICAL CONTRACTOR'S ESTIMATE)

COST OF MAINTENANCE, REPAIR, AND CLEANING OVER ITS USEFUL LIFE*

COST OF RELAMPING OVER ITS USEFUL LIFE*

CURRENT CONSUMPTION AT AN ESTIMATED COST OVER ITS USEFUL LIFE*

ADDITIONAL COST OF AIR CONDITIONING (FIRST COST AND OPERATIONAL COST OVER ITS USEFUL LIFE) TO OFFSET HEAT PRODUCTION OF LIGHTING*

SAVINGS (IF ANY) IN HEATING COST RESULTING FROM HEAT PRODUCTION OF LIGHTING OVER ITS USEFUL LIFE*

---

*This item can only be estimated, since future costs of energy, products, and labor may change (probably upward).

Table 11. Color Temperatures

Source	Correlated Color Temperature in Kelvins (Average)
Clear blue sky	25,000–12,000
Hazy blue sky	9,000
Overcast sky	7,500
Daylight fluorescent	6,500
Cool-white fluorescent	4,200
Metal halide (HID)	4,200–3,900
Mercury vapor	3,900–3,300
High-pressure sodium	3,100–2,100
Warm-white fluorescent	3,000
Incandescent 1,000 watts	3,000
Tungsten-halogen	3,000
Incandescent 150 watts	2,800
Incandescent 60 watts	2,790

Since maintenance and lifetime costs, among other factors, can only be estimated, no exact comparative figures can be produced. Nevertheless, comparing various systems can be helpful in making decisions about large installations, in which even small differences, over a period of time, can have a major impact. Systems are often compared on the basis of a simple calculation dealing only with energy consumption. The total wattage of a planned lighting system is simply divided by the floor area to be lighted:

$$\frac{TOTAL\ WATTAGE\ OF\ LIGHTING}{FLOOR\ AREA\ IN\ SQUARE\ FEET} = WATTS\ PER\ SQUARE\ FOOT$$

For example:

$$\frac{6,900\ WATTS\ (OR\ 6.9\ KILOWATTS)}{3,000\ SQUARE\ FEET} = 2.3\ WATTS\ PER\ SQUARE\ FOOT$$

The resulting figure is a good index of the efficiency of the planned installation. In many areas, building codes now try to reduce energy-wasteful lighting practices by setting a maximum watts-per-square-foot average permitted in new installations. Efficiencies of 3 watts per square foot are considered reasonable; some highly efficient installations achieve levels as low as 2 or even 1.5 watts per square foot.

The carton in which lamps are shipped carries information, not only on wattage but also on average lumen output (how much light is produced) and average life of the lamp. These are all factors in the economic performance of a particular lamp, whatever its type. Certain types of lamp, such as soft-white or long-life, while offering special features, are uneconomical compared to standard lamps. For example, a standard 60-watt lamp delivers 890 lumens over an average life of 1,000 hours, or 890,000 lumen-hours. A typical 60-watt long-life lamp delivers 820 lumens over 1,500 hours, or 1,230,000 lumen-hours. If the cost of the standard lamp is $0.85 and that of the long-life $1.65, one penny buys 10,470 lumen-hours from the standard lamp but only 7,454 lumen-hours from the long-life. The first cost of the standard lamp is $0.85 per 1,000 hours of use, while the cost of the long-life is $1.65 per 1,000 hours. Both lamps have the same (60-watt) rate of energy consumption, but the long-life produces about 8 percent fewer lumens than the standard lamp. Taking these factors into account, we see that long-life lamps will cost about 12 percent more than standard lamps to produce the same amount of light.

Lamps of different wattage also vary in economic performance. The standard 60-watt lamp with its lifetime output of 890,000 lumen-hours may be compared with a standard 100-watt lamp having an output of 1,750 lumens and a life of 750 hours, for a total lifetime output of 1,312,500 lumen-hours. Both lamps cost the same, but the 100-watt lamp consumes 66 percent more electricity. The 100-watt lamp therefore delivers 13,125 lumen-hours per watt, while the 60-watt lamp delivers 890,000 divided by 60, or 14,833 lumen-hours per watt. The impact of such calculations depends on local energy costs. The few lamps used in a typical home make such differences insignificant for residential installation, but they become important in large installations using many lamps.

FIXTURE SELECTION

Once the light source is selected, the next logical step is selecting fixtures. Many fixtures will take a variety of lamps, so the selection depends primarily on the type or types of lighting desired for a particular space. For example, a living space combining such activities as conversation and reading may need both soft, indirect general light and good task lighting, to which may be added spot lighting to display art and provide variety. A torchère (a type of floor lamp) can provide indirect uplight; a couple of well-placed lamps give good light for reading or other concentrated tasks, as well as throwing light upward for more general light; and track lighting emphasizes artwork and rounds off the lighting scheme. Since many different fixtures will work in any specific situation, other factors, including cost, the look desired, and maintenance, then enter the decision-making process.

All lighting devices fall into one of two classes, *architectural* or *portable*.

Architectural and Portable Lighting
Architectural lighting is fixed in place through fixtures built into the structure of the building, often recessed or more or less concealed. Portable lighting includes lamps and other movable lighting devices that are plugged into outlets and can be moved about, removed, and replaced at will.

The lighting of public spaces, factories, and offices is primarily architectural. Residential lighting may combine both types but tends to emphasize portable lighting. The built-in lighting provided in most houses and apartments is of such poor quality and so badly located that it is best replaced, removed, or ignored. Replacement in an existing space can be difficult and expensive. Good architectural lighting is usually planned in advance and installed as a space is built or renovated.

The variety of lamps (portable lighting devices) and fixtures available from the many manufacturers of lighting equipment is considerable, and selection can often be a confusing matter. A high proportion of the lamps and fixtures displayed in lighting stores and other retail outlets are of poor design and shoddy construction. Manufacturers of better lighting equipment maintain showrooms in major cities and produce catalogs and data sheets describing their products and giving accurate technical data. Most designers and architects build up a file of data from preferred manufacturers and use the information when they plan lighting.

Types of Light Produced
There are several ways to classify lighting devices. In addition to size, wattage, type of light source, type of mounting (or portability), and appearance, a classification can be made on the basis of the way in which light is delivered. Luminaires (as fixtures are called in technical terms) and lamps all deliver light in one or a combination of the following ways:

- *CONCENTRATING*, or beaming, usually from a point source:
  Up
  Down

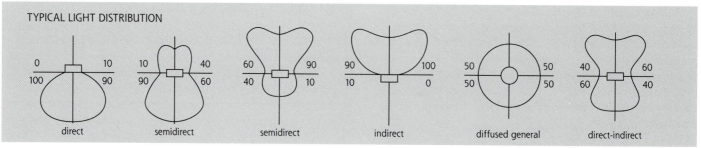

TYPICAL LIGHT DISTRIBUTION

0 10	10 40	60 90	90 100	50 50	40 60
100 90	90 60	40 10	10 0	50 50	60 40
direct	semidirect	semidirect	indirect	diffused general	direct-indirect

10.21

Both up and down

In any direction (adjustable)

• *DIFFUSING*, so as to scatter light in many directions:

Up

Down

Both up and down

In many or all directions

An incandescent reflector spot, flood, or downlight produces a concentrated beam of light. A frosted globe delivers diffused light in all directions. A typical table lamp produces a complex mix of concentrated light from the actual light bulb, somewhat diffused light from the lamp shade, and upward-directed light, which is reflected from the ceiling to become diffused indirect light. Such mixtures tend to create the most satisfactory kinds of lighting, the direct light providing strong illumination for tasks and sharp shadows and highlights that aid clear vision, while the indirect diffused light fills in surrounding areas and prevents excessive brightness contrast. This mixture also most nearly duplicates the light of a sunny day, in which direct sunlight combines with diffuse reflection from the sky and clouds.

The way in which lamps and fixtures direct their light output can be evaluated very exactly by examination of light distribution (photometric) charts provided in the catalogs and data sheets published by manufacturers (fig. 10.22). A circular (or semicircular) graph places the light source at a center point and shows its light output in candlepower at various angles in graphic form. A full circle indicates diffuse light distributed equally in all directions. A direct light (such as the familiar downlight) generates a downward, balloonlike shape. A narrow beam spotlight is indicated by a thin, pointed form on the chart. It is quite easy to become familiar with such charts and to gain an immediate idea of the performance of a particular lamp or fixture at a glance. Another useful chart shows distribution of light on a flat surface as a series of contour lines suggesting the way in which light output will be spread out or concentrated (fig. 10.21).

Many lamps and light fixtures, including some of handsome appearance, are designed so as to form a bright spot. Such fixtures—small globes, bare lamps or tubes, or ceiling fixtures with diffusing surfaces that show up as bright panels—almost always create excessive brightness contrast, causing vision problems even when ample light is present (see page 304). Bare bulbs in ceiling sockets and inferior fluorescent ceiling fixtures are notorious sources of such problems. In general, except for occasional decorative uses, fixtures that leave the bare lamp

or tube open to direct vision should be avoided, as well as fixtures with shades or diffusers that themselves form spots of great brightness in a normal field of vision.

Arranging indirect lighting by beaming all light upward avoids this problem totally, but this gives a light that often seems bland and unattractive in its overall shadowless quality. It also tends to be inefficient, because of the light loss resulting from the round-trip light must make—up from the fixture and back downward—and from a degree of absorption by the ceiling surface, which, even if painted a pure white, will always absorb some part of the light.

The following is a summary of the types of lamps and fixtures in most general use (fig. 10.23).

Floor, Table, and Desk Lamps

SHADED INCANDESCENT LAMPS. These are probably the most familiar and useful of lamp types (figs. 10.24, 10.25, 10.26). The bulb (or bulbs) is surrounded by a shade, which reduces glare but disperses *direct light* both upward and downward. Such lamps, while sometimes of ornate or objectionable design, deliver excellent lighting. Well-designed versions are hard to find but very useful.

GLOBE LAMPS. In these, the shade is replaced by a frosted glass or paper sphere, which reduces the brightness of the enclosed incandescent bulb and delivers *diffuse light*. Such lamps, while often of good

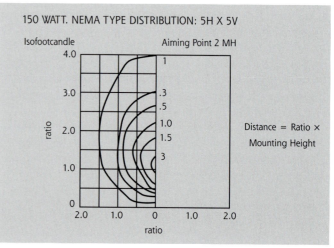

150 WATT. NEMA TYPE DISTRIBUTION: 5H X 5V

Isofootcandle   Aiming Point 2 MH

Distance = Ratio × Mounting Height

10.22

10.21 *Each type of light source generates a different distribution pattern. As illustrated here, distribution diagrams show how much light from a given fixture will be delivered upward, downward, and to the sides.*

10.22 *Manufacturers' catalogs include data on the light distribution of various types of lamps. This chart, from an Osram Sylvania catalog, provides data for a tungsten-halogen lamp, indicating the areas within which specific levels of light intensity will be delivered. (Courtesy Osram Sylvania)*

appearance, tend to form a spot of glare and to deliver unattractive flat lighting. Versions that combine globe and directional shading are particularly useful.

REFLECTOR LAMPS. These enclose a regular or reflector incandescent (type R) bulb in an opaque reflector, which directs light in one direction, usually with adjustability (fig. 10.31). These make good *reading or work lights* but can produce excessive brightness contrast unless fill light is provided from some other source. Small versions make good bedside reading lights.

UPLIGHTS, OR TORCHÈRES. These are usually floor lamps that aim all light output upward to provide *indirect, general lighting* (figs. 10.32, 10.34). The source of light is usually incandescent, but HID or halogen versions are increasingly popular. Floor lamps combining uplight and shaded reading light have been favorites for many years. Small can lights that rest on the floor and direct louver-shaded light upward to

walls and ceilings are also compact and useful. Uplight is also provided by powerful floor-standing tubular, or kiosk, units for ambient (general) lighting in office and public spaces.

Wall-Mounted Units

WALL BRACKETS. Units that use bare lamps (bulbs or tubes) or unshaded globes for *direct light,* these were once widely popular, often in simulated candle form, but are now less used. Simple versions are useful in corridors or at stairs and in bathrooms and dressing rooms (fig. 10.35). Shaded versions, still available, have fallen into disuse.

WALL-MOUNTED REFLECTOR LAMPS. These are similar to the floor and table versions discussed above. Many have swivel or gooseneck mountings, which provide adjustability for *display lighting* and for *reading and bed lamps* (fig. 10.36).

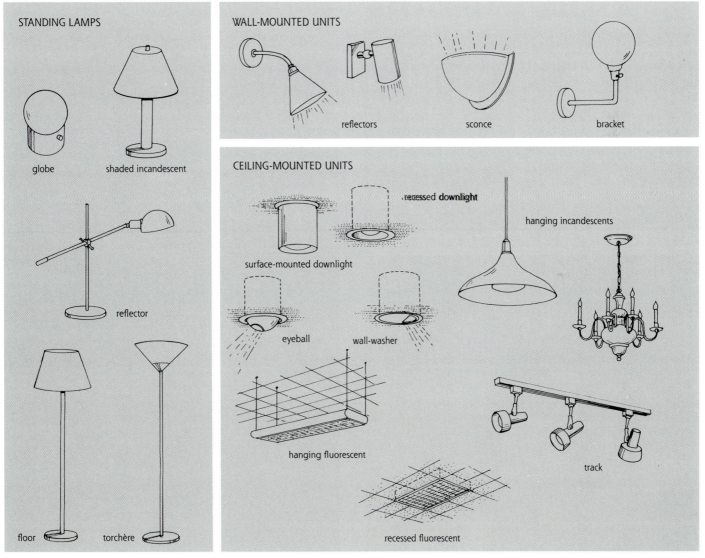

STANDING LAMPS

globe   shaded incandescent

reflector

floor   torchère

WALL-MOUNTED UNITS

reflectors   sconce   bracket

CEILING-MOUNTED UNITS

recessed **downlight**

surface-mounted downlight

eyeball   wall-washer

hanging fluorescent

recessed fluorescent

hanging incandescents

track

10.23

10.23 *Light fixture types in general use are shown here. Standing types are at left; wall-mounted fixtures are pictured above right; and ceiling-mounted fixtures appear below right.*

10.24

10.25

10.26

10.24, 10.25 Because of its size and shape, the *Miss Sissi* lamp (fig. 10.24) lends itself to decorative use as accent lighting. A 1991 design by Philippe Starck for Flos, the lamp comes in violet, opal white, terra-cotta red, and a soft green. (Photograph courtesy Flos, Inc.) In contrast to the background role of the *Miss Sissi* lamp, the *Zink* lamp (fig. 10.25), while also decorative in its design, has sufficient light output to provide foreground illumination for a variety of tasks. The zinc-galvanized steel table lamp is a design of Ron Rezek Lighting & Furniture. (Photograph courtesy Ron Rezek Lighting & Furniture)

10.26 In Tokyo's Hanajuban Restaurant, sconces are used in combination with table uplights and ceiling-mounted lighting, creating a well-lit but soft effect. K.I.D. Associates Co., Ltd., designer. (Photograph: Yoshio Shiratori)

10.27

10.28

10.29

10.30

10.31

10.27 A table lamp in contrasting metals, designed by Robert Sonneman, has a shade of metal mesh with a frosted-glass insert. A 300-watt halogen lamp is the light source, and there is a full-range dimmer. (Photograph courtesy George Kovacs Lighting, Inc.)

10.28 In this 16-inch-high accent lamp by Lanie Kagan for Luz Lampcraft, a woven birchwood veneer shade is wrapped around a structure of metal wire. (Photograph: © Lanie Kagan)

10.29 The Sensu table lamp of anodized aluminum designed by Sean Corcorran and Jorge Freyer incorporates contemporary technology: An infrared sensor activates the lamp, moving the shade up when the light goes on and down when the light goes off. (Photograph: George Hein, courtesy Sointu, New York)

10.30 A leather or rubber base and a double-matte film shade combine to form the playful silhouette of the Zip-Light, a small portable lamp designed by Sigmar Willnauer. The base ships flat but zips together to form a support for the shade. (Photograph courtesy Goods!)

WALL-MOUNTED UPLIGHTS. Often called sconces, these serve the same purposes as floor uplights in fixed locations, providing *indirect, general light* (figs. 10.37–10.39). Popular in the 1930s, units of this type have recently gained new popularity.

Ceiling Units

DOWNLIGHTS. These cans housing an incandescent lamp, usually with a lens or shade to prevent direct glare, are among the most widely used of incandescent architectural lighting devices to give *general light*. They may be recessed, surface-mounted, or hung on a stem. HID versions are coming into use for large spaces with high ceilings.

EYEBALL AND WALL-WASHER ADJUSTABLE UNITS. These are similar to downlights but offer *direct light* that can be *adjusted* to any desired angle. Wall-washers direct light from ceiling level to an adjacent wall to "wash" it with light.

HANGING FIXTURES, OR CHANDELIERS. These widely used fixture types may imitate historic designs or take contemporary forms (figs. 10.40, 10.41, 10.44). They provide *general light*, which may be directed up, down, or both. Various types of globes and shades are used,

10.33

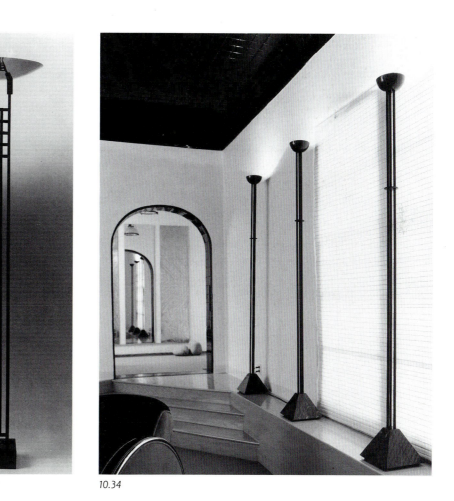

10.32   10.34

10.31 An adjustable table or desk lamp, Condor, designed by Hans von Klier, is suited to task-lighting applications. (Photograph courtesy Bilumen Lighting Ltd.)

10.32 This sculptural floor lamp, a design by Robert Sonneman, directs all light upward for indirect illumination. A 400-watt halogen lamp is used with a full-range dimmer. (Photograph courtesy George Kovacs Lighting, Inc.)

10.33 The classic swing-arm lamp first designed in 1927 by Walter von Nessen has remained popular in both table and floor versions. The floor lamps illustrated are produced by George Kovacs Lighting. (Photograph courtesy George Kovacs Lighting, Inc.)

10.34 Three floor-standing uplights by Ron Rezek are here used in the living space of a Santa Monica, California, house designed by Brian A. Murphy (see fig. 1.5 for another view of this interior). (Photograph: © Tim Street-Porter, courtesy House & Garden)

10.35

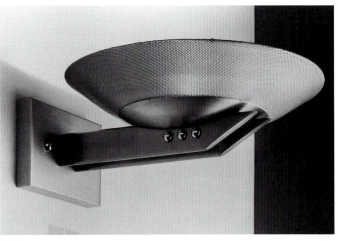

10.37

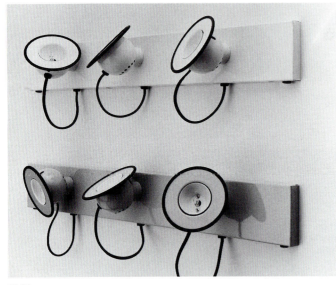

10.36

10.38

and height adjustability is sometimes provided. Versions for residential use are usually incandescent. Fluorescent versions are often used for office and store lighting. Although unattractive and fussy versions abound, excellent designs of this type are also available.

SURFACE-MOUNTED AND RECESSED LUMINAIRES. These widely used architectural lighting devices, usually in fluorescent versions (fig. 10.42), provide *general lighting*. By spacing according to systematic calculation (see pages 328–29), predictable levels of consistent light can be delivered at work-surface levels. Unfortunately, low-cost versions of such fixtures are responsible for the glaring ceiling light all too common in offices, factories, and shops. Glare control requires the use of lenses or louvers that cut off glare at normal viewing angles, making the fixtures appear no brighter than the surrounding ceiling surfaces. Louvers of parabolic cross section do this with a minimum of light loss.

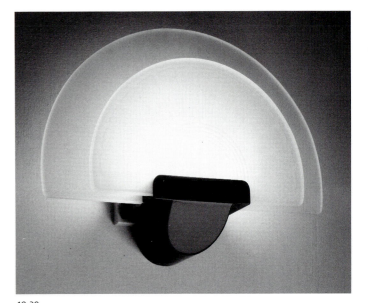

10.39

10.35 A wall-mounted globe lamp, the Aggregato adjustable spot lamp, was designed by Enzo Mari and Giancarlo Fassina. (Photograph courtesy Artemide, Inc.)

10.36 Gae Aulenti designed the Mini-box swiveling wall lamps with built-in transformer. Low-voltage reflector lamps are held in place by magnets. (Photograph courtesy Stilnovo)

10.37 A wall-mounted uplight, or sconce, by Robert Sonneman has a metal-mesh reflector with a frosted-glass insert. It uses a 200-watt halogen lamp. (Photograph courtesy George Kovacs Lighting, Inc.)

10.38 A three-tiered sconce. (Photograph courtesy Trakliting, Inc.)

10.39 The front panel of Diva, a sconce by architect and designer Ezio Didone, is a semicircle of frosted, patterned glass in white or rose. The second, larger semicircle is of unpatterned white glass; both panels provide diffuse light. A textured, white, enameled-aluminum back-plate reflects the light directly from the source, a 100-watt incandescent lamp. (Photograph courtesy Atelier International Lighting)

10.40 Custom-designed, hanging incandescent lighting units illuminate the lobby of the corporate headquarters of Procter & Gamble in Cincinnati, designed by Kohn Pedersen Fox, the architects. (Photograph: © 1985 Peter Aaron/ESTO)

10.43

TRACK LIGHTING. This system uses an electrical track that can be ceiling-mounted or hung (fig. 10.45). Many different types of *adjustable* lighting units, which give both *general and spot lighting,* can be plugged in where desired and moved about as needed. This system is particularly useful for display and gallery lighting (fig. 10.47) and is also commonly used in residential settings.

Built-in Lighting

COVE LIGHTING. This requires a cove, or pocket, built into the ceiling (or, sometimes, wall) construction. Light units, usually fluorescent or cold cathode, are concealed in the cove and provide *indirect light.*

LUMINOUS CEILINGS. With this type of lighting, a false ceiling of louvers or diffusing glass or plastic forms the entire ceiling, with lighting units, usually fluorescent tubes, mounted in the space above. An overall *diffused, shadowless light* results. This form of lighting became popular in the 1950s but has declined in acceptance in recent years. Cleaning of the ceiling louver or diffusing material is a problem, and the quality of light the system gives has proven less satisfactory than originally hoped.

INTEGRATED CEILING SYSTEMS. These systems incorporate *general lighting,* acoustical treatment, and usually air-conditioning supply into their structures. Such systems may be unique to a particular installation, designed by the architect or interior designer, or a manufactured standard product. Use is most common in offices, public spaces, and other large institutional spaces.

Miscellaneous Types

Although the following lighting types belong to one of the groups listed above, they are singled out here for their special characteristics.

CLIP-ON PHOTO LIGHTS. These are a very economical form of incandescent fixture, giving *general and spot lighting,* fully *adjustable,* and available with many different types of reflectors (fig. 10.46). They have become a favorite ad hoc, low-cost solution to many residential lighting needs.

LUXO LAMPS. These are a familiar form of cantilever, *adjustable desk lamp,* available in many colors, base types, reflector types, and sizes. Like photo lamps, they have become a popular, inexpensive solution to

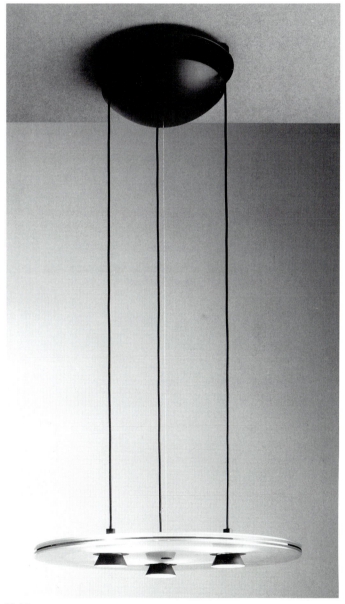

10.44

10.43 From George Kovacs Lighting, these delicate hanging lights with frosted-glass shades—and diameters of only 3 to 5¼ inches—are well suited to contract uses, such as providing concentrated illumination over restaurant tables. They use a 12-volt, 20-watt halogen lamp. (Photograph courtesy George Kovacs Lighting, Inc.)

10.44 Aurora, a hanging fixture by Perry A. King/Santiago Miranda of 1986, uses three 50-watt, 12-volt quartz-halogen lamps in reflectors. The light output is a combination of direct downlight and diffused light from the large, textured-glass disc. (Photograph courtesy Atelier International Lighting)

10.45

10.46

10.47

10.45 Track lighting allows fixtures of many different types to be placed anywhere along tracks that also bear the power line. The two incandescent units illustrated are Manhattan (left), a design of about 1972; and Europa (right) of about 1970. (Photograph courtesy Trakliting, Inc.)

10.46 Clamp-on, pipe-supported, adjustable, reflector incandescent lights were originally developed for theaters and photographic studios to give strong, concentrated light. They now are often adapted to more general interior and architectural uses. Oreste RE is a design of Ernesto Gismondi. (Photograph courtesy Artemide, Inc.)

10.47 Track lighting is ideal for illumination in museums, where it can be almost endlessly adapted to changing exhibits. Shown here is the North Gallery of architect Louis Kahn's Kimbell Art Museum in Fort Worth, Texas.

10.48 In the Creeks Boutique in Paris, small spots of light at the stairway's edge are repeated in similar wall and ceiling units, and all are reflected in the mirrored wall on the left. The store was designed in 1986 by Philippe Starck. (Photograph: Tom Vack)

These might be arranged in 10 rows of 14 fixtures, 5 rows of 28 fixtures, or a different layout suited to the shape of the space. Calculation of this sort is most useful in planning the overall lighting of offices, factories, classrooms, or similar uniformly lighted spaces. Simpler calculation of the same kind can predict the illumination level to be expected from a single lamp or light fixture.

With architectural lighting, the anticipated level of illumination, or brightness, can be calculated quite accurately. This cannot easily be done with portable lighting, since lamps may be moved and wattages changed and since an even illumination level is not usually sought. In residential and other less formal spaces, experience (which can be aided by the use of a light meter) rather than calculation usually guides the placement of lighting.

Switches

It should be remembered that any lighting installation will require switching to provide control from convenient locations. This can be provided by switches at individual fixtures, multiple switches for a single fixture, switching from remote locations or central panels, or, in special cases, switching controlled by clock or light sensors. Switching controlled by sound- or heat-sensitive *proximity* switches turns lighting on when people are present and off when people leave.

Light switches are normally provided at the entry to each room or space. A space that can be entered from two or more directions calls for multiple (upstairs-downstairs) switching. Convenience outlets along walls should be spaced so that an outlet is always available within 6 ⁀t. Wall switches are routinely placed at a height of 50 inches, outlets ⁀ inches from the floor. Although they are minor elements, switch- ⁀h plates, and outlet plates should be selected by the interior ⁀ complement the design of the space, not left to the whim of ⁀⁀⁀ian, who merely installs what he has on hand, regardless of its a⁀ ⁀ropriateness.

Dimmers

Dimmers, a furt⁀ ⁀ification of switching, permit a range of light levels from very lo⁀ ⁀he maximum available, and provide them in a smooth transiti⁀ ⁀incandescent lights are dimmed, they become warmer in col⁀ ⁀effect of coziness is favored in residential spaces and in dining areas generally. Automatic dimmers can alter light levels gradually, in response to time, outside light levels, or an arbitrary program.

CODES AND REGULATIONS

Various legal codes have some, usually limited, impact on lighting design. There are assorted rules in city building codes that require lighting for emergency situations, for signs and other indications of routes to fire exits, and for related passages and stairs. Such lighting may have to be connected to special circuits that are independent of general electrical service, supplied either by back-up battery or by generator circuits that will survive overall power failure.

Another set of requirements deals with minimum levels of lighting required for certain spaces, such as school classrooms, where a mini- mum level of light—50 or 60 footcandles at desktop—is mandated. Such lighting codes unfortunately take no note of lighting quality, and meeting the code at minimum cost often leads to the selection of poor-quality fixtures, which in turn leads to excessive brightness contrast (glaring ceiling fixtures) that results in unsatisfactory seeing conditions in spite of code compliance. Well-designed lighting will comply with such codes and will far exceed their demands in terms of lighting quality. Where codes establish a minimum to be met, it should be recognized that this is merely a floor below which no lighting installation should drop.

Some building codes, particularly in urban areas, now impose restrictions that are opposite in their impact. These are regulations intended to control excessive energy consumption. They establish limits on the electrical consumption that lighting may require in new or renovated construction. Such limits are expressed in terms of watts per square foot that are permissible for a given installation. A common limit is 3 watts per square foot, but some codes have moved to levels as low as 2 or 1.5 watts per square foot. Office lighting of some years back commonly exceeded these limits by a wide margin. Task lighting is an important tool in meeting such codes. When ambient lighting is kept low and higher levels are delivered only at actual workplaces with sources located close to work surfaces, overall energy consumption falls well within such code limits. Designers must be aware of whatever restrictions apply to the lighting design for a specific project. Compliance with regulations will generally not conflict with other design requirements and often results in superior lighting design.

Codes and regulations vary widely among different states and cities and are subject to frequent revision. Professional designers find it worthwhile to become familiar with current regulations applicable in their own communities. When working on a project in another area, it is usually best to consult with a designer or firm active in the location in question to arrange for filing and approval of plans, taking bids, and other aspects of a project, including whatever rules and restrictions apply to lighting.

The complexity of lighting as a technical matter and the constantly increasing variety of lighting sources and devices may tempt the interior designer to turn over all lighting problems to a specialized consultant. It should be remembered that the consultant, however expert, is primarily a technical aid. It remains for the designer to suggest the character, atmosphere, and visual effects desired. The more knowledgeable the designer is about technical issues, the easier it will be to communicate with a consultant, and the greater the probability of a satisfactory result. For modest projects that cannot include the services of a consultant, the designer must accept full responsibility for planning lighting that will balance technical performance with pleasant visual impact.

11.1

TEXTILES

Among the many materials that contribute to the design of a complete interior, textile fabrics have a particularly important role. They introduce a sense of softness, curvature, and flexibility into a space, making a hard- or bare-looking room seem soft, comfortable, and humane. With their vast range of colors, textures, and qualities, they offer unlimited design possibilities.

Fabrics most often appear in interiors as upholstery cover materials for chairs, sofas, and cushions, as bed and table covers, and in window treatment, usually called by the traditional term *drapery*. Lesser uses include curtains in locations other than windows (at door openings, for example) and as wall-covering material. Textiles for interior use are usually divided into two basic groups, upholstery and drapery, with some belonging to both. These are identified in Table 12. (Carpets and rugs, although technically textiles, have been grouped in Chapter 8 with other floor-covering materials.)

In comparison with the basic construction materials (stone, brick, wood, or plaster) that are likely to line a raw space, textiles are less lasting. While this may appear to be a disadvantage, it turns out to be a major reason for textiles' significance to the interior. Since, like paint, they require periodic renewal and are easy to change, they regularly provide an opportunity to do over a space with new color and texture. Indeed, the phrase "to redecorate" implies new paint and new fabrics as the primary means of renewal.

It is probably because of this sense of textiles' impermanence that designers feel free to be somewhat adventurous in their choice of fabric colors, textures, and patterns. This in turn has encouraged designers and manufacturers of textiles to offer a tremendous variety. Fabric design has a close relationship to the world of fashion and shares its constant search for newness and change. Some fabrics, especially prints and other patterned materials, enjoy a brief popularity and then disappear because they come to look dated and out of style. Textile lines reflect changing tastes in terms of color and weave as well. On the other hand, certain basic fabrics will always be available, and any color can be produced on special order, even if color lines change. Fabric selections should always be made after a fresh review of what is currently available.

SELECTING TEXTILES

The selection of textiles often ranks with the choice of furniture, floor coverings, and paint colors as a key element in the designer's contribution to a design project. Textile selection may seem deceptively simple—a matter of casually choosing some attractive colors and textures—but the subject is actually complex and merits more careful attention. For this reason, textiles occupy a full chapter in this book, while other materials are dealt with in the context of their use or together in Chapter 8.

Color

It is most practical to make fabric selections while the color scheme is being developed. This can be approached in two ways. One way is to select approximate colors for the fabric, using colored papers or any other color medium to represent the desired fabric color, while leaving the selection of the actual material to a later time (when visiting various showrooms, for example). However, this creates an extra step when the process can be dealt with all at once. (It is also often difficult to locate a close match for a sample in a particular kind of fabric.) The other approach, to make a final fabric selection when developing a color scheme, saves the extra step but presents other difficulties. It requires having on hand a library of samples large enough to include almost anything that might be desired. Large design firms usually maintain extensive files of samples from the manufacturers they favor, but the individual designer will probably have a much more limited selection on hand.

Dealing with this problem requires building up a sample file large enough to contain at least a few examples of almost anything that may be needed. This involves visiting the showrooms of textile manufacturers in major cities to collect samples. A list of the best-known sources for decorator fabrics can be compiled from advertisements in design magazines. Many furniture manufacturers are also textile distributors, providing fabrics not only for their own products but for general use as well, often offering drapery in addition to upholstery fabrics. Some will provide complete sample swatch sets on request or at a small charge.

11.1 Many historic interiors, particularly residential interiors, use textiles extensively, thereby generating a sense of both comfort and opulence. In the English great house of Chatsworth in Derbyshire (William Talman, architect, 1687–96), Carr of York decorated this Blue Drawing Room *in the 1770s with brocade-covered walls. The rug and upholstery fabrics are more modern, but they perpetuate the original spirit of the room. The large painting is Sargent's portrait of the Acheson Sisters. (Photograph: © James Pipkin)*

Table 12. Textiles in General Use in Interiors

Fabric Name	Fiber(s)	Weight	Weave or Construction	Descriptive Notes	Uses
Antique Satin	S, Syn.	L	Satin	Reversible fabric that imitates silk shantung.	D, U
Batik				Term refers to use of resist-dyeing technique to generate color patterns.	D, (U)
Batiste	C, Syn.	T	Plain	Lightweight; usually light colors, often printed.	C, D
Broadcloth	C, S, W, Syn.	M	Plain or twill	Used for tableclothes, bedspreads, drapery.	D
Brocade	S, Syn.	M	Jacquard	Usually patterned with raised relief design.	U
Burlap	Jute, hemp	L	Plain	Coarse utility fabric. Occasionally used as drapery. Natural tan color, can be dyed.	(D)
Calico	C	L	Plain	Inexpensive, usually printed.	C
Canvas	C, L	M	Plain	Strong, utilitarian fabric. Suitable to outdoor uses, awnings, upholstery.	U
Casement cloth	Various	T	Plain, twill, or leno	Many fibers and weaves; for use as lightweight curtain material.	C
Chambray	C, L	L	Plain	Smooth surface with frosty appearance in various colors.	D
Cheesecloth	C	S	Plain	Very thin utility fabric sometimes used for curtains.	C
Chintz	C	L	Plain	Usually printed and with glazed (glossy) surface.	C, D, (U)
Corduroy	C, Syn.	H	Pile	Pile in ridged textures of wales or ribs.	U
Crash	Various	M	Plain	Rough texture developed from irregular yarns.	D
Cretonne	C	M	Plain or twill	Usually printed in strong patterns. Not glazed.	D, U
Damask	C, S	M	Combination	Jacquard patterns combining two weaves.	U
Denim	C	M	Twill	Inexpensive cotton utility fabric. May have small woven pattern.	U
Dimity	C	L	Plain	Lightweight cotton with a raised warp, giving it a striped effect.	C, D
Drill	C	M	Twill	Sturdy cotton with diagonal twill weave. Normal color gray, but is also dyed.	U
Duck	C	M	Plain	Sturdy utility cotton.	U
Felt	W, Syn.	M–H	Nonwoven	Made by pressing fibers together instead of weaving. Used for table and wall coverings. Cut edges require no hemming. Bright colors available.	(D)*
Fiberglass	Glass	T–M	Various	Glass fibers made into yarn and woven in various weights. Fireproof. Poor abrasion-resistance.	C, D
Flannel	C, W	L	Plain or twill	Woven fabric brushed to produce a soft nap surface.	U
Frieze	C, W, Syn.	H	Jacquard	Rough surface of uncut looped piles.	D, U
Gingham	C, Syn.	L	Plain	Woven from dyed yarns, often in stripes, checks, and plaids. Sturdy; launders well.	D, U
Grass cloth	Jute, hemp, etc.	M	Plain	Woven from grass or similar fibers. Often on paper or plastic backing.	W
Homespun	C, W	L–M	Plain	Coarse yarns in textured weave suggesting hand weaving.	D, U
Hopsacking	C, Syn.	M	Plain	Heavy, coarse, open weave. Durable and economical.	U
Jaspé cloth	Various	L–M	Plain	Sturdy fabric with woven textural striped effect in muted colors.	U
Jersey	W, Syn.	M	Knitted	Knitted with resulting elastic, stretch quality.	(U)
Lace	C, Syn.	L	Machine or handwoven	Fabric of decorative openwork patterns; used for curtains and table coverings.	D
Leather	Animal hide	H	Nontextile	Animal hide finished (and often dyed) for use as upholstery cover, table-top surface, and so on.	U
Linen	L	L–M	Plain	Any fabric woven of linen (flax) fiber. Typically smooth, hard surface. Commonly used for tablecloths.	(D), (U)
Marquisette	C, S, Syn.	S	Leno	Light, sheer, or open weave. Sometimes printed or dyed in light colors.	C, D
Matelassé	C	H	Jacquard	Double cloth with quilted or puckered surface patterning.	D, U
Mohair	Goat hair	M	Twill or pile	Often mixed with cotton or wool. Sturdy and durable. May have a woven pattern.	U
Moire	S, Syn.	L	Plain	Watered textural effect achieved by special finishing.	D
Monk's cloth	C, jute, hemp + C	M	Plain or basket	Coarse and heavy. Usually used in its natural gray color.	(D), (U)

Fabric Name	Fiber(s)	Weight	Weave or Construction	Descriptive Notes	Uses
Muslin	C	T	Plain	Lightweight utility cloth. Economical, often used as underlayer for upholstery cover.	C
Needlepoint	W over backing	H	Hand embroidery or Jacquard	Hand embroidery over canvas or net. Also simulated with Jacquard weave.	U
Net	Rayon or other	S	Plain	Very open (lace) construction. Provides see-through drapery appearance. Many patterns.	C, D
Organdy	C	S	Plain	Crisp cotton sheer. Varied colors, also prints. Primary use in curtains and drapery.	C, D
Osnaburg	C	T	Plain	Strong and durable coarse cotton weave. Often used in its natural color but also dyed or printed.	C, D, (U)
Oxford cloth	C	M	Plain, basket, or twill	Often in stripes or checks. A popular shirt and dress material, also usable for curtains.	C, D
Plastic sheet and film	Plastic	H	Nonwoven	Vinyl or PVC, unbacked or cloth-backed for use as wall covering or as upholstery cover (simulating leather).	U, W
Plush	W (Mohair), Syn.	H	Pile	Cut pile like velvet but with a deeper pile.	U
Pongee	S	T	Plain	Wild silk with irregular texture. Also imitated in cotton and synthetics. Subject to shrinkage.	C, D
Poplin	C	L	Plain	Lightweight fabric with small-scale ribbing.	C, D
Sailcloth	C	M	Plain	Sturdy utility fabric. Suitable to outdoor use.	U, (D)
Sateen	C	L	Satin	Sturdy, glossy surface, similar to satin. Often used as lining for drapery.	D, U
Satin	S, Syn.	L	Satin	Smooth, glossy, rich silk. Often used for luxury draperies.	D, (U)
Scrim	C, L	S	Plain	Loose constructed weave used for curtains and bottom of upholstered goods as dust cover.	D, U
Seersucker	C, Syn.	L	Plain	Light material with a characteristic ribbed surface in various widths of ribbing. Primarily used in apparel.	
Serge	W	M	Twill	Tough, closely woven material primarily used for suiting.	(U)
Shantung	S, Syn.	L	Plain	A heavy grade of pongee. Also imitated in other fibers.	D
Swiss muslin (Dotted)	C	S	Plain	Fine sheer, usually in dotted pattern known as dotted swiss.	C, (D)
Taffeta	S, W, C, various	L–M	Plain	Silky, papery smooth surface, usually with a fine ribbing.	C, D, (U)
Tapestry	W, C, L	H	Jacquard or hand	Hand-woven, usually pictorial, wall hanging or modern Jacquard weave in imitation of handmade tapestry. Usually strongly patterned.	U, (D), (W)
Terry cloth	C, L	M	Pile	Uncut loop pile surface. Much used for toweling, occasionally for bedspreads or drapery.	(D)
Ticking	C, L	M	Twill or satin	Usually light with characteristic stripe. Widely used as mattress covering.	(U)
Tweed	W and various	H	Plain, twill, or Herringbone	Usually a 2-up and 2-down twill in solid color, mixtures, stripes, and checks. Much used for suiting.	U
Velour	Various	H	Velvet pile	Durable cut-pile fabric.	U
Velvet	Various	H	Velvet pile	Cut or uncut loop pile. Rich and luxurious appearance, particularly in silk. Shows wear readily.	U, (D)
Velveteen	C, Syn.	H	Velvet pile	Cotton or synthetic fibers in velvet-type pile weave. Stronger and more durable than actual velvet, but less luxurious in appearance.	U, (D)
Voile	C, S, W, Syn.	S	Plain	Open, sheer drapery material. Varied colors and patterns.	C, D

SYMBOLS

Weight: S = sheer, very thin, T = sheer, thin, L = light, M = medium, H = heavy.

Fiber: C = cotton, L = linen (flax), S = silk, Syn. = synthetic, W = wool.

Use: C = curtains, D = drapery, U = upholstery, W = wall covering. Enclosure in parentheses indicates secondary (unusual or rare) use.

*Felt is used in special applications such as drawer linings and, occasionally, for wall covering.

11.2

11.3

11.2 Small swatches of fabric and larger pieces—called memo squares—are here spread out, along with samples of woods, carpet, marble, tiles, and paint colors. Decorators work with similar selections drawn from large files in order to develop total, coordinated interiors. (Photograph: George Hein)

11.3 A panoply of swatches shows the color ways, or ranges of color, available in various weaves and fibers. Here, a portion of the color way includes, from left to right, cotton velvet, silk, linen, and cotton. Small samples are ideal for filing; larger samples are often requested when decorators make their final selections of the textiles that will be part of the overall color scheme. (Photograph: George Hein)

The designer can usually tell quickly from a showroom visit if it is a source of strong interest. After making a selection of fabrics according to color and other qualities, the designer may request sample swatches, which can be put on file for reference when a scheme is being planned. Swatches, usually small (three or four inches square), are attached to a card identifying the manufacturer and pattern number and giving other data such as width, fiber content, and price (figs. 11.2, 11.3). While small samples give a poor indication of the appearance of large-scale patterns and prints, and may even misrepresent basic colors and textures, the swatch remains a primary selection tool because of its convenience, availability, and low cost. Manufacturers will loan out samples of a square yard, called a *memo square*, of prints and larger patterns. If the scale of the project or the fabric's intended use warrants it, memo squares can be purchased.

Since color is usually the starting point in selection, most designers file samples by color, although they can also be filed under such categories as manufacturer, fiber, or appropriate use. Drapery and upholstery textiles are often filed along with other upholstery cover materials (such as leathers and simulated leathers) and sometimes with other decorative materials, such as plastic wall coverings, window shade and blind materials, and wallpapers. (Because of their greater bulk, carpets and rugs are usually filed separately.) It is often convenient to file favorite fabrics in duplicate so that a file record will remain when a sample is removed for use in planning a color scheme. For a complete color scheme, fabric swatches are grouped with other material samples.

It often turns out that an ideal choice is not on file. When this happens, something close to it can be chosen and marked as a stand-in until another visit to showrooms can be made. In any case, it is a good idea to make frequent showroom visits. They enable the designer to keep up with new patterns as they are introduced and to discuss needs or questions about particular fabrics with the sales staff. Such visits present no problems to residents of major cities. Designers working in small towns or cities routinely plan a visit to a major market center at

11.5

least once a year. Otherwise, less centrally located professionals avail themselves of the services of dealers and traveling representatives who carry several manufacturers' products.

Other Factors

In selecting a fabric, color is only one significant element among many, including durability, resistance to dirt, textural qualities, and, of course, price. A checklist of criteria for fabric selection will include the following items, not necessarily in order of importance:

SUITABILITY OF WEIGHT, WEAVE, AND TEXTURE TO INTENDED USE
COLOR (OR COLORS)
DURABILITY, INCLUDING THE BASIC LIFE OF THE FIBER; RESISTANCE TO WEAR, DIRT, AND SPOTTING; EASE OF CLEANING; AND, WHERE APPLICABLE, EASE OF REPAIR
POSSIBILITY OF SHRINKING OR STRETCHING
EASE OF WORKING (SEWING) INTO FORM FOR INTENDED USE
COLOR-FADING CHARACTERISTICS
FIRE-RESISTANCE
PRICE

The importance of these issues will vary with the intended use. Resistance to fading is vital for curtains at a sunny window, as is fire-resistance for offices and public places, such as restaurants, theaters, or airplane interiors. Price is a more complex issue than it may seem. The initial cost of fabric yardage tells nothing about the fabric's lifetime

11.4

11.4 It is important that fabrics used for contract interiors have good durability. A Teflon finish strengthens this upholstery cloth, a chenille made of 75 percent cotton and 25 percent polyester. The pattern is called Agattu, manufactured by Pindler & Pindler. (Photograph courtesy Lennon and Associates)

11.5 Toiles, cotton with patterns printed from copperplates, first appeared in 1752. Prints from a mill at Jouy, France, near Versailles, came to be known as toiles de Jouy. This example, using designs inspired by a pattern book of

Robert Sayers of about 1772, is a modern version printed on linen. The material, produced by Schumacher, is called Toile Orientale. (Photograph courtesy Schumacher)

cost, which takes into account its durability, cleaning costs, and replacement cost. (This last becomes important with frequent redecoration.) The cost of drapery and upholstery includes the work of making up curtains or covers plus the cost of additional materials such as linings and hardware. (These costs generally do not depend on the type of fabric chosen.) A better fabric at a higher price may be more economical, in the long run, than a cheap material with a short life. However, if the user plans to change fabric frequently, this may not apply. Such intangibles as user satisfaction and aesthetic qualities are important criteria that cannot be priced.

Many fabrics offered for institutional, office, and commercial use have been tested for such things as wear and fire-resistance, and these data can help the designer to select wisely.* However, no such data exist for many other fabrics, in which case, the designer must rely on experience and observation of fabrics in use and on the advice of manufacturers' sales staff. This may, of course, be biased, but reputable suppliers of textiles will usually try to provide good information about suitability for a given use. They have a stake in satisfying specifiers (the people who select or order fabric) and end users (clients or actual users) and will try to prevent such problems as a fragile fabric being specified for a heavy-duty use; unexpected fading or shrinkage; or selection of a fabric that does not clean well.

FABRIC TYPES AND CONSTRUCTION

Knowledge of fabric materials and construction is an important aid in making good fabric choices. This subject becomes constantly more complex as new fibers and manufacturing techniques are developed. The basic information provided here can serve as a point of departure for developing a knowledge of textile technology.

The common names of fabrics—for example, wool, satin, Dacron—are more confusing than helpful since they refer variously to fiber (wool), construction or weave (satin), or even, in some cases, trade names (Dacron). In order to look at fabrics in a systematic way, any given example is best considered in terms of:

FIBER OR FIBERS
YARN OR YARNS
CONSTRUCTION (WEAVE OR OTHER TYPE)
FINISH
DYE OR PRINT
SPECIAL CHARACTERISTICS (IF ANY)

The following summary is a condensed (and by no means complete) listing of the most frequently encountered possibilities within each of these characteristics.

Certified test results for local, county, and state fire codes are routinely supplied by textile suppliers. These tests have been conducted in accordance with specific code requirements by independent certified laboratories. Further discussion on textile testing appears below, page 345.

Fiber

Fiber refers to the basic material from which the cloth is made. It often gives its name to the fabric or to a whole range of fabrics made from that particular fiber. The list of natural fibers in traditional use is fairly short, but modern invention has added many fibers, while the possibilities of combining fibers have become limitless. The most widely used fibers can be grouped into a few categories (see Table 13 on page 338).

Yarn

Yarn is the term for the long, continuous strands or threads made from fiber to prepare it for construction into fabric by such common techniques as weaving or knitting. The yarns themselves can be of various constructions (fig. 11.6); those most frequently encountered include:

MONOFILAMENT. This means a single strand of material, all of the same substance. The most familiar monofilament yarns are those extruded from a plastic (like the much-used fishing lines) and those made by slitting flat plastic sheet. Horsehair can be considered a natural monofilament yarn.

MULTIFILAMENTS. Several monofilament yarns twisted or piled together make a single multifilament yarn. Multifilaments may be used alone or may be spun with other synthetic or natural fibers.

SPUN YARNS. Using a traditional technique, a continuous strand is made from short natural fibers such as cotton and wool. Hand spinning is the ancient way of making such yarns. Spinning machines that took over this function were among the first important inventions of the Industrial Revolution. Synthetic multifilaments cut into short lengths have been blended with natural fibers in an attempt to combine the best qualities of both fiber types.

TWISTED YARN. Spun yarn may be twisted, which increases the strength of the yarn. The tightness of the twist influences the fabric's texture and appearance.

PLIED YARNS. Several yarn strands wound together increase thickness and strength and produce varied textures and appearance. Multiple strands may be plied together. Using strands of more than one color creates special visual effects.

SLUB YARN. Irregular in diameter, slub yarn may be produced either by spinning yarns that have not been combed or by mechanically introducing deliberate irregularities. It gives the fabric a special texture.

STRETCH YARNS. These return to their original length after stretching. They may be constructed with the fiber wrapped around a stretchable core (of latex or similar material) or may be the result of new processes in which synthetic fibers are crimped, giving them a springy, coil form. Fabrics made from stretch yarns, used widely in apparel, are useful in certain upholstery applications.

Construction

Construction refers to the way in which fiber is made into a cloth or textile. The most familiar constructions use yarn as a basic element, but constructions that do not require fiber in yarn form also exist. A list of the most-used fabric constructions follows.

FELT. Fibers, usually wool, that have not been made into yarn can be worked together through pressure, heat, chemical reaction, or other means to produce a homogeneous sheet of tangled-together fiber strands called batting. Some synthetic fibers can be felted with the aid of an adhesive.

FILMS. Synthetic materials such as the plastics polyester and PVC (polyvinyl chloride) can be made into a continuous sheet, familiar in such uses as shower curtains. Films may be laminated over woven fabric to produce plastic sheeting that can be cut and sewn with ease. Plastic wall-covering materials and imitation leathers are often of this construction.

WOVEN FABRICS. The dominant type of textile, these come in a variety of constructions (fig. 11.8). Most are of the sort called *two-element*

weaves, constructed with the familiar technique of the over-and-under interlacing of a lengthwise *warp* and the horizontal *weft*, or *filling*. The strands are normally at right angles, with construction taking place on the weaver's equipment, a loom. The loom holds the warp strands in place and provides a way of lifting some (often alternate) warp strands to open a *shed*, or space, through which the weft strands can be passed, one strand at a time. In hand weaving, the weaver passes the weft strands through the shed, while power looms do this mechanically. Variations in the arrangement of over-and-under strands and in yarn texture and color make possible a vast variety of patterns in woven fabrics.

Weaves may be of two, three, or four elements, each element being a particular kind of yarn. *Two-element weaves* are the most common, the warp and weft each forming one element. In *three-element weaves*,

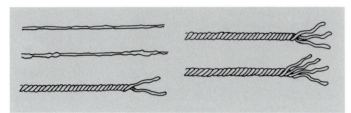

11.6

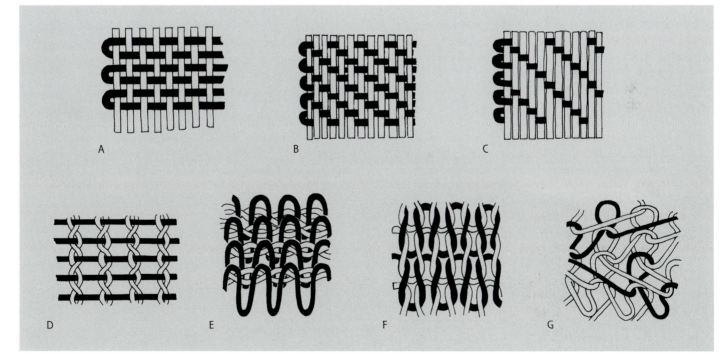

11.8

11.6 From upper left, the following yarn constructions are pictured: monofilament, one-ply, two-ply, three-ply (upper right), and multiple, or cable, ply.

11.7 A complex fabric woven in Ireland, Academia by Jack Lenor Larsen, is suitable for both upholstery and drapery. The recessed squares are of platinum-colored metallic yarn with a

surround of natural-color worsted in a double-twill weave. The fabric can be coordinated with a related design in a Wilton-weave carpet. (Photograph courtesy Jack Lenor Larsen, Inc.)

11.8 The following weaves are illustrated: plain (A), twill (B), satin (C), leno (D), and pile (E). The last two show weft-knit (F) and warp-knit (G) constructions.

Table 13. Fibers

Natural Fibers

IN WIDE USE

WOOL. This is sheared from sheep and processed to various levels of refinement. It comes in only a few natural colors, although it can be dyed. Its performance characteristics are generally excellent.

MOHAIR. This is a goat's hair usually considered a wool.

COTTON. A plant fiber. Under many names, cottons are widely used utility and decorative fabrics.

SILK. Unwound from the cocoon of the silkworm moth, this luxury fiber, while somewhat costly and fragile, is valued for its unique appearance.

LINEN. A plant fiber produced from flax, it provides strong yarns with a characteristic smooth appearance.

IN LIMITED USE

JUTE. A plant fiber of coarse and rough character. Burlap is the most useful product.

HORSEHAIR. A strong, smooth cloth is made from this fiber. It has had significant use as an upholstery cover in traditional design.

CASHMERE. A delicate wool generally too costly and fragile for interior use.

CAMEL'S HAIR. Another fine wool too costly for extensive interior use.

GRASS AND PALM FIBERS. Woven grass cloths are not uncommon as wall-covering materials.

Artificial (Man-Made) Fibers

FROM NATURAL (CELLULOSE) POLYMER

ACETATE. A common economy substitute for various natural fibers, acetate is versatile and inexpensive.

RAYON. Viscose rayon is the type in widest use. One of the most-used economy substitutes for natural fibers, rayon can be processed to resemble many fibers. It has recently been largely displaced in quality fabrics by other synthetics.

FROM SYNTHETIC POLYMERS

ACRYLICS. Wool-like fibers. Modacrylics are so named because they have been chemically modified to offer good flame-resistance. Trade names include (unmodified) Acrilan, Orlon, Verel, Sef, Zefran, and Dynel (which also comes modified).

OLEFIN. This includes the varieties polyethylene and polypropylene. A very light fiber, olefin particularly resembles wool. Herculon is a trade name.

POLYESTER. A light fiber, polyester is often blended with natural fibers. Dacron, Fortrel, Kodel, and Trevira are trade names.

POLYAMIDE (NYLON). One of the first and most useful synthetics, nylon has high strength and good elasticity. Many types are now available. It is frequently used in blends. Antron and Cordura are familiar trade names.

PVC (POLYVINYL CHLORIDE). Familiar under the trade name Saran, it is made into both a yarn and a sheet. Yarns are also made by slitting film. A heat-sensitive fiber, it is suitable for heat-sealing.

POLYURETHANE. A highly elastic fiber, this is used for stretch fabrics such as spandex.

Mineral Fibers

These are technically natural but of nonorganic origins.

ASBESTOS. Formerly valued for its fire-resistance, it has largely dropped out of use because it presents serious health hazards.

METALS. In the form of thin strands, copper, gold, silver, and stainless steel can be used as a fiber, usually in combination with other fibers. Lurex is a trade name for plastic-coated metal strands. Imitation metallics are made by coating a plastic with a metallic finish.

GLASS. Fiberglas (trade name), or fiberglass, is a thin spun strand of glass. It is resistant to fire and moisture but with flexing the fibers tend to break and shed.

Fiber Blends

Two or more fibers are combined in one yarn in order to maximize the strengths and minimize the weaknesses of its component fibers. For example, natural and artificial fibers may be combined to retain the texture and appearance of the natural yarn while gaining the wrinkle- and dirt-resistance and durability of the synthetic.

Dacron and cotton, wool and nylon are useful blends. The different fibers may be spun together into a single yarn or several separate and different yarns may be woven together. More than two fibers may be combined in complex blends, as for example, a blended yarn woven together with a yarn of a third fiber.

11.9 In a showcase model dining room, designer Sig Bergamin used a riot of colorful paisley-patterned textiles for walls, chair seats, and table linens. The opulent scheme achieves coherence through the similarity of the textiles' patterns and the strong color theme of reds and yellows. (Photograph: Michael Mundy)

11.10 Handmade quilts such as this are among the finest products of American vernacular craft. Scraps of fabric are cut, assembled, and quilted, following one of a myriad of time-honored patterns; the result is both unique and traditional. The quilt here covers a four-poster bed of circa 1850 in a 1949 cottage in Castroville, Texas. (Photograph: © 1985 Michael Skott)

11.9

11.10

an additional yarn element is added to either the warp or weft. *Four-element weaves* may be constructed with three warps and one weft, but most are double cloths made up of two warps and two wefts. Within each of these weave types, the pattern of over-and-under interlacing of the elements can vary. The name of a cloth refers both to the number of elements and the pattern of weave. Weave patterns are described as *plain, twill,* or *satin.*

Plain weave is the simple and familiar over-and-under interlace. A one-to-one (warp thread to weft thread) interlace produces gingham, taffeta, monk's cloth, and muslin. A two-and-two interlace (or *basket weave*) is characteristic of canvas and duck, while sailcloth employs a one-to-two relationship. All of these are two-element weaves. Adding a third element produces brocades and the *pile weaves,* which include the cut piles—plush, velour, and velvet—and the uncut piles—terry cloth and velveteen. In pile weaves, the third element projects above the plane of the basic weave, forming loops. These are the uncut piles. When the loops are cut, leaving individual standing strands of yarn, the typically velvety fuzzy surface of the cut piles results. Corduroy is also a three-element plain weave. Four-element construction in double plain weave produces *double cloths,* which are, in effect, two separate cloths woven at the same time and held together by strands that intermittently cross from one surface to the other. The two faces may have different patterns and colors. *Matelassé* combines single and double cloths with doubled areas stuffed to produce a quilted appearance.

Twill weave is produced by passing weft strands over one or more and under one or more warp strands in a shifting sequence to produce an appearance of diagonal pattern. Two-element twills include cheviot, denim, drill, gabardine, herringbone, and houndstooth. Three-element twill brocades and velvets and four-element double twill can be produced.

Satin weave describes a construction in which the warp is carried over four, five, or six weft strands and under one in a staggered pattern that avoids the diagonal patterning of twills. Satin, sateen, and damask are cloths of satin weave.

The term *Jacquard weaving* refers to a mechanical method of controlling a power loom in order to produce woven pattern by means of cards, similar to the punched computer card, that control the interlace of strands. Brocades, damasks, velvets, *tapestry weaves,* and matelassés are often Jacquard-woven.

OTHER CONSTRUCTIONS. Another fabric construction in current use is *knitting,* which is not a weave using warp and weft but a kind of knotting technique in which a single strand is looped or threaded together, in the way hobby knitters make scarves, sweaters, and laces, but now usually produced on complex modern knitting machines. Knits may be of either single- or two-element construction.

Malimo is a modern fabric construction in which many weft strands are laid across the warp and anchored down by a stitch of a third yarn element mechanically knitted into place. *Leno,* or *marquisette,* is a variation on plain weave in which pairs of warp threads cross between strands of weft to discourage the individual strands from slipping. The technique is often used to create open, casement, or drapery fabrics of good strength.

Finishing

The term refers to the various processes that follow basic fabric construction to prepare the textile for use. Many finishing processes, such as boiling, carbonizing with acid, shearing, calendering (pressing between rollers), and fulling (a controlled shrinking), are parts of production that need not concern the designer. Glazing polishes a cloth surface, familiar in the glazed cottons such as chintz. Various finishing processes promise resistance to wrinkling, soil-repellency, and moth-proofing. Widely advertised treatments with trade names such as Scotchgard and Zepel aid in resisting soiling, while other treatments tend to repel water. In recent years, various finishing processes have been developed to aid fire-resistance through a chemical treatment that discourages the spread of flames. Antistatic treatments that reduce the buildup of electrical charge that occurs with some synthetic fabrics have also been developed. The availability of such finishing processes is generally clearly recorded and explained in manufacturers' specifications and advertising. Backcoating of upholstery fabrics with acrylic latex reduces seam slippage and generally improves abrasion-resistance and dimensional stability.

Table 14. Textile Finishes
(Processes and Trade Names)

ANTIBACTERIAL, ANTISEPTIC, OR BACTERIOSTAT Chemical treatment to inhibit the growth of mold, mildew, other fungi, and rot.

ANTISTATIC Chemical treatment to reduce static electricity or conduction.

FIREPROOFING Fiber or chemical treatment providing noninflammability.

FIRE-RETARDANT Chemical treatment to resist ignition and retard flame spread.

FLAME-RESISTANT Chemical treatment to resist ignition.

GLAZING Surface-coating treatment to give high-gloss surface (often used for chintz or cretonne).

MERCERIZATION Chemical process used only on cotton to improve strength and luster.

MILDEW-RESISTANT Chemical process to resist development of mildew, mold, and fungus growth.

MOTH-REPELLENT Chemical process to resist moth damage.

PRESHRUNK Treated to limit shrinkage when wetted.

SANFORIZED A particular preshrinking process limiting shrinkage to 1 percent or less.

SCOTCHGARD The trade name for a chemical process to make textiles resistant to stains.

SOIL-RELEASE FINISH Chemical process making textiles resistant to soiling.

SOIL-REPELLENT Chemical process that coats fibers to make soil removal easier.

ZELAN The trade name for a process to make cotton and rayon water-repellent.

ZEPEL The trade name for a process to increase the stain-resistance of textiles.

11.11

11.12

11.13

11.14

11.15

11.11 This wall covering of polyolefin, a synthetic textile, has been made into a plasticized sheet for excellent stain resistance and easy maintenance. The weaves illustrated are, from top to bottom: plain weave, two plain basket weaves, a twill, and a herringbone twill. The product is called Tek-Wall. (Photograph courtesy Maharam Fabrics)

11.12 The fine, open casement-weave fabric lends itself well to use as curtains or draperies. This one is made from Egyptian cotton, goat hair, and a gold guimpe. (Photograph courtesy Jack Lenor Larsen, Inc.)

11.13, 11.14 The contributions of Vienna Secessionist Josef Hoffmann (see Chapter 4, pages 98–100) to the Wiener Werkstätte craft shops retain a surprisingly contemporary look. Designed in 1908, but once again in production, these are his Zickzack (fig. 11.13) and Orlick (fig. 11.14) fabrics, both viscose, or rayon, and cotton weaves. (Photographs courtesy Bachausen, Vienna)

11.15 This fabric, Saranac, is a cotton Jacquard woven in Belgium. The pattern is based on fabrics seen in old photographs of an Adirondack vacation house and is part of a collection called, appropriately, Adirondack. (Photograph courtesy Gretchen Bellinger Inc.)

11.16

Color

DYEING. This is a primary means of introducing color in fabric, which otherwise has generally neutral gray or grayish tones. (In the trade, *greige goods* refers to undyed and/or unfinished fabrics.) Piece dyeing of woven textiles is a finishing process that produces a solid color. Dyeing yarns before weaving them permits color variation and pattern when variously colored yarn strands are woven together. Traditionally, dyes were made from various natural sources, most of which produce soft colors or colors that tend to be pleasant and harmonious even when more intense. Modern chemically manufactured dyes produce a much wider range of colors and color brightness but tend to be harsher and more garish. Since natural (undyed) yarns and natural dyestuffs rarely produce objectionable effects, they contribute greatly to the excellence of so many traditional woven materials.

Dyed materials are subject to fading from the effects of sun and other light and to fading and running in washing and cleaning. The *fastness*, or lasting quality, of dye color is a significant issue that needs

11.16 *A simply patterned blue-and-white cotton fabric, designed by David Hicks and produced in Paris, is used here for drapery, chair-seat upholstery, and loose cushions. (Photograph: Jacques Dirand, courtesy Elle Decoration)*

to be tested or checked when making fabric selections. Some fading, running, and deterioration through wear is inevitable. These effects are least noticeable when colors are soft rather than bright, patterns are subtle rather than harsh, and textures are rough or coarse rather than smooth. Medium tones are less likely to show fading and wear than very light or very dark shades. However, if a fragile textile subject to rapid wear or fading also has a unique appearance, its use may be justified.

PRINTING. Printing onto a fabric is another widely used way to add color and pattern to textiles. Traditional techniques include *resist printing,* in which a wax or starch applied to the fabric blocks coloring when the cloth is dipped in dye (fig. 11.20). Afterward, the resist material is washed out. It may be reapplied and the cloth dipped again, and so on, to create complex patterns with several colors. This is the technique of *batik,* a well-known craft process. *Block printing,* in which individual wood blocks are coated with color and applied to the cloth, was once an important fabric-printing method in Europe. Its dependence on skilled handwork and the development of modern mechanized printing methods have rendered it generally obsolete in the industrialized world.

Roller printing involves mechanization similar to that of modern printing on paper. Rollers with the pattern for the fabric design embossed onto it are made, one for each color. As the cloth is passed under each roller in turn, the roller prints its color in the proper pattern onto it. The design will repeat on a dimension equal to the circumference of the roller. Fine detail and shading similar to that of imagery printed on paper are possible with roller printing. Although a modern mechanical technique, this method is also passing out of use in favor of screen printing.

In *screen printing,* as in silk-screen printing on paper, a screen of finely woven fabric is used for each color. The screen has blocked-out areas where the color is not to appear. Color is squeezed through the unblocked portions of the screen onto the fabric being printed. Printing may be done by hand, with fabric placed on a flat table; mechanically, onto flat fabric; or with a rotary technique, in which the screens are in roller form, the fabric rolling past printing cylinders for each color required. This is a fast and economical technique for quantity production.

Print design has developed in relation to changing historic styles. Today, many traditional designs are still available, in their original or adapted forms. Floral prints and prints incorporating many kinds of imagery abound. Modern print design includes more geometric and abstract patterns, along with new versions of more representational imagery.

A single design can be varied by altering the colors chosen, by adding or omitting certain color elements, and by changing scale through enlargement or reduction. A print design, usually limited in area, is extended to cover an unlimited yardage through *repeats* of the same design. These are generally planned so that the match line, where one repeat ends and the next begins, is unnoticeable. Print designs have come under copyright protection in order to cut down on the piracy, or imitation, of designs by manufacturers unwilling to pay the expenses and take the risks of commissioning new designs.

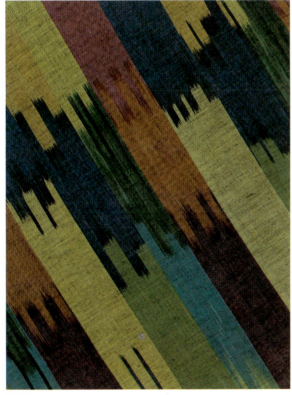

11.17

11.18

11.17 The interiors of the Four Seasons Resort on the island of Bali feature an indigenous ikat fabric with a dyed pattern on untreated cotton. The pattern and colors, as well as the process used to dye the fabric, are typical of Balinese traditions. (Photograph courtesy Four Seasons Resort, Bali)

11.18 The design of a stenciled cotton fabric by Mario Fortuny, produced in Italy in the early twentieth century, is clearly influenced by Venetian Renaissance textiles. (Photograph: Ted Croner)

Special Characteristics

Various specialized forms of textiles also deserve note. These include *embroidery*, familiar as a handwork technique but now mechanically produced, and *quilting*, also best known as a craft technique for layering together several fabrics, possibly with a filling between layers (fig. 11.10). Mechanical techniques for quilting are in current use. *Tufted fabrics* are made on a cloth base with tufts of fiber needled through the base and anchored on the back with a coating.

In *coated fabrics*, a surface material is spread over a woven base, as in oilcloth. Coating is now used to make plastic upholstery materials, which often simulate leather or some other material. These offer good durability at low cost. Coated fabrics have also come into wide use as wall-covering materials more durable than paint or paper and available in a range of textures, in imitation of materials like grass cloth, wood, or even metals, or of original design and texture.

IDENTIFYING TEXTILES

The vast variety of materials and manufacturing techniques used in making textiles and the complex terminology used in describing fabrics can seem intimidating and confusing. By checking manufacturers' suggestions and directly assessing such qualities as texture, weight (density), and feel (or *hand*, as this quality is called in the textile

11.20

trades), the designer can find a range of fabrics appropriate to the intended use. These choices can be further narrowed down by balancing the fabric's aesthetic qualities of appearance, such as color, pattern, and texture, against its practical qualities, such as durability, strength, and colorfastness, and against its price.

While a detailed knowledge of fibers and weaves is not essential to interior design, the designer who wishes to become an intelligent specifier will learn as much as possible about textile technology. It can be an interesting exercise (which can become a useful habit) to take small cuttings of fabrics and pull out the woven strands to identify the fibers and yarns and determine the weave or other construction used. To make a systematic study, the cutting can be attached to an index card and full information entered on the card. For example:

> *FIBER(S)*
>> *Warp*
>> *Weft*
> *YARN(S)*
>> *Type*
> *CONSTRUCTION*
>> *Number of elements*
>> *Type of weave or*
>>> *other construction*
> *FINISH*
>> *Dye (yarn or piece*
>>> *and type)*
> *PRINT*
>> *Manufacturer*
>>> *or supplier*
> *WIDTH*
> *PRICE PER YARD*
> *OTHER DATA*

11.19

11.19 This is a handsome printed chintz, a traditional fabric still in wide use, particularly for draperies, curtains, and upholstery. (Courtesy Brunschwig & Fils)

11.20 Painting and resist-printing were used to produce the pattern on this Indian bedspread of cotton and linen made between 1690 and 1720. These traditional Indian techniques are still in use. This material is in the collection of the Winterthur Museum, Delaware. (Photograph courtesy Winterthur Museum)

The tags that manufacturers attach to samples give some of this information (the name and number of the fabric, width, fibers, finish, and, sometimes, price); further information must come from inspecting the fabric and questioning knowledgeable salespeople who represent the manufacturer.

Fabric Testing

Although the evaluation of textiles by visual inspection and feel is an adequate guide for aesthetic judgments and offers some hints as to durability, the careful designer may also want to obtain data from testing of a more systematic sort. Durability, susceptibility to fading in sunlight, and resistance to ignition when exposed to flame are among those characteristics of textiles that can be evaluated through standard tests.

DURABILITY. Tested by several methods. A *Wyzenbeek testing machine* rubs a fabric sample in two directions with a cloth- or wire-mesh-covered roller. Fifteen thousand cycles of rubbing without breakdown is considered an adequate level of abrasion-resistance. A *Taber test* applies the action of two abrasive wheels rotating in two directions. The number of revolutions before the yarns begin to break is the sample's test rating. A rather crude test for floor coverings involves temporarily mounting an untested sample along with a sample of a material of known durability in a high-traffic area so that both will be walked on equally. By observing the samples at regular intervals over a period of weeks or months, the performance of the unproven material can be compared with the control sample. Similar *use testing* can be devised for upholstery fabrics by placing samples on seating units that will be subjected to heavy wear. While continuing a test to breakdown will take an excessive period of time, comparative observation after a period of weeks or months will give a reasonable indication of expected durability.

11.22

FADING. Tested with a device called a *Fade-Ometer*. A sample is exposed to ultraviolet light at controlled levels of humidity and examined for fading after successive periods of twenty hours. Eighty hours of exposure without noticeable fading is considered an acceptable minimum. There is also an internationally standardized test that rates samples on a scale from one to eight. Four is a satisfactory value, with a rating of five, six, or higher preferred.

FIRE-RESISTANCE. This characteristic is of great importance because fabrics are the most easily ignited materials present in a typical interior. Dropped burning cigarette ashes or stubs commonly cause such fires. Resistance not only to ignition but also to the spread of flame if ignited, to smoldering, and to smoke and toxic-fume production are important safety considerations (fig. 11.21). A standard test places a lighted cigarette on a fabric sample and measures the length of the resultant charring. Letter designations rate fabrics as Class D when charring extends for 3 inches or more; Class C, 1 1/2 to 3 inches; Class B, less than 1 1/2 inches; and Class A when charring extends less than 1 1/2 inches with the sample placed on top of cotton batting. To receive any class rating, the sample must not ignite. Special finishes are applied to fabrics (see Table 14) to achieve required class ratings.

Textile Names

Although by no means complete, the listing of textile names provided in Table 15 on page 346, together with their classification by weight and with notes on their typical uses, can be helpful in clearing up some of the confusion associated with textile identification. It can also provide a basis for classification as one builds up a collection of sample swatches of the materials that will be under consideration for actual interior design projects.

11.21

11.21 *Fabrics can be treated to minimize the risk of flammability. This woven fire-retardant fabric, from the Garden Party Collection of Hoechst Celanese, uses Trevira FR polyester fiber. (Photograph: © Maryanne Solensky, courtesy Pollack & Associates)*

11.22 *Textile design is constantly evolving to develop stronger, more resistant new fabrics that are also of high aesthetic quality. DuPont's polyester Micromattique is a synthetic fiber with the look and feel of silk but of great durability. Designer Jack Lenor Larsen's Cybele, a nylon and polyester taffeta coated with Teflon, is remarkably resistant to stain, water, and fire.*

Also extremely durable are innovative new textiles developed by Japanese designer Reiko Sudo that integrate such metals as copper and iron. The copper cloth uses a warp of a biodegradable fiber called Promix (16 percent) and a weft of copper wire (84 percent). Other fabrics are of 100 percent polyester taffeta coated with powdered metals—including chrome, nickel, and iron—

through a process called splatter-plating; they can be finished to provide rough, embossed, or wave-patterned surfaces. These new materials, which can be bent and shaped, are suitable for such uses as window treatments, screens, and shades. (Photograph courtesy Nuno Corporation)

11.23

Table 15. Textiles

FIBER		TRADE NAMES	CHARACTERISTICS	COMMON USES
NATURAL				
Plant Origins	Cotton		Versatile, widely used, economical. Soils easily. Special treatments and fiber blends provide improved service characteristics.	C, D, U, R, L, S
	Jute (burlap, gunnysack)		Economical, strong. Takes color well but fades easily. Rots if left wet. Burns readily.	C, D, W
	Linen (flax)		Smooth texture with slight gloss. Soils and wrinkles easily. Insect-resistant. Washes well. Sanforizing treatment will limit shrinkage.	C, D, U, R, L
Animal Origins	Silk		Unique texture and surface gloss. Luxurious appearance. Damaged by exposure to sunlight. Good resistance to soiling.	D, U, R
	Wool Also: Mohair Camel's hair		Versatile, high-quality fiber. Good soil- and spot-resistance. Cleans well. Subject to moth damage. Special treatments and blends with synthetics improve service characteristics.	D, U, R, B, S
Mineral Origins	Glass	Fiberglas PPG Fiberglas	Strands of glass flexible enough to be spun into yarn and woven. Noninflammable. Poor resistance to abrasion. Troublesome to sew.	C, D

11.23 West African textiles in vigorous colors were among the design elements chosen for the offices of 40 Acres and a Mule, the company run by filmmaker Spike Lee. The Brooklyn, New York, offices were designed by architect Jack Travis. (Photograph: Ricardo Tegni)

Fiber	Trade Names	Characteristics	Common Uses
Metals	Lurex Metlon	Stainless steel, aluminum, silver, and gold in thin strands or coated on or with plastic to provide a decorative accent. Conductive metal strands may be woven into rugs to eliminate static buildup.	D, R
SYNTHETIC Acetate	Acele Avisco Celanese Chromspun Estron	Economical. Poor resistance to sunlight. Fair soil-resistance.	C, D, U, R, S
Acrylic	Acrilan Creslan Orlon Zefran	Wool-like qualities. Washes and dry-cleans well.	C, U, R, B
Modacrylic	Dynel Verel	Similar to acrylics but better stain-resistance. Texture suited to synthetic furs and some rugs. Flame-retardant.	D, U, R, B
Nylon	A.C.E. Antron Cordura	Silklike, elastic texture. Excellent in fiber blends. Poor resistance to sunlight. Widely used in carpeting. High tensile strength.	U, R, S
Olefin (polypropylene)	Herculon Vectra	Wool-like texture, light in weight, good heat insulator. Soil-resistant.	U, R, B
Polyester	Dacron Fortrel Trevira	Silk- or wool-like. Soils easily but washes well. Used in blends. Dacron used as synthetic substitute for down in cushions and upholstery. Dimensionally stable.	C, D, U, R
Rayon	Avril Enka Zantrel	Economical substitute for cotton or silk. Texture may be glossy or dull; drapes well. Swells when wet. Modifying treatments that improve its appearance qualities are available. Widely used for low-cost apparel, curtains, table linens.	C, D, U, R, L, B, S
Spandex	Cleerspan Glospan Lycra Interspan	Strong and durable. Stretches and recovers. Resists chemicals and sunlight. Easily dyed. Good moisture-resistance. Melts when exposed to flame.	U
Triacetate	Arnel	Drapes and washes well, retains press.	C, D
NONFIBROUS (Textile alternatives) Leather		Animal hides tanned and processed in natural and dyed colors. Textures include suede (matte) and patent leather (high gloss). Sold not by the yard but by the hide. May crack and decay unless carefully maintained.	U, (W)
Plastic Vinyl PVC	Naugahyde Saran	Plastic sheet is usable as curtain (shower curtain) material and as wall covering. Fabric backing improves strength for use as wall covering and for upholstery as a leather substitute. Wide range of colors and surface textures.	C, U, W

SYMBOLS
C = curtains, D = drapery, U = upholstery, R = rugs, L = linens (table), B = blankets, S = bedspreads, W = wall covering, (W) = occasionally used as wall covering.

12.1

in addition to their primary functions. Each available system has its own dimensional characteristics and may influence plan layout by favoring certain arrangements or making others impractical or impossible.

REUSING FURNITURE. Whether or not to reuse existing furniture is another decision to be made before planning begins. This decision may be based on reasons of economy or on a client's desire to retain well-liked or treasured pieces. In residential design, it is probably more common to reuse at least some existing furniture than to start out with everything new. The designer typically inventories and measures existing furniture, noting which pieces *must* be reused and which might be considered for reuse as design develops. New furniture specifically chosen falls into a similar category. A desired seating group or a new grand piano must be planned for as if they already were on hand.

LAYOUT AND PLANNING

Arranging furniture in plan is a vital part of interior-design work. (For a detailed discussion of planning, see Chapter 6.) When this can best be done depends on a number of variables. Usually, basic architectural planning comes before furniture layout. When a project is to occupy existing space, where wall locations as well as room sizes and shapes are predetermined, furniture planning will usually be the first design activity. This is typical of residential projects where a house or apartment already exists and no major architectural changes are contemplated. When the space to be planned is not predetermined, either because architectural planning has not been completed or because the space is an open area without partitions (as on the floors of modern office buildings), some furniture planning can precede final layout of the partitions that will define rooms. In fact, there are situations where furniture planning *must* come before any other step.

An auditorium, a lecture room, or a classroom, for example, can be planned in detail only when an appropriate area has been established. A decision about the number of seats and their layout is a first requirement. The layout of auditorium seats in suitable rows with aisles establishes the general shape and size of the room. In restaurant design, the number and size of tables and chairs and their spacing are key factors in the economic planning that will determine the possibilities for profitable operation. In other projects, the layout of certain spaces may be strongly influenced by furniture layout. The size and shape of a file room, of library stacks, or of stock storage areas are developed by the layout of the required furniture. Hospital rooms and even residential bedrooms must take into account the number and size of the beds to be accommodated. A hotel or motel is planned on the basis of typical room plans, which are, essentially, proposed furniture layouts. Such furniture-first planning does not demand firm decisions on the particular furniture designs to be used—the given dimensions and shapes serve as the basis for the layout of furniture, with room shapes and wall locations following in turn.

The reverse situation, in which partition locations have set room sizes and shapes, may be more common and is certainly typical of many projects where the designer must work with a plan that cannot be changed or that will permit only minor revisions, as for an existing house, apartment, or suite of offices. In such projects, furniture layout must adjust to given circumstances.

Many designers choose to make plan layouts on the basis of square-foot areas assigned to various functions, into which furniture is fit. This approach works best where spaces are not packed with furniture, as in a museum or gallery or in a gymnasium or other sports facility, where furniture is incidental.

Whatever the situation, the designer needs to have in mind the standard sizes and shapes of the furniture types to be used and estimates (or even exact counts) of the numbers of each type to be accommodated. In a large office, for example, it is usual to begin with a listing of personnel (simply by numbers, in groups by function, or even by individual name identity) and then to add to the listing the furniture requirements for each workstation or each group of similar workstations. Workstations are often classified in types designated as A, B, C, and so on, according to size and furniture required. A determination that a certain number—say, 20—"type B" workstations are called for, each with one desk, three chairs, a credenza, and a file cabinet, makes it possible to establish a typical layout for such a workstation and then to group and place the workstations as work patterns may require.

In a restaurant, the number of tables for two or for four or more and the number of booths, tables, or banquettes can be converted to typical layouts for each type as a basis for general planning. In every case, the grouping of furniture clusters must allow for adequate circulation space. Decisions to crowd furniture closely with minimum circulation space or to provide generous spacing will influence the final character of the interior. Ample circulation space and open spacing tend to be convenient and to suggest luxury; close spacing leads to intimacy and, in some situations, to a sense of excitement that may be desirable. Although some furniture groupings are obvious and inevitable—dining tables and chairs, desks and chairs, or beds and bedside units—other groupings need to be planned with careful thought. The placement of furniture in a living room has a strong impact on how the room will be used—where conversation will be comfortable, how people will form into one or several groups, where quiet reading, listening to music, or watching TV will be most comfortable. A floor plan with furniture roughed in can be evaluated by imagining how life will be in the completed space. How will people move about, where will they sit, will the situation be convenient and comfortable, and will it be pleasant visually? Designer and client can each study furniture plans and try to visualize the reality that they suggest. Only when such layouts seem fully satisfactory is it appropriate to move on to the selection of specific furniture.

SELECTING FURNITURE

With a basic plan of the interior space completed, furniture selection can begin. Another decision—which may apply to an entire project or be taken on a piece-by-piece basis—then confronts the designer. Should any furniture for the project be custom-designed and -built, or

12.2 A lively display at the Vitra Factory and Furniture Museum in Weil am Rhein, Germany, features a wide variety of modern chairs. The museum was designed by architect Frank O. Gehry & Associates. (Photograph: © Peter Mauss/ESTO)

should it be purchased ready-made from shops, showrooms, catalogs, galleries, and dealers? The pros and cons of these two approaches deserve some discussion.

Specially Designed Furniture

This can be tailored to suit the precise needs and desires of users and can give an interior a unique visual quality. However, it involves some element of risk; if the finished product turns out to be unsatisfactory in some way, it may be difficult and expensive to change or replace.

In general, special furniture is likely to be more expensive than standard, available products, not only more expensive to produce but also more expensive in terms of design time. Designing a piece of furniture is a major project that cannot be dealt with in a few minutes or hours. Built-in furniture, almost by definition, is specially designed. Simple shelving presents no problem to the designer, carpenter, or cabinetmaker. Other cabinetry, such as dressing-room fittings, a room divider, or special kitchen or bathroom cabinets, can range from fairly simple to extremely complex and costly.

The process usually begins with simple sketches, moves to drafted elevations and cross sections, and, finally, ends with construction drawings for the shop or cabinetmaker that will build the piece or pieces. Scale models are helpful to the design process; even full-size mock-ups are often made before going ahead with a special design. Designing seating is very demanding; chairs in particular have gained a reputation as being difficult to design. The challenge they pose may explain why the design of a special chair has come to be regarded as the signature of a master designer. The designing of a chair proceeds as described above, except that a full-size mock-up or prototype that can actually be sat in is almost essential in order to test for comfort, strength, and stability.

Many fine historic interiors are largely furnished with specially designed elements. An Adam brothers room, an Art Nouveau interior, a Frank Lloyd Wright house can hardly be separated from the special furniture that they contain (see figs. 4.35, 4.55, and 4.63). Many designs now in production originated as "specials" for a specific project. Most of these date from times when fine craft labor was cheaper and more available and budgets more generous than today. The modern tendency is to avoid special furniture design except for simple built-ins or an occasional single piece when no acceptable stock alternative is available. Economic pressures and a client's desire to see a sample before making a decision are probably equal factors in limiting the development of special designs.

Specially designed furniture also includes handcrafted furniture by artisans and furniture by artists (see fig. 12.59).

Ready-Made Furniture

This can include fine antiques, simpler old furniture, modern furniture that has become *collectible*, and any other furniture that is already a valued possession for reuse. However, most selections will be made from furniture in regular production. It can be inspected in a shop, store, or showroom. Manufacturers' catalogs illustrate available pieces and give fairly complete data on dimensions, construction, and available finishes and often include suggestions about planning and layout

12.3

12.3 A complex grouping of built-in furniture, including bookshelves, table surfaces, and seating, accents the bridgelike architecture of a vacation house in Ontario, Canada, designed by Jim Strasman in 1983. (Photograph: © O. Baitz, Inc., courtesy House & Garden)

12.4

as well. Production furniture comes in a wide range of quality and price levels and in a vast variety of styles.

Using a reputable manufacturer and dealer offers some assurance of quality and of repairs, service, and replacements over a period of time. The possibility of both viewing and "trying out" an actual sample in a shop or showroom before making a purchase can safeguard against unhappy surprises, giving both designer and client or user security about a decision that can involve large expenditures.

In exchange for these advantages, one gives up having furniture exactly fitted to specific needs and accepts the closest available standard solution. One must also accept seeing the same designs in other places, in some cases to the point of boredom with what may be a current cliché. Manufacturers do their best to minimize monotony by offering a maximum variety of designs, optional details, and finishes.

12.5

12.4 Gwathmey Siegel & Associates Architects, brought together a pair of Ruhlmann Elephant Noir chairs, contemporary sofas in a related design, and a Josef Hoffmann Vienna Secession screen—an extraordinary mix of objects from diverse times and places—in an East Hampton, New York, interior of 1979. (Photograph: © Norman McGrath, courtesy Gwathmey Siegel & Associates Architects)

12.5 Designed at the height of the Art Deco era (1926–31), Jacques-Emile Ruhlmann's aptly named Elephant Noir chair offers comfort—and a touch of humor. It is now a collector's item. (Photograph: © Editions du Regard, Paris, 1983)

Modular, Knockdown, and Economy Furniture

While any furniture not built into a fixed location is movable, some furniture is designed to permit change by assembling parts in various configurations. Such *modular furniture* is made up of standard units that can be put together in numerous ways. Modular seating, for example, offers individual seats, arms, and often corner and end-table units that can be combined to create sofas or more complex seating groups, including corner and serpentine clusters. Modularity makes it possible to reconfigure groups as needs change or to suit a move to a new location. Modular storage offers similar possibilities for composing a specific arrangement to suit unique needs without turning to custom construction, with the potential for rearrangement as a bonus. Much office furniture is modular; desktops, drawer pedestals, and accessory elements are available separately to be assembled into workstations that can be modified as needs change or totally dismantled and reconfigured when a major reorganization takes place.

Knockdown or *KD* furniture is usually modular but is made and shipped disassembled. Since many furniture units are, when assembled, so large and clumsy as to make shipping and moving difficult, KD construction leads to major savings in costs for warehousing, packing, and shipping. It is most often used for residential furniture of reasonable cost, sold in knocked-down packages that purchasers can take

home in a car. Design of KD furniture is frequently of surprisingly high quality, tending toward simplicity in general form and in detail.

When budgets are limited, furniture products that are well designed and functionally serviceable yet inexpensive are essential. Although it is a common complaint that "good design is too expensive," much expensive furniture is, in fact, poorly designed. Many products of fine design quality at reasonable prices are available. The best sources are neither the mass-market furniture and department stores nor the showrooms that service designers and architects but rather certain specialty "good-design" firms that sell directly to consumers. Many such firms offer mail-order catalogs, and many specialize in KD products. Other good sources lie outside normal supply routes. For years many designers have found economical solutions to their own furniture needs through improvisation. A flush door placed on demountable horses, for example, makes a serviceable table or desk. Steel file units available in larger office-supply shops can substitute for horses to provide more storage. Shelving and storage systems produced for industrial applications can solve problems of storage as an alternative to lumberyard planks cut and assembled with hardware-store brackets and supports. Simple bentwood chairs and inexpensive versions of such classics as the Breuer Cesca chair are of excellent design at minimal price levels. Slipcovers can make secondhand chairs and sofas presentable, and a basic

12.6

12.6 Gustav Stickley, founder of the Craftsman workshops in America, designed this 1911 house in Oradell, New Jersey. The design of the simple oak furniture was influenced by the work of the British Arts & Crafts movement. (Photograph: Ray Stubblebine)

Furniture Selection Checklist

Furniture selection is based on the familiar design criteria of *function, structure and materials,* and *aesthetics* (or *appearance*), as well as a consideration of cost. The intelligent evaluation of available products will normally be based on the following issues:

Function

WHAT IS THE BASIC PURPOSE OF THE UNIT?

Is it a table, desk, chair, sofa, bed, storage unit?

WHAT IS THE UNIT'S SPECIFIC FUNCTION?

Is it a chair for dining, desk use, or lounging? How many people are to be seated on a sofa? How many people, minimum and maximum, are to sit at a table? Is a desk for office or home use, and what must it accommodate and store? What objects will be stored in cabinets or on shelves, and how much are the storage units expected to hold?

WHAT SIZE IS REQUIRED?

This is determined partly by function and partly by available space. What are the clearance dimensions for delivery? (Will it fit through the door to the building, elevator, house, apartment?)

Structure and Materials

WHAT LEVEL OF STRENGTH DOES THE INTENDED USE REQUIRE?

Are materials strong enough and the size sufficient to preclude weakness or breakage? How strong are the joints? Tests include:
Loading for intended use. Do shelves sag, do sofas or beds wobble? Extraordinary stress-resistance. Test for extremes of use, such as moving, dropping, and tipping back a chair.

WHAT IS THE QUALITY OF MATERIALS?

What is the thickness of plywood and solid wood? The surface material and finish? The gauge (thickness) of metal parts? Inspect edges, backs, undersurfaces. Check available written specifications for the quality of hidden elements (as in upholstery).

WHAT IS THE FINISH?

Check the appearance and durability of exposed surfaces. Durability may require testing or checking specifications. Check the scratch- and impact-resistance of surfaces, the rust- and corrosion-resistance of metals, the longevity of plastics exposed to sunlight and air pollutants. Abrasion-resistance and ease of cleaning are important characteristics of cover fabrics and other materials (such as leather and plastics).

IS THE UNIT DURABLE?

Overall, this factor is a product of the factors discussed in the previous section. For demanding situations (such as use in public spaces and institutions), testing to failure (until the product breaks or falls apart) is the best measure of life expectancy. In more general use, the criteria listed above in combination with the reputation of a particular product and its manufacturer provide an adequate standard. Guarantees and warranties may be something of a guide, although failure most often occurs after years of use. Appropriate standards for durability must also be measured against cost (see below).

Design

ARE THE STYLE AND CHARACTER APPROPRIATE BOTH TO THE UNIT'S INTENDED USE AND TO THE OVERALL DESIGN APPROACH DEVELOPED FOR THE SPACE IN QUESTION?

Period styles have obvious characteristics, such as ostentation, rich elaboration, formality, rustic simplicity, even crudity, that must blend in with or work well with their surroundings. Contemporary design must be evaluated in terms of scale, proportion, and other, more subjective qualities. Even in modern design, a particular approach may seem more or less conservative, avant-garde, playful, or dignified.

DOES THE UNIT POSSESS AESTHETIC MERIT?

This is the most problematic of criteria since individual values vary so widely. Still, classics that have wide acceptance can be identified. The reputations of individual designers and manufacturers and the opinions of critics and museum curators offer some basis for evaluation more objective than personal opinion alone.

Cost

WHAT IS ITS COST IN RELATION TO THE AVAILABLE BUDGET?

Few projects are totally free of budget limitations. Decisions on how to apportion budgets can be difficult, but they must be made. Inexpensive items of fine quality and excellent design might be used in some locations to budget for some selected items of higher cost.

WHAT IS ITS LIFETIME COST?

First cost is only one aspect of a unit's true cost. Lifetime cost includes first cost plus the cost of maintenance, energy consumed, cost of disposal, and cost of replacement. These factors must be considered in arriving at realistic comparisons between products at varied price levels. Costly items with a long life expectancy may be more economical than inexpensive products that will need early replacement. Still, available funds will limit the range of products that can be considered.

mattress on springs can take on whatever character its cover establishes. With some thought and ingenuity, inexpensive furniture can yield both functional and aesthetic results in no way inferior to projects with unlimited budgets.

Criteria for Choosing Furniture

The primary issue in choosing appropriate furniture, whatever its source, is *quality*. It is an unfortunate fact that the most widely available furniture tends to be mediocre; badly designed and poorly made, it is intended to sell quickly and serve briefly before being discarded, either because it goes out of style or it physically disintegrates. Furniture only a few years old can be observed in trash piles almost every day, while good furniture can last for a very long time, as demonstrated by antiques still serviceable after hundreds of years. Evaluating furniture quality involves several issues, many easy to evaluate, others more difficult. The primary issues are the same that apply to the evaluation of all design—function, structure and materials, and aesthetics (see Chapter 3, "Design Basics")—but with more particular bearing.

Function relates to the furniture's purpose. Almost all furniture has a practical use, and good furniture serves that use effectively and reliably. Different uses call for specific qualities and characteristics. For example, storage furniture must be sized to hold whatever it will contain efficiently and conveniently, and its drawers and doors must work well and continue to work well over years of use. Chairs and other seating and reclining furniture must fulfill the requirement of providing comfort.

Secondary function is a term sometimes used to describe matters that do not relate to the primary, or main, purposes of an object, but rather to aspects of its performance that may surface only under special circumstances. Safety is not an issue that comes to mind as a major concern when evaluating furniture. Tables and chairs seem benign as compared to automobiles or firearms. Nevertheless, a surprising number of injuries result from circumstances relating to furniture. Chairs can tip over, tables can trip the unwary, and large pieces can overturn with unfortunate results. The hazards relating to furniture can be listed in a number of categories:

SHARP CORNERS AND EDGES. Bumping the corner of a table or cabinet can lead to a bruise or a cut. Soft or rounded edges or corners are safer. Metals are harsher than wood or plastics. Glass is the most hazardous of furniture materials. Glass-topped tables, especially those with sharp corners, are well known to present risks of serious injuries.

CHAIRS. Those that can be easily overturned present dangers. Chairs on casters are especially risky because they can be overturned more easily when tipped. Three-legged chairs are notably dangerous. Four-legged chair bases are now frequently replaced by the safer bases that have five points of floor contact.

FIRE SAFETY. All furniture with fabric covers and upholstery presents this concern. Beds are notorious firetraps for smokers. Cover fabrics that do not flare up or support combustion reduce fire hazards. Cushion and mattress materials that do not burn easily and that do not generate toxic fumes when burning reduce fire-related risks.

CHILDREN AND THE ELDERLY. These two segments of the population are particularly vulnerable to furniture hazards. Small objects that are easily tipped over, as well as sharp edges and corners, are dangerous to older people with reduced visual acuity and physical agility. Children are active, careless, and of a size that often contacts tabletop edges at eye and head levels. Some furniture, such as cribs and chairs, may have spaced members that can catch a child's head in a dangerous grip.

Although total safety is most likely beyond human grasp, it is wise to look at furniture selections in relation to intended use. What might be acceptable in an executive office (a table with a large plate-glass top, for example) may be questionable in a home with young children or in a public lobby where crowds of people may congregate. Fire hazards are most significant in the closed spaces of high-rise buildings or in such special installations as the seating in aircraft. Excessive concern over such issues is probably more valid than the indifference that until recent years has been the norm.

Universal design is a term that has come into use to suggest a goal that would make every designed situation serviceable to those (children or adult) who are very small, those who are taller or otherwise larger than average, and those who are temporarily or permanently physically impaired—whether on crutches, sight-impaired, or with other limitations that make standard heights of chairs and tables, locations of cabinets, heights of beds, and placement of furniture problematic. It is usually true that furniture that accommodates people with disabilities will serve the general population equally well. Considerations of function in furniture should include issues that extend to the full range of human form and performance. (For further discussion of universal design, as well as design for special needs, see Chapter 15.)

Structure and materials concern how the furniture is made. Good furniture is well made of appropriate materials. Examining the broken furniture left on garbage heaps often reveals slick or showy finishes covering flimsy materials and slipshod construction. Since inexpensive furniture of good quality exists, it is clear that the poor quality of such materials and construction stems only partly from an effort to maintain low prices. The difference lies in the maker's awareness of and attention to the kind of construction the furniture calls for and an effort to use affordable materials honestly and to their best advantage.

Aesthetic success is probably the hardest element of furniture quality to evaluate. Furniture that is well designed in terms of function, structure, *and* the expressive qualities that we call aesthetic generally has a long life and gives high levels of satisfaction over that long life. Exactly what aesthetic excellence is remains a matter of disagreement and discussion. To say that furniture should be beautiful seems an easy way of setting a standard, but beauty means different things to different people, in different contexts, and at different times. Many of the greatly valued classics designed a few years ago may not seem beautiful to most people. Designs of the Victorian era considered monstrosities only a few years ago are now valued by collectors. Too often, what people call beauty is a matter of superficial appeal.

A better way to define the aesthetic characteristics of quality furniture is through the strong expression of concepts that were significant when and where the design was developed. Clear expression of functional and structural intent, along with a kind of "spirit of the time," seem to make for furniture design that is lasting and satisfying. Stickley Craftsman furniture of the late Victorian era (fig. 12.6), angular De Stijl designs by Gerrit Rietveld from the 1920s and 1930s (fig. 12.8), and Bauhaus tubular designs by Marcel Breuer (see fig. 12.56) all possess an integrity that makes them just as worthwhile as Georgian Chippendale bureaus, Colonial Windsor chairs (fig. 12.7), or Shaker rockers. Any number of current fashions of the intervening years have become dated and worthless because they lack any comparable integrity of ideas.

Leaving aside aesthetic questions, the more tangible issues of function and construction can be examined in greater detail.

FUNCTION

The usefulness of a piece of furniture relates to its size, shape, and details in fairly clear ways. The functional values of some special-purpose furniture types are described by their names: tea carts, typewriter stands, mobile files, cribs and high chairs, wheelchairs, and outdoor furniture. They are available in considerable variety and tend to be closely suited to their particular function. Other furniture types have so many variables that they can be studied individually.

12.8

12.7

Tables

A table needs to be of a size and shape appropriate to its use. How many people are to sit around it, giving each person 24 to 30 inches of edge space? Is the standard height of 29 to 30 inches appropriate or is a lower height (as low as 25 inches) better for certain uses, such as typing? How do square, rectangular, round, or other shapes relate to use and to the space where the table will go? Are legs or other supports arranged for good stability without interference with users' legs or knees? Is expansion or folding desirable and/or practical for the intended use? Is the top surface serviceable and of suitable color and texture? Is it practical to maintain?

Since tables are made in great variety, the selection of a suitable design for a particular use involves considering a number of factors. Table 16 on page 360 includes most of the available alternatives, with some criteria for selection.

Desks

Desks can be evaluated with a list of questions similar to those for tables, plus questions about storage needs. Does the desk require a file drawer? Surface space for a typewriter? Space for a computer with keyboard and monitor? Desk requirements for office uses can become

12.7 An American Colonial Windsor chair designed and made by J. M. Hasbrouck in the eighteenth century exhibits an ingenious arrangement of thin hardwood turnings of maple and hickory. The result is a remarkably strong structure with a minimum of material and weight—and a clear, pleasing design that does not date.

36¹/4 x 22¹/4 x 22¹/4". The Art Institute of Chicago. Gift of Emily Crane Chadbourne

12.8 Gerrit Rietveld's Red and Blue chair, a design of 1917, is an emblem of the De Stijl movement. Of solid wood and plywood, the frame elements are all painted black except for the ends,

which are bright yellow. The blue-painted seat is of plywood, as is the red-painted back. A modern reproduction is available from Atelier International, Ltd., and a ¹/6-full-size scale model, in kit form, from the Museum of Modern Art, New York. 34¹/2 x 26¹/2 x 26¹/2". The Museum of Modern Art, New York. Gift of Philip Johnson

12.9 Furniture specially designed for an interior can have a strong effect on the atmosphere of the space. In the Moon Soon restaurant in Sapporo, Japan, a 1993 project of architect Zaha Hadid, the unconventional furniture helps to set the mood. (Photograph: © Paul Warchol)

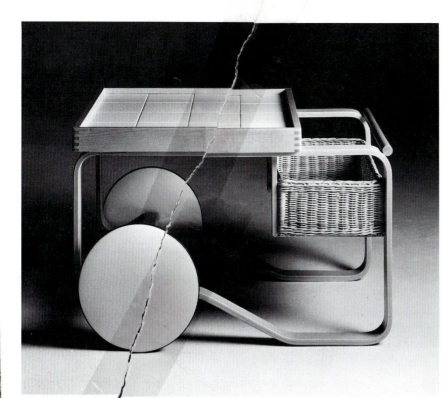

12.10

12.11

12.12

12.10 The Finnish architect Alvar Aalto designed this tea trolley in 1936. The frame is of molded, laminated birch, the top tray has a tile surface, and the basket is of woven wickerwork. The strong visual impact of this special-purpose piece has made it famous in its time—and it is still manufactured today, by Artek in Finland. 35^1/$_2$ x 23^5/$_8$ x 25^1/$_2$".

12.11 The Tippy Jackson is an ingenious folding table that is decorative whether set up or collapsed. Each of the three curved, tubular-steel legs carries a support post and pivots outward from a central hub to open into a stable triangular base. The top is of sheet steel. The design, by Philippe Starck, suggests both Bauhaus and Art Deco influences. (Photograph courtesy Furniture of the Twentieth Century, New York)

12.12 Cini Boeri's Shadow table is in fact a table system. The steel base supports sections of clear glass sandblasted around the perimeter to give a frosted texture. The translucent lower glass shelf is etched. Surfaces of different sizes and shapes—square, rectangular, or with rounded ends—can adapt the table to various purposes. Smaller sizes, for example, are suitable for use as desks or dining tables, while longer versions serve well as conference or boardroom tables. A smaller, low version makes a coffee table. (Photograph courtesy Cadsana)

12.13

complex and quite specific, leading to *workstations* that go beyond a simple desk to become a complete multipurpose working-space unit (see pages 370–72).

Seating Furniture

Seating furniture presents complex problems that are often not well understood.

SEATING COMFORT. It is a truism that a chair should be comfortable, but comfort is, in practice, a very variable thing. One can be comfortable seated on a bicycle or tractor seat, on a picnic bench, or even on a rock. A hard stool is ideal for certain intermittent uses, a contoured chaise for others. The problem is further complicated by the reality that human beings vary greatly in size and shape. If shoes were made in one size only to suit all wearers, a great many people would have uncomfortable feet. Yet chairs (with certain exceptions) are produced in one size for all.

Several issues enter into the consideration of comfort in seating furniture:

- *WHAT KIND OF COMFORT IS DESIRED FOR A PARTICULAR USE?*
  An upright seating posture is best suited to dining and desk work. Lounge seating, in a semireclining position, is a modern concept not recognized in historic furniture. It can range from the slightly lowered and back-tilted posture now preferred for reading, conversation, and the long-term seating in transport vehicles to a near-fully-reclined position suited to rest or even sleep. Reclining seating supports a prone or near-prone position. No single seat can provide for

12.14

12.13 Chairs by Vico Magistretti (in the foreground) make dramatic gestures that echo those of Robert Longo's wall piece and contrast with the more sedate forms of the 1950s-vintage Diamond wire chair by Harry Bertoia, visible to the right of the fireplace. Art and furniture-as-art give the room, in a renovated 1950s California house, its character. Brian A. Murphy, designer. (Photograph: © 1986 Tim Street-Porter)

12.14 A small table by Bruce Tomb and John Randolph comprises an unpolished 3/4-inch-thick glass top on a sandblasted-steel frame supported by four legs of rough, stonelike poured concrete. A larger version is available as a conference table. (Photograph: © Paul Warchol)

12.15

all of these needs, although adjustability can introduce a range of suitability to varied seating postures.

- *HOW WILL THE VARIATION IN HUMAN BODY DIMENSIONS BE ACCOMMODATED?* A chair intended for one particular user can, of course, be selected with that person's requirements in mind, but most chairs and other seating are intended for anyone. Having a different dining chair for each member of a family—not to speak of every guest—would be absurd. In practice, this means making several compromises that, taken together, provide acceptable comfort for most. The "average person" charted from statistics on the general population is in actuality quite rare, but a very large proportion of the population comes fairly close to this theoretical average.

By designing seating with dimensions that favor small users but will not trouble larger users (a shallow seat, for example, is not a problem to people with long legs while a deep seat is not suited to the short-legged), it is possible to arrive at seating dimensions that will suit all but the very largest and smallest users reasonably well. Some seating that will be used by one occupant for long periods of time, such as an office desk chair or an airplane pilot's seat, needs to be adjustable so that the key dimensions can be set to fit the actual occupant rather than an assumed average person.

The concept of universal access for persons with physical disabilities presents a further consideration. Transfer from a wheelchair to other seating calls for a corresponding seat height and form with

12.15 Rattan furniture of the 1930s displays traditional manufacturing techniques. The material is particularly suited to informal, outdoor-related rooms, like this windowed living space in River Oaks, Texas, by Mark Hampton, designer. The fabrics are by Brunschwig & Fils. (Photograph: Feliciano, courtesy House & Garden)

12.16

12.17

12.18

12.19

minimal arm obstruction. Seating in public places, such as waiting rooms (at airports or in hospitals, for example), restaurants, and theaters, ideally will provide access for those with physical limitations to the maximum extent practical.

• *WHAT ARE THE PHYSIOLOGICAL REQUIREMENTS?*

Comfort is too often judged on the basis of a quickly formed first impression. This tends to favor the softness of thick padding and deep cushions. Actually, the body is better accommodated by firm support at certain key points where weight is transferred and limited softness at other locations. The pleasant sensation of "sinking into" a soft seat soon leads to unexpected discomfort—the feet fall asleep and the sitter becomes restless—and can contribute to physiological problems. Long periods of sitting in chairs designed without regard for physical needs can give rise to back ailments and may contribute

12.16 The Eames lounge chair (with ottoman) of 1956 is probably the most famous and most imitated of all the Eames's designs, perhaps because it is a modern design that offers lasting comfort as well as excellent form. Molded rosewood plywood units with fitted leather cushions are supported by a cast-aluminum base. (Photograph courtesy Herman Miller, Inc., Archives)

12.17 The elegant, lightweight Handkerchief stacking chair of 1985 by Vignelli Design has a seat-and-back shell of molded plastic supported by a steel frame. It is available with or without arms and with or without an upholstered pad. (Photograph: Mikio Sekita, courtesy Knoll International)

12.18, 12.19 Ergonomic furniture is designed through careful study of human body mechanics. The office chair in fig. 12.19 was designed by a Swedish physician, Dr. Johan Ullman, for Medical Innovations. (Photograph: Arne Flink, courtesy Medical Innovations Ltd., Sweden) A drawing of the chair (fig. 12.18) reveals that the seat and the back are each made up of two planes, slightly angled so as to permit the user to move into varied positions while maintaining a balanced back. An unusual feature of this chair is the tilted seat, which takes pressure off the lower back. Both the angle of the chair back and the height of the seat can be adjusted. (Drawing courtesy Johan Ullman, M.D./Medical Innovations Ltd.)

12.20

12.21

12.22

12.23

to such major physical problems as varicose veins and heart and circulatory ailments.

In recent years, various seating designs described as *ergonomic*, that is, suited to human body mechanics, have appeared (fig. 12.19). Seating that is truly ergonomic, whether or not so described, will provide comfort in long-term use and will minimize physiological damage that poor seating postures can cause. Many traditional designs, from simple wood stools to old-fashioned rockers, are ergonomically successful, while much "luxury" seating is far less satisfactory.

In selecting seating furniture, then, appropriate comfort with the best possible ergonomic performance is the primary consideration. Suitable size and shape for a particular use follow.

SEATING TYPES. Seating products are available that offer a wide variety of special-purpose features, such as rolling, swiveling, tilting or reclining, stacking, folding, and even conversion to other use—most often in the familiar *convertible* that makes up into a bed.

Multiple seating has developed a terminology of its own that can be confusing. *Sofa* is the generic term; *two-seater* and *three-seater* are self-explanatory. *Love seat* is a charming synonym for two-seater. As most sofas have arms, *armless* is used to designate the occasional exception. Other terms sometimes used include *Chesterfield* for an overstuffed sofa

12.20 The folding Willow piece X-chair, a refined version of the familiar Hollywood director's chair, is now in wide use as a convenient portable armchair. Here, two examples flank an altar table in a San Francisco town house, an unusually formal use for a usually informal chair. (Photograph: Russell Mac-Masters, courtesy the McGuire Company)

12.21 This love seat was handmade of willow, or twig, in a traditional method of simple furniture-making that continues today. It is particularly suited to rural, informal settings. (Photograph courtesy La Lune Willow Collection)

12.22 A 1988 chaise designed by John Mascheroni for Swaim looks back to 1930s precedents. (Photograph courtesy Swaim)

12.23 This type of modular seating is suitable to public spaces, particularly those outdoors. Mounted on a tubular steel support, the contoured, ergonomically designed seats can be grouped as desired with tabletops and other elements in straight-line or curved combinations. The metal parts are coated with weather-resistant polyester. (Photograph courtesy Landscape Forms, Kalamazoo, Michigan)

12.24

12.24 An interesting mix of furniture appears in a New York apartment bedroom, a project of Thad Hayes Design. The modern interpretation of the traditional four-poster is Hayes's own design. The night tables, typical of American Art Deco, were designed and made by Andrew Szoeke of Long Island City, New York, circa 1934. The lamps are also from the 1930s; the desk is an English antique. (Photograph: Michael Mundy)

12.25

12.26

12.27

with padded arms; *Lawson* for sofas with arms lower than the back; and *tuxedo* for sofas with arms the same height as the back.

Modular seating refers to the sectionals that appeared in the 1930s and continue to be popular. These are single units that come armless, with a single arm at right or at left, and as corner units. Several can be assembled in a variety of ways, including straight or angled sofalike groupings; they can be rearranged to suit changing needs or locations. The term *modular* is also used for modern seating systems with a continuous base structure that supports individual seat sections. Arms, corner units, even end-table elements or planters may be added to the basic unit to make up groupings uniquely planned for a specific location. Some modular systems use units less than one seat in width and include tapered units, enabling the formation of curves, circular shapes, and S-shaped groupings. Large modular seating assemblies are particularly useful in public spaces such as lobbies and lounges that call for a large number of seating spaces (fig. 12.23).

Folding and stacking chairs are special designs that offer the functions implied by their names. Folding chairs of simple design and low cost are familiar utility products widely used to provide temporary seating or extra seating wherever needed. While the most basic of folding chairs are often of poor quality and unattractive appearance, many better designs are available, including some that fully equal fixed-chair types. The familiar *director's chair* is a folding unit that has become something of a classic, often used even when the folding feature is of secondary importance (fig. 12.20). Other folding types carefully disguise their portable function with designs that match those of conventional chairs. Any folding-chair design should be checked for its sturdiness in the open position, its compactness when folded, and its ease of opening and closing.

Stacking chairs are designed so that a number of units can be stacked vertically for easy movement or storage (fig. 12.17). The best examples are of fine design and ideal for meeting rooms, ballrooms, and other places where many chairs are needed, and in a form that can be put away in limited storage space when a clear floor is required. Some stacking designs feature extreme compactness, as does the 40/4 chair designed by David Rowland that permits forty chairs to be placed in a four-foot-high stack. Such stacking makes it possible to store all of the chairs from a large hall under a stage or in a small closet or storeroom. The design of stacking chairs has a substantial impact on the ease of the stacking process. Some types require each successive chair being placed in a stack to be lifted up over the top of the last chair added. This can be a significant physical chore and, as a stack grows taller, sets a limit on the height of the stack. The best designs allow stacking from the front, lifting each chair only by the small amount necessary to clear the chair below, usually one inch or less. Such designs are best suited to applications where more than a few chairs are to be stacked.

With many stacking chairs, a wheeled dolly is available for use to support the bottom chair at an angle so that the stack will consistently rise vertically rather than tilt forward. Some stacking chairs that are less compact than others may offer additional comfort through padding or cushioning. When only a small number of removable chairs are needed (about four to eight), such units may be considered. Most stacking

12.25 This bed, headboard, and night table make up a unit called Variations, by Peter Maly of Germany for Ligne Roset. The sleek, floating profile is characteristic of modern sleeping furniture design. (Photograph courtesy Roset USA Corp.)

12.26 A built-in platform bed atop storage drawers is an element in a compact sleeping and study alcove. The 1979 design is by Moore Ruble Yudell Architects & Planners for the Rodes House in Brentwood, California. (Photograph: © 1986 Tim Street-Porter)

12.27 This unit, Flou-flou by De Pas, D'Urbino, Lomazzi, designers, is actually a convertible sofabed. The Dacron-filled, quilted overlay cushioning is removed to give access to the foldout bed underneath. (Photograph courtesy Roset USA Corp.)

chairs are available with arms to separate users within rows of chairs, with tablet arms for classroom use, and with hardware details that permit *ganging,* that is, the locking together of adjacent chairs to make "fixed" rows. The best stacking chairs are of sufficient design quality to be considered for uses in which stacking is not a significant requirement.

Special chair types include the *rocking chair,* a traditional favorite offering comfort through movement that is physiologically highly desirable, particularly for older or infirm persons (see figs. 12.41 and 12.61). Various traditional rocking chairs, some of attractive design, are still in production, and several modern chairs of fine design quality have been produced in rocking versions (a Charles Eames design, unfortunately no longer in production, has become a classic).

Adjustable lounge chairs with tilting backs, and often with leg support, are available in many designs. The traditional *Morris chair* with an adjustable back positioned by moving a metal rod from notch to notch has a history dating back to the 1850s. Modern adjustable chairs commonly use a concealed mechanical linkage that makes it possible to adjust position by simple body movement. Such chairs are great favorites in family or TV rooms, where television viewers may sit for hours watching a screen. Although many designs are distressingly massive and loaded with unnecessary details, a number of versions are simple and reasonable in appearance.

The *wheelchair* is a highly specialized type of chair, rarely selected by a designer but essential to the mobility and convenience of those with temporary or permanent physical disabilities. It has been pointed out that many wheelchairs are of excellent functional design, offering adjustments that would make them highly satisfactory to users with no physical problems. At present there is a certain prejudice against the wheelchair that has blocked development of universal designs that would serve disabled and normal users equally well. It is probable that such designs will surface in the near future.

Sleeping Furniture

Furniture for sleeping can range from simple pads placed on the floor through futons and platform beds to elaborate bedsteads with head- and footboards and auxiliary elements such as bedside stands, lamps, and electronic controls and gadgets. A mattress on a spring unit, varying in size from a narrow single up to roomy king-size, mounted on a scarcely visible metal base has become a near-standard form of bed. The platform bed (mattress or mattress and box spring on a boxlike base) has become a popular alternative (fig. 12.26). As with seating, comfort and physiological serviceability are complex issues that require research and thought. In general, harder beds are probably better than softer, which can cause or aggravate back problems, and simple systems of construction are likely to be more durable than complex inner- and box-spring systems. Such innovative approaches as air-inflated and water-filled beds have not had a very good record of success in continued use. Foam mattresses, however, which came into wide use with platform beds, continue to be popular. In spite of the variety of beds available, the differences between them are mostly superficial. There is probably less variety of basic design in sleeping furniture than in any other furniture type.

Convertible sofa beds are a widely used solution to the furniture problems presented by a one-room apartment or studio (fig. 12.27). Seeing that the designers of such furniture must always compromise the needs of the two functions, it is surprising how well such products, at their best, serve the conflicting needs. They must, of course, be evaluated for both uses. Fold-up or wall beds, once also a popular solution to the space problem, seem to have been largely displaced by improved convertibles, although they have recently become available in a variety of styles and systems.

Other types of sleeping furniture include the loft bed, that is, a bed on a raised platform that frees the space beneath it for other use; the bunk bed, particularly adaptable to children's rooms; and the trundle bed, which is an extra bed hidden under a larger bed.

Hospital beds, commonly used in nursing homes and other health-care facilities in addition to hospitals, are built very high to make it easier for attendants to care for patients and provide a number of adjustments to increase patients' comfort. The adjustments may be manual (with cranks) or powered by an electric motor. Unfortunately, the high mattress position makes access difficult, especially for people with injuries or disabilities. (Conventional beds with very low mattress levels present the opposite difficulty.) Ideally, powered height adjustments should be included on hospital-type beds intended for home use. Such products, which are becoming increasingly accessible, encourage home care as an alternative to nursing homes for those with physical problems that can, with proper equipment and help, be dealt with in a residential setting.

12.29

12.28, 12.29 In the designer's own home in Guilford, Connecticut, Warren Platner has used built-in furniture extensively. Shelves and seating line the hallway (fig. 12.28), while glass shelves store books in the landing space (fig. 12.29). The 1971 house is by Warren Platner Associates Architects. (Photographs: © Ezra Stoller/ESTO)

12.30

Storage Furniture

Storage furniture is logically selected to suit the kind and quantity of materials to be stored. Open shelves and various cabinets with hinged or sliding doors and arrangements of drawers in many sizes and shapes are available in various combinations to suit specific needs. *Storage systems* offer standard related components that can be grouped together to suit a particular set of storage needs.

Modern storage systems often incorporate elements to serve other special purposes, such as desk use, the service of food or drinks, or housing for TV and other electronic devices. Storage can also offer possibilities for display, either for ease in locating specific items, as with open bookshelves, or simply to offer protection while making collections of objects of interest or beauty visible.

Modular or *system* storage furniture is well suited to making up storage walls and room dividers. The former are assemblies of connected storage components that fit from floor to ceiling, often using a custom-fitted insert at the top. They serve the function of a partition wall while providing storage accessible from one or both sides. A storage wall may separate adjacent living and dining spaces, two territorial areas in a shared children's bedroom, or two adjacent office spaces. Room dividers serve similar uses, but do not extend to the ceiling or, in most cases, from wall to wall. They divide a large room into two sections while preserving its sense of unity and providing storage at the same time. Dividing living and dining spaces is one of the most common uses of a room divider. The living side can accommodate books, records, TV, and stereo equipment, while the dining side can hold dishes, glassware, silver, and linens. (See also Chapter 16, "Kitchens, Bathrooms, Storage.")

Contract Design Furniture

Contract design calls for many specialized types of furniture designed to satisfy specific needs. There are special lines of furniture tailored to

12.30 *A console designed in 1933 by Louis Süe is typical of the 1930s modern style, now usually called Art Deco. It is of burl ash veneer with an aluminum structure. (Photograph courtesy Christie's, New York)*

the requirements of hospitals and healthcare facilities, offices, libraries, hotels and motels, restaurants, theaters and auditoriums, and retail shops, to name a few of those most widely available. Among these, the most highly specialized types, such as hospital and laboratory equipment, need only be noted here as areas served by product lines developed to fill such needs.

Other contract furniture products have more varied uses. Theater seats, for example, may also be used in school and college auditoriums and lecture halls. Stacking chairs may be specified for auditoriums, ballrooms, lecture rooms, cafeterias and dining rooms, conference rooms—wherever changing uses call for closely spaced seating at times and clear space at other times. Restaurants demand special tables, attractive and durable when tabletops are left exposed, simple and unobtrusive when tablecloths will virtually conceal whatever is beneath. Banquette seating may be a standard product or may be built to order.

Office furniture has become a very important specialty as office work has become a major part of modern working life. The simple desk and chair continue in wide use, but systems furniture has come more and more to replace the freestanding desk with a complex of work surfaces, screen panels, and storage units that serve as partitioning as well (fig. 12.32). The *workstation* is supplanting the conventional office room, occupying less space while, at best, providing better function (fig. 12.35). The typical office workday of long hours spent sitting in a chair has led to the development of ergonomic chairs offering improved comfort and physiological impact through shape, dimension, and adjustments that minimize muscular stress (see figs. 12.18 and 12.19). Conventional file cabinets have been augmented by lateral files (in which the filed material is stored side by side instead of front to back) and special equipment for microfile materials. Computers require special stands and tables for their keyboards, screens, and printers, all of these connected by wires and cables that must be accommodated in suitable furniture units.

Office-furniture systems have been developed under the influence of open or *landscape* office planning, in which partitioned private offices are avoided in order to open up communication and to allow easy rearrangement of workplaces. Early open office plans often limited privacy too severely by placing conventional desks in totally open space. Most systems now provide for some form of screening to create both visual and acoustical (auditory) privacy. A typical office system offers a continuum ranging from total openness to something approaching a walled private office. Systems can be categorized into two general types depending on the way this flexibility is supplied. Panel or *panel-hung systems* use the panels that provide privacy as their primary structure, with work surfaces and storage components hung from the panels. *Freestanding systems* use desk and storage units similar to conventional furniture as their basic elements and provide panels or screens that can be attached to establish privacy. Many systems offer assorted types of panels of varied height and transparency, some even with doors, to make possible a maximum number of arrangements. Some systems also allow work surfaces to be set at differing heights to suit the physical needs of the individual user. Work surfaces and storage elements set lower than standard heights can be very helpful to

12.31

12.32

12.31 Storage units, a desk, and a chair display the characteristic whimsicality of Memphis design. The Donar Collection, in wood, is an early-1980s project by Italian designer Ettore Sottsass. (Photograph courtesy Furniture of the Twentieth Century)

12.32 The curvilinear panels of the 9000 series office-furniture system by Steelcase can be used to control traffic-flow patterns while also relieving the rectilinear quality typical of most office layouts. (Photograph courtesy Steelcase, Inc.)

workers of less than average height. Others may find it helpful to have work surfaces set at heights for standing work positions. When such flexibility is available, installation must be performed with full instructions about the requirements for each workplace.

The proliferation of electrical equipment in the modern *electronic office* has created the need for extensive wiring to be carried to each workplace. Task lighting (see Chapter 10) is a useful and often necessary element of an office-system installation that requires not only additional wiring and switching but also careful consideration of the quality of lighting that will be delivered at each work surface. Most office systems include ingenious provisions for wiring, with arrangements for concealment, easy service and replacement, and excellent safety ratings.

Planning with systems furniture requires a full understanding of the particular systems to be used because the dimensions of available units determine the possible sizes and shapes of workstations. While some preliminary planning can be done on the basis of typical or generic furniture, an early decision to use a specific system will make it possible to plan realistically and to avoid troublesome later adjustments. Thicknesses of panels and details of how panels and other components meet at corners influence the dimensions of rows or clusters of workstations, as well as the practicality of arrangements of components within workstations. Manufacturers generally provide excellent planning manuals to aid the designer; they also frequently offer a planning service that can take on a considerable share of the detailed planning

12.33

ing a library of current catalogs devoted to suitable furniture products. Some industry manufacturers' associations have established quality standards that are an aid in evaluating available products. The Architectural Woodwork Institute (AWI), for example, produces a quality standards manual that defines three levels of quality, designated as *economy*, *custom*, and *premium*, in detailed specifications. Although meant for built-in woodwork, the same standards are useful in evaluating any wood furniture. BIFMA (Business and Institutional Furniture Manufacturers Association) has published similar standards for performance tests to be used by its member firms.

Children's Furniture

Although children manage to adapt themselves to adults' furniture, their smaller size and varied degrees of strength and mobility make special furniture desirable to improve children's comfort and even aid their physical well-being. Infants require a special bed or crib and, if possible, a unit for bathing called a bathinette. The cradle, popular in earlier times, seems to have disappeared from modern use. As children grow, high chairs and playpens are needed. Interior designers rarely have responsibility for selecting these items, which are thought of as equipment for temporary use, usually more or less portable and, unfortunately, often of poor quality. When a home includes a room

process. Some firms supply computer programs as well to efficiently aid planning and to assist in the production of drawings, specifications, and ordering information on an integrated basis. The selection of a particular system and the use of such aids unfortunately makes the purchaser something of a captive buyer who cannot readily change to an alternative system either at bidding time or in the future when additions or changes to a facility are contemplated. It is desirable to select a manufacturer with a good record of continuing support to users of its products and with excellent prospects for long survival. A system made by a manufacturer who no longer produces that product group or who has gone out of business leaves users orphaned, which can be both inconvenient and costly.

Other contract uses require special versions of ordinary home furniture. Motel and hotel furniture, drawer chests, desks, beds, and bedside tables differ from home equivalents only in having more durable surface finishes, heavy-duty mattresses, and sturdy casters on the bed frames to facilitate movement for bedmaking. Chairs for restaurant service need to be strong and to have spot-resistant cover fabrics. Public lounge furniture is similar to living room furniture except that it, too, demands extra sturdiness and wear-resistant properties. On the other hand, transportation seating (for buses, trains, and airplanes) is of a very special type that must meet exacting performance and safety standards.

The interior designer confronting a specialized contract assignment for the first time will usually need to spend some time visiting special furniture showrooms, talking with salespeople in the field, and collect-

12.34

12.33 Mobile file and storage pedestals for contract use roll on large casters that enable them to be placed easily beneath a table-desk or in any other convenient spot. (Photograph courtesy Howe Furniture Corporation)

12.34 Contract furniture demands a higher level of durability than furniture designed for residential uses. The indoor-outdoor aluminum furniture from the Toledo Collection, designed by Jorge Pensi for Knoll, would be suitable for restaurants and other public spaces. (Photograph courtesy The Knoll Group)

designated as a nursery or child's room, however, it must be furnished with some thought and care. Cribs and playpens may pose a safety problem if their fencelike bars are spaced so that a child's head can be caught. Units using screen mesh in place of bars avoid this problem. Cribs of excellent design are available, including some foldable types that can be stored or passed on for reuse. A well-made high chair of fine design quality can serve successive generations.

As children grow, an appropriate bed becomes a necessity—bunk beds are a favorite provision for two children close in age. Simple shelving, storage chests, and eventually a table or desk round out the basic furniture for a child's room. A number of manufacturers offer furniture that can be adjusted to the changing needs of children as they grow: tables or desks that can be adjusted in height and storage units that can be expanded or rearranged. Designs have been developed that place seat height low for a young child but, when inverted, become appropriate for an older age. Scandinavian designers have been particularly successful in developing home furniture suitable to child use, and some of their lines are available as imports.

In child-care facilities, nursery schools, and elementary schools, special furniture sized to suit appropriate age groups is essential. A number of manufacturers provide lines of school furniture with chairs, tables, and desks of sturdy and durable construction in graduated sizes. Some products are available with adjustable-height units so that smaller and larger children within a specific age group can be comfortably accommodated.

Furniture for children's use is sometimes best accommodated with built-in units that a designer may wish to detail for custom building. In home situations, shelving, clothes storage, and units that combine storage and desk space are candidates for custom detailing, often more economical than purchasing factory-made products. Similarly, in school interiors, built-in shelves, "cubbies," and wardrobes may be detailed to fit a given space, suit a known user group, and still be economical to construct.

Children seem to appreciate furniture that is designed to take into account their sizes and needs, and adults often find that furniture designed for children has a special charm that makes it welcome in whatever setting it may be put to use.

MATERIALS AND CONSTRUCTION

In furniture construction, quality of materials and workmanship has a major impact on both its durability and its proper use. Furniture is made in many ways from a great variety of materials. Generally, the details of construction are at least partially concealed in the finished product. The reputation of a manufacturer, published specifications (when available), and price are all clues to the quality of construction.

Well-made furniture need not be expensive, but cheap duplicates of high-quality products are almost certainly the result of some skimping on materials or details. When evaluated over its useful life, quality furniture is often a better bargain than cheap substitutes. An inexpensive dinette table that must be replaced in five years may, over the long run, end up costing more than a high-priced table that will still be serviceable (and perhaps more valuable) after a hundred years.

The examination of an actual sample, along with some simple testing in the form of shaking, bouncing, pushing, and pulling (particularly if done in comparison with several similar objects), can give some idea of constructional quality. Good furniture is not weak, fragile, or shaky when new and will not develop weaknesses with normal use over long periods of time.

Just how sturdy a piece of furniture needs to be depends on its intended use. Many fine antiques that have held up over centuries are actually quite delicate, but they have been used, as intended, only under conditions that do not impose too much rough usage. In general, home furniture need not be as rugged as furniture used in institutional and public spaces. Delicate materials and finishes can survive in private living spaces or in executive offices better than in hotel rooms, dormitories, or where young children will be regular users. Whatever its intended use, good furniture is characterized by good materials, workmanship, and finishes at an appropriate level of durability.

Although a variety of materials is used for specific details, the primary structure of most furniture is based on three families of materials—wood, metal, and plastics—used alone or in combination. Each material family has its own constructional characteristics.

Wood
Still the most-used furniture material, wood was almost the only material of most historic furniture (see Table 17 on page 378).

SOLID WOOD. The *softwoods* that come from evergreen trees (pine, spruce, fir, cedar, redwood) are the common, easily worked materials of carpentry. They serve well for simple utility furniture and show up in older country tables and chests. They are generally not considered suitable for fine furniture that will hold up well and take attractive finishes. The *hardwoods* of nut, fruit, and other deciduous trees, such as birch, maple, oak, walnut, and more exotic woods, such as cherry, elm, or rosewood, are the materials of good cabinetry. Today, as in much traditional cabinetwork, such solid woods are used for chair frames, table bases, and cabinet legs, although wide surfaces are more often not solid but veneered.

VENEER. Veneer is a very thin slice (usually $1/28$ inch) of a fine solid wood. It is glued to a *core*, which may be a solid wood of lesser quality, a number of layers of thicker veneer, or, in modern practice, *particleboard*. The last is a manufactured board made from chips and sawdust, the scrap of woodworking, held together with a resin adhesive. It is, of course, wood, and very stable against warping, shrinking, or cracking. It is often assumed that veneer is a cheap substitute for solid wood, but this is not its primary reason for being. Solid wood in wide boards will warp and crack with changes in temperature and humidity, a problem that veneer circumvents. A core of solid wood is first covered with a utility veneer, its grain running at right angles to the grain of the core. *Face veneer*, which appears on the surface, is glued on top of the underlayer (called *cross-banding*), its grain running the other way (fig. 12.38). Such a sandwich is far more stable than any solid wood; as an incidental benefit, it contributes to the conservation of the fine wood used for the face veneer. Cross-banding is not needed

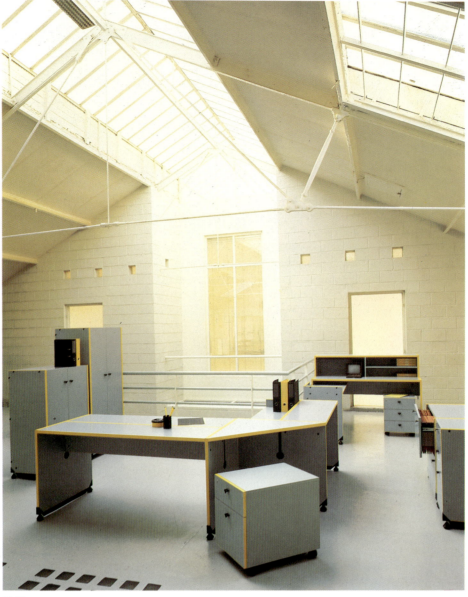

12.35

12.36

12.37

on plywood (veneer) cores or on cores of particleboard. In modern practice, plastic laminates are often used as a surface material over a core where an especially tough and durable surface is required.

PLYWOOD. Plywood, most familiar as a basic construction material, is a number of layers of thin veneer laminated together with the grain of each layer running at right angles to the grain of the layers above and below it. Fir plywood is widely used in carpentry, but it is not generally acceptable for furniture construction uses. The outer surfaces of veneer plywood may be of better-grade woods, but rather than applying good veneer to a plywood core, most furniture uses solid wood or par-

ticleboard cores. An exception arises because it is possible to make plywood in forms other than flat sheets by placing the layers of veneer in a mold while the adhesive between the layers is still wet and applying pressure (in a press) while the glue is setting. The resulting plywood will take the form of the mold, usually curved, to produce parts (seat, backs, or legs) of furniture or even, in some cases, whole chairs or bench sections. The term bent plywood is often used to describe this process, but it is a misleading term since flat plywood is not and cannot be bent; it is more properly called molded. A number of famous and highly successful modern designs use this process (figs. 12.39, 12.40).

12.35 *A workstation grouping using an L-shaped desk assembly with separate file and storage units is part of a modular office system, by the French firm of Rochebrune, using wood-panel surfaces and rubber-cushioned edges. The contrasting color of the edge trim gives the pieces a crisp, linear quality that visually ties the elements of the system together. (Photograph courtesy Club France)*

12.36 *Built-in furniture has a long history on seagoing vessels, where its immobility and compactness have obvious advantages. Philippe Starck was the interior designer of this 1990 yacht. (Photograph: G. Beauvais, courtesy Starck)*

12.37 *Resolutely modern furniture and lighting provide a striking contrast with their Venetian setting. The Palazzo Remer, a fifteenth-century building, has become a hospitality center for the Swiss furniture firm DeSede, whose*

pieces are displayed here. Paolo Piva was the architect for the 1991 building renovation, as well as the designer of the sofa and chairs. (Photograph: © Durston Saylor)

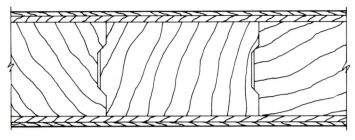

12.38

BENTWOOD. Bentwood is the term for a different process, in which thin strips of solid wood, usually a European beech, are put in a pressure chamber and softened with steam. The strips are then bent around molds or forms and clamped in place until they cool and dry out, when the bent shape becomes permanent. Chairs and other objects can be designed to be made up as assemblies of a number of bentwood parts. Several designs developed near the end of the nineteenth century, when the process was invented, have become classics, collected in their original forms and still produced currently (fig. 12.41).

At its best, bentwood furniture is light and strong, relatively inexpensive, and original and handsome in design. In America, where suitable wood for bending is not easily available, this technique has not been developed extensively, although it is used to produce the curved back rims of some Windsor chairs and other curved chair parts (see fig. 12.7).

Most curved parts in wooden furniture are cut out in curved form from wider planks by *bandsawing*. Because a single strip of wood with the grain running through it is fragile, the curvature must be limited or the part must be made up of several pieces carefully joined. Grain must run close to parallel with the direction of curvature to avoid a weak point subject to easy breakage.

12.39

EVALUATING CONSTRUCTION. The quality of wood construction can be evaluated by inspecting the joints of solid parts and, in cabinet furniture, by observing the joinery of drawers and hidden parts inside, at backs, and underneath the body of a unit. There should be no visible nails or staples, no dripping glue, no bottoms or backs of thin cardboardlike fiber. Drawers should fit and slide well; catches, latches, and pulls should be of good quality and work well. Drawers should have neat and strong joints at all their corners and should withstand tugging and pulling in any direction.

The edges of doors and drawers (including bottom edges) reveal the construction of their panels—whether they are solid or veneered; if veneered, the nature of the core, layers, and veneer; and the character of the machining—and give an idea of the piece's overall quality. Finishes are also a major clue to construction quality. Penetrating oil (*nat-*

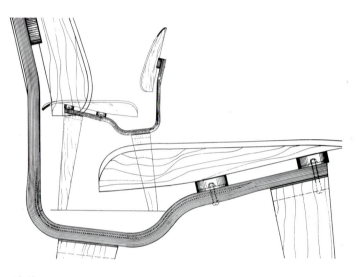

12.40

ural) finishes hold up well and are easy to repair and maintain; they are satisfactory only when applied on good wood construction. Synthetic lacquers are used to produce a hard, smooth finish of high quality. The wood is usually first filled with a wood-filler paste to close the open-grain structure; then several thin coats of lacquer are applied. Poor-quality wood furniture depends heavily on finish to hide what lies below. Beware of strongly toned stained finishes and finishes with shaded color tone or with simulated grain or patina effects. Plastic parts that attempt to simulate wood are a sure sign of cheap and shoddy construction.

A possible exception to this last rule is the use of plastic laminate surfaces in simulated wood-grain patterns. Although generally frowned on by designers, wood-grained plastic tops have come to be widely used in office desks and in institutional furniture, where their resistance to damage outweighs their questionable appearance. There is a range of quality in laminates; the use of a good (that is, highly realistic-appearing) laminate indicates good overall quality. Cheap laminates look like a bad color photograph of wood. Their use signals corner-cut-

12.38 *Illustrated here is a cross section of a veneer panel, a common element of modern wood furniture. The panel is made up of a central core—either solid wood or particleboard—with layers of veneer on each side of the core, the grain running crosswise. (This layer, called cross-banding, is often omitted with a particleboard core because the uniform structure of the grainless mate-* *rial is almost immune to splitting and shrinking.) The layers on each side of the core must be of the same wood to prevent warping. The outer surface, or face veneer, makes up the final, outer layer. If the face veneer is to be concealed inside or under a unit, it may be a wood of inferior appearance. Otherwise, a first-quality veneer will be used, giving the finished product its external appearance.*

12.39 *This armchair by Alvar Aalto represents an early (1930–33) and famous use of molded plywood for a chair's side frames, seat, and back. These parts are often described as being of bent plywood, but the term is misleading because the material cannot be bent after manufacture. 31¼ x 23⅜ x 24⅞". (Photograph courtesy Artek)*

12.40 *This molded-plywood chair, part of a related group, was developed by Charles Eames in association with Ray Eames in 1946. Rubber shock mounts attach the seat and back units to the structural frame. This chair remains among the most admired of American post–World War II furniture designs. (Drawing courtesy Charles and Ray Eames)*

ting throughout. A magnifying glass is helpful in looking at laminate, although the general impression it gives from a distance is also a trustworthy indicator of quality.

Metal

As a furniture material, metal appears in parts (legs, frames, and table bases) and as a primary material for office furniture, kitchen cabinetry, utility shelving, and in some other products as well. Steel, in the form of rods, tubing, and sheets, is the most-used metal. Aluminum appears in tubes and formed sections, such as angles, channels, and Ts, and as a material for cast legs, frames, and small parts. Alloys are used for the casting of small metal parts such as pulls and other hardware elements.

As steel is subject to rusting, it must be finished either by painting or by plating, usually with chrome plating, which can be polished or finished to a frostier (*satin*) surface. Stainless steel requires no finish but is hard to work and therefore expensive and suitable only for certain designs (fig. 12.42). Aluminum is much less strong than steel and is costly relative to its strength. While it does not rust, it requires a finish called *anodizing* to prevent its gradual corrosion, which forms a gray oxide seen on much-used kitchen pots and pans. Anodizing may be done with color, or aluminum can be finished with various types of paints and coatings.

Metal office furniture and utility files, cabinets, and shelving are made of steel sheet. The sheets are cut and then bent to form box shapes or, with bent flanges, shelves or tops. Parts are welded together to make up complete units. The gauge of metal used is a significant factor determining quality. Thin sheet metal can be dented easily and may cause drumming noises, a sign of flimsiness. Flat sheet metal should not "oil can" (pop in and out) and should be difficult to dent with anything less than a hammer blow. It should be impossible to put a bend or kink in any metal part through the stress of normal use. The forming of bent flanges contributes to structural sturdiness; quality sheet-metal furniture often uses nested, doubled-up box forms to produce panels of great strength. Hollow cavity spaces in sheet-metal furniture need to be filled with inert fiber panels to deaden drumming noises and resist denting.

In all metal furniture, the connections are crucial. Joints may be welded or mechanical, that is, held together with screws, nuts and bolts, or other fasteners. Pushing, pulling, bouncing, and shaking with particular attention to joints will give a good idea of sturdiness. Metal tubes and other thin sections, even when amply strong to resist breakage, may be springy. In a chair this may be pleasant; in a desk or shelf unit excessive springiness can be annoying.

Good finishes not only attest to general quality, they also resist rust, corrosion, and damage. Look for chipped paint at edges and corners; if circumstances permit, try to chip a corner or edge in some hidden location (the bottom rear of a drawer, for example). Chrome-plated finishes are harder to evaluate since even the poorest-quality chrome looks bright and resists damage when new. However, after a short time, poor chrome plate permits rust to form, which eventually damages the plating. The best assurance of quality plating comes through the written specifications offered by reputable manufacturers.

12.41

12.42

12.41 True bentwood construction uses lengths of solid wood that are first softened by steam heat and pressure, then bent around molds, where they cool and dry, taking the forms of the molds. This famous rocking chair of 1860 is one of the best known of Austrian Gebruder Thonet's many products. The chair is of bent beechwood with caned seat and back. Height 37 1/2". The Museum of Modern Art, New York. Gift of Café Nicholson

12.42 This Mies van der Rohe armchair was first produced in 1970, although the design concept dates from the late 1920s or early 1930s. The frame is of tubular stainless steel with a polished finish; the upholstery is a channeled-foam cushion resting on straps of saddle leather. 33 x 23 5/8 x 35 1/4". (Photograph courtesy Knoll International)

Table 17. Characteristics of the Most-Used Furniture Woods

A large part of the wood visible in modern furniture is *plywood,* in which only the outermost thin layer of veneer is of the species named. In this case, the only significant characteristics are the color and finish surface of the face veneer. Where *solid* wood is used, as in legs, rails, and stretchers, other characteristics are also important. Woods rarely used as solids but commonly used as decorative veneers are not included in this list.

SPECIES	TYPICAL COLOR	RELATIVE COST	CURRENT AVAILABILITY	TYPICAL USES AND SPECIAL CHARACTERISTICS
HARDWOODS				
Birch	Light beige-tan to near-white	Medium	Good	Hard, strong, compact grain, works and finishes well, generally useful in all furniture applications.
Cherry	Reddish-brown	High	Limited	Works and finishes well, well suited to handcrafting.
Ebony	Brown with near-black grain	High	Limited	Dense and heavy wood with striking grain pattern. Often stained black.
Mahogany	Reddish-brown to red	Medium	Good	Relatively soft, easy to work and finish. Typically red color often deepened with stain.
Maple	Light beige-tan	Medium	Good	Similar to birch (see above), with which it is sometimes combined in one product.
Oak	Light grayish-brown	Medium to high	Good	Hard and strong with marked, coarse grain. Often stained to darker browns.
Poplar	Light tan with pink and greenish streaks	Low	Good	Soft and easy to work. Color and grain not attractive. Much used for hidden parts and panel cores.
Rosewood	Deep red with black graining	High	Very limited	Striking and highly decorative appearance. Most used as veneer, often in matched patterning.
Teak	Warm, light brown	Medium to high	Fair	Close, uniform grain, easily workable. High oil content makes oil finishes desirable.
Walnut	Grayish-brown	Medium to high	Fair to good	Strong, consistent grain and good appearance. Suitable to general furniture uses in solids and veneers. Medium-dark color often further darkened with stains.
SOFTWOODS				
Cedar	Orange to red	Low	Good	Occasionally used in furniture, most often as storage lining because of its pleasant (and moth-repellent) aromatic odor.
Pine (white)	Clear, near-white	Medium	Limited	Soft, even grain and easy workability suited to handcrafting. Limited strength.
Pine (yellow)	Tan, orange to yellow	Low	Excellent	Soft, grainy, and difficult to finish well. Primarily for carpentry. Limited use, low cost, roughly worked applications.
Redwood	Reddish-brown	Low	Excellent	Natural oil content makes it usable outdoors without a finish. Soft and easy to work. Limited strength.

Table 18. Furniture Finishes

PAINT, usually brushed on, hides the color and grain of wood and so is most often used on inexpensive furniture and built-in cabinetry. Several coats are required to hide grain and imperfections. Gloss or semigloss surfaces are best for resisting dirt and abrasion.

ENAMEL is a special type of paint, usually gloss or semigloss, best applied over one or more priming coats. It hides wood color and grain and provides a tough surface that resists abrasion and can be easily cleaned.

BAKED ENAMEL can be used only on metals. It is generally sprayed on and then subjected to sufficient heat to fuse its components into a very hard, glossy surface. It is commonly used on kitchen cabinets, appliances, and bathroom fixtures.

PLASTIC COATING, used on metal parts, is factory-applied by heating the part and then dusting it with plastic powder, which melts and fuses on the metal surface. The resulting leatherlike texture is tough and abrasion-resistant.

CHROMIUM PLATING is a metal surface treatment used for the legs and frames of furniture. It is factory-applied and provides good protection against rust and damage. A silvery metallic finish, a satin grain, or a mirrorlike surface are most often used, although gold, brass, or black are also possible.

LACQUER is a general term for a number of quick-drying synthetic finishes that can be brushed on but are usually sprayed on in several coats, often with heat used to accelerate drying in factory production. Clear lacquer finishes allow the color and grain of wood to show. Fillers are often used to fill the open grain of some woods. Lacquers are also available in a full range of colors that hide wood color and grain.

BLEACH can be used to lighten the color and reduce the grain of wood before applying a clear finish coating. Some woods can be bleached sufficiently to become almost white while still showing a grain pattern. Lacquer is the usual surface coating for bleached wood.

STAIN can be used to darken or color wood before applying a transparent surface finish. Because stains penetrate into woods to some depth, they help to conceal scratches or other damage to the surface coating. The rich colors associated with mahogany are produced by reddish stains; "ebonizing" is achieved by using a black stain.

VARNISH is a gum dissolved in a solvent. As the solvent evaporates, it forms a transparent coating with a brownish color tone. A number of thin coats are usually used to generate a surface that is matte, semimatte, or, most often, glossy. Varnish is used on many antiques and antique reproductions.

SHELLAC is a gum dissolved in alcohol that leaves a light-colored, clear coating as the solvent evaporates. The finish may be satiny or high-gloss. Shellac finish is easily damaged and will show water spots and marks of other liquids. It is often used as a sealer before applying other finishes or is used in combination with other finish materials, such as oil.

OIL finishes penetrate into wood and also form a surface coating. Linseed, tung, and other oils can be used alone or in combination with a solvent to aid application. Oil finishes darken wood somewhat, but they allow grain and color to show through, thus preserving a "natural" surface appearance. Oil may be applied by brushing, spraying, or dipping. Several coats are usually applied, wiped off, and hand-rubbed to the desired level of gloss. Oil finishes are easily damaged but are easy to repair by recoating.

FRENCH POLISH is a term for a traditional furniture finish using oil, shellac, and alcohol applied with cloth pads and hand-rubbed. A variety of mixes and finish processes are used to produce handsome but generally delicate finishes on fine woods.

WAX can be used on wood to provide protection while preserving a natural appearance, although with slight darkening. It is also often used over other finishes (such as shellac, varnish, or oil) to provide protection and aid development of a high gloss.

In evaluating metal furniture, some consideration should be given to the demands the intended use will present. Folding outdoor or camp furniture, intentionally lightweight and built for limited use, cannot be expected to have the toughness and durability that heavier construction can offer. Office furniture, built for a long life of hard use, will stand up against considerable abuse and consequently will be heavy and correspondingly expensive.

Plastics

A relatively new material for furniture construction, plastics come in so many different varieties that generalization becomes difficult (figs.

12.47 and 12.48). Price increases of recent years (most plastics are petroleum-based substances) have somewhat set back earlier expectations that plastics would become the primary material for furniture-making. Still, many modern designs use plastic parts, and certain plastics are widely used for special applications. Its most visible application in furniture is probably as sheet laminate, used as a tough surface material (see above under wood furniture).

PLASTIC LAMINATES. Laminates are composed of layers of heavy paper impregnated with melamine resin. Plain colors, patterns, and imitations of wood grain are common surface finishes. The thickness of

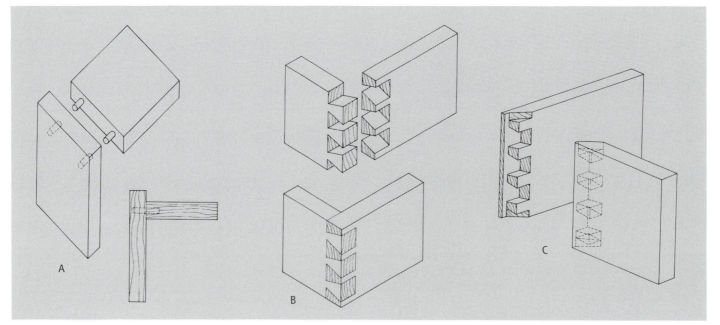

12.43

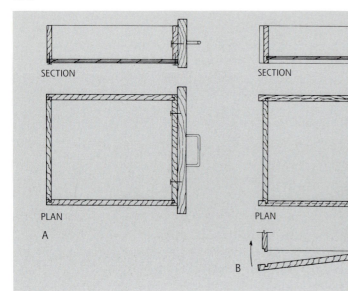

12.44

12.45

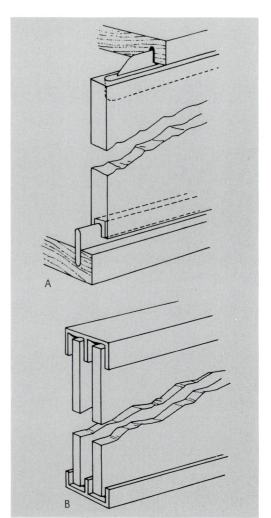

12.46

12.43 Several types of joints are illustrated here. (A) is a dowel joint. Dowels are wood pins glued into bored holes. The ends of dowels are sometimes exposed, but are shown here blind, that is, concealed. (B) is a dovetail joint. Hand-cut with a dovetail saw and chisel and left exposed, these joints are often found as decorative details in both antique and modern crafted furniture.

Machine-cut dovetails, however, are frequently used in modern furniture construction. (C) shows a handcrafted blind dovetail joint.

12.44 This diagram gives two different drawer constructions. (A) shows economical construction of inferior quality. The drawer bottom is glued and nailed or stapled to the sides and back of the

drawer and to an inner front. The front is attached to the inner front with glue and nails or screws. (B) is a superior construction. The sides are attached to the front with dovetails—that is, the sides are slid upward into dovetail grooves in the drawer front. The bottom is then inserted into grooves in the front and sides, and a back is added, trapping the bottom in a groove.

12.45 Some typical furniture hardware is pictured here: (A) A pivot hinge. (B) A pivot hinge, offset for attachment to the top edge of a door. (C) A hinge with an exposed pivot housing—called an "olive knuckle butt." (D) A fully concealed hinge mounted into drilled holes. (E) A spring-clip catch for a door.

12.47

12.48

12.49

12.50

12.46 Sliding door hardware is pictured here. In (A) a fiber strip acts as a lower track; a nylon antifriction block slides along the strip, while a top guide slides within a groove. (B) shows extruded aluminum or plastic track for a sliding glass, plywood, or pressboard door.

12.47 Danish furniture designer Verner Panton took full advantage of molded plastic's malleability in this flowing, strikingly sculptural stacking chair, made as a single unit (1959–60). (Photograph courtesy Herman Miller, Inc., Archives)

12.48 Eero Saarinen designed this graceful pedestal-base armchair in 1956. The shell of molded plastic, reinforced with fiberglass, is supported by a cast-aluminum base. The shell has a lacquer finish, the base a finish of fused epoxy plastic. The removable cushion is of foram foam. (Photograph courtesy Knoll International)

12.49, 12.50 Simple and timeless examples of conventional upholstery, the Mayfair Looseback Chair (fig. 12.49) and the related slipper chair (fig. 12.50) offer excellent comfort in neutral styles that can be adapted to many different situations. (Photographs courtesy Brunschwig & Fils)

the laminate shows as dark brown or black at the edges unless they are trimmed in some way. Some recently developed laminates, of uniform color throughout their thickness, do not create edge appearance problems.

ACRYLICS. Acrylics (such as Plexiglas or Lucite, to mention two well-known trade names) resemble glass in their transparency. They also can be made translucent and colored. While less subject to breakage than glass, they scratch more easily and attract dust and lint with static electrical charges. Acrylics can be bent and molded into curved shapes and are used mostly to make transparent parts and occasionally entire pieces of furniture.

MOLDED PLASTICS. Molded plastics, such as styrene, polyethylene, nylon, and vinyl, are often made into small parts for special purposes, such as glides, rollers, edge trim, and drawer pulls. The only other plastic sufficiently strong and moderate enough in cost to be usable for major furniture parts is *fiberglass,* a hybrid material in which glass fibers are embedded in a molded polyester resin. It is commonly used to make custom auto-body parts and small boat hulls. Fiberglass chair shells can be molded to body-conforming shapes that are very strong and durable when well designed. The plastic may be exposed, painted, or covered with upholstery padding. Fiberglass chair shells can be tested for strength with deliberate rough handling, in testing machines, and through observation of chairs in regular use. The sight of broken plastic shells is common in public spaces, which impose the harsh tests of heavy use and, sometimes, deliberate vandalism. Chair shells made of plastic softer than fiberglass, used in many designs, cannot be expected to stand up to this kind of heavy usage.

A fair test of any plastic chair is to kneel in the seat and try to tear loose the back by pushing back and pulling forward. Also, test leg or base connections to the chair body; they should be unbreakable in any reasonable form of rough treatment.

FOAMED PLASTICS. Foamed plastics have become favorite materials for cushions, mattresses, and padding in upholstery. Foam takes the form of slabs, thin sheets, or molded parts shaped into cushions or fitted to entire chair forms (see fig. 12.48). Upholstery foams vary greatly in degrees of softness, durability, and resistance to fire. Poor-quality foams do not hold up well, and some foams produce toxic fumes when burning. The quality of foams can be verified only through manufacturers' specifications and guarantees since testing calls for laboratory techniques.

Plastic foams can also be made stiff enough to be called rigid. Combinations of soft and rigid foam are used in some modern upholstery, either alone or with embedded frames of wood or metal or with bracing panels of wood, metal, other plastics, or fiber. Evaluating such hybrid plastic furniture is somewhat difficult since the construction is concealed in the finished product. Testing for comfort, durability against hard use, and similar characteristics can be done fairly easily by sitting in each piece, moving in it, and deliberately trying to break it. Durability in service over a long period can be tested only by the

product's service record, so any new construction material should be approached with caution.

Given a structural framework of a stronger material, such as wood or metal, rigid foam, with a plastic surface finish, can also be used as the primary material of storage furniture. This technique is currently used to create mass-produced furniture of minimal quality with surfaces colored to simulate wood. Its potential for use in well-designed furniture of higher quality will probably be developed eventually.

Upholstery

This is a technique using a variety of materials to create softness in seating and reclining furniture (figs. 12.49 and 12.50). Upholstery can range from a thin pad added to a hard seating surface to a complex construction that provides excellent comfort. Since a covering of fabric, leather, or plastic usually conceals all upholstery construction, its techniques and quality are hard to evaluate. Inspecting an upholstered unit before it is covered or watching the upholsterer at work in the shop are the best ways to become acquainted with upholstery techniques.

Traditional upholstery, still used in many quality products, begins with a frame, sturdily made in hardwood, with strong joints (fig. 12.51). This establishes the outer form of the finished unit. The open bottom is laced with an over-and-under weave of heavy webbing. Onto this, a number of coil springs (16 to 25 per seat) are tied and sewn to be pulled down into a partially compressed position. Canvas is placed over the springs and a cushion added on top. The cushion may be a removable unit or sewn down in place. The back is similarly treated, often without the coil springs. Padding is placed on arms and edges, and the whole is covered with the material that will be visible in the finished product. (See Appendix 6, "Estimating Material Requirements.")

Traditional upholstery, which depends on skilled labor, is slow and costly to produce. Most modern variations stem from efforts to reduce this labor cost. For example, flat, sinuous springs or elastic webbing often take the place of coil springs. Plastic foam (discussed above) may replace older cushioning materials, such as down, felt, or cotton, or various grades of foam may make up the entire upholstery construction. The resulting comfort can be evaluated by direct trial. Durability is, again, harder to evaluate. Upholstered furniture made with good workmanship using good materials can have a long life, but upholstery using shortcut methods and cheap materials can be a doubtful economy, leading to the dismembered examples so often seen discarded after a short life. The reputation of a manufacturer is again the best guide to quality.

FURNITURE DESIGN

Furniture design tends to follow the trends in architectural and interior design. Historically, a furniture style displays both the general concept and specific details of its own period (fig. 12.52). The furniture of the Middle Ages exhibits Gothic details, that of the Renaissance elements from classical antiquity. Typical Victorian furniture has a vertical pro-

12.51

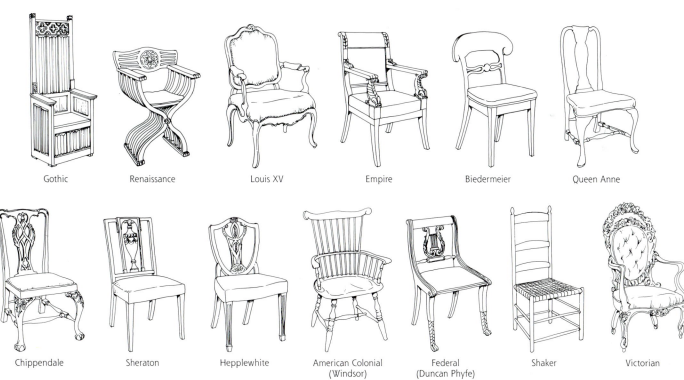

| Gothic | Renaissance | Louis XV | Empire | Biedermeier | Queen Anne |

| Chippendale | Sheraton | Hepplewhite | American Colonial (Windsor) | Federal (Duncan Phyfe) | Shaker | Victorian |

12.52

12.51 This diagram illustrates the construction of conventional upholstered seating as it is now most commonly produced. Coil springs are used for the seat, while the more economical modern alternative, sinuous—No-Sag—springing is used for the back. Rubberized hair or foam has generally replaced the traditional cotton felt and horsehair cushion stuffing.

12.52 Furniture styles display both the general concepts and the specific details of the architecture and interior design of their period. Chairs seem to be the most clearly differentiated representatives of successive historical styles.

12.53

portion and elaborate and fussy details, while modern furniture often appears simple in both form and detail.

The terminology of furniture styles can be confusing, as some terms referring to historic periods and other terms describing an approach to design are used in ways that overlap. The modern habit of reproducing furniture designs from the past generates some of this confusion. The term *Colonial*, for example, describes both actual antiques from the Colonial era and modern reproductions of Colonial designs. *Modern* logically means nothing more than recently produced, but the term has come to designate a style as well. Sorting out this tangle demands careful use of the terms discussed below.

Antiques

This term refers only to furniture made over a hundred years ago (according to the definition used by U.S. Customs) in the particular style then current (figs. 12.53 and 12.54). Dealers and galleries that deal in antique furniture usually reserve the term for examples of good quality, often called fine antiques. As the years go by, old furniture that was once scorned often comes to be appreciated and valued.

Country antiques can still be found at reasonable prices, and good antiques are sometimes, surprisingly, no more expensive than reproductions. Truly fine antiques, considered to be of museum quality, have

12.54

12.53 This Victorian tête-à-tête is an American antique piece of circa 1850. The frame is of rosewood, elaborately carved in keeping with the taste of the time. 44¹/₂ x 52 x 43".The Metropolitan Museum of Art, New York. Gift of Mrs. Charles Reginald Leonard, 1957, in memory of Edgar Welch Leonard, Robert Jarvis Leonard, and Charles Reginald Leonard

12.54 A Queen Anne-style antique wing chair of circa 1725, in walnut and maple, is a product of a New England shop. The cover fabric is the original needlepoint. 46¹/₄ x 31¹/₂". The Metropolitan Museum of Art, New York. Gift of Mrs. J. Insley Blair, 1950

12.55

become very costly; they are selected and bought as much for their investment potential as for their use as furniture. These should be purchased only from reputable dealers, galleries, or auction houses.

Many excellent designs made less than a hundred years ago may be highly valued and sought after. These are generally covered by the term *collectibles*, which also applies to a great variety of old objects, including both very costly one-of-a-kind pieces and inexpensive mass-produced items.

Reproductions of Antiques and Collectibles

These recently made objects reproduce the design of antique originals, more or less accurately. Good reproductions are extremely accurate copies of fine antiques. Makers sometimes go so far as to create finishes (called *distressed* in the trade) that imitate the effects of wear, down to such details as false wormholes.

Many designers frown on the use of reproductions, regarding them as a form of fakery that is dishonest when it truly deceives, foolish when it fails to deceive. Designer and client must judge this issue according to the context. For example, reproduction captain's chairs in a restaurant designed in a particular style may seem easier to accept than a brand-new imitation Chippendale breakfront in a living room.

12.56

12.55 A classic modern sofa of 1928 by Le Corbusier is part of a group that includes an armchair, an extended, or wide, armchair, and a love seat. Polished-steel tubing supports rubber straps with surrounding steel springs for the seat and back, which hold the inserted seat, back, and arm cushions. In modern production, the cushions are of polyurethane foam, latex, and rubberized cocoa fibers and are covered in fabric, vinyl, or leather. $28^7/8$ x $61^1/8$ x $24^3/4$". (Photograph courtesy Cassina)

12.56 The Cesca armchair, a famous classic modern design of 1925 by Marcel Breuer, is usually considered the first tubular-steel chair. It is said that on a visit to a bicycle factory, Breuer was impressed with the possibilities of using steel tubing—a strong, economical, and easily manufactured structural material —for furniture. The photograph shows a modern (1968) reproduction currently available. The seat and back frames and arm pads are of hardwood, the seat and back surfaces of handwoven or machine-made caning. $31^3/4$ x $22^5/8$ x $21^5/8$". (Photograph courtesy Knoll International)

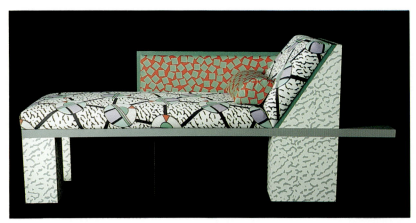

12.57

12.58

12.57 Nathalie du Pasquier's Royal couch of 1983 is a classic example of the Memphis orientation. The surfaces are of plastic laminate in various patterns; the cotton fabric that covers the cushion and armrest is a design by George J. Sowden. (Photograph courtesy Memphis/Milano)

12.58 A grouping of furniture by the contemporary architect Frank Gehry is seen here in a West Hollywood, California, house designed in 1921–22 by the early California modernist Rudolph Schindler. (Photograph: Tim Street-Porter)

12.59

Whatever may be said of quality reproductions, bad reproductions, often called imitations, which are far more common, are an insult to any sensitive observer. Crude designs labeled "Colonial maple," television cabinets of baroque design reproduced in plastic, and the furniture of nonexistent "periods" such as "Mediterranean" are unacceptable for use in interiors of any genuine design quality.

Modern

Logically, this should mean anything new or recent, but it has come to refer to design that is new in concept, particularly the design of the twentieth century related to modern art and committed to simplicity, functional performance, and technology. More specifically, it identifies the stylistic directions (also called *International Style*) exemplified by the Bauhaus. Increasingly, we hear the terms *early modern* (1900 to the 1920s or 1930s) and *classic modern* (for certain famous designs that have lasted for many years; figs. 12.55 and 12.56) to distinguish them from truly recent designs.

Modern furniture (that is, new in concept) has come to be widely used in commercial, institutional, and office interiors. Its residential design use in the United States is still limited to professionals in the design fields and a small public with an aesthetic and intellectual interest in modern art and architecture. After decades of being exposed to it, however, the general public has become increasingly accepting of modern design, as evidenced by the products illustrated in consumer magazines and sold in retail furniture stores.

Contemporary

This simply means "of or in the style of the present or recent times." It should be an umbrella term to refer to whatever is being made now, but it is generally used to refer to designs that, on the one hand, do not reproduce antiques and, on the other, do not belong to the category known as *modern* (fig. 12.60). In the furniture trade, it usually means a current design with no strong stylistic character, furniture that can blend in with almost anything else. The term *transitional*, also

12.59 Furniture is sometimes custom-designed for a specific space by artists or sculptors whose interest in expressive form transcends the merely utilitarian. These tables and chairs, designed by artist and designer Lisa Lombardi, are fantastic elaborations of vegetable motifs. The interior in Santa Monica, California, was designed by Brian A. Murphy. (Photograph: © 1986 Tim Street-Porter)

12.60

12.61

sometimes used, is misleading since such designs are not truly between any two identifiable stylistic directions.

Post-Modern

As a term and a design concept, Post-modern remains somewhat vague. It refers to whatever design trends follow the modern style discussed above, but so far the new directions explored by designers have led to separate paths rather than to a coherent center. More specifically, Post-modern refers to the recent design trend that rejects the strictly functional and logical criteria of the modern movement in order to introduce elements of whimsy, variety, and, at times, absurdity. References to historical precedents in a contemporary vocabulary or context are not uncommon.

Deconstructivist

Since the development of Post-modernism called forth a variety of furniture designs, it is reasonable to ask if there will be a similar out-

12.60 The Stuart sofa, an example of contemporary-style furniture, is in current production but has no characteristics of the modern, or forward-looking, style. On the other hand, it imitates no particular historic period. It is simply graceful and comfortable in appearance and in performance. (Photograph courtesy Brunschwig & Fils)

12.61 In this 1975 handcrafted walnut rocking chair, Sam Maloof of Alta Loma, California, displays both a woodworker's skill and a designer's sensitivity. The result is an object that is both useful and beautiful. 45 x 27³/4 x 46". Museum of Fine Arts, Boston. Purchased through funds from the National Endowment for the Arts and the Gillette Corporation

12.62

12.63

Craft and Art Furniture

Recent years have seen an upsurge in interest in furniture designed and made by craftsmen, either by hand or with limited shop equipment (fig. 12.61). Their furniture displays a wide range of construction and design. Of course, even the finest craft skills do not assure good design skills. At its best, craft furniture is both useful and interesting, and may take on the qualities of an individual work of art as well.

This latter quality comes to the fore when artists choose to make objects of furniture vehicles for artistic creativity (figs. 12.59, 12.62, and 12.63). The level of usefulness varies, as does the quality of the artistic expression involved. While furniture as art is generally costly and often individualistic to the point of eccentricity, it opens up a relatively new and adventurous channel of artistic expression for the interior.

pouring of deconstructivist designs. There are already a number of designs that hint at the broken, torn-apart quality of deconstructivist architecture (see Chapter 4, pages 116–19). Frank Gehry has been an active furniture designer, and his recent works have an inevitable association with the deconstructivist direction (fig. 12.58). His lamps, perhaps more than his chairs, seem to relate to the deconstructivist urge. The work of Philippe Starck, with its sharp points and willful twists, can also be thought of as having connections with this turn in design thinking (see fig. 12.36). It is hard to visualize ways in which the mundane needs of home furniture or office systems and other contract furniture products might be influenced by the deconstructivist direction, but past experience suggests that every development in architectural thinking finds its way into interior design, whether in furniture or in other products.

12.62, 12.63 Furniture-as-art often takes fantastic forms that are only structurally related to a piece's functional purpose. These chairs, although of different design, share an extraordinary visual power. Fig. 12.62 was designed *by Milanese designer Piero Fornasetti. Fig. 12.63, a spidery side chair of scrap metal, is by English designer Tom Dixon. (Photographs: Eric Himmel, courtesy Paul Smith, New York)*

13.1

CHAPTER

THIRTEEN

ART, ACCESSORIES, SIGNAGE

A completed interior of outstanding design with all materials, furniture, and equipment in place will often seem in some way incomplete, in a sense, unoccupied. Spaces come to life with the addition of elements expressive of individual character—the character of the users or occupants of the space or the character developed by the designer to express the less personal individuality of an organization, corporation, or institution. These elements can generally be identified as belonging to one of two classes: works of art or accessories. The dividing line is not absolute; some things fall into an overlapping area.

Works of art are most familiar in the form of mural paintings or two-dimensional pictures hung on walls, but three-dimensional sculpture, bas-relief or in the round, can be fully integrated into interior space. While painting is regarded as the primary art form of a two-dimensional nature, the other two-dimensional mediums, such as the various printmaking techniques, weaving, photography, and other types of graphic art, are probably more often used than original painting to bring visual variety and interest into interior spaces.

The term *accessories* covers a vast variety of objects, usually smaller in scale than furniture, that may be introduced into a space to serve a practical purpose, for ornament or display, or for some combination of these purposes. Stage designers fully realize the importance of appropriate accessories in making a theatrical set express time, place, and character. Photographers photographing interiors often provide their own accessories and make a point of moving—or removing—small objects in order to show the space at its best.

In residential interiors, owners or occupants introduce objects or possessions that may be familiar and beloved or simply necessary and useful. The results vary from charming and interesting to cluttered and messy. The interior designer can affect the outcome by acting as an advisor, helping with placement, perhaps selecting new and different

objects, and, frequently, suggesting the elimination of objects that cannot be successfully placed or that detract from the visual effect of the space because of poor design quality. This last function calls for special tact and persuasive ability.

Although public spaces such as lobbies, restaurants, and shops do not involve such personal issues, providing art or decorative objects is an important way to add warmth. The interior designer may play a role in selecting or suggesting art, as well as useful accessories. Private offices fall in a middle ground between public and personal spaces, with occupants often anxious to differentiate their spaces from identical units by personalizing them. Motivated by a sense of responsibility and pride in a job well done, the designer will usually direct and control the choice and placement of art and accessory elements rather than leave all this to the occupants. Many clients want and appreciate help with these matters.

Both artworks and accessories are often treated as incidentals added almost as an afterthought. This approach may work when only a few practical necessities are required, but it is usually wise to give more design attention to these elements. A major work of art can dominate a space and influence all other design decisions (about color, materials, and furniture placement). An art collection can have a similarly important role, or it can be displayed as a more incidental, background contribution to the totality of a space.

Accessories, especially items such as wastebaskets and ashtrays, are more likely to play a background role, although a large collection of objects or a single object of strong character can also become a major design focus. A handsome clock, a ship model, or a framed map or chart can, like an artwork, dominate an interior.

Of all the elements of an interior, artworks and accessories are among the easiest to relocate, remove, or replace. A painting can be relocated or removed; a ship model can be replaced by a clock; new

13.1 Commissioned for the bathroom of a New York apartment, these paintings by David Fisch are clearly based on ancient Roman motifs as they appear on excavated interior walls in the ruins of Pompeii. (Photograph: © Jeff Blechman)

ACCESSORIES CHECKLIST

ENTRANCE AREAS
Coatracks or hangers
Umbrella and overshoe holders
Protective mats or runners for the floor
Bell pushes, intercom plates, closed-circuit TV
Mailboxes or trays, message board
Signs, bulletin boards
Nameplates

LIVING SPACES
Small tables or stands
Stools, hassocks
Cushions
Bookshelves or racks
Music and video components; record,
    tape, cassette, and CD storage
Ashtrays
Wastebaskets
Flower containers
Planters and plants
Clock
Frames or other display devices
Telephone, intercom
Answering machine

DINING SPACES
Serving cart, trays
Place mats and/or tablecloths
Flatware and hollowware
Dishes and serving pieces, glassware
Candlesticks or holders
Trivets or hot pads

KITCHEN AND PANTRY SPACES
Storage/display for cooking pots and utensils
Storage/display for staples, bottled items
Canisters
Storage/display for dishes, glassware,
    and other tableware
Racks or other holders for towels, potholders
Cutting, rolling, mixing boards
Scales

Spice rack
List and memo pads
Cookbook storage
Clock/radio
Telephone
Small and larger appliances
Special plumbing hardware

BEDROOMS
Bedcovers, quilts, blankets, and so on
Pillows, cushions
Bedside stands or tables
Clock
Radio/TV
Mirror(s)
Dressing accessories (brushes, combs,
    and so on)
Telephone

BATHROOMS (PRIVATE)
Towel rack(s)
Soap dish(es), toilet-paper holder,
    toothbrush and glass holder
Medicine cabinet
Mirror(s)
Scale
Towels, mats

BATHROOMS (PUBLIC)
Paper-towel dispenser, discard container
Liquid-soap dispenser
Coat hooks

OFFICES
Desk accessories (pads, holders for pens,
    pencils, paper clips, scissors, and so on)
Ashtray(s)
Telephone(s)/intercom unit
Clock
Calendar
Computer and associated equipment
Typewriter/business machines
Tackboard/chalkboard
Letter trays

Address and phone number directories
Radio/music and video components

GENERAL (ITEMS THAT MAY BE CONSIDERED FOR ANY SPACE)
Portable lighting (lamps: task, ambient,
    accent)
Telephone and directories
Ashtrays and sand urns
Wastebaskets
Flowers and vases
Plants and planters
Terrarium
Tack (pinup) surfaces
Storage (books, magazines, papers,
    records, tapes, CDs, special purpose)
Fireplace tools, fire screens, wood basket
Display pedestals (plaster or glass
    cases, panels)
Mirror
Clock
Computer
Typewriter/printer

SPECIAL-PURPOSE SPACES/PUBLIC SPACES
Directory, signs, location plan
Graphic materials (brochures, menus,
    wine lists, printed forms)

CHILDREN
Toys and toy storage
Play equipment

PETS
Bird cage
Aquarium
Bed
Litter box
Scratching post
Dishes

MUSIC
Instruments
Music stand
Music storage

13.2

13.3

13.4

vases can replace old. Such flexibility makes decisions about these objects less binding—but no less important than decisions about more lasting elements.

Dealing with artworks and accessories involves several interrelated concerns. It is helpful to anticipate various practical needs and provide for them in order to avoid makeshift and unattractive solutions later on. For example, it is possible to include such items as umbrella holders, coatracks, calendars, bulletin boards, signs, and displays in ways that enhance a design. If these are not planned for, ad hoc approaches to dealing with such needs can be unfortunate.

It is important to provide for specific objects of a personal or sentimental value that occupants of spaces want on view in a way that satisfies their owners without compromising the design. These may include inherited pieces, trophies, or souvenirs that may or may not have aesthetic merit. A collection of shells, boxes, or toys, a hunting or fishing trophy, or a framed document can usually be fitted into an interior if planned for. If not, they may later be inappropriately placed, creating visual clutter.

The introduction of well-chosen artworks and accessories can add to the interest and aesthetic quality of a space while reducing a sense of bareness or incompleteness. Making good choices in these areas is part of the designer's job. A well-chosen artwork placed in an inviting space satisfies everyone who sees it. At the same time, it preempts a less appropriate display.

Accessories

This term refers to the incidental objects, useful, decorative, or both, that may be added to the interior over and above basic furniture and equipment. Such objects are usually portable and subject to frequent change. Many of the items in this class are small, even trivial, so that discovery of sources for well-designed examples may take some searching. Sources may include consumer retail outlets (department stores and mail-order houses), craft shops, and galleries, as well as reputable, design-oriented showrooms. It is helpful to build up a file of sources with brochures, advertisements, and magazine tear sheets. The most

13.2 Roger Zenn Kaufman's Becker desk organizer turns the familiar desktop clutter of calendar, calculator, pencil, pen, and clip holders into an ornamental and positive object—perhaps a bit of a status designator as well. (Photograph courtesy Sointu, New York)

13.3 Many modern designers have come to view minor, functional accessories as worthy territory for the introduction of creative ideas into general circulation. This magazine rack, by Dutch designer Ann Mae, has an active, sculptural quality that enhances its simple utility. (Photograph courtesy Sointu, New York)

13.4 In a bathroom of the Middleton Inn, South Carolina, Clark & Menefee Architects have converted a rather austerely architectural environment into an inviting space by realizing the potential aesthetic value of familiar bathroom

accessories. As arranged here, towels, a basket of washcloths, and the soap and soap dish are vehicles for bringing color and texture into the room. (Photograph: © Tom Crane)

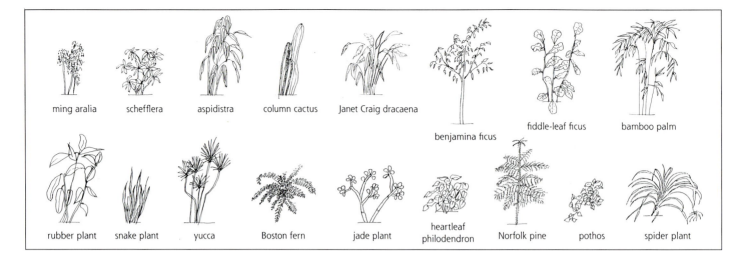

ming aralia   schefflera   aspidistra   column cactus   Janet Craig dracaena   benjamina ficus   fiddle-leaf ficus   bamboo palm

rubber plant   snake plant   yucca   Boston fern   jade plant   heartleaf philodendron   Norfolk pine   pothos   spider plant

Table 19. Indoor Plants

	Plant Name	Height	Width	Pot Diameter	Light Required	Water Required
Floor Plants and Trees	Aralia (Ming)	12–48	8–24	6–14	H	M
	Schefflera	18–96	10–48	6–17	M	M
	Aspidistra	18–40	12–36	6–14	L	M
	Cactus (Candelabra)	4–30	8–18	6–14	M	D
	Cactus (Column)	4–20	6–18	6–17	M	D
	Dracaena (Janet Craig)	16–60	12–28	6–17	M	M
	Ficus (several varieties)	18–240	12–60	6–48	H	M
	Ficus (Fiddle-leaf)	36–84	12–30	10–17	H	W
	Palm (Bamboo)	14–28	8–24	8–21	M	M
	Palm (Dwarf Date)	24–54	18–42	8–21	H	W
	Palm (Kentia)	36–72	12–24	10–17	M	M
	Palm (Lady)	26–120	20–60	10–21	M	W
	Rubber plant	24–96	18–40	6–16	M	M
	Sansevieria (Snake plant)	12–36	8–16	6–14	M	D
	Yucca	15–96	8–24	6–17	M	D
Smaller table and hanging plants	Ferns (various)	12–28	12–36	6–12	H	W
	Ivy (Grape)	6–10+	R	6–10	M	M
	Jade plant	12–30	12–28	5–10	M	D
	Philodendron (Heartleaf)	6–10+	R	6–10	L	W
	Pine (Norfolk)	12–30*	10–24	5–10	M	M
	Pothos	6–10+	R	6–10	L	M
	Spider plant	variable size			M	W
	Flowering plants (various)	variable sizes, range, and requirements				

Heights, widths, and pot diameters are given in inches

Light requirements: L = 50–75 fc (footcandles), M = 75–100 fc, H = 200+ fc

Water requirements: D = less than average, M = average, W = more than average

R = runner plant, variable width and form

*Can grow into full-size tree

13.5 Flowering plants in pots used as a decorative accent combine with bright painted colors to make an otherwise ordinary stairway in a house in New Orleans pleasant and cheerful. R. Clay Markham was the architect and Tom R. Collum, the interior designer. (Photograph: © Jacques Dirand, courtesy House & Garden)

13.6 Live plants often provide decorative accents in an interior. In this dining room an extraordinary display of plants in a pyramidal arrangement becomes the primary visual element. The 1985 project in Valle de Bravo, Mexico, was designed by José de Yturbe. (Photograph: Tim Street-Porter)

13.5

13.6

13.7

13.8

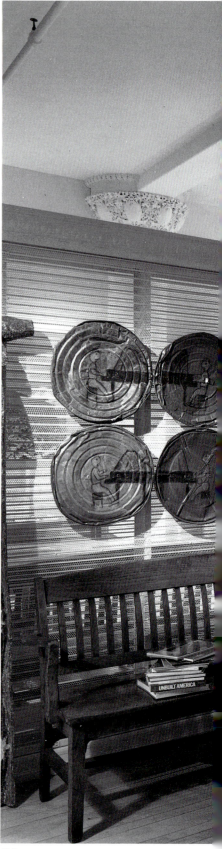

13.9

13.7, 13.8 Wall systems contain and organize the various odds and ends that modern living calls for and that may otherwise turn into clutter. Audio equipment, TV, books, bottles, and glassware become decorative when they fit into the planned wall system made by Cy Mann Designs (fig. 13.8). A sliding, mirrored closure makes them invisible when not in use (fig. 13.7). (Photographs courtesy Cy Mann Designs)

13.9 The offices designed by the innovative architectural design firm SITE Projects Inc. in an older New York loft building are divided by semitransparent screen walls of slats. An eclectic collection of objects and artworks mounted on these dividers gives this space an individuality that expresses SITE's unusual design directions. The project model on the table in the foreground becomes an accessory that connects the creative work of the firm with its setting. (Photograph: © 1985 Peter Aaron/ESTO)

13.10

13.11

serviceable file will include a wide range of stylistic types in every object category. Some interiors, especially true period rooms, demand accessories that match their styles and periods. On the other hand, in many modern interiors, smaller objects from earlier traditions may fit very well. Vases and candlesticks, clocks, or ship models from some past era can be made very much at home in an otherwise contemporary interior.

Practical Accessories

Practical accessories should be considered in relation to the particular functions of each space in which they will be placed. The designer has

13.10 In an authentically traditional interior, period accessories create a consistent character. This is easier to achieve in a museum display than in an environment in daily use. The Federal period room illustrated, from the Phelps-Hathaway House, built circa 1765 and redone in 1788–89, in Suffield, Connecticut, preserves its original details. It is now installed at the Henry Francis du Pont Winterthur Museum, Winterthur, Delaware. (Photograph: Lizzie Himmel)

13.11 In a log house by woodworker Steve Cappellucci, hollowed-out logs are used as window boxes inside the large windows. They are filled with flowering plants and appear to be a natural outgrowth of the overall design concept. (Photograph: © 1985 Michael Skott)

13.12

an obligation to aid in the selection of items that will be fixed in place or built in, and will often have a role in choosing things that will be movable but in regular use. Other, more transient objects may or may not come under the designer's province. The selection of linens and tableware, for example, often an important part of a restaurant's design, may become the designer's responsibility, while residential clients may want to make their own choices of these items, may already own these objects, or may want design help in selecting them.

Reviewing a checklist of accessory items for various kinds of spaces may help to make such objects a planned part of the design rather than intrusions in a space (see the sample checklist on page 392).

Decorative Accessories

Decorative accessories other than works of art exist in infinite variety, often combining some degree of usefulness with a primarily decorative role. Objects may be modern, antique, indigenous, or of craft origins, and they need not always match the style of an interior. Choices may be based on the preferences or interests of the occupants (as with personal collections, trophies, or heirlooms) or may relate to the character and use of the space. A collector of old toys or tools may want to display some or all of a collection; an enthusiastic gardener will want vases and other containers for cut flowers. A ship model might be appropriate in the office of a shipping or engineering company; restaurants often display objects that relate to a national or regional style of cookery or to other menu elements (nets and nautical objects have become clichés of seafood-restaurant design).

13.13

13.12 In a recent renovation of a 1929 cottage in Malibu, California, Andrea Dern has used a variety of accessories, including cushions and paintings with floral motifs that relate closely to the cut-flower arrangements. (Photograph: © Chris Mead, courtesy HG)

13.13 The equipment of dining, particularly formal dining, belongs to a special class of decorative accessories that are also functional. An elaborate table setting is an object display that adds greatly to the ceremony of a meal. In this table setting for two, attractive groupings of plates and napkins, glassware and silver, candles and flowers make it clear that the meal to come will be an occasion. (Photograph courtesy Gourmet)

13.14

Plants

Live plants are a particularly attractive decorative accessory. Even one small plant in a room tends to make the space seem pleasant and civilized. Larger plants, groups of plants, even growing trees can find a place in larger spaces. The provision of containers, planters, plant boxes, even whole greenhouse or conservatory areas is a normal part of the designer's work. Plant selection may be done by the designer alone, the designer and client together, or by a specialized consultant (see Table 19 on page 394).

The obvious aesthetic values of plants are augmented by an increasing realization that they also have a favorable impact on health and the environment. Plants absorb ("breathe in") carbon dioxide and gases considered air pollutants and give off oxygen. It has been shown that a single plant can maintain an atmosphere free of formaldehyde (a common interior pollutant) for each 1,000 cubic feet of enclosed interior space. Plants are also excellent nonmechanical humidifiers, releasing moisture vapor derived from the water they require to survive. A few plants have leaves or berries that can be injurious or toxic if ingested by children or pets and thus are best avoided in residential interiors.

Plants must be located so that they receive light of the intensity and duration appropriate to their species. Each plant type can be classified according to how much daylight or artificial light it requires. Fluorescent light or special *grow lights* can substitute for natural daylight, and many species require only limited light. It is the designer's responsibility to see that light provided, plant location, and species are adjusted to ensure plant growth and survival.

13.15

13.14 *Designed by the owner, a collection of small carved-ivory objects and an ivory model of a ship become a decorative display set out on tables, with a ceramic tureen and candlesticks as background and a framed hunting scene above. (Photograph: Lizzie Himmel, courtesy House Beautiful)*

13.15 *The studio of the famous Italian writer Gabriele d'Annunzio is crowded with possessions that had special meaning for their owner. Their quality and the obvious concern with which they have been collected and displayed turn them into a fascinating reflection of*

personality. A similar density of accessories of lesser quality, chosen at random, would make a space look crowded and busy. (Photograph: © Robert Emmett Bright, Photo Researchers, Inc.)

13.16

Arrangements must also be made for proper and consistent watering. In placing plants, it is important to be sure that watering and maintenance will be practical. Plants placed up high or hanging must be made accessible for watering and other care in some way, possibly with an adjustable suspension so that out-of-reach containers can be lowered for service and returned to their normal positions, much as light fixtures can be lowered and raised for relamping.

When plants are used as design elements in an interior, it is frequently best to arrange for the services of a special supplier who will not only sell plants but who will also provide regular care, rotating or replacing plants as necessary. Such a service may lease the plants or sell them outright while providing a contract for continuing maintenance. Plant suppliers can furnish lists, illustrations, and examples of various species along with information about size range, light, and water requirements. The advice of experienced suppliers can usually be trusted when the supplier will also be performing maintenance. Occupants of a space often wish to buy or bring plants of their own; care must be taken that plant diseases or parasites are not introduced to the detriment of healthy plants already in place.

Artificial plants and flowers are usually regarded as unacceptable in well-designed interiors. Arrangements of dried flowers, leaves, or grasses are sometimes effective as decorative elements, although they offer none of the health benefits of growing plants. Cut flowers make attractive accessories, yet because they are transient they rarely come within the concern of an interior designer. Occupants of an interior may select and place flowers, of course, with the aesthetic effect determined by their taste and budget and the flowers available at local sources. In some spaces a regular program of cut-flower display is established, making the flowers a clear design element in spite of their brief life and need for constant replacement. The presence of flowers can have a strongly favorable impact on a sense of style.

A list of decorative accessories could be endless, and choices are not generally specific to any particular functional use. Arbitrarily introducing decorative accessories for no reason other than to fill space or add interest may well add nothing more than clutter. In doubtful situations, it is usually best to omit display. Errors of omission are far less common than errors of excessive inclusion. Inclusion should perhaps be reserved for times when occupants demand certain objects on display or when the projection of a particular atmosphere or spirit calls for visual support.

ART

The practice of including works of art as integral parts of interiors has a long history. Prehistoric cave paintings, the wall paintings and bas-reliefs of Egyptian tombs, the wall paintings at Pompeii, and the great frescoes of the Renaissance all bear witness to the continuing human urge to make art an important element of our surroundings. During the Renaissance, the framed easel painting became the most popular form of artwork in interiors, and it has remained so, with murals,

13.16 In the home of a professional musician designed by Melvin Dwork, musical equipment plays an essential role. The piano—a strikingly handsome object—becomes an important piece of furniture, here surrounded by music stands and recording apparatus. The library of music scores in this New York apartment strikes a decorative note; the seating furniture is properly angled for listening. (Photograph: Jaime Ardiles-Arce)

sculpture, and a wide variety of art forms other frequent choices.

It seems to be widely felt that an interior is not really complete until the process of "hanging some pictures" has filled up any blank wall areas. In practice, the habit of putting up indifferent or bad works that have no special value or meaning for the occupants of a space often does nothing but add pointless clutter to the visual scenes. Bare walls can be handsome and restful, and a truly fine work of art is usually seen to best advantage displayed in uncluttered surroundings (see fig. 13.22).

Selecting Artwork

The selection of artwork generally follows one or both of two patterns. When works are already on hand—owned, borrowed, or previously chosen for purchase—further selection may be necessary to decide which to display, which to store, which to dispose of. Works to be displayed must then be placed, although available display space may well influence the choice of certain works. Alternatively, works are selected and purchased for specific locations.

The first situation arises when the occupants of a space are art collectors, who may own far more than can possibly be put on view at one time. Other occupants want to display works they are attached to, such as family portraits, works by a friend or relative, or simply favorites, even aside from their artistic merits. In the corporate world, such works as portraits of a founder or former officials, a view of important buildings or events, and similar materials, valued for historic or sentimental reasons over aesthetic merit, may be selected by the client for display.

In private homes or private offices, it is usually possible to find locations where such materials can be put on view to the satisfaction of the occupants. If the spaces are used by visitors or the general public, the designer may try to discourage, exercising ingenuity and tact, display of inferior materials. Failing this, it may be possible to turn such material into something of a historical exhibit rather than an art display. Fortunately, many modern corporations have become major collectors of high-quality artworks. In this case, it is usually easy to place good works in prominent locations and to find more obscure placement for less attractive works that still are wanted on display.

When art is to be specifically acquired for a particular interior project, designer and client must work together to make choices and plan placement. Specialized consultants can help to steer a course through the often confusing world of art markets, both in terms of finding suitable works and giving advice related to costs and budgets. Such consultants may assist significantly in developing a major collection of valuable works. In any case, it is extremely important to verify the consultant's credentials since the art world, like all businesses, has its share of unscrupulous practices.

PAINTINGS. A great variety of artworks may be considered for acquisition and display. Paintings often come to mind as the most suitable works for wall hanging. Certainly, almost any subject matter, size, shape, color tonality, period, or style can be found amid the vast output of artists who have worked or are currently working in this form. Major works by important artists, whether old master or modern, have become very costly. They are sold through art auctions, well-known galleries, and eminent dealers. While no guarantees can be given, they may turn out to be excellent investments.

Works of lesser-known artists, secondary historic figures, and younger living artists who have not made major reputations are more likely to be available at affordable prices. As investments, they carry an even more uncertain future. Even so, modestly priced works selected for their visual merit rather than for name value and price will often be a more workable choice, especially if an unlimited budget is not available.

There is also a seemingly endless supply of inferior work, banal, glibly illustrative, and cliché-ridden. This all too often appeals to the unaware who simply want a spot of color to fill a given space. One can learn to distinguish good art from bad by studying high-quality work directly in museums, major galleries, and through reproductions in books. This does not mean that all the work of unknown artists is bad, but those who have no background in art might do well to avoid the unknown in favor of artists backed by a reputable gallery or by critical approval. This applies to works of art in all other mediums as well.

DRAWINGS AND PRINTS. Works on paper, usually classified as drawings even if they are in watercolors or pastels, are generally smaller in scale and more delicate in character than oil paintings. They are entirely suitable to smaller and more intimate interior spaces. They tend to cost less than larger works by the same artist; in fact, drawings by artists of major reputation are sometimes priced at levels accessible to medium-level budgets.

Prints, or, as they are now often called, *multiples,* are works in one or another medium that permits the making of many copies of a work through some printing technique. Original prints are made from a printing medium such as the copperplate of the engraving and etching, the crayoned stone of the lithograph, or the stencil screen of the silkscreen print worked directly by the hand of the artist or under the artist's direct supervision. The artist signs and numbers each perfect print with figures that indicate the total number of copies printed (the edition) and the order in which the particular print was made (for example, 30/100 indicates the thirtieth impression in an edition of one hundred). After printing, the plate, stone, or screen is destroyed so that additional, possibly inferior, prints cannot be made. Editions are usually small, in the range of 50 to 500 copies. Prints of lesser quality are sometimes produced in large numbers without the participation of the artist, without a signature, with a signature printed from the plate or stone, or even with a forged signature.

A print's monetary value largely depends on the number and signature, but the visual value can be evaluated by simple inspection. Prints produced in large volume, reasonably priced, are often an excellent choice for spaces such as hotels or large office projects that need many artworks. People of average means who wish to start an art collection do well to begin with prints since works of good quality at affordable prices are available and because an extensive collection can be compactly stored in a small space. Such collectors may put a few works on display in rotation.

Photography is another medium that produces prints. The investor should again look for signed and numbered originals printed by the

13.19

13.20

height today brings works down, with their center near average eye level (figs. 13.19, 13.20). If the space has good general lighting, no special lighting is necessary, although special concealed lights or track lights like those used in many galleries might be considered to emphasize the work. Individual lights attached to the tops of frames are now rarely used.

Hanging works from a picture molding or a modern concealed hanging strip is one way to avoid nail holes in a wall, especially if pic-

tures will be rotated. Arrangements of works in symmetrical groups of three or in stepped rows, a traditional placement, now appear forced and unattractive. It is acceptable to cluster a large number of small works together into a kind of mosaic, which serves to display many works in a limited space. Another way to display art in a limited space is to provide a location, perhaps with a ledge or shelf, where individual pieces can be interchanged from time to time. This also avoids putting nail holes in the wall.

13.19, 13.20 In an interesting comparative study, four small drawings have been placed in matching frames and hung as a group: In fig. 13.19, the usual rule of hanging at eye level has been followed, with the result that the works seem to float off upward, unrelated to the other objects. In fig. 13.20, the same four works have been
lowered to a position closer to the chair and table, where they become easy to view from a seated position and enter into a relationship with the real objects placed on the table—the bottles, teapot and cup, and dish of fruits— which are more transitory accessories. (Photograph: Michael Luppino, courtesy Metropolitan Home)

13.21

Sculpture and other three-dimensional works, if they are small, may be simply placed on a table, shelf, or other horizontal surface (fig. 13.21). If the work is too large or it requires protection, a glass or plastic case, which tops a pedestal base of some kind, may be used (see fig. 13.23). Generally, the simplest of frameless cases looks best, with similarly simple boxlike pedestal bases. The moving sculptures called mobiles must be suspended, usually from the ceiling, and need to be located to prevent a possibly dangerous collision that could damage either the mobile or the colliding person. This entails hanging the work beyond human reach or providing a barrier (furniture or a railing) that makes contact impossible. Here, too, the practices of major museums and better galleries are a good guide.

Positioning works of art involves relating the spaces available, the objects to be displayed, and the desired level of viewers' attention. A major work, especially if it is large, calls for a focal location—for example, centered on an uncluttered wall (fig. 13.22). Certain locations, including the chimney breast above a fireplace mantel or the blank wall above a low chest or bookshelf, seem to invite the display of art. Works placed in these locations will tend to draw attention and can even dominate a room. Less important works may be best fitted into locations that draw less attention, such as smaller wall areas, the walls of corridors, or other incidental spaces, or may be grouped so that no one work has a dominant position. A collection can be seen to advan-

tage in a circulation space, where objects come to attention in a planned sequence as the viewer walks past.

Another possibility in acquiring artwork that has not yet been discussed is the commissioning of work for a specific place (see fig. 13.1). The practice boasts a noble history. Some of the great masterpieces—including the Sistine Chapel frescoes by Michelangelo, the metopes of the Parthenon (now known as the Elgin marbles), or Matisse's stained-glass windows in the chapel at Vence—are works commissioned to occupy a particular location. Today, commissioned artwork is most often created for important public spaces; some public buildings built with public funds are even legally required to have it. Occasionally, competitions, more or less formal, are undertaken to select an artist or a work in such situations.

A specially commissioned work always involves some element of risk, since there is no sure way to predict how the end result will actually look in the space until it is complete. Commissions are usually granted on the basis of an artist's reputation and, often, after a preliminary small-scale sketch or model has been considered and evaluated. Murals painted to fit a given space and monumental architectural sculpture are almost always commissioned. They may be executed on site or, when the scale and medium allow, in the artist's studio, to be delivered to the intended location and installed. A specially commissioned work calls for understanding and cooperation among artist, designer, architect, if involved, and client. It may happen that the results disappoint the commissioning individual or agency, possibly leading to conflicts.

While designers expect to have an important role in the selection and placement of artworks and accessories in typical projects, it should be recognized that in some situations the user may have preferences quite different from those of the designer. This pattern arises in large projects where there are many private rooms, including office projects, dormitories, and spaces, such as school classrooms, where users actually produce art and other decoration. In such cases, it is best to provide locations where art and objects can be placed according to the occupants' wishes without doing either physical or aesthetic damage to the space. A tackable surface and an empty horizontal shelf or other surface allow placing a picture without damaging a wall and can be used for a favorite family snapshot, a potted plant, or a souvenir.

Since the desire to have such things about in any space that can be regarded as personal territory seems to be nearly universal, the wise designer accepts this reality and supports it, whether the actual selection and placement are part of the project or are left to the inclinations of occupants.

SIGNAGE AND GRAPHICS

Rarely of significance in residential projects, signs and other graphic elements can be of considerable importance in commercial, office, institutional, and other contract interiors (fig. 13.26). When this material is neglected by the designer, improvised signs will proliferate, ranging from indifferent and awkward to amateurish and unattractive. Many interiors are badly marred by makeshift signs and labels that occupants have created out of necessity.

13.21 In the living room of a house on Long Island, New York, framed antique prints rest on a ledge above a vintage sofa by the late Angelo Donghia. Since these pieces are not hung, they can be easily rearranged, replaced, or re- moved without worrying about wall damage from nail holes. An Indonesian banana-leaf-and-shell box serves as an occasional table. Sherri Donghia was the designer in 1991. (Photograph: © William Waldron, courtesy Elle Decor)

13.22 A truly fine, major work of art such as this Picasso is generally best given an important location in a simple and uncluttered setting. The painting clearly dominates and sets the character of this otherwise subdued, traditionally detailed space, with furniture placed to emphasize the importance of the work, designed by Emily Landau. (Photograph: © Henry Bowles, courtesy House & Garden)

13.23 This 1982 New York apartment highlights a collection of diminutive three-dimensional pieces in a well-designed and -lighted display case. Bromley/Jacobsen Designs was the designer. (Photograph: Jaime Ardiles-Arce)

13.22

13.23

When well designed and appropriately placed, good graphic elements can enhance an interior aesthetically. Several classes of graphic components can be recognized:

MAJOR IDENTIFICATION SIGNS, exterior and interior, aid first-time visitors in identifying their destinations. A house or room number is basic, along with—for most nonresidential projects—a name identification. For business establishments the name identification can also be an effective advertising element. Even if not within the formal responsibility of the interior designer, coordination of exterior signage (even a rooftop sign) with interior character and interior graphics is important.

INTERIOR SIGNAGE may include directories giving locations and room numbers for departments, individuals, or specific functions. Simplified floor plans are often helpful as sign elements in large and complex projects, such as corporate office groups, hospitals, and other institutional facilities, as well as hotels or cruise liners, where strangers can easily become lost. Directional signs are helpful in locating elevators, stairs, restrooms, information counters, and offices that serve the public (fig. 13.25). The first-time users of an airport or bus terminal, an auditorium or healthcare facility need signage to locate counters, stairs, baggage-claim areas, parking access, buses, taxis, and any number of other possible destinations. Clarity and legibility are of vital importance, as is neat and attractive appearance.

CODE REGULATIONS and common sense both require signage to serve emergency needs. Exit signs defining routes to doors and stairs that provide

13.24

13.25

13.24 *Graphic symbols that replace verbal messages with universally understandable visual images have been developed for many frequently used signs and labels. Illustrated here are several variations of symbols for rest rooms. Each was developed for a specific organization; some were designed by the organization's design staff, while* others were designed by outside consultants: (A) Dallas–Fort Worth, Henry Dreyfuss Associates; (B) Transport Canada, design staff of the Ministry of Air Transportation; (C) International Civil Aviation Organization, design staff; (D) German Airport Authority, M. Krampen and H. W. Kapitzki; (E) Port Authority of New York and New Jersey, design staff of the Aviation Department, Owen Scott, graphic designer; (F) Department of Transportation, American Institute of Graphic Arts, Cook and Shanoski Associates.

13.25 *Graphics—typography and layout—for signs has become a specialized phase of design detail called signage.* This section of a New York subway station, the 53rd Street concourse, was designed by Beyer Blinder Belle in 1984. The sign, produced by Whippany Park, is clear and decisive and provides a striking visual accent. (Photograph: © 1985 Frederick Charles)

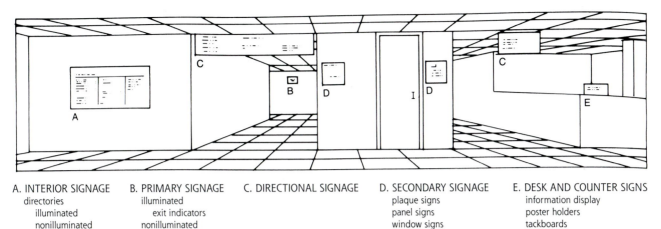

A. INTERIOR SIGNAGE
  directories
    illuminated
    nonilluminated

B. PRIMARY SIGNAGE
  illuminated
    exit indicators
  nonilluminated
    exit indicators

C. DIRECTIONAL SIGNAGE

D. SECONDARY SIGNAGE
  plaque signs
  panel signs
  window signs
  frames
  fixture signs

E. DESK AND COUNTER SIGNS
  information display
  poster holders
  tackboards
  changeable letterboards
  literature organizers
  perpetual calendars

13.26

fire exits are mandated by fire codes. Although their size, coloring, and—in many locales—illumination are specified by code, exact placement and detailed design fall to the designer. Location of such emergency equipment as fire-alarm boxes, fire extinguishers, and hose cabinets must also be identified by appropriate signs. New regulations (as well as a sense of responsibility to the public) call for sign designations of locations where circulation and facilities to serve persons with disabilities can be accommodated. Certain signs and labels useful to those with disabilities also call for modifications or additions, as in the case of elevator floor-call buttons that are made accessible to wheelchair users when placed at appropriate heights and to blind persons with the addition of braille numerals.

GRAPHIC SYMBOLS that replace verbal messages with visual images conveying information clearly and concisely have been developed for many frequently used signs and labels (fig. 13.24). The popularity and ease of international travel would indicate that such signage should be considered in place of, or in addition to, verbal message signs. The use of graphic symbols is particularly appropriate wherever an international user group can be anticipated, as at a major airport.

Provisions for adjustability and revision are important if signage is to maintain its designed quality and accuracy over a period of time. Functions of spaces vary, people change offices or leave, and new names surface. Within a good signage program, directories can be updated and nameplates can be moved to new locations or replaced. Transient items, announcements of events, posters, and notices need suitable places for display in cases, holders, or similar units that permit posting within organized surroundings to discourage the ad hoc treatment that can decline into visual chaos.

Graphic design is a specialized design field that has its own aesthetic and vocabulary. The interior designer should be aware that the selection of lettering styles and typefaces and the layout of graphic elements call for expertise and skill. Many signage systems incorporate components of excellent graphic quality that foster signage programs requiring minimal design effort. A careful listing of every required sign within a project is a basic step in the selection of suitable products that will create an organized graphic program.

In business and institutional projects, the idea of an *identity program* may surface. This concept calls for a coordinated effort to relate all of the visible elements that an organization uses. A corporation may have a trademark or logotype, theme colors, and standardized ways of using typography in advertising, packaging, product identification, publications, letterheads, and other printed materials. Such firms as IBM, Olivetti, Knoll International, Amtrak, and many airlines have developed highly successful identity programs that tie in with the interiors that serve these organizations. A strong identity program should be recognized and supported in interior design work. In projects where no such program exists, the designer may propose the establishment of such a coordinated graphic effort. In a restaurant, for example, a theme that gives the venture its character and style can be carried through signage, menus, ashtrays, matchbooks, and other materials that can be designed in relation to the forms and colors dominant in the interior itself.

Large-scale graphic elements that cover entire wall surfaces present an additional technique that can help to set character, guide circulation, and relieve monotony. Such decoration when introduced a few years ago came to be called *super graphics* and threatened to become something of a fad. But viewed as a tool of the designer, along with the use of artworks, accessories, and the more standard elements of functional interior design, such large-scale graphics are appropriate when they serve clearly defined purposes effectively and economically. When a project calls for extensive signage and other graphic elements, designers specializing in the field can be employed as consultants.

13.26 Signs and other graphic elements have a central role in many contract interiors. The drawing here illustrates the various kinds of signage that may be required to communicate essential information.

14.1

Chapter

Fourteen

Technical Matters

Generally, the interior designer will not have to deal with excessively demanding technical issues in the course of most projects. Many residential and other smaller projects hardly make any technical demands at all. Larger and more complex projects may introduce issues of some importance. While the architect, engineer, and contractors will probably be responsible for resolving these, the interior designer should have a good general knowledge of technical fields, as an aid in talking with these and other professionals and consultants and as a basis for handling the impact these matters have on interiors.

The term *mechanical systems* describes aspects of building technology of major importance. These are the electrical, plumbing, and *HVAC* (heating, ventilation, and air-conditioning) systems. Lighting, a primary technical problem closely associated with interior design, has been covered in Chapter 10. Other technical matters relating to acoustics, safety and security, and communications are discussed here.

Typically, the interior designer faces such technical questions as: Can a new sink be provided here? Can this bathroom be relocated? Can a new bath be added here? Is the electrical service adequate for the new lighting and the appliances? Can the ducts be concealed? These questions may require consultation with specialized experts for firm answers, but a good sense of what such problems involve and of what questions to ask and of whom is an important part of the designer's special skills. The interior designer often acts as a liaison between the architect, mechanical engineer, or contractor and the client.

HVAC

Heating, ventilation, and air-conditioning are the mechanical systems that provide thermal comfort within buildings. The factors that influence bodily comfort are air temperature (the most obvious and easily measured element), humidity level, radiation to or from nearby surfaces, and the movement of air. In addition, good air quality is dependent on HVAC performance. Cleanliness of air and absence of objectionable odors, smoke, and fumes affect both comfort and health.

Human body temperature must be maintained within a narrow range to sustain normal functioning. When body heat is lost to cold surroundings, discomfort is felt in a way that everyone has experienced at one time or another (fig. 14.2). Replacing heat loss is a primary function of HVAC systems. The four ways in which heat can be provided are as follows (fig. 14.3):

CONVECTION. Warmed air conveys heat and warms whatever it touches—objects and human bodies alike. A thermometer measures air temperature and is the most familiar indicator of the thermal comfort level within a space.

RADIATION. Heat energy can be transmitted directly as a form of radiant energy. Heat from the sun reaches the earth in this way. Even with a cold ambient air surround, the human body can be warmed by radiation—a familiar experience in bright sunlight on a cold day. Radiant heat can be supplied by many small, portable heaters and by systems of floor or panel heating that have little effect on air temperature but still maintain body comfort. A reverse effect occurs when cold surfaces cause body heat to radiate outward, as when a cold glass window surface creates sensations of chill even when air temperature is adequate.

CONDUCTION. When a cooler mass contacts one that is warmer, heat flows from the warmer to the cooler mass. Touching a cold surface chills the body part making contact. Bare feet on a cold floor, or hands resting on cold metal or stone surfaces, allow body heat to escape. Contact with a warm surface provides heat to the contacting body. A hot-water bottle or a warm bath provides heat by conduction.

14.1 Air-conditioning ducts—the large tubes visible in the upper portion of this photograph—are normally concealed above dropped ceilings, but in High Tech designs they are often exposed, even painted in strong colors, to become interior design details, as in the Columbus Occupational Health Center in Columbus, Indiana, designed by Hardy Holzman Pfeiffer Associates. (Photograph: © Norman McGrath)

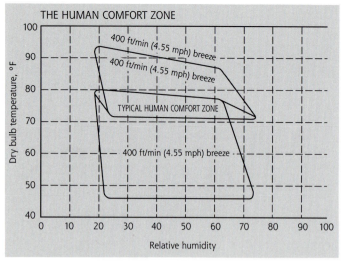

400 ft/min (4.55 mph) breeze
400 ft/min (4.55 mph) breeze
TYPICAL HUMAN COMFORT ZONE
400 ft/min (4.55 mph) breeze

Dry bulb temperature, °F

Relative humidity

14.2

EVAPORATION. This method of heat transfer is effective in removing excess heat rather than in supplying heat. Cooling results as moisture is evaporated from surfaces of the human body. Sweating is a natural means of dissipating heat through evaporation. The level of humidity in the air limits the degree of evaporation that can take place. The discomforts of a hot, humid day relate to the inability of humid air to allow enough evaporation to carry off excess body heat. Evaporative cooling is the basis for the refrigeration used to remove heat for summer air-conditioning.

Cooling is the direct opposite of heating, with the same methods of heat transfer operating in reverse. *Convection* provides cooler air to carry off excess heat. *Conduction* similarly carries off heat through contact with cooler surfaces. *Radiation* of body heat to cool surfaces is also a means of reducing excess levels of heat, while reduction of humidity favors *evaporative cooling*.

The HVAC systems in general use can be considered separately.

Heating Systems

Heating systems are essential in all buildings in any but tropical climates. The interior designer is generally concerned only with the visible elements that deliver heat—radiators, convectors, registers, outlet grilles, and ducts or pipes. These must either be concealed or treated to minimize their effect on the interior design. The common heating systems are:

HOT WATER OR STEAM. In these systems a boiler heats water that is circulated through pipes to the spaces to be heated. Hot-water heating may use a one-pipe system in which water is fed to a single pipe that connects to each radiator or convector unit, a two-pipe system in which separate pipes supply heated water and return the water to the boiler, or a loop system in which the heated water flows through interconnected radiators in a continuous ring (fig. 14.4). One- and two-pipe systems permit individual control of each radiator by valves. Air is heated as it passes over the radiators naturally or as it is blown over

the radiator pipes by blowers in "fan-coil" units placed as needed. Steam heating is similar except that the boiler raises water temperature to a level that generates steam, which is piped to radiators. As the steam cools, it condenses into water and is returned to the boiler by gravity. Radiators or convectors (similar to radiators), are usually located under windows or in baseboards (see fig. 14.15). The concerns are to conceal them with covers of inoffensive appearance, as well as concealing the pipes connected to them.

WARM (OR "HOT") AIR. Such systems require a furnace in which air is passed over a heating unit that warms the air to a temperature controlled by one or more thermostats. A fan blows the heated air through ducts to the spaces to be heated. In older hot-air systems, the heated air rose naturally, without a fan, and returned to the furnace as it cooled and dropped downward (fig. 14.5). Control of temperatures in various rooms was difficult with such gravity systems.

In modern systems, ducts are sized to deliver suitable quantities of heated air to outlet grilles or registers (openings to admit air) in floors, baseboards, or ceilings. Concealment with covers of satisfactory appearance of these outlets is a primary concern. Ducts serving the outlets must also be placed in concealed or unobjectionable locations. When air-conditioning is also provided, heated and cooled air are usually circulated through the same duct and outlet systems. When a suspended ceiling is used, the space above the ceiling (called a *plenum*) may be used to distribute air to supply grilles or may be used to return air to the furnace by means of return grilles and ducts Doors of individual rooms may incorporate vent grilles or be *undercut* (cut short of

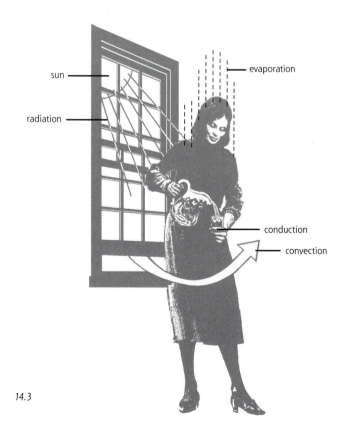

sun
radiation
evaporation
conduction
convection

14.3

14.2 The relationship between temperature, humidity, air movement, and radiation establishes a limited range of conditions under which human comfort is assured.

14.3 Heat and cold move from one medium to another in four ways, as this schematic drawing shows. Conduction transfers heat and cold through direct contact with a physical object. Convection involves transfer through the atmosphere by means of air currents. Evaporation, a cooling process, occurs when moisture vaporizes. Radiation is heat transfer through space.

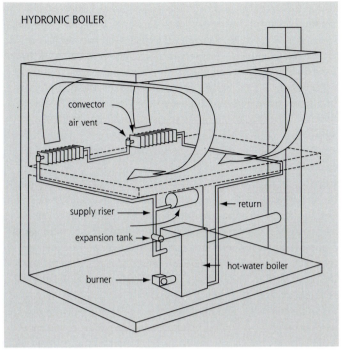

HYDRONIC BOILER

convector
air vent
supply riser
expansion tank
return
hot-water boiler
burner

14.4

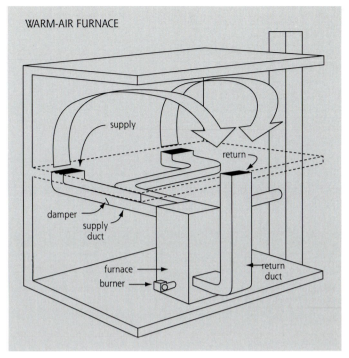

WARM-AIR FURNACE

supply
return
damper
supply duct
furnace
burner
return duct

14.5

the floor by an inch or two) to permit air to move through corridors or open spaces to large return grilles, thus avoiding the need for a separate return from each room.

Warm-air systems can provide controlled humidity along with heating and, since they share ductwork and outlets with air-conditioning, offer simplicity and certain economies as compared to totally separate heating and air-conditioning systems. The sound of air passing through supply grilles and, if it is close by, the sound of the circulating fan may create objectionable background noise, particularly if the fan operates intermittently. Recirculation of air can be a troublesome source of indoor air pollution if filtration and cleaning of returned air is inadequate. Fresh air drawn from outside should be added to recirculated air to improve air quality.

Ducts, grilles, and furnace can all be eliminated through the use of electric heat provided by baseboard or wall units in each heated space (fig. 14.6). Individual room thermostats provide good local control. However, in most locations, the high cost of electrical energy as compared to other fuels makes electric heating costly and, when air-conditioning is also required, a savings in ducts and outlets cannot be realized.

RADIANT HEATING. These systems use pipes carrying heated water or electric heating wires embedded in floors, walls, or ceilings, resulting in few visible elements. However, they make more specific demands in terms of material choices. The heat-supply elements must be fixed in materials that conduct well (embedded in plaster or concrete; placed under stone, brick, or tile) and must not be blocked by elements that act as insulators. For example, rugs absorb heat from a radiant-heated floor, reducing effectiveness.

Radiant heating is often used as the backup system for solar heating (which is another form of radiant heat). The same surfaces that conduct radiant heat can be used to absorb solar heat by day and radiate it back at night. Floors are particularly suited to working in this way since sunlight normally falls on them.

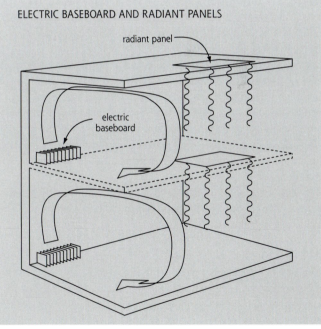

ELECTRIC BASEBOARD AND RADIANT PANELS

radiant panel
electric baseboard

14.6

14.4 A forced hot water (or hydronic boiler) system uses heated water circulating through pipes and convectors to deliver heat.

14.5 A warm-air system heats air in a furnace and circulates it through ducts with the aid of a blower. The ducts also return cooled air to the furnace.

14.6 Electric heating converts electric power into heat and then delivers it either through baseboard units that warm the air or by direct radiation from panels in ceilings or walls. Electric heat is clean and convenient but generally costly, depending on local electricity rates.

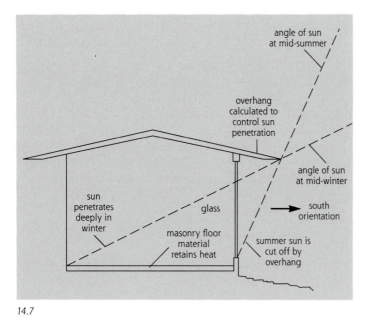

14.7

SOLAR HEATING. This requires some basic architectural involvement in terms of orientation, the size and placement of windows and over-hangs, and the choices of interior materials for floors and, in some systems, for ceilings.

Passive solar heating does not use mechanical equipment. Sun heat enters through windows and heats interior surfaces, primarily floors (fig. 14.7). In some systems, special blinds reflect the heat up to ceilings, where heat-absorbing panels are placed. The heated surfaces radiate heat back into the space, keeping occupants comfortable, and store heat so that the surfaces continue to radiate at night and on dark days (fig. 14.11). A backup heating system, either radiant or conventional, is needed to provide additional heat when solar radiation is insufficient (in very cold weather or during protracted cloudy or stormy periods).

Active solar heating uses sun heat to heat air or water in collector elements. The heated air or water is then circulated by mechanical fans or pumps to deliver heat when and where it is needed. The circulating medium also heats a storage medium (a tank of liquid or, in some systems, a mass of stones), which radiates heat back into the system when solar output is insufficient. The same mechanical system that circulates the radiant heat is also used to distribute backup heat provided by a conventional fuel.

The fuel used for any of the nonsolar heat systems is usually chosen on an economic basis and has no significant influence on interior design considerations.

Ventilation

Ventilation is essential to provide fresh air to replace air made stale by smoking, cooking, and the bodily functions (primarily breathing) of human occupants, as well as to remove pollen, dust, and odors. In the past, the opening of windows and, perhaps, doors and the air leaks of ordinary construction generally provided adequate ventilation of all but totally internal (windowless) spaces. Modern warm-air heating and air-conditioning systems can provide fresh air and filter recirculated air. With other systems, separate mechanical ventilation may be required. Windowless interior spaces always need some provision for ventilation. This is usually a legal requirement for interior bathrooms, but other spaces may need smoke vents or other such arrangements involving ducts and fans (fig. 14.8). Meeting and conference rooms and places where many people gather are especially in need of ventilation. The interior designer must remember to address ventilation needs in the design (fig. 14.9).

Air-Conditioning

This has become a widely demanded comfort, particularly in areas where summer heat tends to be a problem. The term describes systems that provide cooling, controlled humidification (or dehumidification, as required), and air filtration and purification. Many modern buildings are windowless or have sealed windows, making mechanical air-conditioning essential.

The cooling function of air-conditioning systems is provided by mechanical refrigeration, which removes heat from the conditioned spaces and discharges it to the outside in the form of warmed air or water. Water, chilled at a central unit, can be passed through pipes to units distributed through the served spaces where fans blow air over the cooled pipes to provide cooled air. Other systems circulate air over coils carrying cooled water or refrigerants at a central location and then distribute the cooled air through ducts to outlet grilles in the same way that warm air is distributed in cold weather. Dehumidification of the cooled air is an important aspect of establishing reasonable comfort levels since excess humidity is often associated with the excessive heat of summer climates.

Built-in systems, which normally provide central locations for machinery, require only that the designer place the outlet ducts in inconspicuous locations and consider how to handle the return of exhaust air to the system. As in warm-air heating systems, the built-in systems often call for doors with either vents or undercuts to permit air to pass along corridors toward return air grilles. Supply outlets can often be provided as part of ceiling light fixtures described as *air-handling* or can be incorporated into many ceiling systems. Ducts, often large and intrusive, need to be concealed (usually above hung ceilings), unless the designer chooses to expose and treat them as part of the interior design (see fig. 14.1). Such exposed ducts are often prominent in High Tech interiors.

Providing air-conditioning on a room-by-room basis is often the only practical means in older buildings or for projects with a limited budget. Window or under-window units are common, but larger *cabinet units* are sometimes better for such medium-sized spaces as shops, restaurants, or small offices. Finding suitable, unobtrusive locations is a planning responsibility.

While the details of air-conditioning systems are best left to experienced engineers, the interior designer must often act as coordinator in determining how the requirements for space, electrical service, water supply, and duct layout will be accommodated. This involves superim-

14.7 Passive solar heating requires large glass areas facing south and carefully planned overhanging shading. The shading must be placed to permit rays of the low winter sun to enter the space but to block rays from the higher summer sun.

posing proposed layouts for the various systems on one plan drawing (and often in sections as well) to make sure that there is space for each system without any conflict. Lowered (*furred down*) ceilings (fig. 14.10), enlarged columns, thickened walls, and vertical pipe chases are the usual means for providing hidden space for these necessities. Suppliers of equipment often offer technical design services; however, except in the most minimal of projects, the designer must be careful to evaluate such self-serving advice. A better system for less money can often be developed by an independent expert who has no interest in promoting a particular product or brand.

HVAC equipment, when concealed in walls, floors, or ceilings, usually requires access panels located to permit adjustment and repair without breaking into fixed construction. Many suspended ceiling systems provide for access at any point, but access at other locations must be planned for with coordination between mechanical engineering and interior design.

Energy Supply for HVAC

All HVAC systems consume energy. Furnaces and boilers are generally fueled by *oil* or *gas*. *Coal*, in common use in the past, has become obsolete because of the inconvenience of delivery, storage, ash removal, and the air pollutants it creates when burned. *Wood* is used in fireplaces and stoves, primarily for its aesthetic appeal; in rural locations where it is in plentiful supply, however, it also serves as an auxiliary energy source. Wood burning, because it creates air pollutants, is unsuitable for use as a substantial energy source in urban or suburban areas. Although in most locations *electricity* is more costly than oil or gas, the majority of modern systems use it to power the fans and compressors needed for cooling. Electric heat may be considered wherever electric rates are low or where heating is required only for limited time periods, as in warm climates.

Geothermal heat drawn from warm water pumped from deep wells can provide energy, but the high cost of pumping water and extracting the available heat has limited its use. The mechanism known as a *heat pump* uses a compressor to provide cooling in summer and can be reversed to provide winter warmth by extracting heat from outside air or from geothermal sources. In most climates a heat pump can deal with summer cooling with efficiency comparable to other systems, but in cooler climates backup heating, in the form of direct electrical heating (with its attendant costs), is necessary whenever winter temperatures fall to levels of 32 degrees and below.

Solar energy, as used in the solar-heating systems described above, is an economical and appealing possibility currently being used in a variety of systems. The need for large solar collectors and for backup systems for use when solar heating is insufficient, as well as the problems of using solar energy for summer cooling, are all difficulties that have limited the application of solar systems. Active solar systems require fans and/or pumps driven by electricity. Although a fully solar system would generate this power from solar-energy cells or from generators powered by solar energy, such systems remain experimental or even theoretical.

ELECTRICAL SYSTEMS

Modern buildings provide electrical service as required for HVAC equipment, vertical transportation, lighting, and incidental appliances and equipment. Older buildings often have obsolete wiring and inadequate service for modern needs, requiring updating or replacement of their electrical systems. Power is distributed from utility companies as high-voltage alternating current and is reduced to service voltage by transformers that may be located out-of-doors to serve a number of smaller buildings or, in larger buildings, may be located in a basement or other unobtrusive location. A meter and main switch are provided at a panel where fuses or circuit breakers are provided for the separate circuits that serve various parts of the building system. In larger buildings circuit-breaker panels are provided close to the locations that they serve, on each floor of a building, for example, or at several locations on each floor.

Power is further distributed through two or three wire feeders with insulated wires enclosed in conduits or raceways as required for safety under strict code regulations. Rigid metal conduit provides the best protection for building wiring. The flexible metal conduit known as BX makes installation easier because of its flexibility, but it is not permitted under many city codes. A flexible plastic cable known as Romex can be used in residential buildings of three stories or less where local codes permit.

Although wiring is generally concealed in walls, floors, or ceilings, it can also be run in exposed conduits, in flat, floor-level conductors, or in raceways provided in many modern office-furniture systems (fig. 14.12). Wiring for lighting, convenience outlets, and equipment is furnished in separate circuits, with each circuit limited to 20 amps (2,400 watts for the usual 120-volt current). Higher-voltage circuits to serve special equipment (electric stoves, dryers, and mechanical equipment) are also supplied separately. In some large installations of fluorescent lighting, 277-volt current is used for its increased efficiency, requiring additional special circuitry.

The interior designer's involvement in electrical systems includes establishing the requirements for which the mechanical engineers must plan and coordinating the relationship of electrical equipment with HVAC systems and with other interior elements, such as suspended ceilings.

Some electrical details that may fall to the interior designer include the placement of switches, outlets, and circuit-breaker panels; the selection of dimmers, proximity switches, and other special controls; and the appearance of outlets, switch controls, and plates. Code requirements usually specify that convenience outlets be spaced no more than twelve feet apart and must be supplied somewhere on each wall surface where furniture could be located. Computer equipment generally calls for *dedicated circuits*, that is, circuits that serve no other purpose so as to prevent interference that might disturb function. Circuits located in places where dangerous shock hazards can occur, such as in bathrooms or outdoor locations where water pipes or damp earth can provide grounding, require protection by a ground-fault interrupter (GFI). This is a device that cuts off power in case of grounding to limit fire or shock hazards.

Emergency lighting is a code requirement in commercial and institutional buildings. It is intended to furnish sufficient light to permit a safe exit in the event of a general power failure. A one-footcandle light level at floor height is usually stipulated along with light in corridors and stairs and illumination of exit signs. Emergency lighting must use separate circuitry and an independent power source. Telephone and other low-voltage electrical systems, such as intercoms and fire-detection and security systems, also need separate wiring provisions, built-in whenever possible to avoid surface wiring that may be unsightly.

Designers must be familiar with the electrical symbols used on plans and understand how to read wiring diagrams that show the locations of fixtures, outlets, and switches, as well as the functions of switches.

(The standard symbols used are shown in Appendix 3.) In plan diagrams, dotted lines show the relation of switches to the fixtures they control. Studying a few such diagrams will make their meaning fairly clear. Complex wiring diagrams may seem confusing at first glance, but they are different only in the larger number of devices and circuits that they show. By simply following each symbol and line methodically, they can be understood quite readily (fig. 14.13).

Energy Consumption

This issue relates to both HVAC and electrical matters. All electrical uses consume energy at a cost that can be determined from the rate schedules of the local electric company. The primary uses of electrical energy

14.8

14.8 A large window fan provides ventilation, removes cooking odors generated in this open loft kitchen, and acts as a decorative element as well in a New York loft by architect Michael S. Wu. (Photograph: Antoine Bootz)

14.9

in buildings are the lighting and air-conditioning systems and, when electric heat is used, the heating system as well. Electric lighting not only consumes energy directly, it also generates heat as an unwanted by-product, calling for additional air-conditioning in summer. The heat from lighting can reduce winter heating costs, but this positive factor cannot begin to offset the greater burden of the summer heat load. The other primary energy cost is for winter heating fuel.

Energy consumption was not considered an important issue until the price of energy in all forms climbed in the 1960s and 1970s and set off a movement toward energy conservation. Then it became of major significance in larger projects and of more limited concern in smaller, residential, and similar projects. Reducing lighting to reasonable levels and placing it only where needed, a return to the use of available daylight wherever possible, and design that minimizes winter heating and summer cooling loads all help to keep energy costs down. Good insulation and the sealing of windows and other openings can reduce energy requirements, but they call for extra concern for ventilation and filtration to ensure that the air quality remains satisfactory. The interior designer has an obligation to review all of these matters and to make sure that experts and uninformed clients do not arrive at systems that appear to be efficient and practical but instead introduce troublesome problems.

14.10

14.9 Air-supply inlet grilles—the square, louvered units in the ceiling—are standard products widely used in HVAC installations. In this 1980 cafeteria in Ferris Booth Hall, Columbia University, New York, by Robert A. M. Stern Architects, the normally unobtrusive design of the grilles pleasingly echoes the four-sided lighting clusters atop the columns. (Photograph: Ed Stoecklein)

14.10 A ceiling provides acoustical absorption and houses architectural lighting and air-conditioning outlets, while the hollow space above conceals wiring, ductwork, piping, and other mechanical and structural elements. The suspended ceiling is designed to facilitate access. (Photograph courtesy USG Interiors, Inc.)

14.11

14.11 Architect Marlys Hann installed large glass panels in the bathroom of her 1985 home in New York's Catskill Mountains to create a passive solar heat trap. The bathroom receives the sun's heat by day, retaining it in the tiled areas to reduce nighttime energy consumption. (Photograph: © Paul Warchol)

Table 20. Electrical Basics

AMPERE (abbreviated to amp). The unit of measurement of the magnitude of an electrical current. The higher the amperage requirement of any device, the more current it will use.

VOLT. The unit of pressure (intensity) of electric current. In the United States, 115–120 volts is the standard. Heavy-duty appliances, including stoves, air-conditioners, and other machinery, require a 220-volt current, separately wired.

WATT. The unit of power that results when a device uses a certain amperage at a particular voltage. Electrical devices carry a wattage rating that is based on

their ampere requirement at the standard voltage. Electricity is sold on the basis of wattage consumed in relation to time. A device that requires 1,000 watts (1 kilowatt) when used for one hour will consume one kilowatt-hour (KWH). An electric meter measures KWH consumed so that the utility company can bill on this basis.

ELECTRICAL WIRING is normally planned to carry 1,200 to 1,320 watts in one circuit, or wiring loop. The total combined wattages of the devices connected in one circuit cannot exceed this maximum. A fuse or circuit breaker is provided for each circuit to protect

it against an overload, which could cause overheating or fire. Groups of circuits are supplied by heavier wires or copper bars (called busbars), which are, in turn, protected by larger fuses or circuit breakers.

LOW-VOLTAGE (most often 12-volt) SERVICE is used for smaller electrical devices, such as bells and buzzers, and for some types of lamps (bulbs). A transformer is needed to convert normal voltage to the required low voltage. Since batteries deliver low voltages, a transformer is used when a battery device (such as a radio or tape recorder) is to be connected to regular power outlets.

14.12

PLUMBING SYSTEMS

The third of the major mechanical systems of buildings, plumbing systems supply water to baths, kitchens, other sinks, water coolers, and any other situations that require water and, at the same time, provide drains from the same locations for wastewater and sewage. Architects and engineers design building plumbing systems. The role of interior designers in selecting and locating fixtures is covered in Chapter 16. In addition, an interior designer should have some basic knowledge of how plumbing systems are arranged, since this influences decisions about relocating fixtures and moving or providing new baths, kitchens, or other facilities using water, including washer-dryer installations, wet bars, and darkrooms (fig. 14.14).

In most buildings, hot and cold water is supplied by a pressure system geared to the planned number of occupants and use of the building. This usually covers all demands except for the type of air-conditioning equipment that consumes water for cooling. In most

localities, because of concern with conserving water, the consumption of water for air-conditioning is not permitted. However, systems that recirculate the water, since they do not add a major demand for water, present no problem. In older buildings, clogged pipes often reduce the available water supply, a problem that can be solved only by replacing the affected pipes.

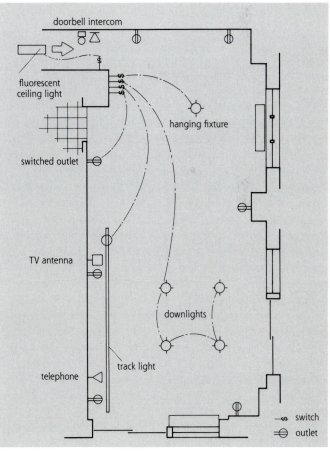

14.13

14.12 Placing such standard office equipment as telephones, computer terminals, desktop electronic devices, and task lighting together can result in an unsightly tangle of dangling wires. Many modern office systems provide neat, unobtrusive, and accessible locations for wiring—such as this trough at the rear of an office desk. (Photograph courtesy Steelcase, Inc.)

14.13 A floor plan with electrical outlet and switch locations uses the standard electrical symbols. The curving lines connect switch indicators with the outlets they are to control.

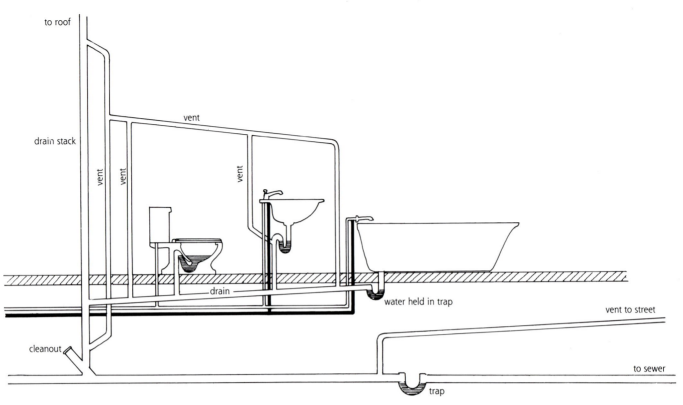

to roof

vent

drain stack

vent

vent

vent

water held in trap

drain

vent to street

cleanout

to sewer

trap

14.14

Since water is supplied under pressure and supply pipes are quite small, it is normally fairly easy to supply water to new locations. *Risers,* the vertical lines of pipes running upward through a building from the basement, must be located (they are usually found adjacent to existing baths or kitchens) and then connected to the new pipes, which run horizontally to the new fixtures. The new pipes may be concealed by running them in walls, under floors, above ceilings, or in specially built enclosures. Since drainpipes pose more difficulties, they will most often determine when and where new *wet facilities* can be provided. Drains use not pressure but gravity to steer waste downward to the pipes leading to a sewer or other disposal arrangement. Therefore, drainpipes must always slope downhill. Drains from basins and sinks need only slope down at a gentle angle, but the large soil pipes serving toilets must slope sharply to discourage clogging. New facilities must be placed close enough to vertical existing drains to make the required down slope possible without damage to spaces below the intended location. The vertical drain that carries wastewater from sinks and washbasins is called a *waste stack* and is normally two or three inches in diameter. A drain carrying human wastes is a *soil stack* and must have an inside diameter of four inches, making it too large to fit within the thickness of a normal partition wall. It must run within a special vertical shaft called a *pipe chase* or through a partition of extra thickness.

Many people fail to realize that drains are also connected to upward stacks that must be carried up through the roof of a building. The stack is part of a safeguarding system that begins with a *trap* at each fixture. The trap holds water in such a way as to form a seal, preventing gases present in drainage pipes from entering living spaces and bringing objectionable odors. Beyond each trap, there must be a *vent* that prevents suction from pulling water out of the trap and that carries gases up and out to the air at roof level. Just as drains angle downward to a vertical stack, vents must angle upward and connect to the same stack as it travels up to the roof. This means that every drain location must allow for the provision (and concealment) of these upward vents without disturbing the spaces *above* it. In a single-story building, it is usually practical to provide water and drainage in almost any location, but in a multistory building, the impact of plumbing changes on spaces above and below can be significant. In tall buildings, it may be out of the question to install pipes, drains, and vents in a new location because of the need to pass pipes through spaces that may be occupied by other tenants or owners. In any case, even when possible, it may be prohibitively expensive.

The interior designer may have to turn to an architect, engineer, or plumbing contractor to arrive at a firm conclusion about whether a certain plumbing change will be easy, possible but difficult (and therefore costly), or virtually impossible, but the designer will find it useful to be able to make a reliable preliminary judgment. In general, it is easiest to locate new fixtures adjacent to walls where pipes already exist, that is, next to existing fixtures; close to pipe chases; or, in large buildings of steel- or concrete-frame construction, close to *wet columns,* structural

14.14 *Plumbing concerns water supply and drainage. Every drain requires a trap, a curved section of drainpipe that always holds water which prevents the backflow of sewer gases and their offensive odors. Every trap also requires a vent, a pipe leading to the open air, usually at roof level, so that a rush of water down the drainpipe does not create suction and pull the water out of the trap. A typical bathroom requires drainpipes and traps for each fixture, as well as vent pipes connected to the drain stack that extends upward to the roof. Unlike drains and vents, which work by gravity and normal air circulation, water-supply pipes are under pressure and can be placed virtually wherever they are needed.*

columns that have an added space for pipes. Piping locations are sometimes difficult to identify on site, but building plans will show them very clearly.

Fire-safety equipment calls for additional plumbing installations. Codes require that taller buildings (whose upper floors cannot be reached easily by fire-company equipment) have various systems to make water available wherever a fire might occur. A *standpipe* system uses a large main pipe that leads to hose cabinets located on each floor, so that a hose can reach any point on that particular floor. The standpipe is filled with city water and may also be connected with a roof-level water tank. Another connection to the standpipe is located on the outside of the building, where fire fighters can connect a hose to supply additional water under pressure from fire hydrants and a pumper fire engine.

Sprinkler systems, however, provide even more effective fire protection since they are fully automatic. Large main pipes are connected to smaller pipes that feed sprinkler heads located at or near ceiling level. In case of fire, heat causes a sprinkler head to release and spray water over the area it covers. Sprinkler systems in larger buildings also provide an outside connection (with two inlets and thus called a *siamese* connection) for fire-company pumpers in case the building water system is inadequate to control a larger fire. An outside (and usually also inside local) shutoff valve can be used to stop the flow of water after a fire has been extinguished. Sprinkler release causes a drop in water pressure in the system that sets off an alarm to a local fire company, facilitating prompt fire fighting and sprinkler shutoff, ideally before major water damage occurs. Sprinkler systems provide the best available fire protection for larger buildings. Modern sprinkler heads of reasonably neat and unobtrusive design are available. Placing the heads to satisfy code requirements (see page 427) and coordinating their locations and piping with other equipment are part of the interior designer's task.

Plumbing systems are subject to strict legal regulation. Plans and diagrams must be filed for approval for any significant plumbing work, which must be carried out by licensed contractors and inspected and approved when completed. Such work can entail high costs, surprising to many clients who have never had extensive plumbing work done before. Finally, it should be mentioned that since, unfortunately, all plumbing is subject to the possibility of leaks, access for repairs must be provided. This can be done by building access panels or locating pipes in closets or other semihidden spaces. This possibility also calls for judgment to avoid locating pipes above places where a leak could cause unusually costly or troublesome damage. Plumbers and engineers may not think of such issues, but a designer will be wise to point out any such problematic situations to a client.

ACOUSTICS

Although not a building system, acoustics can present several technical problems that have direct bearing on interior design. Major acoustical problems may call for the services of specialized consultants, but most can be dealt with by the interior designer quite simply through planning and material selection.

The common acoustical problems are of several types. They concern excessive noise levels; the transmission of noise from one space to another; guarding the privacy of individual spaces; maintaining the intelligibility of speech in relation to background noise; providing suitable background noise in certain situations; and, in the case of auditoriums and larger meeting rooms, the qualities that give the characteristics described as *good acoustics*.

Excessive Noise

Excessive noise can be disturbing in spaces where many people are present and involved in sound-producing activities. Offices, restaurants and cafeterias, and factory production spaces commonly present noise problems. The best way to limit general, ambient noise is through interior design decisions. Sound-absorbing materials for floors, walls, ceilings, and even furniture contribute greatly to reducing noise levels. Taken together, they will most often deal with noise problems at anything less than factory-machinery levels. Hard surfaces such as tile floors, plaster walls or ceilings, and glass and metal surfaces not only reflect noise, they may even generate excess noise as feet and chairs scrape on floors or dishes and silver rattle on tabletops.

Soft and absorbent materials include carpet or rugs for floors, fabric upholstery and drapery, mats or linens on tabletops, and various special acoustical materials for walls and ceilings. Since floors and ceilings are usually the largest surface areas of a space, they become target areas for noise control. Carpeted floors have become widely accepted in offices and even in schools and hospitals largely because of their effectiveness in reducing noise levels. Various ceiling tiles and ceiling systems (fig. 14.16) offer noise reduction to a level of efficiency indicated by a numerical rating called a noise reduction coefficient, or NRC (see Table 21). Some of these acoustical materials, such as the least expensive tiles, are unattractive, but many products of good appearance are now available. Another way to reduce noise levels is to identify major sources of noise (for example, typewriters or printers in an office) and place them in an isolated location or furnish some local sound control, such as an acoustic housing.

Residential spaces rarely need any noise-level controls beyond the carpeting and upholstery that will normally be present. A space with hardwood or tile floors and large glass areas, especially in combination, may warrant the introduction of rugs, wall hangings, or some other absorbent surface to improve its acoustical quality.

Transmitted Noise

Noise transmission from one space to another can be a source of annoyance and distraction. Traffic noise from outside, conversation from an adjacent bedroom, office, or hotel room, piano practice from upstairs, and the sounds from a nearby elevator or bathroom are frequent causes for complaint. Unfortunately, the problems of transmitted noise are more difficult to cope with than noise generated within a space. Despite their common use, acoustical materials on walls or ceilings give little improvement.

The easiest solutions to transmitted sound lie in prevention—through basic building structure and layout and planning decisions (fig. 14.17). Massive, heavy building materials, such as thick masonry or concrete

14.15

Table 21. Noise Reduction Coefficients (NRCs)

An NRC rating is a single number indicating the effectiveness of a material in absorbing sound. With a range from 1.00 to .00, an NRC of .99 would indicate almost total absorption, .01 virtually none. The higher the NRC of a particular material, the more effectively it will absorb sound.

Material	NRC
Bare concrete floor	.05
Tile or linoleum on concrete	.05
Carpet (¹/₈" pile)	.15
Carpet (¹/₄" pile)	.25
Carpet (⁷/₁₆" pile)	.40
Plaster ceiling	.45
Metal pan acoustic ceiling	.60
Partition system surfaces	.55–.80 (.60 typical)
Carpet over padding	up to .65
Acoustical ceiling systems	up to .90

walls, and heavy floor and ceiling construction are the best defenses against sound transmission (see Tables 21 and 22), but interior design usually has little input into such matters. Failing this, double-wall construction, with separate studs for each side and insulation material packed in between, or building a false wall adjacent to but isolated from an existing wall can be useful in dealing with noise from plumbing, elevators, or a noisy neighbor. Radio studios are sometimes built as complete rooms within an outer shell with walls, floors, and ceiling all isolated on rubber cushions, but such a drastic step can rarely be justified or afforded in normal usage.

Double or triple glazing for windows, gaskets at the edges of doors or *sound-lock* double doors, and acoustical treatment inside ductwork can also help to prevent sound transmission. Unfortunately, sound transmission through floors is particularly difficult to eliminate. Carpet and under-carpet padding in the space that is the source of the sound may be of some help, but when the source space is occupied by another tenant or owner, it may not be possible to arrange. Ceiling treatment, such as replacing a ceiling with a hung ceiling with insulation above, may reduce sound levels but cannot totally eliminate the offensive sound.

Sound transmission between spaces can be controlled by planning. Potential sources of loud sounds should be located well away from

14.15 The lighting and acoustic qualities of this 1984 New York media room conceived for video and audio monitoring must meet the standards set by the complex technical equipment. Note the neat design of the radiator enclosure at lower right. The design was done by Bromley/Jacobsen Designs for Kips Bay Decorator Show House, New York City. (Photograph: Jaime Ardiles-Arce)

14.16

Table 22. Sound Transmission Class (STC) Values)

The STC rating of a particular assembly (such as a wall, partition, or screen) is a single number that indicates effectiveness in preventing sound transmission. The higher the STC value, the more effectively the assembly blocks sound transmission.

MATERIAL	STC
³⁄₁₆" plywood	19
Open-plan furniture screen panel (typical)	21
¼" Plexiglas sheet	27
⅝" gypsum wallboard	27
22-gauge steel plate	29
Wood 2" X 4" stud partition	35–39
Staggered stud partition	45
6" concrete block wall	46
Steel stud partition with two layers of wallboard each side	55

spaces where quiet is desired. Bedrooms should not be placed next to TV or recreation rooms. Plumbing should be isolated or adjacent to the space it serves. Corridors and closets can act as sound buffers between spaces (adjacent bedrooms or offices, for example; fig. 14.18). Music practice rooms need to be remote from classrooms or offices. This applies to vertical as well as to horizontal adjacency. A piano in a room above a bedroom can be as much of a problem as in an adjacent space on the same level. Fortunately, noise does not transmit upward as readily as downward, but amplified music, television, or stereo may still be audible from a space below. Control through ceiling or floor treatment is usually inadequate.

Overheard Speech

In spaces that are generally quiet, such as private offices or bedrooms, another problem may develop: overhearing of intelligible speech in an adjacent space. This can be controlled by separating the spaces with partitions or a wall of solid (or double and insulated) construction and carefully plugging "sound leaks" around doors or through ducts, but, again, avoiding adjacency or using buffers such as closets works better. Fear of being overheard, a particular concern in doctors' consulting rooms, lawyers' private offices, and some business offices and meeting rooms where confidential conversations may take place, is the reverse of this problem, to which the same techniques for control apply.

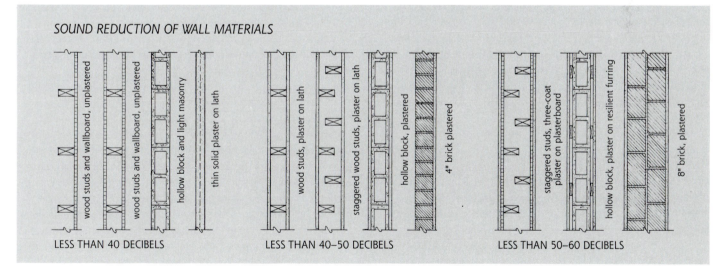

SOUND REDUCTION OF WALL MATERIALS

wood studs and wallboard, unplastered / wood studs and wallboard, unplastered / hollow block and light masonry / thin solid plaster on lath

LESS THAN 40 DECIBELS

wood studs, plaster on lath / staggered wood studs, plaster on lath / hollow block, plastered / 4" brick plastered

LESS THAN 40–50 DECIBELS

staggered studs, three-coat plaster on plasterboard / hollow block, plaster on resilient furring / 8" brick, plastered

LESS THAN 50–60 DECIBELS

14.17

14.16 Sound-absorbent ceiling material is usually in the form of tiles, from 1 foot square to 2 by 4 feet. These, and the metal ribs that support them, make up a ceiling system that may also include light fixtures and air-conditioning outlets in a dimensionally coordinated assembly. The installation shown is typical of systems selected for offices, healthcare facilities, and similar spaces. (Photograph: Bob Shimer, Hedrich-Blessing, courtesy USG Acoustical Products Company)

14.17 How partition walls are constructed determines how effectively they acoustically isolate the spaces on each side. It is hard to achieve perfect acoustical separation, but materials and methods can be rated in terms of an STC (Sound Transmission Class) factor (see Table 22). The types of construction illustrated are ranked by their STC number.

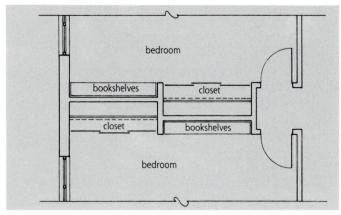

14.18

In modern open-plan offices where no partitions are used, full acoustic privacy is difficult to achieve. Satisfactory conditions depend on the use of carpeting, an acoustical ceiling, screen panels with acoustical value placed between workstations, and a layout that adequately spaces out workstations. If necessary, an artificial, electronically generated background sound may be added to blend into the general sounds of activity to prevent conversation from being overheard. Similarly, in a busy restaurant, the ambient noise makes it possible to talk without fear of being overheard at a nearby table.

Good Acoustics

In concert halls, theaters, auditoriums, and large meeting rooms, an opposite acoustical problem arises—making sound satisfactorily audible throughout the space. Achieving good acoustics in large halls presents complex problems in which the size and shape of the space and the placement of reflecting, absorbing, and diffusing elements play a part (fig. 14.19). An expert consultant is a virtual necessity, and architects and designers need to work closely with the consultant in order to arrive at the best possible results (fig. 14.20). Disappointments are not unusual, and remedial steps can be troublesome and costly.

Amplification systems are usually resorted to in large meeting rooms, ballrooms, and similar kinds of halls. They are, of course, routinely used in film projection and some kinds of music performance. "Sound reinforcement" is objectionable, however, for the performance of classical music and should be avoided in churches, lecture rooms, and conference halls if at all possible. If amplification must be used in such circumstances, expert consultation is called for to make it as unnoticeable as possible.

WIRED SYSTEMS

Aside from electrical systems, discussed earlier, these include telephone, intercom, public-address, wired-music, and other sound systems, such as background sound and amplification (discussed above). Telephone wiring is often installed by telephone company staff as an after-the-fact improvisation. This serves well enough for simple installations, but more complex installations benefit from planning conduit

and outlets, which makes for neatness in all situations. In larger buildings, *risers* are installed in special vertical chases leading to closets where wiring can be connected to horizontal runs, often in special under-floor ducts or, in the case of situations with extensive phone and other wiring needs, in hollow space provided beneath raised flooring. This latter system is particularly helpful in situations with extensive wiring for telephones, computer systems, and other communications needs. The raised floor is often installed in brokerage offices, reservations centers, trading rooms of banks and financial corporations, and computer centers (fig. 14.21). Wiring and speaker locations for sound systems are best planned as part of a project rather than added as an afterthought.

Special, and sometimes elaborate, audiovisual equipment has become a common requirement in business conference rooms and in presentation rooms of the kind required by advertising firms. This dictates special projection facilities for slides, film, and live or taped TV, often with rear projection as well as conventional projection arrangements. Sound and control systems (for switching equipment, dimming lights, and so on) can be quite complex, calling for special consultants to play a role in laying out and selecting equipment and planning wiring.

SAFETY SYSTEMS

The designer should be aware of items required by building codes or that may be otherwise needed for both safety and security concerns. Wiring and plumbing systems as well as separate elements may be involved. A checklist will include:

> ALARMS
>> Fire
>> Burglar
>> Exit door
> EXTINGUISHERS
> LOCKING HARDWARE (INCLUDING MAGNETIC AND COMPUTER-
>> CONTROLLED SYSTEMS)
> SIGNS (EXITS)
> SPRINKLER SYSTEMS (SEE PLUMBING SYSTEMS, ABOVE)
> TV-SURVEILLANCE SYSTEMS

For larger buildings, a centralized control system that integrates safety, security, and other matters at a central console is now widely used.

VERTICAL TRANSPORTATION

Usually of concern only in larger buildings and large public spaces, this refers to elevators and escalators. In residential applications, as well as in many smaller multistory buildings, only one elevator is required. Provision for wheelchair access (see p. 436) is usually the determinant for the size of the cab, which in turn establishes the size of the required shaft. In larger multistory buildings, a number of elevators may be required to handle expected traffic. The number of floors to be served and the speed of the type of elevator to be furnished combine

14.18 One of the best strategies for ensuring acoustical privacy is to avoid shared partitions between adjacent areas. Intelligent design situates bathrooms, corridors, or closets in place of common walls whenever possible. In the plan shown here, two adjacent bedrooms or offices are separated by a line of closets and storage shelves.

14.19

14.20

14.19 Theaters, auditoriums, and concert halls have special acoustical requirements. Walls and ceilings must be shaped so as to blend and distribute sound evenly throughout the audience space. A hall's size and form are also crucial factors in generating both an acoustic intimacy between audience and performers and a warm, well-balanced orchestral sound. Jaffe Acoustics was the consultant to Morris Architects in the 1987 design of the Brown Theater of the Gus. S. Wortham Theater Center in Houston. (Photograph: Paul Hester, courtesy Wortham Center)

14.20 Once used by a Masonic lodge, this small meeting room in New York's Carnegie Hall building renovated in 1984 is now the J. M. Kaplan Space, used for rehearsals and sound recording. The cylinders along the side walls, filled with sand, alternate with acoustical cabinets. Together, they control reverberation and also contribute a strikingly rhythmic design element. The oversized ducts at ceiling height permit air-conditioning to flow at low velocity, thus eliminating any audible hiss. Abraham Meltzer acted as the acoustical consultant to James Stewart Polshek and Partners, Architects. (Photograph: © Brian McNally)

with traffic projections to define the number and size of elevators needed. An inadequate supply of elevators leads to long waiting times that are a source of annoyance to building occupants, yet providing adequate elevators for periods of peak demand (such as lunch hour in an office building or the end of an event in an auditorium) can be excessively costly.

Escalators can move large numbers of people but are impractical for high-rise situations. While a single escalator for ascending traffic and a stair for descent are common provisions, paired up and down escalators, which take up more space and double cost, offer convenience to all building users. Barrier-free access requirements call for elevators as alternatives to escalators, and stairways are always required as alternative vertical circulation in case of power failure. Elevator shaftways and the opening through floors for escalators both create fire-safety problems because the openings permit smoke, toxic fumes, and actual flame to travel upward. Building codes include specific restrictions and requirements to minimize these dangers.

Manufacturers of vertical transportation products provide excellent planning advice to architects. Interior designers are concerned with the location and appearance of escalators and the design of elevator entrances, cab interiors, lighting, and signal systems (fig. 14.22). Coordinating these elements with centralized building control systems now in general use is desirable.

14.21

14.21 In this executive office, carpet squares and floor panels are raised to reveal the area beneath the visible, or access, floor. Access flooring is a surface of removable panels supported some distance—usually 6 to 18 inches—above the structural floor. The space generated can accommodate

wiring, plumbing, and ductwork. Easy access from above makes this system particularly suitable to offices and work spaces where computers and computer-related equipment require complex wiring that needs frequent repair service or upgrading. (Photograph courtesy USG Interiors, Inc.)

BUILDING CODES

Professional interior designers are expected to be aware of the legal restrictions that affect building construction, planning, and equipment. In all urban areas, as well as in many other locations, codes define requirements that affect the safety and well-being of building occupants and the general public. Codes are enforced through the submission to and approval by an appropriate authority of plans for new construction and all but the most minor alterations, following which a building permit is issued. Designers and architects need to be sure that plans comply with codes to avoid the delay and annoyance of rejection, revision, and resubmission. Although meeting code provisions may often seem burdensome, these requirements are essential to establishing basic standards of safety. Common sense may lead to design that satisfies most code requirements, but knowledge of the specific rules applicable to the location where a project is to be executed is necessary to obtain plan approvals.

Unfortunately, codes differ in various locations, each having been prepared and adopted by local authorities. In an effort to reduce the chaos of innumerable differing codes, standard codes have been developed that have been adopted by most local jurisdictions. The *Uniform Building Code* (UBC) is the most widely accepted model in the United States. The BOCA code, used in part of the Northeast; the SBC code, used in the Southeast; and the National Building Code of Canada (NBC) are all similar enough to the UBC to make knowledge of that code generally sufficient. In addition, there are mechanical, plumbing, and electrical codes that deal with those aspects of buildings. Other regulations include federal standards for access for people with disabilities (American National Standards Institute A117.1) and the provisions of the Americans with Disabilities Act (ADA), which are discussed in more detail in Chapter 15.

Table 23. Building Codes and Their Sponsoring Groups	
BOCA Building Officials Code Administrators International	**NBC** Basic/National Building Code
ICBO International Conference of Building Officials	**UBC** Uniform Building Code
SBCCI Southern Building Code Congress International	**SBC** Standard Building Code

The materials and construction techniques specified in codes meet requirements for certain standards established by testing. The American Society for Testing and Materials (ASTM) publishes standards based on tests that lead to ratings for these materials and products. Building construction, for example, must provide safe support for floors, with loadings defined as a pounds-per-square-foot figure for the intended type of occupancy. Typical permissible floor loadings for various uses are:

RESIDENTIAL USE	40 POUNDS PER SQUARE FOOT
SCHOOLS	40 POUNDS PER SQUARE FOOT
HOTELS AND APARTMENTS	40–100 POUNDS PER SQUARE FOOT
HOSPITALS AND NURSING HOMES	50–100 POUNDS PER SQUARE FOOT
OFFICES	50–100 POUNDS PER SQUARE FOOT
PUBLIC ASSEMBLY	50–125 POUNDS PER SQUARE FOOT

Fire-Safety Requirements

Fire safety is a major concern of building-code regulations. Fire ratings indicating the relative flammability of materials or their resistance to fire are typical of such standards. For example, the results of flame-spread tests allow materials to be grouped into classes:

CLASS I OR A	0–25 FLAME-SPREAD RATING
CLASS II OR B	26–75 FLAME-SPREAD RATING
CLASS III OR C	76–200 FLAME-SPREAD RATING

Class I has the greatest fire-resistance. The allowable material class rating is then given in tables that relate types of usage to these ratings as follows:

TYPE OF OCCUPANCY	ENCLOSED VERTICAL EXITWAYS	OTHER EXITWAYS	ROOMS AND OTHER AREAS
A Assembly spaces	I	II	II
B Business uses	I	II	III
E Educational uses	I	II	III
H Hazardous usage	I	II	III
R-1 Residential	I	II	III
R-2 Residential	III	III	III

When occupancy of spaces within a project falls into more than one type, each occupancy must be isolated by fire-rated partitions, and each area treated as codes require for its particular occupancy classification.

Buildings are also classified by type of construction, with each class (from I to V) established by the level of fire-resistance of the system of construction used. Within a building, partitions and floors are considered potential barriers to the spread of fire and ratings are given for each type of constructional assembly. Ratings range from twenty minutes to four hours, and each barrier must have a rating at the level required by codes for its position and function within its building type.

Systems for fire detection, alarming, and suppression are also required by codes. High-rise buildings have special concerns that result from the difficulty of exiting for occupants and the problem of access for fire-fighting equipment. Smoke detectors, wired alarm systems, and automatic sprinkler systems for fire suppression are required for new construction and for older buildings when alterations occur. Sprinklers have proven to be the most effective devices for fire control and should be considered for any spaces where exiting and fire-fighting

access may present problems, even when not legally mandated. Reduced insurance costs and decreased exposure to possible liability suits can often offset the cost of sprinkler systems over a period of time. Sprinkler systems require one sprinkler head per 225 square feet of area with heads spaced no more than 15 feet apart. Each enclosed space, however small, must have at least one sprinkler head.

Other code requirements restrict the use of flammable materials in furniture and fabrics, proscribe the use of glass in locations that may create hazards, and may specify limits on permitted sound transmission (STC rating; see Table 22) through walls and floors.

Exit Requirements

Provision of adequate exits is essential to building-interior safety. In fires or other emergencies, sufficient clearly defined exit routes are vital to prevent panic and to permit rapid escape. For each type of usage, the UBC rules specify that occupancy be estimated on the basis of floor area. This occupant load factor varies from one occupant per 500 square feet in warehouse space to one per 3 square feet in waiting areas outside such assembly spaces as auditoriums and theaters. Typical occupant load factors are:

AUDITORIUMS, CHURCHES, STADIUMS	7 SQUARE FEET
HOMES FOR THE AGED OR CHILDREN	80 SQUARE FEET
RESIDENCES	300 SQUARE FEET
HOSPITALS AND NURSING HOMES	80 SQUARE FEET
OFFICES	100 SQUARE FEET
SCHOOL CLASSROOMS	20 SQUARE FEET
RETAIL STORES	30 SQUARE FEET

The occupancy is estimated by dividing the actual floor area by the specified load factor. A retail store with an area of 4,000 square feet, for example, will have an occupancy estimated as 4,000 divided by 30, or 133. A minimum of two exits is required for each category of use when the number of occupants is estimated to reach or exceed a specified level. Upper-floor areas with 10 or more occupants always require two exits, as do other areas with an estimated occupancy of 50 or more. When there are to be 500 to 1,000 occupants, three exits are necessary; for occupancy over 1,000, four exits. In the retail-store example cited above, with an estimated occupancy of 133, two independent exits are clearly required.

Exits, when two or more are required, must be placed far enough apart to ensure that a fire could not easily block both at once. Distance between two exits must be at least one-half the diagonal dimension of the space they serve. The maximum permitted distance to an exit from any point in a space is 150 feet in an area without sprinklers and 200 with sprinklers. An additional 100 feet of distance is permitted if it goes through an exit corridor with a one-hour fire rating. One exit may be through an adjoining room if the maximum exit distances specified are not exceeded. The width of exits is determined under the UBC code as the occupant load multiplied by .3 for stairs and by .2 for other exits. Thus a space with an occupancy load of 133 would require stair exits with a width of 133 X .3, or 39.9 inches, and other exits of 133 X .2, or 26.6 inches. These are minimums that would normally be

14.22 Elevators can be more than the standardized units provided by a manufacturer. The cabs and entrances can be conceived instead as significant, interesting elements in a multistory building. A glimpse of elevator cab interiors, visible here, shows how they extend the lobby design. The Saddlery Building in Des Moines, Iowa, is the work of Douglas A. Wells, architect. (Photograph: © 1986 Frederick Charles)

exceeded by the widths of stairs, corridors, or doors stipulated by other rules. Corridor widths must equal 36 inches where occupant load is less than 50 and 44 inches for a load over 50. In practice, 48 inches is a usual minimum corridor width, with 60 inches for most corridors in institutional or commercial buildings. Corridors in schools must be at least 6 feet in width.

When the two required exits must use corridors, layout must permit travel in two directions to independent safe exit paths. A dead-end corridor that provides only one route to an exit cannot be more than 20 feet in length and, ideally, should be avoided whenever possible.

Additional regulations stipulate that corridors must have a one-hour fire rating on walls and ceiling and a twenty-minute rating on access doors, which also must be self- or automatic-closing in case of fire. Glass in corridor walls is restricted to 25 percent of the wall of the adjacent space and must have a forty-five-minute fire rating. Doors must swing in the direction of exit travel, must not block corridors when opened, and must have a fire rating determined by code. Revolving and sliding doors cannot be counted as exit routes. Doors to exit stairs and to the out-of-doors must have hardware that permits opening on contact (*panic bolts*).

Exit stairways must have a minimum width of 36 inches, or 44 inches if they serve an occupancy of 50 or more. Stair risers must be more than 4 inches but no more than 7 inches in height, and treads must be at least 11 inches deep. Landings must be provided at the tops and bottoms of stairways, and there must be handrails on both sides plus an additional (center) railing if width exceeds 88 inches.

Exit requirements for single-family houses are less stringent, permitting as few as one exit from a basement or second-floor level. Corridors may be as little as 36 inches in width and doors may swing into rooms. Stairs may have risers up to 8 inches in height and treads as narrow as 9 inches.

When code restrictions are complex (as in many urban areas), it is often helpful to employ a consultant who specializes in advising designers and architects on code provisions. Such consultants are architects or engineers whose services include a review of plans to ensure code compliance and assistance in obtaining plan approvals and building permits.

Environmental Requirements

In addition to legal requirements concerning building construction, fire safety, and mechanical systems, other regulations that may affect interior design relate to environmental concerns. The excesses of urban congestion that developed in major cities early in the twentieth century as tall buildings were built close together led to the adoption of *zoning laws*. These are regulations that divide a city or nonurban region into zones that are each restricted in specific ways. Zoning and other land-use laws usually deal with the following issues:

AREA ZONING. These regulations control the permitted coverage of a particular lot or property and define how much land must remain open. In cities, this may mean requiring open yards as a percentage of total lot area and may call for specific back, front, or side yards adjacent to buildings.

HEIGHT ZONING. The height to which buildings can be built on any site within a zone is often restricted. Many city zoning laws established rules that required that high buildings be designed with *setbacks* to permit light and air to reach streets and lower floors of tall buildings. An unrestricted tall tower was usually permitted on some portion of a site, typically 25 percent of total area. More recent zoning rules provide that a building floor area be limited to a certain multiple of the lot area. In a 2X zone, for example, a two-story building may cover the entire site, whereas a ten-story building would be limited to the same floor area and so would cover only 20 percent of the lot, leaving the balance open to courts or plazas. In a 10X zone, a twenty-story building could cover no more than 50 percent of the site.

USE ZONING. Zones for residential, commercial, and industrial uses are established to avoid mixtures of inappropriate building types within a given district. Factories and gas stations, for example, cannot be placed along residential streets. Strict segregation of different uses has come into question, and many modern zoning rules permit some mixture of uses while blocking potentially objectionable combinations.

Other zoning rules may set controls on various aspects of buildings in an effort to retain neighborhood character, property values, and even aesthetic values (as when all buildings are required to be of a certain style). Some zoning rules have come under criticism as serving the values of specific groups while working against the interests of others and of the population at large.

Zoning laws generally permit application for a *variance*, special permission for a departure from requirements, which is usually given only after public hearings, most frequently in cases where some advantage can be offered in exchange for the right to be excused from a particular zoning restriction.

LANDMARKING. This type of regulation restricts the rights of owners to alter buildings in neighborhoods which are designated as having historical or aesthetic character that deserves preservation. In many locations landmark designation is also given to individual buildings of historic or exceptional aesthetic character. Efforts to obtain landmark protection for interior spaces that call for protection from destruction or ill-advised alteration are increasing. Conflict between the desires (and the economic interests) of the building owner and the interest of the public in preserving outstanding structures makes landmarking and building designation an area for frequent controversy and litigation.

Preservation and restoration of landmark structures and the planning of adaptations to make such buildings useful in current contexts has created a specialty of interior-design practice. Special knowledge and skill are required to work on a landmark building in ways that will be advantageous to an owner, as well as to occupants and users, and yet still preserve the values that make such a structure significant for a larger general public.

15.1

INTERIOR DESIGN FOR SPECIAL NEEDS

Until quite recently interior design—in fact, all design—was based on the idea of serving most people, meaning average people or those close to average. Throughout history, widths of corridors, dimensions of doors, heights of steps, and sizes of furniture have all been determined·by the beliefs that people are generally similar and that whatever will serve any one person will serve everyone else equally well. Convenient as this assumption may be, it is obviously false; no one person is average in every way—height, weight, strength, and health. People who are significantly larger or smaller than average in physical size and weight, including children; people weaker than average in some way, including the elderly; and people experiencing either temporary or permanent physical disability are those most likely to be ill-served by design solutions generated for the public at large. Statistics now show that a sizable percentage of people will fall into at least one of these special-need groups for some portion of their life spans, making awareness of these needs essential to good design. (See Chapter 7, "Human Factors and Social Responsibility," for the many considerations affecting design for the "average" person.)

Many essential guidelines for meeting the needs of people with physical handicaps are set forth in the code of standards known as ANSI A117.1, developed by the American National Standards Institute. These recommendations have become the basis for most state and national codes dealing with accessibility and accommodation of the disabled. The more recent Americans with Disabilities Act legislation discussed below makes these standards mandatory in a wider variety of situations.

AMERICANS WITH DISABILITIES ACT

The Americans with Disabilities Act (generally known as ADA), passed in January 1991 and effective in January 1992, stipulates that all commercial and public facilities be barrier-free, providing access to people with disabilities. Employers with fifteen or more employees may not discriminate against persons with disabilities who are otherwise qualified for a particular job and must accommodate the disabilities of these employees unless doing so will result in undue hardship. State and local governments also may not discriminate against qualified persons with disabilities, and new construction and alteration of existing structures must provide access for disabled people. By July 1995, buses, trains, and their stations must be made barrier-free. Public facilities such as hotels, restaurants, theaters, museums, stores, doctors' offices, and day-care centers may not discriminate in their hiring of employees on the basis of disability, and both new construction and alterations of existing public structures must be made barrier-free.

Although achieving compliance with the Americans with Disabilities Act can be difficult and complex, designers must be aware of the requirements and expert in realizing these goals for any applicable facilities. A broader objective for the designer to consider is the realization of optimum barrier-free service for those with special needs other than the disabilities referred to by ADA, including children and the elderly, as well as those with temporary impairments, and the extension of such provisions to private homes, smaller businesses, and other facilities not covered by the ADA.

UNIVERSAL DESIGN

In response both to the provisions of ADA and to the growing awareness of the needs of the large percentage of the population currently disadvantaged by so many existing facilities, the concept of *universal design* has emerged. The term refers to the idea that all facilities, all spaces, and all products (from vehicles and furniture to appliances and tools) should be designed to accommodate all people with special

15.1 Gallery Tom in Tokyo, Japan, was designed to serve blind and partially sighted visitors as well as the general public. Tactile clues to materials and spatial elements of the gallery are combined with artwork that is meant to be touched. The gallery's baffle arrangements create daylight effects that are stimulating for both partially and fully sighted visitors. Hiroshi Naito was the architect for this 1989 project. (Photograph: Shinkenchiku-sha, Tokyo)

requirements; in striving for this goal, the needs of the total population will surely be better served. There are, of course, limits to the degree of success possible (at least within the boundaries of present knowledge and technology) in making truly universal design a reality. We cannot imagine making it possible for the totally blind to drive an automobile, for wheelchair occupants to climb stairs, or for those confined to bed to cook meals. It is possible, however, to make vehicles accessible to the blind; to provide elevators, lifts, and ramps usable by those in wheelchairs; and to make kitchens and bathrooms practical for those with a wide variety of disabilities. It is a reasonable design goal to press for maximum progress in these directions.

ECONOMIC CONSIDERATIONS

Granted the acceptance of universal design goals, businesses, institutions, government agencies, and private individuals tend, as clients of designers, to focus on the added expense of realizing these goals. Elevators cost more to build, maintain, and operate than do stairs. Wide corridors, ramps, and clearances for wheelchair movement require extra space, which is inherently expensive. The price of meeting the requirements of the Americans with Disabilities Act falls equally on all affected and must be accepted as inevitable if our society is to eliminate the needless limitations placed on so large a part of the population.

Projects on which the ADA does not bear, such as private homes and other nonpublic facilities, require designer and client to determine together the degree to which the objectives of universal design should apply. Ignoring these issues may not in the long run be functionally or economically advantageous. A house designed with no consideration of these issues may be serviceable for average adults, but it may cease to be habitable if one of the occupants suffers an injury or illness that creates special needs. An accident to a child or an elderly visitor may not only be an unhappy disaster but costly as well when medical treatment, nursing-home stays, or paid caretakers—even possible liability damage suits—are considered. Before such matters are dismissed as either insignificant or impossible to resolve, it behooves designer and client to review any applicable special needs, which are further enumerated and discussed below.

CHILDREN

Everyone begins life as a child and spends a number of years with a body smaller and lighter than that of the average adult. As young children develop from crawlers to walkers, their needs differ quite obviously from those of adults, and even well into the preschool years their small and constantly changing body size creates additional concerns relating to safety and comfort that are often overlooked, in part because the remarkable adaptability of young children is often viewed as part of a normal learning process. The phrase "the burnt child dreads the fire" may express a certain truth but ignores the possibility that the burn may be dangerous and quite preventable. Young children cannot articulate their needs in detail, and older children, in their eagerness to achieve adult status, tend to deny such needs, leaving to adults the

responsibility to recognize the problems and hazards that children face in the complex modern world.

Particular considerations for children are those related to safety and comfort. When the designer is planning a residence, whether a house or an apartment, with a client whose family makeup is a known factor, the need for appropriate bedrooms, privacy, suitable storage, and other comfort issues are usually taken into account. When residences are developed for rental or sale, assumptions are made about the number and age of the probable occupants. The near certainty that children will be among the occupants of almost any residence at some time, present or future, suggests that some thought be given to their requirements.

The issue of safety centers on stairways, railings, gates, windows, and doors, where falls are a hazard to the young child learning to walk, as well as to the older child who runs and jumps and may be tempted to try risky adventures. Stairways with long uninterrupted runs, changes of level, and transitions with just one two steps are all obvious problems. Railings on stairs, balconies, or decks present risk of failure, the danger of slipping through or catching small heads between supports, and temptations for climbing or other gymnastics. Sharp corners and the hard edges of steps and adjacent walls and railings can be elements of risk. Glass and mirror, especially in large areas close to steps or in places, such as bathrooms, where hard and slippery surfaces are common, are also dangerous to children. Children need to be protected from open fireplaces, heating stoves, and electrical devices, wires, and outlets. Kitchen-stove controls and bathroom faucets and handles must be located with safety in mind. Medicines and other hazardous items, including chemicals for cleaning or hobbies, guns, and so on, need to be stored in safe, enclosed areas.

Comfort issues for children also have health implications. Although special furniture for infants, such as cribs and high chairs, is widely available, it must be checked for safety regarding distance between railing slats, stability, toxicity of finish, and small breakable parts, among numerous other concerns. Chairs and desks or tables sized for children help to reduce awkward postures that can contribute to physical problems. Play equipment, including swings, slides, and climbing and motion toys, calls for careful attention to safety problems not only

15.2   15.3

15.2, 15.3 A "Lift" system renders a washbasin accessible to persons in wheelchairs and to small children. The sink can be set at normal height or lowered as required. It is available in eleven colors and can be used with basins of several different designs. (Photographs courtesy Villeroy & Boch USA)

in selection but also in placement. Good lighting is important both for safety and to reduce eye strain (see Chapter 10, pages 296–98). The needs of children in a home must, of course, be worked out in relation to the needs of adults and with recognition that these needs change as children grow into adulthood.

In schools, day-care accommodations, and health facilities for children, these needs become primary and can usually be closely adjusted to the particular age group to be served (fig. 15.7). Yet even within a limited age group children vary greatly in size, making provision of appropriately sized furniture difficult. Adjustable chairs and tables or a range of assorted sizes (notably various heights) maximize comfort and limit undesirable physical impacts. Here especially the effects of lighting on visual function and general health issues are significant (again see Chapter 10). Safety issues become extremely important where supervision may be less than ideal and wherever children interact in ways that may promote carelessness.

THE ELDERLY

Modern sanitation, dietary knowledge, and medical advances have continued to increase average life expectancy in the developed countries. The ability to live effectively and happily as one ages is strongly influenced by the environments in which one lives and the facilities one uses for transportation, work, and enjoyment. The needs of the elderly involve issues of safety and comfort quite analogous to many of the requirements of children: reduced strength, changes in body size, limited visual and auditory sensitivity, slowed reaction times, and decreased mobility—although they occur in differing degrees and at differing rates for each individual—are typical of advancing age. The tendency toward serious decline in effective life experience can, however, be greatly reduced by appropriate environmental design.

Just as children can be expected to occupy most residences at one time or another, occupancy by older people at some point is a high probability. Elderly relatives come to visit or may move in with younger family members. Prime occupants may remain in residence until they move into an older age category. Planning that permits one-floor-level living (access to living-dining space, kitchen, bedroom, and

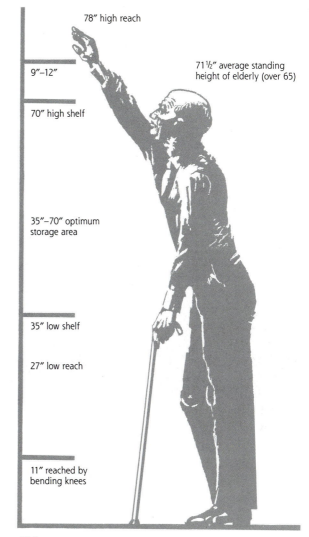

15.5

15.4

15.4 Bathroom fixtures designed for disabled or older users often include handgrips, as in this lavatory in a nursing home with special facilities for the elderly. Sidney Gilbert was the architect for County Manor, Toms River, New Jersey. (Photograph: © 1980 Wolfgang Hoyt/ESTO)

bath on one level) avoids many problems and can often be arranged even in a multistoried house as a possible alternative use of space. The many small level changes often introduced by designers to "add visual interest" are, unfortunately, generally troublesome and even dangerous for elderly occupants. Although the problems of actual disability in old age are of prime interest here, even older people in normal health will usually be best served by design that recognizes some special requirements.

As we consider how to incorporate the needs of older people in declining health into design planning, we must also remember that as a group elderly persons are increasingly mobile and are in fact likely to be among the patrons of restaurants and theaters, the customers of stores, and the users of public transport, hotels, motels, and other facilities. As the percentage of the population in upper age brackets increases, it is reasonable to expect that all such spaces will need to accommodate the special requirements discussed here.

15.5 This diagram gives average reaching dimensions for elderly males.

Reduced visual acuity, decline in muscular strength, and impaired sense of balance all conspire to make accidents an increasing risk to the elderly, with the danger of falling a key safety issue. Environmental obstacles include stairways and level changes of a few steps, elements (such as door saddles or thresholds) that can cause tripping, slippery floor surfaces, and carpets or rugs than can slip underfoot or trip passersby; small mats and throw rugs are particular hazards. Bathrooms bring together hard and slippery surfaces, sharp corners, electrical outlets, running (often hot) water, mirrors, and glass, making them especially dangerous. A shockingly high percentage of accidents occur in homes, with bathrooms and stairways the most common locations.

Stairways are safest when designed with a gradual slope, short runs, intermediate landings, sturdy handrails, and good lighting. Individuals with heart problems need stairs with short runs and gradual slopes and may in some instances require a plan layout that avoids stairs entirely. Ramps are an alternative to stairs and make wheelchair access possible, but they must have a very gradual slope (no more than a rise of 1:12), which makes them excessively space-consuming. Maximum rise between ramp landings should be limited to 30 inches. Ramps are generally most useful for small level changes both because of the space demanded and because moving up a ramp can become extremely tiring. Climbing a full story height by ramp is usually not practical for

15.6

15.6 Thoughtful interior design can create spaces that accommodate the needs of people who are ill or disabled. The living room and kitchen (shown in fig. 16.27) of Friends in Deed, a facility in the SoHo district of New York, provide services for terminally ill patients. Bob Patino was the designer. (Photograph: © Stephen Barker, courtesy Metropolitan Home)

15.7 Rooms and furniture for children must be designed with the user's size in mind. Clear, bright, usually primary colors are generally considered the most appropriate to children's visual orientation. The United States Child Center in Lemoore, California, was designed by Naomi Hatkin and Pamela Helmich of GHI Architects in 1985. (Photograph: Brenner Vandouris)

15.8 Unlike the institutional atmosphere of most healthcare facilities, The Hospice at Mission Hill in Boston, a residential facility for AIDS patients, offers a humane environment. Patients are encouraged to decorate the rooms with their own possessions and to rearrange the furnishings to suit their inclinations.

William Hodgkins and Charles Spada, designers, organized volunteers from the Boston design community to develop The Hospice. Among those who contributed was The Cooper Group, whose 1990 bedroom is seen here. (Photograph: © Donna Paul, courtesy Metropolitan Home)

15.7

15.8

wheelchair users and many others with impaired mobility. Because of cost and space requirements, escalators are practical only in public places where large numbers of people must be moved from level to level; they also cannot serve wheelchair occupants and are unsatisfactory for most people with impaired movement. Although elevators are expensive as well, they are the most effective vertical transport for special-need users and are useful and convenient for all others.

Locating bathrooms for easy access at any time (particularly in relation to bedrooms) provides substantial convenience for the elderly. Bathrooms used by older people (as with those used by children) require numerous safety features: antiskid floor surfaces and tub and shower bottoms; rounded corners on fixtures; safe placement of projections such as towel bars, hooks, and faucet handles; and grab bars to aid safe movement in and out of tubs and showers (fig. 15.4). Tubs designed to permit easy access and bathing in a seated position are helpful to many elderly users. Transfer to bathroom fixtures by wheelchair users, unaided if possible, calls for special design considerations (figs. 15.13–15.15; wheelchair specifications are discussed in greater detail below). Glass shower or tub enclosures are to be avoided. Electrical outlets should be positioned for safety and equipped with ground-fault interrupters (now usually required by codes) to prevent shocks.

Kitchen design requires special attention if independent living for the elderly is to be facilitated. Standard counter heights and cabinet placement too often create problems for older people (fig. 15.5). (Kitchen design for wheelchair users is discussed on pages 442–43.)

In selecting furniture for a household with elderly members, the designer needs to provide seating that is not too low (making seating uncomfortable and rising difficult) and bed heights that are neither too low (making access difficult) nor too high (making falls out of bed dangerous). Furniture that can tip or overturn should be avoided, along with projecting feet or legs that can cause tripping. Other hazardous objects include footstools or low tables, especially those with

sharp edges or corners, as well as glass tabletops, glass doors, and mirrored walls.

Good lighting is an important factor in safety of movement after dark. Special night lighting at stairs and in bathrooms and bedrooms is appropriate, as are switch locations that encourage use of additional lighting when moving about at night; self-illuminated switches are easiest to find in the dark. Switches activated by sound or proximity can be employed in some locations to ensure that adequate light will be turned on automatically.

Retirement homes, healthcare facilities, nursing homes, and other spaces where a high proportion of users will be elderly necessarily demand close attention to the needs of their occupants to comply with legal requirements, to safeguard their managers against liability to legal suits, to make them attractive to their intended clientele in an increasingly competitive market, and to make them safe, convenient, and comfortable to their residents. In the design of these facilities, it should be remembered that in addition to the requirements typical of all older people, many users of such facilities are also burdened with specific disabilities that result from illnesses and injuries. People with lasting disabilities eventually grow old, and those who were without such difficulties in youth and middle age often experience disabling problems in later years. Just as facing the special needs of children leads to design decisions that are helpful to the elderly, it becomes clear that the needs of the elderly and the disabled often overlap.

PEOPLE WITH DISABILITIES

In addition to the demands of the first and last fifteen years of life—in themselves almost 40 percent of a typical life span of eighty years—a high proportion of individuals will spend some part of the intervening "normal adult" years with some form of disability. Although many such problems are temporary—a sprained ankle, perhaps, or a broken leg—they may still be of long duration and require the use of crutches, a wheelchair, or confinement to bed. Other disabilities may be permanent, extending from onset (be it early or late in life) through the remainder of a lifetime. It is estimated that at any given time forty-eight million Americans are to some degree disabled. This surprisingly large figure results from adding together the many types of disabilities mentioned above

Modern medical techniques coupled with the constant invention and improvement of technical devices and therapies have made it possible for an increasing number of people with disabilities to lead effective and comfortable lives. This fortunate reality in turn highlights the growing need for design that acknowledges the special needs created by the many different kinds of disabilities. The most common problems that can influence design include the following:

Extremes of small or large body dimensions and weight
Problems requiring use of a cane (including the light four-footed cane)
Problems requiring the use of crutches
Problems requiring the use of a wheelchair (manual or motorized)
Limited or lacking hand and/or arm function
Confinement to bed, with or without special equipment, such as a respirator

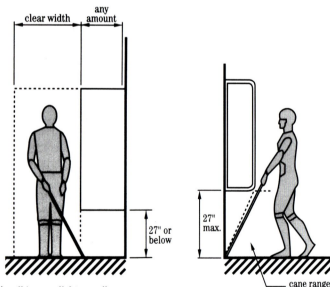

(a) walking parallel to a wall

(b) walking perpendicular to a wall

15.9

15.9 Accommodating blind or partially sighted people calls for specific design provisions in any interior project that will be used by the general public. The diagrams here indicate established restrictions on objects and building elements that project into corridors and other walkways and may present hazards to the sight-impaired.

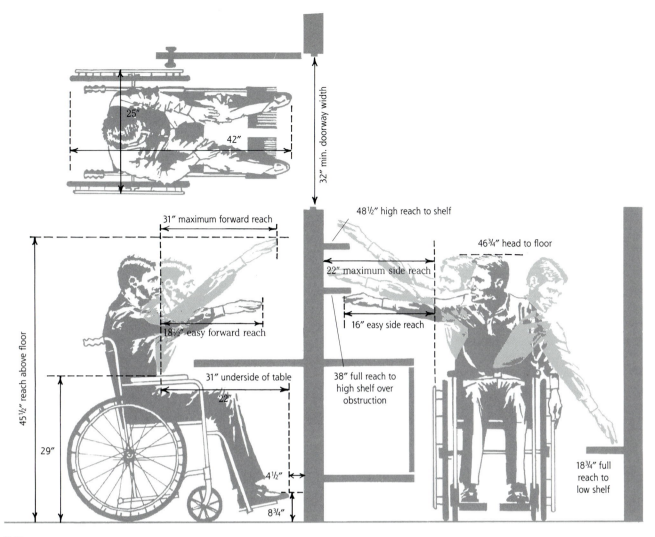

25"

42"

32" min. doorway width

31" maximum forward reach

48½" high reach to shelf

46¾" head to floor

22" maximum side reach

18½" easy forward reach

16" easy side reach

45½" reach above floor

31" underside of table

38" full reach to high shelf over obstruction

22"

29"

4½"

8¾"

18¾" full reach to low shelf

15.10

Vision impairment ranging from minor to total blindness

Hearing impairment

Slowed reaction time, impaired balance, muscular weakness

Heart problems requiring limited activity

Many types of disability are, in their minor forms, extremely common in the general population. Visual impairment, for example, at levels that can be corrected by glasses, is very widespread—almost universal among people of middle age or older. Blindness, on the other hand, affects only a small part of the population and calls for specific provisions in any interior project that will be used by the general public (see fig. 15.9). Although hearing impairment has less direct impact on interior design, it nonetheless calls for specialized accommodations in any space where sound is a significant part of the intended activities. Auditoriums, classrooms, temples and churches, theaters and concert halls, conference rooms, and medical facilities are notable examples of places where people need to hear and where technical equipment must be available either to make hearing possible for the partially deaf or to provide related input through another sense, usually vision.

Mobility-impairing disabilities have the most impact on interior design. Architects and interior designers have for centuries assumed that monumental entrance stairs, stairs connecting floor levels, access routes, doorways, and any number of lesser details were to be introduced for functional reasons or for dramatic effect with no consideration of the large number of people with various disabilities. In response to new legal requirements, special entrances at ground level and ramps, elevators, and lifts are being retrofitted to buildings whose original design made no provision for mobility by those with disabilities, often at great cost and with unfortunate aesthetic results.

The concept of barrier-free access has become a stimulus to encourage the awareness not only that people using canes, crutches, and wheelchairs can function more fully but also that aesthetic quality can be maintained if the initial design process takes account of access requirements in a systematic way (figs. 15.16–15.19). Furthermore, the activities that occur within spaces can be facilitated through design approaches. Cooking in a kitchen, getting in and out of bed, using a bathroom, buying things in a store, and filing papers in an office are a few examples of the activities, difficult or impossible in many current

15.10 The reach of a person in a wheelchair and the clearance for the chair itself are important factors in adapting storage and work spaces to those so constrained. (See also wheelchair clearances in figs. 15.11, 15.12)

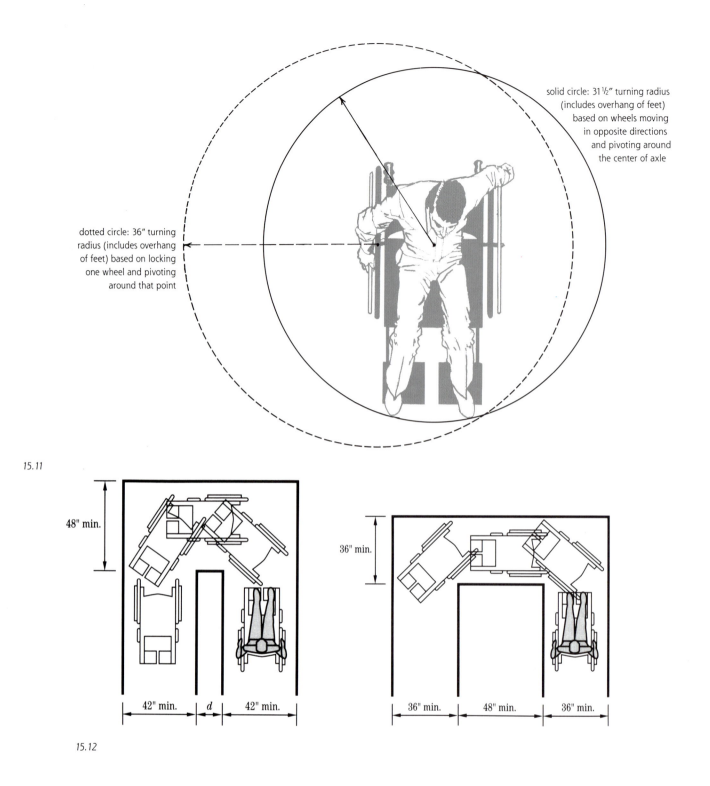

solid circle: 31½" turning radius (includes overhang of feet) based on wheels moving in opposite directions and pivoting around the center of axle

dotted circle: 36" turning radius (includes overhang of feet) based on locking one wheel and pivoting around that point

15.11

48" min.

42" min.   d   42" min.

15.12

36" min.

36" min.   48" min.   36" min.

situations, that can be made practicable through design adjustment.

The impairment of manual functioning—the use of arms and hands—demands greater emphasis on the selection of specific details than on overall planning. Door hardware, for example, often consists of knobs, handles, thumbplates, and other elements that can be quite problematic for people with a hand or arm that is stiff, paralyzed, or

missing. Getting through a closed door can be a difficult challenge for a person thus disabled and can prove impossible if wheelchair use and impairment of hand or arm functions are combined. Suitable hardware is helpful, but a full solution to complex disability may require a mechanized opening device. Similarly, the many knobs and buttons that control innumerable everyday functions need to be chosen with antici-

15.11 This diagram shows dimensional clearances for wheelchairs.

15.12 This diagram illustrates wheelchair clearance standards for movement through corridors.

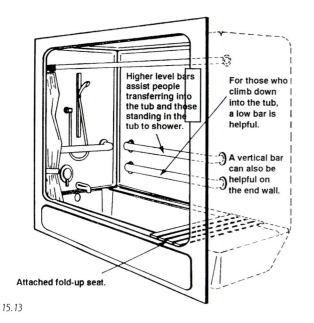

15.13

15.14

pated problems in mind. Light switches, elevator call buttons, telephones, thermostats, and appliance controls frequently are placed too high for wheelchair users and are too small or awkward to operate with limited or absent hand function. Sound- or proximity-activated electric switches may be the best solution for certain locations. In addition, the selection of bathroom faucets and drain controls must be made with care.

A number of safety issues require special attention to the needs of those with disabilities. Fire exits are often poorly located, narrow, and may use stairs or ladders—difficult if not impossible for the disabled to negotiate. Even mild sight impairment calls for signs and lettering large and clear enough to make reading easy; blindness renders standard emergency-exit signs and lights totally ineffective. Signs and labels, such as the floor numbers of elevator controls, can be composed of braille numerals or other markings that convey information through touch (fig. 15.21); audible signals also offer assistance. Objects protruding from a wall or other support pose a hazard to the visually impaired. Projections should not exceed 4 inches, unless the object extends to below 27 inches above the floor, making it detectable by walking cane. Overhead obstructions must be no lower than 80 inches above the floor. Flooring at the edges of such hazards as stairs and other level changes not protected by railings (including platforms and driveways) must have a surface that is noticeably rough, grooved, or otherwise textured to contrast with surrounding surfaces. The handles of doors that open into hazardous areas must be distinguishable by touch from other handles. Emergency warning systems require both audible and visual signals. Details such as the location and workability of fire-alarm boxes, as well as the practicality of exit-door hardware, demand thoughtful consideration and a thorough understanding of current legal requirements (fig. 15.22).

The extent to which barrier-free design can serve every type of disability varies. The provision of ramps, escalators, and elevators, the avoidance of needless level changes, and the allotment of space for

wheelchair movement are all now required by law in the design of public places. These accommodations also turn out to be advantageous to the general public. Other aids for disabled users may have little value to people without physical problems but cause no inconvenience. Tactile labeling of directional signs and elevator controls, for example, assist blind users yet are barely noticeable to others. Still more specialized arrangements, such as kitchen counters, appliances, and cabinets

15.15

15.13 Grab bars provide tub and shower access for disabled users. This diagram illustrates the various standards and requirements for the design of grab bars. (Courtesy Lasco Bathware)

15.14, 15.15 Many conventional facilities that would be difficult or impossible for a person in a wheelchair to use can be made practicable through design adjustments. Two products of the Silcraft Corporation—a side-access

bathtub with hand-held shower (fig. 15.14) and a barrier-free shower unit (fig. 15.15)—were designed for users with disabilities. (Photographs courtesy Silcraft Corporation)

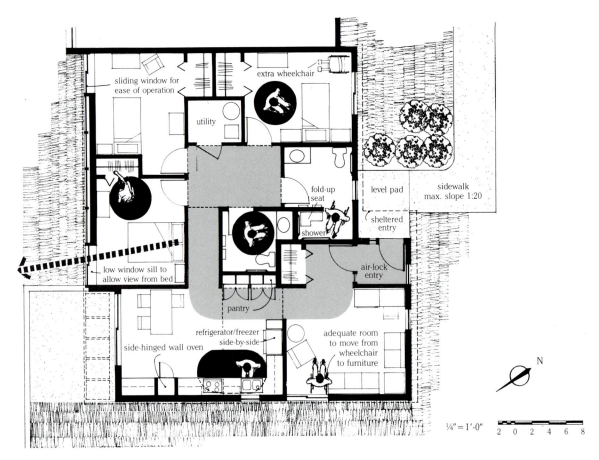

15.16

15.17

15.16–15.19 The floor plan (fig. 15.16) illustrates barrier-free strategies in a residential apartment designed to accommodate a person with a disability. The shaded central zone indicates a circulation path for wheelchairs. The Nutting Apartments for Disabled Persons, Amherst, Massachusetts, was designed by Juster Pope Associates Architects and Planners, 1981. In an interior of the Nutting Apartments, the kitchen area (fig. 15.17) is designed to make appliances and work surfaces easily accessible to residents in wheelchairs. A low oven comes equipped with a pull-out shelf below, to facilitate use by a person in a wheelchair (fig. 15.18). The work surface pulls out from the counter to allow wheelchair clearance and provide a comfortable working height (fig. 15.19). (Photographs courtesy Juster Pope Associates)

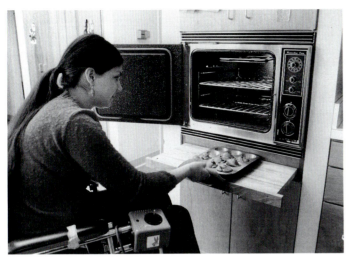

15.18

15.19

15.20

set at heights accessible to wheelchair occupants or bathroom fixtures with variable height adjustments (see figs. 15.2–15.4), are not feasible for every situation but can be made available where it is known there will be a user who can benefit from such equipment. In practice the designer can expect to provide legally mandated and intelligently conceived accommodations for disabled users in every project to the maximum extent that current techniques allow. Further measures to deal with specific problems may be considered when a prospective occupant has special needs that can be defined and dealt with on an individual basis, as with a residential project for a person with a disability—a blind person, perhaps, or a wheelchair user. A private office could be similarly planned to offer optimum conditions for an occupant with specific requirements. Such individualized design for special needs can achieve a remarkably high level of accommodation to disability problems (fig. 15.27).

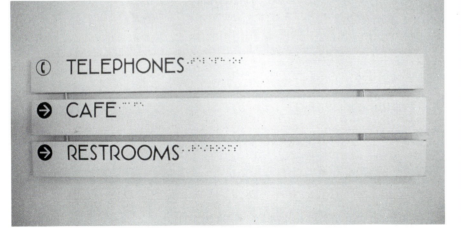

15.21

15.22

15.20 Well-designed alternatives to standard appliances can often accommodate the needs of users with disabilities. A horizontal refrigerator by Penguin Products offers improved accessibility to people in wheelchairs. (Photograph courtesy Penguin Products)

15.21 Directional signs can include equivalent legends in braille to aid sight-impaired visitors. Such signs are mounted at a height of 60 inches from floor to centerline (an ADA standard) to make location by touch easy. The sign shown here was designed by Vignelli Associates Designers for the Solomon R. Guggenheim Museum, New York. (Photograph courtesy Vignelli Associates Designers)

15.22 Fire safety is an important consideration in designing for elderly or disabled persons. The Lodex manual fire-alarm system, an invention of Kevin Jameson, can be adjusted to a height of 48 inches to meet the standard forward reach of a wheelchair user. Its name is derived from the words "low" and "dexterity." (Photograph courtesy Kevcor Limited)

CASE STUDY 4

A CITY APARTMENT

Davis, Brody & Associates, Architects
and Interior Designers
Lewis Davis, Partner in Charge

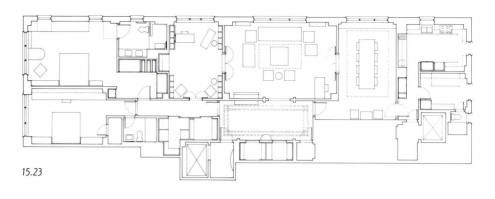

15.23

In presenting their requirements for the design of a newly purchased apartment, the clients of the Davis, Brody firm clearly defined special needs. The apartment was to offer to the wife, partially disabled by multiple sclerosis, maximum wheelchair mobility and overall accessibility. But the clients also wanted the scheme to express the high aesthetic standards appropriate to the husband's work as a design professional. The end result is an apartment that gives visitors no hint that it is accommodating special needs, but one that appears exceptional only in its extraordinary handsomeness and comfort. It is a large (2,500-square-foot) apartment with a linear plan typical of many older apartment buildings in large cities. A straight line through corridor and foyer connects the major spaces of the apartment and provides a barrier-free circulation route.

Wide openings with double doors were added between the three major rooms—living room, dining room, and study—to form a second line of circulation, simultaneously tying those spaces together into a suite that opens up for entertaining. The doors are elegantly detailed with a grid of white-painted wood holding panes of glass sandblasted with a geometric grid pattern. An edge reveal that provides a handgrip at any level is used on doors throughout the apartment. When the sets of glass doors are closed, each room gains privacy while maintaining a sense of spatial connection as a result of the translucency of the glass. Barrier-free movement through the major rooms is provided by ample open floor space, uncluttered by furniture or rugs. A marble band set flush with the wood flooring at each door opening eliminates the hump of a traditional door saddle.

Other details that help to make the apartment highly functional are equally unobtrusive. In the kitchen, generous open space provides maneuvering room for the wheelchair and a shared work area for two or three users. Standard counters and appliances are used on three sides of the room. On the fourth side, a lower 30-inch-high counter has its own sink and burners; clear space beneath is screened by a curtain of metal beading. The master bedroom is reached through a dressing area with rolling pullout units that hold shelves for accessories. Hanging bars for clothing are at two levels, an accessible lower level and an upper bar that swings out and down by a remote control mechanism. In the master bathroom, twin sinks are set in a marble counter with open clearance under one sink, storage under the other. A large roll-in shower area has a teak floor level, with drainage, set flush with the marble bathroom floor.

Shower controls are accessible, and next to the bench seat is a hand-held shower head to supplement the conventional overhead shower. Grab bars are located throughout for easy maneuvering. In the bedroom, push-button controls for lighting, blinds, air-conditioning, and a radio, as well as a battery charger for the motor-powered wheelchair, are mounted in a drawer of the bedside unit. A counter extending from the drawer top provides accessible space for a computer, transforming one corner of the room into a daytime home office.

A checklist of accessible and barrier-free elements used in this apartment could serve any designer facing a comparable project:

CIRCULATION	Barrier-free clearance dimensions
	Freely opening doors
	Finger-grip door edge reveals
	Flush door saddles
MAJOR ROOMS	Open access routes
	Smooth, hard flooring (free of rugs or other obstacles)
KITCHEN	Open central floor area
	Low (30-inch) extra counter with sink and burners
	Double oven with side-hinged doors
	Double refrigerator-freezer with side-hinged doors
	Pull-out lower cabinet drawers with finger-grip pulls
	Built-in mixing bowl in low pull-out
	Roll-out (side access) pantry shelving units
	Pull-out storage shelves for dishes, glassware
BATHROOM	Sink with under-counter knee clearance
	Roll-in shower area with flush floor and bench
	Controls at accessible level (including intercom)
	Toilet at 18-inch height
	Grab bars where appropriate
CLOSETS	Pull out (side-access) storage shelves
	Garment hanging bars at accessible height and/or with remote-controlled swing-out mechanism
BEDROOM	Controls in bedside unit drawer and remote-control units
	Adjacent hospital bed and standard bed with one cover
GENERAL	Individual air-conditioning controls at accessible location and height
	All switches, telephone, and so on at accessible height

The virtually invisible barrier-free features allow the classic modern simplicity of the apartment's design to predominate. Walls are white; color is provided by the natural warmth of the wood floors, accents of black and gray, the tones of Oriental rugs, the colors of artwork, and the green of growing plants. The overall impact of the environment proves, as the clients have commented, "that design for the disabled need not be clinical or sterile."

15.24

15.25

15.26

15.23–15.26 A plan (fig. 15.23) shows the linear circulation pattern of the apartment. (Courtesy Davis, Brody & Associates) The bathroom (fig. 15.24) is equipped with a roll-in shower and a sink with under-counter clearance. One of the counters in the kitchen (fig. 15.25) is only 30 inches high (lower than standard height) and includes its own sink and cooking surface; clear space below the counter makes for easy wheelchair access. The hanging chain screen encloses plumbing without presenting any barrier to movement. Wide openings with specially detailed wood-and-glass double doors link the spacious, uncluttered living room (fig. 15.26) with the dining room and the study, allowing for ease of circulation. (Photographs: Adam Bartos)

HOME NURSING

The staggering costs of hospital and nursing-home care, together with the inevitable discomfort and unhappiness associated with such facilities, have led to a new interest in maximizing home care for health and disability problems. This usually involves personnel—family members, hired aids, or, in many situations, part-time attendants—who can deal with the needs of elderly and/or disabled persons in a home setting if suitable facilities are available. Interior design becomes a factor in providing those accommodations.

The typical basic requirements for satisfactory home care include a room with easy access; an appropriate bed and additional furniture, such as a chair suitable for long periods of sitting; conveniently located appliances, such as lighting, telephone, and television; and a bathroom with close and easy access fitted with suitable fixtures. Food-preparation, serving, and cleanup areas must also be available. An extra room, such as a den or guest room, if location, access, relation to bath, and so on, have been considered, can greatly facilitate home care, as living space either for the ailing person or for a live-in nurse or other caretaker. Because the need for home care often arises unexpectedly (after an accident or sudden illness, for example), suitable interior arrangements may be difficult or impossible to prepare on short notice, suggesting that some degree of contingency planning in residential projects may be wise. The concept of adaptable housing is a step in that direction.

ADAPTABILITY

To make every residential unit fully accessible and usable for the entire range of special needs, no matter how desirable this might be, would involve arrangements that in practice would come into use in only a small percentage of cases. Houses that are not custom built and apartments in multiple dwellings cannot be expected to provide ramps and elevators, full wheelchair access, and all of the other special features discussed above. If original planning and construction take into account such requirements as a future possibility, however, adapting to special needs can become comparatively easy.

In a two-story dwelling, for example, a layout that allows space downstairs for a future, fully accessible bathroom with available plumbing lines may make it possible to provide for an elderly and/or disabled person without major reconstruction. An elevator, an unneeded luxury when a house is constructed, may be extremely difficult to retrofit if a suitable location, perhaps in a stair hall or where closets are placed one over another, has not been planned. A few changes in kitchen and bathroom equipment can make those rooms barrier-free if the basic layout permits. Halls, stairs, and doors of adequate width present no difficulty in regular use and make adaptation to special needs quite simple.

In facilities that accommodate many users, such as hotels, motels, and dormitories, provision of a suitable percentage of fully barrier-free

15.27

KITCHENS, BATHROOMS, STORAGE

Although the basic issues involved in interior design are the same for every kind of space, the areas for food preparation, sanitation, and storage merit special attention from the points of view of both user and designer. In residential design, kitchens and bathrooms attract particular interest on the part of those who will occupy a house or apartment. Builders have long known that an attractive kitchen and bathroom plus adequate closets will do more than any other features to sell a home. Renovation of a kitchen or bath is often the first (and sometimes the only) project that new owners or occupants plan on when moving to a new home.

Bathrooms and kitchens are design problems of unusual complexity because they raise specific and demanding functional considerations, they make use of specialized fixtures and appliances, and they call for special material and finish selections. In most projects, they are the only areas in which the various trades of plumber, electrician, cabinetmaker, and tile installer must all be coordinated and in which so many special details must be worked out. While less technically complex, storage still requires careful thought and planning if it is to be truly convenient and efficient.

Professional kitchens for restaurants, hotels, and other larger dining facilities are so specialized in nature as to fall outside the concern of most interior design work. Therefore, this chapter deals only with residential kitchens. On the other hand, the design of public and semipublic toilet and rest room facilities often falls to the interior designer, so it is discussed here.

The interior designer usually confronts preplanned spaces, that is, already in existence or planned on paper in terms of size, shape, and general layout. The designer's first task is to evaluate the space and decide whether the existing (or planned) spaces can be accepted and worked with in terms of more detailed layout and design or whether more basic replanning should be done. In the latter case, the constraints of walls, doors, windows, adjacent space requirements, and plumbing locations must be taken into account and balanced against the time and budget available.

Common reasons for replanning are given in Table 24. In addition to all the practical reasons to redesign these spaces, there is the desire to make them visually attractive, well lighted, and cheerful. Specific suggestions for dealing with these issues follow.

KITCHENS

Programming

It is unfortunate that a complete, somewhat standardized kitchen is normally built into every house or apartment. The needs of individuals and families differ so widely that such ready-made kitchen spaces are rarely ideal for any user. Therefore, the designer's work properly begins with a careful review of the real needs and desires of the actual users (see Table 25). With these data in hand, the designer works out the amount of space needed, going on to the general plan layout and the selection of appliances and equipment, finally proceeding to the detailed design of counters and cabinets, and choices of finishes, colors, and similar details, as discussed in the following pages.

Planning

Historically, the big Colonial kitchen, with its huge fireplace, had been the main room of the house and the center of family activities (fig. 16.2). The Victorian kitchen, at least in larger houses, provided a spacious work area for servants, as well as (when they chose to use it) for the ladies of a family (fig. 16.3).

Until recently, ideas about kitchen design have been colored by the thinking of the Depression years of the 1930s, when the decreasing use

16.1 In a pleasantly informal farmhouse kitchen in Van Deusenville, Massachusetts, open shelving takes the place of the usual door-fronted cabinets, allowing both physical and visual access to the shelved items. The restaurant range indicates a serious interest in cooking. Peri Wolfman and Charles Gold were the designers for their own 1990 remodeling project. (Photograph: Joshua Greene, courtesy HG)

Table 24. Reasons for Replanning

Kitchens

Older kitchens are often too large, oddly subdivided, and inefficient, having been intended as work areas for a servant or staff. Modern kitchens are often too small, having been planned as "efficiency" units with little conception of family living patterns and modern ideas of gourmet cooking.

The layout of counters and appliances is often ill-considered, impractical, and antiquated.

Modern appliances are often different from their older equivalents: refrigerators are larger; stoves break up into cook tops and wall ovens; multiple sinks and dishwashers have new spatial requirements. New functions may call for new features, including informal dining areas, laundry facilities, or some kind of office-like work area within the kitchen space.

Bathrooms

New bathroom spaces—an additional bath, a new lavatory (toilet and washbasin only), or a powder room (a popular euphemism for a lavatory with some luxury dressing features such as mirrors, counter with washbasin insert, or both)—may be required.

The typical three-fixture bath may need to be replanned into a different configuration to accommodate reorganized or new functions. For example, the compartmented bath, separating toilet from bathing, often works best for family use. Additional or different fixtures (multiple fixtures, counter lavatory, extra stall shower, larger bathtub) may be desired.

Older bathrooms are often crammed into the minimum of space, while modern ideas about hygiene and relaxation suggest more spacious and versatile plans. New functions, such as exercise and rest or recreation, may call for a larger and more luxuriously planned bath.

Storage

Insufficient and badly planned closet spaces are among the most common causes of complaint about house and apartment plans. Finding locations for additional storage space is a frequent interior design problem.

Closet space may be adequate, but often the given shape, layout, and equipment do not work well. Deep, narrow closets are hard to use efficiently. In wide closets with a narrow door, the side spaces are hard to reach. The customary provision of hanging space in all closets—except, perhaps, for one linen closet with shelves—does not answer the varied and specific storage needs of modern living patterns.

General storage space, which used to be provided by the cellars and attics of older houses, is often entirely missing, leaving no place to store such bulky items as bicycles, unused furniture, trunks, and boxes. This need may call for a special planning effort.

Table 25. Programming Considerations for Kitchens

IN PLANNING A KITCHEN, THE DESIGNER MUST TAKE INTO ACCOUNT THE FOLLOWING QUESTIONS.

WHAT MEALS ARE TO BE PREPARED?
Breakfast only
Breakfast plus an occasional dinner
Breakfast and dinner daily
Three meals a day

HOW MANY PEOPLE WILL BE SERVED, NORMALLY AND AT MAXIMUM?
One alone
Two people
A family: how many?
Occasional, or frequent, guests: how many?
Maximum number
Seated
Buffet style
Party service

HOW MANY PEOPLE WILL WORK IN THE KITCHEN, NORMALLY AND AT MAXIMUM?
One person
Two people working together
One or two with helpers (children, relatives, guests)
A servant: normally, or for special occasions only

WILL MEALS BE SERVED IN THE KITCHEN?
Breakfast
Lunch
Snacks
All meals
Occasionally; always

IS THE KITCHEN TO BE AN ISOLATED WORK CENTER; A ROOM ACCESSIBLE TO FAMILY AND GUESTS; TOTALLY OPEN TO DINING OR LIVING AREAS?

IS THE KITCHEN TO ACCOMMODATE ANY SPECIAL FUNCTIONS IN ADDITION TO FOOD PREPARATION?
Laundry
Ironing
Plant and garden care
Sewing
Other

FOR EACH REGULAR USER, WHAT IS:
Optimum counter height (32"–38"; standard: 36")
Maximum high shelf reach (72"–76")
Need for use by person with a disability, if any

DESIRED APPLIANCES (GENERAL TYPE AND ANY SPECIFIC PREFERENCES), STORAGE REQUIREMENTS, SPECIAL NEEDS?

16.2

16.3

16.2 The Colonial American kitchen was a highly functional work center. In New England, it also served as the main living and dining space of the house. In the South, with its warmer climate and highly stratified social system, the kitchen did not function as a social area. Illustrated here is the kitchen of the Wythe House in the restored town of Williamsburg, Virginia. (Photograph: Langdon Clay, courtesy the Colonial Williamsburg Foundation)

16.3 In the kitchen of a large residence modernized in the early 1900s, the tiled floors, walls, and ceiling and the well-organized storage cabinets indicate a high level of concern for sanitation and efficiency, but the utilitarian character of the space is clearly determined by the expectation that only servants will work here. (Photograph courtesy Museum of the City of New York)

16.4

of household help, the need to scale down construction costs and size, and the appearance of more varied and improved appliances and equipment led to the "streamlined" kitchen of minimum size, designed with a laboratorylike neatness for efficient work patterns (fig. 16.4). This small kitchen had been planned for use by one person—the "typical housewife"—whose burden of work, it was thought, would be reduced by the compact, assembly-line layout, with appliances and

16.5

16.6

16.4 In the 1930s, as households employed fewer servants and the kitchen became increasingly the province of the homemaker, kitchens became much smaller and more finished in appearance. At the same time, however, industrial designers of the period focused on efficiency, introducing appliances and cabinetry of almost laboratorylike aspect. The "streamlined" kitchen became a showplace in the modern house, although it did not prove to be the ideal workplace. This example is in the Butler House of 1936 in Des Moines, Iowa, designed by Kraetsch and Kraetsch, architects. (Photograph: Hedrich/Blessing)

16.5 A counter for informal dining wraps around the cooktop in this spacious, comfortable kitchen. Open-shelf storage provides a display of useful supplies, while large windows let in light and view. Peggy Bosley and Jeffrey Biben were the owners and designers of this 1990 project, a drastic reconstruction of an older bungalow in Claremont, California. (Photograph: © Dominique Vorillon, courtesy Metropolitan Home)

sink embedded in a continuous line of counters, favoring neatness and easy cleaning. Storage space was usually enclosed by doors.

This concept still influences modern kitchen design, although its assumptions have come into question. To begin with, a small kitchen is likely to be inconvenient with more than one person working; closed storage makes for the endless opening and closing of doors; and a uniform counter line tends to place storage and appliances too high or too low for many users.

In addition, today's life-styles have outgrown the "laboratory kitchen." The modern tendency is toward open kitchen plans that permit easy communication with family or guests. The standard kitchen layout cannot accommodate other activities, such as eating, children's play or study, sewing, or laundry. Eating habits have become varied, too, ranging from quick snacks and prepackaged frozen dinners to gourmet cooking requiring more space and equipment than the "average" meal uses.

Whatever the functional requirements for a particular kitchen may be, planning will follow some basic concepts. First of all, plumbing limitations must be considered. It is always most economical to stay close to existing piping or, in new construction, to group plumbing fixtures close together, back-to-back when possible. If piping can be run freely below the floor (as, for example, when the basement is below the kitchen space), plumbing can be located as desired, although a close grouping minimizes the cost of plumbing installation. If access to the

space below is difficult or impossible (as in multistory apartment buildings), it is essential to stay close to existing plumbing riser locations. Pipes can extend a few feet in one direction or another, but long horizontal runs are impractical. (See also Chapter 14, pages 419–21.)

The placement of architectural elements usually imposes constraints as well. Planning must take into account window location, for example, to make the best use of it. Most users prefer a window over a sink. Door location is somewhat more flexible, although any change, particularly of an outside door, may be costly. Kitchens designed for those with disabilities call for special consideration (see Chapter 15, figs. 15.16, 15.17).

PRIMARY WORK CENTERS. With these constraints in mind, and with a program of needs established, the designer can consider the different plan layouts possible. All of these, from the smallest to the most elaborate, will feature three primary work centers, each related to one of the basic pieces of kitchen equipment.

RECEIVING AND STORAGE. The refrigerator is the primary item of equipment, with space for unpacking and spreading out groceries and storage for packaged and canned goods close by. Some serving from this center (for ice, cold drinks, and cold foods) can also be anticipated.
FOOD PREPARATION. This center comprises work counter space and the sink (or sinks) for washing, mixing, chopping, and so on (fig. 16.8). After

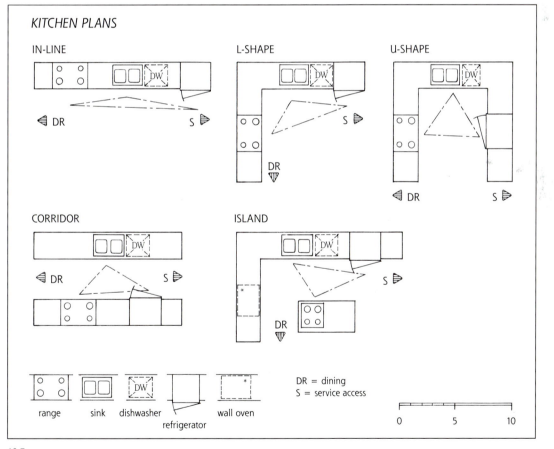

16.7

16.6 *Minimalist purity is the overriding aesthetic in a kitchen designed by architect Richard Rogers for the Royal Avenue House, his own home in London. Note the gas burners mounted on top of the metal counter surface. (Photograph: © Richard Bryant/Arcaid)*

16.7 *Different kitchen layouts are illustrated here, from upper left: in-line, L-shape, U-shape, corridor, and island. The work triangle outlines the walking path created by the layout of the three centers. The arrows point to service access and dining room. The architectural plan symbols for the major fixtures and appliances are given below.*

16.8

meals, it becomes the center for cleanup. Dishwasher and disposal unit, when they are provided, logically belong here, along with conventional trash and garbage containers. Adjacent storage holds utensils, cleaning supplies, and possibly some cooking and serving items.

COOKING. The range and/or cook top and oven plus, possibly, a microwave oven are the obvious equipment. Adjacent counter space is used for some preparation and for serving. Storage for pots and pans and serving dishes should be at hand.

Storage for dishes and glassware may relate to either food preparation or cooking. Secondary functions (such as laundry equipment and eating space) are logically given peripheral locations.

KITCHEN LAYOUTS. Ideally, kitchen planning places the three centers in sequence, starting with receiving and storage, proceeding to preparation, and ending with cooking and serving, with the idea that this corresponds to the actual sequence of meal preparation, thus minimizing wasted movement (fig. 16.7). This leads to a typical layout with refrigerator, sink, and range in that order, spaced out with work counters and storage between the major appliances.

The most favored arrangements are:

STRAIGHT LINE. The three centers are lined up in order, ideally with service entrance at one end and access to dining at the opposite end (fig. 16.9).

16.9

16.8 In this 1984 kitchen designed by John Caulk for a house in Bryn Mawr, Pennsylvania, the island holds the primary preparation surface with a sink, with a secondary surface and another sink in the counter space on the left. The cooking area is straight ahead; a wall oven is on the right. The laboratory-like, continuous counters of the 1930s have now been humanized, and natural wood finishes have replaced white enameled metal. (Photograph: © Tom Crane)

16.9 This three-center, in-line kitchen graces a California house. Here, the refrigerator is not in the line but facing it on the left. (Photograph: © Philip L. Molten)

This is the most common plan for a minimal or very small kitchen or kitchenette. An in-line plan in a larger facility may stretch the elements out across an overly long walking path.

L-SHAPE. The centers, in the same sequence as above, are bent around a corner to fit the space available and to reduce paths of work movement. This plan places two of the centers in a line with the third at a right angle. Occasionally, the preparation center is placed at the bend, sometimes with an L-shaped or diagonal sink.

U-SHAPE. This plan, in which the three centers make up the three sides of the layout, is probably the most popular and most often recommended (fig. 16.11). This plan is particularly efficient for one person working alone who stands within easy reach of a work triangle formed by the three sides. Its problems include the two corner areas, often difficult to use well, and the somewhat constricted space within the U if more than one person will work in the kitchen.

OTHER PLAN TYPES. More or less variations on the basic layouts, these include the *parallel,* or *corridor, plan* and plans incorporating an *island.* In the first, a straight line is cut into two parts, placed to face one another across the work aisle, or a basic straight line is paralleled by a storage line opposite (fig. 16.12). An island is usually added to an L or U plan to make either the range or the sink accessible from several directions. It is particularly suitable to larger kitchens and situations in which several people will work together at meal preparation.

Elements and Materials

After selecting a basic plan layout and incorporating additional elements, such as laundry or eat-in table or counter, the designer moves on to the detailed planning of work surfaces, storage, and equipment selection and placement. A number of kitchen systems offer excellent counter and storage products (fig. 16.24) and, often, an advisory service as well, making solutions almost certain of success. Some appliance manufacturers offer related storage elements. The many cabinet lines, in wood, metal, and combinations of materials, vary from excellent to indifferent in both design and construction quality.

It is also entirely possible to custom design all kitchen installations, incorporating only a sink and appliances of standard manufacture. While it takes considerable effort, this latter course makes it possible to provide for specific, even unusual needs. It is often more economical than high-quality standard product systems.

This phase of design involves the following choices:

COOKING APPLIANCE. The common choice is between a unit range, or stove, or separate cook top (fig. 16.21) and oven or ovens. Large restaurant, or professional, ranges have come into use in kitchens designed for serious cooks (fig. 16.16). Cooking devices such as microwave ovens, electric frying pans and casseroles, toaster ovens, and so on often serve as auxiliaries to the basic range.

Ranges are made in several standard sizes in two basic types: those that stand on the floor, usually placed with counters of matching shape on one or both sides, and *drop-in* versions that are inserted into a cutout in a counter with the counter base carrying through uninterrupted at floor level. Restaurant ranges, special ranges such as the AGA cooker (fig. 16.23), and traditional stoves that burn coal or wood (as

well as gas) typically stand free of counters. Built-in cook tops and ovens (wall or under-counter) are at the opposite extreme, fitting unobtrusively into continuous counter and cabinet installations.

Users with disabilities may be aided by cook tops situated lower than standard height and by ovens with side-hinged doors placed at an appropriate level. (For further discussion of special-need kitchen considerations, see Chapter 15.)

FUEL. The choice between gas or electric fuel depends upon both economics and the cook's personal preference. Even the obsolescent wood stove can be considered, usually with a gas backup, in rural locations where wood is an economical fuel.

REFRIGERATOR TYPE. Models come with freezer space at the top or, more convenient but requiring more space, alongside. When space permits, a separate freezer of cabinet or chest type may be a good choice. Wall-recessed refrigerators of fine design are also available.

For people with disabilities the choice of a refrigerator requires special consideration. The upper freezer compartment common in many refrigerators may be too high for convenient access. The side-by-side freezer compartment is better, although some upper parts of both compartments may be unreachable. A special low refrigerator with top access has been developed to provide improved access for wheelchair users (see fig. 15.20).

SINK TYPE AND MATERIAL. Types may be single, double, or multipurpose; of stainless steel or enameled cast iron; with or without a drain board configuration (fig. 16.14). Faucet type and design must also be selected (fig. 16.13), as well as dishwasher and disposal unit, if included. Space, budget, and user preferences are determinants in selection.

STORAGE PROVISION. Closed cabinets are a favorite, but open storage deserves consideration for items that are not messy and require no protection. Open shelves and hanging pots and utensils avoid the inconvenience of constantly opening and closing doors. Open wire shelves and baskets (fig. 16.25) and systems for hanging pots and tools (fig. 16.15) are convenient and inexpensive storage alternatives. Dish and glassware storage may be part of a kitchen plan or may be placed in or adjacent to the dining space. Drawers, cabinets with rotating shelves, and ingenious special units for specific storage needs, including cleaning supplies and equipment, are available in most kitchen systems (figs. 16.22, 16.26).

The choice of wood or metal as a primary material is not a simple one, as each material offers its own advantages. Wood doors and drawers, with their quiet operation and their warm feel, texture, and appearance, may create a more comfortable, or homelike, atmosphere. Metal is stronger, easier to clean, and suggests sanitation and durability. Finishes on metal are usually tough, but once damaged they are hard to repair, with the possibility of rust developing. Natural finishes on wood are less likely to show damage and are easier to repair. Paint finishes on wood are less durable than similar metal finishes, but repainting is comparatively easy. Plastic laminate is a durable alterna-

16.11

tive. Since neither material has an overall clear advantage, selection is primarily a matter of personal taste. A possible compromise is the use of metal cabinets with wood door and drawer fronts.

COUNTERS. The standard height of 36 inches will not serve all tasks and all users, but it is widely adopted as a compromise norm. When a kitchen is planned for a particular user, it may be appropriate to consider counters higher or lower than standard to suit that person. Wheelchair occupants need counters placed at 34-inch height or adjustable from 28 to 36 inches. Open space at least 30 inches wide is required under counter tops for knee clearance.

Many surface materials are possible, each with various advantages and disadvantages. Favorite choices include plastic laminate, wood (butcher block), linoleum, tile, stainless steel, and special synthetic composition materials such as Corian.

Counter tops present special problems at front and back edges, where a crevice that may be unsightly and hard to keep clean will occur if materials must be joined at these points. Front edges may be of laminate or may use a trim molding of plastic or metal. The best treatment results when the top material is thick enough to form its own edge (as with wood or granite) or when the material is rolled over to form an edge, as provided with some laminates and with metal. A similar problem occurs at the rear of counters, where it is usual to provide a *back-splash* of easily cleaned material 4 to 6 inches high. Here also a continuous material, rolled upward from the top, avoids a crevice (laminates are available with such integral back-splashes). When sinks or cook tops are recessed into counters and wherever counters meet other elements—walls, appliances, or counters with different top materials— special attention is required to avoid cracks that are difficult to clean and maintain.

FLOOR MATERIALS. Linoleum, resilient tile, ceramic tile, quarry tile, and slate all lend themselves to the kitchen environment. Wood and carpet specially made for wet-location use may also be considered.

Hard-surface floor materials such as tile and slate, while easy to keep clean, can be noisy and may chip easily when objects are dropped. Some users may also find them tiring to stand on for extended periods of time. Although more resilient materials are quieter and may feel more pleasant to stand on, they do not wear as well and may prove difficult to keep clean. Color and pattern of floor material also have an impact on ease of maintenance. Plain colors, especially light tones, show every spill and foot mark and demand constant cleaning. Medium colors and small-scale textures or patterns conceal minor spotting but for that very reason do not express perfect cleanliness. The attractive gleam of glossy surfaces is harder to maintain than matte finishes, and many such surfaces create an actual slipping hazard. Floor tile with a dimpled surface has become a popular choice even though soil tends to collect at the edges of the raised discs, presenting some difficulty in cleaning. Points where the flooring meets walls, cabinets, or appliance bases call for special attention to ensure a neat joint without a hard-to-clean crack; a cove baseboard treatment is ideal.

WALL SURFACES. Paint, plastic sheet material, plastic laminate, and tile are popular choices.

CEILING MATERIALS. Sheetrock, plaster, and acoustical materials are possible choices.

MISCELLANEOUS ITEMS. Other details that call for consideration include lighting, ventilation, and a variety of accessories and gadgets. A central globe light, often provided for general illumination, tends to

16.10 *A harmony of natural colors is established in this kitchen through the use of wood flooring and cabinets, granite for countertops, and brushed stainless steel for the oven front and the custom-designed range hood. Fu Tung Cheng was the architect for the house, located in Portola Valley, California. (Photograph: © Alan Weintraub, courtesy Metropolitan Home)*

16.11 *Glass block and stainless steel establish the High Tech character of this U-shape kitchen in a Southern California house. Francisco Kripacz was the architect. (Photograph: Tim Street-Porter)*

16.12

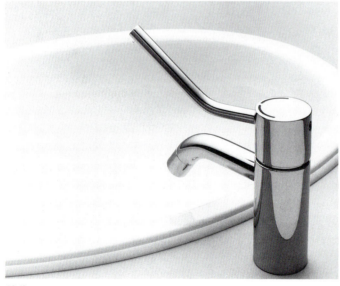

16.13

16.14

16.12 In a corridor kitchen, the work space is between two parallel lines of counters, appliances, and storage units. Service access is usually at one end of the corridor, access to the dining room at the other end. This kitchen was designed for maximum efficiency by its owners, Jim and Christopher

Hirsheimer, the latter a caterer. (Photograph: John Waggaman, courtesy Metropolitan Home)

16.13 A single-control, or mixing, faucet displays an exceptionally neat and elegant design. (Photograph courtesy Kroin

16.14 A double kitchen sink of acid-resistant enameled cast iron supports, in one basin, a removable wooden cutting board. The person working pushes scraps through the hole into a container in the sink below. A single-control, or mixing, faucet is an alternative to the two-control installation shown. (Photograph courtesy Kohler Co.)

16.15 In this unusual, glass-roofed kitchen by James Rossant, racks of tinlined copper pots and pans become accessories on display—and in handy reach. The stainless-steel cabinets are rubber-lined to deaden noise. (Photograph: © 1985 Wolfgang Hoyt/ESTO)

16.19

16.20

16.21

16.19 This unusual kitchen is part of a house in Tokyo constructed entirely of prefabricated, industrially produced elements. The long counter serves as both a work surface and a place for eating. Small wheeled units roll under the countertop to provide movable storage; the long suspended bar is used to hang lighting units that can be moved about as needed. The house was designed by architect Toyo Itoh. (Photograph: Gilles de Chabaneix)

16.20 A collection of baskets inside a glass-front under-counter refrigerator has been put to use for food storage in a Southern California project designed by Kitty Bartholomew. Tile (at left) and hand-painted decorative panels (above the refrigerator) are used behind counter-tops. (Photograph: Michael Mundy, courtesy Crown Publishers, Inc.)

16.21 In this "kitchen idea" from Abaco, designed by Giovanni Offredi, cupboards make up an unbroken wall at the far end of the counter. Sinks and burner top are set into the counter; its curved back-splash is surmounted by a continuous luminous band that provides working light directly above the work surface. (Photograph courtesy Abitare)

16.22

16.23

16.24

16.25

16.22 Roll-out shelves make items stored near the rear of an under-counter storage unit easily accessible, forestalling the need for stooping and groping. The small spice shelves above the countertop at the rear store the diminutive jars neatly. (Photograph: Diane Padys)

16.23 Although standard ranges are usually surrounded by counters, restaurant or other special ranges are generally freestanding. One such range is the AGA cooker, a British alternative to the usual kitchen range, developed more than fifty years ago. Its heavily insulated construction conserves heat from a central gas burner, which serves all of the cooking functions. (Photograph courtesy AGA Cookers, Vermont)

16.24 The most compact possible kitchenette: a single unit incorporates sink and burners in the countertop, refrigerator below, and microwave oven above. (Photograph courtesy Dwyer Kitchen Products)

16.25 An open wire-grid storage system, used here to hold a food processor's attachments, can accommodate a variety of hooks, holders, racks, and shelves, making it possible to arrange a custom-storage assembly for almost any imaginable collection of small items. (Photograph courtesy Heller Designs, Inc.)

place the user in his or her own shadow and gives an overall effect of bleakness. The most effective lighting comes from strips concealed under wall cabinets or shelves. Downlights directed at counters also work well. A range hood, ideally outside-vented, is the best cure for kitchen smells and deposits of cooking fumes and grease. A window fan or ceiling fan is an inferior alternative. Accessories such as towel racks, pinup boards, clocks, spice racks, and many other popular gadgets will become items of clutter if not planned for.

Appearance

It is a curious fact that the appearance of residential kitchens is most often spoiled by efforts at beautification, usually realized in one or both of two ways: by importing an artificial charm, which may derive from inappropriate period decor and fussy elements such as patterned curtains, overdecorative tile, and other ornamental materials, or by using imitative materials. Modern cabinets faced in imitation—or even real—knotty pine or with French provincial details; linoleum that imitates Spanish tiles, flagstone, or brick; wallpapers that simulate Dutch (or any other) tiles—all these set a tone of falseness and visual clutter. Such elements are all too often featured in consumer publications that provide advice on kitchen design. In fact, a more practical and straightforward design will hold up better, both in use and in attractiveness, over a period of time. This approach eliminates neither comfort nor, at best, genuine beauty.

BATHROOMS

Like kitchens, bathrooms are usually given a minimum of space and designed according to formula, with a few "special features," such as a counter lavatory, possibly added to soften the effect. While bath functions are less complex than those of kitchens, they deserve more attention than the formula layouts devote to them

Residential

The modern bathroom has its origins in the Victorian introduction of modern plumbing (fig. 16.32). The toilet owes its alternative name of *water closet* to its frequent introduction, quite literally, into an existing closet. The bathroom most often began as an existing room, perhaps a small bedroom or storage room, and was converted by the installation of the three standard fixtures (toilet, washbasin, and bathtub).

Placing these fixtures together in one room has a certain logic since the privacy of all three functions is ensured with one closable door to the room. The disadvantage, of course, is that one user ties up the entire room as long as the door remains closed. Moreover, modern bathroom use often calls for, in addition to the basic three fixtures, a shower (or substitutes this for or combines it with the bathtub), twin washbasins, perhaps a bidet (common in France but unusual elsewhere), provision for exercise, rest, or special bathing facilities (such as a sauna or Jacuzzi), and, occasionally, laundry facilities.

One bathroom can hardly accommodate all of these elements. Also, if there will be more than one user, two or more units have clear advantages. A number of possible combinations can be considered (fig. 16.38), including adding a *lavatory* or *powder room* (without tub

16.26

or shower) accessible to guests as well as family; creating a *split bathroom,* for example, with toilet or toilet and washbasin in a unit separate from a bathing unit; and providing two or more complete bathrooms.

Whatever their layout, all bathroom spaces must connect to plumbing, most economically with pipes shared by another bath or kitchen, ideally back-to-back. The toilet requires a larger drainpipe called a *soil stack,* which can pass through only a thick partition wall or pipe chase space. Efficient plans usually line up all fixtures with pipes along one wall. Minimal dimensions are well-known standards, widely published. However, these make for rather cramped facilities; actual use patterns give a better guide to dimensions. Easy access for people with disabilities, particularly for wheelchair users, requires additional clearances, as well as consideration of fixture and cabinet heights and provision of grab rails in certain locations (see Chapter 15, pages 436–41).

TOILETS. (*Water closet* or W.C. is the plumbing-trade designation.) Toilets are made with either separate or integral tanks. In modern high-rise buildings, a *syphon-jet* flush does not require a tank. Bowls are now made in a variety of shapes, some more attractive than the traditional oval. Although seat and cover must be chosen to suit the bowl form, assorted colors and texture patterns are available.

16.26 The doors of this kitchen storage unit have glass inserts to provide a glimpse of the items stored within. The solid faces of the cabinet are of Color-core laminate, a plastic surface material in which the face color is carried through the thickness of the laminate so that the edges are the same color as the face. (Photograph courtesy Formica Corporation)

16.27

16.28

WASHBASINS. (*Lavatories*). These vary from complete units with a pedestal base or with legs to bowls that can be wall-hung. It has become popular to set bowls into a counter top to provide generous surrounding space for soap dishes and other accessories. Bowls are available in a range of sizes, shapes, and finishes. The surround can be of plastic laminate, marble, tile, or any other material that is reasonably water-resistant. Twin basins are a favorite luxury in a master bathroom.

BATHTUBS. Tubs are made in various shapes and sizes, and manufacturers have vied with one another to develop luxury units in unusual shapes. Some provide a rim wide enough to serve as a seat; others suggest opulence by approaching a small pool in size. Whirlpool Jacuzzis and hot tubs remain popular. Even the old-fashioned tub on legs continues to seem attractive and appropriate in certain settings. Many tubs provide their own exterior front or front and end surfaces, while others are designed to be recessed into a constructed surround or platform. Tubs sunken into the floor require clearance below or an elevated platform into which the tub can be recessed. Materials include porcelain-enameled iron, a lighter enameled sheet steel, and some modern units in fiberglass plastic. As the population grows to taller average heights, tub lengths beyond the standard 60 inches deserve consideration.

All tubs call for safety precautions. Getting into and out of a tub with wet and slippery surfaces both inside and possibly outside can be hazardous, particularly for the elderly and those with disabilities (see Chapter 15, page 439). Textured bottom surfaces and suitable handrails can reduce the danger of slipping.

SHOWERS. Commonly provided with tubs, showers can also be separate units. Standard shower stalls are available as complete units, or shower areas can be custom-built from appropriate materials that must, of course, be water-resistant. At floor level, a shower stall may use a manufactured bottom pan with coved edges and center drain, or a base can be custom-built with surfaces sloping to a drain. Shower enclosure is needed to confine spray and steam. A simple shower curtain on a rod works well but may not seem as luxurious as a sliding or swinging door. Glass enclosure, however attractive, is hazardous. In addition to spray, showers produce steam that condenses on surrounding surfaces, requiring special attention in material selection and detailing within the entire bathroom.

BIDETS. Sanitary fixtures long accepted in France and some other European countries, bidets are rarely used in America. The units are roughly similar in size and shape to a toilet.

All standard bathroom fixtures are available in various designs and in a range of colors, in addition to the ubiquitous white.

All bathroom spaces require ventilation as well as heat. The former may be by means of either a window or skylight or a fan and duct, or by a combination of the two. Details of a bath include provision for soap, towels, toilet-paper dispensers, medicine cabinet, mirror, and suitable lighting. Materials need to be selected for water-resistance.

16.29

16.30

16.27 *Restrained color and a simple design characterize the communal kitchen of Friends in Deed, a facility established in a loft space to serve terminally ill residents of the SoHo area. Bob Patino was the designer. (Photograph: © Stephen Barker, courtesy Metropolitan Home)*

16.28 *In a traditional Litchfield, Connecticut, house, the kitchen combines the functions of food preparation, eating, and storage. A collection of majolica pottery displayed on open shelves acts as a decorative element. The house is owned by designer Bunny Williams. (Photograph: John Vaughan, courtesy Crown Publishers, Inc.)*

16.29 *White tile walls and glass-enclosed storage compartments for towels and linens add to the clean lines of a Hollywood, California, bathroom designed by Brian Murphy (see also fig. 16.36). (Photograph: © Tim Street-Porter, courtesy Elle Decor)*

16.30 *Executive washrooms have become favorite status symbols in business office complexes. Handsome materials and details add to the sense of opulence in this example, designed by Gwathmey Siegel & Associates Architects, for the offices of FDM Productions, New York. (Photograph: O. Baitz, Inc., courtesy Gwathmey Siegel & Associates Architects)*

16.31

Tile, slate, and marble are more durable than plaster, wood, and wallpaper, which, although commonly used, must be regularly renewed.

Bathrooms have a bad record as locations for accidents. The presence of slippery surfaces, water (particularly hot water), soap, electric outlets, and, often, glass-enclosure elements, alone or in combination, creates a variety of hazards, especially for children, the elderly, and people with disabilities. As mentioned above, glass shower enclosures should be avoided, mirrors placed with care to prevent accidental breakage, nonskid surfaces and grab rails provided, and electrical outlets using a ground-fault interrupter specified.

Space and budget permitting, bathrooms can become outstandingly attractive, with good daylight, night lighting, growing plants, space and equipment for rest and exercise, and handsome materials and colors. Small details such as faucets, soap dishes, and towel racks—even the towels themselves—can add to the design quality of a bathroom. Storage space for towels, soap, and similar items can be provided within or adjacent to a bath. Dressing and makeup facilities can be combined with or located adjacent to a bathroom.

Nonresidential

Bathrooms for hotels and motels, dormitories, hospitals, and the "executive washroom" now often provided in office facilities (fig. 16.30) follow home practice, with appropriate modifications for the special needs of these situations. Bathrooms in hotels and motels are important expressions of the level of quality and luxury that a particular establishment offers. An elaborately luxurious bathroom can play a

16.31 An Eileen Gray mirror is an elegant feature of an uncluttered bathroom designed by Andrée Putman. Note the band of decorative tile and the glass-block wall of the shower alcove. (Photograph: © Grant Mudford, courtesy House & Garden)

16.32

16.32 This luxurious, late-Victorian bathroom dates from the beginning of this century. Note the fireplace with stained-glass window above, the chandelier, and the marble washbasin counter and back-splash. The extraordinary arrangement at the left offers seated comfort while showering. Museum of the City of New York. Wurts Collection

16.33

16.34

very substantial role in guests' satisfaction with the room or suite they are staying in.

Public toilets, or *rest rooms*, for offices, stores, restaurants, and other public situations demand more complex planning (fig. 16.33). One basic planning issue concerns how the size of public rest rooms is to be determined. Ideally, the size and type of facilities provided should relate in some logical way to the number of people using a space. Although some rules have been suggested, this is not a simple problem. The area of a floor is not a reliable guide to the number of people who will use the space—that number may change over a period of time, as in offices or industrial structures where the number of workers may vary as tasks are changed. In many situations there is a problem of peak loading, as in theaters and auditoriums where intermissions lead to heavy use of facilities that may be almost unused at other times. In schools or college buildings, use may be maximal during periods between classes. In addition, it is difficult to predict the proportion of men and women who will be using public rest rooms. While it has been customary to allot similar floor areas to men's and women's rest rooms, this is quite illogical when the user population can be predicted to not be equally mixed. In addition, women's rest rooms require more space for a given user population to ensure an adequate number of stalls and to allow for the longer time women tend to take using the facilities.

In public rest rooms the basic fixtures of home bathrooms—toilets and washbasins—are augmented by provisions of urinals in men's rooms and by the need for stalls and screens for privacy. Rest-room stalls are standard manufactured products available in many colors and finishes, supported from walls and floors or wall-hung without floor support. The latter, particularly when used with other wall-hung fixtures, permit clear floors that are easily cleaned and maintained. Public rest rooms also require soap dispensers, towel holders, trash containers, and, in some locations, hot-air hand dryers and various vending machines. Details of faucets and other hardware need to be carefully considered for practicality and appearance. In many locations, including theaters, better restaurants, and corporate office buildings, spacious rest rooms of high aesthetic quality express organizational respect for the comfort of users.

Rest rooms accessible to a large general public may be designed to be more strictly utilitarian. Such facilities must also provide maximal protection against vandalism (the ever-present graffiti) and crime. The selection of materials that are resistant to damage and easily cleaned aids maintenance, while a thoughtful plan layout (one that avoids areas of isolation, for example) can discourage trouble. Guidelines for barrier-free access must also be adhered to (see Chapter 15, pages 437–39).

Storage

Residential

Closets make up the primary storage provision in modern residential practice, although shelving, cabinets, files, and even entire storerooms may also be called for. Intelligent design begins with a careful estimate of what is to be stored and a consideration of where suitable storage

16.35

16.36

16.33 At the Phoenix Level Restaurant (1985) of the Garden State Racetrack, Cherry Hill, New Jersey, a richly detailed public toilet displays strong colors and opulent materials, which transform a necessary utility into a dramatic space. Ewing, Cole, Cherry, Parsky was the designer. (Photograph: © 1985 Tom Crane)

16.34 A bathroom sink that stands above the marble counter, rather than being sunk into it, has both functional and aesthetic merits: it is located at a convenient height for adult use, but its unusual placement also highlights its decorative quality. Eva Jiricna was the architect for the modern renovation of an 1820s vintage building in Knightsbridge, London. (Photograph: © Richard Bryant/Arcaid)

16.35 An oval lavatory sink of handcrafted metal with a polished nickel finish becomes a striking design element. (Photograph courtesy Eljer Plumbingware)

16.36 In a bathroom designed by Brian Murphy for a Hollywood, California, house, sandblasted glass forms the side enclosures for the washbasin (see also fig. 16.29). The exposed pipes, which allow for easy cleaning, are also decorative in effect. (Photograph: © Tim Street-Porter, courtesy Elle Decor)

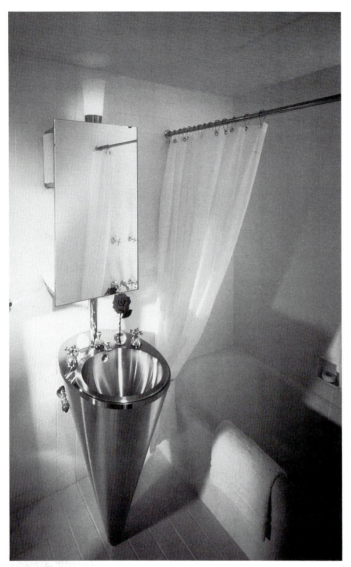

16.37

and other storage fittings on both sides of an aisle, and the dressing room, in which closets and other storage are combined with space and equipment for dressing, grooming, and makeup, including good mirrors and lighting (fig. 16.39). A dressing room is often used as a transitional element between bedroom and bath.

There are several ways to introduce extra storage space into a plan that lacks adequate closets:

REPLACING A WALL BETWEEN TWO ROOMS WITH A LINE OF CLOSETS. The storage wall usually goes between two bedrooms and is divided so that each room gains half (or some other fraction) of the total. Each space loses only one-half the total closet depth while otherwise retaining its shape.

STORAGE FURNITURE. This can be placed (or built-in) where needed (figs. 16.41–16.43). Wardrobes and armoires, widely used in Europe in place of built-in closets, are available as imports, often as elements of storage systems that also provide drawers, shelving, and special-purpose elements such as desks, bars, and TV/audio equipment arrangement.

ROOM DIVIDER AND WALL UNIT. These are also furniture approaches to adding storage. (See Chapter 12, fig. 12.31.) They are best suited to the storage of smaller objects such as books, records, dishes, and glassware

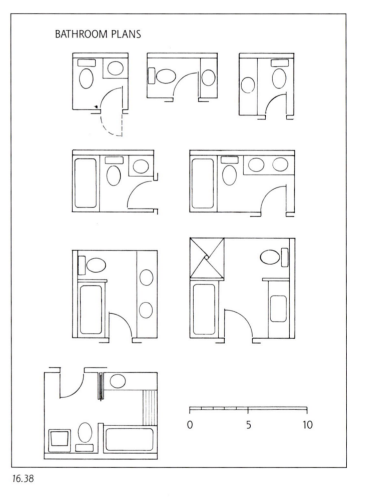

16.38

spaces should go. Commonly, a coat closet is needed near each primary entrance to a dwelling, a clothes closet for each bedroom (ideally double for double occupancy), and at least one linen closet to hold bedding, blankets, and bathroom linens. In addition, the great variety of things that modern families accumulate—sports gear, toys and games, photography equipment, records, tapes, CDs, luggage, and even such bulky items as bicycles, snow tires, and skis—demands general storage space.

Conventional closets must be large enough to provide hanging space for clothing and require full front access through sliding or accordion doors. Shelves, shoe racks, built-in drawer units, and other specialized provisions can make storage space more efficient and convenient. Such storage arrangements can be specially detailed and built or can be developed through the use of widely available ready-made systems of closet accessories (fig. 16.45). More extensive storage arrangements include the walk-in closet, actually a small room with hanging space

16.37 A gleaming stainless-steel cone forms the support of the washbasin in a guest bath of the Paramount Hotel in New York. The sink is one of several unusual elements in Philippe Starck's interior renovation of the Paramount. (See fig. 18.30 for another view of this project.) (Photograph: Tom Vack, courtesy Starck)

16.38 Here are layouts of typical bathrooms, ranging from the lavatory or powder room to complete baths, in minimal, simple, and split-bath arrangements. Pipes are hidden in the walls indicated with a double line.

rather than clothing. A room divider is used, as the name implies, between two spaces—where there is a large opening, where an opening can be created by the removal of a wall, or where one large space can be divided to serve multiple functions. The most usual locations are between living and dining areas and between dining area and kitchen. Wall units stand against, and may be attached to, a blank wall. Both types of units are usually made up of modular elements, available in a range of sizes and with varied functions. This means that the complete unit can be custom-designed to fit particular needs, even though the elements are factory-made. Similar units can also be specially designed and custom-built, often at a lower cost than a similar installation of ready-made elements. Storage walls can often accommodate bulky items—sporting gear, hobby equipment, and so on (fig. 16.44).

WHERE SPACE IS LIMITED, INGENIOUS WAYS TO USE SPACE CAN OFTEN PROVIDE EXTRA STORAGE. Drawers or rolling box units under beds are one example (see fig. 12.26). Closets often contain waste space above the normal hat shelf that can be developed for dead storage of rarely used objects. Shelves or cabinets high up on walls, while inconvenient, can hold items needed only occasionally if a suitable stepladder or stool is accessible. Space above standard kitchen wall cabinets may be used in this way, thus avoiding the problem of dirt collecting on cabinet tops at the same time. In a garage, it is often possible to develop storage space at an upper level over the hood of a parked car or over the entire car with some arrangement for a rack or container that can be lowered and raised as needed.

16.41

16.42

16.40 A guest house bathroom in Ormond Beach, Florida, uses mosaics and colorful tile in wild, playful patterns. Steven Harris & Associates were the designers. (Photograph: Timothy Hursley)

16.41 In a New York studio apartment, storage is ingeniously fitted into every possible space underneath and surrounding the access stair to a loft bed. Special drawers were designed to fit under the stair, where they accommodate objects of various sizes. Andrew M. Tuller of Tuller-McNealus Architects was the designer. (Photograph: Charles Maraia, courtesy Metropolitan Home)

16.42 The most traditional wall storage—bookcases—can be installed wall to wall, floor to ceiling, or both. Shown here is a 1981 New York apartment designed by Gwathmey Siegel & Associates Architects. (Photograph: Norman McGrath, courtesy Gwathmey Siegel & Associates Architects)

16.43

Nonresidential

Storage provisions for hotels, motels, and dormitories follow residential practice, although, obviously, it is impossible to design for unique, individual needs. Office storage in executive and managerial offices also follows similar patterns in providing closets and space for books and equipment. For general and open offices, hanging space is necessary for outdoor clothing and for smaller items, jackets, handbags, and personal possessions. Wardrobe units are often placed close to general work spaces, with a lockable drawer or locker compartment nearby. Larger coat rooms located near entrances pose security problems that have discouraged their use.

Offices present special problems in the storage of records, documents, computer-related materials, and supplies. File cabinets, the traditional basis of office storage, are produced in a great variety of sizes and types by a number of manufacturers. Most file systems also offer utility cabinets, wardrobes, and other storage units in modular sizes that make it possible to assemble neat banks of storage elements, which may also be used as space dividers. For file rooms and archives, systems with banks of files on roller tracks are available; the units are

16.44

16.43 Eileen Gray's ingenious storage cabinet with pivoted swinging bins in place of conventional drawers is here realized in lacquered wood and nickel-plated metal. (Photograph courtesy Ecart International/Palluco)

16.44 The doors of a compact storage-wall installation open to provide access to drawers, bookshelves,

and spaces for paper and other supplies. The open shelf permits display of some objects, while other items can be enclosed in storage above. Designed by The Finished Room, New York. (Photograph: Zindman/Fremont)

16.45 A closet system provides drawers, shelves, and multilevel hanging spaces. Such planned fittings can multi-

ply the usable space of conventional closets. (Photograph: Rothschild, courtesy Closet Systems)

16.46 When storage is made from transparent plastic, it becomes easy to locate any stored item. Sliding trays in a see-through box are a practical and attractive part of this 1968 wardrobe by Leonardo Fiori, designer, and

Zanotta Poltrone, Italy, manufacturer. (Photograph courtesy The Design Counsel)

16.47 These children's storage units with architectural silhouettes, painted with decorative geometric patterns, were designed by Fernando Martinez of MISMA Productions. (Photograph courtesy MISMA Productions, Inc.)

16.45

16.46

16.47

16.48

16.49

solidly packed with no aisle space except at a single location where the banks are rolled apart to permit access. When file cabinets are closely banked, the weight of the files can build up heavy floor loadings that may exceed the limits permissible for the structural system of the building. In new construction, engineers can provide extra support for dense file locations. In existing buildings, it is important to know what structural limitations may influence the placement of files.

Adequate provision of general storage—for supplies, equipment, and odds and ends such as sample products—is important if office spaces are to maintain a sense of neatness and order. Papers and objects that cannot be discarded but do not fit any available storage space contribute greatly to the chaos that all too often characterizes office interiors.

Kitchens, bathrooms, and storage facilities are special-purpose spaces—spaces used for specific purposes, with their own unique set of design problems—that appear in almost every interior project. Most residential interiors include other special-purpose spaces. The following chapter deals with a variety of such project types.

16.48 Executive workstations at American Capital, Houston, in a semiopen plan are separated by large, custom-built wall units, some with central openings. The units, designed by ISD Incorporated, provide storage as well as defining individual offices. (Photograph: Charles McGrath, courtesy ISD Incorporated)

16.49 A mobile system of double-banked bookcases can greatly expand the storage capacity of a given lateral space. The front unit rolls in tracks to give access to the units behind. (Photograph courtesy Punt Mobles, S.L.)

17.1

CHAPTER

SEVENTEEN

SPECIAL PURPOSE SPACES

SPECIAL TYPES OF INTERIOR SPACES

The interior designer occasionally encounters special types of interior spaces. Some of these gain their special character from a particular kind of building or plan type, others from a special function. The following section presents a survey of such spaces.

Lofts

A loft is simply an open space, usually unfinished in detail, intended for utilitarian uses such as manufacturing or storage. In larger cities, loft buildings provide space in multifloor configurations similar to the open areas typical of large office buildings. Artists in search of studio space were the first to recognize that, with the addition of kitchens and baths, loft space could serve as living space as well as for studio use. As manufacturing and warehousing activities have tended to move out of central city locations, first artists and then others looking for spacious city living space have gradually taken over loft buildings and whole loft neighborhoods, converting them to studios and/or living space.

A typical loft is large, high-ceilinged, often generously windowed, and has one or more details characteristic of older industrial or mill buildings (figs. 17.2 and 17.3). There may be large exposed wood or cast-iron columns, exposed beams or so-called tin (pressed-metal) ceilings, sprinkler pipes, rather crude heating and lighting arrangements, and, of course, no partitioning into rooms for normal residential use. The new occupants, with their designer and (often) architect, must introduce the kitchen, bath, storage, and partitioning to make the space useful and comfortable, all in ways that comply with building laws and the occupants' budget.

The results can range from open studio space with a minimal bath, kitchenette, and sleeping alcove or raised platform tucked away in a corner of the space to the luxury loft, which, aside from its unusually large space, can be quite similar to a conventional apartment. The big spaces characteristic of lofts, which lend themselves to social gatherings, performances, and exhibits, call for special attention to suitable furniture and finishes. Many typical residential elements (furniture, textiles, wallpapers) are on a small scale that looks out of place in open loft spaces. Simple materials, strong colors, and unpretentious kinds of furniture tend to work well in lofts. Large paintings and other works of art appear to advantage.

Studios

The term has come to designate a one-room apartment, generally small, but the studio in its original sense is discussed here—an actual work space for an artist, musician, dancer, or other creative person who needs a special and fairly large place to work. Lofts often are studios or incorporate studio space, but a studio may also be a special room in a house or apartment. Traditionally, the studio of an artist or photographer is placed to make north light available through large windows or, best of all, from a north-facing skylight.

The interior design of a typical artist's studio is totally simple (fig. 17.4). White walls and ceiling are the norm, with a floor of neutral color. Even the floor is often painted white, to reflect light and minimize any visual impact from a particular chromatic color. Furniture, usually minimal, may be improvised or "found" in character. Visual interest often derives solely from the work in progress and the artist's props and collection of necessary materials. It is surprising how often this direct and unplanned interior becomes a beautiful and exciting space. The studios of well-known artists are often photographed; those

17.1 A passage connecting living room and bedrooms, previously a wasted space, has been converted into a compact home office. Books on cherry wood shelves create the atmosphere of a library. Files and a computer printer are housed behind wood paneling on the right. Carl Pucci of BumpZoid architects was the designer of this home in New York. (Photograph: Charles Maraia, courtesy Metropolitan Home)

17.2

17.3

17.2 Many large loft buildings erected in American cities around the turn of the century for manufacturing and warehouse purposes are now often recycled for residential or office use. This space is in the Puck Building of 1885, originally designed by Albert Wagner for the printing presses of a publishing company. The undivided floors, with their large windows, sprinkler systems in place, and vast open areas, will be subdivided for architects, designers, filmmakers, and other commercial purchasers. (Photograph: © Langdon Clay)

17.3 The northern exposure—ideal for artists' studios because of the consistent light—and the pleasant view of a public park make this double-height loft space particularly attractive. It was designed by Bray-Schaible Design and Joseph Paul D'Urso in 1978 to house the designers' studios. (Photograph: © 1979 Peter Aaron/ESTO)

of some earlier famous artists can be visited as museums (for example, the studios of Cézanne, Monet, and Renoir). Such studios, with their lively and simple but expressive qualities, provide fine examples of studio space at its best.

Workshops

With do-it-yourself and other hobby activities becoming increasingly popular, the demand for home workshop space has increased (fig. 17.7). For many years, homeowners have commonly devised some sort of basement workshop. Now, more and more inhabitants of small houses or even apartments have begun to insist on having workshop space. Although the interior designer is rarely responsible for the design of such space, some thoughtful planning can have a significant effect on making a workshop useful.

For hobbies that require a large area—such as serious woodworking, boat-building, or work on cars—basements, garages, or, when they exist, barns are often used as workshops. It is important to plan the space around shop equipment so that tools and materials have ade-

quate clearances. A circular saw in a woodworking shop, for example, requires clearance for feeding and removing work, calling for a considerable clear area when such large pieces as 4-by-8-foot plywood or 16-foot lengths of wood are being cut. The size of projects must also be taken into account beforehand. Jokes about boats built in spaces too small to permit their removal are not so farfetched. Noise from power tools and fumes from painting and work with plastics and the fire risks associated with such materials also need attention.

Some hobbies do not need a large space but call for equipment that many home spaces cannot easily accommodate. The minimal requirement for firing pottery, for example, is an electric kiln that may need special heavy-duty wiring. Gas or wood-burning kilns need a chimney. Many craft hobbies, such as woodcarving, making model airplanes or boats, making guitars or violins, printing on a small scale, and weaving, make more modest demands on space and equipment but still deserve some thought if suitable workshop space for any one or any combination of these activities is called for. Such hobbies may even use a closet, a storage wall grouping, or a foldaway piece of furniture as a

17.4

17.4 The vast proportions of Willem de Kooning's studio are appropriate to the large scale of the artist's work. The signs of creative activity become the source of the space's aesthetic quality. (Photograph: Jaime Ardiles-Arce)

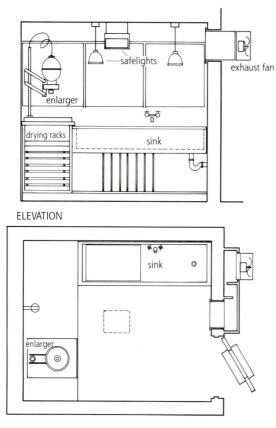

safelights

exhaust fan

enlarger

drying racks

sink

ELEVATION

sink

enlarger

17.5   FLOOR PLAN

17.6

17.7

17.8

workplace, arranged to make work convenient. Although the work space is clearly limited, it concentrates and confines equipment and the mess associated with the hobby.

Sewing Rooms

Ideally, this activity receives its own room, but it is most often combined with a laundry room, utility room, or, occasionally, a kitchen. Sewing requires good task light, good placement for a sewing machine with ample surrounding work space, a cutting table, an ironing board (a foldaway board may be used), and suitable storage.

Darkrooms

Many professional and serious amateur photographers require a home or studio darkroom (fig. 17.5). A bathroom or kitchen may serve as a makeshift space, but the most practical darkroom has its own space and facilities. An extra bathroom or a large closet can sometimes be successfully converted to a darkroom (fig. 17.9), but a space planned for the purpose works out best.

The need for darkening is obvious, with special arrangements at window and door to assure full light-tightness. Since excluding light usually means cutting off ventilation, some mechanical ventilation (or air-conditioning) is essential. Running water and drainage are highly

desirable, although improvised ways of doing without can be considered. Manuals addressed to photographers and photo technicians give comprehensive advice on the suitable arrangement of work counters, storage, electrical outlets, and similar matters, on which the user will have specific ideas.

Home Offices

As a result of the ways in which computers and facsimile machines permit information access and rapid communication between a home office and a traditional business facility, many regularly employed people whose work is office-based are discovering that it is possible to work at home part-time or perhaps close to full-time. Independent contractors and other small-business entrepreneurs, including writers, editors, and other creative professionals, as well as investors and agents, are all finding that a home office needs the same thoughtful design that would be provided in an office building. Even the office-like chores of everyday life (writing letters, paying bills) can be facilitated by having a special place for doing paperwork and for keeping files and a typewriter or personal computer.

A home office may be a single piece of furniture sharing space in a bedroom, library, living room, or kitchen. It may be a special built-in grouping in a study, an extra bedroom, or even a closet (figs. 17.1,

17.5 A photographic darkroom is a highly specialized workshop much prized by both amateur and professional enthusiasts. While makeshift spaces in bathrooms and kitchens are not uncommon, a complete, custom-designed facility—like the one shown in this drawing—is ideal for serious photographic work.

17.6 This home office was carved out of a living room wet bar, and doors were added. A walk-in bedroom closet could provide a similar space. A roll-away file, a pull-out work shelf, and a wire-rack storage system on the right wall all expand the utility of the small room. (Photograph: Steve Smith, courtesy Metropolitan Home)

17.7 A special-purpose home workshop is equipped to serve the needs of professional textile designer and weaver Jack Lenor Larsen. Both the worktable and loom are well lit and placed to allow a pleasing view of the garden outside. The workshop, designed by Larsen, is part of his home in Connecticut. (Photograph: Karen Radkai, courtesy House & Garden)

17.8 Work space, storage, and a tiny conference area are all accommodated in the small, spare home office of designer Ken Hsia's Toronto, Canada, apartment. Note the creative use of stacked magazines as room dividers. (Photograph: Fraser Day, courtesy Ken Hsia)

17.9

17.6). If extended use is anticipated, it may become a room not unlike a typical private office in a larger office grouping (fig. 17.8).

A checklist of issues to be considered includes:

Isolation from other household activities

Adequate work surfaces

Provision for computer equipment with monitor in proper viewing position, keyboard at correct height and angle (or adjustable), and space for "mouse" or input slate if needed

Space for computer printer and (if required) typewriter

Suitable location for telephone(s), answering machine, facsimile machine, and copying machine as required, plus any other special equipment

Good general lighting and suitable task lighting with avoidance of glare, veiling reflections, and reflections from monitor screen (for a thorough discussion of office lighting needs, see Chapter 10)

Files as needed

General storage for supplies, reference books, and magazines

A carefully selected ergonomic office chair

Provision for any special needs such as display of objects, pictures, pin-up tackboard or chalkboard, drafting table, computer plotter, flat storage (for drawings or layouts), TV or audio equipment, intercom, clock

Basic amenities such as adequate space, suitable ventilation, heat, and air conditioning are, of course, as necessary as in any other room of a home.

Media Rooms

This new and developing functional room type is based on the special conference/meeting rooms utilized by many office facilities. The media room is really a small theater designed to provide a comfortable and convenient setting for viewing and listening to television and projected film and slides (figs. 17.10, 17.11). A special space for these purposes is obviously a luxury only possible in a large house or apartment, although to someone who is professionally active in television, film, and related advertising fields, it may be a necessity.

Ideally, the media room is a specially dedicated space with arrangements for its own equipment, seating, and acoustics. If this is not possible, the required equipment may be built into or incorporated into the living room or entertaining space. Specialized consultants can be very helpful with technical requirements. Besides making the space attractive, the interior designer must deal with positioning complex equipment so that it can be easily concealed, if desired, as well as used.

17.9 Photographer Dianne Blell solved the difficult problem of combining a bathroom with a photo darkroom in her home without compromising design quality. A ceiling fan and vent remove chemical fumes, and dials above the tub faucets control temperatures for color processing. A stainless-steel sink stored outside the room is wheeled in to fit beside the tub during printing. (Photograph: Dianne Blell, courtesy Elle Decor)

17.10, 17.11 An elliptical conference room for the New York offices of Elektra Entertainment also serves as a media demonstration theater (fig. 17.11). (Photograph: © Peter Mauss/ESTO) The table was custom-designed by the architects, Bausman-Gill Associates. As indicated on the axonometric drawing (fig. 17.10), the walls and panels of the room are movable. (Courtesy Bausman-Gill Associates, New York)

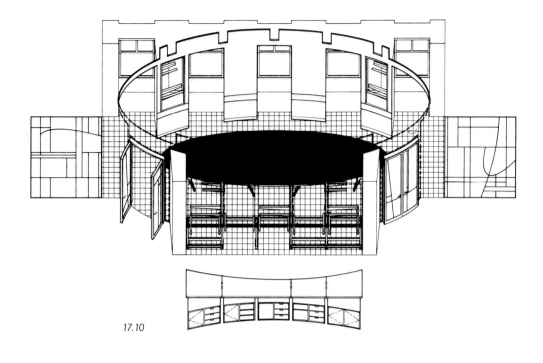

17.10

17.11

Conservatories

A special room or alcove for plants has been a desired feature of many residential spaces at least since the Victorian era (fig. 17.12). Big windows, preferably south-facing, are the basic requirement for a conservatory. Shelves for plants and, for larger plants, a suitably water-resistant floor are needed. A conservatory that houses tropical plants must be isolated from other interior spaces and have its own separate controls to maintain the proper levels of heat and humidity. Glass partitions accomplish isolation without giving up visibility.

Greenhouses

A greenhouse is a special type of conservatory that has glass walls and roof to maximize the entrapment of solar energy for plant growth. Adaptations of the freestanding greenhouse used by professional nurseries, in forms that can be attached to a residence, have become popular. Adding a greenhouse to other living spaces by extending it into garden space or onto a deck or patio is a pleasant way to open up the interior to light while providing space for growing plants. In fact, many people add greenhouse space simply to gain living area with a particular feeling of brightness and openness.

In order to put in a greenhouse, sufficient south-facing space with unobstructed light must be available. Issues that must be considered are how to handle the connection between greenhouse and existing walls; the type of opening for access and closure; and the type of flooring, taking into account the damp conditions. A greenhouse addition works well as an extension of living, dining, or kitchen areas. The greenhouse used for serious plant cultivation, like the conservatory, needs isolation and separate atmospheric controls. At the other extreme, when no space is available for a larger, walk-in unit, tiny greenhouse units that fit into a window opening offer a limited greenhouse function.

Courtyards

A court is, in effect, an outdoor room, surrounded by adjoining enclosed spaces and differing from them only in being roofless. Courts have been a traditional element in home design in Mediterranean regions since ancient times, and they continue to be an attractive possibility in larger residential plans. A court is normally an element in a one- or possibly two-story building, but it is technically feasible at the top level of a taller building, too.

17.12

17.12 This conservatory porch doubles as an informal living area. The hydraulically operated windows can be retracted into the basement, thus opening the space to the outdoors. The West Porch of Westbury House, Old Westbury Gardens, Old Westbury, New York, is a modern renovation of the 1906 mansion. (Photograph: Richard Cheek)

A court may have a primarily gardenlike character, or one closer to that of an interior room, or any possible mixture of these characteristics. Pools and fountains are favorite elements for inclusion in a courtyard (fig. 17.14). With the modern availability of glass or window walls, an open court can be seen and enjoyed even in the cold months in more northern climates. The materials and furniture used in a courtyard, like those for terraces, decks, and patios, must be selected for the special qualities that outdoor service demands. In addition, unless the courtyard is at ground level, the construction must ensure that there is no water leakage into spaces below. Some kind of lighting may be desired for nighttime use.

Atriums

The word *atrium* (its preferred Latin plural is *atria*) is simply Latin for *courtyard*. It has recently come to refer to a large interior space roofed over with glass—an interior courtyard that is actually a special kind of interior room. The atrium has become a much-favored element in large new hotels and in some corporate office headquarters buildings. In a private house, an atrium plays almost the same role as the courtyard, with the difference that it is independent of the effects of weather and climate (fig. 17.15). Introducing an atrium into an older, conventional row house is one way to open up the interior into a more modern set of spatial relationships. Incidentally, it can also help to bring daylight into what might otherwise be dark interior spaces. An atrium is often used as an indoor garden or conservatory, where growing plants up to the size of small trees can thrive.

Pools

A swimming pool has become a popular luxury feature of homes located on sufficient land to make space available (fig. 17.18). Most pools are out-of-doors, but enclosure is a possibility that makes a pool, at least occasionally, an interior element, perhaps in combination with a gym or other exercise facility. A fully indoor pool in a room of its own is possible, but usually an outdoor pool is enclosed with a glass housing similar to a greenhouse. This makes the pool available in all seasons and all weather conditions and minimizes the cleaning problems typical of outdoor pools.

A glass enclosure may pick up excessive solar heat in summer, making some means of shading (with blinds, awnings, or special heat-resistant glass) desirable. The pool space should have its own source or controls for heat, cooling, and humidity. Materials for floor surfaces and furniture must be water-resistant. Floors should also be nonskid.

Terraces, Patios, Roofs, Decks

Although these are not, strictly speaking, interior spaces, their function as outdoor living rooms and their close relationship to adjacent interior spaces often bring them into the concern of interior design (figs. 17.16, 17.17). The concept of indoor and outdoor space flowing together, primarily through the use of large glass window walls, has been a favorite idea of modern architecture. This concept can be strengthened by choosing floor and/or wall materials suitable to both indoor and outdoor use, so that the space appears to pass through the window wall and continue into the out-of-doors. In general, masonry materials, such as brick, stone, and tile, serve best. While wood can be used out-of-doors, it will weather and eventually decay unless it is kept painted or treated with a special preservative.

Furniture for decks and terraces also presents some special problems. Sun, rain, winter weather, and dirt are all hard on furniture. Even furniture made especially for outdoor use will eventually deteriorate if left out year-round. A special class of *indoor-outdoor furniture* has been developed that is intended to hold up with moderate outdoor exposure, to be suitable in appearance for indoor use, and to be sufficiently portable to be pulled or rolled in or out as needed (fig. 17.13). The most durable materials include metals (aluminum stands up best), some plastics, glass, marble, tile, and certain woods. Cedar, redwood, and teak have an oil content that makes them more weather-resistant than most other woods. Cushions and other upholstery elements are best made removable and brought indoors when not in use.

Outdoor spaces can also be designed to include permanent, built-in-place elements, such as benches, seats, tables, pools, and fireplaces (favorite elements for cookouts), of durable architectural materials. The familiar interior elements such as walls, ceilings, and doors are joined, out-of-doors, by additional elements such as fences, hedges, gates, awnings, and umbrellas. The profession that has special concern with this vocabulary of design is landscape architecture, a field usually asso-

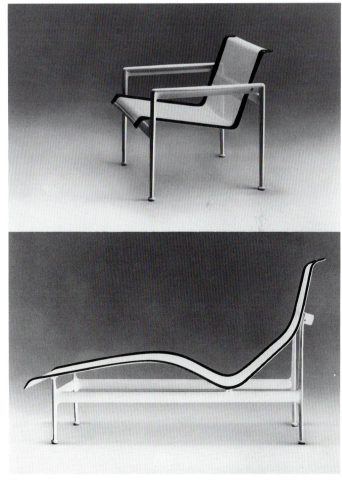

17.13

17.13 Outdoor furniture must be both weather-resistant and suited to the relaxed style associated with open-air living. In this armchair and lounge, part of a group designed in 1966 by Richard Schultz, plastic-coated frames of cast and extruded aluminum support seating surfaces of woven Dacron mesh with vinyl straps. Rainwater runs off through the mesh, and all of the materials are conceived to withstand exposure. (Photograph courtesy Knoll International, Inc.)

17.14

17.15

17.16

17.17

17.14 Architectural elements, such as the spiral staircase and the overhead beams, mediate between a pool in an open atrium and the residential structure itself. The result is an area that is both outdoor and indoor. The house in Del Mar, California, was designed by Batter Kay Associates, Inc., Architect, in 1983. (Photograph: © Mary E. Nichols, courtesy House & Garden)

17.15 A skylight surmounts an atrium with a central pool in a monumental space that acts as a formal focus for a multiple residence, the Colonnade Apartments in Philadelphia, renovated in 1985 by David Beck, Architects. (Photograph: © Elliott Kaufman)

17.16 Tennessee twig chairs bring the rural outdoors to a New York roof terrace. (Photograph: © 1985 Michael Skott)

17.17 This porch of a landmark Victorian house on Long Island, New York, was renovated in 1983 by Mark Hampton, designer. Like many traditional porches, this one functions as an outdoor room, for which the choice of furniture and fabrics is no less important than for an indoor living room. (Photograph: Peter Vitale, courtesy House & Garden)

ciated with the use of plant materials in garden and landscape design. The landscape architect works with paving, steps, walls, and fences, as well as outdoor lighting, and will often be a helpful consultant or collaborator in dealing with outdoor spaces as they become of concern to the interior designer.

HISTORIC PRESERVATION AND ADAPTIVE REUSE

Interior design for buildings with historic detail presents a special set of interesting problems. Many excellent older buildings survive, displaying either the styles of design current at the time of their construction or imitations of older historic styles. In Europe, structures built as far back as the Middle Ages, as well as buildings ranging through all the historic styles since, can be found. In America, all of the historic styles are represented, sometimes in combination, in the eclectic, imitative architecture of the late nineteenth and early twentieth centuries, while genuine examples of Colonial, Federal, and Victorian periods are not uncommon.

For many years, it was common practice to gut older buildings and reconstruct them in an entirely new way. Old farmhouses, older city row houses, and many stores and office buildings have been given such "face-lifts." Some of the results were of excellent quality, but too often fine older work was replaced with inferior modern substitutes. Many older buildings were designed with detail of fine aesthetic quality and built with craftsmanship that is now difficult or impossible to equal. When such older buildings become neglected, it is often tempting to modernize them totally, but in many cases it is wiser and cheaper to restore existing work, making appropriate changes to adapt it to modern uses and needs.

Recent years have seen an upsurge in historic preservation and what is called *adaptive reuse*, that is, the preservation of structure and some details with modifications to permit ongoing modern use. Many places now designate historic buildings or districts as *landmarks*, legally protecting them against destruction or inappropriate modernization. Although the landmarking of interiors has increased, generally only exteriors are protected. Nevertheless, the preservation and intelligent adaptation of interior space in preserved buildings, even when not required by law, are usually advisable. The modern movement toward professional specialization in historic preservation includes interior design as an important aspect.

Dealing with preserved interiors presents several special problems. These include adaptation to modern uses, needs, and expectations, and the practical matters of obtaining appropriate materials and workmanship. These problems appear in various ways depending on the functional purposes of the particular space. The answers to the following questions will influence and guide the interior design approach to buildings with historic detail:

Is the historic detail of such good quality and in sufficiently good condition that it should be preserved?

Is the detail of basic merit, but in bad condition? If so, can it be and should it be restored?

17.18 In the 1979 pool house of a residential project in Llewellyn Park, New Jersey, whimsical Post-modern elements give the space a playful quality appropriate to its recreational function. Robert A. M. Stern Architects was the designer. (Photograph: © 1981 Peter Aaron/ESTO)

17.19

CASE STUDY 5

ADAPTIVE REUSE
ALUMNI HALL
ALFRED UNIVERSITY,
ALFRED, NEW YORK

Project Designer: Philip B. Prigmore,
Architectural Consultant
Architects and Engineers:
Fred H. Thomas Associates, P.C.
Interior Designer and Furniture Consultant:
John Pile

The center edifice of the Alfred University campus—an 1851 Greek Revival structure—was originally built as a church that served the university and town. Over the years, however, it underwent several changes in purpose, its final incarnation being a gymnasium. With the arrival of a new university president, it was decided to rehabilitate the building and endow it with a function appro-

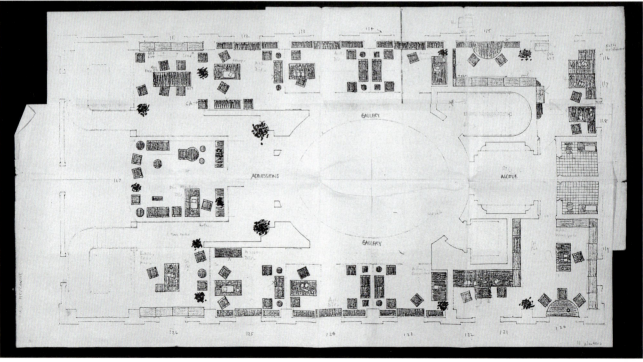

17.20

17.19 In this detailed model of the project the exterior shell can be lifted off to reveal the complete planned interior.

17.20 Rough furniture plans were developed by the designer after he conducted extensive interviews with the staff members, deans, and faculty members who would be the future users of the space. Having obtained comprehensive data on work and storage needs, he surveyed with a consul-

tant the roughly two hundred office systems available and narrowed them down to ten product lines. The final selection was made on the basis of versatility: it offered both conventional furniture for partitioned offices and system furniture for open spaces.

priate to its focal location on campus. Today, Alumni Hall is a reception center for prospective students and also houses the admissions and related offices, as well as exhibition and meeting spaces.

The exterior of the building was painstakingly restored; the interior, long in decay, was gutted and totally reconstructed. The result is a new structure nested into the old shell. While the new interior does not attempt to reproduce the historic original, it retains a relationship to the 1850s design in its quiet symmetry and its choices of materials and colors. The twin winding stairs to the four upper levels were the pride of the original building, while the double-height rotunda embodies the monumentality of the period.

The completed project forms a striking physical theme for the institution as a whole, a warm and welcoming starting point for incoming students and their parents and an active center for internal administrative functions.

17.21

17.22

17.21 Samples of actual materials—color swatches for paints, wood finishes, and drapery material—are spread out here on prints of the architectural construction plans. The colors and textiles convey tradition and stability along with an energetic and forward-looking orientation that reflects the present character of the university. (Photograph: George Hein)

17.22 This view of the main area in the finished project is from the first-floor rotunda toward the entrance, which is flanked by twin stairways. The contemporary furniture—Circolo sofa and Acorn chairs designed by Massimo Vignelli—strikes a modern note but also harmonizes with the restored and reconstructed details of the historic building. (Photograph: Bill Kontzias, courtesy Sunar Hauserman Systems and Furniture)

17.23

Should the style of the interior design elements—furniture, color, lighting, and so on—follow the style of the building, as a type of *restoration* interior similar to the period rooms in many museums? Is this technically and economically practical? Will it be possible to obtain actual antique elements of the appropriate period, or will reproductions be used?

Will it be best to retain and restore the existing historic elements while introducing modern elements (furniture, lighting, color) for reasons of econo-

my, practicality, and comfort? How can this be done to avoid conflicts of style?

Is the existing older work of such mediocre or poor quality or in such bad condition that the best solution is to totally reconstruct it into a modern space?

These questions must be worked out with the owner or client after the condition of the given space has been evaluated.

17.23, 17.24 Original architectural details have been preserved and emphasized in a 1984 adaptive reuse of an older building for modern office purposes. Here, a bank building of the 1880s has been reconceived by architect Glave Newman Anderson to house the information and processing center of a state-run money-management facility for retirees, the Virginia Supplemental Retirement System, in Richmond. Among the more startling and amusing touches of the project is a bank vault—complete with its massive door—that has been turned into a conference room. (Photographs: Whitney Cox)

Residential Projects

In residential projects, while basic living patterns remain largely unchanged, many of the details of day-to-day living are quite different from those of the past. For example, the Colonial interior tends to have small windows, big fireplaces, and very limited storage facilities. Bathrooms, modern kitchens, and modern lighting, not to mention any kind of electronic equipment, were all unknown until recent years. Most people today do not find ladder-back chairs and hard benches for dining seating adequately comfortable. As a result, a genuine Colonial house poses problems about what to preserve and what to modify. Total preservation, with a giant cooking fireplace and candle and oil-lamp illumination, is usually possible only in museumlike exhibition situations. To use such buildings for actual living, ways must be found to introduce more comfortable furniture, bathrooms, and modern heating and lighting. Kitchens must be totally renovated, tucked away in some hidden place, or, possibly, placed in a modern wing.

Victorian and later periods, with ideas of comfort and convenience closer to present-day standards, are less problematic. Victorian kitchens and baths may have outmoded equipment, but otherwise they are often quite practical, permitting modernization without much visual change. Gas lighting can be electrified (it often already has been) without greatly changing its appearance.

Whatever its age, the historic interior has probably been subjected to some unfortunate changes. Over the years, different owners remove fireplaces, alter windows, paint over woodwork, damage plasterwork and wood moldings, and destroy other period details while making repairs. Decisions about what to restore, replace, or simply accept depend on an evaluation of the space's condition, budget limitations, and practical issues. Fortunately, many new techniques and products make it possible to restore old detail, remove inappropriate finishes, and generally refurbish historic interiors to the limit of the owner's desires and budget.

Many difficult decisions remain. Should furniture be genuine antiques, which tend to be rare, expensive, and not the most practical choice; antique reproductions, which are also expensive and cannot avoid a quality of artificiality; or modern, which carries the danger of clashing with the space's period? The last alternative often works out surprisingly well, with the modern movable objects forming a pleasant

17.25

17.26

contrast with the period background. Should dark Victorian woodwork be preserved and complemented with dark and florid Victorian wallpaper, or should brighter modern colors and finishes be used? There are no absolute answers. The judgment and taste of the owner and designer will enter into the resolution of every such question that arises in a particular project.

Nonresidential Projects

Nonresidential historic buildings present some other problems, depending upon the building type (figs. 17.25, 17.27). Houses of worship can usually be preserved or restored without much change, except to heating and lighting systems. Introducing modern levels of lighting without resorting to inappropriate fixtures or excessively dramatic effects requires discretion and judgment. Theaters and auditoriums often need improved and more comfortable seating, but care must be

17.25 Union Station in Washington, D.C., a monumental building designed by Daniel H. Burnham in 1908, was rescued by historic preservation and adaptive reuse. The vast spaces of the old station had become underutilized as rail travel decreased in recent years. With the introduction of new retail spaces and a variety of restaurant facili-

ties, the building has been converted into an attractive and popular commercial center while retaining its usefulness as a station. Harry Weese Associates with Benjamin Thompson & Associates were the architects and designers for this project. (Photograph courtesy Osram Sylvania)

17.26 The former loading dock of a beer warehouse in Brooklyn, New York, is the unlikely setting for this project of 1989. Daylight floods into the living room through windows at the top of what were once entrances to the shipping docks. Mary Evelyn Stockton and Frank Lupo were the architects for their own home. (Photograph: © Andrew Garn, courtesy Metropolitan Home)

taken not to harm acoustics when making changes. Safety requirements dealing with exits, stairs, and certain materials may also be an issue.

Many public buildings include large and monumental spaces that may seem depressing (creating a gloomy atmosphere that can be corrected by improved lighting) or simply wasteful in terms of modern economics. How to deal with such spaces in courthouses, post offices, and banks, for example, is a special concern, but it is clear that making new ceilings, carving out commercial shop space, and similar courses of action can be destructive and unwise. Some building types—such as the railroad station—have become largely obsolete. An appropriate new use must first be found for them before design issues can be addressed. Many good examples of intelligent adaptive reuse are appearing.

17.27

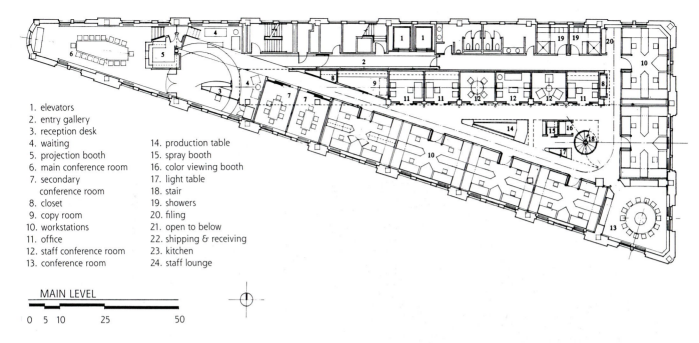

1. elevators
2. entry gallery
3. reception desk
4. waiting
5. projection booth
6. main conference room
7. secondary
   conference room
8. closet
9. copy room
10. workstations
11. office
12. staff conference room
13. conference room
14. production table
15. spray booth
16. color viewing booth
17. light table
18. stair
19. showers
20. filing
21. open to below
22. shipping & receiving
23. kitchen
24. staff lounge

MAIN LEVEL

0 5 10   25   50

17.28

17.29

17.27, 17.28 Adaptive reuse has turned an unusual triangular space— formerly a printing and production facility for the Seattle Times—into highly original offices for the firm of Herring/Newman. The floor plan (fig. 17.28) shows the lower level, seen in fig. 17.27 through the open well from the floor above. NBBJ Architecture Design Planning were the designers for this 1991 project in Seattle, Washington. (Photograph: Robert Pisano, plan courtesy NBBJ Architecture Design Planning)

17.29 A studio-office space occupies a Roman building with rich historic detail. The interior design incorporates an eclectic collection of furniture and objects, serving modern uses effectively, and was by Adriano Magistretti, of Pediment Design, Inc., for his own home. (Photograph: Isidoro Genovese)

18.1

CHAPTER

EIGHTEEN

PUBLIC INTERIORS

As mentioned earlier, interior design work separates into two main fields described as *residential* and *contract*. The first term is self-explanatory, but the second term merits a closer look. It comes from a semiobsolete business practice in which nonresidential projects were often taken on under an inclusive contract to provide all the needed elements, similar to the kind of contract usually entered into for building construction. The term has come to refer to all interior design work that is *not* specifically related to private residential space — that is, the kinds of spaces that are discussed here as *public interiors*.

Residential design is characterized by relatively small-scale projects and a close working relationship with the client (in fact, the client may even be his or her own designer). The resulting space has been carefully tailored to the needs, desires, and tastes of the individuals who will be the occupants and users of the completed project.

Nonresidential interior design tends to have a different character. Projects are generally larger, sometimes huge. More often than not, users are not the clients of the designer but some segment of a public that may include staff, workers, employees, executives, and professionals, plus, in many projects, outsiders from a general public of customers, visitors, travelers, guests, and casual passersby. Their relationship to the project may vary from quite close (occupants of a dormitory, patients in a hospital, or workers in an office) to very tenuous (customers in a shop, visitors to a museum or gallery, or passengers in a depot or terminal).

Public interiors are accessible to a large range of users and include highly visible, even spectacular spaces that attract interest and excitement. Professional interior design has, in recent years, come to focus on contract work, partly because it includes large and lucrative projects, partly because such projects almost always require the services of design professionals. A high proportion of residential spaces are still put together, for better or for worse, without help from any trained specialists. This used to be the case with public spaces as well. Some

years ago, a typical office was simply furnished with whatever the office manager thought necessary to make work possible. A restaurant was often designed by the contractor who built the installation, while major public buildings (courthouses, churches, libraries, and museums) received furniture and lighting almost as incidental details.

Various factors have brought an increasing number of public spaces into the sphere of interior design. These include a new awareness of environmental influences on human behavior: the way in which an office interior influences work performance, for example, or the way in which the design of a restaurant fosters the satisfaction of the restaurant's customers. Design has come to be seen as an important factor in the commercial success of many enterprises. The good design of a store, bank, hotel, or office makes an impression on the people who visit the spaces, raising their confidence and encouraging a return visit. Bad design can have an opposite and highly negative impact.

Designers aim to make public spaces serve their purpose well, that is, to be comfortable and convenient for both the public and the staff. A second, equally important goal is to create pleasant, exciting, and memorable spaces. This may serve strictly commercial ends in bringing in (or bringing back) customers, or it may serve wider purposes in building morale and confidence in an institution, an organization, a town, or a nation.

In working on such projects, the interior designer is guided by the same concerns that govern residential projects: the functional issue of having a space work in a practical way; choosing materials and construction techniques to serve the practical requirements; and resolving the first two issues in a way that makes an aesthetic impact.

Contract design is often quite specialized. Some designers concentrate on certain fields, such as offices, hotels, restaurants, or hospitals. While specialization tends to build efficiency and skill in a particular field, it can also lead to repetitious formula design. A designer who tackles a new kind of project for the first time is more likely to come

18.1 The New York headquarters for Ebel, a Swiss watchmaking firm, include a double-height showroom designed by Andrée Putman, who also designed the custom furniture of oak ceruse. (Photograph: © Peter Mauss/ESTO)

18.2

18.2 The Esprit store in West Hollywood, California (1985), with High Tech
accents in the fans and lighting and its
use of Memphis furniture (foreground),
suggests a lively and energetic orientation. Joseph Paul D'Urso was the
designer. (Photograph: Tim Street-
Porter)

up with a fresh approach than a designer who works on an endless stream of similar projects. Still, many modern assignments have such specialized technical requirements that some specialization seems necessary. Hospitals and healthcare facilities, for example, demand technical expertise, but a specialized consultant or an association with a designer experienced in such a field can bring the necessary skills into a firm taking on such a project for the first time. The skills that lead to first-rate work in one kind of project are generally transferable to even highly specialized projects when all the necessary specialized knowledge is drawn into a design team.

The increasing variety of projects that come to the attention of interior designers has extended the range of practice in this field to make it a more varied and lively profession than it was only a few years ago. Such seemingly unlikely interiors as those of spacecraft, submarines, laboratories—even jails—are now appropriate areas for professional design concern. An extensive literature deals with the specialized problems of various interior types, including offices, hotels, restaurants, hospitals, museums, and retail stores. It is impossible to go into detail about every one of these fields here. Instead, this section offers a survey of typical projects in a wide range of types, with some brief comments about each area of practice.

Shops, Shopping Centers, Showrooms

In the modern, aggressively commercial world, shopping is an important activity, and shops form the setting for a wide range of practical and emotional experiences. People expect to be lured, charmed, and entertained in the process of selecting and buying goods.

SHOPS. The design of a shop should convey a variety of messages about style, quality, and attitudes toward its products and services at the same time that it provides a practical setting for the display, storage, and actual sale of goods. The shop designer is expected to grasp the special character of a particular store—sometimes even to help invent that character—and then project it visually in a concrete way that the customer and potential customer can feel, remember, and enjoy.

All of these features can be studied in some fine older shops in many of the world's great cities. The special qualities of these stores have been arrived at through tradition and the individual shopkeeper's sense of what appeals to a particular type of customer. Lacking a tradition, the shop designer must find ways to put across comparable impressions and to do it with the more impersonal realities of most modern merchandising.

The nature of the goods to be sold, their price level, and the style of marketing will all influence the design. A shop may be conservative or avant-garde, it may present a masculine or a feminine aspect, or it may impart a sense of bargains waiting to be snatched up in a hurry or a feeling of leisurely and careful service. Small shops can convey a highly distinctive and personal feeling, while larger stores, such as major department stores, must provide varied settings for different departments and still suggest an overall character that can catch and hold customer loyalty. Along with all of this, display techniques, color, and lighting are deployed to make merchandise look its best and, for shops

that sell apparel and related goods, to flatter the customer as well. Even fitting or dressing rooms call for consideration in this respect.

In planning a retail shop (whether a small specialty shop, a section of a larger department store, or a large mass-marketing outlet) the designer will need to anticipate the customer's experience of the space, as well as the related roles of staff and management. A shopper will first encounter the space from outside. The storefront, open to the interior or composed of display windows, offers a preview of the shop's character. Big windows loaded with merchandise express the bargain outlet of mass marketing. Closed windows, each with a display planned like a stage set, characterize high-end specialty stores. Even the shopper who comes to a known store with a set purpose needs reassurance that the store is of the kind, in terms of pricing and quality, that is expected. A storefront can serve as a major advertising vehicle with signs, display, and lighting that lure the chance passerby and reinforce the intentions of the purposeful customer (fig. 18.3).

Once inside, the shopper's experience will be considerably more positive if needed information (where to go, what is available) is close at hand and if circulation paths are clear and obvious. The open displays of mass marketing invite the customer to inspect, compare, and make choices among goods on open shelves, in bins, or on racks. When merchandise for sale is more costly or specialized and the customer requires the help of salespeople, the character of the shop must establish the territory of movement open to the shopper, by means of counters or displays and other boundaries to indicate work spaces for staff. With qualified sales help increasingly difficult to find and expensive to staff, retailers are constantly seeking to maximize the ways in which shoppers can find and select merchandise on their own.

Cashier and checkout locations need to be intelligently planned and clearly marked, as do areas of special services, such as packing and wrapping, placing special orders, and information booths. Certain kinds of retailing call for special elements that relate to the goods in question. A shoe store calls for chairs for customer fitting and appropriate mirrors. Clothing stores need fitting rooms and large, even triple, mirrors. Food shops are usually divided into open shelving or rack areas for general packaged products, refrigerated cases for perishables, and serviced areas where attendants behind counters cut meat or serve delicatessen items.

The spacing of components within a shop must relate to the pace of activity, the price and quality level of merchandise, and the type of customer desired. The clutter and bustle of a discount shop encourage quick buying decisions but discourage the questions, comparisons, and thoughtful choices associated with the selection of costly items in a luxury store. The purchase of fine jewelry, an expensive rug, or a fine camera is aided when the setting provides both space and time for careful selection (although such items may also be effectively sold, if offered at very low prices, within a "bargain" setting). In any setting, efficiency and orderly organization will work to the advantage of both customer and management, while chaotic layout will only irritate and frustrate.

Almost all retail outlets require backstage areas for stock, for lockers and rest rooms for staff, and, possibly, for offices, wrapping, and shipping and receiving areas. In addition to considering circulation pat-

18.3

18.4

terns of customers, it is useful to consider the movement of goods through a shop. Where do goods arrive, where are they stored, how are they brought into display and customer contact, and how do they leave the shop? How is money handled and protected and what security provisions are required to minimize shoplifting, mischief, and "shrinkage" (pilferage by employees)? Along with these planning issues, the considerations of color and finishes, lighting, and graphic elements are all significant in showing merchandise to best advantage and making the customer's experience pleasant, possibly even exciting, to ensure return visits.

SHOPPING CENTERS. The shopping center, plaza, and mall are relatively recent types of commercial centers that have rapidly become extremely popular public gathering places. At their best, they offer pleasant, even beautiful interior spaces that easily attract crowds, although many people come without intending to shop. This makes it highly advantageous for the individual shops within the shopping center or mall to develop designs that will offer special attractions in such a highly competitive environment.

SHOWROOMS. The use of design as a tool for competitive selling has also become an important factor in the showrooms maintained by manufacturers of products and materials used by the design professions in their architectural and interior projects and in the showrooms serving the fashion trades. The showroom not only displays goods, it is also a source of design stimulation, an expression of company attitudes and philosophy, and almost a kind of theater for the projection of new ideas associated with products that often have a strongly fashion-related character. A well-designed showroom or display space may be as important to sales as the design of the actual products offered for sale (fig. 18.1).

Offices

Modern business now generally regards the drab and often depressing quality displayed by business offices in the early part of the twentieth century as unacceptable. It has been realized that appearance makes a

1. elevator lobby
2. reception
3. board room
4. conference
5. legal assistants
6. word processing
7. secretarial stations
8. lawyers
9. copy/printer/coffee

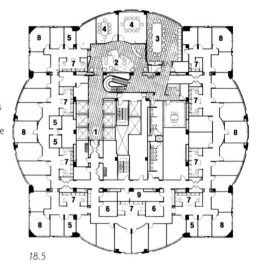

18.5

18.3 The storefront windows of the L-S Collection shop in New York offer a partial view of the attractions inside, serving as an invitation for passersby to enter. Bob Patino Ltd. were the architects and designers of this 1988 project. (Photograph: Peter Vitale)

18.4, 18.5 Office workstations are arranged along a circulation route (fig. 18.5) in the law offices of Perkins Coie in Seattle, Washington. Beechwood grid screens give a partial sense of enclosure

(fig. 18.4). Gensler and Associates Architects were responsible for the interior design. (Photograph: © Peter Aaron/ESTO)

18.6

18.7

difference: visitors to an office form impressions and draw conclusions about the business's character and quality based on the design of the offices they see; in addition, the setting in which employees spend their regular working days heavily influences their attitudes toward their employers.

The offices of major corporations and other big modern organizations (such as government agencies) have become large, even vast complexes sometimes occupying many floors or entire buildings. Planning such office projects is a demanding and specialized activity, and office design and planning has become an important field of interior design practice. Decisions about layout, the sizes of offices, and the provision for privacy through partitioning (fig. 18.6) or (often in modern practice) without partitioning (fig. 18.7) must be balanced against the requirements of the work function, the projection of individual rank and status, and the overall style and objectives of the organization.

The many design firms that have chosen to specialize in office planning (often called *space planning*) have developed highly systematized ways of dealing with such projects. Over time, the typical single room with a door that served the solitary lawyer, manager, or executive grew in larger organizations to an unwieldy agglomeration of private spaces. Secretaries were often placed in an outer office, in effect guarding access to the private-office occupant. Stenographers, typists, bookkeepers, and clerks were all thrown into larger rooms (often called "bull pens"), entirely without privacy. A typical office plan of this sort placed managers and executives in private rooms along the outside walls,

18.6 Semiprivate work conditions surround two informal conference areas. Playful accents in unusual colors suggest cheerful creativity in this toy manufacturer's office. ISD Incorporated designed the offices for Mattel Inc., in Hawthorne, California. (Photograph: Toshi Yoshimi, courtesy ISD Incorporated)

18.7 Through stepped-height screen partitions, designer Sanford Stein provided degrees of privacy for a group of designers' workstations in the Minneapolis office of SteinDesign, Sanford Stein, principal. (Photograph: © 1986 Philip Macmillan James. All rights reserved)

18.8

with assistants, secretaries, and other staff in central, usually window-less spaces. While many offices are still planned and built in this general way, modifications have come into use that make most modern offices both more attractive and more functionally effective.

About 1951, a concept often called *office landscape,* or *open planning,* emerged. Traditional walled private offices were abandoned, and all personnel—managers and staff alike—were placed in an open space with movable storage units or screen panels to provide limited privacy where necessary. The result was simplified communication among all workers, ease in making layout changes as work processes might require, and a reduced emphasis on hierarchical status. Although many open-plan offices have been highly successful, there has been a retreat from this stance toward something that might be described as a mixture of open and conventional planning.

It must be recognized that some office work calls for privacy, quiet, and freedom from interruption. The nearly universal acceptance of

computers as vital to office work, requiring a small computer or computer terminal (CRT—cathode-ray tube—unit) at almost every work-place, has led to the development of furniture systems that provide screen panels, partition elements, and work and storage components that can create every sort of work space without resorting to fixed partition walls. Such systems (see Chapter 12, pages 370–72) are now basic to most office planning. Techniques for developing layout through surveys of needs, matrix charts, and link and bubble diagrams have been discussed in Chapter 6. In addition to the layout of actual workstations, office design includes such special-purpose spaces as conference, board, and meeting rooms, reception areas, dining facilities, lounges and rest areas, mail and shipping rooms, and file spaces.

The need to make any office comfortable and attractive to its workers as well as to visitors involves logical plan layout, suitable lighting, and sound choices of materials, finishes, and colors, so that the completed project expresses the nature of the user organization in a way

18.8 *The Winston & Strawn President's Room, in the facilities of the Chicago Bar Association, is used for meetings, seminars, and dining. A wall of photographs of past presidents serves as a decorative focus in the double-height space, which has wall panels of teak* *and recessed ceiling panels of brushed steel. Greg Landahl of the Landahl Group was the interior designer; the building was designed by Tigerman McCurry, architects. (Photograph: Jon Miller/Hedrich-Blessing)*

that builds efficiency and staff loyalty. Dreariness and monotony are constant dangers in the offices of large corporations or any sizable organization in which hundreds of workers may feel lost in a vast hive. Efforts to break up expansive spaces into smaller units, to use spaces with more individual character (such as those in older existing buildings), and to encourage personal expression in the vicinity of the individual work space have produced many positive results.

Some offices are primary contact points with the public. This is true of ticket offices, the consumer service offices of insurance or loan companies, brokerage offices, and the public offices of different organizations where people come to apply for credit, make complaints, or confer about other matters. In all of these situations, the ambience of the office itself conveys a strong impression about the nature and quality of the organization.

The design of all offices includes the selection of suitable work equipment and seating. Modern office furniture and equipment are available in great variety and are, at best, of very high design quality. Modern computer and communications equipment has brought new efficiency to office work, creating what is often called the *electronic office,* but it has created new problems as well. The need to maintain a fixed seating position can result in physical problems (muscular or back pains), while long hours working with the computer terminal under unsatisfactory lighting can cause eyestrain. A work pace set by the electronic equipment rather than by the worker's own normal habits can generate nervous and emotional problems. Research has shown that these can be minimized with careful design. Spatial arrangement, color, lighting, and acoustics influence the ease and efficiency of work and establish an atmosphere that can reduce stress, make work easier and less tiring, and support morale. The office designer has an opportunity (and an obligation) to achieve some of the best interior design work currently being produced.

Banks

The tradition of formal, templelike architectural structures for bank facilities has been upset by the new competitive struggle among banks to attract depositors. The "friendly banking" movement has drawn banks toward the liveliness and attraction of a retail shop or display pavilion for their public spaces (fig. 18.10). This is no easy goal, considering that banks have no merchandise or products to display and that the growth of automation is gradually replacing human tellers and counter attendants with machines.

At its best, the interior design of today's banks ranges from a modern but still dignified formality to visually spectacular displays of light and color. Some of the most interesting of bank designs involve older bank buildings of fine design quality, even of landmark status. These have been modified internally to improve convenience and project a sense of contemporary vitality while still retaining and respecting the older setting with its architectural dignity (fig. 18.11).

In addition to the public banking room spaces, banks usually include semipublic spaces, such as a safe-deposit box area, and an office area with formal executive quarters and more utilitarian "backstage" work areas. All of these spaces can be examples of design excellence.

The planning of a bank combines some of the elements of a retail shop with aspects of office design and yet other considerations unique to banking. The major space of a typical bank or bank branch is a public area where depositors may fill out forms at a counter, stand in line near the tellers' windows, and, with as little waiting as possible, conduct a transaction at the tellers' counter. This traditional pattern has been modified with the introduction of automated teller machines (ATMs) that can deal with the vast majority of banking transactions without human contact. At the same time, most banks offer a number of special services, such as loans, mortgages, and brokerage and insurance services, that require more complex customer contacts either at counters, in semiprivate or private offices, or in conference rooms.

The planning of a banking space must begin with estimates of the number and kinds of customer transactions that will take place. Brief use of an automated device calls for a treatment different from that required by personalized service (whether at a teller's window or in a more extended meeting with staff at a counter, desk, or table). Although the need for nonpublic areas in a bank has been greatly diminished by computerization, these spaces remain necessary and their requirements are frequently no different from those of other office spaces. The area directly behind the tellers' counters, however, demands particularly tight security, including internal control, as well as protection from the public.

Many banks offer a safe-deposit service requiring public access to the vault. Access to this area (often in a basement location) of course requires special security control, with booths for customer use adjacent to the vault within a secure area. In smaller banks the vault is also used by the bank itself, creating a complex problem of circulation for both staff and customers, who must retain separate but equally secure access. Banks also commonly offer drive-up window service, complicating planning with the further need to make both human tellers and ATMs available at an external driveway.

Brokerage Offices

These constitute another special office type that mixes public service with internal functional needs. The typical brokerage office has a public space (either at street level or on an upper floor) where customers can watch the *board* that displays transactions, consult literature, obtain services at a counter, and request conversation with an individual broker or customer representative. In a generally open area, brokers have workplaces that include a desk surface with an array of electronic screens and keyboards, along with a visitor's chair to accommodate a customer. Other areas not accessible to customers include managerial office spaces, private offices and conference rooms, and areas called *trading rooms,* unique to financial institutions, where by means of electronic devices brokers or *traders* buy and sell securities and other financial instruments. Traders must have eye and voice contact with one another while using a variety of screens, telephones, and keyboard-communication devices (fig. 18.15). Large trading rooms are spaces that call for highly specialized, technologically oriented design.

Public Buildings

Courthouses, city halls, capitols of states, and legislative buildings of nations have usually been designed to include some monumental and

18.9

ceremonial spaces of strong architectural character. Offices and public service spaces (information counters, cashiers' windows, registries of public documents, and so on) in the same buildings are often drab, inconvenient, and unattractive. In recent years, public buildings of more modern design have appeared, and many of these have more functional, comfortable, and attractive interior spaces (fig. 18.19). In many older public buildings, improvements have been made through superior interior renovation. In some situations, a change in use has stimulated an interior renovation that greatly improves the building while preserving the best aspects of its traditional character. For instance, the Jefferson Market Courthouse in New York has been successfully turned into a public library.

Museums, Galleries, Libraries

These public and semipublic facilities often suffered in the past from an emphasis on monumentality at the expense of utility. Newer buildings invite creative solutions to providing genuine service to the public, while the renovation of older buildings can often greatly improve both the function and attractiveness of their interior spaces.

MUSEUMS. In recent years, many museums have launched an aggressive effort to attract a large public to exhibitions planned and designed with a sense of showmanship comparable to that of the commercial world. Dramatic settings and use of color and lighting can convert a museum from a dusty warehouse of antiquities to a lively and exciting space in which educational values merge with entertainment (fig. 18.12).

GALLERIES. Private galleries for the exhibition and sale of works of art and related objects are generally smaller in scale than museum spaces and do not attempt to serve as large an audience. They share the need to show off exhibited objects to best advantage through intelligent planning of space, color, and lighting.

LIBRARIES. Libraries may be public institutions varying from very small to large and complex (fig. 18.18); they may also be specialized parts of a larger project such as a school, an office, or an institution. All must provide book storage and protection (plus provision for modern book alternatives, such as microfilm materials) along with space for the users of the facility to read, study, and take notes. Specialized

18.9 Simple furniture and brilliant colors (in wall frescoes by Dorothea Rockburne) seem appropriate in the monumental "sky lobby" of the Sony headquarters in New York (formerly the A.T.&T. Building). Philip Johnson and John Burgee were the architects of the building and Gwathmey Siegel & Associates Architects designed the interior. (Photograph: © 1993 Durston Saylor)

18.10 A neighborhood branch of the Chase Manhattan Bank in New York's SoHo district, a favorite location for artists' lofts and studios, features artwork in a gallery atmosphere in order to express a kindred orientation. Plants add another "friendly" touch. Skidmore, Owings & Merrill were the designers. (Photograph: © Wolfgang Hoyt/ESTO)

18.11 Many bank facilities are designed to project a sense of dignified conservatism. This space, designed by John F. Saladino for the Chase Manhattan Bank of New York, is in a building constructed circa 1933 and was renovated in 1986.

The atmosphere suggests a Georgian residence or club, while the modern electric lighting from recessed ceiling fixtures provides illumination for contemporary working conditions. (Photograph: © Langdon Clay)

18.10

18.11

18.12

18.12 In a remarkable conversion, a disused turn-of-the-century Paris railroad station was transformed into an exciting museum. The Gare d'Orsay in Paris was redesigned as the Musée d'Orsay by architect Gae Aulenti in 1986. (Photograph: J. Purcell, © Établissement public du Musée d'Orsay)

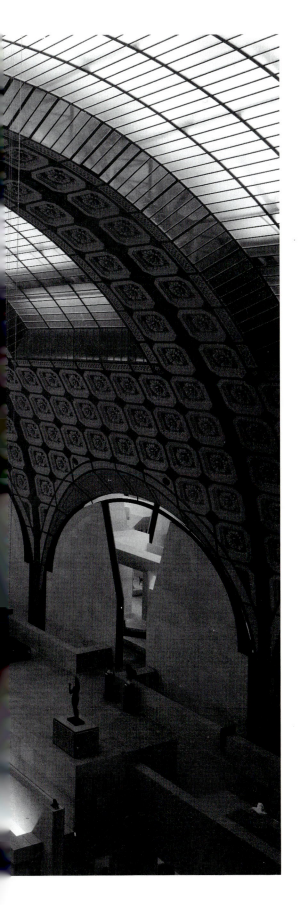

18.13

18.14

18.13 New York's Carnegie Hall, built in 1891 to the designs of William B. Tuthill (with William Morris Hunt and Dankmar Adler as consultants), has an international reputation for its fine acoustics. In a 1986 renovation and restoration, the firm of James Stewart Polshek and Partners, Architects, brought the building up to modern standards of safety and performance while preserving and refurbishing the period opulence of the interior. (Photograph: Jan Staller)

18.14 Circulation spaces in the Greater Columbus Convention Center were designed for the efficient movement of large crowds. Trott/Eisenman Architects were the designers of the project in Columbus, Ohio, in 1993. (Photograph: © Jeff Goldberg/ESTO)

18.15

libraries (law, music, or for children, for example) modify library basics to suit a particular need.

Exhibition Design

Exhibits ranging from small to vast are a ubiquitous part of the modern commercial and institutional world. Shows of automobiles, boats, various kinds of manufactured goods, even military hardware take place in exhibition halls built for the purpose (fig. 18.20). These structures are simply empty shells that shelter the material on display and the crowds of visitors that come to view it. Exhibits range from a small booth setting in such a structure to entire buildings with all their contents, as in the major exhibit pavilions at a world's fair.

The exhibit designer is a highly specialized kind of interior designer who must create settings that can be constructed quickly, that will communicate effectively in a competitive and sometimes confusing environment, and, often, that employ standard and reusable elements. The temporary nature of exhibits sometimes offers the designer an extraordinary freedom to try out experimental and adventurous approaches

that might seem too risky for more lasting projects. Exhibit design can be an experimental showcase for future-oriented design directions, as it has proved to be in the past.

Theaters, Concert Halls, Auditoriums, Arenas

Auditorium spaces present special and interesting interior design problems. An audience numbering in the hundreds or even in the thousands must be seated in reasonable comfort within a space that provides good sightlines and satisfactory acoustical conditions for all. In addition, safety considerations impose very stringent demands, usually expressed in legal codes, on lengths of seating rows, aisle widths, arrangements of steps, and exit doors.

Along with the solution of these technical problems, the designer is expected to create a visual ambience appropriate to the events that will take place in the facility. The traditional opera house or theater is expected to present an atmosphere of festivity and opulence without overwhelming the performance that takes place within it (fig. 18.13). A more modern approach gives the hall a totally neutral and simple

18.15 In one example of the highly specialized office facility called a trading room, the floor is raised six inches to provide for communication cables, while ductwork and sprinklers are left exposed overhead to accommodate the existing low ceiling height. The facility serves the American Stock Exchange in New York. Swanke Hayden Connell Architects were the designers, with Altan Gursel, design director of the American Stock Exchange. (Photograph: Robert Miller Photography)

setting that focuses all attention on the performance event taking place. Ancillary spaces such as lobbies, lounges, bars, and cafés present a wide range of related design problems. Specialized consultants have an important part in dealing with the problems of sightlines, acoustics, and lighting, as well as the complexities of backstage mechanics.

Large performance spaces, convention halls, and sports arenas tend to be more strictly functional in character, with the enclosure, seating, and performance space dominating interior design elements (figs. 18.14 and 18.16). In such projects, however, color, lighting, and the design of access spaces present interior design problems of considerable scope.

Houses of Worship

Religious buildings have a tradition of monumentality and pure architectural expression. In referring to the great cathedrals or other historic religious buildings, one can hardly speak of interior design indepen-

18.17

18.16

dent of the basic structural form. It is interesting to note the ways in which modern interior design ideas have come to play a part in the design of contemporary religious buildings (fig. 18.17). The same thoughtful interior design that goes into other, secular spaces has greatly influenced the success of many new religious buildings. The renovation and restoration of older buildings often call for new thinking about color, lighting, and functional issues concerning both ritual and public accommodation.

Along with the actual sanctuary space, religious buildings often include related spaces for teaching, social functions, and similar secondary uses that present design problems closely related to those of similar secular building types. Interior design can have a significant and creative role in making houses of worship both serviceable and inspiring in visual character.

Institutional Buildings

To say that the design of a building is *institutional* is not normally a compliment. The word suggests dreary corridors and drab color schemes of green and brown. There is no reason, however, why institutional buildings should be any less attractive than other buildings; in fact, it is increasingly acknowledged that interior design of high quality can improve the function and morale of every institutional type. Even so unpromising a type as the modern jail, or correctional facility,

18.16 *The Ingalls Hockey Rink was designed by architect Eero Saarinen in 1958 for Yale University in New Haven, Connecticut, with an innovative structural system that gives the interior an exciting spatial quality. (Photograph: © Ezra Stoller/ESTO)*

18.17 *Symmetry and a sense of ceremonial procession generate an atmosphere suitable to a space for religious observances. The Marty Leonard Community Chapel of the Lena Hope Home in Fort Worth, Texas, was designed by E. Fay Jones + Maurice Jennings Architects. (Photograph: © R. Greg Hursley)*

18.18

18.19

can be shown to be more effective when its interiors avoid depressing grimness. Schools too often seem rather like jails, although the most modest thought and effort could easily make them pleasant, even stimulating places.

Interior design has met with considerable resistance in many institutional areas. Government agencies often feel that a demonstration of respect for economy requires the most austere and unattractive treatments that can be produced, while the design of public facilities and jails (figs. 18.24, 18.25) has often followed the even more oppressive view that such places should contribute to the suffering of occupants rather than to their needs. Modern research has demonstrated that superior design for such places can improve their effectiveness while making the life of staff and professionals easier, pleasanter, and more productive.

Historically, college and university buildings have often included beautiful and inspiring spaces. The interior design of these buildings, which include dormitories, lounges, small classrooms, lecture halls (fig. 18.29), auditoriums, offices, dining halls (fig. 18.27), and libraries, should satisfy the minimum requirements of making the spaces function well, with good lighting, seating, acoustics, and color. It can go a lot further to create memorable, exciting, and inspiring spaces.

Residential facilities, dormitories, nursing homes, and facilities for the elderly also invite design treatment that will support the morale of their occupants, make for comfort and convenience, and allow users a degree of personal expression by providing a suitable balance between preestablished or fixed design elements and design details that can be modified, changed, and adjusted. The quality of life in such places is strongly influenced by the design of both private spaces (such as bedrooms) and the shared spaces of living or common rooms, dining halls, and circulation spaces.

Healthcare Facilities

The field of healthcare includes a wide variety of facilities, ranging from the relatively simple doctor's or dentist's office to the quite complex modern general hospital. Offices for group medical practice, for specializations such as pediatrics, radiology, or dialysis, and for medical laboratories have emerged as separate units, some of which also appear as elements within the larger hospital. All healthcare facilities share a common problem in that they must serve a number of user groups whose requirements differ and may sometimes conflict. These groups include doctors, nursing and other support staff, patients and companions, visitors, maintenance personnel, and management and business staff.

The basic units of a medical office include a reception desk, waiting area, doctor's consulting room (office), examining and/or treatment rooms, business office with files, and additional service areas, notably bathrooms and suitable storage space.

The waiting rooms, office or consulting rooms, and treatment rooms of the professional offices of doctors (fig. 18.26), dentists, and similar individual practitioners (whether in practice alone or as part of a group) can strongly influence the patient or client. An ugly, cramped, or depressing waiting room and office can add to a patient's nervousness and tension. In the end, professional competence is more impor-

tant than appearances, but an appropriate and attractive setting reinforces confidence in professional skills and improves the patient's experience.

In a hospital the basics found in a doctor's office are expanded and duplicated to serve such departments as admitting, emergency care, and outpatient treatment; other components that support the major areas of patients' rooms and associated nursing services are grouped to relate to the various departments concerned with surgery, pediatrics, maternity, and general medical care. Depending on the type and size of a particular hospital, there may be various other departments, each with its special needs. An emergency room, intensive care, radiology, cardiology, neurology, ophthalmology, and physical therapy are among the functions present in many larger hospitals. In addition, hospitals associated with medical schools and schools of nursing, so-called teaching hospitals, require facilities for their students, including lecture rooms and classrooms similar to those of other colleges and universities. Many hospital departments require special facilities, among them the delivery rooms and nurseries for maternity care, as well as the operating rooms, doctors' dressing and scrub rooms, and patient

18.20

18.18 The New York Public Library, a famous work of 1911 by John Merven Carrère and Thomas Hastings, formerly draftsmen in the office of McKim, Mead and White, remains an outstanding example of classicism in the American architecture of its day. The area illustrated was restored and modernized in 1985 by Davis, Brody & Associates. Now the D. Samuel and Jeane H. Gottesman Hall, it is a monumental circulation space also used to display exhibitions. The original wood ceiling was carved by Maurice Grieve. The arches and columns are of Cipollino marble, the walls of white Danby marble. The modern, unobtrusive track lighting is easily adapted to the changing exhibits. (Photograph: © 1985 Peter Aaron/ESTO)

18.19 The City Hall built in 1969 in Boston, Massachusetts, is one of the most striking public buildings built in

any American city in recent years. The interiors make no reference to any historic style. They convey a sense of dignity and permanence in an entirely modern idiom. The architects—who won the commission in a competition—were Kallmann, McKinnell & Knowles, in association with Campbell, Aldrich & Nulty. The engineers were LeMessurier Associates, Inc.; interior space designers were ISD Incorporated. (Photograph courtesy ISD Incorporated)

18.20 At the Montreal World's Fair, Expo '67, the United States pavilion was a giant geodesic dome built according to Buckminster Fuller's patented system of construction. The design firm Cambridge Seven developed exhibits on platforms that seemed to float in the vast space within the largely transparent structure. Escalators moved visitors from level to level. (Photograph: John Pile)

18.21

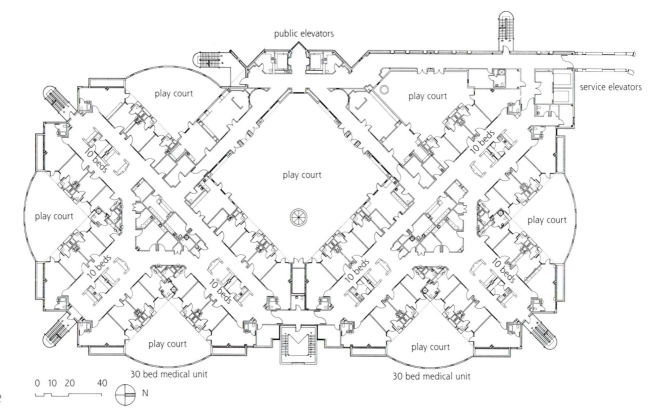

public elevators

service elevators

play court

play court

play court

10 beds

10 beds

play court

play court

play court

10 beds

10 beds

10 beds

10 beds

10 beds

play court

play court

30 bed medical unit

30 bed medical unit

0 10 20 40

 N

18.22

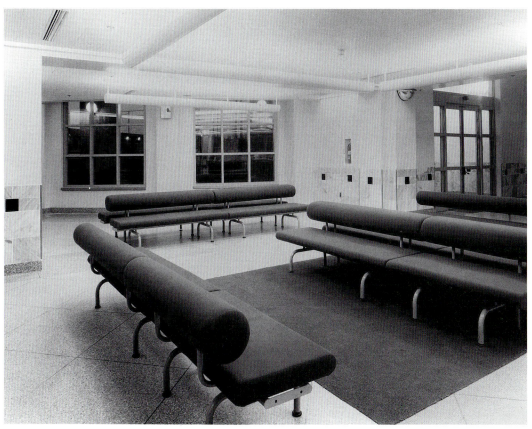

18.24

18.23

18.25

18.21, 18.22 Unlike the sterile and depressing atmosphere of so many hospital interiors, the Children's Hospital and Health Center in San Diego, California, offers a dynamic, cheerful ambience. As indicated in the plan, thirty-bed nursing units are subdivided into three "neighborhoods," each with ten "houses," or beds, and play courts. Each of the nurses' stations resembles a house, complete with peaked roof,

chimney, and garden wall. Pastel colors are used throughout to distinguish individual rooms, and at night fiber optics in the ceilings create sparkling constellations. The hospital was a project of NBBJ Architecture Design Planning, with David Noferi as design director. (Photograph and plan courtesy NBBJ Architecture Design Planning)

18.23 The black-and-white checked floor and yellow overhead ducts relieve the austerity of a laboratory at the Center for Molecular Recognition, College of Physicians and Surgeons, Columbia University, New York. Freeman & Pizer were the architects. (Photograph: © 1992 Michael Moran)

18.24, 18.25 A jail cell may seem an unlikely professional design project,

but the value of intelligent planning in such facilities is receiving increasing recognition. The cell (fig. 18.25) and the public seating area (fig. 18.24) were designed in 1986 by Ehrenkrantz & Eckstut, architects, in collaboration with Jacob/Wyper Architects (Philadelphia) for the Philadelphia Industrial Correctional Center. (Photographs: © 1986 Paul Warchol) recovery rooms associated with surgery. Other hospital spaces include waiting rooms, laboratories, storage areas, and offices, as well as such ancillary services as food-preparation areas, dining rooms, and gift shops.

Many existing hospitals occupy facilities that are to some degree outmoded and in constant need of renovation, expansion, or replacement. Recent developments that have had an impact on healthcare facilities include the introduction of new technologies, some of which demand extensive facilities to accommodate large pieces of equipment, such as CT scan and MRI machines. Modern medical practice has turned toward the reduction of long hospital stays, with an increased emphasis on outpatient care and greater reliance on home and nursing-home care. Many medical procedures, including minor surgery, medical tests, X-ray, and CT and MRI examinations, do not require hospitalization and when possible can be performed in specialized facilities apart from a hospital.

When working on healthcare projects, the designer must be aware that the client, usually a doctor, dentist, or hospital administrative personnel, represents just one set of requirements. However important these concerns may be, they frequently do not take into account the needs of the other people the facility is intended to serve, particularly patients, who often feel that their needs are treated as secondary to the requirements of technology and the professionals who deal with that technology. Designers have an opportunity to act as advocates for the patients' needs, as well as for the concerns of staff, visitors, and others who are users of healthcare facilities but who may lack input at the planning stage.

Two issues call for special design attention. The first is the need during planning to minimize the conflicts that result from shared circulation and occupancy by too many activities. In the corridors and elevators of the typical hospital, doctors, nurses, visitors, staff, patients (ambulatory or on stretchers), and carts of food, as well as trash, are all jumbled together in confusion. Patients are continually moved to and from their rooms to various locations for tests and treatment. Crowding and the ensuing delays raise tension levels, which can interfere with treatment and convalescence.

The second issue derives from an increasing realization (supported by research) that patients' recoveries are influenced by the quality of convenience and comfort a facility provides. Pleasant rooms decorated in suitable colors, outdoor views of pleasant surroundings, accommodation of visitors, and minimization of the annoyances generated by noise and disturbing activity are all desirable and all considerably affected by the design of the facility (figs. 18.21, 18.22). A grim and depressing hospital filled with noise and conflict tends to influence the behavior of doctors, nurses, and staff and to increase the anxiety and stress felt by patients. A sense of calm and order, pleasant surroundings, and well-organized treatment are important aids to patients' well-being and recovery.

A good plan for any healthcare facility is best generated by charting the experience of each typical user, whether patient, doctor, visitor, nurse, or other staff member. What are the sequential steps from arrival through treatment, work, or visit to departure, and how are these steps related to suitable spaces? Once this is determined, the

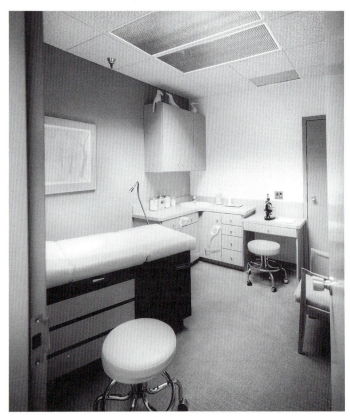

18.26

spaces can then be assigned areas, arranged with appropriate adjacencies, and organized into plans. Tracing the movement of the different user groups on a diagrammatic plan is the primary tool for simplifying circulation patterns and minimizing conflicts.

Child-Care Accommodations

The need for child-care facilities outside the home has risen greatly in recent years, propelled by the increase in both two-career families and single-parent families. Day-care centers are now provided in many housing developments, in some business and industrial facilities, and in independent locations. The typical day-care facility is similar to a kindergarten or nursery school except that it must provide for longer daytime stays and, in some establishments, for night care as well. A typical facility will include the following elements:

ENTRANCE AREA. Space for arriving children and parents and for taking off and putting on outer clothing, including some seating with benches and stools, and possibly some seating for waiting parents, is required. Compartmented hanging space for children's outer garments and one space ("cubby," for cubbyhole) for each child's belongings should be provided.

MAIN PLAY AREA. Good lighting, pleasant color, adequate space (New York code requires 30 square feet per child), and suitable play equipment are called for, including storage shelves and cabinets for blocks, toys, and other equipment. According to the ages of children to be accommodated, appropriate tables and chairs or stools of easily movable types are necessary. Wall surfaces should provide for the display of children's artwork and other visual materials.

18.26 Pale pinks and greens soften the otherwise clinical atmosphere of an examining and consulting room in a gynecologists' office suite in Texas by Kenneth Jorns & Associates, Inc., Kenneth Jorns, designer. (Photograph: R. Greg Hursley)

18.27 The interior of Gordon Wu Hall, Butler College, Princeton University—an unusual university dining hall—was designed by Venturi, Rauch and Scott Brown in 1983. The hanging lighting fixtures of curious shape are a strong visual element, while the tables and chairs recall more traditional academic interior spaces. (Photographs: Tom Bernard, courtesy Venturi, Rauch and Scott Brown)

18.28 The austere simplicity of a dormitory bedroom at the School of American Ballet, New York, is relieved by a quilt bedspread. Davis, Brody & Associates were the architects, with Mark Hampton as interior designer. (Photograph: © Jennifer Lévy)

18.29 This university lecture hall derives its striking visual impact from the stepped, sweeping curves of the functional writing surface. It was designed by Peter L. Gluck and Partners for Uris Hall, the Business School, Columbia University, New York (1985). (Photograph: © Paul Warchol)

18.27

18.28

18.29

Movable cots for rest periods need suitable storage space, along with compartmented storage for sheets and blankets.

KITCHEN OR KITCHENETTE. Refrigerated storage, sink, and equipment for food preparation are necessities.

CHILDREN'S BATHROOM. A minimum of one toilet and one washbasin mounted at appropriate height for every fifteen children is required.

SEPARATE ADULT BATHROOM. For staff use.

SERVICE FACILITIES. Space for janitor supplies, trash collection, and general storage should be provided.

ACCESS TO OUTDOOR PLAY SPACE.

CRIBS. For each child under one year of age, space for cribs and diaper-changing shelves are necessities.

Safety matters, such as protection from hazardous steps, sharp edges, and window and door openings, are essential. Codes require safe fire-exit provisions, usually two separate means of egress not counting fire escapes. Fire extinguishers, alarms, exit signs, and other safety devices are required by codes; sprinklers are necessary in child-care spaces located in nonfireproof structures. Normal provisions for HVAC to provide satisfactory air quality are, obviously, also required.

In selecting materials and colors, the designer should consider the need for a bright and cheerful atmosphere, as well as for easy cleaning and maintenance. The customary use of bright primary colors in spaces for young children is based on the finding that such colors are readily recognized and enjoyed by children. Some researchers now suggest that less aggressive color—pleasant but restrained—may be less distracting and may encourage the use of children's own work as a visual stimulus.

Restaurants, Hotels, Clubs

For these spaces, the importance of excellent interior design has long been understood.

RESTAURANTS. The aim of restaurant design is to create an atmosphere or ambience that supports the character of the food and service being offered and that makes the experience of dining memorable, encouraging the customer to return and to recommend the restaurant to others (figs. 18.31, 18.32). Restaurants vary from simple to elaborate, from frenzied to leisurely, from cheap to staggeringly expensive. All of these possibilities have their usefulness and their own particular clientele.

Although they may be clichés, certain familiar practices serve to make prospective patrons aware of the character of a restaurant and can help to satisfy their expectations. A fast-food shop should *look* fast, with bright lights and colors, slick surfaces, and an atmosphere of efficiency. A luxury restaurant calls for richer colors and materials, soft lighting, carpets, and a quiet atmosphere. The style of food served can also be expressed through choice of color, materials, and detail. One expects blue and yellow colors in a Swedish restaurant, red and white if the establishment is Danish. Seafood is associated with solid-oak tabletops and nautical accessories, while formal service and haute cuisine are better expressed in a setting of traditional elegance. It is all too easy to overdo restaurant theme expressiveness with decor so exotic as to approach absurdity.

18.30 *The lobby of the recently renovated Paramount Hotel in New York, designed by Philippe Starck with architect Anda Andrei, serves as a striking backdrop for the comings and goings of guests. Furniture is placed on an angled area of carpet in large squares of contrasting tones. The floor is of pietra serena marble, and the wall adjacent to the astonishing tapered stair is surfaced in platinum leaf. (Photograph: © Peter Mauss/ESTO)*

18.31

18.32

18.31 Total restaurant design often includes tableware, linens, and glassware, as well as graphic designs for menu covers, coasters, and matchbooks. A consistent theme helps to place a unique and memorable stamp on a dining environment. The tableware illustrated here was designed by Vignelli Associates for the Palio restaurant illustrated in fig. 18.32. (Photograph courtesy Vignelli Associates)

18.32 In the spectacular, high-ceiling bar area for an elaborate—and expensive—New York restaurant called Palio, designed by Skidmore, Owings & Merrill in 1986, the large mural by Sandro Chia is the dominant design element. (Photograph: © 1986 Wolfgang Hoyt/ESTO)

18.33

The involvement of the interior designer in restaurant projects is usually limited to the public spaces, which will include some or all of the following:

WAITING AREA

CHECKING AREA OR HANGING SPACE FOR COATS

BAR (POSSIBLY COMBINED WITH A COCKTAIL LOUNGE)

COUNTER SEATING

SERVING COUNTER (FOR CAFETERIA SERVICE ONLY)

DINING ROOM WITH TABLE SEATING, POSSIBLY WITH BANQUETTES OR BOOTHS

PRIVATE DINING ROOM(S)

REST ROOMS

CASHIER'S STATION

The kitchens and other service portions of a restaurant not accessible to the public are usually not part of the interior designer's concern. An area comprising between 20 and 50 percent of the dining space is allocated to services; detailed planning of this part of the restaurant is often provided by the makers of kitchen equipment, working closely with the restaurant's management and chefs. The dining areas of hotels and motels are, of course, also restaurants. In larger hotels there are often several different dining areas, perhaps a coffee shop, a service restaurant and bar, and private dining and banquet facilities. Hotel

kitchens and other services are usually grouped for efficiency, posing complex problems in planning.

Design must reinforce the best aspects of a restaurant's qualities while promoting functional efficiency, ensuring the comfort and pleasure of the diner and serving the economic needs of the management to make the place a business success.

HOTELS, MOTELS, AND INNS. Hotels, motels, and inns range from the simplest of small guest houses to vast complexes, complete resorts, or urban meeting places on a major scale (figs. 18.30, 18.32, 18.42). At a minimum, hotel guests seek comfort. They have come to expect entertainment as well—the active entertainment of sports facilities, casino, or nightclub or the more passive entertainment of using interesting or exciting public spaces and occupying guest rooms that are more than mere places to sleep. Modern hotels and motels serve a variety of guests, ranging from the vacationer through the expense-account business traveler to celebrities who expect their lodging place to set off their personalities and styles.

CLUBS. Clubs combine, in various proportions, the qualities of meeting halls, restaurants, hotels, and residences. Their design needs to

18.33 The famous Villard Houses, palazzo-like dwellings for wealthy New Yorkers, were built in 1882–86 to designs of McKim, Mead and White in what is now a central midtown site. When they were incorporated into a new hotel complex, the Helmsley Palace, in 1980, the lavish traditional interiors were restored, converted, and preserved. Sarah Tomerlin Lee of Tom Lee Limited turned spaces such as this salon—now a lounge—into rooms answering contemporary requirements. (Photograph: Jaime Ardiles-Arce)

Case Study 6

Restaurants in Small Spaces

In many large cities tiny ground-floor spaces, often of irregular shape, have recently been discovered as ideal locations for fast-food shops featuring a particular item or style of cooking. These spaces present an interesting challenge to the interior designer, who must make efficient use of a very limited area while projecting a forceful image that will attract customers as well as identify the shop's specialty. The three projects featured here, each with its own unique character, are located in New York.

Of the three shops, TacoMadre is the only one clearly based on a specific traditional cuisine. To anyone who has been to Mexican cities, the references to the shops there are obvious, but even the passerby who has not traveled south of the border will recognize clues to a regional style. There is a certain intended naiveté in the white tiles with blue and white decorative banding, the menu board with its ornamental yellow frame

18.34

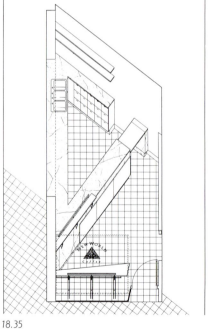

18.35

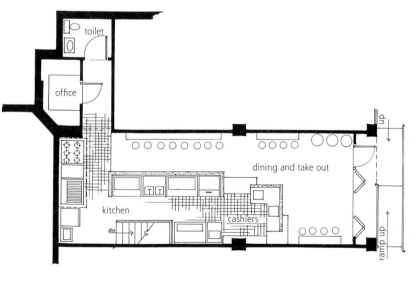

FIRST FLOOR

18.36

18.34, 18.35 The angle of the rear wall in New World Coffee is repeated in the triangular counter arrangement, as well as the store's logo (fig. 18.34) (Photograph: Otto Baitz) An axonometric drawing (fig. 18.35) shows the plan layout with the front window elevation superimposed. It was designed by Ronnette Riley Architect. (Drawing courtesy Ronnette Riley)

18.37

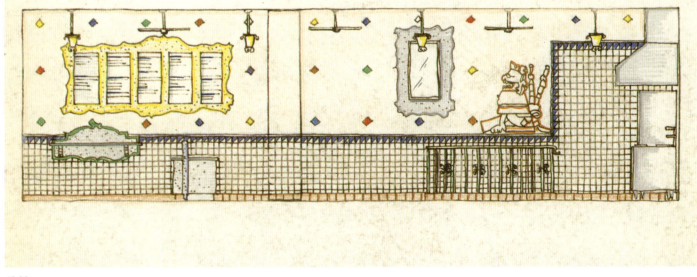

18.38

18.36–18.38 TacoMadre Mexican Kitchen uses tiled counters and colorful menu boards to establish a distinctive character (fig. 18.37), which will be maintained in the future TacoMadre restaurants planned as part of a chain. A sketch by the architect, Denise A. Hall, shows the design concept under development (fig. 18.38), while the plan shows the efficient use of limited space (fig. 18.36). (Photograph: Ken Schles, sketch and plan courtesy D. A. Hall Architects)

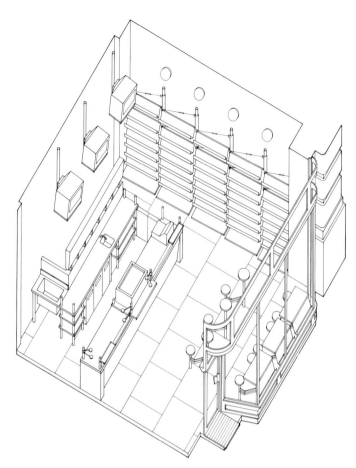

18.39

18.40

mounting, the framed mirror, the lanternlike light fixtures, and the ceiling fans. In a space of only 750 square feet (with services in the basement), architect Denise A. Hall has managed to fit in eighteen counter seats and small tables and chairs as well as to provide for wheelchair accessibility. The shop's take-out service is a major attraction for customers in a hurry, who can sense the promise of speed from a glimpse in the streetfront window. This space was developed as a prototype for a chain expected to grow to some thirty stores within three years.

In contrast to the homey character of Taco-Madre, Turett Collaborative Architects have given Newsbar urban sophistication and a High Tech flavor by using glass and metals as materials, bright, focused spotlighting, and gleaming wall-mounted television monitors.

The TVs suggest the rapid pace of breaking news, while the store's magazine racks invite a scan of the latest publications. A few stools invite a brief stop for coffee and a snack; take-out customers can consider adding a magazine to a food purchase. The glassy open front puts the entire shop—including food and publications—on display from the street, luring customers interested in either coffee and snacks or magazines.

New World Coffee also presents an open-front view of the entire shop. The lettering and trademark on the window, the bagged coffee beans on display, and the coffee-brewing machinery behind the counter act together to set off the prospective customer's urge to taste the special coffee flavors the shop offers. The angled rear wall, an oddity of the tiny space, has been turned into an

advantage: the green-gold wall is brightly lit to pull attention into the depth of the shop. The architect, Ronnette Riley, has also used the wall as the basis for the angled counter, generating a triangular form that suggests movement and activity while also maximizing length. The eight lights hanging in a closely spaced row above the counter further emphasize the angle. The triangular theme is reinforced in the window logo, a triangle containing a globe, with rays suggestive of steaming coffee rising from it.

A common denominator of these three shops is the use of thoughtful and skillful design to generate a visual impression that is both attractive and memorable, a strong contrast to the cluttered and chaotic image that is all too common in typical fast-food outlets.

*18.39–18.41 Newsbar offers coffee, snacks, magazines, and papers in a very small store. Gleaming metal details, sparkling lighting, and active TV screens make the interior lively and inviting (fig. 18.39). The use of space is illustrated in an axonometric draw-*ing *(fig. 18.40), while preliminary sketches by the architect, Wayne Turett, of Turett Collaborative Architects, record concept development (fig. 18.41; see page 525). (Photograph: © 1992 Paul Warchol, drawings courtesy Turett Collaborative Architects)*

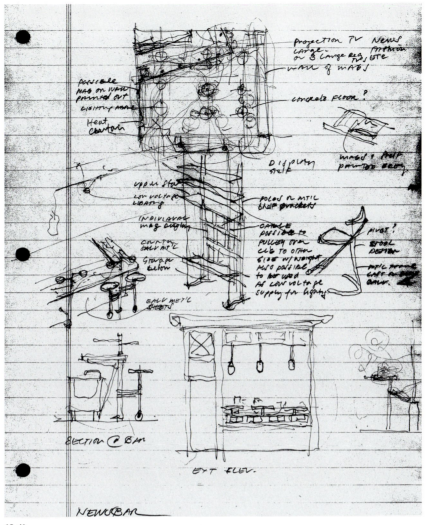

18.41

express the particular quality that has brought together a specific membership. The clubhouse is something of a secondary home at the same time that it serves the needs of such groups as golfers, business people, gamblers, yachtsmen, or whatever group has chosen to band together. The interiors of some older clubs are showcases of fine traditional design that modern design cannot easily equal.

Gymnasiums, swimming pools, and other kinds of health and exercise facilities formerly were of a strictly functional character. Today, their design has more and more come to emphasize their value as places for recreation and social contact. The growth of these facilities, in connection with hotels, clubs, and institutions or independently, and the increasing importance of giving them a strong visual character have made them another field for interior design expression.

Transportation

Transport calls for two kinds of interior space: the interiors of stations, terminals, ticket offices, and other fixed-base locations that serve transport; and the interiors of the transport vehicles themselves: buses, trains, airplanes, ships, and private automobiles. Some of these, for

example, cars and planes, may seem to fall more in the professional territory of the industrial designer; nevertheless, as interiors they receive careful professional design attention.

While the day of the great ocean liners is drawing to a close, cruise ships prosper and proliferate, and their interiors receive the same kind of design attention called for by resort hotels. The interior space of aircraft is extremely limited and restricted by the shape and size of the craft, by the need to pack in the maximum number of passengers, and by complex weight and safety restrictions. Despite these design limitations, intense competition among airlines and the increased use of private jets have led to an extraordinary effort to make airplane interiors special, attractive, and, insofar as possible, luxurious.

Long-distance passenger trains present similar design problems in a slightly less intense form, while commuter and subway trains and buses present special problems resulting from constant, long-term use and the threats of vandalism and other mischief.

Great railway terminals with dramatic interior spaces have become relics of the past, but modern rail and urban transit stations present challenging problems in aesthetics, functional utility, and security (fig.

18.41 See figs. 18.39 and 18.40 on page 524.

18.43). Airport terminals vary from the strictly utilitarian to those with a monumental expressivity rivaling that of the older railway terminals. Practical issues of functional efficiency, economics, and new problems of security make these exciting projects with possibilities for impressive and user-satisfying results.

Interior design can even contribute to such unlikely spaces as the interiors of naval vessels and spacecraft. Long time spans in the cramped and sealed spaces of ships (submarines in particular), airplanes, and spacecraft generate psychological stresses that intelligent design, including its aesthetic considerations, can do much to limit, through what is sometimes called *habitability*. This promotes efficient performance by maximizing functional convenience and comfort and by minimizing the discomfort and stress involved in such spaces, thereby conserving human energy for the tasks that must be performed.

The design of automobiles, often called *styling* in the industry, contributes greatly to the product's commercial success. It is widely recognized that, in addition to the basic engineering design and the external form, a car's interior is a major factor in purchase decisions and in user satisfaction. Even the employment of famous designers, who contribute visual improvements (and, perhaps, an element of snob appeal), has become commonplace with some automotive manufacturers.

Design issues obviously include comfort, ease of operation for the driver, and appearance. Safety considerations, long neglected in the auto industry, are receiving increasing attention. Interestingly, at its best, the design of the family car's interior is often far superior to that of the same family's house or apartment!

Work Spaces

The interiors of factories, workshops, laboratories (fig. 18.23), and power plants rarely receive professional interior design attention. Their strictly functional purposes have kept them within the province of engineers and technicians. The exceptions suggest that there can be benefits in considering the aesthetic possibilities of such spaces. In industrial plants, color and lighting can be used to aid vision and to promote efficient work and safety. Interested visitors are always

18.42

18.42 In the Mansion on Turtle Creek, Dallas, the tropical and elaborate decorative treatment creates an atmosphere of luxury in a guest room. The hotel, attached to the original 1925 structure, was built by Shepard & Boyd in 1979–80 and renovated by Hirsch/Bedner & Associates. (Photograph: Jaime Ardiles-Arce)

18.43

impressed by a steel mill, an auto factory, or a powerhouse, and the impression is heightened when the space is treated visually to make it understandable, provocative, and even beautiful.

Utility companies have found that inviting public inspection of power plants and control rooms is good policy. The power plants of the Tennessee Valley Authority have been consistently admired as examples of the beauty possible in industrial settings (fig. 18.44). The power plant at Kennedy airport in New York City occupies an all-glass building, displaying its colorfully painted equipment to those driving by. The engine room of a ship is often one of the most handsome parts of the vessel. In all of these instances, strict engineering needs are, of course, primary, but concern for visual design can help to make the technical realities attractive, interesting, and exciting in a way that helps public understanding while supporting staff pride and morale.

18.44

18.43 Passengers using big-city transportation often have to deal with noisy, unattractive, even dangerous conditions. In stations of the Washington, D.C., Metro (subway) system, spacious, well-lighted interiors help to make the traveler's experience pleasant. The curving, coffered ceiling reflects the reinforced-concrete structure of the underground space. This is the Stadium-Armory Station (1977), designed by Harry Weese Associates. (Photograph: Phil Portlock, courtesy Washington Area Transit Authority)

18.44 An aesthetic of industrial technology, developed in the Tennessee Valley Authority projects of the 1930s, is evident in this generator room at the Pickwick Dam Powerhouse. Roland Wank of the Tennessee Valley Authority headquarters in Knoxville, Tennessee, was in charge of design. (Photograph courtesy Tennessee Valley Authority)

19.1

PROFESSIONAL DESIGN/ BUSINESS MATTERS

PROFESSIONAL PREPARATION

An interest in interior design usually begins with familiar problems in a home or office. Young people often design their own rooms at home or in a dormitory. Householders make choices of furniture, color, and materials for their own apartments or houses. Books such as this one can often provide the information needed to deal with home projects of modest extent. If the results of such efforts are admired and if the process has been interesting and enjoyable, thoughts of turning professional may come to mind. There are several routes into professionalism, and all involve training of one sort or another. Historically, the most common training involved working for a successful interior designer. Whether through a formal apprenticeship or simply by getting a job as an assistant to a designer, the real-life experience of working on projects can gradually build up the skills that professional design work demands.

The path to professional practice more frequently begins with training at the college level in an art or design school or at a university. Although almost every college offers some courses in interior design, a few courses taken as electives or in an adult-education program can do no more than give a general overview of what full professional training involves. Institutions that grant a bachelor's degree in interior design usually require four years of regular college courses, including some liberal-arts subjects and art history, in addition to a variety of courses in design itself. The content of such a program includes "design" studied through the use of a sequence of problems, as discussed in Chapter 5, plus a number of courses in such specific subjects as color, materials, furniture, lighting, construction, and professional practice. A complete degree program of this kind is offered by many institutions with an art or architecture department and by some schools that teach design only but have an affiliation with a liberal-arts college.

The quality of programs and their emphases vary considerably. Accreditation by the Foundation for Interior Design Education and Research (FIDER) indicates that a school program meets certain minimum standards of excellence. Correspondence courses and programs that do not meet FIDER standards are generally inadequate. Anyone who has received a bachelor's degree in some other field can consider graduate programs in interior design offered by some institutions. These programs usually require two or more years of work and stress design subjects presented at a more advanced level than in undergraduate courses. A master's degree in interior design offered in such programs can also be obtained by students whose undergraduate degree is in interior design.

Another road to professionalism involves study in an architecture school leading to either a bachelor's or master's degree in architecture. Architectural training emphasizes building construction and technology and concentrates on the design of complete buildings, which leads to limited treatment of the more specialized aspects of interior design. Many graduate architects become interested in interiors and make up for what their training omitted through their own study and experience. Although a number of architects feel fully qualified to design interiors, most focus on the total design of buildings and often refer the interior design aspects of projects to specialists, either designers employed by their offices or independent interior designers.

Successful completion of interior design training is normally followed by a period of employment in an interior design firm or in the interior

19.1 The calculator joins other tools of the designer in the business aspects of project realization.

design department of an architectural office. The experience of working on real projects under supervision rounds out training and prepares a designer to take on professional assignments.

LICENSING AND REGISTRATION

Until recently each designer was free to decide when training and skills were sufficient to justify entering professional practice. Although this remains true in some states, a number of states, including those with major concentrations of population, have since the early 1980s adopted laws that provide for the licensing of interior designers and that restrict the use of the title "interior designer"—and in one state the practice of interior design—to those who have met the formal requirements for a license. Registration acts are spoken of as *title* or *practice laws*. At present twelve states and the District of Columbia have registration or licensing laws, but only the District of Columbia restricts practice. More states will no doubt pass licensing laws in the near future, and as time goes on title acts will be upgraded to restrict practice. Requirements vary from state to state, with each state setting its own regulations. By meeting the requirements of the states setting the highest standards, a professional designer can feel free to work in any state, now or in the future.

The typical requirements of the strictest states are:

Two to four years of formal design education after high school

A total of six to eight years of combined design education and work experience

Passage of the examination administered by the National Council for Interior Design Qualification (NCIDQ)

Compliance with these requirements not only satisfies the states with registration laws but also establishes the designer's level of competence in a way that offers reassurance to potential clients both in those states and in the states that as yet have no such requirements. Most of the professional organizations for interior designers have also made passage of the NCIDQ exam a requirement for membership.

NCIDQ EXAMINATION

Because the basis for licensing laws is the protection of the safety, health, and well-being of the public, the examination developed by the NCIDQ concentrates heavily on areas that impinge on these matters most directly. The training offered in design schools tends to focus on the aesthetic aspects of design and to deal with technical matters secondarily, leaving study of building codes and business matters to the students' postgraduation experience. It is often a surprise to examination candidates to find that aesthetic abilities are, for the examination, subordinate to these more mundane considerations. Even work experience is not necessarily an adequate preparation for the exam. The NCIDQ provides a manual that details the format and content of the exam, and various books have appeared that are useful study aids for those preparing to take the exam. "Cram courses" are also offered by some schools to help candidates brush up on subjects in which they may need special preparation.

Examination Format

The NCIDQ requires that applicants for the examination have a four- or five-year degree in interior design plus two years of work experience; a three-year certificate in interior design plus three years of experience; or a two-year certificate plus four years of experience. The examination is given twice a year at more than sixty locations in the United States and takes two full days. The six sections of the exam can be taken all at once or at different times. Although a failed section can be repeated until passed, all six sections must be passed within a five-year period. The six parts of the exam are as follows:

FIRST DAY   Identification and Application: Two parts of
1 ½ hours each
Programming: 2-hour session
Three-Dimensional Exercise: 1 ½-hour session
SECOND DAY   Problem Solving: 1 ½-hour session
Building and Barrier-Free Codes: 1 ½-hour session
Project Scenario: 2 ½-hour session

Multiple-choice questions are used in the Identification and Application, Problem Solving, and Building and Barrier-Free Codes sections; an essay answer and a drawn diagram are required in the Programming section; and drawings are required for the Three-Dimensional Exercise and Project Scenario sections. For the Project Scenario, the candidate may choose a project that falls into one of the five areas of corporate, residential, retail, institutional, or hospitality design.

Examination Content

The subject matter covered in the various sections of the NCIDQ exam are as follows:

IDENTIFICATION AND APPLICATION. Questions deal with theory, programming, contract documents, furniture, equipment, finishes, building and interior systems, sketching, drafting, perspective, business and professional practice, project coordination, and history.

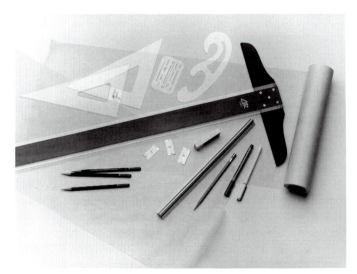

19.2

19.2 The tools of the designer's trade include a T-square, triangles, scale, French curve, eraser and eraser shield, an assortment of pencils, markers, and razor blades, and a roll of yellow tracing paper for sketching or preliminary drafting. (Photograph: George Hein)

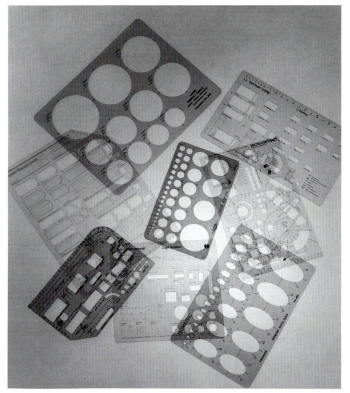

19.3

PROFESSIONAL ORGANIZATIONS

Many professional interior designers elect to join one or more of the professional organizations that have been created to represent the profession and provide various services to their members. A listing of these organizations and a summary of their activities are presented in Appendix 8. Membership usually entails meeting certain standards that give evidence of qualifications. In states where licensing is not yet required, membership in a major professional organization serves as an alternative means of establishing the professional standing of an interior designer.

EMPLOYMENT OF INTERIOR DESIGNERS

As mentioned above, most designers acquire work experience after their school training by taking a job in the office of an established designer. Entrance-level positions (often called *junior*) are sometimes available while a student is still in school—during summers or on a part-time basis. Although working while in school may lead to a work overload, most students find it helpful to establish early contact with the professional world through some work experience. The junior designer is often given chore work, including gathering samples, mounting presentation items, and even filing, but he or she can also hope to be given creative work from time to time, such as designing and developing color schemes. Making construction drawings under supervision is an invaluable form of on-the-job training.

A large office presents opportunities to participate in a variety of bigger projects, whereas a small office is more likely to offer varied experience in seeing a particular project go through all of the steps from beginning to end. A junior designer who does good work can expect advancement to greater responsibility, leading to a major role in projects, possibly with the title of *associate*. Office jobs in design can be volatile from the expansion and contraction that follow fluctuating work loads. Changing jobs for this reason does not reflect on a junior designer's abilities, and it is often wise to make a voluntary change when an ongoing job ceases to offer varied experience or advancement.

Work in a firm can develop into a satisfying long-term career position with major design responsibilities without the burdens of running a business. A role as partner in a firm can make it easier to get credit for work done and provides many of the advantages of individual practice. A number of designers grow into positions where they are in charge of an interior design department within a larger firm. Some architectural offices operate an interior design department or have established an affiliated interior design organization. Other possibilities include facilities-planning or space-planning departments within large corporate organizations. Some hotel and restaurant chains have in-house design groups that supply interior design services to their facilities; organizations with large office facilities often maintain similar in-house services. Furniture manufacturers or dealers have occasionally established *planning units* that provide interior design services to cus-

PROGRAMMING. A simulated client interview is presented in words. The candidate writes out questions to be asked of the client and then prepares a schematic or bubble diagram based on given program requirements.

THREE-DIMENSIONAL EXERCISE. A short design problem is given in words. On one of two 17-by-22-inch sheets, the candidate must draw either two elevations, a section, a plan, and a reflected ceiling plan *or* an axonometric, a plan, and a reflected ceiling plan. A brief written description is also requested.

PROBLEM SOLVING. The candidate is given project drawings and a written description and must answer questions on the basis of the given material.

BUILDING AND BARRIER-FREE CODES. Questions relate to contract documents, building and interior systems, safety, building and barrier-free codes, and testing standards.

PROJECT SCENARIO. A design problem from the category selected by the candidate (from among the five alternatives listed above) is presented in written form. Two preprinted sheets are provided showing a plan of the space to be dealt with at a scale of ¼" = 1'-0". The candidate must draw a floor plan of the design solution complete with furniture on one sheet and a reflected ceiling plan on the other.

19.3 Templates are employed in design and drafting to draw much-used forms to scale without measuring. Among the dozens available are circle and ellipse templates, shown here along with others provided by various furniture companies with cutouts geared to specific products. (Photograph: George Hein)

19.4

tomers. Although a designer is somewhat captive to the organization in such positions, he or she can nonetheless have the advantage of a secure job with a flow of interesting work. Some planning services have produced work of very fine quality, quite comparable to that of the best interior design firms.

SETTING UP A WORKPLACE

Most designers start out by working at home. While some modest work can be done in the corner of a living room or bedroom, active work will usually soon demand a room of its own. As a design practice grows, so will the need for an outer office with reception desk and waiting space, a place for meetings and conferences, and workplaces for assistants, drafting, models, sample storage, and filing. If there are to be partners or senior associates, each will probably require an office. Such a professional office commonly occupies rented space in an office building in a suitable location. Eventually a design firm may choose to build a building of its own that can be an effective demon-

stration of the quality of the firm's work. The need to expand and contract office facilities as the volume of work changes tends to make rental space the most practical choice for the majority of designers.

Whether it is the solitary beginner or the staff designer in a larger organization who needs a suitable place to work, setting up a workplace where drawings can be made, samples and catalogs stored, and work in progress kept together is a wise preparatory step to the design process (fig. 19.4). The essential piece of furniture is a sturdy desk or table for drawing. A drafting table made for the purpose is ideal, but a separate drawing board placed on a table or desk also works well and has the advantage of being portable so that it can be put away or moved easily. A large board on the sawhorses used for carpentry is an inexpensive way to make a drafting table. Drawing-board or drafting-tabletops must be large enough to accommodate the largest drawing to be made, preferably 30 by 50 inches, with 24 by 36 inches as a practical minimum.

A suitable chair or stool and good lighting are also needed. Windows give the best light, but a lamp will be needed for dark days and

19.4 In this designer's office and studio, drafting equipment, lighting, and storage are all well placed to create effective—as well as pleasant—working conditions. Note the generous work surface, angled for efficiency. Charles Damga designed his own workplace in New York. (Photograph: © Peter Paige)

for evenings. The widely available adjustable Luxo lamp is a great favorite. The best version has a large reflector and a long arm and takes a 75- or 100-watt lamp (bulb). A large board may call for two Luxos. There must also be a straightedge whose length matches the width of the board. A T-square is traditionally used for the purpose. Parallel rules attached more or less permanently to the board also answer this need. They may seem easier to use since, unlike the T-square, they have no head (the crosspiece of the T-square) to be held in place while drawing. The yet more elaborate drafting machine, highly favored for engineering drafting, is expensive and unnecessary for interior work but will serve well if available.

The other necessary tools and equipment are all fairly simple and inexpensive to acquire. Several will probably be found at hand already (figs. 19.2, 19.3).

- *TRIANGLES.* Two are needed, one of 45° and a second of 30–60°, each of 8- or 10-inch size. A single adjustable triangle may be substituted.
- *SCALE.* An architect's scale is needed. The triangular variety with various scales along its three edges is the usual choice.
- *TEMPLATES.* A circle-guide template is the most useful. A template with squares and hexagons in small sizes may be helpful, as will an ellipse guide with various ellipse shapes in a range of sizes. A furniture template with typical furniture units in plan at scale can be a convenience, as long as it does not tempt the user to avoid drawing furniture in more varied ways. Furniture manufacturers often give away templates for their own product lines.
- *MEASURING TOOLS.* A yardstick, a carpenter's folding footrule, and a 6-foot tape are essential. A 100-foot tape may be wanted eventually.
- *PENCIL SHARPENER.* A good crank-type is best, plus a small pocket-type for portability. An electric sharpener is also a common choice.
- *ERASER AND SHIELD.* Staedtler Mars No. 526 50 is the ideal plastic eraser. Bad erasers can damage or ruin a drawing and should be avoided. An eraser shield makes it easy to erase small details.
- *MISCELLANEOUS ITEMS.* The drawing board should be covered with sturdy paper or illustration board. An accessory metal edge for the board's left side is helpful if a T-square is used. A roll of drafting tape and a few thumbtacks and pushpins should be at hand. An adjustable curve or several *French curves* may be helpful, and a drafting compass may be needed occasionally. Drafting instrument sets in neat boxes, while attractive, will rarely be used and hardly justify their cost. Good scissors and a matte knife are vital.

Consumable materials can be acquired as needed. A basic stock for starting out would be the following:

- *PAPER.* Tracing paper in rolls is most common. Thin yellow (or *canary*) tracing paper is the norm for rough sketching. Twelve- or 18-inch rolls are convenient; stock plenty since it will be used in quantity. For more finished drawings, a good-quality white tracing paper in 36- or 42-inch rolls is standard. Avoid vellum papers. A pad of tracing paper and a white drawing pad may also be useful. Illustration board, in white on one side, gray on the other, is often used for presentation drawings and for color charts. Twenty by 30 inches is a convenient size.
- *PENCILS.* Good-quality pencils are necessary. A few ordinary No. 2 pencils are useful, but drafting is usually done with special pencils that come in grades of hardness. Stock a few in grades H, F, HB, B,

and 2B. Berol Turquoise is a good brand, with Dexel Cumberland a fine English alternative. Berol Draughting Pencil No. 314 is a favorite for sketching (not, in spite of its name, for drafting). A few colored pencils, or a set in a range of colors, can be useful; the Berol brand Prismacolor is a good choice.

- *PENS.* Since ink drafting is rarely used for interior design work in the United States, special pens and the technical pen sets widely available are not needed. Felt-tip marker pens, however, are widely used. A few thin-line markers in black will be useful, and color markers are a favorite sketching medium. Staedtler Mars 3000 series color markers have a convenient flexible foam point and a fine color range. A good fountain pen with nonclogging black ink is a good sketching medium, but a disposable felt-point pen can serve as well and is more convenient than keeping a fountain pen in working order.
- *MISCELLANEOUS SUPPLIES.* Colored papers may come in handy. Color-Aid paper is a good brand; a book of samples is available and full sheets can be bought as needed. Transfer lettering in a few styles may be helpful in making neat titles. Duco cement is a good adhesive. Avoid rubber cement. A box of single-edge razor blades is often useful.

Normal office supplies will also be needed from time to time. Standard typing paper, lined yellow pads, index cards, file folders, labels, tape, and similar supplies will be used constantly. A typewriter or computer is basic to a working setup. Papers, catalogs, and samples, which can expand to alarming proportions all too easily, call for filing space. Drawings can be rolled and stored in tubes until the quantity of work builds up and calls for a flat file made for the purpose—an expensive item. In another category, a camera, an exposure meter (built-in or separate), a tripod, and photo lights will be useful. Almost any kind of camera can serve, but the most versatile choice is a 35-millimeter single-lens reflex.

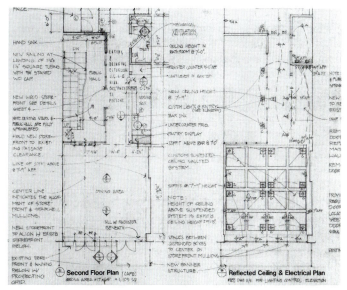

19.5

19.5 Shown here are typical construction drawings, a floor plan and a reflected ceiling plan, for a small restaurant project. The restaurant, Cafe Word of Mouth, was designed by Alfredo De Vido Associates in 1992. (Courtesy Alfredo De Vido Associates)

INTERIOR DESIGN DRAWINGS

With a workplace set up and tools and materials assembled, it is possible to turn to the most specialized aspect of interior design work, the making of drawings.

Everyone has made decisions about color choices or selected a piece of furniture and ordered it, and it is easy to understand how expanding such choosing, selecting, and ordering to include everything that will make up an interior can turn into a complete project. Many such interior design steps actually rely on the everyday exercise of judgment combined with what might be called good business practices. Few people, however, have the training or skill to make drawings, especially the rather special sorts of drawings that the interior designer uses in planning and carrying out a project.

Drawings fall into two major categories. *Design drawings* develop the conceptual approach and visual form of a space. *Construction drawings* are made for use in taking bids and directing and controlling the work of contractor and workmen. Books and courses devoted to drafting, or (as it is often called in schools) *mechanical drawing*, are widely available. With a suitable book or two and the necessary tools at hand, it is possible to teach oneself to draw. However the skills are acquired, every interior designer will find some drawing ability helpful and useful. The two types of drawings used by designers, design drawings and construction drawings, are discussed in greater detail below.

Design Drawings

In large measure the design process is, in fact, a matter of making drawings. Ideas, however valuable and exciting, only begin to relate to reality when they are made visible—to the designer and, at appropriate times, to others, including colleagues and possibly clients. An emerging design concept is first expressed visually in sketches. Concept sketches may be abstract or tiny, sometimes made in a notebook or on any available piece of paper. At the drawing board the usual medium is the inexpensive yellow tracing paper described above, used in quantity and perhaps discarded as sketches are developed. A soft pencil is the most-used tool because it produces a flowing line, a series of tones from pale gray to black, and is easily erased. A felt-tip marker is an alternative, to which color tones from colored pencils or markers can be added. For most projects sketching begins with plans, but elevations, sections, and perspectives can be useful as well. First sketches may not be to scale, but bringing concepts into scale form as soon as possible helps to discipline ideas and relate them to reality. The concept of drawing to scale is basic to all design communication. (For a complete discussion of drawing to scale, see Chapter 6, pages 148–53.)

Sketching on graph paper or on tracing paper placed over graph paper also facilitates drawing to scale without constant measuring and helps to keep lines straight and angles as they are meant to be. Sketching is sometimes done in three dimensions with bits of either white or gray paper or card stock bent and folded, then taped or glued together to create a *sketch model*. Such a model is easily revised as the design develops and can help evaluate how forms relate in space.

As ideas evolve and choices are made among alternatives, sketches tend to become less "sketchy," meaning more specific and more literal.

At some point in design development it becomes appropriate to move from freehand drawing to the use of instruments. A drafted plan begins to elucidate a design. One or more sections or elevations follow along. Color can be added to drafted preliminary design drawings either on the original tracing paper or on a print, which leaves the original uncolored. Colored pencils and markers are favored mediums. Perspective drawings can be sketched *by eye* or, once plans are drawn to scale, can be constructed geometrically, as detailed in Appendix 5, pages 551–55.

Carefully drafted design drawings, with or without coloring, is the usual medium for presentation of preliminary designs to a client. Perspectives can also be used for this purpose, sometimes in the form of colorful and realistic *renderings,* virtual paintings of the spaces being proposed. The drawings made to show a completed design to a client are normally called *presentation drawings* and are often grouped with material and finish samples, as well as photographs of proposed furniture and other purchased-item selections.

Construction Drawings

Once a design has been set and approved, drawings must be made for use in obtaining estimates or bids and for the use of the contractors who will execute the work. These *working drawings* are a key part of the *contract documents* that define the work that a construction contract calls for (see fig. 19.5). Working drawings differ from design drawings in that they show all necessary information about construction and materials in great detail. The skills involved in making working drawings are not limited to draftsmanship; they must include full knowledge of the materials and techniques of construction. These skills are not easily taught either in school or in texts. They are usually learned in an office while working under the supervision of an experienced master—most often an "old timer" who has been making such drawings for many years.

Every designer needs to learn to make working drawings, if only as a way of learning to *read,* that is, to understand, such drawings. A set of drawings for a major project can appear overwhelmingly complex, and an interior designer working on a space in an architect-designed building must understand the architectural drawings as a starting point for interior work. Construction drawings are organized in a set of several, even many, sheets. A typical set of drawings will include:

A COVER SHEET. This identifies the project, gives a list of the sheets that make up the set, and carries general notes that apply to the project as a whole.

FLOOR PLANS. For multifloor projects, several floors may appear on one sheet, if there is space. Each floor may be on a sheet of its own or, for a very large project, may be shown broken up to fit on several sheets.

ELEVATIONS AND SECTIONS. These drawings show height relationships and other information not clear from plans.

DETAILS AND SCHEDULES. These include drawings for windows, doors, and wall sections.

FURNITURE PLAN(S) AND SCHEDULE.

FINISH PLAN AND SCHEDULE.

REFLECTED CEILING PLAN(S) AND FIXTURE SCHEDULE.

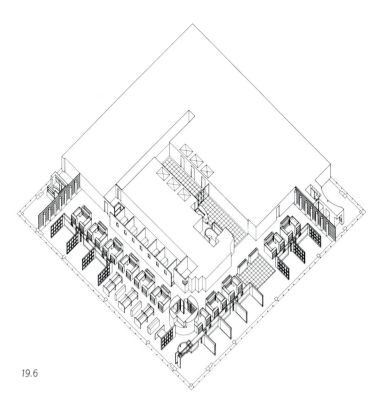

19.6

SPECIFICATIONS

In addition to drawings, contract documents normally include written specifications that spell out information not readily conveyed in drawings, such as verbal descriptions of materials, methods of work, and standards that are to be met in the quality of both materials and workmanship. Specifications are particularly important when competitive bidding is to take place, so that all bidders will base their estimates on the same precise basis of quality. Standard specifications are available for many materials, products, and construction techniques. Such model specifications can be used when appropriate or modified to apply to a given project.

MODELS

Models are helpful devices in presenting design concepts. They convey a sense of reality, are readily understood by clients who may find drawings confusing, and generally have a certain toylike charm that helps to make a proposal attractive to a client or sponsor. Many designers make their own models (the technique is much used and therefore taught in design schools) or have a staff member who is expert in this medium. There are also professional model builders who work from drawings and color and finish samples to build models with a high level of finish. Interior models are usually built without a ceiling or with a removable ceiling so that they can be viewed from above to give a bird's-eye view of a project. A scale of $1/4'' = 1'-0''$ is suitable for models of groups of rooms or of a whole floor. Models of a single room are often made at a scale of $1'' = 1'-0''$ to show detail (many materials, accessories, and even some furniture are available ready-made for architectural modeling and for the use of dollhouse hobbyists). Larger scale models also make it easier to view the interior at normal eye levels, either through openings or removable walls. Photographs of models can be very effective in conveying a sense of realism. Color slides of larger scale models, when projected, may be hardly distinguishable from actual interior views. Special equipment has been developed to permit photography or videotaping of spaces within smaller scale models. A videotaped *walk-through* of a model interior can be impressive and convincing. Although such techniques are highly specialized and very costly, they can be extremely effective in presenting designs to client organizations in which committees or various groups are involved in viewing and accepting design proposals.

COMPUTERS AND DESIGN

Computer-based techniques can be of great usefulness in design. CAD (computer-aided design) and CADD (computer-aided design and drawing) are now widely accepted methods in design offices. The specifics of equipment (hardware) and the programs to be used (software) are in constant flux as improved techniques are developed and costs decline.

Interior design is particularly well suited to computer applications because it so often makes use of repeated elements that are fairly well standardized (furniture, appliances, plumbing fixtures, doors, closets,

If the project requires it, additional sheets will show electrical, plumbing, and HVAC work. Although these sheets are usually prepared by a mechanical engineer, they must be checked and coordinated with the interior design drawings. Sheets prepared by a structural engineer showing basic constructional elements also appear in any complete set of architectural drawings for building construction.

Plan drawings are developed by making a *base sheet* that shows the basic layout of spaces. For each final plan drawing, a fresh piece of tracing paper or vellum is laid over the base sheet so that the basic plan can be traced to provide the general floor plan, reflected ceiling plan, and other special-purpose plans. To save tracing, prints of the base sheet can be made on tracing paper or vellum so that it is necessary to draw in only the information for each of the other plans not on the base sheet. The numerous symbols, figures, and words indicating materials, dimensions, door types, and the locations of details can make a basic floor plan look quite complex. Similarly, a reflected ceiling plan showing lighting, electrical layout, HVAC, and, possibly, ceiling systems, sprinklers, and related data can become extremely complicated. Schedules are the best way to convey information about door types, finishes, equipment, light fixtures, and, if furniture has been selected and ordered at the time the drawings are completed, furniture location. Details make use of elevations and sections, often at large scale to show construction. Axonometric drawing may be used for some details. In many firms, frequently used details are kept on file, ready to be transferred to the detail sheets for future projects when they apply. Standardized sizes for drawings and uniform borders and title blocks make a set of construction drawings appear orderly, organized, and professional.

19.6 An axonometric drawing illustrates an office design project. Building-standard interiors furnish a floor covering, utility-quality lighting, and a minimum linear footage of partition walls with doors. The glass-block walls, special partitions, and workstation units shown here raise the interior far above the building-standard level; the tenant must either pay for the enhancements or, if they are provided by the building owner, negotiate a higher rent than the base rent charged for building-standard space. This largely open office space was designed by Tod Williams for B.E.A., an investment banking firm in New York, in 1979. (Courtesy Tod Williams and Billie Tsien Associates, Architects)

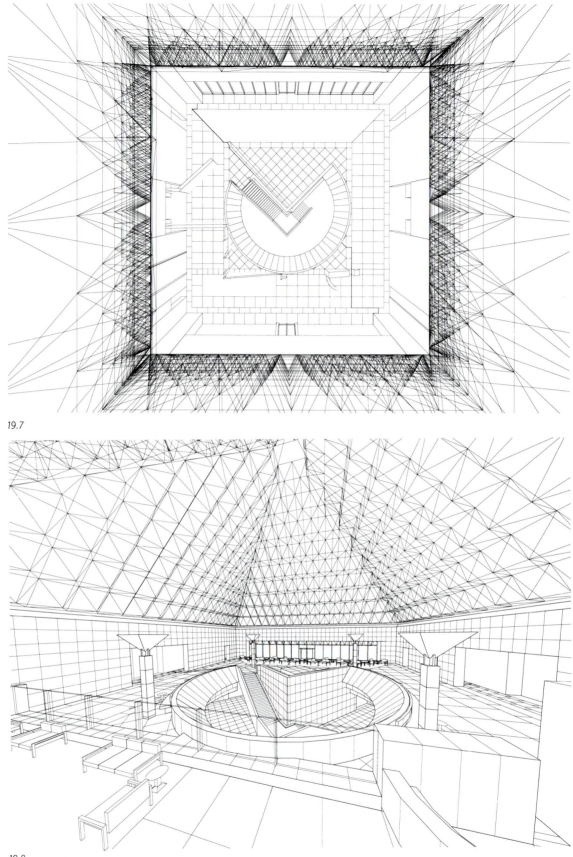

19.7

19.8

19.7–19.9 These three drawings were computer-generated. Once the basic data about an interior have been entered into the computer, any number of perspectives can be generated instantaneously, either on a screen or on paper, as required. In fig. 19.7a one-point perspective looks straight downward into a space—the floor plan of the atrium of an IBM building at Somers, New York, designed by I. M. Pei & Partners, 1986. Fig. 19.8 shows the plan at eye level. Fig. 19.9 shows the atrium in axonometric projection. (Courtesy CAD/East, Inc.)

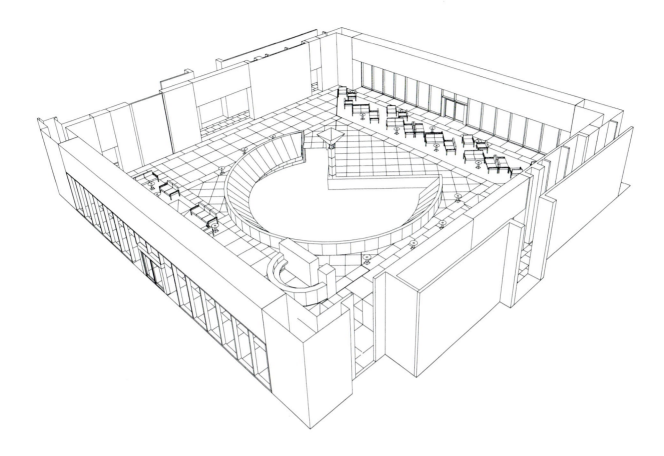

19.9

and so on). By storing in computer memory such elements as plans and three-dimensional views and such data as catalog numbers, manufacturers' identifications, and prices, this information can be called up as needed instantaneously for incorporation into drawings, specifications, estimates, and purchase orders.

The often expressed fear that computers will push aside human designers and make design work a mechanistic process seems to be subsiding as familiarity convinces more and more designers that computers are merely a tool to make routine work easier and more rapid and to aid human memory with reliable backup. Computers also have the potential to extend the capabilities of the designer, making larger projects more practical for the individual designer and small firms, thus giving them a wider variety of outlets.

The design-office tasks that computers can aid range from mundane business and clerical chores through drafting, specification writing, and perspective drawing to assistance in the actual planning process. The more complex tasks demand large and powerful computer equipment, but the ever-expanding capacities of even the smaller machines, plus the ability of personal computer terminals to tap into larger networks over telephone wires, are making it possible to use highly sophisticated computer techniques with comparatively small and simple equipment.

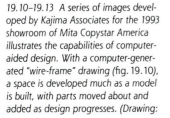

19.10

19.10–19.13 A series of images developed by Kajima Associates for the 1993 showroom of Mita Copystar America illustrates the capabilities of computer-aided design. With a computer-generated "wire-frame" drawing (fig. 19.10), a space is developed much as a model is built, with parts moved about and added as design progresses. (Drawing: Shoko Maetani) The CADD program used to generate such drawings allows the designer to eliminate the hidden lines of the diagrammatic perspective, converting it into a conventional line drawing suitable for client presentation. Fig. 19.11 (following page) shows a computer-generated color study based on the line drawing in fig. 19.10; an alternative color scheme, using warmer tones, is presented in fig. 19.12. (CADD drawings courtesy Kajima Associates, Inc.) A color photograph of the completed project (fig. 19.13) demonstrates the accuracy of the computer-generated image. (Photograph: © Peter Paige)

19.11

19.12

19.11–19.13 See previous page.

Table 26. Computer Tasks

PERFORM OFFICE TASKS. *Computers can expedite bookkeeping, payrolls, billings and purchase orders, tax returns and filing, and, through word-processing techniques, a considerable proportion of ordinary correspondence.*

MAKE DATA BANKS OF INFORMATION INSTANTLY AVAILABLE. *The information in manufacturers' catalogs and literature and the data in handbooks and journals, together with legal codes and restrictions, often difficult to locate, use, and store, can be kept in compact memory and called up as needed (fig. 19.14). Central data banks can store vast amounts of such information and make it available to any subscriber over telephone lines. The centralized data will usually be kept constantly up-to-date to prevent the unintentional use of outmoded information.*

DRAFTING. *Placing and moving points and lines on the computer terminal screen, or monitor, builds up a constructed drawing similar to one done with pencil and instruments but accomplished with great rapidity and ease in making changes (figs. 19.7–19.9). Standard elements, plans of architectural elements, furniture items, and fixtures can be drawn from computer memory, moved about, and fixed in place. Lettering and dimensioning can be added with the same ease. Once com-pleted at the computer, the drawing can be printed out by a printer or actually drawn by pen by a plotter, entirely mechanically, with a high level of precision and at great speed. Changes can readily be introduced in the computer memory and new prints produced as needed.*

PERSPECTIVE DRAWING. *Programs are now available that generate perspectives from basic plan and elevation data. The position of station point and angle of view can be changed, with the resulting varied perspective views instantly available on the monitor. As with other types of drafting, prints can be produced. Images of objects (such as furniture items) can be held in computer memory, to be called up and inserted into a perspective view, moved about, and shifted into the desired position. An interior thus developed in perspective can be redrawn as a plan or elevation and printed out in that form. Color tones can be added into such drawings for diagrammatic or realistic effect (figs. 19.10–19.13). Lighting can be inserted into a perspective and the visual effect of various positions and intensities of light sources studied in quite realistic images.*

PLANNING. *While this function remains at present largely a human monopoly, current programs will convert information about required areas and relationships into plan proposals. Although somewhat diagrammatic, these can form the basis for conventional planning. The ability of computers to hold and manipulate vast amounts of information makes these techniques particularly useful for very large and difficult projects such as airport terminals, hospital complexes, and large corporate and government offices.*

ESTIMATING. *With cost data in computer memory, it is possible to convert plan proposals into cost estimates almost effortlessly and instantaneously. As design progresses and various alternatives are considered, an ongoing estimated total, reflecting every new idea under consideration, can be constantly calculated.*

SPECIFYING AND ORDERING. *Catalog data, numbers, and prices held in computer memory, much as in estimating, can be used to prepare specifications and orders for products and goods such as furniture, light fixtures, carpeting, and fabrics. Orders can then be transmitted electronically directly to suppliers. This kind of electronic data transfer, in wide use in such fields as banking, financial markets, and even in the stock and inventory control of retail chains and mail-order houses, is still limited in the design world, but its application is rapidly increasing.*

A list of the things that computers can do now or will soon be able to do for interior designers is given in Table 26. Taken together, these possibilities suggest that the typical design office will gradually become less a room filled with drafting tables and more a group of computer terminal workstations, with the drafting table an adjunct for occasional use. Many designers with a heavy investment in their knowledge of conventional planning and drafting skills fear that computer techniques will be unfamiliar and difficult and therefore resist this idea.

In practice, these fears seem to have little basis. Many routine computer skills tend to become the province of specialists who work from the verbal or sketched instructions of designers, much as draftsmen now translate the ideas of architects into finished construction drawings. The aspects of computer use that serve creative design are generally quite easy to learn and, once the learning begins, turn out to be a source of pleasure and satisfaction to those willing to take the step. Computers and their associated programs constantly become less abstruse and more accessible to the nonspecialized user. The tasks desired are selected from a *menu* of choices displayed on a screen in easily understandable form, and processes that are slow and demanding when done by hand become quite easy and almost amusing with the aid of a computer.

Design schools are making computer techniques increasingly available to students, offering them basic familiarization, with a corresponding reduction in fear. The computer field is subject to such rapid development and change that techniques learned in school are virtually certain to be obsolete by the time the graduated student is in office practice. Fortunately, learning current techniques takes only a few weeks of specialized study and practice at present, and as equipment and programming grow ever more accessible, it will become even easier.

For the designer who is not a full-time professional directing or working for a design office—the individual consultant designer, or the nonprofessional who wants to deal only with smaller private projects—computer techniques may seem to have little significance. There is a strong possibility that some of these techniques will become available even at this level through connection into centralized equipment provided by manufacturing firms or by independent services. The typical home computer, for example, is not capable of producing complex interior perspective drawings, but access over phone lines to more sophisticated equipment enables the individual designer working at home to make occasional use of computer perspective drawing.

The showrooms of the larger manufacturers of interior-related products may offer computer services to customers, either directly or with the aid of specialists that the showroom might have on staff (fig. 19.15). When working with a client, the designer and salesperson will often find it helpful to sit at a computer terminal and make immediate visual comparisons between various possibilities, instantaneously calling up appearance data and relative costs.

BUSINESS MATTERS

While interior design is primarily a field for artistic creativity, every project involves some business matters. Large interior projects may demand substantial business management. Problems, misunderstandings, even lawsuits are far more likely to arise from business than creative issues. Interior design benefits from employing sound practices applicable to all types of businesses. At the same time, it introduces several unique considerations. Of the issues discussed here, some will be important only for large and complex projects and larger design firms, some will apply to smaller projects and to individual designers, while a few are important even to the individual who is his or her own client for a do-it-yourself project.

BUDGETS

Any project that goes beyond shifting furniture already at hand will involve costs. Planning for those costs—estimating and controlling them—is a primary need for almost every interior project. Since costs vary from place to place and change rapidly with the passage of time, it is not practical to provide specific figures here. The general basis for budgeting is, however, easy to review.

Estimating Budgets

A preliminary budget is usually calculated on the basis of the area, expressed in square feet, involved in a project. Once the extent of work to be done and the general level of quality desired are known, it is possible to arrive at an approximate cost for a project. The dollar cost per square foot may come from the designer's recent experience with similar projects; from costs for completed projects published in professional magazines; or from contractors or other professionals active in the field. Generating a cost range of low, average, and high figures can

aid in setting the price goals for a project and in beginning to plan ways in which the project will be financed.

Clients often initiate a project with unrealistic ideas of prices and may need a period of adjustment to get accustomed to the realities of current costs, either by modifying the project concept or rethinking the way they will handle the financing. With an approved preliminary budget in mind, design can be undertaken with a clear idea of the work to be done and the range of materials and products to be selected. An economy budget restricts the design in terms of both work and selection; a luxury budget places few limitations on design.

As design decisions are made, a detailed budget can be developed on an item-by-item basis. Construction work can be estimated (possibly with the help of a contractor) on the basis of the square or linear footage of each item (ceiling, partitioning, plumbing and electrical work, and so on). Items to be purchased are selected and priced, with the cost multiplied by the number of units desired and added up to give a reasonably firm final total. A cushion, or contingency allowance, should be included to allow for unexpected on-site developments, price changes, and similar surprises, almost certain to be in the upward direction. A skeleton outline for a typical budget follows:

BASIC CONSTRUCTION (CONTRACTS)
   Demolition
   General construction
   Electrical
   Plumbing
   HVAC
   Painting
DECORATIVE ITEMS (PURCHASES)
   Floor covering (plus installation)
   Wall treatment (paper, vinyl, and so on)
   Furniture (plus cover fabrics and installation)
   Drapery (fabric plus makeup and installation)
   Lighting fixtures and lamps
   Accessories
   Art
FEES
   Architectural and engineering
   Consultants
   Interior design
OTHER
   Permits, insurance, and other items not included above
   Contingencies

Estimates and Bids

Following such budget estimating, actual prices are usually obtained from contractors. One general contractor or each trade separately can provide a figure based on time (the working time of employees on the job) and materials, plus allowances for profit and overhead, typically added as a percentage of time and materials. This is called a *firm estimate* if it is based on specific plans and specifications and put in writing. Similarly, suppliers of furniture and other purchased items will quote firm prices in writing.

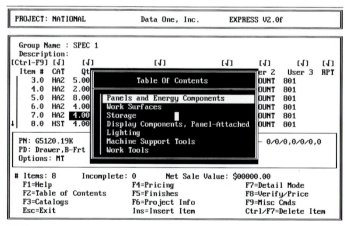

19.14

19.14 Software developed by Data One allows a designer to work with a manufacturer's data base to keep a running account of total costs as product selections are made. (Courtesy Data One, Inc.)

Table 27. Budgeting

A sample budget, proposed for the renovation of a living room in an apartment in 1994, is given below. Since prices vary in different regions and are subject to change, the costs given here cannot be considered a reliable guide, but the items and proportionate costs will probably remain stable.

GENERAL CONTRACT:	Demolition (remove existing closets)	$ 800
	Repair walls and floor	975
	Supply and install built-in bookshelves	850
	Electrical: new outlets and wiring	460
	Painting: walls and ceiling	920
	Refinish floor	475
FURNITURE AND FURNISHINGS:	Sofa (existing, reupholstered)	825
	3 lounge chairs	1,125
	Dining table	920
	4 dining chairs	1,160
	Desk	825
	Desk chair	340
	Stereo/TV cabinet (custom-made)	825
	Rug (existing, cleaned)	310
	Blinds (2 windows)	400
LIGHTING:	Fixtures	832
	3 lamps	630
		12,672
DESIGN FEES (ESTIMATED):		1,600
CONTINGENCIES:		1,067
	TOTAL:	$15,339

In theory, the total of all such firm estimates will be the total cost of the project. In practice, this figure often turns out to be low, with time and material costs rising to well beyond estimated levels. To obtain tighter controls, estimates must be converted to firm prices, or *bids*. This involves asking for prices from several potential contracting firms (usually three), each of which is provided with identical plans and specifications. All the bidders, chosen on the basis of reputation and recommendations, must be acceptable, ensuring that the low bidder's price and quality of work will be satisfactory. Taking bids for very small projects is rarely practical; even larger projects are often contracted on the basis of a firm, or *guaranteed*, estimate rather than through bidding.

Once bids or firm estimates have been accepted, it might seem that the cost of construction work would be fixed. In practice, design changes—additional or altered items; new choices of materials or finishes; even major replanning—may be necessary for one or another reason, each change entailing a cost adjustment, usually in an upward direction. Once the job has been contracted for, the contractor is under no pressure to minimize the pricing of such *extras*. Making many changes in design after work is under way will almost certainly lead to cost overruns. While some changes will undoubtedly be necessary, minimizing them is an important factor in keeping project costs under control.

The purchase of such items as furniture, floor covering, fabrics, and lighting fixtures normally does not involve bidding since such items are unique. Those offered to the interior design and decoration fields are generally assigned a *list price*, which is subject to a large discount when purchased by trade or professional buyers, usually ranging from 25 to 50 percent, with 40 percent common. The availability of such discounts is significant in encouraging clients to turn to a professional design service rather than making direct purchases. Materials and objects available at retail are not subject to such discounts, a factor leading to the sharp separation between retail and "to the trade" suppliers. The same products are rarely offered in both markets.

Traditionally, interior decorators acted as specialized retailers, purchasing items at *trade*, or discount, prices and reselling them to their clients at marked-up prices. The difference between the purchase and selling prices provided the decorator's fee or profit. This way of working has been largely supplanted by the more professional practice of offering all trade or discount prices directly to the client and billing a designer fee clearly separated from the cost of products or construction services. The designer offers access to showrooms and trade sources, but the client, or end user, makes purchases, either directly from the manufacturer or through authorized dealers who provide installation and other services figured into a firm price.

Suppliers are generally prepared to sell directly to clients on the basis of purchase orders written or authorized by designers. It is important to clarify credit responsibility since suppliers are sometimes concerned about large orders when placed by designers or firms with limited financial responsibility. Payment in advance (with an order) by the client directly or through the designer's firm will usually allay any fears and make orders fully acceptable to trade sources.

Design Fees

Designers' professional fees can be arrived at in several different ways. A percentage of the cost of work—usually in the range of 10 to 15 percent—has some traditional standing but is now generally regarded as illogical. Simply choosing the color of a carpet may lead to a large purchase and, therefore, a large fee, while demanding work over small details may entail no purchases, therefore generating no fees. There is also always the concern that a percentage fee may motivate the designer to urge more rather than less costly solutions to every problem.

For these reasons, a fee based on working time expended, or *hourly rate*, has become more widely accepted as most truly professional. Such charges combine the actual salary costs for each person involved in a project with overhead and profit margins. Charges are billed on the basis of time-sheet hours and agreed-upon standard rates. A billing rate of between two and a half and three times the actual salary cost is usual. The solitary designer must establish an hourly rate related to this basis. Expenses (travel, telephone, making prints, and so on) are billed in addition.

For the many clients who are unwilling to enter into open-ended fee arrangements, designers will calculate an estimated fixed maximum

19.15 Showroom displays of products used in interiors help designers and clients make the most suitable choices. Small samples of tile, for instance, do not give an accurate image of a total installation, and the nature of the material makes it awkward to move, file, or store. Here, the United Ceramic Tile Showroom in New York, designed in 1986 by Paul Haigh, architect, exhibits large areas of tile in many different colors and patterns. (Photograph: © Elliott Kaufman)

based on anticipated working time. Such estimates often turn out to be the effective total fee, making them similar to fixed fees, an alternative basis for design service compensation in which an agreed-upon figure is established on the basis of the work involved. It is a good idea to bill design fees on a monthly basis, so that any dissatisfactions with performance or billings will surface before the sums in dispute become major.

CONTRACTS

Two kinds of contracts are involved in interior design projects: between designer and client and between client and contractor or supplier. The latter is made for work or a product after a bid or purchase price proposal is accepted. The designer has a role in supervising such contracts to ensure that the terms are fair and carry no ambiguities that could later lead to disputes.

The contract between designer and client may take the form of a standardized agreement as developed by the various professional organizations or a simple letter of agreement in which the designer sets forth the terms on which work will be billed and the client makes an acceptance in writing. Strictly verbal agreements can be valid contracts, but since the terms are not recorded, they can readily become subject to dispute. Experience suggests that some agreement in writing is always best. For larger projects, a review of contractual documents by a lawyer familiar with the field is generally advisable.

It is important that the limits of the designer's responsibility be made clear to the client, since disputes often arise over such issues as perfection of work done or conformance to time schedules, which the designer cannot guarantee. Designers are also wise to carry insurance against being held liable for product failures or any risks that can possibly arise out of the complex events that a major design project can involve, from peeling wallpaper to major injury to a workman. The specifics of written designer-client agreements should establish the obligations that the designer assumes and the limits of these obligations.

If designers retain the services of consultants and other professionals, such as architects and engineers, and bill the consultants' fees to clients as expenses, they can become involved in any problems arising from such services. Therefore, while the designer will often aid the client in selecting consultants, financial arrangements are best made directly between client and consultant.

In general, the professional designer will find it best to limit all financial dealings with a client to direct professional fees while arranging for the client to pay for all purchases, professional fees, and any other costs directly, without going through the designer. This eliminates possible tax liabilities and many bookkeeping problems while keeping the possibilities for financial disputes to a minimum.

PROJECT MANAGEMENT

In addition to taking bids and awarding contracts, complete project management involves negotiating lease terms, scheduling, and expediting—that is, coordinating the work of different trades, scheduling the delivery and installation of purchased items, and reviewing and approving all bills and invoices as they are received. The aim is overall control of performance in terms of both time schedule and costs. For large projects, project management may be assigned to a special person or a firm with experience in this field. Employing sophisticated control systems such as CPM (Critical Path Method) or PERT (Project Evaluation and Review Technique), which make use of charts and, sometimes, computer techniques, can be helpful for complex projects (see Chapter 5, page 131). Interior designers and space planners may take on all or part of project management responsibilities in connection with smaller projects.

When space is to be leased in an office or loft building, project management most often begins with the negotiation of lease terms. Most such leases require the building owner to provide elements of interior finish (finished floors, ceiling, partitions, and lighting) to create usable space of a quality defined as *building standard*. Such standards normally allow for a minimal, utilitarian office installation, including a specified amount of partitioning, number of doors, and level of lighting. If the client accepts building-standard work, the designer usually has no role beyond making a plan layout and selecting paint colors. In practice, most offices are designed for a quality level far above this standard (fig. 19.6).

A negotiated lease defines the work to be done by the owner, with costs covered by the negotiated rent, and the items to be paid for by the tenant. Tenants unfamiliar with interior projects often accept highly disadvantageous terms, exposing them to unexpectedly large costs for work that could have been covered under terms of the lease. A document called a *work letter* defines exactly the details of the work to be provided under a lease. Drawings and specifications are often made part of the lease terms. Once a lease is signed, any additional work becomes an *extra*, which is billed on the basis of time and materials plus overhead and profit (a *cost-plus* basis). This poses another hazard for the unwary tenant, since the contractors are employed by the building owner and no restraints exist to keep the costs of extras down. As a result, such costs can easily mushroom, to disastrous effect on the project budget.

Good project management strives to minimize extras by establishing lease terms that define building-standard work as accurately as possible and by setting firm prices for all work beyond the standard covered in the lease. Changes in requirements that develop while a job is in progress and unforeseen conditions that surface after the lease is signed usually make some extras inevitable, but good planning keeps these situations to a minimum, thus avoiding cost overruns and many disputes as well.

Another major source of disputes is scheduling, an issue that involves move-in dates, when rent payments begin, and, if delays occur, the payment of double rents. When a project is in the planning stage, designers tend to be optimistic about rapid completion. Contractors anxious to be assigned work often give unrealistic completion dates. Whether acting as or working with project managers, designers have a responsibility to develop realistic schedules, leaving provision for the delays that always seem to occur, whether through late delivery of materials, the need to correct errors, changes made while work is in progress, or such unpredictable events as strikes, accidents, and storms.

While small projects involve lesser sums of money and fewer complexities of scheduling, the same problems may arise. Careful and realistic project management is just as important to the residential client undertaking a minor renovation as it is to a large corporation engaged in a vast project. The reputation of a designer often rests as much upon efficient handling of time schedule and money matters as upon the aesthetic success of the completed project

HUMAN PROBLEMS

In addition to the many technical and practical problems already discussed, there is another group of problems rarely discussed in design schools. These are the problems created by people—by clients, by the designers themselves, and by the relationships between them—that arise in the course of a design project. Any design professional will admit, at least unofficially, that people problems are more common and more difficult than technical problems. Among themselves, designers often grumble, "Design would be easy if it weren't for clients." While the human problems of design work have no clear solutions, they are worth reviewing in order to avoid or minimize them.

Every client-designer relationship—except when the designer takes both roles—begins with two strangers who have different backgrounds, training, and objectives. The client wants a design problem dealt with quickly, economically, and, often, in accordance with some preconceived ideas. The designer wants a project that will be, above all, a credit aesthetically, a source of professional satisfaction, and, perhaps, a link to additional projects. No designer wants to lose money or have a disgruntled client to deal with, but many designers consider publication in a respected professional magazine a more significant measure of success than monetary profits or even client satisfaction.

For many clients, the design project is their first such experience; in fact, it may be their only one. Clients face difficult decisions, perhaps involving troubling compromises and large sums of money. At the same time, they harbor desires and expectations that are likely to be a mix of realism, hopes, and ideas, dreams, and notions that may be anything from useful to absurd. Projects are usually more complex, slower, and more expensive than they expect. In the modern world, it seems to be an unfortunate reality that the quality of workmanship constantly declines while costs and delays constantly increase. Clients' past experience of the lower prices and better-quality performance that were the norms of a few years ago tends to generate expectations that often cannot be justified under present conditions. Designers often find the temptation to tell the clients what they want to hear at the start of a project all too strong, inevitably resulting in disappointments and recriminations.

It cannot be denied that some clients and designers are difficult—demanding, unrealistic, quarrelsome, arbitrary, and inconsistent. Every experienced designer can tell stories of clients who change their minds endlessly, who have wildly unrealistic ideas about money, who blame every trouble on their designer, and who fly into unreasonable rages, often leading to lawsuits. Stories of designers with comparable tendencies who make promises that cannot be kept, who overrun budgets by

appreciable amounts, and who hide behind the screen of "artistic temperament" also have some unfortunate basis in fact. For a project to run smoothly, both client and designer must act reasonably, making an effort to understand the other's point of view, to cooperate together, and, above all, to be honest in terms of communication, expectations, and actual dealings of every sort.

First meetings between client-to-be and designer are very important. Issues of taste and aesthetic preferences can be explored by looking at published illustrations of completed projects by the designer and others in magazines and books and by making on-site visits to the designer's previous projects. If marked differences of opinion emerge in such sessions, they should be regarded as danger signals. At the same time, qualities of personality and compatibility can be assessed to see if designer and client can set up a cooperative relationship. For the designer, any hint that a prospective client is contentious, suspicious, devious, mean, or cranky suggests that it is best to leave the project to someone else. It is not easy to pass up an interesting assignment voluntarily, but the strain of following through on a project under those circumstances promises to worsen rather than improve the relationship.

The term *client* implies an individual person, but many interior design clients are families, firms, organizations, or other groups of people. Dealing with groups multiplies the probabilities of human problems and calls for considerable tact. A business may be represented by an owner, by several partners, by one or more top executives, or by a committee representing various aspects of the client organization. These people are subject to change (through retirement, resignation, firing, illness, and death), and replacements may not be as sympathetic and cooperative as their predecessors. Committees and groups often have members with differing points of view or even direct conflicts. Steering a course between such members without succumbing to the politics involved can be very complex. The success of many well-known designers of large projects comes as much from their skill in this territory as from their design talent.

Residential clients present a less complex pattern but similar hazards. Many appear as couples who may approach a long-awaited new house or apartment with the expectation that both parties have totally matching desires, only to discover unexpected differences. Every designer with residential experience can tell stories of difficult and painful sessions, even quarrels and breakups, generated by planning a home. Early discovery of such possible frictions is another danger signal to be heeded. The designer's tact and skill may be stretched to the limit in dealing with such problems.

Given reasonable and cooperative people on both sides of a client-designer relationship, avoiding problems is largely a matter of exercising good professional skills with particular emphasis on all matters relating to time schedule and to budget. Not surprisingly, money is one of the most common causes of difficulties and disputes. Following good business procedures meticulously and making sure that the client understands them are probably the most important keys to satisfactory client relationships. Even when inevitable differences occur, good business practices will help to minimize the strains and avoid the unhappy problems of litigation.

DESIGN BUSINESSES

Every designer or design firm is a business that follows one of several organizational structures.

Sole Proprietorship

The individual designer usually starts out, and may continue throughout a career, as a *sole proprietor.* The designer simply owns his or her business and receives fees and pays bills out of a personal bank account or, often, from a separate business account maintained as an aid in keeping personal and business funds identifiable as clear entities. Sole proprietorship has the advantage of simplicity and directness; it requires no formal steps to start up and may serve well for many design businesses. A sole proprietor can, of course, hire employees and even build up a large organization.

An owner can even retire while retaining ownership of the ongoing business. In practice, however, the continuation of a business usually works out better through one of the other forms of ownership. A sole proprietorship is, at least in the design fields, most often difficult to sell if the owner wants to retire or give up the business for any other reason. Reputation and "good will" are usually so firmly attached to the person of the owner as to leave the business with little else of value beyond any outstanding contracts and some furniture and equipment.

Partnership

When a sole proprietor decides to share ownership with another person (perhaps an employee, another designer, or a business aide) or several people decide to establish a joint business, a *partnership* is the

19.16

obvious form of organization. Several partners may bring various projects into a firm or may contribute a variety of complementary skills. Few individuals demonstrate equal abilities as designer, salesperson, office manager, and financial manager, while partners often represent such varied skills. A *silent partner* is someone who simply invests money in a partnership for profit, taking no part in the operation of the firm. Since design businesses rarely need large sums of money to start up, such investing partners are not common in design firms.

Typically, each partner invests some funds or contributes something else of value (such as a contract with a client) to the setting up of a partnership. This establishes each partner's share of ownership and forms the basis for the division of profits from the business. Partners may be equal, each with a half share, or may own different percentages of the business. The concept of junior and senior partnerships (with smaller and larger shares of ownership) is often used to give some share of ownership to employees who make a significant contribution to a firm. Partners normally take funds from the business through a *drawing account,* which provides regular payments similar to a salary for normal living expenses. At a longer interval, usually once a year, an accounting is made and any profits divided according to the terms of the partners' agreement. In small partnerships, the partners often adjust their rate of draw so as to take out profits on a continuing basis, leaving little to be divided annually.

Even when partnerships are started on a very informal basis, it is best to draw up a written agreement (with the help of a lawyer) that spells out the terms of the partnership in detail and covers such matters as the division of profits, the basis on which new partners may be taken in, and the terms for withdrawal of a partner or dissolution of the firm. Many design and architectural firms are partnerships, sometimes with the name of the founder (as in Peter L. Gluck and Partners) or with the names of all (or several senior) partners. A partner may retire while retaining an interest in the business or may sell an interest according to whatever terms may be agreed upon. Many partnerships have remained in business for many years, retaining the original name (for example, Skidmore, Owings & Merrill) after new partners join the firm and the founders retire.

The advantages of partnerships result from the adaptability of this form to group efforts and the ease with which ownership interest can be offered to new partners, allowing a firm to carry on almost indefinitely, even long after its founders have withdrawn. A matching disadvantage arises from the need for partners to get along well and agree about business decisions. Small partnerships (two or three partners) are particularly subject to trouble when a major disagreement occurs among the partners, often leading to the breakup of the firm. Differences in interests and styles, often the basis for making a partnership work, also commonly lead to problems that develop with the passage of time.

Incorporation

The third important format for a design business is *incorporation.* It is possible for one person to form a corporation, but it is a more generally used format for a firm with several principals or large firms with

19.16 This workplace answers all the professional and business requirements of a sole proprietor—a designer who works alone. Antine Polo designed his own office, in Englewood, New Jersey. (Photograph: © Peter Paige)

19.17

many owners. A corporation is an organization recognized by law as having an identity apart from its owners. Owners hold stock that represents their individual shares of ownership in the corporation. Profits are distributed as dividends, paid out at regular intervals. Most large businesses are *public corporations* whose stock is held by many investors and traded in a public stock market. Small corporations are generally *closely held*, that is, the stock is sold only to a restricted group—the original incorporators perhaps, or employees of the firm, or certain investors who have provided financial backing.

A corporation is controlled by a board of directors elected by the stockholders. The board elects officers who are usually the corporation's top executives. In a small corporation, the officers, the board, the stockholders, and the managers are often all the same people, perhaps those who would have been the partners if that form of organization had been chosen. Compensation to managers (as to employees) is generally through a salary and, possibly, bonuses instead of dividends. A corporation can accumulate undistributed income in ways that may have tax advantages and can provide funds for expansion, ownership of assets (such as cars or a building), investment in new ventures, and retirement income for managers. The corporate form of structure also shields the private assets of stockholders against any liability suits that may be brought against the firm.

Incorporation of small professional businesses has become increasingly popular in recent years because of the tax and other financial advantages that it can provide. It is important to consult legal and accounting advisers before deciding whether to incorporate a design business and to help in working out the details of incorporation. As in the case of partnerships, corporations can offer ownership shares to staff or to others and enable a business to continue beyond the involvement of any particular people. As prospective clients, big businesses and other large organizations are often reassured by this form of organization, which parallels their own organizational structures and avoids the more personal involvement of smaller firms. All of these factors tend to encourage the formation of design corporations.

Many designers are inclined to regard business matters as annoying and intrusive interruptions to creative work. They may therefore be tempted to deal with them grudgingly and carelessly. This attitude can all too readily lead to truly troublesome and intrusive problems on a major scale. Time and effort devoted to the relatively small demands of good business practices pay off, in the long run, by making projects go smoothly, by *freeing* time for creative work, and by helping to build a reputation for skillful professional performance.

19.17 In the drafting room of the office of Robert A. M. Stern Architects, the typical layout of workstations with adjustable cantilever lamps over each drawing table is transformed by the addition of whimsical large, shaded lamps and an Ionic column, visible in the distance. (Photograph: © Peter Aaron/ESTO)

APPENDIX 1. ARCHITECTURAL SYMBOLS

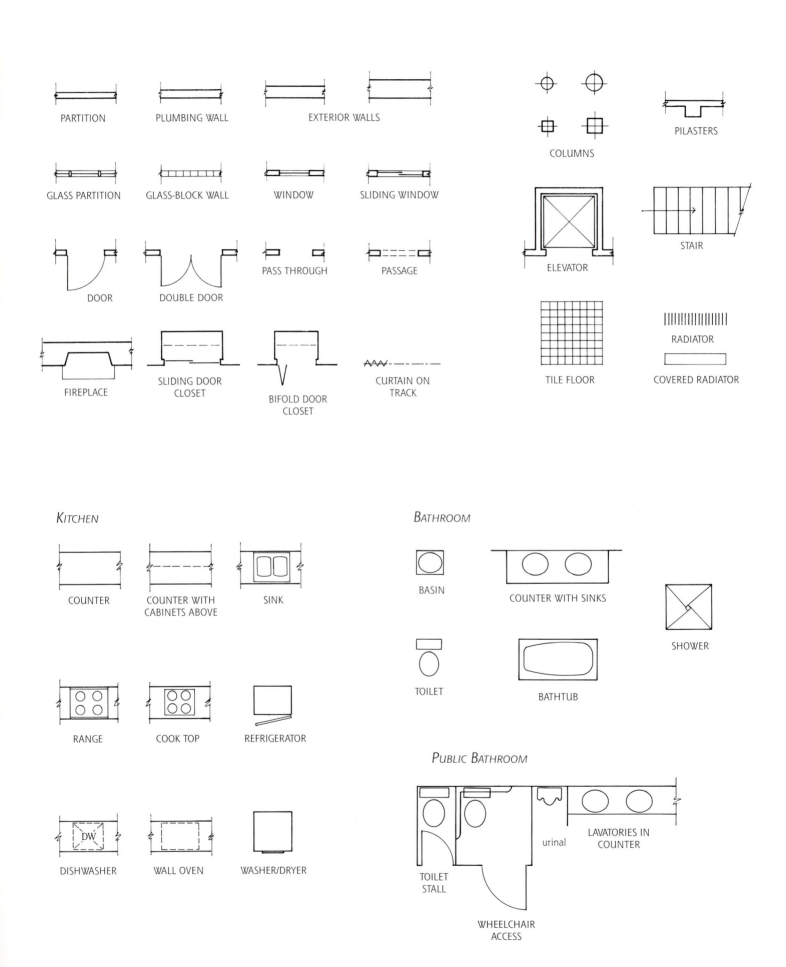

PARTITION

PLUMBING WALL

EXTERIOR WALLS

COLUMNS

PILASTERS

GLASS PARTITION

GLASS-BLOCK WALL

WINDOW

SLIDING WINDOW

ELEVATOR

STAIR

DOOR

DOUBLE DOOR

PASS THROUGH

PASSAGE

FIREPLACE

SLIDING DOOR CLOSET

BIFOLD DOOR CLOSET

CURTAIN ON TRACK

TILE FLOOR

RADIATOR

COVERED RADIATOR

KITCHEN

COUNTER

COUNTER WITH CABINETS ABOVE

SINK

RANGE

COOK TOP

REFRIGERATOR

DISHWASHER

WALL OVEN

WASHER/DRYER

BATHROOM

BASIN

COUNTER WITH SINKS

SHOWER

TOILET

BATHTUB

PUBLIC BATHROOM

TOILET STALL

WHEELCHAIR ACCESS

urinal

LAVATORIES IN COUNTER

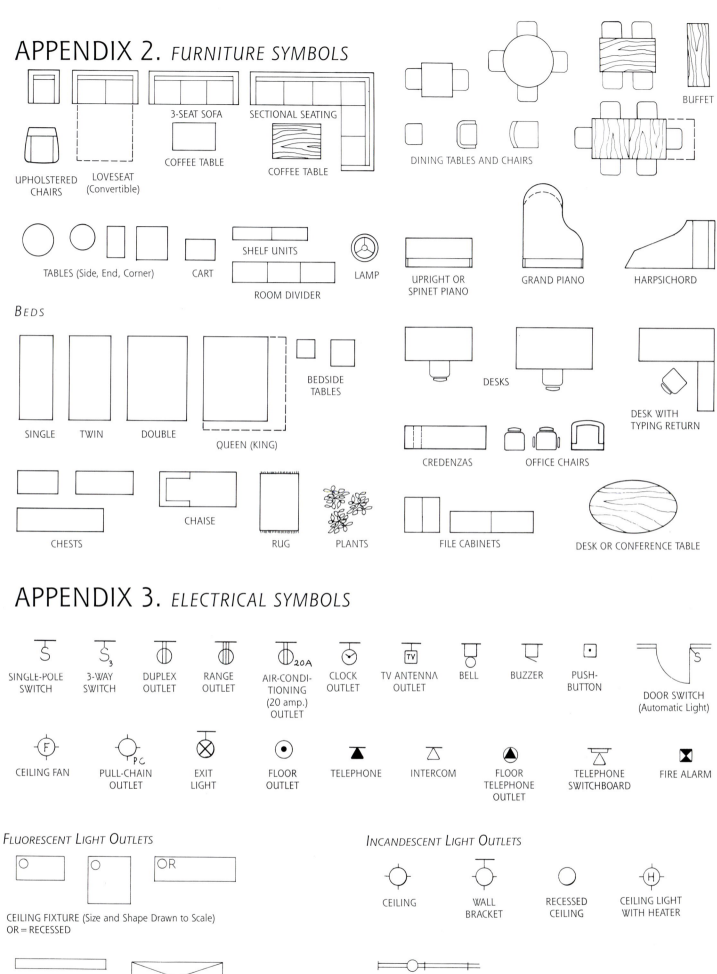

APPENDIX 2. FURNITURE SYMBOLS

UPHOLSTERED CHAIRS

LOVESEAT (Convertible)

3-SEAT SOFA

COFFEE TABLE

SECTIONAL SEATING

COFFEE TABLE

DINING TABLES AND CHAIRS

BUFFET

TABLES (Side, End, Corner)

CART

SHELF UNITS

ROOM DIVIDER

LAMP

UPRIGHT OR SPINET PIANO

GRAND PIANO

HARPSICHORD

BEDS

SINGLE

TWIN

DOUBLE

QUEEN (KING)

BEDSIDE TABLES

DESKS

DESK WITH TYPING RETURN

CREDENZAS

OFFICE CHAIRS

CHESTS

CHAISE

RUG

PLANTS

FILE CABINETS

DESK OR CONFERENCE TABLE

APPENDIX 3. ELECTRICAL SYMBOLS

SINGLE-POLE SWITCH

3-WAY SWITCH

DUPLEX OUTLET

RANGE OUTLET

AIR-CONDITIONING (20 amp.) OUTLET

CLOCK OUTLET

TV ANTENNA OUTLET

BELL

BUZZER

PUSH-BUTTON

DOOR SWITCH (Automatic Light)

CEILING FAN

PULL-CHAIN OUTLET

EXIT LIGHT

FLOOR OUTLET

TELEPHONE

INTERCOM

FLOOR TELEPHONE OUTLET

TELEPHONE SWITCHBOARD

FIRE ALARM

FLUORESCENT LIGHT OUTLETS

CEILING FIXTURE (Size and Shape Drawn to Scale)
OR = RECESSED

STRIP LIGHTS (Exposed Tubes)

SPECIAL FLUORESCENT FIXTURE

INCANDESCENT LIGHT OUTLETS

CEILING

WALL BRACKET

RECESSED CEILING

CEILING LIGHT WITH HEATER

TRACK LIGHTING

APPENDIX 4. *MATERIAL INDICATIONS IN SECTION*

WOOD

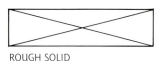
ROUGH SOLID

FINISHED SOLID

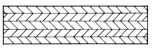
PLYWOOD

PLYWOOD VENEER FACE

SOLID-CORE PANEL

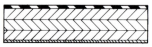
PARTICLEBOARD-CORE PANEL

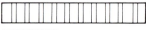
PLASTIC LAMINATE OR PLYWOOD

HARDBOARD

MASONRY

STONE

TERRAZZO

SLATE/BLUESTONE/SOAPSTONE

BRICK

TERRA-COTTA OR CLAY TILE

PLASTER

GYPSUM BLOCK

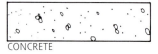
GYPSUM WALL BOX

CONCRETE

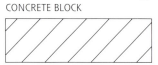
CONCRETE BLOCK

CONCRETE BLOCK CALTER NOTE INDICATION

METAL

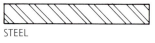
STEEL

BRASS/BRONZE

ALUMINUM

SMALL-SCALE METAL

OTHER

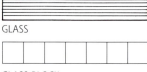
GLASS

GLASS BLOCK

CARPET

INSULATION

RIGID INSULATION

ACOUSTIC TILE

TWO-WAY DRAPERY

VERTICAL BLINDS

APPENDIX 5. *INTERIOR PERSPECTIVE DRAWING*

It is quite possible to work in interior design without making perspective drawings, and, indeed, to the uninitiated, what is merely a matter of technique may appear obscure and difficult. There are many excellent how-to books on the subject, but most emphasize drawings of objects or building exteriors rather than interiors. Since drawing in perspective is the most realistic and, hence, persuasive way to illustrate design proposals, it is a skill well worth acquiring.

In nature, objects far away appear smaller than nearer objects of the same size—an effect produced by the manner in which the lens of the eye projects an image on the retina. A camera lens similarly projects an image on film, resulting in the highly realistic quality of photographs, which are, themselves, accurate perspectives. Close observation of any scene can also, as artists know, be translated into accurate perspective. The familiar example of a road moving away across a barren landscape until its lines meet at a point on the horizon, while the telephone poles on either side become smaller and closer as they move into the distance (fig. A1), illustrates one of the basics of geometrically constructed perspectives: parallel lines converge toward a point on the horizon.

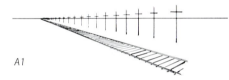

A1

When the aim, however, is to illustrate an interior, possibly not yet built and certainly not yet furnished, direct observation will not serve. Instead, a specific, methodical process produces the desired drawing. Although the process may be followed entirely freehand, better results are obtained at a drawing board using the appropriate drafting instruments (see Chapter 19, pages 532–33). Going through the following routine with a few different examples will soon make the technique familiar.

1. Obtain a floor plan of the space to be illustrated. This may be an architect's construction drawing, a printed plan of the kind often provided by real-estate firms, or a plan drawn for the purpose—even in freehand. Whatever its source, the plan must be to scale. Although ¼" = 1'-0" is often convenient, a ½" scale may be preferable for a very small space and ⅛" for a large area. If the available plan has been drawn accurately to a scale other than these common scales, it can still be used. Note down the

ceiling height of the space and any other significant heights (such as windowsill and head [top], door height, or heights of shelves or mantels).

2. Decide where the imagined viewer will stand and mark this spot with a circled point or cross (fig. A2). This is the *station point,* usually marked SP. For most rooms, it is best to locate the station point near the corner farthest back from the part of the room to be shown so as to produce the most inclusive view possible. It can even be placed outside the walls of the room, although this will produce a view that cannot be seen in reality.

3. Decide on the direction in which the imaginary viewer will look and mark this direction with an arrow. An angle of 30° on either side of this arrow gives the widest view that can be drawn without distortion; this 60° cone of vision approximates normal vision. An angle of up to 90° (45° on either side of the line-of-vision arrow) may be used, if a bit of distortion at the edges of the finished drawing is not a problem. Several possible locations for the station point and several directions of viewing should be tried; it is often helpful to draw station points, viewing direction arrows, and indications of the 60° to 90° cones of vision on separate pieces of tracing paper so that they can be moved about the plan experimentally to ascertain the advantages of each.

4. Once the station point and direction of view have been marked, rotate the plan until the viewing direction arrow is vertical—that is, until it points straight up on the drawing board (fig. A3). Tape the plan down, making sure to leave ample space above it for the final drawing.

5. Draw a horizontal line across the sheet that touches the topmost corner of the rotated plan. This line represents the *picture plane,* or surface upon which the final drawing will be projected in the following steps.

6. Draw a line vertically upward from the topmost corner of the plan into the area where the final drawing will be made. This will serve as the line along which all heights will be measured.

7. Along this *height line,* at a short distance above the plan, measure off the floor-to-ceiling height of the space to the same scale as the plan. This height will represent the most distant corner of the space that will be visible in the final drawing.

8. Measure upward from the bottom of this height line, to the same scale as the plan, a height that represents the eye level of the imagined viewer. This is usually about 5'0" to 5'6" for a standing person, less for a seated person, more for a raised point of view.

9. Draw a horizontal line through the eye-level point right across the drawing. (It will be parallel to the picture plane.) This is the *horizon line.* In an outdoor view it is the line where earth and sky seem to meet—hence the name—but in an interior it is simply an important construction line, that is, a line used in the process of drawing a perspective that will be removed from the final drawing. (It will, however, give the level of the horizon should it be visible through a window or other opening.)

10. It is now possible to locate two *vanishing points,* one each to the right and left. This is done in two stages. First, in the plan, draw a line through the station point parallel to the side walls pictured in the plan, extending it to the picture plane line. Next, draw another line from the station point parallel to the front wall of the room in plan until it, too, reaches the picture plane. Mark these points.

11. From these two intersection points on the picture plane, carry a vertical construction line up

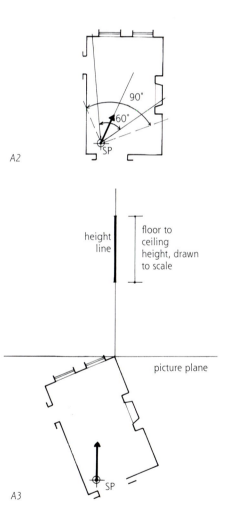

A2

A3

A1 The lines of the tracks seem to converge and the poles appear progressively smaller and closer together until all lines seem to meet at a point on the distant horizon.

A2 A plan drawn to scale shows the space to be drawn in perspective, and the point marked SP indicates where an imagined viewer stands. An arrow indicates the direction in which the viewer is looking. Light lines indicate a 60° cone of vision, dotted lines the maximum 90° cone of vision.

A3 The plan on the drawing board is rotated to render the direction of viewing vertical; a picture plane line is added. The heavy vertical line above the plan is a height line drawn to scale.

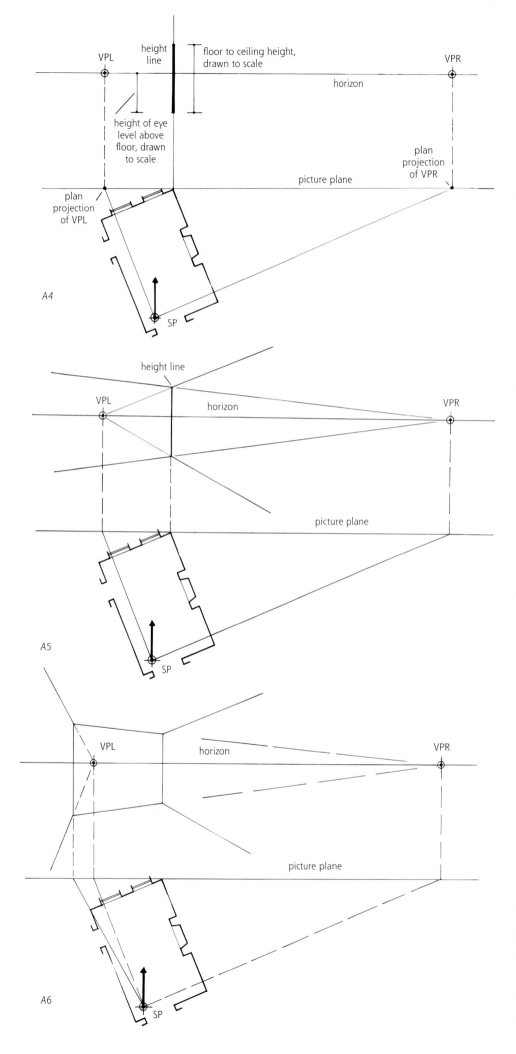

height line

VPL

floor to ceiling height, drawn to scale

VPR

horizon

height of eye level above floor, drawn to scale

plan projection of VPR

picture plane

plan projection of VPL

A4

SP

---

height line

VPL horizon **VPR**

picture plane

A5

SP

VPL horizon **VPR**

picture plane

A6

SP

to the horizon (fig. A4). These intersections are the two vanishing points that will be used to define the perspective. Mark them VPL and VPR. It often happens that one or the other of these points is so far to one side as to be off the drawing board. The point can still be marked on the desk top or even on an adjacent desk or table. If this is too inconvenient, however, go back to Step 4 and turn the plan to an angle that will keep both vanishing points on the drawing board.

12. Using the vanishing point developed by the line parallel to the front wall of the space, draw lines from the vanishing point extending toward the top and bottom of the height line (fig. A5). These lines will represent the intersections of the back wall with the floor and ceiling.

13. The height line forms one corner of the back wall; to find the other corner, draw a light construction line from the station point through the second back wall corner in plan to the picture plane (fig. A6). Extend a construction line vertically upward from this point across the perspective. The portion of this line that runs from the floor-to-ceiling lines of the back wall may be drawn in heavily; it represents the second corner of the back wall and completes the trapezoid that depicts this wall in the final perspective.

14. From the second vanishing point (VPL), four lines can now be drawn outward to show the intersections of the side walls of the space with the floor and ceiling. The box image of the room is now complete.

15. Elements in or against the walls of the space, such as windows, doors, or fireplace, can now be added. The right and left sides are found by using construction lines in plan, the *sight lines*, that begin at the station point and run from each of the edges of the element to the picture plane, just as the corner was found in Step 13 (fig. A7). The top and bottom lines are found by measuring the required heights on the height line—the back, right-hand corner of the space—and carrying a line from the appropriate vanishing point through the intersection of the element's height on the height line to the element (fig. A8). The outline of these elements may now be drawn in heavily.

16. Objects adjacent to a wall and extending into the space are drawn by developing their intersection with the wall, as in Step 15 above, and extending lines outward until they meet the construction lines that locate the other corners (fig. A9). These are found with sight lines in plan that radiate from the station point, pass through those corners in plan, and continue to the picture plane. Verticals are then brought up into the perspective to locate the required corners. The corners are connected by lines radiating from the appropriate vanishing point.

A4 The viewer's eye level is measured, to scale, from the height line. This point fixes the horizon line, parallel to the picture plane. Lines pass through the station point parallel to each set of walls in the plan and extend to the picture plane. Dotted verticals from these points up to the horizon locate the right and left vanishing points, VPR and VPL.

A5 Lines radiating from each of the vanishing points and extending to the top and bottom of the height line and beyond it are drawn to represent floor and ceiling intersections with the back and right-hand walls.

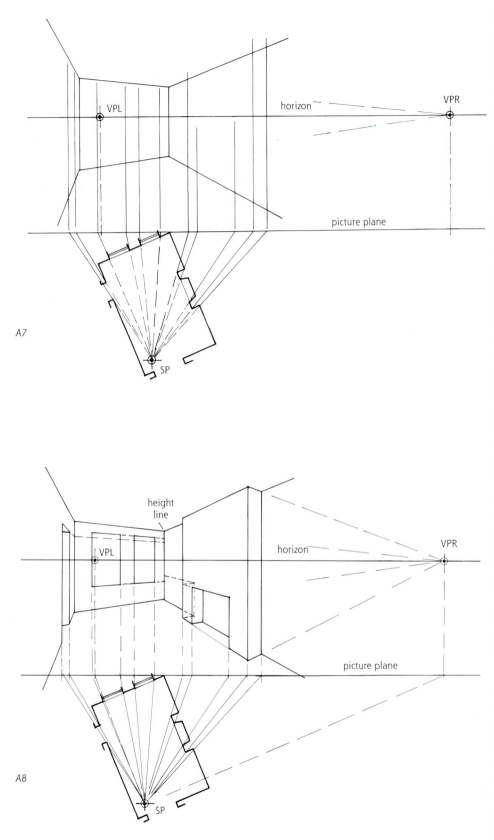

A7

A8

The object's corners on the floor (for example, the table legs in fig. A9) are found by taking the sight lines through each corner in plan and finding their intersection with the wall. This gives two of the lower corners. These points are extended in lines running toward the farther vanishing point, and their points of intersection with the vertical sight lines from the opposite corners in plan locate the remaining lower corners on the floor.

Objects that do not touch any walls can, similarly, be drawn by tracing out imaginary lines along the floor to an adjacent wall, establishing a height at the wall, and extending horizontal lines outward at this height.

17. Objects at angles to the main walls of the space can be drawn by running sight lines through the corners of the object to the picture plane and thence upward vertically into the perspective (fig. A10). Imaginary lines from corners of the object intersect at right angles with the nearest wall. These intersections are given sight lines to the corresponding wall in the perspective. These lines will intersect with the dotted line radiating from the height line and extending down the same wall, and then they will be extended toward the opposite vanishing point until they meet the sight lines drawn from the actual location of the object in plan and extended upward into the perspective. These intersections give the location of two of the object's corners. Once these corners are thus located, the other corners can be similarly located. When the corners are connected, a rectangle results that appears to stand in the space at an angle.

If the drawing has been made accurately, the edges of the rectangle will converge toward additional new vanishing points. This feature can be used as a shortcut in drawing or to check the accuracy of the drafting. Irregularly shaped objects, such as chairs or a piano, are best drawn by developing an enclosing box of lines within which the curved forms can be drawn freehand.

18. Circles require particular attention because the eye discerns even minute errors in perspective. A circle drawn in perspective appears as an ellipse, a geometric figure having longer and shorter dimensions—the major and minor axes—which divide it into four matching quarters. Ellipses vary from almost circular to almost linear, but they are always smooth, continuous curves. Even a very thin, or flat, ellipse does not come to a sharp point at the ends. The form of the ellipse can be studied with ellipse-guide templates, which provide a range of sizes and proportions, but it is unusual to find a template for the specific ellipse required for a particular perspective. The most practical way to put a circular form in perspective is to enclose it in a square, put the square in perspective, and then fit the appropriate ellipse into the resulting quadran-

A6 The left rear corner of the space is obtained by drawing a line from the station point through the top left corner in plan to the picture plane. A vertical carried upward from that intersection locates the left corner. Lines can now be added radiating from VPL extending to the top and bottom of the new corner line to represent the top and bottom lines of the left wall, completing the basic box of the space.

A7 Elements in or adjacent to the walls are located by drawing lines from the station point through the edges of the elements in plan and extending these lines to the picture plane. Verticals carried up into the perspective locate the left and right edges of these elements.

A8 Top and bottom lines for these elements are located by measuring the element to scale along the height line and carrying lines outward from the vanishing points through the heights established on the height line.

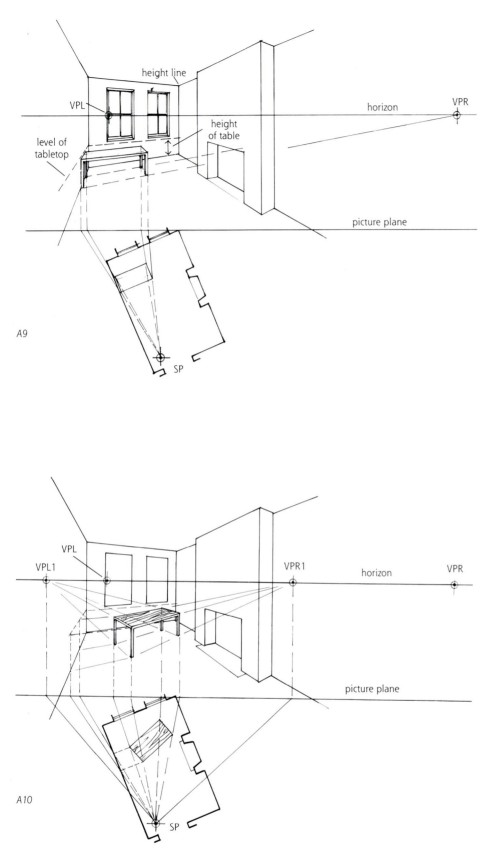

A9

A10

gle (fig. A11). In doing this, however, it is important to observe the following two axioms:

The major axis of any circle that lies in a horizontal plane will be horizontal; the minor axis will be vertical. This applies to tops of round tables, lamps, ceiling lights, round rugs, and all such elements.

Any circle that lies in a vertical plane will have a minor axis that, extended, will pass through the vanishing point that serves the system of lines at right angles to that which represents the surface on which the circle lies. The major axis will be at a 90° angle to the minor axis. This rule applies to round windows, mirrors, clock faces, the portion of a circle that forms an arch, and similar elements.

If these rules are neglected, tabletops will run downhill and arches will be oddly distorted. It may seem impossible to fit an ellipse into a constructed square, but it is preferable to have the ellipse correct than to have a fit that uses a skewed or mispositioned ellipse.

All problems of perspective—including a sloping ceiling, walls at angles, reflections in water or mirrors—can be solved by variations on the basic method described here and above. Angled walls or ceilings, for example, are drawn by locating their beginning and ending edges and completing the figure by connecting the ends of the edges. Reflections are simply images that duplicate the actual space depicted in reverse, right to left or top to bottom.

19. The basic method described above is called *two-point perspective* because it uses two vanishing points, at right and left. *One-point perspective,* often recommended to beginners as being easier to learn, is merely a special case of the two-point method in which the second vanishing point has moved so far away as to be at the theoretical location of infinity, and is therefore unavailable. All lines that move toward this infinitely remote vanishing point are parallel.

In practice, a one-point perspective is drawn by placing the plan in use on the board with its main lines horizontal and vertical (fig. A12). Heights can be measured anywhere on the back wall; in fact, the back wall appears in true elevation. The single vanishing point, as in two-point perspective, is identified by running a line through the station point to the picture plane and bringing that line up to the horizon. (Like the two side walls of the plan, this line, which parallels these walls, will intersect the picture plane at a right angle.) All the other steps are the same as for two-point drawing, except that

A9 *Objects adjacent to a wall and extending into the space, such as the table shown here, are placed by establishing their points of intersection with the wall and by bringing a level from the height line along the walls, here shown dotted. Outer corner locations are found with lines from the station point through the corners of the object in plan to the picture plane and vertical lines carried upward into the perspective. Horizontal lines can now be added that radiate from the vanishing points to complete the top and bottom lines of the object. The bottom lines are used here to locate the points at which the legs touch the floor.*

A10 *Objects at angles to the walls are placed by locating each corner as above and establishing height by bringing imaginary lines outward from one wall. Lines representing the horizontals of the object will be found to converge toward new vanishing points, VPL 1 and VPR 1.*

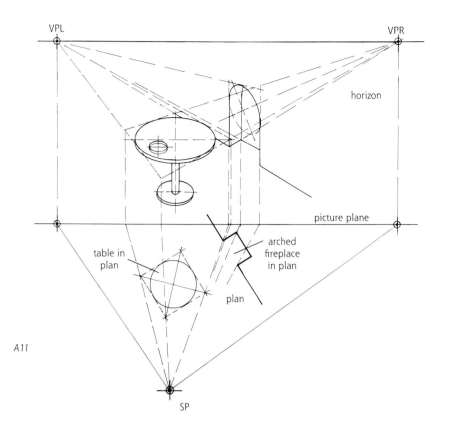

VPL

VPR

horizon

picture plane

table in plan

arched fireplace in plan

plan

A11

SP

one set of horizontal parallel lines can be simply drawn as horizontals without concern for their vanishing point. One-point perspectives work well for formal, symmetrical spaces, but they can be monotonous and limiting if used indiscriminately.

Familiarity with geometrically constructed perspective techniques makes it easier to draw freehand perspectives that are reasonably accurate and look right. Once the essential procedure has been grasped, elements may easily be drawn by eye within a constructed drawing. The ability to design in perspective, beginning with sketches that show spaces as they will actually appear, is a fundamental technical skill for an interior designer.

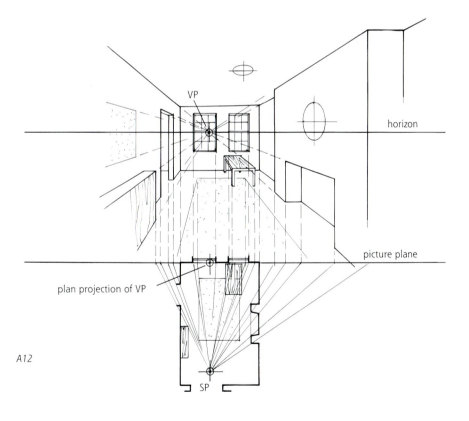

VP

horizon

picture plane

plan projection of VP

A12

SP

A11 Circles are represented by ellipses or sections of ellipses. In horizontal planes—the tabletop and base here—they will have horizontal major axes and vertical minor axes. In a vertical plane—such as the fireplace arch—a minor axis radiates from one vanishing point, with a major axis at right angles to the minor axis. Circular forms are most often located by enclosing the circle in perspective into a square and then fitting a suitable ellipse into the square as it appears in perspective.

A12 In a one-point perspective, the plan is spaced so that the wall lines are horizontal and vertical. Given a station point, the single vanishing point is located by a vertical line that runs upward from the station point to the horizon, intersecting at a right angle. Heights can be measured anywhere on the back wall, which is actually an elevation. Lines moving forward and backward in the space are drawn radiating from the vanishing point; lines that move sideways are drawn as horizontals. Elements are located with construction lines as described above for two-point perspectives.

APPENDIX 6. *ESTIMATING MATERIAL REQUIREMENTS*

Fabric

Before ordering drapery or upholstery fabrics or carpet, it is best to obtain an estimate of the quantity required from the firm that will install the material. A *drapery workroom* and installation contractor will take measurements and calculate the required yardage when quoting a price for the installation. Furniture manufacturers note in their price lists the correct yardage needed for "COM" (customer's own material) cover fabrics for each individual product. The contractor who will install the carpet computes the yardage needed and takes responsibility for making a correct estimate.

Interior designers must often make preliminary estimates for budget purposes before precise figures can be obtained. The budget may have to include the cost of upholstery fabrics before final selections of furniture have been made; or the approximate carpet yardage may be a factor in selecting carpet—or in comparing it with another floor covering. A pocket calculator can help in making such budget estimates.

DRAPERY YARDAGE

Drapery fabrics come in a number of widths, the most common being 36, 42, 45, 50, 52, 54, 56, and 118 inches. Since prices are quoted in linear (lengthwise) yards, it is necessary to determine, or at least assume, the width of the fabric to be used. Curtains are made up with *fullness,* that is, extra width to allow them to hang in folds; this means that the fabric must always be wider than the window or other space to be covered by the closed curtains. This fullness is expressed as a percentage; for example, 100 percent fullness means that the actual flat fabric will be twice the width it will cover when hung. Fullness usually ranges from 100 to 200 percent. Thin and sheer materials require more fullness than heavier materials. Estimating will follow these steps:

1. Measure (on site or from drawings) the width of the space the closed drapery will cover.
2. Multiply that width by the factor that gives the desired percentage of fullness: e.g., by 2, or twice the width, for 100 percent fullness, and by 3 for 200 percent.
3. Divide the resulting total width by the width of the fabric to be used. This gives the number of widths, or panels, required.
4. Measure (on site or from drawings) the total height of the drapery—from floor to ceiling, floor to window head, or sill to window head, according to the design planned. Add to this dimension an allowance for hems at the foot and head of each panel of made-up drapery. This will range from 6 to 16 inches, according to the details selected and the nature of the fabric. The result gives the total length, or height, of each panel *(width)* in inches.
5. Multiply this height dimension by the number of widths. Add a factor to allow for waste (usually 10 percent). Divide the total figure in inches by 36 to obtain yardage. If the pattern requires matching, allow an extra percentage factor for waste.

In addition to estimating the required fabric, the installation firm will quote a price for making up the curtains, including the cost of lining material, if any, and any decorative elements such as fringe, cords, and tassels. It will also price the hardware (track, traverse rods, and so on) and any related elements, such as valances or lambrequins, plus the cost of labor for on-site installation. Having drapery made up and installed usually costs at least twice the cost of the fabric (of average price) alone.

UPHOLSTERY COVER FABRIC

Even before making final furniture selections, it is possible to estimate the fabric yardage needed to cover a piece, given its general type and size, by looking in a manufacturer's catalog or price list. This will enable the designer to estimate cost before making final furniture selections. Typical requirements will be in the following ranges:

Small side chair (armless) . . . . 1–2 yards

Small armchair
  (unupholstered arms) . . 2–3 1/2 yards

Executive office armchair . . . . 4–5 yards

Fully upholstered chair . . . . 3–4 yards*

Fully upholstered
  two-seat sofa . . . . 6–8 yards*

Fully upholstered
  three-seat sofa . . . . 8–12 yards*

Ottoman . . . . 2–3 yards

*Add 1 1/2 yards for each fully upholstered arm.

• • •

Most upholstery fabrics are made in 52-inch widths. An allowance must be made for narrower widths. The matching of stripes or patterns calls for an extra allowance. Natural leather is priced in hides, not by the yard. The leather supplier can indicate the approximate yield in yards per hide, equivalent to yards of 36- or 52-inch-wide fabric, for any particular leather.

CARPET YARDAGE

Carpet, priced by the square yard, used to be made in widths of 27 or 36 inches. Now it is usually manufactured in various *broadloom* widths, commonly 6, 9, 12, and 15 feet. Since many room dimensions do not easily accommodate broadloom widths, it may take some ingenuity to work out an economical way to lay out widths so as to minimize waste. The easiest way to estimate the yardage required is to make a tracing paper overlay with lines spaced to indicate the bands of width and to move this about over the actual space plan to arrive at the best layout of widths and seams.

Once a rough layout is made, measure the length of each band in feet and add all the band lengths together. Multiply the total of the band lengths by the broadloom width in feet. Divide by 9 to convert the area in feet to yards. Add 5 to 10 percent for waste (the larger the area, the smaller the allowance) plus an allowance for matching if there is a pattern. Carpet squares or tile can be estimated simply by figuring the area to be covered and adding a small allowance for waste.

To the cost of the carpet alone, it is necessary to add the cost of any underlay or other installation materials and the cost of installation, which will vary with the location and size of the project. When quoting price per yard, a carpet manufacturer can usually give a fairly accurate estimate of the total cost, including installation in a particular location.

Wallpaper

Wallpaper is priced in units called *single rolls,* although it is produced and distributed in larger (double or triple) rolls as well. Allowing for waste, one single roll will cover 30 square feet of surface, found by measuring the actual ceiling or wall area and subtracting the dimensions of any openings. Very large patterns may call for 10 to 20 percent extra waste allowance to match the pattern properly.

APPENDIX 7. *METRIC EQUIVALENTS*

LINEAR MEASURE

10 millimeters (mm) = 1 centimeter (cm)
10 centimeters = 1 decimeter
10 decimeters = 1 meter (m)
10 meters = 1 decameter
10 decameters = 1 hectometer
10 hectometers = 1 kilometer

1 inch (in.) = 2.54 centimeters
1 foot (ft) = 12 in. = 0.3048 meter
1 yard (yd) = 3 ft = 0.9144 meter
1 rod = 5 1/2 yd or 16 1/2 ft = 5.029 meters
1 furlong = 40 rods = 201.17 meters
1 mile (statute) = 5280 ft or 1760 yd = 1609.3 meters
1 league (land) = 3 miles = 4.83 kilometers

SQUARE MEASURE

100 sq millimeters = 1 sq centimeter
100 sq centimeters = 1 sq decimeter
100 sq decimeters = 1 sq meter
100 sq meters = 1 sq decameter
100 sq decameters = 1 sq hectometer
100 sq hectometers = 1 sq kilometer

1 sq inch = 6.452 sq centimeters
1 sq foot = 144 sq in. = 929 sq centimeters
1 sq yard = 9 sq ft = 0.8361 sq meter
1 sq rod = 30 1/4 sq yd = 25.29 sq meters
1 acre = 43,560 sq ft or 4840 sq. yd =
                0.4047 hectare
                or 160 sq rods
1 sq mile = 640 acres = 259 hectares or
                2.59 sq kilometers

CUBIC MEASURE

1000 cu millimeters = 1 cu centimeter
1000 cu centimeters = 1 cu decimeter
1000 cu decimeters = 1 cu meter

1 cu inch = 16.387 cu centimeters
1 cu foot = 1728 cu in. = 0.0283 cu meter
1 cu yard = 27 cu ft = 0.7646 cu meter

FORMULAS FOR COMPUTING CONVERSIONS

When you know		You can find	Multiply by
Liquid	ounces	milliliters	30
Volume	pints	liters	0.47
	quarts	liters	0.95
	gallons	liters	3.80
	milliliters	ounces	0.034
	liters	pints	2.10
	liters	quarts	1.06
	liters	gallons	0.26
Mass	ounces	grams	28
	pounds	kilograms	0.45
	short tons	megagrams	0.90
	grams	ounces	0.035
	kilograms	pounds	2.20
	megagrams	short tons	1.10

When you know		You can find	Multiply by
Length	inches	millimeters	25.40
	feet	centimeters	30.48
	yards	meters	0.90
	miles	kilometers	1.60
	millimeters	inches	0.04
	centimeters	inches	0.40
	meters	yards	1.10
	kilometers	miles	0.60
Area	square inches	square centimeters	6.50
	square feet	square meters	0.09
	square yards	square meters	0.80
	square miles	square kilometers	2.60
	acres	square hectometers	80.40
	square centimeters	square inches	0.16
	square meters	square yards	1.20
	square kilometers	square miles	0.40
	square hectometers	acres	2.50

An example:
When you know square yards, multiply by .80 to convert to square meters: 10 square yards x .80 = 8 square meters

Another example:
To determine linear meters from linear yards, multiply by .90: 12 yards x .90 = 10.8 meters

APPENDIX 8. *PROFESSIONAL ORGANIZATIONS*

Several organizations set standards for the profession by offering membership to individuals qualified in interior design and providing various services. The following organizations are national in scope:

AMERICAN SOCIETY OF INTERIOR DESIGNERS (ASID)
608 Massachusetts Ave. N.E.
Washington, D.C. 20038
Membership in this primary professional organization attests to the qualification of its members, who may use the initials ASID. It conducts programs, monitors legislation, and coordinates interior design concerns with those of related professions.

FOUNDATION FOR INTERIOR DESIGN EDUCATION RESEARCH (FIDER)
60 Monroe Center
Grand Rapids, MI 49503
This organization is concerned with design education and the accreditation of design schools and their programs.

INSTITUTE OF BUSINESS DESIGNERS (IBD)
341 Merchandise Mart
Chicago, IL 60654
An organization of designers primarily involved in the office and contract fields.

INSTITUTE OF STORE PLANNERS (ISP)
24 North Broadway
Tarrytown, NY 10591
An organization of designers concerned with retail shop design.

INTERIOR DESIGN EDUCATORS COUNCIL (IDEC)
14252 Culver Drive
Suite A331
Culver City, CA 92714
An organization of teachers and others involved in design education.

INTERIOR DESIGNERS OF CANADA (IDC)
Ontario Design Center
260 King Street East
Suite 504
Toronto, Ontario M5A 7K3
Canada
The Canadian equivalent of the ASID.

NATIONAL COUNCIL FOR INTERIOR DESIGN QUALIFICATIONS (NCIDQ)
50 Main Street
White Plains, NY 10606-1920
The organization that administers and scores the interior design qualification examination.

The following organizations serve the professions most closely related to interior design:

AMERICAN INSTITUTE OF ARCHITECTS (AIA)
1735 New York Avenue N.W.
Washington, D.C. 20006
The primary American architectural organization.

INDUSTRIAL DESIGNERS SOCIETY OF AMERICA
1142-E Walker Road
Great Falls, VA 22066
The professional organization of the American industrial design field.

There are, in addition, state and local organizations concerned with various aspects of design, national organizations in other countries, and several international organizations that coordinate the activities of the national organizations.

Words or terms in *italics* within the definitions are also defined in the glossary.

ABSORPTION Dissipation of sound-wave energy within a material. The absorption coefficient of a material indicates the percentage of sound energy that will be absorbed on contact.

AC (ALTERNATING CURRENT) The form in which electrical energy is commonly delivered to buildings.

ACCESS FLOOR/CEILING Systems of manufactured elements that provide accessible hollow spaces below floors or above ceilings, where any combination of wiring, piping, and *ducts* may be placed.

ACCESSIBLE ROUTE A path within a building that permits movement by disabled (including wheelchair-bound) persons.

ACHROMATIC A term used to refer to light or objects reflecting light without chromatic color content; in practice, white, grays, and black.

ACRYLIC A transparent *thermoplastic*, usually made up into sheets, rods, or tubes. It can also be thermoformed into complex curved shapes, made translucent, or colored. Plexiglas and Lucite are trade names.

ADA The abbreviation for the Americans with Disabilities Act, the legislation most significant in mandating *barrier-free* access.

ADAPTABILITY The suitability of interiors to the accommodation of occupants with disabilities.

ADAPTIVE REUSE The conversion of older buildings or spaces to serve current uses.

ADDITIVE COLOR In lighting, color mixing that involves the addition of colors. The mixing of dyes or pigments, on the other hand, *subtracts* color through absorption. The additive *primary* colors are red, green, and blue.

ADJACENCY The nearness of various elements to one another within an interior space. Adjacency studies develop criteria for planning based on the need for nearness between elements.

AMBIENT LIGHT Also called general lighting, this is the overall level of light in a space, which should be adequate for comfortable movement and for seeing people and objects.

ANALOGOUS COLORS Colors that are adjacent or close in their position in the *spectrum* or on the *color wheel*.

ANTHROPOMETRICS The study of the dimensions and articulation of the human body by means of systematic, statistical observation of large numbers of people.

ARCHITRAVE In the classical *orders* of architecture, the horizontal *molding* just above the capital of a column. Also, the molding around a doorway or other opening.

AREA DIAGRAM A chart in which spaces are shown as blocks whose size is determined by the area requirements for each space.

ART DECO A popular term for the stylistic development of the 1920s and 1930s that stemmed from Paris exhibitions called "Les Arts Décoratifs." These included interiors, furniture, and other objects designed in a modern style that came to influence architecture as well. At the time, this style was called Moderne or, in English, Modernistic.

ART NOUVEAU A stylistic development of the late nineteenth century centered in Belgium and France. Abandoning all historical references, this genuinely modern style used instead elaborately curved decorative detail, generally based on natural forms.

ARTS & CRAFTS MOVEMENT An aesthetic inspired by the desire to reform design by closing the gaps between fine arts, crafts, and design in architecture, interiors, and decorative objects. It developed in England in the latter half of the nineteenth century, with William Morris as its primary spokesman. Subsequent design directions have close ties to Arts & Crafts theory and attitudes.

ASBESTOS A mineral fiber with excellent insulating and fire-resistant properties. Loose asbestos fibers present serious health hazards, which have led to a marked decrease in the use of this material.

ASHLAR Building stone cut into square or rectangular blocks; masonry construction made up of such stone blocks.

ASYMMETRICAL BALANCE Balance achieved through means other than *symmetrical* placement.

ATRIUM In classical Roman architecture, the central courtyard of a house; by extension, any central courtyard or open space around which a house is built. In current usage, the term describes an interior space roofed over with glass, as in more recently built hotels, office buildings, or other large projects.

AWNING WINDOW A window with a sash that pivots at the top and swings outward.

AXMINSTER A traditional carpet construction using a jute back and wool cut pile. Made by a now-obsolete mechanical weaving process, these carpets display a wide variety of colors and patterns.

AXONOMETRIC A system of drawing projection in which a three-dimensional illusion is generated by lines representing horizontals drawn at a consistent angle (such as 30 or 45 degrees). *Isometric* drawing, in which all lines can be drawn at true scale dimensions, is a special case of axonometric drawing.

BALLAST In electrical parlance, a *transformer* that converts the current in a circuit to that required by *fluorescent lamps*.

BALLOON-FRAME CONSTRUCTION A method employed primarily in building small houses of wood. Structural members are placed close together as framing; exterior sheathing and interior finishes create hollow spaces within walls and beneath floors that provide locations for pipes, wiring, and insulation. This simple, economical system was developed in mid-nineteenth-century America.

BALUSTER A vertical post or support for a railing, most often a stair rail.

BANQUETTE A continuous, benchlike seat, usually upholstered.

BAROQUE The design of the latter part of the Renaissance, characterized by complex forms and elaborate decorative detail. Baroque design originated in Italy and was widely accepted in Germany, Austria, and related European regions, but less so in northern Europe. Most significant Baroque work dates from the seventeenth century.

BARRIER-FREE SPACE A space or *circulation* route that permits movement by disabled persons.

BASEBOARD A band of protective or decorative trim or *molding* along the bottom of a wall where it meets the floor.

BAUHAUS A German school of art and design that operated from 1919 to 1932. Under the direction of Walter Gropius, the school exerted a profound influence on the development and practice of *modernism* in art, architecture, and design. The name of the school has come to describe work in the severe, functional, and often mechanistic style favored at the school.

BEAM A horizontal structural support element. The bending stresses generated in a beam include both tensile and compressive stresses.

BEAUX ARTS A term referring to the Ecole des Beaux-Arts (School of Fine Arts) in Paris and, by extension, the style of design based on an ornate form of classicism taught at that school.

BENTWOOD The product of a technique in which thin strips of solid wood are softened by steam and bent around molds. Furniture made by this method was developed in the latter half of the nineteenth century by Michael Thonet.

BRIGHTNESS The intensity of light level produced by a light source or reflected back from a lighted surface. The *footlambert* (fL) is the unit of measurement for brightness.

BROADLOOM Carpet woven on a loom at least 54 inches wide so as to avoid the need to seam narrow strips.

BUBBLE DIAGRAM A drawing in which elements of an interior are drawn as soft, bubblelike shapes whose sizes are proportional to the various area requirements and whose placement is determined by *adjacency* requirements.

BUILDING STANDARD The basic interior elements,

such as partitions, floors, ceilings, doors, and light fixtures, provided without additional charge to tenants of large modern office buildings by the building owners.

BURL A marked irregularity in a wood grain resulting from abnormal tree growth. Burled wood is most often used to make a *veneer* with striking color and pattern.

CABRIOLE A furniture leg with a double, or S-shaped, curvature, often decoratively carved and ending in a more or less elaborate foot. The shape is used in many traditional furniture styles.

CAD The abbreviation for computer-aided design.

CADD The abbreviation for computer-aided design and drafting.

CALENDERING A process for finishing textiles or forming thin sheets, for example, of plastic, by passing the material between rollers under pressure.

CANDELA A unit of light intensity approximately equal to the more commonly used *footcandle* (fc), the level of light falling on a surface with an area of one square foot placed at a distance of one foot from a standard candle.

CANDLEPOWER A unit of light intensity equal to the output of a standard candle.

CANTILEVER A horizontal projecting beam or structure anchored at one end only.

CASEMENT WINDOW A window hinged at the side and swinging open like a door, most often used in pairs.

CHAIR RAIL A molding, usually of wood, that runs along a wall at the height of chair backs, thus protecting the wall from being scraped or otherwise marred.

CHAISE LONGUE A reclining chair with a seating surface long enough to provide support for the sitter's legs. (Often corrupted to "chaise lounge.")

CHASE A vertical shaft that holds *ducts*, piping, or wiring.

CHROMA A color's purity, or saturation, in the *Munsell* color system, it is measured by a range of numbers from 1 to 14. The highest numbers indicate maximum intensity, although different hues reach maximum chroma at different numbers.

CIRCULATION The movement patterns of a space's occupants. The study of circulation patterns is particularly important in planning complex interiors made up of many rooms, corridors, or other areas.

CLERESTORY An outside wall, pierced with windows, carried above an adjoining roof, as in the upper walls of the nave of a *Gothic* church; also, a wall with a window or band of windows placed high.

COFFER Originally a chest or other box. By extension, coffers are the recesses that form three-dimensional decorative patterns in ceilings, vaults, or domes.

COLD-CATHODE LIGHT A light source that uses thin, luminous, gas-filled tubes similar to those of neon signs but that produces normal white light. The tubes are often custom-designed and permanently installed, usually in ceiling *coves*.

COLONIAL A term applied to early-American architecture, including a version of English *Georgian*. The same term is used, rather loosely, to describe

more modern imitations of that design.

COLOR TEMPERATURE A single number expressed in degrees Kelvin (°K)—or, more currently, in kelvins (k)—that indicates the relative warmth or coolness of lighting.

COLOR WHEEL A circular arrangement of *hues* in their spectrum, or "rainbow," order of red, orange, yellow, green, blue, and violet. When colors are thus organized, each *secondary* color falls between the *primaries* that make it up, and all colors are directly opposite their *complementaries.*

COMPLEMENTARY COLORS Colors placed in opposite locations on a *color wheel,* such as red and green.

CONDUCTION The transfer of heat through contact between elements of different temperatures.

CONSTRAINT In design, any restriction that influences planning.

CONSTRUCTION DRAWING A drawing made to aid in taking bids and for contractors or artisans to use in executing work; also called a working drawing or blueprint.

CONTEMPORARY DESIGN Current or recent design work. The term commonly describes work that neither refers to historical precedent nor displays the strong stylistic austerity and simplicity associated with *modernism.* The term "transitional" is sometimes used, mistakenly, as a synonym for "contemporary" in a design context.

CONTINUOUS-SPECTRUM LIGHT Light that contains all of the energy wavelengths—colors—that make up white light. When viewed through a prism or spectroscope, such light reveals a continuous rainbow band of colors. Sources of continuous-spectrum light include the sun, candles, *incandescent* electric light, and oil lamps.

CONTRACT DESIGN All non*residential* interior design. Contract design includes the production and distribution of elements such as furniture, textiles, and light fixtures used primarily in larger commercial and institutional projects. These elements are purchased under contracts rather than through retail channels.

CONVECTION The transfer of heat through the movement of heated air.

CONVECTOR A heat-supply device similar to a *radiator* but designed to maximize the effective flow of heated air by *convection,* that is, the circular motion of air at nonuniform temperatures.

CORNICE A horizontal band of projecting decorative *moldings* at the top of a wall or building. In the classical orders of architecture, the uppermost of the three bands that make up the *entablature.* Also, a projecting horizontal band placed above a window to conceal curtain rods.

COST-PLUS A system of charging for construction work in which the final charge represents the actual costs of materials and labor, plus an established percentage for overhead and profit.

COVE 1) A trough or other recess, often part of a ceiling design, occasionally built into a wall. The cove conceals an *indirect light* source (cove lighting), usually *fluorescent* or *cold-cathode;* 2) a concave molding, particularly one placed where the wall meets the ceiling or floor.

CPM (CRITICAL PATH METHOD) A system for charting a sequence of operations against a time base

so as to show their interdependence.

CREDENZA A horizontal chest or cabinet common in interiors of the Italian Renaissance. In modern usage, the term describes an office storage cabinet of dimensions similar to those of a desk, with doors and sometimes drawers.

CRI (COLOR RENDERING INDEX) A measure of the ability of light of a particular kind to permit accurate evaluation of the color of objects.

CROSS-BANDING In the construction of veneered *panels* for furniture, doors, paneling, and other interior elements of wood, the layer beneath the exposed, or face, *veneer.* The grain of the cross-banding runs at right angles to the grains of both the solid-wood core and the face veneer, preventing splits and warping.

CRT (CATHODE-RAY TUBE) The element providing the screen of a television set or computer monitor. A computer unit including a screen is often called a CRT unit.

DADO 1) The lower part of an interior wall treated with paneling or other special surface materials; 2) in classical architecture, the middle band of a pedestal.

DECIBEL (DB) A unit of sound intensity or loudness.

DECONSTRUCTIVISM A recent approach to design in which elements are taken apart and reassembled in partially disconnected relationships.

DESIGN DRAWING A drawing made to illustrate or aid in the development of design. Normally, design drawings emphasize visual concepts and do not include the dimensions and details needed for construction.

DE STIJL A movement (1917–29) in the development of *modernism.* Centered in Holland, it took its name from the magazine that was its primary organ. Gerrit Rietveld, Theo van Doesburg, and Piet Mondrian were the most active in defining this style.

DISCONTINUOUS-SPECTRUM LIGHT Light in which only some wavelengths—colors—are present. Although such light appears to be white, a spectroscope shows bright lines of certain colors and blanks elsewhere along the spectrum. Gaseous-discharge lamps, such as *mercury* or *sodium* lights, produce discontinuous-spectrum light. *Fluorescent* light is a mixture of discontinuous- and *continuous-spectrum* light.

DISTRESSED FINISH A trade term for a finish of reproduction antique furniture that has been deliberately damaged to imitate wormholes and other signs of age.

DOUBLE GLAZING The insertion, in a window, door, or skylight, of two panes of glass with a dead-air space in between to provide insulation; the principle is that of the storm window.

DOUBLE-HUNG WINDOW A window sash made up of two separate panes that slide vertically.

DOVETAIL JOINT An element of wood joinery, made up of two interlocking pieces. Dovetails may be hand cut, as in fine traditional cabinetry, or machine cut. A through, or slip, dovetail uses a lengthwise, wedge-shaped tab that slides into a matching groove.

DOWEL A round pin, usually of wood. A dowel (or doweled) joint uses one or more dowels fitted into bored holes to form a wood joint widely used in cabinetmaking.

DOWNLIGHT A can-shaped housing that directs light from an *incandescent lamp* downward for general lighting. Downlights may be surface-mounted, recessed into a ceiling surface, or hung from a stem. *HID* versions are increasingly available for larger spaces.

DRYWALL A technique in general use for building interior partitions. Large panels or sheets of *wallboard*, *gypsum* board, plasterboard, or Sheetrock are used in place of plaster to cover *studs* or other structural wall-support materials.

DUCT An air passage, usually made of sheet metal and usually rectangular, but sometimes round. In *HVAC* systems, ducts carry heated or cooled air to inlet grilles.

ECLECTICISM Generally, the borrowing of ideas from many sources. In design, the term describes an architectural and interior design direction of about 1900–40, which referred to historic precedents from the distant past, imitating them with considerable accuracy.

ELEVATION An orthographic drawing showing a front, side, or *oblique projected* view in true or consistently scaled dimensions.

ENTABLATURE The part of a classical architectural *order* that extends horizontally above the columns. It is made up of three bands, from bottom to top: the *architrave*, the *frieze* (sometimes omitted), and the *cornice*.

ERGONOMICS The study of human body mechanics and sensory performance in relation to the designed environment, especially in work situations.

EYEBALL An *incandescent* lighting fixture, usually recessed into a ceiling. The *lamp* is installed in a pivoting, spherical element that permits direct light to be focused as desired.

FACILITIES PLANNING A specialized interior design activity concerned with planning of commercial and institutional projects.

FEDERAL An American decorative and furniture style associated with the *Greek Revival* movement in the first half of the nineteenth century.

FIBERGLASS A hybrid material that uses glass fibers to reinforce a polyester *thermosetting plastic*. In translucent form, fiberglass is often employed for skylights or roofs. Other applications are automobile bodies, small boat hulls, chair bodies, and other furniture parts.

FILL LIGHT Background, *ambient*, or diffused light that reduces the contrast between dark areas or shadows and primary or *task light*.

FLOCKING A velvet-like surface made by applying fibers to an adhesive backing, often creating a pattern in relief. Flocking is sometimes used in the manufacture of economy-grade carpeting.

FLUORESCENT LIGHT A combination light source that gives off light both from glowing gas inside a sealed *lamp* and from fluorescent phosphors that coat the inner surface of the lamp. The lamp is usually tubular, and, occasionally, circular, although fluorescent bulb shapes are also produced.

FOOTCANDLE A unit of light intensity. The illumination of a surface at a distance of one foot from a standard candle equals one footcandle.

FOOTLAMBERT (fL) A unit of measurement of light reflected from an illuminated surface.

FRIEZE In the classical *orders* of architecture, the section, often decoratively sculpted, of the *entablature* between the *architrave* and the *cornice*; hence, any horizontal ornamental band such as that often placed at the top of a wall.

FULL-SPECTRUM LIGHT Light that contains the complete range of wavelengths present in daylight, including the invisible radiation at each end of the visible spectrum.

FURRING The lining of a wall with wood, brick, or metal strips to support interior finish material, such as plaster or *wallboard*. The term also describes the strips of metal that support a lowered ceiling, which is then referred to as "furred" or "furred down."

GATELEG TABLE A drop-leaf table in which a hinged leaf is supported by a leg unit that swings out in the manner of a gate.

GEORGIAN The mid-to-late English Renaissance style developed approximately concurrently with the reigns of George I to George III, about 1714–1800. The term is also used for the parallel American design of the same period.

GIRDER A structural member, a large beam supporting other beams.

GLARE Excessively bright light reflecting from a surface in such a way as to obscure observation of detail.

GOLDEN MEAN A proportional relationship expressed numerically as 1:1.618—and used in various historic periods and by some modern designers as an aid to aesthetic excellence in design.

GOTHIC The architectural and decorative style of the latter half of the Middle Ages (about 1150–1500). Its most striking characteristic is the pointed arch and *vault*, used in stone construction and, in similar forms, other design work.

GREEK REVIVAL An architectural and decorative style developed in imitation of ancient Greek design and paralleling the interior *Federal* style. It was popular in America, England, and Germany, and, to a lesser extent, other European countries from about 1800 to 1840.

GROUND-FAULT INTERRUPTER A safety device for electrical circuits that shuts off power in case of a short circuit in order to prevent shocks. Its use is suggested where electrical outlets or devices are close to water or metal pipes, as in bathrooms or near pools.

GROUT A cement mortar, or other material with similar properties, used to fill holes or as an adhesive for setting tiles.

GYPSUM A mineral substance used to make plaster, block for building interior partitions, and gypsum board, a sheet wall-surface material also known as plasterboard, *wallboard*, or Sheetrock (a trade name), used in *drywall* partition construction.

HALF-TIMBER CONSTRUCTION Large-scale timber framing with an infilling of panels of brick rubble and plaster, resulting in a characteristic exterior of exposed dark wood beams against a lighter material. This was the primary system of wood construction in northern Europe from the Middle Ages until well into the eighteenth century. The same structure, but with an exterior facing, was continued in the American colonies.

HALOGEN LIGHT See TUNGSTEN-HALOGEN LIGHT

HAND The textural feel of a fabric.

HARDBOARD A generic term for any of various types of fiberboard, made from pressed wood fibers and hardened in manufacture by heat and pressure. Masonite is the trade name for one kind of hardboard.

HID LIGHT The abbreviation, in current use, for high-intensity discharge. HID *lamps* employ *mercury*, *metal halide*, or high-pressure *sodium* in a sealed globe to produce an efficient type of electric lighting.

HIGH TECH A recent design direction that incorporates elements from industrial, aerospace, and other advanced technologies, giving it a characteristically sleek and gleaming mechanistic look.

HUE The distinctive characteristics of a color described by a basic color name and assigned a particular position in the spectrum. There are three *primary* hues (red, yellow, and blue) and three *secondary* hues (violet, orange, and green).

HUMAN FACTORS The aspects of design that relate to human comfort and convenience.

HVAC The abbreviation in current use for heating, ventilating, and air-conditioning systems.

INCANDESCENT LIGHT The most common light source, from a *lamp* that produces light by means of an electrically heated wire filament within a sealed globe.

INDIRECT LIGHTING Lighting directed against a reflecting surface, most often a ceiling. Such an arrangement generates diffuse, *ambient* lighting.

INLAY A decoration set into the surface of an object and finished flush. Inlays of variously colored wood veneers and, occasionally, other materials such as mother-of-pearl or metals are elements in many traditional furniture styles.

INSULATION Materials that block the transfer of energy from one material or space to another. The undesirable transfer of heat or sound is commonly limited by appropriate insulation.

INTERNATIONAL STYLE A direction of post–World War I architecture and related interior design characterized by an absence of ornament, large glass areas and flat roofs, and an emphasis on functionalism. It originated in 1920s Europe, was developed by the *Bauhaus* school, and became the dominant modern style worldwide from about 1930 until recent years.

ISOMETRIC A special form of *axonometric* drawing in which an illusion of three-dimensionality is created by lines representing horizontals drawn at a 30-degree angle or at 30- to 60-degree angles. True scale dimensions can be measured on lines at the angled axes and on vertical lines.

JALOUSIE A window or door with an arrangement of overlapping, adjustable, horizontal slats, which controls ventilation, light, or both. Jalousie doors for interior use—such as closet doors—often have fixed slats.

JAMB A vertical element at the side of a door, window, or other opening.

JOIST A horizontal structural member supporting a floor. Joists are, in effect, small, closely spaced beams.

JUGENDSTIL The German term for the style that is more generally referred to by the French term Art Nouveau.

KNIT A fabric construction in which yarn is interlaced by means of needles. Hand-knitting is a traditional craft technique, but knitting machines have been developed for the industrial production of knitted fabrics.

LAMBREQUIN A boxlike, usually fabric-covered trimming that holds and decorates drapery at the top or top and sides of a window or door. Also, a short decorative drapery along a shelf edge or window.

LAMINATE Any product of the process of *lamination,* but the term most often describes a plastic sheet made of layers of paper soaked with *melamine* resin. The result is a tough surface material used for table and counter tops and other furniture that calls for resistance to wear and impact damage. Common trade names include Formica, Micarta, Colorcore, and Nevamar.

LAMINATION The process of adhering layers of thin material to make up a thicker sheet. *Plywood,* flat or molded, is made by lamination. Plastic *laminate* is widely used as a tabletop, counter top, and general furniture surface material.

LAMP In nontechnical usage, any portable lighting device, such as a floor or table lamp. In the lighting trades and professions, the term refers to the light source itself, the bulb or tube that converts electrical energy to light.

LATE MODERN A term for recent work that continues the concepts of the modern movement of the 1920s to the 1950s.

LATH Thin strips of wood nailed to the *studs* of a wall to support a plaster or other surface. The term is now also used for metal mesh and perforated sheet serving the same purpose.

LICENSING The regulation of design practice through legislation requiring that work affecting safety, health, and well-being be done only by holders of a professional license.

LINTEL A short, horizontal member spanning an open space between columns or over a door, window, or other opening.

LOAD-BEARING WALL A wall that provides structural support for a floor or roof.

LUMEN A unit of light flow generated by the light of one standard candle.

LUMINAIRE In the lighting trades or professions, a complete light fixture, including the *lamp* or lamps, power connections, and any enclosures, reflectors, lenses, baffles, or other elements.

LUX A metric unit of light intensity equal to one lumen per square meter. One lux equals 10.76 *footcandles.*

MANTEL A horizontal shelf above a fireplace opening.

MAQUETTE An interior plan with related elevations—representing walls—placed around and adjacent to it; when the group is cut out and the elevations folded up, a boxlike model of the interior is formed.

MARQUETRY Inlaid decorative detail on furniture and flooring using variously colored woods or other materials.

MATRIX CHART A chart in which the relationship between two lists of items is displayed in numerical or symbolic form.

MELAMINE A highly resistant *thermosetting plastic*

used to make *laminates* for table or counter tops or other furniture applications.

MERCURY LIGHT A type of gaseous-discharge *lamp* that uses mercury gas in a sealed tube. It is highly efficient, but its *discontinuous-spectrum light* is an unpleasant bluish color unsuitable for all but utilitarian purposes such as highway lighting.

METAL-HALIDE LIGHT An economical *HID lamp* that provides high output.

MITER A joint made by fitting together two pieces of material cut to meet at matching angles, usually 45 degrees, to form a corner, usually 90 degrees.

MODERNISM A general term for design styles developed in the twentieth century that make little or no reference to earlier historic periods, characterized instead by functional simplicity.

MODULE 1) A standardized unit of measurement used in planning and construction, such as 8-inch bricks or 2-by-4-inch studs, to facilitate convenient and economical usage; 2) one of a set of standardized units in an integrated system that allows numerous combinations, as in a furniture set (a modular couch or storage system).

MOLDED PLYWOOD *Plywood* that is shaped under pressure while the adhesive between its component layers is still malleable. Molded plywood is used in many modern furniture products.

MOLDING An architectural band that covers and trims a line where parts or materials join or that creates purely decorative linear patterns. Moldings are often of wood, sometimes of metal, plaster, or plastic.

MONOCHROMATIC COLORS Colors of a single hue.

MORTISE AND TENON In woodworking, a joint in which a projecting element, the tenon, is fitted into a corresponding cavity, the mortise.

MOSAIC Very small stones or tiles arranged to create patterns or images.

MULLION A vertical member dividing *panels* or panes of a door or window.

MUNSELL COLOR SOLID In the Munsell color system, the mass that results when the steps of *value* are arranged in a vertical axis, the *hues* form a sphere in the horizontal planes around the axis, and the steps of *chroma,* or saturation, radiate from the axis (least saturated) to the circumference (most saturated).

MUNTIN A vertical member dividing *panels* or panes of a door or window.

NEOCLASSIC A stylistic development based on a return to the principles of classic—ancient Greek and Roman—architecture and design. For example, neoclassicism characterizes French design of the period following the French Revolution and extending into the nineteenth century, including the Directoire and Empire interior styles.

NOSING The projecting front edge of the *tread* of a stair.

NRC (NOISE REDUCTION COEFFICIENT) A decimal number that indicates the ability of an interior surface material to absorb sound by giving the percentage of sound that will be absorbed. Hard materials have a low NRC, while materials with good sound-absorbent qualities have high NRC ratings, up to a maximum of about .90.

OBLIQUE PROJECTION A system of drawing projection in which one plane (usually a *plan* or an ele-

vation) is drawn orthographically while receding lines are drawn at an angle (30, 45, or 60 degrees) to give a three-dimensional effect.

OPEN PLAN A layout with few or no walls or partitions. The term has become associated with a system of office planning that, instead of separate, enclosed offices, uses screens or other furniture elements to provide some degree of privacy within a single, open space.

ORDERS The classical systems of architectural detail and ornament based on columns supporting an *entablature.* Developed in ancient Greece and Rome, the most commonly found orders are Doric, Ionic, and Corinthian, named after their supposed places of origin.

ORIENTATION The placement of a building, room, window, skylight, or other relevant element in relation to the points of the compass.

ORTHOGRAPHIC see OBLIQUE PROJECTION

OSTWALD COLOR SOLID In the Ostwald color system, steps of *value* are arranged in a vertical axis; the steps of *chroma,* or saturation, radiate outward from the neutral center (least saturated) toward the *hues* (most saturated), which form the outer layer on a horizontal plane. Unlike in the *Munsell* system, steps of variation in chroma are equalized to form a smooth, double-conical solid.

PANEL A rectangular unit of material, usually framed by some sort of border. Wood paneling is a popular wall treatment. Rail-and-panel construction is a system of making doors or parts of furniture by setting thin wooden panels into a frame of *rails.*

PARQUET *Inlaid* woodwork made up of small blocks of hardwood arranged to form a geometric design or pattern, often in contrasting colors, primarily used in flooring.

PARTICLEBOARD A sheet material made up of wood chips, sawdust, or both, bonded with a resin adhesive. Painted or *veneered,* particleboard provides a finished surface equal to *plywood* or solid wood.

PEDIMENT A triangular gable over a door, window, or portico; also, the *molding* edging on a gable roof.

PERSPECTIVE The system of realistic pictorial drawing representing objects and spaces in relative distance or depth. Distant objects appear smaller than nearer objects, and horizontal lines move into the distance, converging toward "vanishing points" on the horizon.

PILE A cloth or carpet surface of raised yarns, looped or cut flush. Velvet and terry cloth are two pile fabrics.

PLAN A depiction, drawn to scale, of a horizontal section of a building or other unit taken at or near ground or floor level. Such "ground plans" or "floor plans" are the most important drawings used in architectural and interior design. The term "planning" refers to the development of such plans and, by extension, any subsequent systematic design actions.

PLASTERBOARD See WALLBOARD

PLENUM A hollow space above a ceiling or below a floor, often used for return air circulation in an *HVAC* system or for placing architectural lighting fixtures.

PLYWOOD A sheet material made by *laminating* layers of *veneer* (veneer plywood) with their grains running at right angles. Some types of plywood contain a solid-material core and are finished with a good veneer. The first is most commonly used for carpentry or, *molded,* for furniture; the second, for furniture.

POINT-SOURCE LIGHT Lighting that comes from a concentrated source virtually identical to a point in space. The sun, the flames of candles and oil lamps, and the filaments of *incandescent lamps* give point-source light, as distinguished from the diffuse light of cloudy skies, *fluorescent* tubes, and luminous or *indirectly lit* ceilings.

POST AND LINTEL A system of construction in which upright members—posts—support horizontals—*lintels*—to form a structural frame or grid, usually in timber or stone masonry.

POST-MODERNISM A term recently coined to describe stylistic developments in architecture and design that diverge from the precepts of *modernism.* Eccentric ornament, historicism as metaphor, and a certain whimsical quality are characteristic of this direction.

PRIMARY COLOR One of a group of colors from which all other colors may be generated, but which itself cannot be made by mixing. The *subtractive* (pigment or dye) primaries are red, yellow, and blue; the *additive* (colored light) primaries are red, green, and blue.

PROGRAM An initial, verbal statement of objectives and requirements for a design project.

PROXEMICS A recently coined term for the systematic study of the psychological impact of space and interpersonal physical distances.

QUARTERED Wood from a log that has first been cut into lengthwise quarters in order to maximize the yield of boards at or close to a radial position in the log.

QUOIN A large stone at the corner of a building that provides visual emphasis.

RABBET A cut or groove in the edge of a material, usually wood, that fits a corresponding cut in another piece so as to form a joint.

RADIANT HEAT A system in which surfaces are heated by water passed through warming coils or by electric heat elements. Unlike *convection,* which circulates heat throughout a space, this system radiates heat directly into a space. Radiant heating is often used in combination with solar heating.

RADIATION The transfer of energy (heat or light) by direct electromagnetic wave action.

RADIATOR A heating device made up of a coil, pipes, or a hollow metal unit through which hot water or steam is passed, radiating heat into the surrounding air and space. The term is somewhat misleading, since the common radiator distributes heat more by *convection* than by *radiation.*

RAIL A horizontal element such as a stair rail or a wooden frame member combined with *panels* in rail-and-panel construction.

REFLECTANCE The proportion of incident light reflected from an illuminated surface, expressed as a percentage.

REFRACTION The bending of light as it passes from one medium to another of different density.

REGISTRATION The regulation of design practice

through legislation requiring that practitioners meet certain standards of competence to obtain a registration certificate.

REINFORCED CONCRETE A hybrid structural material combining concrete, which resists compressive stresses, with embedded steel rods and mesh, which resist tensile stresses.

RESIDENTIAL DESIGN The design of houses and other residential projects and their interiors as distinguished from *contract design,* which addresses commercial and institutional spaces.

RESTORATION The reconstruction of an older room, building, or neighborhood to re-create its original state.

RETURN AIR Air that returns to air-conditioning equipment after circulating through a space. Grilles, for example, permit air to return to *ducts,* a *plenum,* or through corridors.

REVERBERATION Successive reflections of sound (echoes) that cause a gradual decrease in intensity after production of the sound has stopped. Reverberation time is the time required for a sound to die away to inaudibility.

RISER 1) In stair construction, the vertical element of a step; 2) in plumbing or wiring, a vertical stretch of equipment, usually serving the upper floors of a building.

ROCOCO The stylistic developments in eighteenth-century French and, to a lesser extent, German and Austrian interior design, and decorative detail typical of the latter part of the French Baroque. Rococo, although characterized by very elaborate surface decoration, retains relatively simple basic forms.

ROMANESQUE The architectural style of the early Middle Ages in Europe (circa 800–1150). Despite its name, it is not a Roman style, but is so called because of its prominent use of semicircular—or "Roman"—arches. In England, such design is commonly designated "Norman."

SADDLE A slightly raised element at the bottom of a doorway or other opening; also called a threshold.

SATURATION See CHROMA

SCALE 1) A measuring rule, such as an architect's scale, graduated in units applicable to scale drawing; 2) the system of representing objects or spaces in a compact drawing by reducing them by a certain proportion (e.g., 1/4" = 1'-0"); and 3) the concept that all objects and elements of a design should convey proper and true size relationships.

SCONCE A wall-mounted lighting fixture, which generally directs light upward.

SECESSION (or Vienna Secession) A design movement in Austria at the end of the nineteenth century, parallel with Art Nouveau.

SECONDARY COLOR A color that results from mixing two *primaries.* The *subtractive* secondaries are orange, green, and violet.

SHADE A darkened form of a color *hue* produced by the addition of black or gray.

SHEETROCK See WALLBOARD

SILL 1) In construction, a horizontal structural member; 2) the horizontal shelflike surface below a window, door, or other opening.

SOCLE A base, pedestal, or plinth at the bottom of a surface or column.

SODIUM LIGHT A gaseous-discharge light source that uses sodium gas in a sealed tube. Sodium light has a *discontinuous spectrum,* giving it a strong orange tone that makes it unpleasant for general use. Because of its high efficiency, however, it is sometimes used for street and highway lighting.

SOFFIT A lowered portion of a ceiling, or, generally, the underside of a structural element.

SOLAR HEATING Heating using sunlight as a source of energy.

SPACE PLANNING A specialized aspect of interior design concerned with the layout of rooms or other spaces in plan.

SPECTRUM The band of colors, ordered from longest wavelength (red) to shortest (violet), visible when light passes through a prism, as in a spectroscope. Daylight and other white, *continuous-spectrum* light produce a complete rainbow spectrum.

STACK In plumbing, a vertical waste pipe that extends downward to a sewer connection and upward to the open air to permit the venting of gases.

STACKING PLAN A chart or diagram showing the assignment of various functional units to the floors of a multifloor project.

STC (SOUND TRANSMISSION CLASS) A number rating that indicates the effectiveness of a material or structure in preventing sound transmission. Low STC values (15–20) denote a poor sound barrier, higher values (40–60), a superior ability to block sound transmission.

STILE A vertical member in a door or window, usually combined with *rails* and *panels* in rail-and-panel construction.

STRETCHER A horizontal brace, or crosspiece, such as the member set between two legs of a chair or table.

STUDS Vertical frame elements in the construction of walls and partitions. Wood studs are usually 2-by-4-inch members placed 16 inches apart. In modern practice, metal studs are also used.

SUBTRACTIVE COLOR The colors of pigments and dyes absorb—that is, subtract—some of the light that strikes them, reflecting the color that results from this subtraction. Mixing pigments to produce *tints* and *shades* is a subtractive process.

SYMMETRY The placement of identical elements in matching positions on either side of one or more axes.

SYSTEMS FURNITURE Furniture that is designed to combine with other elements. Furniture systems are most often developed in terms of storage walls and office *workstations* that may double as partitioning.

TAMBOUR A furniture front or top made with strips of wood adhered to a fabric backing that allows it to roll in curves. A tambour door slides in a track or groove, often into a hidden trough, to open.

TASK LIGHT Light necessary for specific kinds of work, or tasks, and installed close to a work surface so as to illuminate the area with minimal spill and thus with maximum energy efficiency.

TEMPLATE A guide used in drafting to trace given outlines. The templates most common in the design trade are cut-out plastic sheets with drafting forms such as circles, ellipses, or furniture shapes in scale.

TERRAZZO A flooring material using small chips of marble embedded in cement and given a polished surface.

TETRAD COLOR A color scheme using four hues equally spaced on a color wheel.

THERMOPLASTIC Any plastic material that softens with the application of heat and hardens on cooling. *Acrylics,* vinyls, and polyethylene are thermoplastics.

THERMOSETTING PLASTIC A soft plastic that permanently sets, that is, hardens, with the application of heat. Phenolics, *melamines,* and polyesters are thermosetting plastics.

TINT A form of a color made lighter by mixture with white or light gray.

TITLE LEGISLATION A form of legal registration or licensing that restricts the use of a professional title but permits practice without restriction.

TONGUE AND GROOVE A joining technique used with wood and other materials in which a projecting lip, or tongue, is slipped into a corresponding channel, or groove. In wood boarding, the line of the joint is often emphasized with a cut *molding* to give a pattern or parallel lines.

TRACK LIGHTING A system of lighting in which a continuous fixed band, or track, supplies current and supports movable fixtures.

TRANSFORMER An electrical device that converts an electrical current to a lower voltage, in the case of such elements as doorbells or intercom units, and to a higher voltage for *fluorescent* and *HID* lighting units.

TRAP In plumbing, a curved section of pipe that connects a fixture to a drain. The trap permanently holds water, thus forming a seal that prevents sewer gases from escaping back into a bathroom.

TREAD The horizontal step surface of a stair.

TRIAD COLOR A color scheme using three hues equally spaced on a color wheel.

TROMPE L'OEIL Painting on a flat surface that gives an illusion of three-dimensional reality.

TRUSS A structural framework made up of triangles that span wide spaces, supporting a floor or roof. Trusses may be of wood, steel, or a combination of these.

TUNGSTEN-HALOGEN LIGHT A recently developed *incandescent* light source that uses *metal halides* in compact, highly efficient *HID* bulbs, tubes, or reflectors. Because they generate a great deal of heat, halogen *lamps* require specially designed fixtures.

TURNING A round element, usually of wood, produced on a lathe.

UNDERCUT A clearance at floor level that is larger than normal, created by shortening a door to permit air in an *HVAC* system to return along corridors.

UNIVERSAL DESIGN The design of objects, interiors, and buildings to permit convenient and safe use by all users, regardless of body size, age, or physical disabilities.

UPLIGHT Light directed upward toward ceilings or the upper sections of walls. The term is also used to describe floor lamps, or torchères, that cast all light upward.

VALANCE A short drapery concealing the tops of curtains. The term also describes any trim, of drapery or other material, hanging from an edge.

VALUE The lightness or darkness of a color in relation to a scale of grays ranging from black to white. Light values are *tints,* dark values, *shades.*

VAULT An arched roof or ceiling masonry construction. A barrel vault derives from the horizontal extension of an arch, a groin vault from the intersection of two arches.

VDT (VIDEO DISPLAY TERMINAL) The keyboard and *CRT* screen unit used to control a computer.

VEILING REFLECTION Glare produced by the reflection of a light source off a glossy surface.

VENEER Wood (or other material) cut in very thin sheets for use as a surface material (face veneer), usually of fine quality, or as a component layer of *plywood.*

VENT An air inlet. In plumbing, a vent connects to a drainpipe just beyond each *trap,* to prevent suction from removing water from the trap and to provide an outlet for gases into the open air.

VERNACULAR DESIGN Design developed traditionally without professional participation.

WAINSCOT A surface treatment of the lower part of an interior wall.

WALLBOARD A thin, manufactured sheet material used in the construction of interior walls and ceilings. The term is often used interchangeably with plasterboard or Sheetrock (a trade name).

WALL-WASHER A ceiling-mounted, adjustable lighting fixture that directs light sideways toward an adjacent wall, which is thus washed with more or less uniform light.

WELT A thin tube or cord of fabric used as a decorative trim and reinforcement along the edge of a cushion or other upholstery element.

WERKSTÄTTE Design- and craft-oriented studios and workshops active in Vienna in the late nineteenth and early twentieth centuries.

WORKSTATION Any of several systems of office furniture and equipment, often incorporating screens or other partitions to provide some degree of enclosure and privacy.

BIBLIOGRAPHY
Many of the books listed under the heading "General" may be consulted for information on specific topics.

GENERAL

Abercrombie, Stanley. *Architecture as Art*. New York: Harper & Row, 1985.

——. *A Philosophy of Interior Design*. New York: Harper & Row, 1990.

Ballast, David K. *Interior Design Reference Manual*. Belmont, Calif.: Professional Publications, 1992.

Bayley, Stephen, ed. *Conran Directory of Design*. New York: Random House, Villard Books, 1985.

Brown, Erica. *Sixty Years of Interior Design*. New York: Viking Press, 1982.

Ching, Francis. *Interior Design Illustrated*. New York: Van Nostrand Reinhold, 1987.

Conran, Terence. *New House Book*. New York: Random House, Villard Books, 1985.

Diamonstein, Barbaralee. *Interior Design*. New York: Rizzoli International, 1982.

Dreyfuss, Henry. *Designing for People*. New York: Simon & Schuster, 1955.

Faulkner, Ray, et al. *Inside Today's Home*. 5th ed. New York: Holt, Rinehart & Winston, 1986.

Friedmann, Arnold, John F. Pile, and Forrest Wilson. *Interior Design: An Introduction to Architectural Interiors*. 3d ed. New York: Elsevier, 1982.

Garner, Philippe. *Contemporary Decorative Arts*. New York: Facts on File, 1980.

Jencks, Charles, and William Chaitkin. *Architecture Today*. New York: Harry N. Abrams, 1982.

Kilmer, Rosemary, and W. Otie Kilmer. *Designing Interiors*. Fort Worth: Harcourt Brace Jovanovich College Publishers, 1992.

Kurtich, John, and Garret Eakin. *Interior Architecture*. New York: Van Nostrand Reinhold, 1993.

Mumford, Lewis. *Technics and Civilization*. New York: Harcourt, Brace and Co., 1943.

Ozenfant, Amédée. *Foundations of Modern Art*. Translated by John Rodker. Reprint. New York: Dover Publications, 1952.

Rasmussen, Steen Eiler. *Experiencing Architecture*. Translated by E. Wendt. Cambridge, Mass.: MIT Press, 1962.

Sparke, Penny. *An Introduction to Design and Culture in the Twentieth Century*. New York: Harper & Row, 1986.

Tate, Allen, and C. Ray Smith. *Interior Design in the 20th Century*. New York: Harper & Row, 1986.

Venturi, Robert. *Complexity and Contradiction in Architecture*. New York: Museum of Modern Art, 1966.

Weale, Mary Jo, et al. *Environmental Interiors*. New York: Macmillan, 1982.

Whiton, Sherrill. *Interior Design and Decoration*. 4th ed. New York: Harper & Row, 1974.

DESIGN QUALITY

Deasy, C. M., and Laswell Thomas. *Designing Places for People*. New York: Whitney Library of Design, 1985.

Kaufmann, Edgar, Jr. *What Is Modern Design?* New York: Museum of Modern Art, Simon & Schuster, 1950.

——. *Introduction to Modern Design: What Is Modern Design & What Is Modern Interior Design*. Salem, N.H.: Ayer Company Pubs., 1953. Reprint. New York: Museum of Modern Art Publication in Reprint Series, 1970.

Kepes, Gyorgy, ed. *The Man-Made Object*. New York: George Braziller, 1966.

Lynes, Russell. *The Tastemakers*. New York: Harper & Bros., 1954. Reprint. New York: Dover, 1980.

Museum of Modern Art. *Machine Art*. New York: Museum of Modern Art, 1934. Reprint. New York: Arno, 1969.

Papanek, Victor. *Design for Human Scale*. New York: Van Nostrand Reinhold, 1983.

——. *Design for the Real World*. New York: Pantheon Books, 1971.

Pile, John F. *Design: Purpose, Form, and Meaning*. Amherst, Mass.: University of Massachusetts Press, 1979. Pap. New York: W. W. Norton, 1982.

Read, Herbert. *Art and Industry*. London: Faber & Faber, 1934.

DESIGN BASICS

Arnheim, Rudolph. *Art and Visual Perception*. Berkeley, Calif.: University of California Press, 1960.

De Sausmarez, Maurice. *Basic Design: The Dynamics of Visual Form*. New York: Van Nostrand Reinhold, 1983.

Doczi, György. *The Power of Limits*. Boulder, Colo.: Shambhala, 1981.

Huntley, H. E. *The Divine Proportion*. New York: Dover Publications, 1970.

Itten, Johannes. *Design and Form*. New York: Van Nostrand Reinhold, 1964.

Kepes, Gyorgy. *Language of Vision*. Chicago: Paul Theobold, 1944.

DESIGN HISTORY

GENERAL

Adelmann, Jan Ernst. *Vienna Moderne, 1898–1918*. New York/Houston: Cooper-Hewitt Museum/ Sarah Campbell Blaffer Gallery, 1978.

Ball, Victoria Kloss. *Architecture and Interior Design: Europe and America from the Colonial Era to Today*. 2 vols. New York: John Wiley & Sons, 1980.

——. *The Art of Interior Design*. 2d ed. New York: John Wiley & Sons, 1982.

Banham, Reyner. *Theory and Design in the First Machine Age*. New York: Praeger, 1960.

Clark, Robert Judson. *Design in America: The Cranbrook Vision: 1925–1950*. New York: Harry N. Abrams, 1983.

Copplestone, Trewin, ed. *World Architecture*.

London: Hamlyn, 1963.

Drexler, Arthur, ed. *The Architecture of the École des Beaux-Arts*. New York: Museum of Modern Art, 1977.

Eidelberg, Martin, ed. *Design 1935–1965: What Modern Was*. New York: Harry N. Abrams, 1991.

Ferebee, Ann. *A History of Design from the Victorian Era to the Present*. New York: Van Nostrand Reinhold, 1970.

Fitch, James Marston. *American Building*. 2d ed., rev. and enl. Boston: Houghton Mifflin, 1966.

Fletcher, Sir Banister. *A History of Architecture on the Comparative Method*. 19th ed. Edited by John Musgrove. London: Butterworth, 1987.

Gere, Charlotte. *Nineteenth-Century Decoration: The Art of the Interior*. New York: Harry N. Abrams, 1989.

Giedion, Sigfried. *Space, Time and Architecture*. Cambridge, Mass.: Harvard University Press, 1941.

Heyer, Paul. *American Architecture*. New York: Van Nostrand Reinhold, 1993.

Hiesinger, Kathryn B., and George H. Marens, eds. *Design Since 1945*. Philadelphia: Philadelphia Museum of Art, 1983.

Hine, Thomas. *Populuxe*. New York: Alfred A. Knopf, 1986.

Kouwenhoven, John A. *Made in America: The Arts in Modern American Civilization*. Rev. ed. Garden City, N.Y.: Doubleday, 1962.

Lucie-Smith, Edward. *A History of Industrial Design*. New York: Van Nostrand Reinhold, 1983.

McCorquodale, Charles. *A History of Interior Decoration*. New York: Vendome Press, 1983.

McFadden, David. *Scandinavian Modern Design*. New York: Harry N. Abrams, 1982.

Pevsner, Nikolaus. *High Victorian Design*. London: Architectural Press, 1951.

——. *Outline of European Architecture*. New York: Penguin Books, 1943.

——. *Pioneers of Modern Design from William Morris to Walter Gropius*. 2d ed. New York: Museum of Modern Art, 1949. Rev. ed. Harmondsworth, Eng.: Penguin Books, 1960.

——. *The Sources of Modern Architecture Design*. New York: Praeger, 1968.

Phillips, Lisa, ed. *High Styles: Twentieth-Century American Design*. New York: Whitney Museum of American Art and Summit Books, 1985.

Pile, John. *Dictionary of 20th-Century Design*. New York: Facts on File, 1990.

Praz, Mario. *An Illustrated History of Furnishing*. New York: George Braziller, 1964.

Schaefer, Herwin. *Nineteenth Century Modern*. New York: Praeger, 1970.

Schönberger, Angela, ed. *Raymond Loewy: Pioneer of American Industrial Design*. Munich: Prestel Verlag, 1990.

Smith, C. Ray. *A History of Interior Design in 20th*

Century America. New York: Harper & Row, 1987.

Thornton, Peter. *The Italian Renaissance Interior: 1400–1600.* New York: Harry N. Abrams, 1991.

Trachtenberg, Marvin, and Isabelle Hyman. *Architecture from Prehistory to Post-Modernism.* New York: Harry N. Abrams, 1986.

Varnedoe, Kirk. *Vienna 1900: Art, Architecture and Design.* New York: Museum of Modern Art, 1986.

Wiffen, Marcus, and Frederick Koerper. *American Architecture, 1607–1976.* 2 vols. Cambridge, Mass.: MIT Press, 1981.

ART DECO

Bush, Donald J. *The Streamlined Decade.* New York: George Braziller, 1975.

Sembach, Klaus-Jürgen. *Style 1930.* New York: Universe Books, 1971.

ART NOUVEAU

Amaya, Mario. *Art Nouveau.* New York: Dutton, 1960.

Brunhammer, Yvonne, et al. *Art Nouveau Belgium/France.* Houston: Institute for the Arts, Rice University, 1976.

Rheims, Maurice. *The Flowering of Art Nouveau.* New York: Harry N. Abrams, 1966.

Selz, Peter, and Mildred Constantine, eds. *Art Nouveau.* New York: Museum of Modern Art, 1960.

ARTS & CRAFTS MOVEMENT

Cathers, David M. *Furniture of the American Arts and Crafts Movement.* New York: New American Library, 1981.

Volpe, Tod M., and Beth Cathers. *Treasures of the American Arts and Crafts Movement 1890–1920.* New York: Harry N. Abrams, 1988.

BAUHAUS

Naylor, Gillian. *The Bauhaus.* New York: Dutton, 1968.

———. *The Bauhaus Reassessed.* New York: E.P. Dutton, 1985.

Whitford, Frank. *Bauhaus.* New York: Oxford University Press, 1984.

Wingler, Hans. *The Bauhaus.* Cambridge, Mass.: MIT Press, 1969.

MARCEL BREUER

Wilk, Christopher. *Marcel Breuer, Furniture and Interiors.* New York: Museum of Modern Art, 1981.

DE STIJL

Baljeu, Joost. *Theo Van Doesburg.* New York: Macmillan, 1974.

Jaffé, Hans L. C. *De Stijl, 1917–1931.* New York: Harry N. Abrams, 1967.

Overy, Paul. *De Stijl.* New York: Dutton, 1968.

CHARLES AND RAY EAMES

Drexler, Arthur. *Charles Eames: Furniture from the Design Collection.* New York: Museum of Modern Art, 1973.

Neuhart, John, Marilyn Neuhart, and Ray Eames. *Eames Design: The Work of the Office of Charles and Ray Eames.* New York: Harry N. Abrams, 1989.

EILEEN GRAY

Adam, Peter. *Eileen Gray.* New York: Harry N. Abrams, 1987.

WALTER GROPIUS

Fitch, James Marston. *Walter Gropius.* New York: George Braziller, 1960.

Giedion, Sigfried. *Walter Gropius.* New York: Reinhold, 1954.

HECTOR GUIMARD

Graham, F. Lanier. *Hector Guimard.* New York: Museum of Modern Art, 1970.

Rheims, Ferré. *Hector Guimard.* New York: Harry N. Abrams, 1988.

HIGH TECH

Kron, Joan, and Suzanne Slesin. *High Tech.* New York: Clarkson N. Potter, 1978.

JOSEF HOFFMANN

Sekler, Eduard F. *Josef Hoffmann: The Architectural Work.* Princeton, N.J.: Princeton University Press, 1985.

LE CORBUSIER (CHARLES-ÉDOUARD JEANNERET)

Besset, Maurice. *Who Was Le Corbusier.* Translated by Robin Kemball. Cleveland, Ohio: World Publishing Co., 1968.

Blake, Peter. *Le Corbusier.* Baltimore: Penguin Books, 1964.

Le Corbusier. *1929 Sitzmöbel.* Zürich: Galerie Heidi Weber, 1959.

———. *Towards a New Architecture.* Translated by Frederick Etchells. London: The Architectural Press, 1927. Reprint. New York: Praeger, 1970.

LOUIS I. KAHN

Brownlee, David B., and David G. De Long. *Louis I. Kahn: In the Realm of Architecture.* New York: Rizzoli, 1991.

ADOLF LOOS

Rukschio, Burkhardt, and Roland Schachel. *Adolf Loos.* Salzburg and Vienna: Residenz Verlag, 1982.

CHARLES RENNIE MACKINTOSH

Barnes, H. Jefferson. *Some Examples of Furniture by Charles Rennie Mackintosh in the Glasgow School of Art Collection.* Glasgow: Glasgow School of Art, 1969.

Howorth, Thomas. *Charles Rennie Mackintosh and the Modern Movement.* New York: Wittenborn, 1953.

MEMPHIS

Horn, Richard. *Memphis.* Philadelphia: Running Press, 1985.

Radice, Barbara. *Memphis.* New York: Rizzoli International, 1984.

LUDWIG MIES VAN DER ROHE

Blaser, Werner. *Mies van der Rohe—Furniture and Interiors.* London: Academy Editions, 1982.

Glaeser, Ludwig. *Ludwig Mies van der Rohe: Furniture and Furniture Drawings.* New York: Museum of Modern Art, 1977.

Tegethoff, Wolf. *Mies van der Rohe: The Villas and Country Houses.* New York: Museum of Modern Art, 1985.

WILLIAM MORRIS

Clark, Fiona. *William Morris: Wallpapers and Chintzes.* New York: St. Martin's Press, 1973.

Day, Lewis F. *Decorative Art of William Morris and His Work.* London: H. Virtue and Co., 1899.

Morris, William. *Selected Writings and Designs.* Edited by Asa Briggs. Baltimore: Penguin Books, 1962.

Parry, Linda. *William Morris Textiles.* New York: Viking Press, 1983.

Wilhide, Elizabeth. *William Morris: Decor and Design.* New York: Harry N. Abrams, 1991.

POST-MODERNISM AND DECONSTRUCTIVISM

Johnson, Philip, and Mark Wigley. *Deconstructivist Architecture.* New York: Museum of Modern Art, 1988.

Klotz, Heinrich. *Postmodern Visions.* New York: Abbeville Press, 1985.

SHAKER DESIGN

Andrews, Edward Deming. *Religion in Wood: A Book of Shaker Furniture.* 2d ed. New Haven, Conn.: Yale University Press, 1939.

Rieman, Timothy, and Jean M. Burks. *The Complete Book of Shaker Furniture.* New York: Harry N. Abrams, 1993.

THONET

Wilk, Christopher. *Thonet: 150 Years of Furniture.* Woodbury, N.Y.: Barron's, 1980.

LOUIS COMFORT TIFFANY

Couldrey, Vivienne. *The Art of Louis Comfort Tiffany.* Secaucus, N.J.: Wellfleet Press, 1989.

Duncan, Alastair, et al. *Masterworks of Louis Comfort Tiffany.* New York: Harry N. Abrams, 1989.

HENRI VAN DE VELDE

Osthaus, Karl Ernst. *Van de Velde.* Hagen: Folkwang Verlag, 1920.

FRANK LLOYD WRIGHT

Gill, Brendan. *Many Masks: A Life of Frank Lloyd Wright.* New York: G.P. Putnam, 1987.

Hitchcock, Henry-Russell. *In the Nature of Materials.* New York: Duell, Sloan and Pearce, 1942.

Wright, Frank Lloyd. *An Autobiography.* New York: Green and Co., 1932.

THE DESIGN PROCESS

Shoshkes, Ellen. *The Design Process.* New York: Whitney Library of Design, 1989.

PLANNING

American Institute of Architects. *Architectural Graphic Standards.* 8th ed. Edited by Charles G. Ramsey and Harold R. Sleeper. New York: John Wiley & Sons, 1988.

Callender, John Hancock, ed. *Time-Saver Standards for Architectural Design Data.* 6th ed. New York: McGraw-Hill, 1986.

DeChiara, Joseph, Julius Panero, and Martin Zelnik.

Time-Saver Standards for Interior Designers. New York: McGraw-Hill, 1992.

HUMAN FACTORS AND SOCIAL RESPONSIBILITY

Bennett, Corwin. *Spaces for People.* Englewood Cliffs, N.J.: Prentice-Hall, 1977.

Diffrient, Niels, et al. *Humanscale One–Two–Three.* Cambridge, Mass.: MIT Press, 1974.

———. *Humanscale Four–Five–Six.* Cambridge, Mass.: MIT Press, 1981.

Gutman, Robert, ed. *People and Buildings.* New York: Basic Books, 1971.

Hall, Edward T. *The Hidden Dimension.* Garden City, N.Y.: Basic Books, 1971.

———. *The Silent Language.* Garden City, N.Y.: Doubleday, 1959.

Harrigan, J. E. *Human Factors Research.* New York: Elsevier Dutton, 1987.

Lang, Jon, et al. *Designing for Human Behavior.* New York: McGraw-Hill, 1974.

Lee, Terence. *Psychology and the Environment.* London: Methuen, 1976.

Panero, Julius, and Martin Zelnick. *Human Dimensions and Interior Space.* New York: Whitney Library of Design, 1979.

Perin, Constance. *With Man in Mind.* Cambridge, Mass.: MIT Press, 1970.

Proshansky, Harold M., et al., eds. *Environmental Psychology: Man and His Physical Setting.* New York: Holt, Rinehart & Winston, 1970.

Sommer, Robert. *Design Awareness.* San Francisco: Rinehart Press, 1972.

———. *Personal Space.* Englewood Cliffs, N.J.: Prentice-Hall, 1969.

———. *Social Design.* Englewood Cliffs, N.J.: Prentice-Hall, 1983.

———. *Tight Spaces.* Englewood Cliffs, N.J.: Prentice-Hall, 1974.

Sykes, Jane. *Designing Against Vandalism.* New York: Van Nostrand Reinhold, 1980.

MATERIALS AND ELEMENTS

Eiland, Murray L. *Oriental Rugs: A Comprehensive Study.* Greenwich, Conn.: New York Graphic Society, 1973.

Hornbostel, Caleb, and William J. Hornung. *Materials and Methods for Contemporary Construction.* 2d ed. Englewood Cliffs, N.J.: Prentice-Hall, 1982.

Katz, Sylvia. *Plastics.* New York: Harry Abrams, 1944.

Manzinai, Ezio. *The Material of Invention.* Cambridge, Mass: MIT Press, 1989.

Radford, Penny. *Designer's Guide to Surfaces and Finishes.* New York: Watson-Guptill, 1984.

Riggs, J. Rosemary. *Materials and Components of Interior Design.* 2d ed. Englewood Cliffs, N.J.: Prentice-Hall, 1989.

Rupp, William, and Arnold Friedmann. *Construction Materials for Interior Design.* New York: Whitney Library of Design, 1989.

Smith, R. C. *Materials of Construction.* 3rd ed. New York: McGraw-Hill, 1979.

COLOR

Albers, Josef. *Interaction of Color.* New Haven, Conn.: Yale University Press, 1971.

Birren, Faber. *Color and Human Response.* New York: Van Nostrand Reinhold, 1984.

Evans, Ralph M. *An Introduction to Color.* New York: John Wiley & Sons, 1959.

Itten, Johannes. *The Art of Color.* New York: Van Nostrand Reinhold, 1961.

Mahnke, Frank H., and Rudolph H. Mahnke. *Color and Light in Man-Made Environments.* New York: Van Nostrand Reinhold, 1987.

Munsell, A. H. *A Color Notation.* Baltimore, Munsell Color Company, 1981.

Munsell Color Company. *Munsell Book of Color.* Baltimore: Munsell Color Company, 1929.

LIGHTING

Egan, M. David. *Architectural Lighting.* New York: McGraw-Hill, 1983.

Grosslight, Jane. *Light: Effective Use of Daylight and Electric Lighting in Residential and Commercial Projects.* Englewood Cliffs, N.J.: Prentice-Hall, 1984.

Kaufmann, John E., and Jack F. Christensen, eds. *IES Lighting Handbook.* 5th ed. New York: Illuminating Engineering Society, 1972.

Nuckolls, James L. *Interior Lighting for Environmental Designers.* 2d ed. New York: John Wiley & Sons, 1983.

Ott, John. *The Effects of Natural and Artificial Light on Man and Other Living Things.* New York: Pocket Books, 1976.

Phillips, Derek. *Lighting in Architectural Design.* New York: Holt, Rinehart & Winston, 1968.

Rooney, William F. *Practical Guide to Home Lighting.* New York: Van Nostrand Reinhold, 1980.

Smith, Fran Kellogg, and Fred J. Bertolone. *Bringing Interiors to Light.* New York: Whitney Library of Design, 1986.

Sorcar, Pratulla C. *Architectural Lighting for Commercial Interiors.* New York: John Wiley & Sons, 1987.

TEXTILES

Albers, Anni. *On Weaving.* Middletown, Conn.: Wesleyan University Press, 1965.

Hardingham, Martin. *The Fabric Catalog.* New York: Simon & Schuster, Pocket Books, 1978.

Harris, Jennifer, ed. *Textiles, 5,000 Years: An International History and Illustrated Survey.* New York: Harry N. Abrams, 1993.

Hollen, Norman, and Jane Saddler *Textiles.* New York: Macmillan, 1964.

Jackman, Diane, and Mary Dixon. *The Guide to Textiles for Interior Designers,* 2d ed. Winnipeg, Can.: Peguis, 1986.

Larsen, Jack Lenor, and Jeanne Weeks. *Fabrics for Interiors.* New York: Van Nostrand Reinhold, 1975.

Thorpe, Azalea Stuart, and Jack Lenor Larsen. *Elements of Weaving.* New York: Doubleday, 1967.

FURNITURE

Ambasz, Emilio, ed. *Italy: The New Domestic Landscape.* New York: Museum of Modern Art, 1972.

Boger, Louise Ada. *Furniture, Past and Present.* Garden City, N.Y.: Doubleday, 1966.

———. *The Complete Guide to Furniture Styles.* New York: Charles Scribner's Sons, 1969.

Boyce, Charles. *Dictionary of Furniture.* New York: Roundtable Press, 1985.

Bradford, Peter, and Barbara Prete, eds. *Chair.* New York: Peter Bradford & Thos. Y. Crowell, 1978.

Butler, Joseph T. *Field Guide to American Antique Furniture.* New York: Holt, 1986.

Chippendale, Thomas. *The Gentleman & Cabinet-Maker's Director.* Reprint. New York: Dover Publications, 1966.

Emery, Marc. *Furniture by Architects.* New York: Harry N. Abrams, 1983.

Gandy, Charles D., and Susan Zimermann-Stidham, *Contemporary Classics: Furniture of the Masters.* New York: Whitney Library of Design, 1989.

Garner, Philippe. *Twentieth-Century Furniture.* New York: Van Nostrand Reinhold, 1980.

Hanks, David A. *Innovative Furniture in America from 1800 to the Present.* New York: Horizon Press, 1981.

Hepplewhite, George. *The Cabinet-Maker and Upholsterer's Guide.* Reprint. New York: Dover Publications, 1969.

Kaufmann, Edgar, Jr. *Prize Designs for Modern Furniture.* New York: Museum of Modern Art, 1950.

Larrabee, Eric, and Massimo Vignelli. *Knoll Design.* New York: Harry N. Abrams, 1981.

Logie, Gordon. *Furniture from Machines.* London: Allen & Unwin, 1947.

Lucle-Smith, Edward. *Furniture: A Concise History.* London: Thames and Hudson, 1985.

Mang, Karl. *History of Modern Furniture.* New York: Harry N. Abrams, 1979.

Meadmore, Clement. *The Modern Chair.* New York: Van Nostrand Reinhold, 1975.

Noyes, Eliot F. *Organic Design in Home Furnishings.* New York: Museum of Modern Art, 1941. Reprint. New York: Arno Press, 1969.

Ostergard, Derek E., ed. *Bentwood and Metal Furniture 1850–1946.* New York: American Federation of the Arts, 1987.

Page, Marian. *Furniture Designed by Architects.* New York: Whitney Library of Design, 1980.

Pile, John F. *Furniture: Modern and Postmodern.* New York: John Wiley & Sons, 1990.

Russell, Frank, Philippe Garner, and John Read. *A Century of Chair Design.* New York: Rizzoli International, 1980.

Russell, Gordon. *Furniture.* West Drayton, Eng.: Penguin Books, 1947.

Sembach, Klaus-Jürgen. *Contemporary Furniture.* New York: Architectural Book Publishing Co., 1982.

Sheraton, Thomas. *The Cabinet-Maker and Upholster's Drawing Book.* Reprint. New York: Dover Publications, 1972.

Walker Art Center. *Nelson, Eames, Girard, Propst: The Design Process at Herman Miller.* Minneapolis: Walker Art Center, *Design Quarterly* (no. 98/99), 1975.

Wanscher, Ole. *The Art of Furniture.* New York: Reinhold Publishing Corp., 1967.

ACCESSORIES, ART, SIGNAGE

Emmerling, Mary Ellisor. *American Country.* New York: Clarkson N. Potter, 1980.

Furuta, Tok. *Interior Landscaping.* Reston, Va.: Reston Pub. Co., 1983.

Gaines, Richard L. *Interior Plantscaping.* New York: Architectural Record Books, 1977.

McLendon, Charles, and Mick Blackstone. *Signage.* New York: McGraw-Hill, 1982.

TECHNICAL MATTERS

American Society of Heating, Refrigeration and Air-conditioning Engineers. *ASHRAE Handbook of Fundamentals.* New York: ASHRAE, 1981.

Ching, Frances. *Building Construction Illustrated.* New York: Van Nostrand Reinhold, 1975.

Egan, M. David. *Architectural Acoustics.* New York: McGraw-Hill, 1988.

Flynn, John E., A. Segil, and G. Statly. *Architectural Interior Systems.* 2d ed. New York: Van Nostrand Reinhold, 1988.

Loftness, Robert L. *Energy Handbook.* New York: Van Nostrand Reinhold, 1978.

Wilkes, Joseph A., ed. *Encyclopedia of Architecture Design, Engineering and Construction.* New York: John Wiley & Sons, 1988–89.

INTERIOR DESIGN AND SPECIAL NEEDS

American National Standard for Buildings and Facilities Providing Accessibility for Usability for Physically Handicapped People. Washington, D.C., U.S. Department of Housing and Urban Development, 1986.

American National Standards Institute, Inc. *Specifications for Making Buildings and Facilities Accessible To and Usable by Physically Handicapped People.* New York: American National Standards Institute, Inc., 1986.

Goldsmith, Selwyn. *Designing for the Disabled.* 2d ed. New York: McGraw-Hill, 1967.

Harkness, S., and J. Groom. *Building Without Barriers for the Disabled.* New York: Whitney Library of Design, 1976.

Kearney, Deborah. *The New ADA: Compliance and Costs.* Kingston, Mass.: R. S. Means, 1993.

Leibrock, Cynthia. *Beautiful Barrier Free: A Visual Guide to Accessibility.* New York: Van Nostrand Reinhold, 1992.

Minimum Guidelines and Requirements for Accessible Design. Washington, D.C.: U.S. Architectural and Transportation Barriers Compliance Board, 1982.

Raschko, Bettyann. *Housing Interiors for the Disabled and Elderly.* New York: Van Nostrand Reinhold, 1982.

U.S. Department of the Interior. *The Secretary of the Interior's Standards for Rehabilitation and Guidelines for Rehabilitating Historic Buildings.* Washington, D.C.: U.S. Department of the Interior, National Park Service, 1979.

KITCHENS, BATHROOMS, STORAGE

Brett, James. *The Kitchen: 100 Solutions to Design Problems.* New York: Whitney Library of Design, 1977.

Conran, Terence. *The Bed and Bath Book.* New York: Crown, 1978.

———. *The Kitchen Book.* New York: Crown, 1977.

Kira, Alexander. *The Bathroom.* 2d ed. New York: Viking Press, 1976.

Nelson, George, ed. *Storage.* New York: Whitney Library of Design, 1954.

Wise, Herbert. *Kitchen Detail.* New York: Quick Fox, 1980.

SPECIAL-PURPOSE SPACES

Insall, Donald W. *The Care of Old Buildings Today.* London: The Architectural Press, 1972.

Kramer, Jack. *Garden Rooms and Greenhouses.* New York: Harper & Row, 1972.

Slesin, Suzanne, et al. *The International Book of Lofts.* New York: Clarkson N. Potter, 1986.

Tresidder, Jane, and Stafford Cliff. *Living Under Glass.* New York: Clarkson N. Potter, 1986.

PUBLIC INTERIORS

Backus, Harry. *Designing Restaurant Interiors.* New York: Lebhar-Friedman, 1977.

Harris, David A., et al. *Planning and Designing the Office Environment.* New York: Van Nostrand Reinhold, 1981.

Ketchum, Morris. *Shops and Stores.* New York: Reinhold, 1957.

Klein, Judy Graf. *The Office Book.* New York: Facts on File, 1982.

Mazzurco, Philip. *Media Design.* New York: Quarto, 1984.

Pile, John. *Open Office Planning.* New York: Whitney Library of Design, 1978.

Pulgram, William L., and Richard E. Stonis. *Designing the Automated Office.* New York: Whitney Library of Design, 1984.

Rutes, Walter A., and Richard H. Penner. *Hotel Planning and Design.* New York: Whitney Library of Design, 1985.

PROFESSIONAL DESIGN/BUSINESS MATTERS

ASID Professional Practice Manual. Edited by Jo Ann Asher Thompson. New York: Whitney Library of Design, 1992.

Ballast, David Kent. *Practical Guide to Computer Applications for Architecture and Design.* Englewood Cliffs, N.J.: Prentice-Hall, 1986.

Ching, Frank. *Architectural Graphics.* New York: Van Nostrand Reinhold, 1975.

Diekman, Norman, and John F. Pile. *Drawing Interior Architecture.* New York: Whitney Library of Design, 1983.

———. *Sketching Interior Architecture.* New York: Whitney Library of Design, 1985.

Haviland, David, ed. *Handbook of Professional Practice.* New York: A.I.A., 1988.

Hornung, William J. *Architectural Drafting.* 4th ed. Englewood Cliffs, N.J.: Prentice-Hall, 1966.

Interior Design Educators Council. *Interior Design As a Profession.* Richmond, Va.: IDEC, 1983.

Kennedy, E. Lee. *CAD Drawing, Design, Data Management.* New York: Whitney Library of Design, 1986.

Knackstedt, Mary U. *The Interior Design Business Handbook.* New York: Whitney Library of Design, 1988.

Morgan, Jim. *Marketing for the Small Design Firm.* New York: Whitney Library of Design, 1984.

Murphy, Dennis Grant. *The Business Management of Interior Design.* North Hollywood, Calif.: Stratford House Publishing Co., 1988.

National Council for Interior Design Qualification. *NCIDQ Examination Guide.* New York: National Council for Interior Design Qualification, 1994.

Pile, John F. *Perspective for Interior Designers.* New York: Whitney Library of Design, 1985.

Piotrowski, Christine M. *Professional Practice for Interior Designers.* New York: Van Nostrand Reinhold, 1988.

Ratensky, Alexander. *Drawing and Modelmaking.* New York: Whitney Library of Design, 1983.

Reznikoff, S. C. *Interior Graphic and Design Standards.* New York: Whitney Library of Design, 1986.

———. *Specifications for Commercial Interiors.* New York: Whitney Library of Design, 1979.

Rose, Stuart W. *Achieving Excellence in Your Design Practice.* New York: Whitney Library of Design, 1987.

Siegel, Harry, and Alan M Siegel. *A Guide to Business Principles and Practices for Interior Designers.* Rev. ed. New York: Watson-Guptill, 1982.

Staebler, Wendy W. *Architectural Detailing in Contract Interiors.* New York: Whitney Library of Design, 1988.

Teicholz, Eric. *CAD/CAM Handbook.* New York: McGraw-Hill, 1985.

Wakita, Osamu A., and Richard M. Linde. *Professional Handbook of Architectural Working Drawings.* New York: John Wiley & Sons, 1984.

Wallach, Paul I., and Donald E. Hepler. *Reading Construction Drawings.* New York: McGraw-Hill, 1981.

Wright, Lawrence. *Perspective on Perspective.* London: Routledge and Kegan Paul, 1983.

PERIODICALS

Abitare (Milan)

American Craft (New York)

Architectural Record (New York)

Designers West (Los Angeles)

Domus (Milan)

Interior Design (New York)

Interiors (New York)

Progressive Architecture (Stamford, Conn.)

Restaurant and Hotel Design (New York)

28–29; hardware for, *380*; in historic interiors, 493–95; historic styles of, 358, 382–89; importance of, in Western world, 349; indoor-outdoor, 485; joints, 377; knockdown, 355–57; low-cost, 355–57; materials and construction, 357, 373–82, 487; medieval, 71; modern, 111, 493–95; modular, 355–57; newly purchased vs. reused, 351; outdoor, 485, *485*, 487; planning of, 349–51; quality of, 373, 376, 377–79; reproductions and imitations of, 385–87, 493; safety considerations, 195, 357; scale models of, 170; selection of, 103, *104*, 107, 351–58; showrooms, *27*; sources of purchase, 355–57; specially designed vs. ready-made, 352–54; standards for, 372; strength of, testing, 382. *See also specific rooms,* e.g. bedrooms; *specific styles,* e.g. American Colonial style; *specific types,* e.g. chairs
furniture manufacturers, planning units of, 531–32
furniture placement, 158, 351; checklist for, 169; drawings for, 170, *170, 172, 172–173, 534*; levels of mobility, 169–73; plan of, *490*; on plan drawings, *135, 137*; safety considerations, 193
furniture symbols, Appendix 2
furred (hung) ceilings, 250, 414
furs, 257
futons, 369

gabardine, 340
Gabriel, Ange-Jacques, 83, 86, *87*
galleries, 506; in the home, *93*
Gallery Tom (Tokyo), *431*
garages: safety considerations, 195; size of, 158
garden city, 196
Garden Party Collection, *345*
Garden State Racetrack, Phoenix Level Restaurant (Cherry Hill, N.J.), *467*
Garnier, Charles, 101
gas fuel, 415
Gaudí, Antonio, 98
Gehry, Frank O., 118, *171*, 240, 251, 268, 386, *389*; *See also* Frank O. Gehry & Associates
general lighting, 325
Gensler and Associates/Architects, *222, 502*
George, Philip, 53
George Kovacs Lighting, *321, 325*
Georgian style, 85, 120
Georgis, William T., *136*
geothermal heat, 415
Gerritsen, Frans, color system, 266, *266*
GHI Architects, *434*
Gilbert, Sidney, *433*
gingham, 332, 340
Gismondi, Ernesto, *326*
Giulio Romano, 77–78
glare, 306, *306*; dealing with, 298
Glaser, Milton, 53, *159*
glass, 204, 205, 207, 215, 257; building code requirements, 427; ceilings, 251, *456*, 485; doors, *193, 225, 233*; for furniture, 485; light- and heat-controlling, 300; partitions, 226; safety considerations, 193, 195, 464; special types of, 215; walls, *217*, 485; windows, 234, 485
glass block, 226, *226*
glass fabric, 346
glass fibers, 338
Glass House (New Canaan, Conn.), 111–13, *112*
glazing, multiple, in window glass, 300
globe lamps, 316–17, *317, 322*

gloss enamels, 229
glues, for wood, 209
Goethe, Johann Wolfgang von, 264, 266
Gold, Charles, *447*
golden ratio, 54, 55, 62, 66
Goldman, Sachs & Co., *192*
Gothic art, 71–74; architecture, 11–12, 49, 62, 71–74, *75*, 126, 210; furniture, 74, *75*, 382, *383*; influence of, 89, 92
Gothic Revival style, 90–92
government buildings, interior design of, 513
grab bars, *439*
granite, 210, 240
Granvelle, Christian, *268*
graphic design, 409; symbols, 408–9, *408*
graphics, 254
grass cloth, 332
grass fibers, 338
Graves, Michael, 116, *253*
Grawunder, Johanna, *63*
gray axis, 282
Gray, Eileen, *17*, 111, *464, 472*
gray scale, 265
Greater Columbus (Ohio) Convention Center, *509*
Great Exhibition of 1851 (London), 94, 97
Great Mosque (Damascus), *126, 127*
Greek art, 67–69, 89; architecture, 67–68, 90; furniture, *90*
Greek Revival style, 89–90, *90, 92*
green, psychological associations with, 270
Greenbelt, Md., planned community, 197
Greene (Charles) and Greene (Henry), *96, 97*
greenhouses, 484
Gregotti, Vittorio, *254*
grid plans, 167
grilles, ventilation, *417*
Grinstein Daniels, *307*
Gropius, Walter, 100, 105, 106, *106*, 111
Grotta House (N. J.), *21*
Guarini, Guarino, 82
Guggenheim Museum. *See* Solomon R. Guggenheim Museum
Guimard, Hector, 97
Gwathmey, Charles, 113
Gwathmey Siegel & Associates, *227, 354, 463, 471, 506*
gymnasiums, interior design of, 525
gypsum block, 205, 206, 226

Haas, Richard, *324*
Hackley School, Kaskell Library (Tarrytown, N.Y.), *294*
Hadid, Zaha, 358
Hadley, Albert, 35
Hagia Sophia (Constantinople), 71, *72*, 127
Hagmann Mitchell Architects, *235*
half-timber construction, 71–74, *76*, 204
Hall, Denise A., *523, 524*
Hall, Edward T., 63, 186
hallways, 181, *369*
halogen lighting, 309
Hampstead Garden Suburb, 196
Hampton, Mark, *42, 46*, 229, 276, *363*, 487, *516*
Hanajuban Restaurant (Tokyo), *319*
Hancock Shaker Village (Mass.), 98
handcraft, 92, 97
handicapped. *See* disabled
Handkerchief stacking chair, *364*

hanging lighting fixtures, *322, 325*; classification of, 321–22
Hann, Marlys, *211, 418*
hardboard, 205, 208
Hardouin-Mansart, Jules, 82
hardware, 254, *254, 380, 381*; locking, 424
Hardwick Hall (England), 84, *84*
hardwoods, 205, 206, 208, 373, 378; endangered species, 258; environmental issues, 257
Hardy Holzman Pfeiffer Associates, *411*
harmony, as design concept, 54
Harris, Harwell Hamilton, 280
Harry Weese Associates, *495, 527*
Hasbrouck, J. M., 358
Hastings, Thomas, *513*
Hatkin, Naomi, *434*
Hayes, Thad, *366*
health: interior design and, 23–24, 193–94, 293, 314, 393; materials hazardous to, 193–94
healthcare facilities: color schemes for, 285–86; furniture for, 370; interior design of, 433, 513–16; lighting for, 308–9; patients' needs, design for, 436, 516. *See also* hospitals
hearing impaired, design for, 437
heat, ventilation, and air-conditioning (HVAC), 250, 251, 256, 411–15; energy consumption of, 415; plans of (layout), 415, 535
heaters, portable, 411
heating: physics of, 411–12, *412*; systems, 412–14, 418
heating stoves, 252
heat pumps, 415
Heller Designs, *460*
Hell's Angel chair, *50*
Helmich, Pamela, *434*
Helmsley Palace (New York City), *521*
Henry Dreyfuss Associates, *408*
Hepplewhite, George, 86, *86*, 383
Hering, Ewald, 266
Herman Miller, Inc., 35, *222*
herringbone, 340, *341*
Herring/Newman offices (Seattle), *497*
hickory, 208
Hicks, David, *342*
HID (high-intensity discharge) lighting, 279–80, 309, 312, 313, 314
Hidden Dimension, The (Hall), 63, 186
high-pressure sodium HID lights, 312, 314
High Tech style, 113–14, *116*, 250, 411, *455*, 500, 524
Hildebrandt, Johann Lukas von, *81*
Hilton Hotel (Los Angeles), Cardini restaurant, *152*
Himmel, Richard, *248, 298*
Hints on Household Taste (Eastlake), 97
Hirsch/Bedner & Associates, *526*
Hirsheimer, Jim and Christopher, *456*
historic interiors: furniture, 352, 493–95; lighting, 328; textiles, *331*
historic preservation, 429, 489–97, *497*
historic styles: of architecture, 489; decorators' use of, 16; of furniture, 358, 382–89, *383*, 493–95; mixed (eclectic), 58; quoting of, 116
Hodgetts + Fung Design Associates, *220*
Hodgkins, William, *434*
Hodsoll, Christopher, *403*
Hoechst Celanese, *345*
Hoffmann, Josef, 98, 100, *235*, 341, 354, 469
Holl, Steven, 39

McLaughlin, John, *21*

McMillen, Inc., *290*

Mead, Chris, *238*

mechanical drawing (drafting), 534

mechanical engineering, 20, 535

mechanical systems, 411–21

media rooms, 170, 171, *174*, 482, *482*; furniture in, 369; noise control in, *422*. See also family rooms

Medical Innovations, *364*

medical offices, 513, *516*. See also healthcare facilities

medieval art, 71–74, *75*, 280

meeting rooms, 504

Meier, Richard, *21*, 113, *114*

melamines, 217

Meltzer, Abraham, *425*

memo squares, *334*, 335

Memphis style, *28*, 116, *242*, 371, 386, 500

Merchant & Main Bar & Grill (Vacaville, Calif.), *253*

mercury, 194

mercury lamps, 313

mercury vapor HID lights, 312, *313*, 314

metal, 204, 205, 206, 213–15; ceilings, 251; color affected by, 277; doors, 233; fibers, 338, 345, 347; finishes for, 377; furniture, 377–79, 485; interior use of, 215; in kitchens, 453–55; structural use of, 213–15

metal chain drapery, *236*

metal halide HID lamps, 312, 314

metopes, *68*

metric equivalents, Appendix 7

Metropolitan Museum of Art (New York City), *27*

Metropolitan Tower (New York City), *50*

Michelangelo, 77

Michelozzo di Bartolomeo, 76

Micromatique fabric, *345*

Middleton Inn (S.C.), *393*

Mies van der Rohe, Ludwig, 100, 106–7, *107*, 111, 147–48, 225, *283*, 377

Millard House, 127

Miller, R. Craig, *27*

millwork, 209

mineral fibers, 338, 346

Minibox swiveling wall lamps, *322*

mirror glass, 215, 227, *227*

mirrors, *464*; effect on space, *174*

Miss Cranston's "The Willow" tearooms (Glasgow), *349*

Mission (Golden Oak) furniture, 97, *203*

Miss Sissi lamp, *318*

Mita Copystar America showroom, *537*

mixed use zoning, 429

Miyawaki, Mayumi, *181*

mobile furniture, *372*, 475

mobiles, 406

mobility impaired, design for, 437

modacrylic, 347

models, *135*, 138, 535; slides and videotaped walk-throughs of, 535

modernism, 100; in architecture, 12–13, 100, 105–8, 386; color schemes associated with, 283; criticism of, 116; early and classic periods, 387; in furniture, 111, *385*, 387, 493–95; Japanese influence on, 126; Late, 113; meaning of term, 384; postwar, 111–13

modular furniture, 355–57, 375; seating, 365, 367

modular plans, 167

Modulor system, 53–54, *55*

mohair, *332*, 338, 346

moire, 332

Mondrian, Piet, 105, 282

monk's cloth, 332, 340

monochromatic color schemes, 272, *277*

monofilaments, 336, *337*

monotone (neutral) color schemes, 270, 272, *277*

Monticello (Virginia), 89

Montoya, Juan, *44*, *174*, *233*, *240*

Montreal World's Fair (1967), United States pavilion, 113, *513*

Moon Soon restaurant (Japan), *358*

Moore, Charles, *243*, 445

Moore Ruble Yudell Architects & Planners, *243*, 367

Moorish style, 89, 92

Morphosis, *226*

Morris, William, 94, 96, 97, *229*

Morris chair, 369

Morse, Edward S., 123

mortar, 210

mosaic, 71; tile, *242*

mosques, 126–27

Moss, Eric Owen, 217

motels: accommodations for disabled, 444–45; bathrooms in, 464; color schemes for, 286–87; furniture in, 351, 370, 372; interior design of, 521; storage in, 472

move-in, supervising and evaluation of, 143

Muennig, Mickey, *14*, *220*

multifilaments, 336, *337*

multiples (prints), 402

multiple seating, 365–67

Munsell, Albert color system, 264–66, *282*

murals, 406

Murphy, Brian A., *14*, *321*, *362*, *387*, *463*, *467*

Musée d'Orsay (Paris), *508*

Museum of Modern Art (New York City), 358

museums, 506, *508*; lighting in, *326*, 328

music, piped-in, 424

musical equipment, 392, *401*

music rooms: acoustics in, *425*; and noise control, 423

muslin, 333, 340

Naggar, Patrick, *50*

Naito, Hiroshi, *431*

Naomi Leff and Associates, *13*

Narita Express (Japanese train), *20*

Nash, John, 89, *89*

National Audubon Society headquarters (New York City), 199–201, *199–201*, 303

National Building Code of Canada (NBC), 426

National Council for Interior Design Qualification (NCIDQ), examination, 24–25, 530–31

National Gallery of Art (Washington, D.C.), East Wing, 63, 113, *114*

Native American art, 37, 127, *127*

natural color schemes, 280–82

natural gas, 453

nature, design in, 36–37, *39*

NBBJ Architecture Design Planning, *497*, *515*

NCS (Natural Color System), *267*

Neas, Richard Lowell, *300*

needlepoint, 333

Neoclassical style, 86–90, *86*, *88*

neon lighting, 312

Nessen, Walter von, *321*

netting, 205, 333

Neue Staatsgalerie (Stuttgart), *116*

Neumann, Johann Balthasar, 82

neutral and neutral-plus color schemes, 282–83, *282*

neutral colors, psychological associations with, 271

Newman, Oscar, 193

Newsbar (New York City), *523*

New World Coffee (New York City), *522*, *524*

New York Bar Association, library, *219*

New York Public Library, Gottesman Hall, *513*

New York University: library, *302*; Midtown Center, *324*

Nieto, John, *54*

Noferi, David, *515*

noise: ambient, 424; building code requirements, 427; control of, 421–24; discomfort from, 195

Noise Reduction Coefficients (NRCs), 422

Normandie (ship), 111

Norman Foster Associates, *254*

Notes on the Synthesis of Form (Alexander), 133

Notre-Dame-du-Haut (Ronchamp, France), 107, *109*, 147

nurseries, 372–73

nursing homes, 436, 513

Nutting Apartments for Disabled Persons (Amherst, Mass.), *440*

nylon, 217, 245, 347, 382

oak, 205, 208, 373, 378

occupant load factor, building code requirements, 427

occupants. See users

office furniture systems, 504

office planning, 17. See also space planning

offices: accessories in, 392, 406; artworks in, 399–401, 406; case study, 177–79; circulation routes in, *502*; color schemes for, 283–84; electrical systems in, 371, *419*, 424; expressive of an organization's character, 505; floor plans of, *135*, *161*, *176*; furniture in, *103*, 349–51, 355, 370–72, 377, 504, 505; furniture placement in, *135*, *172*; home (see home offices); interior design of, 372, 502–5; layout of, 503–4; lighting in, *303*, 306–8, 315; noise control in, 421, 423–24; open plan layout (office landscape), 370, 424, 504; privacy in, *231*, 370, 503, *503*, 504; signage and graphics in, 406; size of, 158; space planning of, 155; storage in, 472; traditional layout (with private offices), 503–4

office systems, 370–72, *371*, 375

Offredi, Giovanni, *459*

Ohno, Hidetoshi, *296*, *324*

okoume, 258

oil finish, 379

oil fuel, 415

Olbrich, Josef, 98

Old Hickory Chair Company, 97

olefin, 338, 347

Oliver, Richard B., *445*

one-floor-level living, 433

on-site checks, 154–56

open (free) plans, 167. See also kitchens; offices

open-web joists, 214–15

Opera House (Paris), 101

Opus One Winery (Oakville, Calif.), *248*

Opus Restaurant (Santa Monica, Calif.), *307*

orange, psychological associations with, 270

orders of architecture, classical, 56–57, *68*, *68*, 76

in, 308, 309, *326*; small, design of, *523*
Strasman, Jim, *352*
streamlining, 111
stress: computer usage and, 505; and habitability, 526
structural elements, 203–4; exposed, 250; materials used for, 204–7, 213–15, 220
structural engineering, 20, 535
structure, in design, evaluation of, 34, 41
Stuart, James, 90
Stuart Moore Jewelers (New York City), 308
Stuart sofa, *388*
Stubbs, Del, *21*
stucco, 212
studio apartments, *30*
studios, artists', *300*, 477–79, *478*, *479*
studs, 224, 226
Stumpf, William, *222*
styles. *See* historic styles
styrene, 382
Suarsu, Putu, *217*
subways, *408*, 525, *527*
Sudo, Reiko, *345*
Süe, Louis, *370*
Süleyman I, mosque of (Istanbul), 127
Sullivan, Louis, 100, *100*, 101
sunlight. *See* daylight
Sunnyside Gardens (Queens, N.Y.), 197
super graphics, *409*
surfaces: color affected by, 277; physical attributes of (texture, etc.), 48; treatment of, *18*, 220–22
surveillance systems, 256, 424
surveys, of clients' requirements, 157–58
Sussman & Prejza, *232*
Swaim company, 365
Swanke Hayden Connell Architects, *510*
swatches, 331–35, *334*
Swedish NCS (Natural Color System), 266
swing-arm lamps, *321*
swinging doors, 233
switches: for lights, 329; sound- and proximity-activated, 439
symbols: for furniture, Appendix 2; for materials, Appendix 4
symmetry, 56, *56*, 63
synthetic materials, 205; color of, 280; environmental issues, 259
Syon House (England), 86
systems furniture, 349–51
Szoeke, Andrew, *366*

Taber test, 345
table lamps, 316, *318*, *320*
tables, *361*, *362*; folding, *361*; functional analysis of, 358; selection of, 360
table settings, *399*
TacoMadre restaurant (New York City), 522–24, *523*
taffeta, 333, 340
Taj Mahal (India), 127
Talman, William, *331*
Tange, Kenzo, *126*
tapestry weave, 333, 340
Tapiola (Finland), 197
task-ambient lighting, 306
task lighting, 302–3, *302*, 306, 371
Tatlin, Vladimir, 118
Taylor, Michael, *18*, *273*
teak, 258, 378, 485

Tech Center office complex (San Diego, Calif.), *176*
technological design, 36, 39–41; influence on designers, 113–14
technology, overreliance on, by designers, 185
Tek-Wall, *341*
telephones, wiring for, 424
television, placement of, 170
Telford, Thomas, 94–97
templates, 349, *531*
temples, ancient, 68
Tennessee Valley Authority, power plants, 527, *527*
terraces, 485–89
terra cotta, 205, 212
terrazzo, 206, 240
terry cloth, 333, 340
tête-à-tête couch, *384*
tetrad color schemes, 276, 277, *277*
textile designs, copyrighting of, 343
textiles, 207, 331–47; color of, 280, 331–35, 342–44; color affected by, 277; construction of, 337–40; durability of, *335*, 345, *345*; dyeing of, 342–43, *343*; economic issues, 335–36; fading of, 345; finishes for, 340; fire safety of, 336, 340, *345*, *345*; function of, in interiors, 331, *331*, *338*; natural, 346; printing of, 343, *343*; selection of, 331–36; soil-resistance of, 340; types and uses of, 245, 332–333, 336–47
textile samples, collecting, 331–35, *334*, 344–45
texture, 48; color affected by, 277
Thad Hayes Design, 366
Thaxted Guild Hall (England), *74*, *76*
theaters: accommodations for disabled, 445; acoustics in, 424, *425*; adaptive reuse of, 495–96; furniture in, 370; interior design of, 510–11
Theory and Practice of Color (Gerritsen), 266
thermal shades, 235
thermoplastics, 217
thermosetting plastics, 217
Thonet, Michael, 208
Thonet furniture, *377*
Tibetan rugs, *235*
ticking, 333
Tiffany, Louis Comfort, 100
Tigerman, Stanley, *305*
Tigerman McCurry, architects, *504*
tile, 204, 205, 206, 212, 227, 455; acoustical, 207, *421*; asphalt, 207; color of, 280; for floors, 240, *242*, *243*; for outdoor use, 485; resilient, 455; shapes and patterns of, *213*
Tilghman Gallery (Boca Raton, Fla.), *282*
Times Mirror office (New York City), *231*
tints, 264, *265*, *268*
Tippy Jackson table, *361*
Tizio lamps, *293*
Toile Orientale, *335*
toiles, 335
toilets (water closets), 461
Toledo Collection, *372*
Toltecs, 127
Tomb, Bruce, *362*
Tom Lee Limited, *521*
Tooke, James and Robert, *253*
torchères, 317, *317*
Towards a New Architecture (Le Corbusier), 107
toxic fumes, 259, 382
track lighting, 317, 325, *326*
trading rooms, 505, *510*

traditional design, 37
trains, interiors of, 283, 525
transitional design, 387
transparency, 48
transparent finishes, 230
transportation: terminals, design of, 525–26; vehicles, design of, *20*, 525–26; seating in, 372
traps (plumbing), 420, *420*
travertine, 240
Travis, Jack, *346*
triacetate, 347
triad color schemes, 272–77, *275*
triglyphs, 68
trim, 254
trompe l'oeil, 77, 219, 230, *268*
Trott/Eisenman Architects, *509*
trundle beds, 369
trusses, 204
Tschumi, Bernard, *116*, 119
tubular-metal furniture, 377, *385*
tufted fabrics, 344
tufted rugs, 246
Tugendhat House (Brno, Czechoslovakia), 107, *225*
Tuller, Andrew M., *471*
Tuller-McNealus Architects, *471*
tungsten-halogen lighting, 310, 314; bulbs, *310*
Turett, Wayne, *523*
Turkish window treatment, *236*
Tutankhamen, throne of, 66
Tuthill, William B., *509*
tuxedo sofas, 367
TWA terminal (New York City), 213
tweed, 333
twig furniture, 365, *487*
twill weave, 340, *341*

Ullman, Dr. Johan, *364*
underlayment, 244–46
Uniform Building Code (UBC), 426
Union Station (Washington, D.C.), *495*
United Crafts, 96
United States Child Center (Lemoore, Calif.), *434*
unity, as design concept, 55
universal design, 357, 431–32; economic benefits of, 432
upholstery, 331, *342*, 382, *383*
uplights, 317, *319*, *321*, *322*; wall-mounted, 321
Upper Belvedere Palace (Vienna), *81*, 82
Urasenke Tea Ceremony Society (New York City), *219*
urban sprawl, 196
urethanes, 217
urinals, 467
users: do-it-yourself design by, 12–13, 23, 26–27, 406; participation of, in design process, 187–88, 406; personal possessions of, decorating with, 391–99, *399*, *400*, *402*, 406; of public spaces, 499
use zoning, 429
Usonian Houses project, *149*
utile, 258
utility rooms, evaluation of, for planning, 181

Vallinby (Sweden), 197
value (color), 48, 264
variances, building, 429
Variations bed, *367*
variety, as design concept, 55

ACKNOWLEDGMENTS

The author is indebted to innumerable people and organizations who have contributed ideas, advice, photographs, and other materials to make this book possible.

Thanks are also offered to Norman Diekman; Susan Forbes and Joel Ergas of Forbes-Ergas Design Associates; Philip B. Prigmore, architecture consultant to Alfred University; Kirsten Childs; Lewis Davis; Wayne Turett Collaborative; Denise A. Hall of Denise A. Hall Architects; and Ronnette Riley, Architect, all of whom provided the information and illustrative materials for the case studies.

The many designers, architects, manufacturers, and photographers who have provided information, illustrations, and permission to use material have also made an appreciated contribution to this book.

At Harry N. Abrams, Inc., the efforts of many dedicated editorial and design staff members have been of essential importance to this project. Among these, the author is particularly indebted to Director of Textbook Publishing Julia Moore who, as project director, suggested areas of change to this edition and orchestrated the various elements that are part of a complex book. Editors Cynthia Clark, Kate Norment, and Elisa Urbanelli were exceptionally diligent and tireless in editing text and in coordinating the relationship of words and images. Picture editor Susan Sherman, responsible for the selection and organization of the visual materials that are central to the content of this book, once again made an extraordinary contribution through her special understanding of the ways in which illustration can support the framework of words. Ms. Sherman was ably assisted by photo researcher Colin Scott, who obtained permissions and photographs. Bob McKee, this book's designer, gave graphic form to the combination of words and images with a special skill that makes a totality superior to the sum of its component parts.

John Pile

PHOTO EDITOR'S NOTE

In the course of the lengthy and complex process of putting together *Interior Design*, the publishers have incurred several debts of gratitude.

The formidable task of gathering photographs was immeasurably aided by the patience and generosity of designers and photographers who opened their files to us, especially in this second edition: Tim Street-Porter, Peter Paige, Paul Warchol, Bob Patino, John F. Saladino, Kajima Associates, Inc., and Kent Larson.

The following people and organizations went out of their way to be helpful, and we are indebted to them: Phyllis Fleiss of Crown Publications, Betty Boote of *House Beautiful*, Arabella Mills of *Metropolitan Home* magazine, Diana Edkins of *HG*, Jodi Lahaye of *Elle Decor*, and Marjorie McNaughton of Schumacher.

ILLUSTRATION CREDITS

Our grateful thanks to the many photographers, publications, companies, and individuals, including those mentioned in the picture captions or listed below, who provided us with material and kindly permitted its reproduction.

Fig. 1.17 Copyright Meredith Corporation, 1987. All rights reserved; fig. 2.2 from *Mary Emmerling's American Country West*, Copyright ©1985 by Mary Ellisor Emmerling. Used by permission of Clarkson N. Potter, Inc.; fig. 2.5 Copyright ©1991 by The Conde Nast Publications Inc.; fig. 3.4 Copyright ©1984 by The Conde Nast Publications Inc.; fig. 3.17 from *Mary Emmerling's American Country West*, Copyright ©1985 by Mary Ellisor Emmerling. Used by permission of Clarkson N. Potter, Inc.; fig. 3.36 Reprinted with permission from *Metropolitan Home* Magazine ©1990. Hachette Filipacchi USA Inc.; figs. 4.8, 4.20 from *Andrea Palladio: The Four Books of Architecture*, published by Dover Publications, Inc., New York, 1965; fig. 4.44 Copyright ©1983 by The Conde Nast Publications Inc.; figs. 4.92, 6.18, 6.19, 6.43, 6.53 from *Japanese Style* by Suzanne Slesin, Stafford Cliff, Daniel Rozensztroch, and Gilles de Chabaneix. Copyright ©1987 by Suzanne Slesin, Stafford Cliff, Daniel Rozensztroch, and Gilles de Chabaneix. Reprinted by permission from Crown Publishers, Inc. All rights reserved; fig. 7.22 Adapted from *The Visual Handbook of Building and Remodeling* by Charles G. Wing. Rodale Press, PA. Copyright ©1990 Charles G. Wing; fig. 8.4 from *Interior Graphic and Design Standards* by S. C. Reznikoff. Copyright ©1986 by S. C. Reznikoff. Reproduced by permission of Whitney Library of Design, New York; figs. 8.5B, 8.6B–6D Adapted from *Construction Materials for Interior Design* by William Rupp and Arnold Friedmann. Reproduced by permission of Watson-Guptill Publications. Illustrations copyright © by Philip Farrell; fig. 8.9 Adapted from *The Visual Handbook of Building and Remodeling* by Charles G. Wing. Rodale Press, Pa. Copyright ©1990 Charles G. Wing; fig. 8.10 Adapted from *Construction Materials for Interior Design* by William Rupp and Arnold Friedmann. Reproduced by permission of Watson-Guptill Publications. Illustrations copyright © by Philip Farrell; fig. 8.11 Adapted from *The Visual Handbook of Building and Remodeling* by Charles G. Wing.

Rodale Press, PA. Copyright ©1990 Charles G. Wing; fig. 8.12 Adapted from *Construction Materials for Interior Design* by William Rupp and Arnold Friedmann. Reproduced by permission of Watson-Guptill Publications. Illustrations copyright © by Philip Farrell; fig. 8.22 from *Mary Emmerling's American Country West*, Copyright ©1985 by Mary Ellisor Emmerling. Used by permission of Clarkson N. Potter, Inc.; fig. 8.45 from *Mary Emmerling's American Country West*, Copyright ©1985 by Mary Ellisor Emmerling. Used by permission of Clarkson N. Potter, Inc.; fig. 8.47 from *Caribbean Style*, Copyright ©1985 by Suzanne Slesin, Stafford Cliff, Estate of Jack Berthelot, Martine Gaumé, Daniel Rozensztroch, and Gilles de Chabaneix. Used by permission of Clarkson N. Potter, Inc.; figs. 8.55–57 from *Interior Graphic and Design Standards* by S. C. Reznikoff. Copyright ©1986 by S. C. Reznikoff. Reproduced by permission of Whitney Library of Design, New York; fig. 8.59 Copyright ©1986 by The Conde Nast Publications, Inc.; fig. 9.11 from *Theory and Practice of Color* by Frans Gerritsen. Uitgeverij Cantecleer BV, The Netherlands; fig. 9.17 Copyright ©1990 by The Conde Nast Publications Inc.; fig. 9.21 Copyright ©1986 by The Conde Nast Publications Inc.; fig. 9.27 Copyright ©1984 by The Conde Nast Publications Inc.; fig. 9.30 from *Theory and Use of Color* by Luigina De Grandis, Copyright ©1984 Arnoldo Mondadori Editore SpA, Milan; fig. 10.6 Copyright ©1986 by The Conde Nast Publications Inc.; fig. 10.51 adapted from *The Visual Handbook of Building and Remodeling* by Charles G. Wing. Rodale Press, Pa. Copyright ©1990 Charles G. Wing; fig. 10.52 from *Interior Graphic and Design Standards* by S. C. Reznikoff. Copyright ©1986 by S. C. Reznikoff. Reproduced by permission of Whitney Library of Design, New York; fig. 11.10 from *Mary Emmerling's American Country West*, Copyright ©1985 by Mary Ellisor Emmerling. Used by permission of Clarkson N. Potter, Inc.; fig. 12.15 Copyright ©1986 by The Conde Nast Publications, Inc.; figs. 12.26, 12.59 from *Freestyle* by Tim Street-Porter, published by Stewart, Tabori & Chang; fig. 13.13 Copyright ©1986 by The Conde Nast Publications Inc; fig. 13.14 Reprinted by permission from *House Beautiful*, copyright © August 1986. The Hearst Corporation. All Rights Reserved; fig. 13.17 from *Italian Style*, Copyright ©1985 by Catherine Sabino

and Angelo Tondini. Used by permission of Clarkson N. Potter, Inc; fig. 13.18 Copyright ©1990 by The Conde Nast Publications Inc; figs. 13.19–20 Copyright Meredith Corporation, 1986. All rights reserved; fig. 13.26 from *Interior Graphic and Design Standards* by S. C. Reznikoff. Copyright ©1986 by S. C. Reznikoff. Reproduced by permission of Whitney Library of Design, New York; figs. 14.2, 14.4–6, Adapted from *The Visual Handbook of Building and Remodeling* by Charles G. Wing. Rodale Press, PA. Copyright ©1990 Charles G. Wing; fig. 14.8 from *The International Book of Lofts*, ©1986 by Suzanne Slesin, Stafford Cliff, Daniel Rozensztroch. Used by permission of Clarkson N. Potter, Inc.; figs. 15.9, 15.12 taken from the *Interior Design Reference Manual* by David K. Ballast, with permission from the publisher, Professional Publications, Inc., copyright 1992; fig. 16.1 Copyright ©1990 by The Conde Nast Publications Inc.; fig. 16.12 Copyright Meredith Corporation, 1986. All rights reserved; fig. 16.16 from *Collecting American Country* by Mary Ellisor Emmerling, Copyright ©1983 by Mary Ellisor Emmerling. Used by permission of Clarkson N. Potter, Inc.; fig. 16.19 from *Japanese Style* by Suzanne Slesin, Stafford Cliff, Daniel Rozensztroch, and Gilles de Chabaneix. Copyright ©1987 by Suzanne Slesin, Stafford Cliff, Daniel Rozensztroch, and Gilles de Chabaneix. Reprinted by permission from Crown Publishers, Inc.; fig. 16.20 from *Kitchens* by Chris Casson Madden. Copyright ©1993 by Interior Visions, Inc. Reprinted by permission from Crown Publishers, Inc.; fig. 16.22 from *Creative Kitchens*, Copyright ©1984 by Knapp Communications Corp. Courtesy of *Home* Magazine; fig. 16.28 from *Kitchens* by Chris Casson Madden. Copyright ©1993 by Interior Visions, Inc. Reprinted by permission of Crown Publishers, Inc.; fig. 16.41 Reprinted with permission from *Metropolitan Home* Magazine ©1991. Hachette Filipacci USA Inc.; fig. 17.1 Reprinted with permission from *Metropolitan Home* Magazine ©1991. Hachette Filipacci USA Inc.; fig. 17.6 Copyright Meredith Corporation, 1986. All rights reserved; fig. 17.7 Copyright ©1985 by The Conde Nast Publications Inc.; fig. 17.16 from *Mary Emmerling's American Country West*, Copyright ©1985 by Mary Ellisor Emmerling. Used by permission of Clarkson N. Potter, Inc.; fig. 17.17 Copyright ©1983 by The Conde Nast Publications Inc.